Neurobehavioral Toxicology

Neurological and Neuropsychological Perspectives

Volume III
Central Nervous System

Studies on Neuropsychology, Neurology and Cognition

Series Editor

Linas Bieliauskas
University of Michigan

Studies on Neuropsychology, Neurology and Cognition provides state-of-the-art overviews of key areas of interest to a range of clinicians, professionals, researchers, instructors, and students working in clinical neuropsychology, neurology, rehabilitation, and related fields.

Topics cover a broad spectrum of core issues related to theory and practice concerning brain and behavior, including: practical and professional issues (e.g. diagnosis, treatment, rehabilitation); cognitive development over the lifespan (e.g. child, geriatric); domain-specific cognitive issues (e.g. sport, toxicology); methodology related to brain and behavior (e.g. functional brain imaging, statistics and research methods); as well as relevant allied issues (e.g. ethics, minorities and culture, forensics)

The authors, editors, and contributors to each title are internationally recognized professionals and scholars in their field. Each volume provides an essential resource for clinicians, researchers, and students wanting to update and advance their knowledge in their specific field of interest.

Forthcoming

Dunkin – *Geriatric Neuropsychology Casebook*
Fujii – *Neuropsychology of Asian-Americans*

Published

Anderson, Jacobs, & Anderson – *Executive Functions and the Frontal Lobes*
Crowe – *The Behavioral and Emotional Complications of Traumatic Brain Injury*
Morgan & Ricker – *Textbook of Clinical Neuropsychology*
Kalechstein & van Gorp – *Neuropsychology of Substance Use*
DeLuca & Kalmar – *Information Processing Speed in Clinical Populations*
Stern – *Cognitive Reserve*
Tuokko & Hultsch – *Mild Cognitive Impairment*
Poreh – *Quantified Process Approach to Neuropsychological Development*
Leon-Carrion, von Wilde, & Zitnay – *Brain Injury Treatment*
Bush & Martin – *Geriatric Neuropsychology*
Berent & Albers – *Neurobehavioral Toxicology, Vols. I, II, and III*
Bush – *A Casebook of Ethical Challenges in Neuropsychology*
Ciccetti & Rourke – *Methodological and Biostatistical Foundations of Clinical Neuropsychology and Medical and Health Disciplines, 2nd Edition*
Lovell et al. – *Traumatic Brain Injury in Sports*
Wilson – *Neuropsychological Rehabilitation*
Lamberty, Courtney, & Heilbronner – *The Practice of Clinical Neuropsychology*
Ferraro – *Minority and Cross-cultural Aspects of Neuropsychological Assessment*
Rourke, Rourke, & van der Vlugt – *Practice of Child-clinical Neuropsychology*
Sweet – *Forensic Neuropsychology*

For continually updated information about published and forthcoming titles in the Neuropsychology, Neurology, and Cognition series, please visit: www.psypress.com/nnc

Neurobehavioral Toxicology

Neurological and Neuropsychological Perspectives

Volume III
Central Nervous System

Stanley Berent

James W. Albers

Taylor & Francis
Taylor & Francis Group
New York   London

Taylor & Francis is an imprint of the
Taylor & Francis Group, an informa business

Psychology Press
Taylor & Francis Group
270 Madison Avenue
New York, NY 10016

Psychology Press
Taylor & Francis Group
27 Church Road
Hove, East Sussex BN3 2FA

© 2009 by Taylor & Francis Group, LLC

Printed in the United States of America on acid-free paper
10 9 8 7 6 5 4 3 2 1

International Standard Book Number-13: 978-1-84169-494-8 (Hardcover)

Visit the Taylor & Francis Web site at
http://www.taylorandfrancis.com

and the Psychology Press Web site at
http://www.psypress.com

Contents

Contents of Volume I

Contents of Volume II

Dapsone
Disulfiram
Ethyl alcohol
n-Hexane
Lipid-lowering medications (HMG-CoA reductase inhibitors)
Nondepolarizing neuromuscular blockade and corticosteroids
Nitrofurantoin
Penicillamine
L-Tryptophan
Vaccination—A/New Jersey (swine flu) vaccine
Summary

12   CONDITIONS WHICH SOMETIMES MIMIC PERIPHERAL NERVOUS SYSTEM DISEASE

The influence of aging on clinical and electrodiagnostic examinations
Neurologic examination
Electrodiagnostic examination
The influence of anthropometric factors on the clinical
    and electrodiagnostic examinations
Neurologic examination
Electrodiagnostic examination
Nerve biopsy results
Physiologic or emotional conditions producing symptoms
    suggestive of neuromuscular disease
The influence of normal physiology on the nervous system
Functional or psychological factors
Non-neurologic conditions suggestive of peripheral neuropathy
    or myopathy
Symptoms due to connective tissue or skin
Vascular disorders
Metabolic/endocrine disorders mimicking neuropathy
Disorders of the spinal cord and nerve roots mimicking
    peripheral neuropathy
Conditions suggesting myopathy or defective neuromuscular
    transmission
Case presentation
Summary

13   CONSEQUENCES OF AN INCOMPLETE DIFFERENTIAL DIAGNOSIS

Case presentations
Lead-exposed painter with arm weakness
Patient with acute sensory loss and ethylene oxide exposure
Patient with an acute reaction to an organophosphorus pesticide

About the Primary Authors

Stanley Berent, PhD is a psychologist with specialties in clinical psychology and clinical neuropsychology. He is affiliated with the University of Michigan, where he is Professor Emeritus of Psychology and Psychiatry at the University of Michigan Medical School. He was the founding director of the Neuropsychology Programs at the University of Michigan Health System and the Ann Arbor Veterans Administration Health Center, and he is currently the codirector of the Neurobehavioral Toxicology Program at the University of Michigan Medical School.

James W. Albers, MD, PhD is a neurologist who specializes in neuromuscular diseases and electrodiagnostic medicine with a special interest in clinical neurotoxicology. He was the founding director of the Neuromuscular Program at the University of Michigan, director of the Electromyography Laboratory at the University of Michigan Health System for over 25 years, and codirector of the Neurobehavioral Toxicology Program at the University of Michigan Medical School.

Guest Contributors

In addition to the primary authors, a number of individuals were asked to contribute to the present volume, based upon their expertise in specialized areas. These contributions are indicated by the contributing authors' names listed with their specific section in the text. The primary authors of the book acted as editors for these contributions. The guest contributors include the following:

Kenneth M. Adams, PhD: V.A. Healthcare System and the University of Michigan, Ann Arbor, Michigan

Linas A. Bieliauskas, PhD: V.A. Healthcare System and the University of Michigan, Ann Arbor, Michigan

Henry G. Buchtel, PhD: V.A. Healthcare System and the University of Michigan, Ann Arbor, Michigan

Christopher J. Graver, PhD: Western State Hospital, Tacoma, Washington

Sherri L. Provencal, PhD: Sargent Rehabilitation Center, Warwick, Rhode Island

Victor S. Roth, MD, MPH: General Motors Powertrain, Livonia, Michigan, and the University of Michigan, Ann Arbor, Michigan

Christine L. Trask, PhD: Rhode Island Hospital and Brown Medical School, Providence, Rhode Island

Acknowledgments

The authors owe a debt of gratitude to many individuals for their support, encouragement, and patience during the long periods of effort required to bring this work to completion. We wish to especially acknowledge our students and colleagues who motivated us to obtain and remain current in the knowledge needed for this work. A special thank-you to our families, who sacrificed along with us while we completed this project (Joy, Melissa, Alison, and Rachel [SB]; Janet, Jeffrey, Matthew, Katherine, and Elizabeth [JWA]).

Stanley Berent
James W. Albers

Disclosures

The authors have at times been retained as consulting experts by companies concerned with the manufacture or use of solvents, pesticides, pharmaceuticals, or other substances with the potential for toxicity; or by firms representing those companies in litigation. Also, the authors have at times received funding support for research from government agencies, foundations, and private industry.

From the Series Editor

It is indeed a great pleasure to introduce this final volume of the series, *Neurobehavioral Toxicology, Neuropsychological and Neurological Perspectives: The Central Nervous System*. Combined with the grounding in theory and science in volume I, and covering the impact of neurotoxins in the peripheral nervous system in volume II, this volume completes what may be the most comprehensive treatment of the clinical neurological and neuropsychological effects of neurotoxins in humans. In this volume, Professors Albers and Berent cover commonly encountered neurotoxic agents, including industrial and environmental substances, as well as medications that can have neurotoxic consequences. The interaction of potential neurotoxic effects with psychological/psychiatric and medical conditions is also addressed, which is seldom seen in most texts on this topic. Case examples are described to illustrate how exposure to various substances is manifest in behavior and how potential etiology for presenting can be evaluated. The text concludes with a frank discussion of state-of-the-art understanding of the complex interactions between changes in the central nervous system and the factors that influence its evaluation and description. Specific attention is given to well-known controversies concerning subtle expressions of clinical conditions associated with neurotoxic exposure.

As with the other volumes in this work, the depth and completeness of addressing the neurological and neuropsychological changes in neurotoxic conditions will be impressive and rewarding to the reader. This flagship series on neurobehavioral toxicology deserves a space in any reference library dedicated to neurotoxic conditions and will be a most valuable resource for further research and teaching, as well as clinical formulation, for students, scientists, practicing physicians, psychologists, and other health care professionals. I am extremely proud of this volume of work and recommend it to all.

Linas A. Bieliauskas
Ann Arbor

Authors' Preface to Volume III

This book represents the final volume in a three-volume work that has addressed and critiqued the scientific methodologies relevant to neurobehavioral toxicology and, in the authors' view, are necessary in developing a clinical neurobehavioral diagnosis and in establishing a toxicological cause. We have applied these methodologies in case presentation and narrative formats to peripheral and central nervous system disorders that hold the potential for neurotoxic etiologies. The first of these three volumes focused on basic concepts and methodologies in the field of neurobehavioral toxicology. The foundations and methods described in volume I are seen by the authors as necessary for achieving a complete understanding of the concepts and case materials covered in volumes II and III. Consideration of the peripheral nervous system provided the focus in volume II. The present volume (i.e., volume III) addresses the central nervous system.

Volume III begins with a presentation and discussion of the major substances that are commonly used in industrial settings and that often, as a result of such use, find their way into the general environment. Information concerning specific substances and their effects is presented via narrative and a descriptive case method. Chemicals have multiple applications. Intent often determines if a given substance is considered by the public to be helpful or harmful. In reality, the toxic nature of a given substance is determined largely by a variety of factors. Some of these factors relate to the physical properties of the chemical or compound (e.g., anticholinesterase) while others pertain to the organism (e.g., absorption) or interaction between the two (e.g., metabolism). All substances have the capacity to be toxic, depending on dose and other factors such as those just listed. As a result of these same factors, many substances, on the other hand, might be used therapeutically or even recreationally. Whether or not a given substance can be described as a medicine, a recreational drug, or a poison often depends on a careful balance between adverse and intended effects. Such issues are routinely attended to in decisions regarding the use of chemical agents by industry, research, government regulators, and the general public. Individuals in clinical practice, likewise, often deal with problems associated with these same issues, and an individual cost–benefit analysis is implied or is overtly manifest in every clinical decision that involves the medicinal use of a chemical substance.

Whether toxicant exposure is intentional or inadvertent, the clinical manifestations of toxicant-induced disorders are often nonspecific; and a differential diagnosis in a given instance will need to include a number of normal and abnormal conditions that have the capacity to influence the individual's response to exposure or to produce symptoms and signs in common with the suspected causal substance. Therefore, a comprehensive differential diagnosis is essential to an accurate final diagnosis and statement of causality. In the research setting, analogously, potentially confounding variables need to be identified and properly controlled in order to establish an accurate understanding of neurobehavioral responses to a given substance.

As in the previous two volumes in this series, we emphasize in the present volume an applied approach to diagnosis and causal determination in neurobehavioral toxicology. Volume III begins with a presentation of frequently encountered industrial and environmental agents and the known central nervous system effects of these substances. A variety of chemical substances are employed for medicinal and at times recreational purposes, and these are covered next. The idea that nontoxicant considerations can be critical to an accurate conclusion regarding a suspected toxicant-induced disorder is consistently emphasized in the present volume. The central nervous system is complex, and chemicals that are often viewed as toxic can also represent normal functional components of the nervous system. Normal and abnormal behavioral conditions such as anxiety and other aspects of mood or thinking can be mistakenly identified as symptoms induced by exposure to a toxicant when they are not. In instances of abnormal psychological conditions or medical disease, the clinical manifestations can be erroneously attributed to a toxicant unrelated to the condition. Following a review of these medical and psychological considerations, we present examples of instances when a differential diagnosis has been inadequately considered and of the different result from pursuing a more complete list of possible explanations for the patient's condition.

Volume III concludes with a review of the complex issues involved in the neurobehavioral toxicological evaluation of the central nervous system and some of the controversies that can arise as a result of that complexity. Many issues that must be dealt with in clinical neurobehavioral toxicology reflect factors that are associated with the methods employed and the knowledge base to which these methods relate. When our knowledge about a given area of inquiry is incomplete, controversies can develop. When knowledge of relevant and potentially explanatory factors is inadequately considered, error is likely to result.

Stanley Berent
James W. Albers

15 Industrial and environmental agents

Although the story may no longer be familiar to most people, it occupied the attention of whole nations in the mid- to late 19th century (Beattie & Geiger, 1988). The story is that of Sir John Franklin, who in 1845 led an expedition to complete the Northwest Passage, the arctic water route connecting the Atlantic and the Pacific Oceans. This adventure is well known to historians, and it has been succinctly described by Richard Bayliss (Bayliss, 2002). As presented by Dr. Bayliss, "Sir John" commanded the *HMS Erebus* and, along with Captain Crozier who commanded the *HMS Terror* and an expedition of 129 officers and sailors, set sail from London on May 19, 1845. Nothing further was heard directly from the Franklin expedition. In an approximate 30-year period (from about 1850 to 1880), some two dozen expeditions were sent to discover what happened to Franklin and his men. Through these, and later expeditions, some as late as the 1980s, bits and pieces of information slowly came to light (Amy, Bhatnagar, Damkjar, & Beattie, 1986; Bayliss, 2002; Beattie & Geiger, 1988; Savours, 1990). The story that emerged was one of mystery, desperation, and tragedy.

It is believed that no one from the expedition survived, and eventually, the aim of the searches shifted from rescue to solving the mystery of how the crew died. It is this part of the story that makes it relevant in the present context. As it came to light, the Franklin expedition experienced a prolonged period of unusual winters, with summers too brief to allow the Arctic pack ice to melt. Bayliss described some of the events as follows. The explorers became trapped in the ice in the winter of 1846–1847, somewhere west of Boothia Peninsula. Many members of the crew became ill and began to die, including Sir John Franklin. The pack ice and wind carried the two ships south until they came to rest around King William Island. Captain Crozier made the decision in 1848 to abandon the ships in hope of reaching help at the Hudson Bay Company outpost. Accounts are that the men who had survived to this point were very ill, with symptoms suggestive of scurvy, e.g., bleeding gums, loose teeth, weight loss, weakness, shortness of breath, ecchymoses, and subcutaneous hematomas. Although some members of the crew made it as far as the mainland, none is believed to have survived the journey.

Aside from evidence of scurvy, tuberculosis, frostbite, and other problems related to the cold, other explanations regarding what killed the men on this expedition remained a mystery for over a century. The expedition was noteworthy, among other things, for its technological sophistication at the time. The ships involved were hybrids, combining steam driven screws with traditional sails and equipped especially for traversing frozen seas. Also, the engines allowed for central heating. Medical knowledge at the time progressed to allow recognition of how to prevent scurvy, and enough citrus fruit had been stocked to prevent the disease. However, it may be that the longer-than-anticipated trip led to a breakdown of the ascorbic acid in the fruit or some other event that interfered with the fruit's effectiveness, as the men did come down with scurvy despite their adequate knowledge of prevention. Most importantly, and while it might not seem today to be "high-tech," the expedition capitalized on the process of preserving food for long periods using the "tin can," the can being invented earlier in the 19th century by Peter Durand (Can Manufacturers Institute, 2000). This packaging, as it appears to have happened, was both a boon and a liability.

Bayliss (2002) looked at earlier work by Beattie and Geiger (1988) and considered several diverging trends in research that included autopsy results on bodies found from the Franklin party. Bayliss observed that, especially in comparison to Eskimos in the area, the crew members showed evidence of scurvy but also very high bone lead content (229 ppm, about ten times the amount in Eskimo controls). On the basis of the entire record, Bayliss concluded that the Franklin party suffered the effects of several diseases, including tuberculosis, scurvy, exposure to cold, and most important here, lead poisoning. Bayliss postulated that the source of lead contamination was the soldering of the cans used to keep the preserved meats. It was not that the lead poisoning directly killed the explorers, but, rather that the metal led to weight loss, fatigue, weakness, gastrointestinal difficulties, and eventually to psychological abnormalities like anxiety and paranoia. The combination of these symptoms and signs served to enhance the already compromised health of the crew, leading ultimately to their demise.

The Franklin story is interesting, but here it underscores issues associated with postindustrialization and the modern society. Various substances, synthetic and naturally occurring, are used alone and in unique combinations in our modern society. As in the case of the Franklin expedition, our knowledge regarding how to employ some new technology can be advanced beyond our understanding of all of the liabilities associated with such use. While many of the substances discussed in this chapter do occur naturally in the environment, our use of these agents for various primary and secondary industrial purposes contributes ultimately to their presence in the environment. Because of the relatively closed aspect of the Franklin expedition environment, it is easy to see in retrospect the impact of contamination. In the larger general environment, such recognition may be long-coming, despite the fact that, ultimately, it is no less a closed environment, no less real, and no less a threat to our survival than it was to the Franklin party. Knowledge is a prerequisite for control. If the planners of the Franklin expedition had all of the knowledge (e.g., that the lead content of the solder could poison as well as help preserve the contents by preventing the escape of air from the container), they might have been able to make adjustments and avoid the ultimate lead poisoning that occurred. In the remainder of this chapter, we present a number of, what we see as, important industrial and environmental agents. We have chosen the specific topics because of such factors as the frequency with which they are encountered, the seriousness of their risk, or because they serve as a model for understanding some aspect of neurobehavioral toxicology. We hope to increase the reader's understanding of these substances and, in so doing, contribute to safe and productive use of our environment to better the quality of our lives.

Selected presentations

Carbon monoxide poisoning

Stanley Berent

Carbon monoxide (CO) is a by-product of incomplete combustion. It is colorless, odorless, and nonirritating (Feldman, 1998). CO is ubiquitous, occurring as a result of both natural (e.g., forest fires) and man-made sources (e.g., combustion for purposes of heating or cooking, burning of tobacco products, and energy production). This gas is so prevalent in our environment that newspaper accounts reporting an incident of CO exposure are commonplace. CO has been reported to be the most common cause of fatal poisoning in the United States (Easley, 2000).

The initial symptoms of CO poisoning are similar to the flu (although without fever) and often can be misattributed to flu, at times with tragic consequences. These include such nonspecific symptoms as headache, fatigue, shortness of breath, nausea, and dizziness (Raub, Mathieunolf, Hampson, & Thom, 2000). Even exposure to CO at a relatively low level (resulting in a carboxyhemoglobin (COHb)[1] level of 10%) can produce symptoms (Goldman & Bennett, 2000). Exposure at this relatively low level can lead to transient impairments in visual perception, manual dexterity, learning, attention, and driving performance (Raub & Benignus, 2003), critical functions considering that likelihood of exposure is increased when inside a car. Also, purposeful exposure to CO is a method commonly used to attempt suicide (Trimble & Krishnamoorthy, 2000). It has been estimated that over 200 people in the United States die each year from CO that results from fuel-fired appliances like furnaces, water heaters, and space heaters, and thousands more are treated for CO poisoning in hospital emergency departments (U.S. Consumer Product Safety Commission, 2004).

Case presentation[2]

A 27-year-old, single male was referred for neuropsychological evaluation about 1 month following hospitalization and hyperbaric treatment for acute CO poisoning. The referral asked for documentation of behavioral and cognitive deficits in the face of continuing complaints of depression, memory, and other cognitive difficulties.

The patient had been hospitalized initially when one of his two roommates came to their apartment and discovered the patient "sleeping" and unresponsive on the couch. The roommate detected the smell of "gas" in the apartment,[3] dragged his friend to an outside hallway, and called the police from a neighbor's apartment. The police alerted emergency medical services (EMS), who, upon arriving at the scene, were able to revive the patient and, then, transport him to the emergency department (ED) of a nearby hospital. He was described by EMS personnel as having been unconscious for an undetermined length of time. The gas company was called as well and discovered an improperly vented space heater as the source of the CO. Ambient CO in the air inside the apartment was measured at 77 ppm. The patient's COHb at time of admission was 29.1%, a level consistent with severe poisoning, with a COHb of 0.8% following hyperbaric treatment.[4] Complaints at the time of the ED admission included nausea, headache, and a sense of "light headedness." He was described as "anxious" and drowsy but oriented to person, place, and time upon examination. He was able to recall two of three objects with delay but was unable to perform serial sevens. In response to questioning, the patient recalled that he had come home from school and that the apartment felt cold. He could not remember turning on the space heater or lying down on the couch. The next thing he could remember was someone calling his name and telling him he needed to go to the hospital. His memory for the ride to the hospital was said to be "fuzzy." The EMS arrived at the apartment about 5:00 p.m., and the patient said he usually arrived home about 4:00 p.m. The roommate arrived at about 4:30 p.m. Given this information, the period of unconsciousness could have been up to an hour but probably less.

INITIAL CLINICAL DIAGNOSIS

The patient's primary physician concurred with the emergency physician's diagnosis of acute CO poisoning and referred the patient for the present examination.

ADDITIONAL INFORMATION

The patient reported that he had never been married but was hoping to meet the "right person" at some point. At the time of the described incident, the patient was a graduate student in his second year of working toward a master's degree in business management. He reported that he had done well in high school and undergraduate college where he had graduated with a GPA of 2.66 (of 4). He further reported that he had been doing well in his current educational program, and that he worked about 3 days a week as a waiter in a fast-food restaurant in order to supplement the limited funding he received from a teaching assistantship at the school. Review of actual school transcripts revealed information that was consistent with his self-report and also indicated that he was earning a combination of "A" and "B" grades in his full load of graduate courses. His high school transcripts contained an IQ estimate of 118. The CO exposure occurred at the beginning of the heating season, just short of 2 months into the fall semester of his graduate program. He reported that he returned to class but was finding it difficult to concentrate and believed he was not doing as well as he had before the exposure incident. He had not yet returned to his part-time restaurant job. He felt that he was getting better and reported that his teachers and his employer have been very understanding and cooperative.

Despite his report that he was better in comparison to immediately after the CO exposure, the patient complained at the time of the present evaluation of difficulties with memory, sleep, headaches, fatigue, lack of interest in his usual activities, and a sense of "anxiety," the anxiety being attributed to concerns he had about his history of CO exposure and the subsequent symptoms he had experienced. There was no personal or family history of emotional, substance abuse, or other psychiatric diagnoses or treatment. He neither drank nor smoked.

Neuropsychological test results. Selected results from the patient's neuropsychological examination are presented in Table 15.1. These scores reflect mild difficulties

Table 15.1 Selected neuropsychological examination scores for a patient with a history of carbon monoxide exposure.

Test administered	Domain measured	Test results
MMSE	General mental status	27 of 30
WAIS-R, VIQ	Verbal intellect	99
WAIS-R, PIQ	Performance intellect	84
WAIS-R, Vocabulary	Vocabulary level	12
WAIS-R, Similarities	Abstract conceptualization	11
WAIS-R, Block Design	Visual-motor problem solving	7
WAIS-R, Digit Symbol	Psychomotor problem solving	7
WAIS-R, Picture Completion	Attention/concentration and visual problem solving	9
WMS, MQ	General memory and orientation	99
WMS, Passages	Verbal recall, percent retained	72%
WMS, Visual Reproduction	Visual recall, percent retained	82%
WRAT-3, Reading	Reading recognition	115
Self-Rating Scale	Clinical ratings of depression	Mild depression
MMPI-2	Personality/psychopathology	L = 60 F = 55 K = 58 Hs = 57 D = 64 Hs = 55 Pt = 72 All other scales within normal

across a range of cognitive abilities. General intellectual level appeared to be lower than estimated levels of functioning before his exposure. Language functions were preserved, with normal vocabulary, abstract conceptualization, and reading recognition level. Mild difficulties were noted in areas of problem solving, both verbal and nonverbal mediated tasks in this area. Psychomotor performance may have been slowed but only mildly so. Both concentration and memory appeared to be relatively impaired in comparison to estimates of prior ability. There were no dramatic differences between verbal and nonverbal memory tasks, although percentage of retained material was slightly better in the nonverbal than in the verbal area. The patient's general mental status was normal; however, the three points lost on the MMSE were on tasks that demand adequate concentration, i.e., two errors on serial sevens subtraction and one error on delayed memory.

In the portion of the examination that looked at emotional functioning, the patient reflected a valid MMPI-2. His highest score was on psychasthenia (T = 72), reflecting an obsessional approach that was only partially successful in dealing with a mild level of anxiety. Although the patient's demeanor contained an element of depression, his MMPI results (Scale D, T = 64) suggested that depression, as reflected in his MMPI performance, remained within normal limits, albeit at the border between normal and pathological.

Brain imaging studies. A report of the results of magnetic resonance imaging (MRI) done about 2 months after the patient's ED admission concluded bilateral, slightly asymmetrical with left greater than right, hyperintensities in the periventricular white matter and centrum semiovale and mild necrosis of the basal ganglia, with possible involvement of the hippocampus bilaterally.

Comment. It has already been mentioned that the common source of CO exposure is incomplete combustion. In addition to endogenous CO, mentioned earlier, that results from oxidation of organic molecules and heme degradation (Raub & Benignus, 2003), CO can be produced via metabolism of some other chemicals. The solvent, methylene chloride, e.g., can metabolize to CO and contribute to the body burden of COHb (Bleeker, 1994). CO has been toxicologically termed as an *asphyxiant* because it attaches to hemoglobin (Hb) with greater affinity than oxygen (O_2) (Raub & Benignus, 2003) to form COHb and prevents oxygenation of the blood for systematic transport to organs, such as the brain and heart (Klaassen & Watkins, 2003). Thus, the primary mechanism by which acute CO exposure produces adverse effects is *hypoxia* (Raub & Benignus, 2003). The reader is referred to *hypoxic encephalopathy* in chapter 17 of the present volume for further discussion of *hypoxia*. Although hypoxia is viewed as the primary mechanism by which CO induces damage to the nervous system, biochemical mechanisms also are known to exist. A number of studies of the intracellular effects of CO have been completed (e.g., inhibition of hemoproteins). Most of these studies have been in vitro and with animal models and have supported the idea of physiological effects via nonhypoxic mechanisms; however, the direct relevance to humans has not yet been shown (Raub & Benignus, 2003). Raub (Raub & Benignus, 2003) described CO poisoning as not being a "pure pathological process" since damage to the nervous system from CO can be the result of a number of processes, including consequences to the brain from cardiac damage.

The levels of exposure at which CO becomes toxic are relatively low. Steady state exposure to concentrations of CO in atmosphere at 10 ppm leads to an estimated COHb blood level of 2%, COHb—about 30% COHb at 220 ppm, and 40–50% COHb at 350–520 ppm (Raub & Benignus, 2003). Klaassen (Klaassen & Watkins, 2003) reported that while no overt human health effects have been noted for COHb levels below 2%, levels above 40% can lead to death from asphyxia. According to Klaassen (Klaassen & Watkins, 2003), changes in perception can occur at COHb levels as low as 2.5%. However, the threshold at which changes in neurobehavioral function occur has not been precisely determined. In their review of the literature on this topic, Raub and Benignus (2003) estimated that COHb levels of 15–20% are likely required to produce a 10% reduction in any behavioral or visual measurements. Nevertheless, the World Health Organization set the guideline for levels for CO in ambient air using a system of ratios of time to amount of CO to prevent blood COHb from rising above 2.5% (World Health Organization, 1999). These ratios range from exposure to CO concentrations of 8.7 ppm CO for 8 hr to 81 ppm for 15 min (Townsend & Maynard, 2002). Although documentation of exposure to CO and determination of an elevated COHb are required to diagnose CO poisoning, the severity of the patient's illness has a higher correlation with exposure amount and duration than does COHb (Piantadosi, 2000).

Regardless of the exact threshold, and to put the level of COHb resulting from exposure in perspective, CO concentrations above 87 ppm have been reported to be present in such common places as underground garages, tunnels, and buildings (Klaassen & Watkins, 2003). Over a relatively short period (e.g., minutes), an exposure at this level is sufficient to produce a COHb level that is within the range at which adverse effects are seen, regardless of whether the higher or lower threshold limits are used. These effects are independent of loss of consciousness and likely to be reversible.

Symptoms of CO poisoning vary widely, are related to dose, and include acute, chronic, and delayed development of central nervous system dysfunction (onset of symptoms 1–3 weeks following exposure) (Raub & Benignus, 2003; Raub et al., 2000). Depending on the extent and type of damage from acute CO exposure, symptoms can be reversible (Goldman & Bennett, 2000). On the other hand, residual impairments can persist and in some instances become permanent (Feldman, 1998). In the latter circumstance, previously unrecognized impairments may be mistakenly labeled as delayed even years after initial exposure. While CO poisoning can follow a course that includes a period of symptom resolution, only to be followed by a recurrent onset of symptoms (Choi, 1983; Ginsberg, 1979), such recurrence occurs within days, weeks, or, in some cases, months following initial symptoms (Kim et al., 2003).

REVISED CLINICAL DIAGNOSIS

Based on the patient's history, examination results, and other aspects of the patient's current evaluation, a revised clinical diagnosis was made: 1. Cognitive disorder, not otherwise specified (NOS) and 2. adjustment disorder, with anxiety (American Psychiatric Association, 1994). The patient's initial diagnosis was not disputed, and the revised diagnosis can be viewed as additional to the accepted initial diagnosis of CO poisoning and the implied hypoxia producing an acute encephalopathy.

Discussion

The clinical emphasis in a particular case may vary depending on the nature and objectives of the setting. When first seen in the ED, the objective would have been to determine what had likely happened to the patient and what should be done clinically to correct it. As such, consideration of cause, i.e., CO, most likely took precedent over many other considerations. In the present evaluation, the primary emphases were on the patient's current functioning, with a secondary, though still important, consideration with regard to cause. In the following paragraphs, we discuss the various diagnostic and related factors we considered in reaching our conclusions in presentation of this case.

NERVOUS SYSTEM LOCALIZATION

The proposed initial diagnosis for this patient's problem raises the possibility of central nervous system dysfunction. In concluding that the patient was "poisoned" as a result of exposure to CO, the unstated conclusion would be that the patient suffered some period of reduced oxygenation. Since any organ system that requires oxygen for normal function could be adversely affected by anoxia, the diagnosis of CO poisoning does not in itself document that damage to the central nervous system has, in fact, occurred. Further tests would be required to determine the involvement of the central nervous system. In the present case, other tests were conducted, e.g., MRI and psychometric examination. The results of these additional tests did document involvement of the central nervous system and more specifically, involvement of subcortical and possibly cortical regions of the brain as well.

The brain imaging studies demonstrated abnormalities that were consistent with anoxic damage to the brain. The results of neuropsychological evaluation resulted in findings that also were consistent with the conclusion of abnormal central nervous system function. The neuropsychological results provided further information about the level of functional impairment but also these results indicated a pattern of dysfunction that was consistent with areas that had been identified by MRI as compromised. In other words, the behavioral measurements enhanced the findings from brain imaging in three ways. First, the findings strengthened the MRI conclusions through independent replication; second, these results provided a basis for documenting a change from estimated baseline functional level; and third, the neuropsychological findings provided a functional viewpoint that allowed for grading of severity of the patient's condition.

VERIFICATION OF THE INITIAL CLINICAL DIAGNOSES

The original diagnosis of "acute CO poisoning" was accurate but contained an effect, "poisoning," as well as the cause of the poisoning, i.e., CO. This diagnosis is appropriate for the ED setting and easily meets criteria for verification. A clinical diagnosis of CO poisoning requires only documentation of exposure and an elevated COHb, after ruling out other possible explanations for the patient's symptoms and signs, e.g., poisoning by an agent other than CO, stroke, etc. (Goldman & Bennett, 2000). All of these conditions were met in the present case.

VERIFICATION OF THE REVISED CLINICAL DIAGNOSIS

Although it was not stated specifically in the revised diagnosis, the initial diagnosis of CO poisoning was accepted as valid. The emphasis in the present evaluation was on the patient's neurobehavioral status and the relationship of this status to his history of CO exposure. Neuropsychological evaluation has been recommended in cases of CO poisoning in order to document functional abnormalities (Abelsohn, Sanborn, Jessiman, & Weir, 2002).

Although the initial diagnosis reflected the presumed cause for the patient's condition, i.e., CO, and could be viewed as appropriate for the setting of the ED in which he was evaluated, that causal attribution might or might not have been accurate in terms of his current neurobehavioral functioning. Therefore, and in keeping with the theme in these present volumes, we have treated the diagnosis as distinct from causal attribution.

The revised diagnosis in the present instance accounts for all of the patient's history and complaints as stated at the time of this evaluation. These complaints included anxiety, problems with memory, and other cognitive difficulties. In terms of the patient's cognitive function, a history that documented clearly, by recorded observation (e.g., school performance) and psychometrically (past intelligence test results), that the patient functioned at a higher level prior and up to the time of his exposure aided in the conclusion that his present functioning represented a change from baseline and was impaired. The affected areas in his psychometric results were consistent with functions known to be mediated by areas of pathological findings reported in his MRI results. Also, these areas are those known to be especially sensitive to damage from his purported exposure to CO. Emotionally, the patient complained of anxiety, and the results from MMPI-2, as well as clinical observation, were consistent with anxiety. He described his sense of anxiety as manifesting primarily in "worry" about his having been injured as a result of his CO exposure.

DSM-IV (American Psychiatric Association, 1994) criteria allowed for the more specific diagnoses with regard to type of cognitive and emotional disorder, and the levels of scores from the psychometric examination, as well as the patient's report of history since his exposure incident, allowed for a statement as to the severity of his condition, i.e., mild.

CAUSE/ETIOLOGY

The patient's condition at the time of his initial evaluation was attributed to CO exposure.

VERIFICATION OF CAUSE/ETIOLOGY

The cause for the patient's condition that was proposed in this *case presentation* met all verification criteria such as those proposed by Hill (1965). For instance, and more specifically, the timing of exposure and onset of illness were appropriate. The risk of such exposure is well documented, and the relationship between exposure and response was biologically plausible. The adverse effects were modified by removal from exposure.

Comment

We have repeatedly stressed the importance of separating the diagnostic enterprise from the process of causal attribution. However, many diagnostic systems present the clinician with choices that demand consideration of cause in rendering a final diagnosis, depending on the vagaries of the particular diagnostic system employed. The diagnosis in the present instance, "cognitive disorder, not otherwise specified (NOS)," is designed for disorders that presume an underlying medical condition. In the present case, that condition would be presumed to be CO poisoning. With regard to the second diagnosis of "adjustment disorder, with anxiety," this designation also calls for a decision that the condition is in response to a stressor, and that the stressor, in this case, is related to the patient's history of CO poisoning. A differential consideration in this case would be "anxiety disorder due to a medical condition." This alternative requires that the anxiety be judged as the direct physiological consequence of the medical condition (American Psychiatric Association, 1994). In fact, symptoms of emotional disturbance have been reported to occur as a consequence of CO poisoning (Feldman, 1987; Trimble & Krishnamoorthy, 2000). Also, and as we discussed in the opening chapter of volume I, the important role that chemicals play in central nervous system mediated behaviors, including anxiety, leaves these behaviors especially vulnerable to disruption as a result of toxic damage to the brain. Nevertheless, and since we cannot resolve the issue of specific causal event in this specific instance, i.e., to what extent the anxiety is the direct result of the medical condition versus a response by the patient to the experience of his illness as being stressful, the diagnosis of adjustment disorder was appropriate.

With regard to the issue of dealing with causality in rendering the diagnosis, the clinician should keep these two considerations as separate as possible, for as long as possible, even if the final diagnosis reflects both components. In the present instance, it was fairly easy to determine that the patient manifested difficulties with cognition and in his emotional functioning without having to know anything about the cause of these conditions. It was only at the time of applying a specific DSM-based diagnosis that any consideration of cause became relevant.

The diagnoses given in the case presentation are completely verifiable using evidence-based criteria (Richardson, Wilson, Williams, Moyer, & Naylor, 2000). The diagnoses are adequate, coherent, and parsimonious. They best fit the pattern revealed in the clinical evaluation.

Conclusion

The results of CO poisoning can vary widely, depending on factors such as amount and duration of the exposure and a variety of individual differences in physiology (Gale & Hopkins, 2004; Raub & Benignus, 2003) and personal habits (e.g., smoker or nonsmoker) (Piantadosi, 2000). Despite such variability, the diagnosis of CO poisoning is straightforward because of the relative specificity of the biological effects of CO on the organism (Goldman & Bennett, 2000). With regard to neurobehavioral evaluation of a patient with suspected CO poisoning, the task may not be quite as uncomplicated as it may be for the emergency physician, and the task is quite different, although no less important (Abelsohn et al., 2002). Some of the complications derive from the myriad effects exposure to CO can have on the central nervous system, again depending on differences in exposure and individual difference variables. While certain brain structures are particularly sensitive to the damaging effects of CO and its accompanying hypoxia, damage is not necessarily limited to these areas of the nervous system (Asai & Toru, 1969; Choi, 2001; Dunham & Johnstone, 1999; Gale et al., 1999; Kim et al., 2003). As a result, it is unlikely that a diagnosis of CO intoxication can be accomplished solely on the basis of some identifiable pattern of neuropsychological impairment. The presence of a confirmed diagnosis of CO poisoning, as was the situation in the present *case presentation*, is welcome and helpful. In this case, the independently diagnosed CO poisoning was critical in determining the etiology of the patient's complaints as well as in helping to refine the DSM diagnosis that was employed.

But, what if the diagnosis of CO poisoning had not been available? We have emphasized repeatedly the need to proceed independently in determining the diagnosis and, then dealing with the matter of cause. More than anything else, the present case serves to emphasize the value of this clinical approach. For instance, and to address the question posed, the diagnoses of cognitive dysfunction and anxiety would have been made even without the CO information. The clinician would still have been able to address issues such as the pattern of cognitive impairment as well as level of severity and other aspects of the patient's neurobehavioral functioning that we listed and discussed in volume I of the present work. On moving to the topic of cause for the patient's condition, the information from the patient's history (patient's self-report as well as objective records) would have allowed the clinician to determine that the presently observed functioning represented a change from the past. With the patient's report of a specific incident that occurred at a specified time, the clinician could determine that this behavioral change occurred at that time. In following the course of symptoms over time and since the specified incident, the clinician could determine that the patient's behavior improved and his complaints lessened during that time. These incidents combine to meet many of the criteria presented by Hill (1965) and needed to verify a causal connection between the reported incident and the current diagnosis. These include timing of the incident and onset of impairment, modification of the effects following the incident, analogous problems that result from a number of substances, and elimination of other potential causes. In other words, the clinician could conclude that the present diagnoses probably resulted from something that happened in that particular incident, even though the proof that the "something" was CO might be lacking.

Lead in adults

Victor S. Roth

Occupational and environmental lead poisoning has been a recognized health hazard for more than 2,000 years. Characteristic features of lead toxicity, including anemia, colic, neuropathy, nephropathy, sterility, and coma, were noted by Hippocrates and Nikander in ancient times, as well as Ramazzini and Hamilton in the modern era (Landrigan, Silbergeld, Froines, & Pfeffer, 1990). In Germany in 1473, Ulrich Ellenbog wrote on the occupational hazards faced by goldsmiths and metalworkers, describing how to avoid lead and mercury poisoning. The brochure, written for smiths, included advice on measures to reduce exposure by "opening windows" and "covering the mouth with a cloth." This reportedly was the first published work on industrial hygiene (Gochfeld, 2005).

In the early 1900s, Alice Hamilton, a pioneer in occupational medicine, documented lead hazards among American workers in the pigment manufacturing, battery, painting, plumbing, ceramics, pottery, and other industries. A recently published paper prepared in tribute to Dr. Alice Hamilton on her 120th birthday, reviewed her pioneering studies of occupational lead poisoning and its control, her largely unheeded warnings about the possible consequences of widespread lead exposure to the general public through the use of leaded fuel, and the results of recent studies of human exposure to and health effects of lead in the general environment (Lippmann, 1990). In 1921, the president of the National Lead Company, Edward J. Cornish, wrote that lead manufacturers, as a result of "50–60 years" experience, agreed "lead is a poison when it enters the stomach of man." Dr. Hamilton eventually concluded, "the total prohibition for lead paint for use in interior work would do more than anything else to improve conditions in the painting trade." By the early 1930s, a consensus developed among specialists that lead paint posed a hazard to children. Physicians have gained an extensive understanding of the causes, the clinical presentations, and the means of preventing lead poisoning. However, it remains one of the most important occupational and environmental health problems (Saryan & Zenz, 1994).

The continued occurrence of occupational lead overexposure and lead poisoning in the United States remains a serious problem despite awareness of its adverse health effects and despite the conception that lead exposure is arguably the oldest known occupational health hazard. It is a particularly insidious hazard with the potential for causing irreversible health effects, including hypertension, central nervous system problems, anemia, and diminished hearing acuity before these conditions are clinically recognized (Staudinger & Roth, 1998). Scientific evidence of subclinical effects of lead toxicity continues to accumulate, making further reduction in workplace exposure, regular surveillance screening, and early diagnosis and treatment of lead toxicity of critical importance in the prevention of this occupational hazard.

For the most part, the diagnosis of lead poisoning in the adult worker is based on the integration of data obtained from the history, a physical examination, laboratory tests, and tests of specific organ function. A blood lead level of 40 μg/dl (1.95 μmol/L) or greater requires medical intervention; a level of 60 μg/dl (2.90 μmol/L) or three consecutive measurements averaging 50 μg/dl (2.40 μmol/L) or higher necessitate the employee to be removed from the workplace exposed to lead. The decision to initiate chelation therapy is not based on specific blood lead levels but depends on the severity of clinical symptoms. For adults, various studies have produced associations between blood pressure and blood lead concentrations below 35 μg/dl, suggesting possible effects on cardiovascular health. Even though the biological mechanisms responsible for these effects remain poorly understood, recent and current efforts to reduce exposure to lead by the virtual elimination of lead in gasoline and food packaging clearly demonstrate Dr. Hamilton's teaching that a most effective means of reducing excessive exposures is control of environmental sources.

Lead serves no useful biologic function in the human body. Over the past several years, concern has increased over the health effects of low-level lead exposure and the "normal" body burden of lead. In the occupational setting, the present "no-effect" level for lead exposure is currently being reevaluated as more sensitive measures of the physiologic effects of lead are made available through clinical investigations On the basis of the current knowledge of the health effects of lead in adults, the U.S. Public Health Service declared a health objective for the new millennium: the elimination of all exposures that result in blood lead concentrations greater than 25 μg/dl (1.20 μmol/L) in workers (Kaufman, Burt, & Silverstein, 1994).

Lead and lead compounds play a significant role in modern industry, with lead being the most widely used nonferrous metal (Fischbein, 1992). A wide variety of industrial populations are at risk of occupational exposure to lead. According to estimates made by the National Institute of Occupational Safety and Health (NIOSH), more than 3 million workers in the United States are potentially exposed to lead in the workplace (Staudinger & Roth, 1998).

Chronic lead nephropathy: Case presentation (Ahn et al., 2000)[5]

A 50-year-old man, a lead-smelting worker, was admitted to the local hospital because of persistent renal insufficiency and intermittent gouty arthritis. Four years earlier, his serum creatinine was noted to be elevated, at 2.5 mg/dl, his creatinine clearance was decreased to a level of 54 ml/min, and his uric acid was elevated at 12.3 mg/dl. This patient had worked at several lead-smelting plants for 17 years. Ambient air lead levels at the work site were in excess of the threshold limit value (TLV) for lead. The patient was removed from further exposure to lead at the work site after he was diagnosed as having lead poisoning through a required surveillance examination. His annual health examination, which began 6 years earlier, noted that the patient had no specific symptoms of lead poisoning and had no abnormal laboratory findings related to renal function. The findings noted that the patient had the nonspecific symptoms of fatigue, dizziness, numbness, facial edema, and polyarthralgia for several years before admission. He denied headache, wrist drop, or abdominal pain. The remainder of the patient's medical and family history was noncontributory.

On physical examination, his blood pressure was elevated at 150/96 mmHg with other vital signs being normal. He appeared pale, had mild edema on both legs, and red nodules on the left ankle and left great toe. Laboratory studies were found to be consistent with a normocytic normochromic anemia (hemoglobin, 10.7 g/dl) with the additional finding of basophilic stippling of erythrocytes; albumin, 4.2 mg/dl; total cholesterol, 225 mg/dl; sodium, 140 mEq/L; potassium, 5.0 mEq/L; blood lead, 62.0 μg/dl; and zinc protoporphyrin, 218 g/dl.

Renal ultrasound revealed bilaterally normal sized kidneys. Renal biopsy showed focal moderate atrophy or loss of proximal tubules with prominent interstitial fibrosis. Also, 22% of glomeruli showed global sclerosis and arterioles exhibited patchy hyaline deposits. An ultrastructural study revealed an absence of immune complex depositions. A Lead Mobilization Test (LMT) was completed. Baseline urinary excretion of lead was 106 g/dl. After the first intravenous infusion of 1 g calcium disodium ethylenediamine tetraacetic acid (CaEDTA), urine lead increased to 3,934 μg/dl. Cortical bone lead was assessed in units of grams of Pb per grams of bone mineral. Tibial bone lead level was 337 g Pb/g bone mineral. After treatment with CaEDTA over 11 months, serum creatinine has fallen to less than 2.0 mg/dl (1.5–1.9 mg/dl) and CaEDTA chelatable lead has decreased to 3,028 μg/dl. Blood lead has remained high at a level of 59.3 μg/dl.

Lead intoxication from a ceramic mug: Case presentation (Ziegler et al., 2002)[6]

A 16-year-old female patient was admitted to the hospital with a 4-month history of colic-like abdominal pain, hypertonia, anemia, weight loss of more than 10 kg during the last 6 months, and general deterioration of her general physical condition. Several differential diagnoses, such as hepatitis, Gilbert's disease, and anorexia nervosa, were suspected. When she developed intermittent hypertonia and tachycardia, she was transferred to cardiology. Laboratory testing revealed red blood cell basophilic stippling and an elevated blood lead concentration of 91.9 μg/dl. Electrocardiography, echocardiography, chest radiograph, and cranial computed tomography were normal.

Further investigation revealed the patient's brother to be the only other family member with an elevated blood lead concentration (59 μg/dl). Analyses of the drinking water from the patient's household did not reveal an elevated lead content. No other environmental source of lead could be identified. The patient later admitted that she used to drink up to 2 L of lemon tea, served from a pot that had a ceramic inner glaze.

Analysis of the inner surface of the teapot revealed a layer of lead glaze. Elution of the teapot glaze with 10 ml of diluted nitric acid over a period of 2 hr liberated 1.27 g/L of lead. The findings of lower lead levels in the patient's brother were in accordance with the fact that he claimed that he drinks less tea than his sister. The parents did not drink any tea, and as such had normal blood lead concentrations. Following chelation therapy with EDTA (20 mg/kg per body weight per day) for 3 days, the patient's blood lead level decreased to 62.7 μg/dl. The patient recovered and was discharged.

Lead poisoning presenting a difficult diagnosis: Case presentation (Hettmansberger & Mycyk, 2002)[7]

A healthy 57-year-old man developed abdominal pain and lower back pain over the course of several days. He had no significant medical history, took no medications, and had no known allergies. He denied having any antecedent trauma and reported no other symptoms. His vital signs were normal and physical examination was unremarkable. Rapid office tests revealed a hemoglobin level of 9.7 g/dl (97 g/L) and blood on urine dipstick. The patient was admitted to the hospital for nephrolithiasis work-up and treatment. Despite an extensive 3-day hospital evaluation, work-up was inconclusive.

At follow-up after discharge, the patient continued to have the same symptoms; he then revealed that he was a welder exposed to lead fumes. A whole-blood lead level obtained at that time was greater than 100 μg/dl (4.83 μmol/L), and he was readmitted to the hospital for chelation therapy with dimercaprol (or BAL) and edetate calcium sodium (CaNa^{2}EDTA). Chelation was continued for 5 days. The patient's symptoms resolved, and the work-site evaluation was completed.

Adult lead encephalopathy: Case presentation (Tuzun et al., 2002)[8]

A 28-year-old man was admitted to the hospital with a 7-year history of memory impairment, weakness, and weakening of concentration. He had worked in the manufacture of storage batteries for nearly 15 years. His clinical examination revealed cooperation impairment. Psychological testing showed weakening of short-term memory, weakening of concentration, emotional imbalance, drowsiness, and fatigue. His blood lead level was 90 μg/dl.

Discussion

The sources of adult lead exposure are many and varied with the main exposure source being occupational (U.S. Department of Human Services, 1992). The professions that carry increased risk of lead exposure include (but are not limited to) plumbers, pipe fitters, lead miners, auto repairers, glass manufacturers, shipbuilders, printers, plastic manufacturers, lead smelters and refiners, police officers, steel welders or cutters, construction workers, rubber product manufacturers, gas station attendants, battery manufacturers, bridge reconstruction workers, and firing range instructors. Environmental sources of adult lead exposure include lead paint, soil/dust near lead industries, roadways, older homes with lead paint, leached lead from plumbing pipes and ceramic cups and bowls, and leaded gasoline. There are also many hobbies, recreational activities, personal medications, and substance use and abuse activities, which have risk of increased lead exposure. These include glazed pottery making, target shooting at firing ranges, lead soldering, painting, preparing lead shot, preparing lead fishing sinkers, stained-glass making, car/boat repair, home remodeling, folk remedies, health foods, cosmetics, moonshine whiskey, and gasoline "huffing."

Lead poisoning in adults can cause a variety of nonspecific symptoms involving the neurologic, renal, hematologic, gastrointestinal, and musculoskeletal systems. Given the variety and subtlety of lead poisoning, it is easy for clinicians to incorrectly assign these symptoms to entities other than lead poisoning (Morgan, Todd, & Moore, 2001). It can be seen in all four cases presented that arriving at the diagnoses of lead toxicity based on the evaluation of the presenting symptoms did not result in a straightforward diagnosis. In the first case, the patient had findings of renal insufficiency and intermittent gouty arthritis. In the second case, the patient described a chronic colicky abdominal pain, hypertonia, anemia, and weight loss with first liver disease and then cardiac disease as differential diagnoses. The patient in the third case complained of abdominal pain and lower back pain and with a finding of blood on urine dipstick, underwent an inconclusive work-up for renal calculi, was discharged and then readmitted to the hospital. The fourth (encephalopathy) case describes a patient who continued to work in an industry with known lead exposure even though he demonstrated progressive symptoms of lead toxicity ongoing for at least seven years. The common thread running through all of these cases is the nonspecific type of symptoms that adults can display when they have lead toxicity.

Unlike lead toxicity in children, in adults, even in cases where lead toxicity is not part of the initial differential diagnosis, a thorough occupational and environmental history will, at least in most cases, bring lead into the picture and lead to appropriate diagnostic testing. Because the most common exposure to lead among adults is occupational, the first and the third cases illustrate that a thorough occupational history is essential in any patient who presents with a constellation of unexplained symptoms. An occupational history would most likely have revealed important diagnostic clues regarding the nature of both these patient's illnesses and may have prevented a lengthy diagnostic work-up and delay in treatment. Furthermore, an exposure history should be elicited with a particular focus on personal hygiene, such as eating or smoking on the job, and the habits and general health of coworkers who also may experience similar exposures. Ideally, a work-site evaluation should include a walk-through of the patient's work area, paying particular attention to engineering and administrative controls. An inspection of the patient's personal protective equipment would ensure that it is functioning properly and is appropriate for the type of work that is performed.

In the case reports noted in this chapter, fortunately, the second and third cases recovered completely with proper treatment. This was not true for the first and the fourth cases, which included a patient with nephropathy and chronic pathologic changes in the kidney on the biopsy report and a patient with a 7-year history of decreased central nervous system function.

In the first *case presentation*, the early recognition of the etiology of this patient's nonspecific symptoms (which eventually led to his renal abnormalities) should then have been followed by implementing industrial hygiene controls or removal of this employee from occupational lead exposure, which could have prevented the development of chronic kidney disease in this patient.

Chronic lead nephropathy occurs as a result of years of lead exposure. This disease has been prevalent throughout human history. It is important that primary care providers and internists recognize this disorder because it can contribute to progressive loss of kidney function. Diagnosis is made by a thorough history in combination with physical examination. A history of lead intoxication often requires knowledge of the various sources of lead exposure. Laboratory tests, many previously known and some newly described, are available to further support this diagnosis. Therapy to reduce lead burden may be useful when employed early in the disease; new data shed more light on which of the patients should be treated and when such patients should undergo chelation therapy. In particular, treatment with calcium EDTA chelation may benefit certain patients with chronic kidney disease by slowing the progression to end-stage renal disease (Brewster & Perazella, 2004).

Lead encephalopathy is rare and is much less common in adults than it is in children. The fourth case describes the irreversible central nervous system effects of lead toxicity in an adult with occupational lead exposure (Tuzun, Tuzun, Salan, & Lu, 2002). Lead encephalopathy is almost always associated with a blood lead concentration of >100 $\mu g/dl$, although it has been observed at levels as low as 70 $\mu g/dl$. Encephalopathy is a rare but severe complication of lead poisoning. It is sometimes lethal and, as in the chronic case noted above, can result in serious neurologic sequelae.

The major pathologic finding in acute encephalopathy is brain edema. The symptoms of acute encephalopathy usually evolve over several days and ataxia, headache, vomiting, convulsions, paralysis, stupor, and coma may occur.

In chronic lead encephalopathy, lack of sensory perception, learning disorders, disorientation, weakening of memory and concentration, depression, headache, drowsiness, insomnia, diminished libido, dizziness, syncope, tremor, irritability, seizure, ataxia, restlessness, and behavioral abnormalities may be noted. With progression of the disease, development of cerebellar or cerebral edema, vomiting, apathy, stupor, coma, paralysis, and death may occur.

Other than physician specialists in occupational medicine, most physicians are not trained in workplace evaluations. Thus, a work-site inspection should be performed in conjunction with a certified industrial hygienist or a health and safety officer familiar with health and safety protocols, the Occupational Safety and Health Administration regulations for lead exposure and surveillance and whether appropriate personal protective equipment should be used and if so, is it the proper equipment for the exposure and is the equipment being properly used (Suls, 2003).

Chronic inorganic lead toxicity is an insidious illness with variable manifestations (Lewis, 1990). Symptoms may include arthralgias, headache, weakness, depression, loss of libido, impotence, and vague gastrointestinal difficulties. Late effects may include chronic renal failure, hypertension, gout, and chronic encephalopathy (Landrigan, 1994).

Arriving at a diagnosis of lead poisoning in an adult requires a high index of suspicion and a careful history. The infrequency of classic diagnostic signs and the nonspecific nature of the symptoms frequently contribute to misdiagnosis (Keogh, 1992). The diagnosis of inorganic lead intoxication in adults requires the demonstration of excess lead absorption, documentation of impairment in an organ system consistent with the effects of lead, and exclusion of other causes of disease. At present, the blood level concentration is the single best indicator of recent, acutely elevated lead absorption. This level provides good information on lead absorption in persons with relatively brief exposure, such as construction workers or new entrants into the lead industry. The blood lead level rises rapidly within hours after an acute exposure and remains elevated for several weeks (Landrigan, 1994).

Zinc protoporphyrin (ZPP) has been used both as a screening and diagnostic test for overexposure to lead for nearly 30 years, although limitations of using ZPP for both purposes are recognized. ZPP elevations in both chronic and acute exposure settings lag behind elevations in whole-blood lead by approximately 8–12 weeks. Therefore, ZPP measurement, in conjunction with whole-blood lead determination, has clinical utility in cases of substantial overexposure by providing information on how long an individual may have been overexposed to lead (Martin, Werntz, & Ducatman, 2004). However, while ZPP levels do correlate with whole-blood lead measurements in aggregate, the considerable individual variability of ZPP measurements, poor sensitivity at lower ranges of lead exposure, poor specificity and delayed changes in unstable exposure conditions indicate that this test contributes little to screening programs. The results of the study cited (Martin et al.) also confirm that basophilic stippling is seen in acute as well as chronic lead intoxication, and may provide the first indication of lead intoxication.

Conclusion

The cases presented here were those with high lead exposure and with classical though nonspecific (and thus unrecognized) symptoms of lead toxicity. Understanding of lead toxicity has advanced substantially over the past three decades, and focus has now shifted from high-dose effects in clinically symptomatic individuals to the consequences of exposure at lower doses that cause no symptoms (Needleman, 2004).

The availability of more sensitive analytic methods has made it possible to measure lead at much lower concentrations. This advance, along with more refined epidemiological techniques and better outcome measures, has lowered the least observable effect level until it approaches zero. As a consequence, the segment of the population who are diagnosed with exposure to toxic levels has expanded. At the same time, occupational efforts by OSHA and environmental efforts mandated by federal and state regulations, most importantly the removal of lead from gasoline, have dramatically reduced the amount of lead in the workplace and in the biosphere.

The toxic effects of lead and lead compounds have been extensively studied for over a century. One of the cases described in this section had a chronic lead encephalopathy associated with occupational exposure to lead and a high blood lead level that most likely was present in this individual over several years. However, despite knowing that these clinical findings occur, there is still insufficient information on the mechanisms of action that account for neurotoxic effects of lead, particularly in terms of impaired intellectual ability.

Current research on lead toxicity in industrial populations is focusing on the definition of dose–response relationships, particularly at low levels of exposure. Major interest surrounds the development of biochemical and physiologic markers of subclinical toxicity. There is a need to better delineate the toxicity of lead on the peripheral and central nervous system, the kidneys, the cardiovascular system, the endocrine system, the liver, and the male and female reproductive organs using newly developed markers. To obtain more accurate information on cumulative individual exposure to lead, future research on lead toxicity will increasingly use x-ray fluorescence analysis (Landrigan, 1990).

The potential teratogenicity and carcinogenicity of lead, as well as its effect on pregnancy outcomes and neonatal growth and development, also require further study (Moreira & Moreira, 2004).

Despite intensive study, a vigorous debate remains about the toxic effects of lead, from low-level exposure in the general population owing to environmental pollution and the use of lead in the occupational setting. In most industries, blood lead levels have declined below levels at which signs or symptoms are seen. Thus, the current focus of attention is on subclinical effects of exposure. Legislation to reduce lead exposure in the general population and in working environments must be based on scientific evaluation of the available evidence (Gidlow, 2004).

Lead in children

Christine L. Trask

For pediatric neuropsychologists, lead exposure is the most commonly encountered neurotoxic issue (Dietrich, 2000). Although lead is toxic for both adults and children, children are at greater risk. Children are more often exposed to sources of lead dust because of developmental behaviors (e.g., hand-to-mouth, crawling, oral exploration of objects). Children, more likely than adults, are exposed to lead from contamination of the environment (e.g., in dust or soil), whereas adults are more likely to be exposed through occupational exposures (Bellinger, 2004). In addition, developmental metabolic factors and the vulnerability of the developing brain increase the risk for children, especially those under 6 years of age. Lead levels in children have continued to decline over the last several decades, and according to data from National Health and Nutrition Examination Surveys (NHANES), the number of children with blood lead levels above 10 μg/dl declined from 88.2% of children aged 1–5 years (13,500,000 children) during 1976–1980 to 2.2% of children (434,000 children) aged 1–5 years during 1999–2000 (CDC, 2004). Nevertheless, state and local surveillance data reported to the CDC indicated that despite targeting the year 2000 for national elimination of blood lead levels greater than 25 μg/dl, a total of 8,723 children out of 2,422,298 children tested in the United States still had blood lead levels greater than 25 μg/dl in 2000 (Meyer et al., 2003). This is a small number in terms of percentage, and the reduction in numbers of children reflecting what now are considered to be high levels of lead is impressive. Nevertheless, the data just presented indicate that a relatively large number of children continue to exhibit unacceptable lead levels. The Centers for Disease Control (CDC, 2004) is currently working toward a goal of eliminating instances of blood lead levels greater than 10 μg/dl in children aged 1–5 years by 2010.

Due to secondary prevention efforts, children with elevated lead exposure are often first identified through community-based routine screening. As a result, the challenge to clinicians is to assess the relative influence of low levels of lead exposure on a child's cognitive and behavioral functioning in the absence of acute neurological symptoms. Moreover, lead exposure is often associated with adverse social and biological conditions, including nutritional deficiencies, anemia, poor caretaking, poverty, and substandard housing (Dietrich, 2000). As a result, one of the major challenges in assessing pediatric lead exposure is to determine the relative contributions of a variety of potential causal agents that compete as explanations for an individual child's difficulties.

Case presentation[2]

The parents of a 3-year-old boy had not sought medical or psychological evaluation or treatment for their child before a routine health screening at age 3 years, which detected an elevated level of blood lead. In particular, the initial blood work revealed a blood lead level of 18 μg/dl. Subsequent blood

Table 15.2 Repeated blood lead levels (BLL in µg/dl) in a case of suspected lead poisoning.

	2/94	4/95	5/95	6/95	*Family moved to new home*	9/00
BLL	18	23	13	16		<5

lead levels peaked at 23 µg/dl and ultimately fell to less than 5 µg/dl (see Table 15.2). There was no reported history of pica, although his mother described the child as "impulsive" and noted that he frequently mouthed objects as a toddler. Environmental testing in the home revealed moderately elevated levels of lead in dust in window wells and on baseboard areas. In addition, there were more pronounced concentrations of lead in the soil around the home.

The mother sought an evaluation for her child at 4 years because of "lead poisoning," with specific complaints of poor sleep, loss of weight, headaches, stomachaches, shortness of stature, irritability, lack of concentration, difficulty playing with peers, and low frustration tolerance, as well as a newly developed fear of insects. His mother stated that she did not believe her child was "delayed," but added that he was scheduled to enter "HeadStart," a federally funded child development program that focuses on increasing school readiness of young children in low income families (U.S. Department of Health and Human Services, 2005; www.acf.hhs.gov/programs/hsb/about/index. htm). She also noted that he appeared to be losing interest with preacademic tasks, such as puzzles or drawing.

The history indicated that the child was born during the 8th month of pregnancy. His mother reportedly did not obtain regular prenatal care, and medical records reflected suspicion for intrauterine growth retardation and oligohydramnios. At birth, the child was described as appearing "postmature" with "very loose and wrinkly skin." Birth weight was 5 lb, 11 oz. Nevertheless, Apgars were reported as 9 and 9, and the neurological examination after delivery was normal. Developmental milestones were achieved within normal intervals (e.g., walked at 12 months, pedaled tricycle at 4 years, spoke at 12 months, toilet trained at 2 years; see Table 15.3). The medical history was otherwise nonsignificant, except for mild physical trauma, primarily frequent cuts and scrapes.

The child lived with his parents and two older siblings. Blood lead testing on the siblings did not yield any detectable levels. Both of the child's parents are high school graduates. The child's father has had periods of unemployment, but he was currently working as a cook in a fast-food restaurant. The child's mother worked as a waitress. The mother described the older children as "doing well in school," although review of their school records reflected grades mostly in the "C" and "D" range, with multiple comments about trouble staying on task, not working to potential, having difficulty listening, and displaying a bad attitude. In addition, one brother was noted to have a speech and language disorder and required 3 years of speech therapy.

Table 15.3 Developmental milestones (Sears & Sears, 1993).

3 months	Rolls back to side
5 months	Transfers objects from hand-to-hand and hand-to-mouth Babbling
6 months	Sitting alone briefly
6–9 months	Crawls on hands and knees Babbles consonant and vowel combinations Separation anxiety begins
9–12 months	Cruises while holding onto furniture Stacks blocks
12–15 months	Walks alone First words
15–18 months	Scribbles Sorts shapes
18–24 months	Runs Completes simple puzzles Telegraphic speech with two to three word phrases

It should be recognized that there is variation in the age at which these developmental milestones are achieved.

INITIAL CLINICAL DIAGNOSIS

Brief neuropsychological testing was completed when the child was 4 years old. The child was described by the neuropsychologist as being slightly restless and appearing to have limited ability to identify shapes or colors. In general, the test results obtained during this evaluation reflected low-average to borderline intellectual functioning, and borderline-to-impaired receptive language skills (see Tables 15.4 and 15.5). The child was diagnosed with lead poisoning, impaired auditory attention, expressive language, and lack of adequate behavioral control. Although visual–constructional abilities commonly apparent in lead encephalopathy were not noted, the clinician indicated that, given the young age of the child, the medium-to-long-term effects of lead were not yet known for this young child. Repeat assessment in 2 years was recommended. After this evaluation, the family moved out of the home, the suspected source of lead exposure.

INITIAL CAUSE/ETIOLOGY

The initial cause for this child's difficulties was attributed to lead exposure; however, this causal attribution was confounded with the diagnostic statement.

VERIFICATION OF THE INITIAL CLINICAL DIAGNOSIS

With any clinical assessment, the first consideration is to determine if the child's reported difficulties fall within the range of normal development. Although the child's mother reported developmental milestones being

Table 15.4 Neuropsychological (cognitive) test results in a case of suspected lead poisoning.

Domain/Measure	Standard score at age		
	4 years	*8 years*	*9 years*
Intellect	WPPSI-R	WISC-III	WISC-III
VIQ	82	90	99
PIQ	81	91	102
FSIQ	80	90	100
Academics			
WIAT Basic Reading		101	91
WJ-R Broad Reading			99
WIAT Spelling		95	98
WIAT Math Reasoning			103
WJ-R Broad Math		93	89
Language			
PPVT-R	70		83
NEPSY Language			100
WISC-III Vocabulary			11 (scale score)
Visual–Spatial			
WISC-III Block Design			9 (scale score)
NEPSY Visuospatial			94
Attention			
WISC-III FFDI			96
WISC-III Digit Span			8 (scale score)
WISC-III Number–Letter			5 (scale score)
NEPSY Auditory Attention			10 (scale score)
Memory			
WRAML General Memory		100	97
WRAML Verbal Memory		83	79
WRAML Visual Memory		98	98
NEPSY Memory			109
Executive			
NEPSY Tower			15 (scale score)
Trail Making		Low average	93
Children's Category Test			81
Sensory-Motor			
NEPSY Sensorimotor			98
Tapping, dominant hand		Low average	100
Grip strength, dominant hand			112

achieved within age-appropriate intervals, the child had a significant number of somatic symptoms, including poor sleep, loss of weight, headaches, stomachaches, and decreased growth. In addition, he demonstrated below-average attentional abilities, weaknesses in verbal cognitive skills, and maladaptive behaviors. This constellation of signs and symptoms can be associated with a variety of medical and psychological disorders in addition to lead

Table 15.5 Neuropsychological (behavioral) test results in a case of suspected lead poisoning.

Domain/Measure	T-Score at age		
	4 years	*8 years*	*9 years*
CBCL			
Withdrawn			72
Social problems			72
Thought problems			78
Somatic complaints		Elevated	82
Aggressive behaviors		Elevated	87
Attention problems	Elevated	Elevated	90
Conners CPRS-R:L			
Social problems			69
Oppositional		Elevated	73
Cognitive problems/inattention		Elevated	74
Hyperactivity			80
Psychosomatic		Elevated	90
Vineland Adaptive Behavior Scale			
Communication		65	43
Daily living skills		66	33
Socialization		51	31

Table 15.6 Differential diagnosis.

Variant of normal development
  Slow learner
Developmental
  Intrauterine growth retardation
Psychopathological
  ADHD
  ODD
  Anxiety
  Specific phobia
  Depression
  Bipolar disorder
Neurological
  Migraine headaches
  Anemia
  Sleep disorder
Educational
  Specific learning disorder
  Mild mental retardation
  Cognitive disorder, not otherwise specified

(see Table 15.6). The differential diagnosis includes attention-deficit/hyperactivity disorder (ADHD), oppositional defiant disorder (ODD), anxiety disorder, depressive disorder, a specific learning disorder, mild mental

retardation, and a speech–language disorder. In addition, conditions such as migraine headaches, anemia, or a sleep disorder may also be implicated. Also, it is possible that these behaviors still fall within the range of normal, including what has been previously associated with children described as "slow learners" (e.g., Shepherd, 1976).

VERIFICATION OF INITIAL CAUSE

Results from the initial clinical assessments commented only on the relevance of particular symptoms to lead exposure. From a scientific perspective, this reflects a confirmatory bias, and reflects confusion between a "diagnosis" and a "cause." Although laboratory testing had revealed an elevated level of lead, the clinicians failed to consider the expected level of problems associated with this level of lead exposure and other possible contributing factors. In particular, very little attention was paid to family history and home environment.

Mental disorders, such as ADHD, ODD, or bipolar disorder, reflect a clinically significant behavioral or psychological pattern that is associated with significant impairment or distress (*DSM-IV*, American Psychiatric Association, 1994). It is noted that medical conditions may have a direct etiological relationship to the syndrome or may have a less clear relationship with the behavioral and psychological symptoms (*DSM-IV*, American Psychiatric Association, 1994). In particular, the diagnosis of a behavioral disorder may be used across a wide variety of situations with different etiological factors. After determining that this child demonstrated significant impairment in functioning related to moderate behavioral symptoms and some mild cognitive symptoms, the next question to examine relates to the etiology, or etiologies, of these difficulties. There is evidence of a low-level lead exposure for at least 1-year duration, as well as reports of limited prenatal care and other family variables that are often associated with behavioral disturbances and mild cognitive symptoms.

ADDITIONAL INFORMATION

Neuropsychological examination at age 8 years. Follow-up testing was completed when the child was 8 years old (see Tables 15.4 and 15.5). At that time, he demonstrated average to low-average intellectual abilities with low-average visual-motor skills. Mild-to-marginal impairments also were noted in concentration, spatial recall of tactually learned information, and verbal memory. Behavioral ratings completed by the child's mother were consistent with a wide range of maladaptive behaviors. The psychologist concluded that the child continued to demonstrate inattention and visual–spatial deficits, consistent with lead exposure.

Additional assessment was completed by an occupational medicine physician. At this time, blood lead levels were reported as <5 μg/dl. In terms of interim history, the child had been treated with ferrous sulfate from age 4 years until 7 years, presumably for an iron deficiency, with no clear benefit in terms of amelioration of behavioral symptoms. In general, there was no significant interim medical history, although the child was said to have sustained a wrist fracture on the playground when he was 6 years old. On the neurological examination, there were no abnormal signs. Laboratory evaluation showed slightly reduced white cell count, but the remaining routine laboratory studies were otherwise normal. A urinalysis was also reported as normal. The occupational medicine physician also concluded that the child demonstrated cognitive impairment from lead exposure.

Review of school records. Educationally, the child repeated the second grade and records noted that the primary reason for retention was his lack of completed work and his poor attitude toward school. On report cards, there were multiple teacher comments referring to difficulty maintaining attention and completing work. His mother indicated that he had not received any special education services, explaining that the school told her he was "too smart for special education."

Neuropsychological assessment at age 9 years. The child was seen for a third neuropsychological evaluation at age 9 years when he was in the third grade (see Tables 15.4 and 15.5). Current symptoms at that time included sleeplessness, nose bleeds, poor concentration, mood swings, absent appetite, and angry attitude. His mother said that he typically slept 10 hr a night, but awoke two times during the night, and occasionally took 1 hr to fall asleep in the evening. With regard to appetite, his mother stated that it was "fine until he was four," and that he continued to have limited food preferences, enjoying macaroni and cheese and candy, but hating vegetables. He continued to be relatively small for his age, and his mother expressed ongoing concerns about his growth. He reportedly had few friends and had gotten into several physical fights. His mother stated that he will not listen to her, although he is somewhat more compliant to his father.

Results from neuropsychological testing completed at age 9 years reflected generally average intellectual abilities (see Tables 15.4 and 15.5), with limited variability between individual scores. Academic skills were relatively consistent with measured intellect. Memory testing reflected generally average abilities, with some variability in verbal memory skills. In particular, his verbal memory score decreased in comparison to his earlier examinations because of difficulties on an auditory attention span task. In general, there was some variability in his performance across measures of attention and executive skills. Performance on other measures of language functioning was average, with the exception of a low-average score on a measure of receptive vocabulary. Visual–spatial skills were generally average. Sensorimotor skills were average for age. Behavioral rating scales completed by the child's mother continued to reflect a wide range of maladaptive behaviors. In addition, the child's mother reported significant delays in the development of adaptive skills and continued difficulties at school.

REVISED DIFFERENTIAL DIAGNOSES

Given the generally average scores across a wide variety of measures, one of the first questions that needs to be answered is the following: Does this child's functioning differ significantly from what would be normally expected? This question relates to diagnosis. Although the child had demonstrated some improvement in intellectual scores over repeat examinations, there were continued signs of subtle difficulties with attention regulation and increasingly marked impairments in behavioral control. He was reported to have difficulties with behavioral control both at home and at school, fulfilling the *DSM-IV* criteria for significant disruption in functioning (American Psychiatric Association, 1994). As to the specific nature of the pattern of difficulties reflected in his examination results, the primary focus appears to be on behavioral issues, as well as some subtle findings of cognitive impairment. Over the intervening years, academic skills appeared to have made age-expected gains, ruling out the possibility of a specific learning disorder. In addition, intellectual test scores improved, ruling out the possibility of mild mental retardation. According to his mother's report, there were no significant symptoms of anxiety, although she continued to describe his mood as "irritable" and noted significant mood swings. The differential diagnosis continued to include ADHD, ODD, conduct disorder, bipolar disorder, or other nonspecified cognitive disorder.

FINAL DIAGNOSIS

This child's pattern of cognitive and behavioral symptoms is most consistent with ADHD, primarily inattentive and mild.

VERIFICATION OF THE FINAL DIAGNOSIS

According to the criteria established by the *DSM-IV* (American Psychiatric Association, 1994), this child demonstrates a significant number of symptoms associated with an attentional disorder (see Table 15.7). In particular, he demonstrates a wide range of symptoms of inattention which have interfered with his functioning at school, at home, and with friends. Common associated features of ADHD include low frustration tolerance, temper outbursts, mood lability, and rejection by peers (American Psychiatric Association, 1994). The symptoms have been present since early childhood and have remained fairly constant despite changes in his affect or mood.

Richardson et al. (2000) have also developed a set of criteria for verifying a clinical diagnosis, which can be applied to this case. The diagnosis of ADHD is adequate because it encompasses the majority of his symptoms and signs. ADHD is associated with both cognitive, behavioral, mood, and social impairments. Some of the somatic symptoms, such as decreased appetite and shortness of stature, are also specifically found in children with chronic lead exposure.

The diagnosis of ADHD is coherent because it captures this child's difficulties with sustained attention and the symptoms of behavioral dyscontrol. Moreover, the absence of continued laboratory abnormalities or overt neurological signs on examination is also consistent with a diagnosis of ADHD.

Table 15.7 DSM-IV (1994) criteria for attention-deficit/hyperactivity disorder.

A. Either (1) or (2)

   (1) Six (or more) of the following symptoms of inattention have persisted for at least 6 months to a degree that is maladaptive and inconsistent with developmental level:

   Inattention

     (a) Often fails to give close attention to details or makes careless mistakes in schoolwork, work, or other activities

     (b) Often has difficulty sustaining attention in tasks or play activities

     (c) Often does not seem to listen when spoken to directly

     (d) Often does not follow through on instructions and fails to finish schoolwork, chores, or duties in the workplace (not due to oppositional behavior or failure to understand instructions)

     (e) Often has difficulty organizing tasks and activities

     (f) Often avoids, dislikes, or is reluctant to engage in tasks that require sustained mental effort (such as schoolwork or homework)

     (g) Often loses things necessary for tasks or activities (e.g., toys, school assignments, pencils, books, or tools)

     (h) Is often easily distracted by extraneous stimuli

     (i) Is often forgetful in daily activities

   (2) Six (or more) of the following symptoms of hyperactivity–impulsivity have persisted for at least 6 months to a degree that is maladaptive and inconsistent with developmental level:

   Hyperactivity

     (a) Often fidgets with hands or feet or squirms in seat

     (b) Often leaves seat in classroom or other situations in which remaining seated is expected

     (c) Often runs about or climbs excessively in situations in which it is inappropriate (in adolescents or adults, may be limited to subjective feelings of restlessness)

     (d) Often has difficulty playing or engaging in leisure activities quietly

     (e) Is often "on the go" or acts as if "driven by a motor"

     (f) Often talks excessively

   Impulsivity

     (a) Often blurts out answers before questions have been completed

     (b) Often has difficulty awaiting turn

     (c) Often interrupts or intrudes on others (e.g., butts into conversations or games)

B. Some hyperactive–impulsive or inattentive symptoms that caused impairment were present before age 7 years.

C. Some impairment from the symptoms is present in two or more settings (e.g., at school [or work] and at home).

D. There must be clear evidence of clinically significant impairment in social, academic, or occupational functioning.

E. The symptoms do not occur exclusively during the course of a pervasive developmental disorder, schizophrenia, or other psychotic disorder and are not better accounted for by another mental disorder (e.g., mood disorder, anxiety disorder, dissociative disorder, or a personality disorder).

ADHD provides the best fit (i.e., primacy) to the specific pattern of neurobehavioral strengths and weaknesses for this child. Fluctuations in attention can also affect efficiency in memory and learning, thereby significantly impairing a child's performance in school. The mood disorders typically have more of a waxing and waning presentation than was observed here, whereas symptoms associated with ADHD tend to be more constant, as was true of this child.

A diagnosis of ADHD is *parsimonious* in that it provides explanation for the range of symptoms reported. Any alternative to ADHD would need to reflect multiple diagnoses (e.g., language processing problem plus a behavioral disorder). In addition, although the diagnostic criteria for ADHD require the presence of symptoms in more than one setting, it also recognizes that the severity of symptoms manifested may vary based on the unique environmental demands. For example, it is common for children with ADHD to have particularly prominent symptoms at school, during classes that require sustained attention, although overt indicators of inattention may be less obvious when working in a highly structured situation or in one-on-one activities, such as during formal testing (*DSM-IV*, American Psychiatric Association, 1994). The diagnosis is robust in that attentional deficits were shown to be a core problem consistently across three separate examinations. Finally, the diagnosis of ADHD is predictive.

Particularly common in boys (*DSM-IV*, American Psychiatric Association, 1994), ADHD is often first diagnosed when a child is in elementary school, although symptoms can be reported in early childhood (e.g., preschool years) as well. Children with ADHD often continue to demonstrate ongoing symptoms through early adolescence (*DSM-IV*, American Psychiatric Association, 1994).

FINAL CAUSE/ETIOLOGY

It is most likely that this child's difficulties are the result of multiple etiological factors. Lead exposure is one of them. As noted in the *DSM-IV* (American Psychiatric Association, 1994), a history of neurotoxin exposure (e.g., lead poisoning) can be associated with ADHD. Also, and with respect to lead poisoning, the published literature also suggests relatively enduring patterns of deficits (e.g., Bellinger, 2004; Tong, 1998). In addition to lead exposure, there appears to be a family history of some similar behavioral difficulties, suggesting a genetic or familial predisposition or other common environmental factor influencing the behavior of multiple family members. Research has supported a familial pattern for ADHD, with first-degree biological relatives of children with ADHD often having similar problems (*DSM-IV*, American Psychiatric Association, 1994). Moreover, records suggest that the child had an early history of iron deficiency, as well as limited prenatal care. Nutritional factors are also a likely contributor to this child's clinical presentation.

As previously noted, mental disorders, such as ADHD, reflect a clinically significant behavioral or psychological pattern that is associated with significant impairment or distress, which may have a direct medical etiology (*DSM-IV*, American Psychiatric Association, 1994). Nevertheless, the diagnosis of a behavioral disorder may be used across a wide variety of situations with different etiological factors. After determining that this child demonstrated significant impairment in functioning related to inattention and moderate behavioral symptoms, the next task is to examine the etiology of these various difficulties.

VERIFICATION OF FINAL CAUSE/ETIOLOGY

Did lead play a role in the child's neurobehavioral impairments? From a neuropsychological viewpoint, it is most likely that there were multiple contributions to this child's behavioral difficulties. On the basis of history, symptom course, and neuropsychological test results, exposure to lead is likely one of the etiological factors involved in this child's presentation. As the child's blood lead levels declined, there appeared to be some modest improvement in general intellectual and verbal skills, with a continued deterioration of behavioral functioning. Although lead exposure likely made some contribution, there appears to be a strong environmental or genetic predisposition for learning and behavioral difficulties. The child's siblings did not have any discernible lead exposure, yet school records indicate a history of similar behaviors and average to below-average grades.

In terms of objective criteria for verifying cause such as those developed by Hill (1965) (see Appendix), the timing and onset of the child's difficulties are relatively consistent with the child's exposure to lead. Children under the age of 5 years are at highest risk for lead exposure (Banks, Ferretti, & Shucard, 1997). Average blood lead levels appear somewhat higher in children aged 1 to 2, in comparison to older children (Pirkle et al., 1998). Behaviors of early childhood, including crawling and mouthing of objects, increase the risk for ingestion of lead-contaminated dust (Bellinger, 2004). Research has suggested that there is a "time lag" between blood lead levels and neurodevelopmental sequelae, with previous blood lead levels often exhibiting a stronger association to a child's current neurodevelopmental functioning than current blood lead levels (Bellinger et al., 1991; Bellinger, Stiles, & Needleman, 1992). This may reflect the time required for lead to exert an effect on central nervous system processes, or it may also reflect that lead tends to affect high-order cognitive functions that do not fully emerge until later in life (CDC, 2004).

For this child, there is no clear onset for either lead exposure or neurodevelopmental symptoms, although there is evidence of exposure. The first confirmation of lead exposure occurred when the child was 3 years old, and blood lead levels suggest that lead exposure continued until he was at least 4 years of age. Cognitive functions and developmental status were not evaluated until he was 4 years old. Although this child appropriately achieved early developmental milestones, he appears to have had significant difficulty developing appropriate levels of behavioral control and sustained attention. With very young children, it is often difficult to establish an accurate "baseline" on which to compare potential effects from lead exposure. The acquisition of developmental milestones is a very gross indicator of neurobehavioral functioning, and is not sufficiently sensitive to reflect issues associated with low levels of exposure. Symptoms of weight loss, shortness of stature, and headaches, however, are consistent with an ongoing, low-level exposure to lead.

There is a substantial body of literature on the effects of lead in children demonstrating its role as a developmental toxicant, although the magnitude of the effect is small and the research is limited by differences in measurement tools and a plethora of uncontrolled confounding variables. In research that adjusted for confounding factors, studies have consistently found a relationship between lead exposure and decreased scores on intellectual measures (Dietrich, 2000). The effect of low-level lead exposure, however, tends to be small in magnitude. For example, based on meta-analytic studies from cross-sectional and prospective data, it is estimated that an increase in blood lead levels from 10 to 20 μg/dl is associated with a decrease of two points in full scale IQ score (World Health Organization, 1995). The most often cited longitudinal studies have been conducted in Boston, USA; Cincinnati and Cleveland, USA; Port Pirie and Sydney, Australia; and Yugoslavia (Koller, Brown, Spurgeon, & Levy, 2004; Ris, Dietrich, Succop, Berger, & Bornschein, 2004). Specifically, in the Port Pirie cohort study, which was initiated in 1979 and monitored 375 children over time, the full scale IQ declined an average of 3.0 points for an increase in lifetime average blood lead concentration from 10 to 20 μg/dl (Tong, Baghurst, Sawyer, Burns, & McMichael, 1998). In the prospective Boston study, increased blood lead levels were associated with lowered intellectual and academic achievement scores (Bellinger et al., 1992). Despite information from studies just listed, the accounting of potential confounding variables continues to be one of the greatest areas of controversy in the assessment of the effect of lead exposure on children (Dietrich et al., 2004). The NHANES, for instance, yielded one of the largest sample sizes (4,853 children) but lacked information on key confounding variables, such as home environment and maternal intellectual level, seriously limiting the usefulness of the results (Koller et al., 2004).

Nevertheless, epidemiological studies have shown a consistent association between increased neurodevelopmental effects and increased lead concentrations. For example, analysis of the NHANES III data discussed previously showed an association between increased blood lead levels and decreased reading scores, specifically for children with low blood lead levels (<10 μg/dl; Lanphear, Dietrich, Auinger, & Cox, 2000). Moreover, a dose-dependent relationship between increased blood lead levels and decreased cognitive function has also been extended to a group of children whose peak blood lead levels remained below 10 μg/dl (Canfield et al., 2003). The association between increased lead levels and increased neurobehavioral deficits is seen in indices of behavioral observations in addition to formal psychometric results. Scalp hair specimens were taken from 277 first-grade students with hair lead concentrations ranging from <1 to 11.3 ppm. There was a strong dose–response relationship between levels of hair lead and negative teacher ratings for attention-deficit behaviors, even after controlling for age, ethnicity, gender, and socioeconomic status (Tuthill, 1996).

Although it is generally accepted that increased lead concentration is associated with decreased intellectual scores, the specific bases for these deficits have not been fully determined. Although findings across studies have been fairly consistent, there has been controversy regarding the idea of a "behavioral signature" for lead. In general, the behavioral domains typically reported as vulnerable to lead have been attention, executive function, cognitive efficiency, visual-motor reasoning skills, vestibular-proprioceptive control, and social behavior (Chiodo, Jacobson, & Jacobson, 2004; Hansen, Trillingsgaard, Beese, Lyngbye, & Grandjean, 1989; Winneke, Brockhaus, Ewers, Kramer, & Neuf, 1990). This pattern has been reported to be present even in children with very low blood lead levels. For example, in a sample of children with a lifetime average blood lead level of approximately 7.2 μg/dl, deficits in spatial working memory, spatial memory span, and executive functions were reported (Canfield, Gendle, & Cory-Slechta, 2004). Some inconsistency persists, nevertheless, between reported specific findings, with other studies suggesting that verbal skills are more impaired than visual-motor skills (Hansen et al.). For example, in a longitudinal study, which assessed children at ages 6.5, 11, and 15 years, it was reported that children with higher lead levels at age 15 had reduced growth in verbal comprehension abilities, with no effect noted on perceptual organization scores (Coscia, Ris, Succop, & Dietrich, 2003). Similarly, in a group of children with low-level lead exposure (mean 4.3 μg/dl, upper 95 percentile value 8.9 μg/dl), there was an association between level of lead exposure and deficits in attention, but no relationship with performance on measures of visual perception, visual memory, finger-tapping, or reaction time (Walkowiak et al., 1998). Nevertheless, other studies have failed to find a relationship between elevated blood lead levels in early childhood and language impairment (Ernhart & Greene, 1990).

Some people have suggested that the discrepancies between studies in identifying a behavioral signature may be the result of different periods of vulnerability for different cognitive domains or "endpoints" (Bellinger, 2004). It is theorized that different cognitive domains are more or less susceptible to the effects of lead at different points during development. Discrepancies between studies may reflect differences in the age of the children and their age at exposure. For example, Rice (1990, 1992a) used a primate model to demonstrate that the timing of developmental lead exposure affected the nature and severity of cognitive tasks. Similarly, Morgan et al. (2001) found that the timing of lead exposure resulted in different types of attentional problems in rats. Gilbert, Mack, and Lasley (1999) noted that in rats lead exposure restricted to the lactational period was less disruptive to long-term potentiation in the dentate gyrus than continuous exposure to lead beginning around birth or weaning.

In terms of dose–response relationships, epidemiological studies have documented a consistent dose-dependent relationship, but the magnitude of the effect tends to be small statistically. As a result, for a given child, it can be difficult to differentiate dose–response changes from changes associated with error variance.

For the child in the current *case presentation*, his highest blood lead level was 23 µg/dl, and it eventually fell to less than 5 µg/dl. Chelation was not used, although nutritional iron supplementation was provided for several years. Over the course of time, he demonstrated a slight improvement in his intellectual test scores, which would be consistent with a dose–response change. There was also some improvement in his symptoms of stomachache, although he continued to have a limited appetite. Behavioral problems appeared to persist and intensify over time.

Did removal from exposure to lead modify the adverse effects in the *case presentation*? Adults with occupational exposure to lead can demonstrate a reversal of effects of peripheral nervous system after cessation of exposure (See *lead in adults* in the present chapter and *lead* in chapter 10, volume II). However, the central nervous system effects associated with childhood lead exposure appear to be more enduring despite removal from further exposure (Bellinger, 2004; Tong, 1998). Nevertheless, there does seem to be some amelioration in effect that appears to be interactive with environmental factors. For children in higher socioeconomic groups, for instance, there appears to be some reversal of neurobehavioral effects with reduction of lead levels in early childhood (Bellinger, Leviton, & Sloman, 1990). Similarly, for animals, long-term deficits in spatial learning associated with lead exposure were at least partially reversible by provision of an enriched environment (Guilarte, Toscano, McGlothan, & Weaver, 2003). In contrast, lead-exposed young rats raised in an impoverished environment demonstrated spatial learning deficits and decreased neurotrophic factor gene expression in the hippocampus when compared with rats raised in an enriched environment. The latter condition was reported to be associated with a protective effect against lead toxicity (Schneider, Lee, Anderson, Zuck, & Lidsky, 2001). In addition, nutritional variables may also have a mediating influence for the reversal of lead exposure effects. Ruff, Bijur, Markowitz, Ma, & Rosen (1993) noted that there was an improvement, particularly in perceptual-motor performance scores, associated with decreases in blood lead levels for children that were iron sufficient at the onset, whereas there was no relationship in iron-deficient children.

Evidence about the persistence of central nervous system effects has been found in research on the effects of chelation in children. Current treatment guidelines indicate the use of inpatient chelation therapy in children if blood lead levels are greater than 70 µg/dl or if the child exhibits symptoms of clinical encephalopathy. Chelation therapy has also been suggested when blood lead levels fall between 45 and 70 µg/dl (Committee on Drugs. American Academy of Pediatrics, 1995). Chelation therapy, however, is generally not recommended for children with moderate elevations of blood lead. Although blood lead levels may decline following chelation treatment, this decline is not always associated with improvements in cognitive or behavioral functioning. For example, in a group of children with moderate exposure levels, the addition of chelation therapy to abatement interventions lowered blood lead levels, but was not associated with improvement in cognitive functioning (Ruff, Markowitz, Bijur, & Rosen, 1996). In another group, for children with blood lead levels between 20 and 44 μg/dl, chelation therapy with succimer was able to lower blood lead levels for 6 months, but there was no improvement found in cognitive, behavioral, or neuromotor skills over that same time (Dietrich et al., 2004; Rogan et al., 2001). Some have even suggested that succimer impairs cognitive performance in children (Liu et al., 2002). Moreover, in children with moderate blood lead levels, there appears to be no benefit from treatment with succimer on growth parameters, and there is even some suggestion of adverse effects from such treatment (Peterson et al., 2004).

There were possible slight improvements in intellectual scores following lowered blood lead levels in the current *case presentation*, but other central nervous system symptoms persisted despite these lowered levels. In particular, behavioral symptoms appeared to continue and even intensify over time. Although the findings in this area are not consistent with Hill's (1965) criteria, they are consistent with the published scientific literature that has reported the persistence of central nervous system effects in children exposed to low levels of lead.

What about the biological plausibility that lead caused the impairments found in the *case presentation*? Lead has been found to be disruptive to every organ system. As a result, it can produce varied and diverse neurodevelopmental effects. Silbergeld (1992) has suggested that lead can act as both a neurodevelopmental toxicant, interfering with the "hard wiring" and differentiation of the central nervous system (nonreversible or "structural" changes), and as a neuropharmacological toxicant, interfering with the ionic mechanisms of neurotransmission (reversible or "functional" changes). The direct effects of lead are reported to include apoptosis, excitotoxicity, influences on neurotransmitter storage and release processes, mitochondria, second messengers, cerebrovascular endothelial cells, and both astroglia and oligodendroglia (Lidsky & Schneider, 2003). Although there are multiple mechanisms for injury to the nervous system, lead's ability to compete with and act as a substitution for calcium, and perhaps zinc, has been reported to be common factors in lead's toxicity (Lidsky & Schneider, 2003). In particular, it has been suggested that lead affects two specific protein complexes: protein kinase C and the N-methyl-D-aspartate subtype of glutamate receptors, both of which are involved in learning and cognitive functions (Marchetti, 2003).

Indirect effects of lead include disruption of heme synthesis, induction of anemia, and disruption of thyroid hormone transport into the brain (Lidsky & Schneider, 2003). For example, increased lead exposure was associated with difficulties in maintaining adequate serum erythropoietin concentrations (Graziano, Slavkovich, Liu, Factor-Litvak, & Todd, 2004). In a group of individuals with normal MRI examinations of the brain, those with elevated blood lead levels demonstrated a significant reduction in the N-acetylaspartate/ creatine and phosphocreatine ratios in frontal gray matter in comparison with the non-lead-exposed controls. There was no difference in white matter measures (Trope, Lopez-Villegas, Cecil, & Lenkinski, 2001). Lead-induced damage occurs primarily in the prefrontal cerebral cortex, hippocampus, and cerebellum (Finkelstein, Markowitz, & Rosen, 1998), which is consistent with the clinical symptoms of disruption in attention, learning difficulties, and motor coordination.

Research has also suggested that some individuals may be genetically more vulnerable to the effects of lead. Three genes have been identified that may play a role in lead neurotoxicity: the ALAD genes (codes—aminolevulinic acid dehydratase), the vitamin D receptor gene, hemochromatosis gene coding for a defective protein, known as HFE (Lidsky & Schneider, 2003). For example, children with the ALAD-2 genotype had significantly higher blood lead levels than noncarriers (Perez-Bravo et al., 2004). Nutrition can also be a significant moderating effect. For example, children consuming diets low in calcium and iron may be prone to greater absorption of lead than children consuming well-rounded diets (Wigg, 2001). Children appear to be at greater risk for nutritional deficiencies (e.g., iron, calcium) than adults (Bellinger, 2004).

There is evidence that lead can pass through the blood–brain barrier, as reflected in the strong correlations obtained between maternal and cord blood lead levels (e.g., Al-Saleh, Khalil, & Taylor, 1995; Marchetti, 2003). The mechanism for transport of lead through the blood–brain barrier may be due to its ability to substitute for calcium ions (Lidsky & Schneider, 2003). Lead disrupts the structural components of the blood–brain barrier by injury to astrocytes with secondary damage to the endothelial microvasculature (Finkelstein, Markowitz, & Rosen, 1998). This provides further evidence for lead's ability to disrupt brain functioning.

In addition, research has supported a biological explanation for the finding of greater vulnerability in children. The half-life of lead in blood is approximately 35 days, while in the brain it is roughly 2 years, and reportedly decades in bone (Lidsky & Schneider, 2003). Children are more vulnerable to damage from lead exposure than are adults because a greater proportion of lead is absorbed from the GI tract, a greater proportion of circulating lead gains access to the brain in children under the age of 5 years, and the developing nervous system is more vulnerable to the adverse effects of lead (Lidsky & Schneider, 2003). With regard to the special vulnerability of the developing central nervous system, children under the age of 3 years are presumed to be at increased risk for effects of lead than are older children due to the presence of immature capillaries, resulting in increased permeability of the blood–brain barrier, cerebral edema, and reduced cortical perfusion (Goyer, 1993).

There is a wide body of literature demonstrating the effects of lead exposure in a variety of animal models. Animal studies have also demonstrated effects in paradigms of reversal learning, delayed response disinhibition, and perseveration (Banks et al., 1997). Animal studies have suggested that complex cognitive tasks, particularly ones that require shifting of cognitive set, are sensitive to the effects of lead (Rice, 1992b). Recall of spatial information and tasks requiring delay of or inhibition of a response have also been sensitive to the effects of lead in animals (Munoz, Garbe, Lilienthal, & Winneke, 1989; Rice, 1992a).

In summary, this review indicates that most of the major, objective criteria for verifying a cause are met in the case presentation, including presence of an animal model, biological plausibility, consistency of a dose–response relationship found in the literature, support for risk based on sound epidemiological studies, and appropriate timing and onset of symptoms. In addition to determining that lead exposure was a causal factor for some of the symptoms, this review also highlighted the multifactorial nature of assessing children, noting potential causal contributions from other genetic and environmental influences.

Discussion

Lead exposure in children has been a major issue in public health during the later half of the 20th century. Although cases of lead poisoning in children were first described in Australia in the late 19th century (Gibson, Love, Hardine, Bencroft, & Turner, 1892), the potential impact of lead exposure on children's long-term learning and behavioral functioning was not appreciated until the mid-20th century (Byers & Lord, 1943).

Blood lead levels have been the most often used measure of exposure (De Gennaro, 2002). The clinical picture of "classic lead encephalopathy" was initially reported to occur with lead levels greater than 60 μg/dl (Weitzman & Glotzer, 1992), and blood lead levels of 70–80 μg/dl or higher are associated with a serious risk of encephalopathy in children (Agency for toxic substances and disease registry [ATSDR], 1999). The clinical consequences of classic lead encephalopathy associated with excessive lead levels (>60 μg/dl) are indisputable, with a clear progression of neurologic symptoms and signs including ataxia, lethargy, seizures, coma, and death. Blood lead levels have been described as "moderate" if falling above 30 μg/dl (American Academy of Pediatrics, 1998) or between 25 and 55 μg/dl (Ruff et al., 1996), and as "low" if falling between 10 and 25 μg/dl (Weitzman & Glotzer, 1992). There remains some debate if blood lead levels that are less than 10 μg/dl reflect an "elevated" level of lead, and some have argued that there is no threshold for the toxic effects of lead. In 1986, the World Health Organization set the acceptable lead limit at 20 μg/dl. The Centers for Disease Control revised the intervention level of lead limit for children downward to 10 μg/dl in 1991 (Centers for Disease Control and Prevention, 1991).

As noted earlier, there is ongoing debate about the potential effects on children from very low levels of lead exposure (<10 μg/dl). Koller and colleagues (2004) remarked that the magnitude of cognitive effects in humans is small on a population basis, and some well-designed studies have failed to find any significant cognitive effects. The association between lead exposure and intellectual functioning for lower levels of exposure has been described as borderline (Winneke et al., 1990), with meta-analyses suggesting that an average IQ decrement of two to three points is associated with every 10 μg/dl increase of blood lead (Winneke, 1995; World Health Organization, 1995). Nevertheless, there has been some research that suggests that a reduction in lead levels in early childhood might be associated with only partial reversal of adverse neurobehavioral effects already acquired (Bellinger et al., 1990; Tong, Baghurst, McMichael, Sawyer, & Mudge, 1996; Tong et al., 1998).

Environmental exposures from contaminated soil or dust in a home often result in ongoing or "chronic" lead exposure, with blood lead levels remaining elevated across several measurements over time. Chronic lead poisoning in adults is associated with behavioral changes, nephritis, anemia, abdominal pain, blood pressure abnormalities, and peripheral neuropathy (Banks et al., 1997; Koller et al., 2004). Frank anemia typically is present only when blood lead levels remain elevated for prolonged periods of time (Agency for toxic substances and disease registry [ATSDR], 1999). For adults, neurobehavioral toxicity from occupational lead exposure has not consistently been found when blood lead levels are less than 40 µg/dl, whereas effects for children are reported, even at very low levels, such as less than 10 µg/dl (Winneke & Kramer, 1997).

Central nervous system effects from exposure to lead are more prominent in children than in adults (Bellinger, 2004). In general, lead exposure is believed to be associated with cognitive, behavioral, and perceptual-motor sequelae for children (Hansen et al., 1989; Winneke et al., 1990). In addition to these cognitive effects, an association between lead exposure and physical development has been reported. There are reports, for instance, that increased lead exposure during development is associated with decreased height in comparison to normal expectations (Rahman, Maqbool, & Zuberi, 2002).

In the United States, based on the data from the NHANES, the blood lead levels in children have continued to decline since first measured in 1976. In the 1976–1980 data collection, approximately 88% (95% confidence interval: 83.8–92.6) of children aged 1–5 years had blood lead levels greater than 10 µg/dl, with a geometric mean for the sample falling at 14.9 µg/dl (95% confidence interval: 14.1–15.8). In comparison, from 1999 to 2000, only 2.2% of preschool children had blood lead levels greater than 10 µg/dl, with a geometric mean for the sample falling to 2.23 µg/dl (95% confidence interval: 1.99–2.49; www.cdc.gov). Grosse Matte, Schwartz, and Jackson (2002) estimated that the economic benefit for each year's cohort of 2-year-old children was between $110 and $319 billion as a result of these declines. Moreover, although there have been significant reductions in overall blood lead levels in the United States, the subgroups that continue to be at increased risk include children who are less than 5 years of age, African-American children, and children who live in central cities (Banks et al., 1997). Also, there is a higher prevalence of increased blood lead levels in children from lower socioeconomic status, immigrants, and refuges (Geltman, Brown, & Cochran, 2001). For example, in 2003, approximately 6.3% of children below 6 years of age in Detroit, Michigan, had blood lead levels greater than 10 µg/dl (Wayne State University, College of Urban Labor & Metropolitan Affairs, 2002–2003). During the same time period, approximately 29% of children aged 6 months to 5 years in New Orleans, Louisiana, had blood lead levels greater than 10 μg/dl (Rabito, Shorter, & White, 2003). In contrast, the average blood lead levels for children in England (UK) and some parts of Europe, such as Sweden and Germany, are approximately 3 μg/dl (Koller et al., 2004). In contrast, children in developing countries, such as South Africa and Bangladesh, are at increased risk for lead exposure (Falk, 2003; Fewtrell, Pruss-Ustun, Landrigan, & Ayuso-Mateos, 2004; see Table 15.8). But for many countries, there are no data available about the prevalence of childhood lead exposure (Falk, 2003). Therefore, the actual exposure to children could be much higher than indicated by the few surveys reported, especially since such surveys are often done in places where efforts have already been made to reduce the amount to which children might be exposed.

Blood lead levels in children are influenced by multiple factors. Age at time of exposure, for instance, is a potentially significant moderating variable. In general, postnatal blood lead levels often increase when children reach 6 months of age, and presumably this is due to the onset of greater crawling and coordinated hand-to-mouth behaviors, and these levels began to fall after the age of 2 years (Ris et al., 2004). There has been some evidence to suggest that children between the ages of 18 months and 5 years may be most vulnerable to demonstrating effects from lead exposure. For example, a longitudinal study in Mexico assessed children at 6-month intervals from 36 months of age to 60 months of age (Schnaas et al., 2000). Mean blood lead levels were calculated for the children at three different age periods: 6–18 months, 24–36 months, and 42–54 months. Results were analyzed with a repeated measures ANCOVA, controlling for 5-minute Apgar scores, birth weight, birth order, sex, socioeconomic level, maternal IQ, and maximum maternal educational level. There was not a significant relationship between a measure of global cognitive functioning and blood lead levels at 6–18 months. Nevertheless, increasing blood lead levels at 24–36 months were associated with decreased global cognitive functioning at 48 and 54 months of age. Increased blood lead levels at 42–54 months were also associated with decreased scores on a measure of global cognitive functioning at 54 months of age. The authors suggested that the pattern of associations reflected a maximum association between blood lead levels and cognitive functioning 1–3 years later, identifying 4–5 years of age as a critical period for the manifestations of earlier elevated blood lead levels (Schnaas et al., 2000). In another study that followed children prospectively from birth, Bellinger et al. (1991, 1992) found that blood lead levels at 24 months of age were predictive of decreased intellectual performance for as long as until 12 years of age. Blood lead levels before and after 2 years of age did not have the same predictive power. Moreover, Pocock, Smith, and Baghurst (1994) reported that elevated blood lead levels in children aged 1–3 years appeared to be most predictive of the development of problems later in childhood.

Gender and socioeconomic factors are also moderating factors. For example, data from the Cincinnati Lead Study (Ris et al., 2004) reflected a significant gender interaction, suggesting that males are more vulnerable to

Table 15.8 A sampling of average international blood lead levels (BLL, μg/dl) for children.

Citation	Country	Ages of children (years)	BLL geometric mean	BLL range	Children with >10 μg/dl (percent)
CDC, 2004	United States	1–5	2.2		2
Wayne State University, 2002–2003	Detroit, USA	<6			6
Rabito, Shorter, & White, 2003	New Orleans, USA	0.5–5			29
Geltman, Brown, & Cochran, 2001	Refugees/USA	1–11			11
Golding, Smith, Delves, & Taylor, 1998	United Kingdom	2.5	3.44		
Kordas et al., 2004	Mexico	6–8	11.5		50
Schnaas et al., 2004	Mexico City, Mexico	2 10	10.1 6.4		
Espinoza et al., 2003	Callao and Lima, Peru	9.9		1–64	64
Jarosinska, Peddada, & Rogan, 2004	Poland	2–7	6.3	0.6–48.0	13
Falk, 2003	India	<12			50
Gao et al., 2001	Wixo City, China	1–5			27
Li, Zhenyia, Lon, & Hanyun, 2004	Zhejiang, China	3–6	9.5[a]	2.5–43.7	29
Ruangkanchanasetr & Suepiantham, 2002	Bangkok, Thailand	6	5.03		
Lee, Lee, Yoo, & Kim, 2002	Korea Industrial Suburban	8–11 8–11	5.41 4.93		
Rahman, Maqbool, & Zuberi, 2002	Karachi, Pakistan	6–10			80
Khan, Khan, Ghani, & Khurshid, 2001	Karachi, Pakistan	1–12	7.9		25.2
Mathee et al., 2002	Johannesburg, South Africa	School-aged			78
von Schirnding et al., 2003	South Africa Mining town Control town	6–10 6–19	16 13	9–27.5 6–22	98 85
Kaiser et al., 2001	Dhaka, Bangladesh	4–12			87

[a] Arithmetic mean.

the effects of lead on attention than are females. In this study, there was also a significant interaction for gender and lead exposure on tasks utilizing visual–constructional skills, with males demonstrating greater vulnerability than females. The authors also noted a trend toward a significant interaction on intellectual and academic tasks with children from lower socioeconomic groups appearing more vulnerable to lead exposure than children from higher socioeconomic groups (Ris et al.). Lastly, there also appear to be seasonal variations in blood lead levels, with children often demonstrating increased blood lead levels during warmer months (Jarosinska, Peddada, & Rogan, 2004; Haley & Talbot, 2004). This may reflect increased exposure to contaminated soil when playing outside.

For children, the primary sources of lead exposure are from deteriorating lead-based paint, lead-contaminated dust, and lead-contaminated soil (U.S. EPA, 2005). As noted above, there appears to have been a decline since the 1970s and 1980s in the prevalence of lead poisoning in children, at least in the United States, and this decline is believed to be at least partially attributable to the discontinuation of leaded gasoline, reductions of lead in drinking water due to replacement of lead water pipes and water tanks, increased air pollution controls for lead, and bans or limitations on lead used in consumer products like paint (U.S. EPA, 2005). Indoor floor dust is the primary source for a young child's (up until age 2 years) total lead intake (Institute for Environment and Health, 1998), with lead-contaminated windowsills in older homes a more common source of lead intake for older children (Koller et al., 2004). More recently, concerns related to lead exposure from candy and children's jewelry have also been reported (Medlin, 2004; Van Arsdale, Leiker, Kohn, Merritt, & Horowitz, 2004). Candy may be contaminated from lead by certain ingredients (e.g., chili powder, tamarind) from improper drying, storing, or grinding of the ingredients, as well as from the ink on the wrappers that leaches into the candy (CDC, 2005; www.cdc.gov/nceh/lead/faq/candy.htm). With regard to children's jewelry, the U.S. Consumer Product Safety Commission (2005; www.cpsc.gov/cpscpub/prerel/ prhtml05/05097.html) currently recommends that pieces of jewelry be less than 600 ppm lead, noting that if the accessible lead in the jewelry exceeds 175 μg/dl, it could result in elevated blood lead levels in children, particularly if the children place the jewelry in their mouths.

It is estimated that young children ingest approximately 50 mg/day of soil (Stanek & Calabrese, 1995). Blood lead levels appear to peak in children at about 2 years of age, when hand-to-mouth behaviors are common (Lanphear et al., 2002). In particular, children with pica, the habit of eating nonnutritious substances, are at increased risk for lead exposure. Children with pica may ingest more than 5 g/day of soil (Mielke & Reagan, 1998). There has been some evidence to suggest that iron deficiency increases a child's desire for nonfood items (Buchanan, 1999; Singhi, Ravishaker, Singhi, & Nath, 2003) and that iron deficiency is desired at the same time and associated with increased risk for lead poisoning (Kwong, Friella, & Semba, 2004). Severe iron deficiency in infants and young children has also been associated with delays in mental and motor development (Cook & Lynch, 1986;

Lozoff, Wolf, & Jiminez, 1996). Moreover, although pica appears to remit after iron therapy, these mental and motor deficits appear to persist despite extended dietary supplementation (Federman, Kirsner, & Federman, 1997; Lozoff et al.).

Although blood lead testing can confirm an ongoing exposure to lead, it is not sufficient to determine the influence of that exposure on a child's cognitive and behavioral functioning. It is rare that a child's cognitive functioning and behavior is unifactorial, and the result of a single causal event. As a result, one of the tasks of the clinician is to determine and assess the relative contributions of a variety of potential causal variables. Moreover, the neuropsychological symptoms of lead exposure can often appear nonspecific and somewhat subtle. For example, as illustrated in a case study from the literature (see Table 15.9; Chin & Charlton, 2004), even children with marked elevations of blood lead may present with only neurodevelopmental symptoms and no clear "medical" or somatic signs. As Chin and Charlton (2004) noted, children with blood lead concentrations greater than 70 μg/dl are generally considered to be a "medical emergency," presenting with symptoms such as lethargy, constipation, and vomiting. When blood lead levels are in excess of 100 μg/dl, signs such as ataxia, seizures, or coma may be present. Nevertheless, in children with blood lead concentrations greater than 100 μg/dl, approximately 50% of them present without any medical signs (Chin & Charlton, 2004).

With the discovery of an elevated blood lead level, there is a tendency to ascribe all of a child's current difficulties to lead exposure. For the family in the *case presentation*, when elevated levels of lead were detected during community-based routine screening, behaviors that had typically not generated concern, became identified by the family as "sequelae" of lead exposure. During the initial evaluation, there was a cursory review of family history, but no attempt to discuss the likely contributions of family history or other environmental factors. Moreover, there was no discussion of the difficulties in applying epidemiological and group research data to an individual person. In particular, the relative influence of low levels of lead exposure was not presented with regard to its explanatory power. Even in larger studies, the influence of maternal intellectual status has a greater contribution to the child's ability level than do the effects associated with elevated lead levels. For example, current lead exposure accounts for a very small percentage of variance in cognitive ability (1–4%), whereas social and parenting factors account for at least 40% of the variance (Koller et al. 2004; Weiss, 2000). In the Cincinnati Lead Study (Ris et al., 2004), the best model only accounted for 21% of the variance of cognitive scores, suggesting that factors not represented in the study might have had greater contribution to the cognitive factors measured than did lead itself. Moreover, this issue is also seen in the findings related to behavioral disturbance. Similarly, in the Yugoslavia Prospective Lead Study, a measure of lifetime lead exposure accounted for 4.2% of the variance in IQ scores at age 7 years, whereas social and parenting covariates (i.e., quality of the home; maternal age, intelligence, education, and ethnicity;

Table 15.9 Estimated time line of a comparison case of severe lead exposure in a child, reported in the literature by Chin and Charlton (2004).

Birth: Born at term, weighing 5 lb and 13 oz
  No known delivery or perinatal complications

Preschool: Preschool developmental milestones achieves within age-appropriate intervals
  Described as "bright" by his mother during preschool
  Moved into an older home

1st grade: Began to fall behind in school
  Onset of pica, by child's report

2nd grade: Falling further behind in school
  More aggressive and argumentative with teacher

3rd grade: Emotionally volatile
  Frequent arguments with teachers regarding completion of his work
  Begins to receive special education services
  Described as being unable to read or write
  Diagnosed with a visual learning disorder
  Demonstrates good learning potential by auditory memorization

Middle school: Child confessed to mother of 5-year history of pica.
  Mother consults primary care physician.
  Initial venous blood lead level $= 173$ μg/dl

Background history: Child has been in good health.
  Family history of one sibling with an auditory learning disorder who is receiving special education services.
  No other family history of neurodevelopmental disorders.

Current symptoms: No somatic symptoms
  Severe neurodevelopmental delays, including high level of motor activity, short attention span, low frustration tolerance, poor impulse control, aggression, and poor school performance

Home study: Found high levels of lead in paint chips (15–19 mg/cm^2; reference value: >1.0 mg/cm^2).

Laboratory studies: Normal white blood cell count and platelets
  Hemoglobin slightly low (10.5 μg/dl)
  Repeat venous blood lead $= 175$ μg/dl
  Free erythrocyte protoporphyrin > 600 μg/dl

Radiographic films: Of long bone $=$ "lead lines" of radiodense signal at metaphyseal plates
  Similar sclerotic bands at other sites

Treatment: Initially chelated with dimercaprol calcium disodium edentate (CaNa$_2$ EDTA) and Succimer. On Day 9, repeat blood lead level $= 52$ μg/dl. Toward the end of first course of chelation, blood lead levels stabilized at 27 μg/dl, but rebounded to 54 μg/dl 2 weeks after completion of treatment. Eventually had four courses of chelation. After the last course (at 6 months later), blood lead level $= 39$ μg/dl.

---

birth weight; gender) accounted for approximately 50% of the variance in IQ scores (Factor-Litvak, Wasserman, Kline, & Graziano, 1999).

This pattern of a limited role for lead exposure in contrast to larger contributions from socioenvironmental variables is also found when the outcome measure is focused on behavioral disturbances. For example, in Yugoslavia, children in a lead smelter town and a non-lead-exposed town were followed from pregnancy to age 3 years to study the possible development of behavior problems. Approximately 7–18% of the variance on the Child Behavior Checklist (CBCL), a behavioral rating scale, was explained by socio-demographic factors. Another 2–5% of the variance was explained by an early difficult temperament. In contrast, concurrent blood lead level explained only 1–4% of the variance on the Destructive and Withdrawn subscales on the CBCL. Increases with blood lead level were associated with increases in scores on the Destructive subscales, with increases from 10 to 20 µg/dl in blood lead being associated with increases in subscale scores by approximately 0.5 points (Wasserman, Staghezza-Jaramillo, Shrout, Popovac, & Graziano, 1998).

Comments

This case presentation serves as a reminder of the limitations of generalizing from epidemiological and large-scale research findings to an individual case without conducting a sufficient and individualized evaluation of the individual child before making diagnostic and etiological conclusions. Richardson et al. (2000) developed some guidelines to be used to help evaluate the potential of the scientific literature to use for a particular instance. As they noted, one of the considerations is to evaluate how closely the patient's presentation resembles others with the disorder reported in the literature. For the child in our *case presentation*, there was similarity in the reported ongoing difficulties with attention regulation, behavioral control, growth parameters, iron insufficiency, stomachaches, and headaches. Nevertheless, there are other multiple possible etiological factors, including family genetic factors, family environment, and early iron insufficiency. In the United States, it is becoming less common to see children with markedly elevated blood lead levels. Rather, clinicians are more often asked to assess the relative contributions of a variety of factors on a child's cognitive and behavioral functioning, including very low levels of lead exposure. As noted by Kaufman (2001), even if low levels of lead might result in slight decrements of cognitive functioning, the estimates of change are so small as to make them indistinguishable from chance variation and may have little clinical meaning.

For the *case presentation*, the effects of lead exposure were quite modest. The changes seen in some intellectual and language measures between the first and last assessment may reflect some improvement in performance associated with his declining blood lead level. In addition, lead exposure may also have an etiological role for his small size and frequent stomachaches in early childhood. Nevertheless, it is likely that genetic and environmental factors are more salient issues to be addressed when trying to formulate effective interventions for this child.

Although the effects from lead exposure may be quite subtle in an individual child, others have noted the potential negative influence of this effect in large populations. For example, Wigg (2001) noted that a downward shift of three to five points in intellectual scores associated with lead exposure would result in an increase of intellectual disability within that group by two- or threefold. The public health implications of very low levels of lead exposure are salient and highlight the importance of continued work on the prevention of lead exposure in young children. The role of the clinician, however, is to remain sensitive to detecting subtle effects of lead exposure, but also recognizing the limited relative contribution that exposure might have on a single child's presentation.

Organic mercury

Stanley Berent

Mercury (Hg), also termed *elemental mercury* and *quicksilver*, is abundant in the earth's crust (0.5 ppm) and extracted from ore (cinnabar [mercuric sulfide, HgS]) through roasting or agitation (Merck Research Laboratories, 2001). Hg converts into many forms as a result of oxidation or other chemical transition. In its initial state, Hg is an inorganic metal that is unusual for being a liquid at room temperature (Klaassen & Watkins, 2003). At room temperature, Hg releases mercury vapor (Hg^0) and also forms inorganic salts in its Hg^+ (mercurous) or Hg^{2+} (mercuric) valence states (Life Sciences Research Office, 2004). Mercury vapor is considered to be much more hazardous than the liquid form of mercury and is prevalent in the atmosphere as a result of natural degassing of the earth's crust (Klaassen & Watkins, 2003). Hg has a number of industrial uses (e.g., in thermometers, barometers, hydrometers, ultraviolet and fluorescent lamps, mirrors, extraction of gold and silver from ores, dental amalgams, batteries, etc. [Merck Research Laboratories, 2001]). In addition to being the result of natural processes, Hg^0 derives from these various industrial activities such as mining and the burning of fossil fuels or waste products containing mercury (U.S. Environmental Protection Agency Office of Air Quality Standards, 1997). Also, Hg has been used widely as a major component in dental amalgams (approximately 50% Hg combined with other metals), which is known to emit Hg^0 that is absorbed into the bloodstream (Clarkson, Magos, & Myers, 2003) (see discussion on *dental amalgams* in chapter 18 of the present volume). While human exposure to Hg^0 as a result of its background presence in the atmosphere is considered to be negligible (U.S. Environmental Protection Agency Office of Air Quality Standards, 1997), industrial accidents and other human activities have the capacity to increase the amount of exposure.

Also, inorganic Hg (see discussion of *Hg* in volume II) can be converted to organic forms, methyl or ethyl mercury compounds (Clarkson & Strain, 2003). Because organic forms of Hg are no longer used as a fungicide, the potential exposure to ethyl mercury has been reduced considerably and is now limited mostly to its inclusion as the vaccine preservative, *thimerosal* (Clarkson et al.). The use of thimerosal as a preservative in vaccines has been discontinued in the United States, although it continues to be used in some other countries. Ethyl and methyl forms of Hg are chemically related and considered to be similar in their health effects; however, of the two forms, *methylmercury* (MeHg) is considered to be the more toxic (Clarkson et al., 2003). Thus, MeHg is seen as the most important organic form of Hg for the present discussion. MeHg can be of several compound types (e.g., monomethylmercury or dimethylmercury) and dimethylmercury is found together with monomethylmercury compounds as environmental contaminants in fish and fish-eating animals (Merck Research Laboratories, 2001). Here, we will use the more generic term (MeHg), except when identifying a more specific type of organic compound is indicated. Mercury is converted to MeHg by bacteria in the environment and enters the food chain primarily via fish (Life Sciences Research Office, 2004; National Research Council, 2000; U.S. Environmental Protection Agency Office of Air Quality Standards, 1997).

Consuming seafood is a major source of human exposure to MeHg (Klaassen & Watkins, 2003), although other routes of exposure have been reported (Bakir et al., 1973; Davis et al., 1994). Two mass exposures of MeHg included an incident in the Minamata Bay area of Kumamato Prefecture, Japan, in the mid-1950s (1953–1956) (Eto, 2000) and in a 1972 epidemic in Iraq (Bakir et al., 1973). The Minamata Bay exposures occurred when waste containing MeHg was discharged from a chemical plant into the bay (Clarkson et al., 2003). More than 2,000 people were affected when they consumed seafood taken from the waters surrounding Minamata City (Igata, 1993). In a separate incident, more than 6,000 people were affected throughout Iraq in 1972 when they consumed homemade bread that was made unknowingly from wheat that had been treated with a MeHg fungicide and intended to be used as seed grain (Bakir et al., 1973; Clarkson et al.).

The Minamata, Iraq, and other instances of MeHg exposures of greater and lesser magnitude have sensitized us not only to the potential hazards of MeHg but also to the need to maintain a careful balance between human activities and nature. MeHg has become the most widely studied of the organic Hg compounds. This focus may have resulted from the publicity surrounding the incidents of mass exposure just mentioned, the fact that MeHg may be the most toxic of the mercurial compounds (Sanfeliu, Sebastia, Cristofol, & Rodriguez-Farre, 2003), that the developing nervous system (i.e., children) is especially vulnerable to its toxicity (Mahaffey, 2000), that exposure to MeHg is practically unavoidable, or to a combination of these factors. For these or other reasons, poisoning from MeHg is now considered to be rare (Clarkson et al., 2003). However, according to Clarkson et al., there have been two reports of MeHg poisoning in the United States in the last 35 years.

A group of people who continue to be at special risk for organic mercury poisoning are researchers who synthesize or work with MeHg compounds. In fact, Clarkson and Strain (2003) noted that following the compounds first synthesis in the 1860s, the chemistry profession for many years avoided the study of MeHg as the technicians who had worked with these compounds all died.

Case presentation[9]

Nierenberg and colleagues (1998) described a 48-year-old female chemistry professor who was admitted to the hospital following a 5-day history of progressive worsening of gait, balance, and speech. Over a period of 2 months, she also had experienced a 15-lb weight loss, with brief episodes of nausea, diarrhea, and abdominal discomfort. The patient described an incident from work that occurred about 4 months before her admission in which she had spilled several drops of liquid dimethylmercury she was working with onto her hand. She had been wearing latex laboratory gloves at the time of the spill and subsequent cleanup. The patient was described as noticeably thin and appropriately concerned about her problems, but otherwise healthy appearing at the time of admission. The results of clinical neurological examination revealed, "moderate upper-extremity dysmetria, dystaxic handwriting, a widely based gait, and mild 'scanning speech.'" Routine laboratory tests were reported as normal.

Over the course of days, the patient complained of, "...tingling in her fingers, brief flashes of light in both eyes, a soft background noise in both ears, and progressive difficulty with speech, walking, hearing, and vision (constricted visual fields)." Her neurological condition continued to deteriorate, with "marked deficits in all areas" on "neuropsychiatric testing."

WORKING DIAGNOSIS

Possible methylmercury neurotoxicity.

ADDITIONAL INFORMATION

The results of routine laboratory tests at the time of admission were normal, as were CT and MRI images of the head, with the exception of a (1 cm in diameter) "probable meningioma." Cerebrospinal fluid was said to be clear, with no cells, and a protein concentration of 42 μg/dl. Whole-blood Hg was preliminarily reported to be >1000 μg/L (normal value reported as 1–8 μg/L [Clarkson, 1997]). The Hg content of a strand of the patient's hair was measured segmentally (in 2 mm segments from the patient's scalp). These measurements confirmed a lag time of approximately 17 days following the date of reported exposure, followed by a rise in Hg hair content over a period of about 22 days, and subsequent decline in Hg hair content over a period of about 131 days (Nierenberg et al., 1998). The patient was transferred to another hospital, and a repeat CT and MRI were again read as normal. Audiometry showed sensorineural hearing loss, and neuro-opthalmological evaluation showed constricted fields concentrically and no evidence of papilledema.

The patient was chelated with oral succimer (10 mg/kg every 8 hr), and laboratory values the day following the initiation of chelation included whole-blood Hg (4,000 mg/L) and urine Hg (234 μg/L, normal value reported as 1–5 μg/L [Clarkson, 1997]).

Twenty-two days after the onset of her neurological symptoms, the patient became unresponsive. She was transferred back to the original hospital and chelation therapy was continued in addition to aggressive general clinical support. Her general condition was described as having the appearance of a persistent vegetative state with episodes of crying and agitation. The patient died about 3 months later, about 10 months after her exposure.

An autopsy was done, and findings included dehydration and bronchopneumonia. Findings with regard to brain included diffuse thinning of the cerebral hemispheres, grossly gliotic tissue around the calcarine fissure and superior surface of the temporal gyri, and diffuse atrophy in both vermal and hemispheres of the cerebellum. Also noted were extensive neuronal loss and gliosis bilaterally in the primary visual cortex and auditory cortex. Other widespread cell loss in the brain was noted. Extremely high levels of Hg were reported in frontal lobe and visual cortex (3.1 mg/g) and also in liver and kidney.

Discussion

NERVOUS SYSTEM LOCALIZATION

The proposed initial diagnosis for this patient's problem implicates the central nervous system and primarily the cerebral and cerebellar cortices of the brain.

VERIFICATION OF THE WORKING CLINICAL DIAGNOSES

The original diagnosis of "possible methylmercury neurotoxicity," as we have often discovered, reflected the hypothesized cause for the patient's condition. The clinicians' actual and final clinical diagnosis appeared to be "delayed cerebellar disease" (Nierenberg et al., 1998). Since this case was adapted from the published literature, the entirety of the patient's file was not available. The published case report focused on the cerebellar aspects of the case; however, the description of the case left it clear that the central nervous system was widely affected beyond the cerebellum. This would leave the diagnosis of cerebellar disease only one of perhaps several diagnoses, e.g., "clinical encephalopathy" and dementia, for instance. These additional diagnoses would need to be presumed in order to verify the final diagnosis as it was presented.

CAUSE/ETIOLOGY

The patient's condition was attributed to exposure to dimethylmercury.

VERIFICATION OF CAUSE/ETIOLOGY

While dimethylmercury was proposed specifically as the causal substance of illness in the *case presentation*, this level of specificity is probably not relevant to the patient's subsequent disease and course of illness. As pointed out by the authors in their description of this case, dimethylmercury converts rapidly to MeHg following exposure (Nierenberg et al., 1998). Dimethylmercury is a lipophilic mercurial that has been shown in mice to convert rapidly in liver to methylmercuric ion, described by Hanlon as a "toxic species" (Hanlon, 1998; Ostlund, 1969). The importance of the dimethylmercury specification in the present instance would seem to be limited to the implications that it is a potent neurotoxicant, that it has the capacity to enter the body transdermally, that its toxic effects mirror those of MeHg, and, as objectively determined in the referenced study, standard laboratory latex gloves are not sufficient to prevent exposure when working with this material.

Assuming that MeHg can be referred to interchangeably with dimethylmercury in this case, the majority of objective criteria for establishing causality have been met (Hill, 1965), with a few caveats. Certainly, the evidence of high risk associated with MeHg is well documented. The effects described in the *case presentation* are biologically plausible and consistent with descriptions we summarized in our comments. An intriguing exception to this is the lack of positive findings on CT and MRI, on two different occasions and during the time that the patient was symptomatic and evidencing positive findings on psychometric examination (Nierenberg et al., 1998). The findings from brain imaging studies reported in the scientific literature have been straightforward and consistent anatomically with later findings from autopsy (Korogi, Takahashi, Okajima, & Eto, 1998). In the *case presentation* as well, the reported findings from autopsy were positive and revealed damage to the brain that was consistent with damage reported for Minamata disease, e.g., gliosis around the calcarine fissure, superior temporal gyri, extensive neuronal loss, and diffuse atrophy in the cerebellum. The identification of Hg deposits in liver, kidney, and brain also was consistent with published scientific findings (Eto, 2000). Why the brain imaging studies in the *case presentation* failed to show such extensive neurological involvement appears at first to be a mystery. A possible explanation is that although the patient was symptomatic at the time these scans were made, gross structural damage to the nervous system had not yet occurred. From this viewpoint, one might predict positive findings on PET or some other measure of metabolic activity (see chapter 7 in volume I). Such measures were not administered in the present instance.

Animal models exist that document effects of MeHg exposures, which are similar to and consistent with those described in the *case presentation*. Studies of MeHg have been very consistent in their reported findings, and the cause–effect relationship in MeHg exposure has been shown to be quite specific. It is not clear that all causal criteria have been met unequivocally, however. Hanlon (1998), for instance, raised questions regarding what appeared to be an extraordinary length of time between the presumed exposure to dimethylmercury and the onset of neurological symptoms. Hanlon cited several sources (Bakir et al., 1973; Davis et al., 1994) to argue that manifested toxic effects from MeHg occur much sooner than the 5 months reported by Nierenberg et al. On the other hand, delays between MeHg exposure and onset of illness have been described by others as being measured in days to months (Weiss, Clarkson, & Simon, 2002).

Also, Hanlon questioned the amount of dimethylmercury that could have been received by the patient and whether the amount calculated would have been sufficient to cause the reported illness. The question of sufficiency of dose has been raised by others. Byard and Couper (1998) agreed with the conclusion reached by Nierenberg and colleagues but argued for the possibility that the patient had experienced other exposures, perhaps before the reported spill. The information regarding analyses of hair segments that was presented in this case is powerful and suggests that if other exposures were involved in the patient's illness, these exposures would need to have occurred before the suspected incident.

With regard to the criteria of modification of effect with removal from exposure, MeHg intoxication is somewhat unique among the toxicants discussed in these volumes in its unfortunately frequent irreversibility of damage. The information provided does not allow for a critical appraisal as to whether or not all other potential explanations for the patient's illness were sufficiently investigated and eliminated. While the publication's authors stated that other conditions had been eliminated, no details were provided as to how this was accomplished. For instance, mention was made of both a "probable brain meningioma" as well as "other causes of acute cerebellar dysfunction," but further information about these possible conditions was not conveyed.

Overall, and with regard to causality, this patient's presentation and eventual course do appear to reflect poisoning from organic mercury. This conclusion will have to be tempered, however, by the considerations mentioned.

Comment

Each oxidation state of Hg (Hg^0, Hg^+, and Hg^{2+}), as well as each organic form of Hg, has different toxic properties and can produce unique health effects (Klaassen & Watkins, 2003; Sanfeliu et al., 2003). All Hg compounds are considered to be hazardous to human health, but the organic forms of Hg are considered to be the most harmful (Clarkson et al., 2003; Sanfeliu et al.). Although the exact mechanisms of toxic injury are not yet understood fully, primary mechanisms are believed to include inhibition of protein synthesis, disruption of microtubules, increase of intracellular Ca^{2+} with disruption to neurotransmission, oxidative stress, and increased excitotoxicity (Sanfeliu et al.; Tsuzuki, 1982). Some animal data suggest that apoptotic processes may play a key role in cellular damage as a result of MeHg poisoning (Nagashima et al., 1996). From a developmental perspective, results from a study of the developing cerebellar cortex in mice led the study's authors to conclude that the antimitotic effects of MeHg exposure were the most likely mechanism that explained reductions in numbers of cells in treated mice (Sager, Aschner, & Rodier, 1984).

Pathology differs as a function of Hg state as well as exposure characteristics, e.g., whether acute or chronic (Eto et al., 1999). On the basis of autopsy, Eto et al. described differences in pathological findings between organic- and inorganic-poisoned individuals. Those patients exposed to MeHg who presented with acute onset of symptoms and died within 2 months and those with acute onset who lived for more than 10 years following exposure showed similar patterns of neurological damage to the brain. In those patients with acute onset and who died within 2 months, findings included more or less symmetrical neuronal loss with reactive proliferation of glial cells, microcavitation, vascular congestion, petechial hemorrhage, and edema of the cerebral cortex that was predominant in precentral and postcentral calcarine layers, transverse temporal regions, and the cerebellum. A later study by the same author (Eto, Tokunaga, Nagashima, & Takeuchi, 2002) reported more widespread lesions in the brains of patients who died from MeHg poisoning than reported in the earlier study, lesions not limited to the calcarine cortex. In the group with acute onset of symptoms but who lived longer than 10 years after exposure, brain pathology included neuronal loss and reactive proliferation of glial cells in an anatomical distribution similar to that found in the patients who died relatively quickly. Findings in patients who died from acute inorganic mercury poisoning, in contrast, showed the patients to have diffuse pneumonia, necrosis of renal cortex, disseminated intravascular coagulopathy, and infarction in brain and kidney (Eto et al., 1999). In contrast to the central nervous system findings related to MeHg, examinations of two mine workers who were chronically exposed to Hg over a 10-year period revealed no specifically identifiable brain lesions (Eto et al., 1999). Whether Hg or MeHg was involved and regardless of duration of clinical signs or presence or absence of brain lesions, inorganic mercury was found to be present in the brain. Histochemistry studies have also shown Hg to be present in kidney and liver in addition to brain in individuals acutely poisoned by MeHg (Eto, 2000). Hg does not cross the blood–brain barrier easily, and it may be that MeHg is biologically transformed to Hg once in the brain (Davis et al., 1994).

The symptoms of MeHg intoxication are dose dependent and relatively consistent across studies (Bakir et al., 1973; Eto, 2000; Goldman & Bennett, 2000), although the developing brains of the fetus and young children appear to be especially vulnerable to the damaging effects of mercury exposure (Davis et al., 1994; Life Sciences Research Office, 2004). For example, Davis et al. retrospectively reported findings related to a family 22 years after they had been exposed to MeHg contaminated pork. The family's four children, aged 20, 13, 8 years, and a neonate were all exposed, and all developed signs of neurological impairment at the time of exposure. The signs of neurological illness appeared about 4 months after the family began eating the contaminated pork and primarily consisted of ataxic gait, involuntary movements, constricted visual fields, slurred speech, seizures, and hyperactive reflexes (Curley et al., 1971; Pierce et al., 1972). Interestingly, the pigs that were the source of the contaminated pork also became ill, with neurological problems similar to those seen in the family members. The pigs developed blindness, lack of coordination, and posterior paralysis about 2 months after they started to be fed seed grain contaminated with an organomercurial fungicide (Curley et al.). Within another month, 12 of the

14 pigs had died (Curley et al.). Twenty-two years later, the two oldest children were found to have deficits of attention, restricted visual fields, poor coordination, slowed intellectual processes that included slowed word finding, and hyperactive reflexes (Davis et al.). The youngest child was found to have severe mental retardation, blindness, and quadriplegia. The third child died at age 30, and autopsy showed cortical atrophy, with neuronal loss and gliosis, most pronounced in paracentral and parietal–occipital regions of the brain (Davis et al.).

In adults, there may be a latent period of weeks to months between MeHg exposure and onset of symptoms (Bakir et al., 1973; Weiss, Clarkson, & Simon, 2002). The reason for a long latency period between exposure and manifestations of MeHg poisoning is not known (Feldman, 1998), although it may be related to body concentrations of MeHg. Also, as emphasized by Feldman, the relatively long latency period may postpone the recognition of MeHg exposure, delay an accurate diagnosis, or lead to a wrong diagnosis. Any of these failures might result in continued unrecognized exposures, causing more serious neurological damage to the patient or to others being exposed than might otherwise be the case (Feldman, 1998). Paresthesia appears to be an early manifestation of MeHg intoxication, followed by changes in vision (even blindness in severe cases), hearing, ataxia, dysarthria, tremor, spasticity, paralysis, coma, and death (Bakir et al.; Eto, 2000; Goldman & Bennett, 2000; Klaassen & Watkins, 2003; Life Sciences Research Office, 2004). To the list of symptoms that can result from MeHg poisoning, Klaassen and Watkins (2003) have described *neurasthenia*,[10] which they define as a general feeling of weakness, fatigue, and difficulty concentrating. Bakir et al. studied 93 individuals who were admitted to hospitals following the 1972 Iraq exposures. He reported a dose–response relationship that was reflected in types and severity of symptoms and signs. The periods of ingestion ranged from 41 to 68 days, and latencies between ingestion of contaminated food and onset of illness ranged from 16 to 38 days, and the clinical manifestations included paresthesia, ataxia, visual changes, dysarthria, hearing defects, and death (Bakir et al.). The deaths were limited to those patients whose blood levels of Hg were >3000 ng/ml at time of admission (Bakir et al.).

Uchino et al. (1995) studied 80 patients, mean age being 63 years, with documented MeHg poisoning. They reported that sensory impairment was the most often observed finding (98.8% of cases), with impairment of lower extremity coordination in 60% of cases. The next highest occurring impairment was constriction of visual fields (51.9%), followed by retrocochlear hearing loss (41%). Korogi et al. (1998) studied the victims of the Minamata exposures using MRI and reported finding significant atrophy in visual cortex, cerebellar vermis and hemispheres, and the postcentral cortex that resulted in visual field constriction, ataxia, and sensory disturbance, respectively, which the Korogi group described as the three most prevalent functional impairments found among patients diagnosed with *Minamata disease*. The cause of death as a result of MeHg poisoning is variable and cannot be stated as being specific to the disease; however, published studies (Tamashiro, Arakaki, Akagi, Futatsuka, & Roht, 1985; Tamashiro, Arakaki, Futatsuka, & Lee, 1986) have reported an excess mortality for cerebral hemorrhage (not further specified) with multiple risk factors from hepatic-related diseases (nephritis–nephrosis–nephrotic syndrome). The mortality rate between 1954 and 1981 from all causes in the areas affected in the Minamata exposures was reported by Tamashiro and colleagues as 29.6%, which was said to be significantly higher than the general population ($p < 0.05$), with significantly lower survival rates in males in comparison to females and for older persons (Tamashiro et al., 1985). A standardized mortality ratio was employed in the Tamashiro studies, leaving a direct comparison between exposed persons and the general population impossible. Also, the authors admit to weaknesses in their method in terms of being able to make a direct link between MeHg poisoning and death. For instance, the exposed persons were identified from death certificates, which failed in many instances to include MeHg exposures and other factors in a given individual's history. A follow-up study (Tamashiro, Fukutomi, & Lee, 1987) reported a gain in life expectancy years over three periods: 1969–1972, 1973–1977, and 1978–1982. The 1987 study concluded that there was no appreciable difference in life expectancy between the exposed and control populations (Tamashiro et al.).

The central nervous system is the primary target organ for MeHg (Clarkson, 1997; Eto et al., 2002; Igata, 1993). High levels of MeHg are known to adversely affect the kidneys and the developing fetus as well (Agency for toxic substances and disease registry [ATSDR], 2005a). Within the central nervous system, it is the cerebral hemispheres and cerebellum that appear to be most adversely affected by MeHg. However, there is some evidence from animal models that subcortical regions of brain are affected as well. Tsuzuki (1982), for instance, studied the effects of MeHg exposure on different neurotransmitter systems in rat brain. In addition to other changes in brain, Tsuzuki reported marked decreases in 5-hydroxytryptamine (5-HT) in hypothalamus, brain stem, and striatum (Tsuzuki, 1982).

The peripheral nervous system is not usually mentioned as a target for MeHg damage. For example, Eto et al. (2002) reported that MeHg-induced damage to peripheral nerves has not been universally accepted. Despite this, Eto presented data that were based on autopsy and sural nerve biopsy of a 64-year-old male with autopsy findings characteristic of MeHg poisoning to conclude that peripheral nerve degeneration does occur as a result of MeHg poisoning. A sural nerve biopsy done 1 month before the patient's death revealed endoneurial fibrosis, axonal loss, and the presence of "Bungner's bands," a nonspecific finding associated with axonal regeneration of any cause, consisting of clusters of axonal sprouts and Schwann enclosed in a Schwann cell basement membrane. At autopsy, Wallerian degeneration was found within the fasciculus gracilis of the spinal cord, with relative preservation of sensory ganglia neurons (Eto et al., 2002). On the basis of an epidemiological study of victims of the Minamata disaster, Igata (1993) concluded that peripheral neuropathy is a cardinal feature of Minamata disease, with "glove-stocking" type of impaired sensation of the extremities that reflects biopsy and autopsy documented generalized loss of myelinated fibers and other pathology of the peripheral nerves. Symptoms may be expressed as complaints such as numbness, tingling, or hyperesthesia (Igata, 1993). No mention was made by Igata regarding abnormal reflexes, considered to be the most objective clinical sign of neuropathy. Still others have found that peripheral involvement in MeHg intoxication remains unresolved (Bromberg, 2000) or maintain that all of the effects of MeHg, including sensory disturbances, are explainable on the basis of central nervous system damage (Korogi et al., 1998). The literature on Minamata disease appears to be the primary place where peripheral neuropathy has been seen to be a consequence of MeHg exposure. It may be that there is something unique to this population that does not necessarily generalize to all instances of MeHg poisoning.

The central nervous system remains the primary focus of concern associated with MeHg intoxication producing encephalopathy (Bromberg, 2000), and ensuing neurobehavioral manifestations that include psychiatric and cognitive symptoms that may be reversible or persistent (Feldman, 1998; Goldman & Bennett, 2000; Rowland, 1989). While MeHg toxicity appears to be selective for certain cell types and brain structures (Sanfeliu et al., 2003), central nervous system damage can be extensive and widespread, especially in the developing brain (Bromberg, 2000; Clarkson, 1987, 1997; Sanfeliu et al.). As a result, no specific pattern of neuropsychological impairment is likely to be identifiable, beyond that associated with the nature and extent of neurological damage in the individual case being examined at a given time. That is, neurobehavioral symptoms and neuropsychological test findings can be expected to reflect the areas of underlying neurological damage and the severity of that damage in the individual case. Some common neurobehavioral manifestations that have been reported to occur in MeHg poisoning include impaired concentration, memory loss (short- and long-term), depression and emotional lability, more generally, decreased intellectual function (including mental retardation in children and dementia in adults) and abnormal mental status changes in vision and other senses, ataxia and movement disorders, spasticity and paralysis, and hyperreflexia (Bromberg, 2000; Davis et al., 1994; Feldman, 1998).

EXPOSURE TO LOW LEVELS OF METHYLMERCURY

What about the effects of chronic and low-level exposures to MeHg? The data presented by Bakir et al. (1973) leave it clear that the effects of MeHg are dose dependent. As per Bakir's studies, people who consumed contaminated bread for only a short while experienced symptoms often limited to paresthesia, while others who ate more experienced a greater number of clinical manifestations of greater severity and duration (Bakir et al., 1973). Eto (2000) in reference to Minamata disease advanced the idea that continuous ingestion of "small doses" of MeHg would over time lead to what he termed "chronic Minamata disease" even though there might have been no earlier observation of acute signs of toxicity. For most people, according to Gochfeld (2003), eating fish is the only significant source of exposure to MeHg. Gochfeld surmised that people who eat large amounts of fish can accumulate sufficient amounts of MeHg to cause symptoms of MeHg poisoning and, further, that pregnant women who consume these fish can pass on to their offspring amounts of MeHg sufficient to cause disorders of the nervous system (Gochfeld, 2003). The world is dependent on fish as a food source. MeHg binds to proteins in fish and the amount available becomes magnified up the food chain, such that fish at the highest predatory levels (e.g., shark, swordfish, pike, bass) may have MeHg concentrations that are up to a million-fold greater than the water surrounding them (Clarkson et al., 2003; Gochfeld, 2003; Wooltorton, 2002). Once ingested, MeHg is readily absorbed and retained, with a half-life of about 44 days, and fecal elimination as inorganic mercury (Wooltorton, 2002). Blood tests are a useful measure of acute exposure while analyses of hair segments can reflect exposure history (Wooltorton, 2002). The current EPA reference dose (RfD) for MeHg intake is 0.1 mg/kg/day, which is viewed as sufficient to protect the most sensitive endpoint, fetal development (Gochfeld, 2003; Mahaffey, 2000). This dose is more stringent than the previous reference dose of 0.3 mg/kg/day for adults, and this increased strictness reflects the growing concern regarding the possible adverse developmental consequences from MeHg exposures.

The establishment of the RfD can be said to reflect the presumption that low-level exposures to MeHg are detrimental. Clarkson et al. (2003) has pointed out that the current threshold of allowable intake of MeHg (0.1 mg/kg/day) translates to one 7-oz can of tuna a week. He contrasts the more general health and economic benefits of eating tuna to what he views as the speculative conclusion that such small amounts of MeHg are harmful and concludes that the debate on this topic is likely to continue with some intensity (Clarkson et al.). The proponents of tight control of fish consumption, and consequently limitation of MeHg ingestion, argue that small, subtle decrements in neurobehavioral functions, similar to those identified in learning disabilities can be attributed to low-dose MeHg exposures (Mahaffey, 2000). The data fueling both sides of the debate derive from laboratory animal studies as well as the findings of developmental abnormalities in the poisoning episodes in Japan and Iraq. Most importantly, data come currently from three prospective cohort studies: one in New Zealand (Crump, Kjellstrom, Shipp, Silvers, & Stewart, 1998), a second study in the Seychelles Islands (Davidson et al., 1998), and the third in the Faroe Islands (Grandjean et al., 1997). The results of these studies have not been consistent, however, and potential confounders are still being discussed. All of these studies have employed sensitive psychometric approaches to longitudinally measure the development of children born into these cultures.

In the New Zealand cohort, Crump et al. (1998) used regression analyses to report a relationship in 6- and 7-year-old children between their performances on scholastic and psychological tests and mercury concentrations in the mother's hair during pregnancy. In the Faroe Islands study, Grandjean et al.

(1997) measured Hg concentrations in cord blood and maternal hair. Nine hundred and seventeen children of age 7 years were administered a battery of neuropsychological and other tests. While clinical examination and neurophysiological testing did not reveal "clear-cut mercury-related abnormalities," neuropsychological impairments were noted (Grandjean et al.). Dysfunctions in these children were said to be most pronounced in language, attention, memory, and, to a lesser extent, visuospatial and motor functions. The impairments were related to indices of maternal mercury levels. Grandjean concluded that the effects on brain function associated with prenatal MeHg exposure were widespread, and that early detection of dysfunction could be accomplished at exposure levels previously considered to be safe (Grandjean et al.). The results of the Seychelles study differed from those of the two studies previously discussed. As in the last study, a battery of neuropsychological and developmental tests was administered in the Seychelles study. Davidson et al. (2001) reported an association among both prenatal and postnatal exposure and scores from some of the tests administered, e.g., Woodcock–Johnson Applied Problems. However, and in contrast to the other studies mentioned, these results suggested beneficial effects that were associated with increasing levels of Hg levels. This was interpreted by the study's authors as reflecting the dietary benefits of fish consumption, and they concluded that they found no evidence of adverse effects from exposure to MeHg in the population studied (Davidson et al., 1998).

Why such a difference in findings between the studies just reviewed? As pointed out by Clarkson and colleagues (Clarkson et al., 2003; Clarkson & Strain, 2003), there was a major difference between the Seychelles and the Faroe Islands in terms of diet. Whale was a major food source in the Faroes while the Seychelles population consumed only fish (Clarkson et al.). As a result, the Faroe Islands cohort was likely exposed to higher levels of polychlorinated biphenyls (PCBs) than was the Seychelles population (Clarkson et al.; Mahaffey, 2000). The bottom line is that the issue of adverse effects from low-dose exposures to MeHg remains unresolved.

Conclusion

Unlike many of the other toxicants discussed in these volumes, removal from exposure to organic mercury does not ensure reversibility of illness. There is essentially no "cure" for MeHg poisoning and no single effective treatment. Bakir et al. (1973), for instance, noted that although many of the patients in the 1972 Iraq exposures were chelated with penicillamine and thiol resin and exhibited a drop in Hg body burden, these patients did not show any dramatic improvement in clinical signs and symptoms of their disease. Even in milder cases, recovery is often accompanied by residual impairments (Davis et al., 1994).

Also, the exact steps to take in prevention are not always clear, or they involve trade-offs that may not be desirable. The main source of MeHg exposure, e.g., is food, and more specifically fish. The results of studies in the

Seychelles and Faroes reviewed earlier have taught us that the risk–benefit ratio between the nutritional benefits of eating fish and the developmental risks that might be associated with this source of food has not yet been determined. Hopefully, these ongoing studies will resolve some of these questions.

While psychometric methods have begun to be employed in research on the effects of MeHg, their involvement is noticeably minimal in past studies of mass exposures. From the nature of damage to the nervous system that has been documented in previous studies, one can assume an important role for formal neurobehavioral evaluation in these cases. Since, however, the extent of neurological damage may be variable, especially, in cases of mild MeHg intoxication, no one pattern of neuropsychological strengths and weaknesses can be presumed. Clinically, it will be important to consider the results of other medical tests, e.g., the results of imaging studies, to fully understand the individual patient's neurobehavioral condition. Nevertheless, the clinical neurobehavioral evaluation can provide baseline information that will aid in clinical diagnosis as well as in measuring recovery and determining residual impairments. Also, it may aid in separating primary effects of intoxication versus pre-existing and secondary manifestations. In research, especially with regard to questions about low-level exposures, such methods are likely to prove invaluable. An area of research that might profit enormously from the neurobehavioral approach is the emotional consequences of MeHg intoxication, an area that appears to be under-represented in the published literature.

The *case presentation* underscored the difficulty in confirming an accurate diagnosis in cases of MeHg poisoning. Documentation of actual exposure and exclusion of exposure to other substances will be an important challenge to the clinician.

Pesticides

Stanley Berent

Simply defined, a pesticide is any substance or device that is used to eliminate a pest. The targets of pesticides include insects, rodents, botanicals, or other biological organisms. The term *pesticide* is generic, and the types of pesticides are usually more specifically defined either on the bases of the target organism (e.g., insecticide), a substance's primary mechanism of action (e.g., anticoagulants, anticholinesterases), or the chemical class to which the substance belongs (e.g., organophosphorous esters). On the basis of primarily the target organism, the various types of pesticides have been organized by Ecobichon (2003) as including insecticides (organochlorine compounds, anticholinesterase agents, pyrethroid esters, avermectins, and "newer" chemicals), botanicals (e.g., nicotine), herbicides (e.g., chlorophenoxy compounds), fungicides (e.g., hexachlorobenzene), fumigants (phosphine), and rodenticides (e.g., anticoagulants).

Most present-day pesticides rely on some mechanism for disrupting the normal function of the nervous system, although adverse effects may occur in other organ systems as well. Since the nervous system functions similarly across species from insect to humans, insecticides are not selective to one species. Human exposures to these substances can, and do, occur in a variety of ways: in the manufacturing of these substances, in agricultural occupations, in pest control applications, through accidents or intentional ingestion (e.g., suicide), or even as a consumer of pesticide-treated products or as a member of the general public passively coming into contact with pesticide residue. Children may be especially at risk as they tend to engage in activities that bring them into contact with pesticides, e.g., playing on floors and outside on the ground, putting things in their mouths (Weiss, 2000). In addition, the developing nervous system is believed by many to be especially vulnerable to environmental toxicants (Koger, Schettler, & Weiss, 2005; Weiss, 2000).

Pesticides are viewed by most as essential for our survival. For example, they aid in the control of pest-born diseases and help to ensure ample crops for food production. Their use, nevertheless, poses a risk to humans and our environment more generally. This potential for harm demands that we understand the risks involved and how to minimize such risk, e.g., through regulation and education to enhance proper use, through development of less toxic but still effective substances, and through conservative use of pesticide products.

Chemical compounds are used extensively for pest control. Organophosphorus (OP) compounds represent the largest group of pesticides at present, with estimates of more than 100 individual OP compounds used in thousands of commercial products around the world (Bleeker, 1994; Ecobichon, 2003). OP compounds were derived originally from the highly toxic "nerve gases" such as sarin, soman, and tabun that have been used at times as weapons of war (Ecobichon, 2003). Even recently, these gases have been employed as weapons in terrorist acts (Morita et al., 1995) (also, see chapter 1, volume I). The OP insecticides used today, however, are several generations removed from their notorious roots and less highly toxic (Ecobichon, 2003). These products have varying levels of toxicity in themselves, nevertheless, and often they are combined with other pesticide chemicals (e.g., carbamates) and other inert ingredients that also can be toxic (e.g., *n*-hexane) (Feldman, 1998). Because of its widespread use and the importance to public health that derives from that use, the remainder of this section will focus on OP pesticides.

Case presentation[2]

A 36-year-old man was found unconscious by his girlfriend an estimated 2–3 hr after he ingested an unknown amount of an OP pesticide with the intent to commit suicide. He was comatose on admission to the hospital. He was hypotensive (blood pressure 70/40 mmHg), tachycardic (pulse rate of 140 bpm), and tachypneic (respiratory rate greater than 30/min) with ineffectual, shallow respirations. He was intubated and placed on a ventilator. Neurological examination showed that he was unresponsive to voice but responded symmetrically with nonpurposeful arm flexion and leg extension (decorticate posturing) to painful stimuli. His pupils were small but responded to light. Brain stem function was intact, including corneal, oculovestibular, and gag reflexes. Muscle stretch reflexes were brisk, and he showed bilateral Babinski signs. On the basis of the presence of profuse sweating, excessive tearing, and diffuse fasciculations, he was judged to be in cholinergic crisis. He was treated with atropine and pralidoxime (2-PAM), a cholinesterase reactivator. Laboratory studies included arterial blood gases prior to intubation showing a severe respiratory acidosis and markedly reduced butyrylcholinesterase (BuChE) and RBC acetylcholinesterase (AChE) levels, consistent with OP poisoning. The patient remained unconscious for about 12 hr, after which he regained consciousness and recovered to baseline over a period of 2 days. Neurological examination at that time was unremarkable, other than being amnestic for the events surrounding the suicide attempt or the first 24 hr of hospitalization. He remained hospitalized for another 3 weeks for psychiatric evaluation. He also was monitored for organophosphorous-induced intermediate syndrome or delayed neuropathy (OPIDN) (see chapter 10, volume II), but he never developed evidence of impaired neuromuscular transmission or signs of peripheral neuropathy. He was discharged from the hospital asymptomatic, with normal strength and no evidence of neuropathy or abnormal neuromuscular transmission on nerve conduction studies (which included repetitive motor nerve stimulation).

Because of the nature of the patient's OP exposure (i.e., attempted suicide), a psychiatric consult was obtained. In response to questions regarding the events that led him to attempt suicide, he replied that his girlfriend had wanted to break up with him. He had been through a divorce in the past, and he said that suddenly life did not seem worth living. He assured the psychiatrist that he no longer felt this way, that he had been given another chance in life. The psychiatry report included a diagnosis of major depression, and the patient was referred for psychiatric treatment on an outpatient basis.

INITIAL CLINICAL DIAGNOSIS

The patient's presentation on admission to the hospital included coma, severe respiratory insufficiency, and hypotension. The combined presentation was thought to reflect an acute hypoxic encephalopathy. There also were signs of overactivity of cholinergic synapses that indicated cholinergic crisis. The history included his attempted suicide through ingestion of an OP insecticide that helped to identify the presence of cholinergic crisis, and the laboratory findings of depressed BuChE and RBC cholinesterase activity confirmed OP intoxication. The patient also was diagnosed with major depression, in remission.

ADDITIONAL INFORMATION

The patient was seen for outpatient psychiatric treatment, with sessions once a week for about a 6-month period. Since the patient's depression no longer appeared to be overt, no antidepressant medications were prescribed. Treatment consisted of clinical evaluation and psychotherapy. No comprehensive neuropsychological examination was conducted in the initial clinical evaluation, but the patient complained of persisting difficulty with concentration and memory, stating that he was having problems remembering things he was supposed to do and following what others were saying to him. He had returned to his job as an electrical engineer and computer programmer but described trouble performing his duties. Past medical records verified that he had never evidenced similar performance problems in the past. The results of an MMSE that was administered included a score of 23 of 30, with points lost for delayed recall (three errors), carrying out a multiple stage command, and orientation items (e.g., mis-stating the date). As the patient was no longer manifestly depressed, depression that was in remission was included along with a diagnosis reflecting amnestic disorder.

The patient's mild cognitive difficulties improved over the course of treatment, and at his last treatment session, he reported that he was doing much better at work. His MMSE score on repeat testing was 28 of 30, within normal limits and reflecting improved orientation, delayed recall, and following commands.

REVISED CLINICAL DIAGNOSIS

The initial diagnosis of depression, in remission, was further refined as major depressive disorder, single episode, severe and in remission. Amnestic disorder due to a general medical condition (OP intoxication) was added.

NERVOUS SYSTEM LOCALIZATION

This patient's coma and cholinergic signs at the time of hospitalization implicate both the central and peripheral nervous systems. Specifically, the altered consciousness implicates involvement of the bilateral supratentorial level. The intact brain stem function on neurological examination argues against involvement of the posterior fossa level, although the initial impaired respiratory function could reflect involvement of the medullary respiratory center or the neuromuscular junction of the peripheral nervous system. Fasciculations are a nonspecific finding, but in this setting reflect cholinergic overactivity at the neuromuscular junction. Depression and amnestic disorder are consistent with involvement of the bilateral supratentorial level.

Discussion

The potential effects of OP pesticides on the peripheral nervous system are well established, as discussed in volume II. In the current *case presentation*, the only signs of peripheral nervous system dysfunction reflected presumed neuromuscular blockade, although only supportive treatment (respiratory support) was administered. He received treatment for the acute cholinergic effects at muscarinic receptors, as well as treatment with pralidoxime. The patient was appropriately clinically monitored for late effects of OP intoxication (which never developed), and he recovered without sequelae. The primary remaining question has to do with the potential effects of OP intoxication on the central nervous system.

The toxicity of anticholinesterase pesticides (e.g., OP compounds and carbamates) results from their disruption of normal cholinergic neurotransmission. The inhibition of AChE, the enzyme responsible for termination of and, therefore, regulation of acetylcholine (ACh) activity, allows continued stimulation of cholinergic nerves in the autonomic, peripheral, and central nervous systems (Ecobichon, 2003). The subsequent, unchecked ACh stimulation can continue to the point of physiological crisis, medically termed *cholinergic crisis* when associated with bulbar or respiratory dysfunction. The primary clinical effects of OP intoxication result from inhibition of AChE and the cholinergic overstimulation that results from such inhibition. The symptoms of excessive ACh include diaphoresis, nausea, vomiting, diarrhea, bradycardia, visual disturbance, headache, dyspnea, paresthesias, pulmonary edema, fasciculations, salivation, lacrimation, and incontinence (Agency for toxic substances and disease registry [ATSDR], 1998; Rowland, 1989). Neurobehavioral and neurophysiological manifestations have been reported as well, including giddiness, anergia and psychiatric disturbance, electrophysiological disturbances, coma, convulsions, and death (Agency for toxic substances and disease registry [ATSDR], 1998; Ecobichon, 2003; Rowland, 1989). With some variations across species, the effects of AChE inhibition have been reliably reproduced in animals (Agency for toxic substances and disease registry [ATSDR], 1998). The physiologic importance of the cholinergic system to human survival leaves the organism extremely vulnerable to OP poisoning. Overdose of OP pesticides may result in death, often as a result of cardiorespiratory dysfunction. It may be that individuals who have been exposed to OP pesticides in amounts sufficient to develop signs of central nervous system dysfunction die of respiratory failure before the disorder can be documented. For example, Richardson, Moore, Kayyali, and Randall (1993) used an animal model (the hen) to conclude that chlorpyrifos (an OP pesticide)-related OPIDN would be expected to occur only at doses that would be fatal if not aggressively medically treated, including respiratory support. This same phenomenon, i.e., inability to observe adverse effects on the nervous system because of the patient's death, has interfered with the knowledge base concerning the specific effects of OP intoxication on the central nervous system since the patient may be lost to study before central nervous system symptoms become known. As a result, much of what is known about the adverse effects of OP pesticides on the central nervous system has been derived from case reports or cross-sectional studies of insecticide applicators or workers involved in the use of pesticides and at exposures less than associated with OPIDN. It has been difficult to control the many potential confounders in such studies or to accurately quantify the amounts of exposure involved. Also, such populations often have had contact with a variety of pesticides, not unitary in their mechanisms of toxicity, and the reported studies have usually been limited to subjects with chronic and low-dose pesticide exposures. The following review should be considered with these limitations in mind.

Despite the fact that no specific neurobehavioral syndrome or pattern of strengths and weaknesses has been associated with repeated or chronic, low-level exposure to OP compounds, a number of cognitive and emotional impairments have been reported. Outcome variables, unfortunately, have often been vague, with specific impairments differing between studies. Blain (2001), for instance, commented on work done to that time that had attempted to better understand the effects of long-term, low-dose OP exposure on human neurobehavioral function. In his editorial, Blain expressed the opinion that these studies universally lacked information on historical exposure data or employment of validated behavioral measures. The studies referred to by Blain dealt with a multitude of neurobehavioral and electroencephalographic changes, including neuropsychiatric disorders (e.g., depression, anxiety, and irritability), as well as neuropsychological functions (e.g., memory, attention, and concentration). Although he recognized the importance of the societal concerns surrounding these issues, he was critical of the fact that these studies relied almost entirely on questionnaire reported symptoms, with no clinical examination-based determination of objective signs (Blain, 2001). A study by Pilkington (2001), e.g., relied heavily on questionnaires to conclude a strong association between OP compounds and neurological and neuropsychological symptoms. The investigators reported only "weak evidence of a chronic effect" for low dose, cumulative exposure and "neuropsychological abnormalities." However, the specific abnormalities were not reported in detail. The investigators in this study of sheep herders and dippers also acknowledged that their findings depended on the inclusion of the four highest exposed subjects in their sample and, further, that few of the workers they studied used the recommended personal protection equipment.

Whether OP exposure has been acute or chronic, the published literature to date fails to establish a clearly documented, specific neurobehavioral syndrome or neuropsychological pattern. Rosenstock and colleagues (1991), for instance, identified multiple neuropsychological impairments they associated with acute OP pesticide intoxication. This retrospective, cross-sectional study examined and compared 36 men who had been hospitalized for what was termed "organophosphate intoxication" 2 years earlier and to a "matched" control group (Rosenstock, Keifer, Daniell, McConnell, & Claypoole, 1991). The exposed subjects were more likely than controls to report symptoms that included difficulties in auditory attention, visual memory, visual-motor speed, "sequencing," problem solving, motor steadiness, reaction time, motor dexterity, and other neurobehavioral abnormalities. On the basis of the questionnaire results, Hogstedt, Anderson, and Hane (1984) reported findings similar to the findings by Rosenstock.

In a retrospective cross-sectional study of 100 agricultural workers previously poisoned with OP pesticides and matched in pairs with controls, Savage and colleagues (1988) found significantly more neurological and neuropsychological abnormalities among the exposed subjects than among their matched controls. Serious concern can be raised about the results and the interpretation that those results reflect OP pesticide exposures, however. With regard to their neurological findings, the authors stated that of the more than 50 scores from the neurological examination, abnormalities were demonstrated among the cases only on measures of "memory, abstraction, and mood, and on one test of motor reflexes" (Savage et al., 1988). There were no other neurological signs reported. The neuropsychological results were presented as more widespread and better able than the neurological findings to differentiate exposed from control subjects. Unfortunately, the many tests that were said to be impaired included measures of "intellectual functioning" and "academic skills," raising important questions about the premorbid status of the subjects in the exposed group. In addition, the exposed subjects were said to be in more distress, on the basis of MMPI results, than control subjects, and more complained of disability by questionnaire results, raising questions regarding motivation. A methodology that relies heavily on self-report may be especially vulnerable to selection bias. Also, the disproportionate presence of emotional disturbance in one or another group can differentially affect the approach to tasks between groups and would need to be controlled in some fashion.

Other studies have reported finding neurobehavioral impairments associated with OP exposure, but, the specific types of impairments have often differed between studies. In contrast to the results reported by Rosenstock, Keifer, Daniell, McConnell, and Claypoole (1991), Stephens and colleagues (1995) reported that sheep farmers showed poorer performance in areas of sustained attention and speed of information processing and an increased propensity for emotional disturbance in comparison to controls, but there were no observed effects on short-term memory and learning as reported by Savage et al. (1988).

After reviewing the literature on the effects of chronic exposure to OP pesticides, Baldi and colleagues (2001) concluded that there were only a few studies that would allow for some conclusion regarding the adverse effects on humans as a result of long-term occupational exposure to pesticides. They narrowed the effects that they derived from their review to "attention and flexibility, visual-memory, visual-motor and motor function, intellectual functioning, and abstraction" and proceeded to study a relatively large sample of vineyard workers in order to investigate a possible association between long-term exposure to pesticides and neuropsychological performance (Baldi et al.). These investigators modified standard neuropsychological instruments to test workers. A sophisticated regression analysis research design was employed that attempted to control for a host of potential confounders among Bordeaux vineyard workers in France. The results of this study included consistent differences between the exposed and nonexposed workers, and they found a negative association between performance and their measures of pesticide exposure (i.e., higher exposure associated with poorer performance).

However, Baldi's *Phytoner* study, as it has been called, is of little or no value in increasing our understanding of the potential effects of OP insecticides on neurobehavioral function. Baldi's study has been sometimes referred to as lending support for the adverse effects of chronic pesticide exposures on neurobehavioral function. In fact, and as its authors acknowledged, a number of potential confounders might have eluded complete control in the research design employed by Baldi. In terms of education level, for instance, many of the workers had a history of very limited education. Also, the national origin among the workers varied considerably. A major weakness in the study was the absence of a toxicological explanation for their epidemiological findings since the chemicals the workers could have been exposed to included a range of fungicides, herbicides, and insecticides. This fact was pointed out by the authors, who cited their own unpublished survey suggesting that OP represented less than 5% of pesticides used in the areas from which they drew their study participants. Nevertheless, Baldi and colleagues listed the most impaired functions they found among their "exposed" workers as including selective attention and information processing, working memory, associative memory, verbal fluency, and abstraction. The strongest association with exposure, they indicated, was with the Benton Visual Retention Test, a test involving both selective attention and working memory.

In their study of Egyptian cotton field pesticide applicators, Farahat and colleagues (2003) reported an association between occupational exposure to OP and multiple, "deficits in a wider array of neurobehavioral functions than previously reported by others." However, the pesticides involved were not limited to OP compounds and included carbamates and pyrethroids, as well. Controlling for age and education, these authors reported significantly lower performance by exposed workers in comparison to controls on six neurobehavioral measures. They concluded that "moderate chronic OP exposure negatively effected "visuomotor" speed, verbal abstraction, attention, and memory" (Farahat et al., 2003). Although they attempted to control for age and education, other potential differences between the two groups may have been left unaccounted for in their study. The exposed group, for instance, was reported to have more "neuroticism" than controls as measured by personality testing. Possibly unrelated to the effects of exposure or even likely, related to job selection, such as personality trait, could have explained test performance in other areas of the Farahat study, e.g., on speeded psychomotor tasks, in particular. Also, the authors concluded that there were difficulties in attention demonstrated by the exposed group in comparison to controls. However, performance appeared to be normal on two tests included in the study that are identified as specific for attention (i.e., PASAT and Letter Cancellation). At the least, and to avoid a Type II error, conflicting test findings within a given study should be explained, especially in studies that employ multiple measures with overlapping performance demands. Memory test results, too, were not consistently found to be lower in the exposed group. For example, the exposed group's performances on Digit Span and the Benton Visual Retention Test were lower than the control group's performance; however, initial learning and story delayed recall performances were not. In addition, and although an attempt was made to control for educational level, differences in job type between the two groups were not inconsequential. Workers in the control group were involved in clerical and administrative positions, occupations with notably different demands than those required of the cotton field pesticide applicators. The differences in these work demands hold unknown implications for performance on tests such as those measuring verbal abstraction, especially in the absence of measures of reading comprehension or general ability.

The neurobehavioral effects that have been attributed to chronic exposure to OP pesticides, often on the basis of studies with poorly identified chemical substances with varying and often poorly characterized dose levels, have failed to establish a specific relationship between such chronic exposure and central nervous system dysfunction. Mostly, the studies in this area have included individual case reports, individual reports using small numbers of exposed individuals, cross-sectional studies with inadequately controlled confounders, or studies that suffer from one or more methodological problems. Typically, the reported adverse effects have been nonspecific in precise neurological terms and inconsistent between studies. Unlike the well-established peripheral nervous system syndrome associated with massive acute exposures to OP compounds, no similar neuropsychological occurrence in response to these exposures has been documented. Reporting on the conclusions from the 1999 United Kingdom working group on organophosphates, e.g., Woods et al. (1999) indicated that the balance of evidence to that time suggested that chronic OP exposures at doses lower than those causing overt acute toxicity either do not cause neurological or neuropsychological abnormalities, or do so only rarely. Final answers to these questions will require analytic epidemiological studies. Such studies will be essential for clarifying the specific nature of neurobehavioral changes that result from exposure to OP pesticides.

VERIFICATION OF THE INITIAL CLINICAL DIAGNOSIS

The arterial blood gases showing a severe respiratory acidosis confirmed the presence of acute hypoxia, and supported the diagnosis of acute hypoxic encephalopathy. The history of ingestion of OP pesticide, together with presenting signs of cholinergic overactivity, substantiated with laboratory findings consistent with depressed cholinesterase and hospital course, satisfies all criteria for establishing the diagnosis of an acute cholinergic crisis.

The diagnosis of "major depression, in remission" can be verified only in a generic sense since no information was presented with regard to possible differential psychiatric manifestations, e.g., history of manic episodes, recurrent or cyclical variations in psychiatric manifestations, the presence of psychotic features, etc. (American Psychiatric Association, 1994). Certainly, the history of suicidal attempt and feelings of worthlessness reported by the patient at the time do justify a diagnosis of depression, and the absence of symptoms of mood disturbance at the time he was seen also justifies the "in remission" designator.

VERIFICATION OF THE REVISED CLINICAL NEUROBEHAVIORAL DIAGNOSIS

The patient met *DSM-IV* criteria for *major depressive episode,* and the diagnosing psychiatrist appropriately excluded other conditions that appear in the differential diagnosis for this disorder, including adjustment disorder, manic or mixed episodes, bereavement or sadness, and attention disorder. Also appropriately, the clinician did not attempt to relate the patient's depression to a general medical condition, in this case, to the history of cholinergic crisis or to the patient's ingestion of OP pesticide. The history clearly documented that the patient's depression existed before the medical condition and, in fact, led to his ingestion of OP pesticide.

With regard to the patient's diagnosis of amnestic disorder, the diagnosis chosen, amnestic disorder due to a general medical condition (OP intoxication) appropriately excluded dementia, another condition in the differential diagnostic list for major depression. A more comprehensive neuropsychological examination than was undertaken would likely have provided more detail with regard to the patient's cognitive status than was reported. Nevertheless, the results of MMSE did meet criteria for abnormal mental status (MMSE score <24 [Albers et al., 2004]), and the history and clinical observations were sufficient to establish mild cognitive difficulties and to determine that criteria for dementia were not met (e.g., no indication of aphasia, apraxia, agnosia, or disturbance in executive function) (American Psychiatric Association, 1994). The onset, following ingestion of OP insecticide, and subsequent course of improved memory function were consistent with the type of cognitive dysfunction that was diagnosed as well.

CAUSE/ETIOLOGY

This patient's coma and respiratory failure were attributed to cholinergic crisis due to an overdose of OP pesticide, ingested in an attempt to commit suicide. No cause was specified for the depression listed in the initial diagnosis. The revised clinical neurobehavioral diagnosis, while not specifying an exact cause for the depression, did not causally associate this pre-existing disturbance to either the OP intoxication or to the medical condition resulting from the ingestion of pesticide. On the other hand, the mild amnestic disorder was attributed to a general medical condition, i.e., cholinergic crisis and coma as result of OP intoxication.

VERIFICATION OF CAUSE/ETIOLOGY

The patient's acute encephalopathy and cholinergic crisis were appropriately attributed to his ingestion of OP pesticide. Although the cholinergic crisis was a direct result of the OP exposure, the encephalopathy could have reflected either a direct effect of the OP insecticide or a consequence of hypoxia. Importantly, there was nothing unusual about the acute neurological presentation or the subsequent recovery that was atypical for an hypoxic encephalopathy. The availability of biochemical tests to detect cholinesterase inhibition leaves verification of OP intoxication and its biological plausibility relatively straightforward in this case. This conclusion meets all formal criteria for establishing causality, including timing of exposure and onset of expected and specific signs, and modification of the adverse effect following removal from exposure and appropriate treatment.

For similar criteria-based reasons, the exclusion of OP intoxication as causal to the patient's depression is appropriate as well. If for no other reason, the temporal relationship is not causally sensible. OP pesticides have been said to be causally associated with depression. These claims have been based theoretically on known associations between serotonin and depression and data from animal studies that related OP exposures to changes in central nervous system serotonin (London, Flisher, Wesseling, Mergler, & Kromhout, 2005). In this case, however, the patient had no history of depression and no known exposure to OP pesticide before ingesting the substance in a suicide attempt.

With regard to a causal association between OP intoxication and the patient's diagnosis of amnestic disorder due to a general medical condition (OP intoxication), this conclusion fits most of objective criteria for establishing causality (Hill, 1965). The timing of exposure and onset of amnestic symptoms (e.g., complaint of difficulty with memory) and signs (e.g., objective test findings of memory impairment) were appropriate. Memory difficulties have been said to occur following OP intoxication (Agency for toxic substances and disease registry [ATSDR], 1998; Feldman, 1998). The cause–effect relationship is biologically plausible (e.g., disruption of neurotransmission), and mild signs and symptoms were present that were likely consistent with *acute cholinergic crisis*, without development of *intermediate syndrome* or OPIDN (see chapter 10, volume II for a more detailed discussion of the various OP-induced clinical stages). These memory difficulties improved over time, fitting with expectations of symptom resolution following removal from exposure. However, there is a far more compelling explanation for this patient's mild cognitive problems, namely the acute hypoxic encephalopathy. Although the respiratory dysfunction and the subsequent hypoxia prior to intubation were directly related to the OP ingestion, the initial acute central nervous system abnormalities and the residual findings related to impaired memory are explained sufficiently and completely by hypoxia, independent of cause. Other possible causes in the differential diagnosis for the patient's memory impairment were excluded, e.g., depression, progressive dementia.

From this phenomenological viewpoint, the patient's memory impairment fits almost all of these objective, causal criteria; and it can be concluded with substantial certainty that the patient's amnestic disorder resulted from the event of his OP intoxication and subsequent cardiopulmonary arrest. What is not known is the exact biological mechanism through which this occurred. That is, the present state of our knowledge about the effects of OP intoxication on the central nervous system remains incomplete. As mentioned in the earlier review, attempts to document a cause and effect relationship using chronic OP exposures have to date not been successful. Attempts to use an acute exposure model also have presented substantial challenges, in animal models as well as in potential serendipitous study of acutely poisoned patients. The patient's who do survive acute poisoning and who show residual impairments on recovery very likely have a number of competing explanations for their symptoms and signs, as in this case (e.g., hypoxic encephalopathy as result of respiratory arrest; cardiac insufficiency; and pulmonary, cardiac, or neurological infarcts). In the present case, the patient evidenced pulmonary insufficiency, went into coma, and had to be maintained on a respirator for some 12 hr, with unknown consequences to the integrity of his nervous system. While the onset and course of his memory problems fit with acute injury from OP intoxication, they fit also with any other hypoxic encephalopathy that might have been secondary to that intoxication.

Conclusion

This case presentation reflects an area that is both extremely important and at the same time incomplete in terms of our scientific understanding. It reflects the distinction we have made multiple times in these volumes between diagnosis and causal determination. Also, it adds another dimension to this distinction. That is, attribution of cause will be limited by the extent to which we have developed a scientific understanding of a given chemical substance and its effects on the nervous system. Here, it was possible to make a comprehensive diagnosis, and it was possible to conclude a phenomenological statement regarding causality. What could not be fully explained was the exact mechanism of action that produced the entire spectrum of the patient's symptoms and signs of impairment. Was it the direct consequence of chemical disruption of the cholinergic system or did that disturbance set into motion a series of events, one or more of these secondarily responsible for the patient's impairment in other functional areas, e.g., amnestic disorder?

Solvents

Stanley Berent, PhD

The category, *solvents*, lends itself to controversy as much as any topic in neurobehavioral toxicology. One reason for this is that the term itself is imprecise, referring only to, "...any liquid in which another substance can be dissolved" (Anderson, 1994). In terms of current practice, the term *solvent* is used often in a more limited fashion to refer to *organic solvents*, primarily petroleum distillates containing hydrogen and carbon, *hydrocarbons*, or *chlorinated hydrocarbons* when the molecule contains chlorine (Anderson, 1994). Such substances are used as solvents in the manufacture of a host of products that are in turn used for various industrial and domestic purposes. These applications range from agricultural (e.g., solvent mixtures containing *n*-hexane to extract vegetable oils from soybean crops) and industrial (e.g., use of xylene as a solvent in paint thinners or cleaning agents) to household uses (e.g., trichloroethylene [TCE] as a spot remover) (Agency for toxic substances and disease registry [ATSDR], 2005b). Some frequently encountered solvents and their uses include 1,1,1-trichloroethane (TCA), a synthetic chemical now strictly controlled because of its affects on the ozone layer, it was among other things used in the past as a degreaser, spot cleaner, and as a component in glues and aerosol sprays; tetrachloroethylene (also referred to as perchloro-ethylene [PERC or PCE] and used for dry cleaning, metal degreasing, and in the making of other chemicals); and TCE (metal degreasing and as a solvent in typewriter correction fluids, spot removers, and adhesives) (Agency for toxic substances and disease registry [ATSDR], 2005b; Feldman, 1998; Merck Research Laboratories, 2001).

The constituents of solvents vary in composition as well as in their relative toxicity, directly and as a result of metabolic processes and products that differ from one substance to another. PERC, for instance, has been described, along with TCA, as relatively low among the organic solvents in terms of toxicity, and this has been given as one reason for the preference of these substances over other solvents such as TCE and carbon tetrachloride for use in dry cleaning (Feldman, 1998). PERC, like TCE, also has been used medically in the past as an anesthetic (Carmel, 1970; Farman, 1981; Feldman, 1998). In short, while both TCE and PERC are classified as solvents, they are different from one another in terms of their chemical properties, with different effects on the human nervous system. The reasons for these differing effects are not known completely; however, it is known that each of these two substances is metabolized differently by the human body. In terms of PERC, 80–90% of inhaled PERC is exhaled unchanged, while less than 15% of TCE is exhaled unchanged (Feldman, 1998). Most (approximately 80–95%) of the PERC that remains after exhalation stays in the body unchanged prior to its metaboliza-tion and elimination in urine, mostly as trichloroacetic acid (TCAA) and trichloroethanol glucuronide; whereas 50% or more of an absorbed dose of TCE undergoes biotransformation (Agency for toxic substances and disease registry [ATSDR], 1997a, 1997b; Feldman, 1998). Both TCE and PERC produce *trichloroethanol*, a metabolite that has been shown in animal (mouse) models to enhance inhibitory neurotransmission while inhibiting excitatory mechanisms (Peoples & Weight, 1994, 1998), and the presence of trichloroethanol has been suggested as a basis for any acute neurotoxic effects that might result from exposure to these compounds (Agency for toxic substances and disease registry [ATSDR], 1997b; Feldman, 1998) as well as the sedative effects of TCE, PERC, and related compounds, e.g., chloral hydrate (Pershad, Palmisano, & Nichols, 1999; Scheibler, Kronfeld, Illes, & Allgaier, 1999). Differences in the rates of metabolism between TCE and PERC may play an important role in toxic effects as well, explaining at least in part the difference mentioned earlier in relative toxicity between these two substances.

Toluene, another organic solvent, has received considerable scientific and clinical attention not only because of its widespread application and availabil-ity but also because of its propensity for abuse. For these reasons, we have dealt with toluene separately from its applications in industry (see *toluene* in chapter 16 and also *other psychological/psychiatric considerations* in chapter 17). Much of the discussion in the present section is relevant to these other referenced sections and vice versa.

For the most part, and despite the incompleteness of our scientific understanding regarding the adverse effects of these various organic solvents on neurobehavioral function and the central nervous system, governments worldwide have attempted to reduce the use of these substances and to replace them with various less toxic materials. These governmental actions have been based in part on neurotoxic considerations, but they also have been prompted by concerns about carcinogenicity, adverse effects on organ systems other than the nervous system, as well as effects that may be detrimental to the environment (e.g., effects on the ozone). While these efforts to reduce the use of organic solvents have been increasingly successful, the presence of these chemicals is likely to persist for many years; in land fills, contamination of underground wells, in agricultural locations, and around industrial sites. The continuing concerns regarding such contamination are well known to the public in general, as reflected in frequent news reports concerned with the topic and popular books, such as Jonathan Harr's 1995 book, *A Civil Action* (Harr, 1995). This book and the movie by the same name described events related to a neighborhood whose drinking water was contaminated with industrial waste containing TCE, among other substances. Separate from the occurrences depicted in the movie, 28 people from 8 families who used water from this neighborhood over about a 15-year period were examined clinically, and 24 of these individuals were said to have been diagnosed as having mild-to-moderate encephalopathy (Feldman, 1998; Feldman et al., 1994).

As is the case with all substances, exposure to solvents in sufficient dosage can cause central nervous system injury, whether through direct neurotoxicity, consequences secondary to direct mechanism of action (e.g., hypoxia), or by way of indirect effects that result from damage to other organ systems (e.g., heart or lung).

Case presentation[2]

A 22-year-old male was admitted unconscious to the ED following his attempted suicide by inhalation of fumes from a household cleaning solvent. He was found by a friend, who called 911. EMS was alerted and found the victim on the floor, unconscious and not breathing. Cardiopulmonary resuscitation (CPR) was administered, and the patient was resuscitated, intubated, given O_2 by face mask, and transported to the hospital. The cleaning solution and trash bag he had used to administer the fumes were found nearby and later found to contain TCE as its primary active ingredient. At the time of admission to the ED, he was intubated but breathing on his own. His vital signs were normal, other than tachypnea. He was deeply comatose, responding only with nonpurposeful decorticate posturing to painful stimuli. His pupils were small but reactive to light. Corneal and oculovestibular reflexes were intact. Deep tendon reflexes were diffusely brisk, and he showed prominent palmomental, Chaddock, and Babinski responses. Shortly after admission, he exhibited several major motor seizures. He was treated with anticonvulsants, and no further seizures were noted.

On admission, laboratory tests of blood and urine were normal, including arterial blood gases. An EEG showed generalized slowing in the theta range, bilateral epileptiform activity, and poor activation. A cranial CT was normal.

He remained deeply comatose for about 24 hr, making occasional but incomprehensible vocalizations. Thereafter, he began to open his eyes and show more purposeful movements in response to tactile and verbal stimulation. As he improved, he began to speak in response to simple questions and follow simple commands. He rapidly became oriented to his surrounding, but he had no memory of the early hospitalization or of the events leading to his hospitalization. An MRI done about 2 weeks after admission revealed poor gray–white matter differentiation on T-1 weighted sequences and mildly hyperintense areas bilaterally in the globus pallidus, putamen, and caudate nuclei. Increased signal was noted bilaterally on T-2 weighted images in occipital areas bilaterally. Mild supratentorial cortical atrophy was noted.

Over the course of the next 3 weeks, the patient showed continued steady improvement. He voiced few complaints, other than fatigue, mild confusion, difficulty concentrating, and memory difficulties. At the time of his discharge, approximately 6 weeks after his admission, he felt weak but relatively well. Although he was unable to explain the reasons for his suicide attempt, he agreed to referral for psychiatric treatment.

INITIAL CLINICAL DIAGNOSIS

The patient was diagnosed with "suicide attempt and TCE intoxication, possible cardiorespiratory arrest, major motor seizure, possible encephalopathy." A diagnosis of *depression* or other psychiatric condition was deferred pending further outpatient evaluation.

Following his discharge from the hospital, he was seen by his primary care physician who diagnosed *toxic-induced encephalopathy* and referred him for psychiatric and neuropsychological evaluations.

ADDITIONAL INFORMATION

The report of psychiatric evaluation indicated that the patient had been in his senior year of college when the suicidal attempt occurred. He had become acutely disturbed when his girlfriend of 2 years declined his proposal for marriage. In response, he became withdrawn and stopped going to his classes. He had never abused substances in the past, but he recalled that an acquaintance had some years before told him about someone killing themselves by pouring household cleaning fluid into a plastic garbage bag and tying it over their head. He decided to do the same, securing the bag to ensure that his mouth and nose were covered. The patient reported that he no longer felt this way, nor even depressed, and that he believed that he had done a dumb thing and wanted to get on with his life. He planned to look for a temporary job and to return to school and complete his college work the following fall. His long-term goal was to teach English in public school.

The patient underwent neuropsychological evaluation approximately 6 weeks after his discharge from the hospital. At that time, he reported that he felt much better in most areas, but he complained that he felt "slow" in mental activities that required him to think or to concentrate. He was on no medications. Scores from the formal psychometric portion of that evaluation are contained in Table 15.10. Results were interpreted as reflecting mild cognitive disturbance, with general ability lowered from estimates of his premorbid functioning, which was estimated to be above average on the basis of past educational performance and above average language scores on WAIS-III Vocabulary and WRAT-3 Reading. While most of the scores reported in the

Table 15.10 Case presentation: Results of neuropsychological testing.

Test administered	Domain measured	Test results
WAIS-III, FSIQ	General intellect	101
WAIS-III, VIQ	Verbal intellect	110
WAIS-III, PIQ	Performance intellect	92
WAIS-III, Vocabulary	Vocabulary level	12
WAIS-III, Similarities	Abstract conceptualization	9
WAIS-III, Block Design	Visual-motor problem solving	7
WAIS-III, Digit Symbol	Psychomotor problem solving	8
MMSE	General mental status (including orientation, recall, attention/calculation, language, and visual construction)	25/30 (Errors on serial sevens [×2], recall [×2], and copying)
WMS-III, Working Memory	General working memory	73
WMS-III, Auditory Immediate/Delayed	Verbal recall	102/98
WMS-III, Visual Immediate/Delayed	Visual recall	90/72
WRAT-3, Reading	Reading recognition	115
MMPI-2 (selected scales)	Personality/emotional functioning	Scales (T-Scores): Hs = 65 D = 65 Hy = 66 PD = 56 Pt = 63 Sc = 62 Ma = 44 Validity scales: All normal
Rey 15 Item	General effort	12/15 (normal)

table remain within the normal range, he performed relatively better in verbal than nonverbal areas. Also, relative difficulty was noted in tasks that required good attention and short-term memory, especially nonverbal recall.

His scores on the MMPI-2 reflected a repressive coping style, with very mildly depressed mood that remained at the border of normal in terms of his formal score on the MMPI. Validity indicators were all normal. Primarily at normal levels, he reflected relatively elevated scores on 5 of 10 clinical scales on the MMPI.

The patient also reflected good insight and a positive and realistic plan for the future. A repeat of his suicidal behavior was felt to be unlikely, and his prognosis was listed as good.

REVISED NEUROBEHAVIORAL DIAGNOSIS

Adjustment disorder, with depressed mood was added to the initial clinical diagnoses.

Discussion

Determining that a person has been injured as a result of acute exposure to a given substance, e.g., TCE, can be relatively straightforward when there is a clear history of the exposure together with clinical and laboratory findings that are consistent with such an event as was the situation in this *case presentation*. Things are not always this clear, however, and in the case of chemical solvents, there are peculiar obstacles that can confound a complete under-standing in general and in a given case.

Despite the vagueness that results from classifying various chemical com-pounds under the rubric of one common characteristic, i.e., that they can occur in the form of solvents, the scientific literature is replete with articles on the "effects of solvents" on some aspect of the nervous system, neurobehavioral functioning, or human health, more generally. This tendency to combine a host of unspecified substances and to use the resulting combination as an independent variable in a research design was given impetus by a series of articles that appeared in the literature in the 1970s. These reports referred to what came to be called *chronic painters' syndrome* (Gade, Mortensen, & Bruhn, 1988). Also called at times *painters' encephalopathy, psycho-organic syndrome*, or *solvent encephalopathy*, studies on this proposed syndrome sought to address the question of whether occupational exposure by workers to a host of solvents (including TCE and PERC, but also TCA, mineral spirits, other solvents, as well as at times other potentially toxic substances, e.g., lead) primarily at low doses over long periods of time had produced permanent neurobehavioral dysfunction in the subjects studied (Albers & Berent, 2000; Baker & Fine, 1986; Herskowitz, Ishii, & Schaumburg, 1971; Maizlish, Fine, Albers, Whitehead, & Langolf, 1987; Spencer & Schaumburg, 1985; Spencer, Schaumburg, Raleigh, & Terhaar, 1975) (also, see *case presentation*, solvent-exposed machinist with behavioral and neurological complaints in chapter 18 for further discussion on the topic of *painters' encephalopathy*). The inclusion of the term *encephalopathy*, which is itself a general term denoting only an abnormal condition of the brain (Anderson, 1994), in reference to the proposed solvent-induced condition did nothing to enhance its exactness, and the disorder has been surrounded by controversy almost since its inception. Vagueness associated with these studies went beyond nomenclature, however, with primary problems being associated with study design and methodology. The initial reports on this topic described a syndrome that included symptoms of memory and other cognitive complaints, altered mood, and imbalance; however, these descriptions were based on case reports and cross-sectional designed studies that were incapable of addressing issues of causality conclusively (Albers & Berent, 2000). Weaknesses were evident in important aspects of study design and methodology, including subject selection and description, documentation of exposure variables, selection of control subjects, and control of potentially intervening variables that would be necessary to explain the reported outcomes. In fact, initial findings were later revised by some authors who participated in the initial work and who reanalyzed the original data using a more appropriate referent group that allowed better control of such individual difference variables as age, education, and intellect (Gade et al., 1988).

Also, the progressive dementia that was initially speculated to occur in chronic painters' syndrome was not found on retesting of these same subjects several years later (Edling et al., 1990; Errebo-Knudsen & Olsen, 1986). Nilson and colleagues addressed the question of disease progression in workers previously exposed to solvents through follow-up examinations 18 years after their initial evaluations (Ekberg, Barregard, Hagberg, & Sallsten, 1986; Nilson, Backman, Sallsten, Hagberg, & Barregard, 2003; Nilson, Sallsten, Hagberg, Backman, & Barregard, 2002). They compared 40 carpenters with 41 floor layers, the latter presumed to have been more highly exposed to solvents than were the former. While they found no indication for greater neurobehavioral deterioration in the floor layers than in the carpenter controls, they did find that among those subjects who were over 60 years of age, the floor layers showed the greatest decline in visual memory (Nilson et al., 2002). They concluded that their results were consistent with the view that adverse effects of "heavy" solvent exposure may interact with age to produce greater cognitive deterioration than would otherwise be the case. These studies suffer from a number of methodological problems that limit the conclusions, however. For one thing, they rely on self-report as a means for determining further exposures that might have occurred between initial and follow-up examinations. The fact that the floor layers evidenced greater neuropsychiatric disturbance (e.g., history of depression) than did carpenters in the initial examination could have reflected some unspecified initial difference between these two groups with implications for performance later in life. Also, floor layers were said to have reported more "other health problems" than did carpenters. The study authors raised the possibility that these reported illnesses could have been initiated by their solvent exposures, but it is equally likely that this was not the case. Tateyama et al. (2003), for instance, reported an association between early cognitive (visual-motor) functioning in schizophrenia and worsening of psychopathology with aging that was greater than that seen in normal aging alone.

The research design employed by Nilson et al. (2002) relied on the presumption of limited initial differences between the two occupations studied in factors other than nature and extent of exposure. In fact, there could be any number of differences that were left unaccountable (e.g., selection bias) that could explain any observed differences in magnitude of performance decrement with aging. Finally, a number of tests were administered in these examinations, with only one, Block Design, showing a significant difference in the primary analysis (main effect for exposure group). Interestingly, the only significant three way interaction (group $\times$ time $\times$ age) showed the referent group to have deteriorated more over time in "reasoning" than did any other group. The study authors reported that their "older floor layers" evidenced a mean decline in "abstract visual–spatial reasoning (unfolding)" and in "two handed motor speed performance (bolt);" however, these differences were not statistically significant. More importantly perhaps, one might expect the differential decline with aging to reflect in Block Design since this was an area found initially to be lower in the exposed group than in the referent group. This type of decline did not occur. When all analyses reported are considered, it is difficult to accept the biological plausibility that progressive neurological deterioration resulting from toxic-induced neurological dysfunction 18 or more years before would eventuate in the one statistically significant finding on Block Design, perhaps especially since the original study had concluded that the "disease" appeared to be reversible and that all participants had "essentially recovered" at the time they were evaluated initially (Ekberg et al., 1986). Also, the between group difference in Block Design in the follow-up work had been observed in the initial examination as well, and this would fit, as conceded by the study authors, with selection bias, perhaps based upon subtle differences in occupational demands or even psychological factors (Spurgeon, 2002). Speaking speculatively for the moment, carpentry might demand visualization skills than include three-dimensional conceptualization in a manner that differs from floor layers who work with two-dimensional grids. With the passage of time, one might predict a difference in ability between these two groups, whether through differential selection on the basis of pre-existing skill at the time of entry to the occupation or the result of prolonged occupation-specific practice, or a combination of factors.

What about clinical signs? Objective and subjective signs as well as clinical test findings can result from exposure to organic solvents. Signs vary depending on the specific solvent and also on extent and duration of exposure as well as regional neuroanatomical site vulnerability to a specific solvent or its metabolites. As in the case of symptoms, not all signs are specific to a given disorder or its cause. Some signs may not be specific to pathology at all, occurring normally in some portion of the population, especially with advancing age. Even when abnormal signs result from exposure to a specific toxicant, these abnormalities may be reversible following removal from such exposure (see chapter 6, volume I for further discussion). Consider, e.g., a group of printing press workers studied initially by Wang et al. (1986) and later described by Feldman (1998). The workers who were studied developed progressive muscle weakness, numbness, and other symptoms and signs that were ultimately attributed to their occupational exposure to *n*-hexane (Wang et al.). The clinical neurological examination of these workers was reported to include, among other findings, decreased deep tendon reflexes. The workers were followed with repeat clinical examinations over a period of years, and it was found that reflexes improved gradually in all patients, with ankle reflexes being the last to reappear. Ten of 11 workers who were followed clinically reportedly showed good recovery at 30 months following the cessation of their exposure to *n*-hexane (Chang, 1990).

In terms of imaging findings, these are too often nonspecific to a given underlying disease. del Amo, Berenguer, Pujol, and Mercader (1996), for instance, reported MRI findings in a 17-year-old male who was acutely exposed to TCA following purposeful inhalation of correction fluid. They reported finding mild bilateral T-1 and T-2 weighted hyperintensities in globus pallidus, poor gray–white matter differentiation on T-2 weighted images, and increased T-2 signals in putamen, caudate nucleus, and occipital hemispheres. These findings are those of a leukoencephalopathy and are characteristic of those reported following intoxication with solvents other than TCA (e.g., toluene [Filley, Halliday, & Kleinschmidt-DeMasters, 2004]). But, it is important to note that such MRI findings are not specific to organic solvent intoxication. del Amo et al. (1996), for instance, likened the findings from two MRI studies done 6 months apart on their patient to findings described for toxicants other than TCA (e.g., methanol and carbon monoxide) as well as to hypoxic injury involving cortical and basal ganglia areas.

What about neurobehavioral test findings? Neuropsychological testing in general represents a method that is impressively accurate in measuring behavior. This statement may appear surprising in light of our repeated emphasis on the lack of specificity of such measures (see, e.g., chapter 5 in volume I). How are these two seemingly contradictory statements reconciled? By specificity, we are referring not to the accuracy of measurement, which for neuropsychological testing competes favorably in terms of reliability with any number of physical tests used routinely in medicine (see chapter 7, volume I). Since neurobehavioral alterations are common in toxicant-induced dysfunction, frequently representing a major area of disability for the patient, the inclusion of the psychometric examination can be expected to document the presence, type, and severity of neurobehavioral impairment (Dixit, Nadimpalli, & Cavallino, 1999; Filley & Kleinschmidt-DeMasters, 2001). Also, serial testing of the individual patient can establish a baseline and allow for determination of important clinical information such as disease progression, chronicity, or resolution. In research, neuropsychometrics can be used to objectively quantify behavioral variables.

In short, the neurobehavioral symptoms and signs of toxicant-induced central nervous system dysfunction are likely to be both nonspecific and highly variable between individuals (Jin, Haut, & Ducatman, 2004). They are nonspecific because behaviors mediated by the central nervous system often can be multiply determined. Trimble (Trimble & Krishnamoorthy, 2000), e.g., described an association between exposure to TCE and depression; however, depression is certainly not specific to this solvent. Also, while depression may occur in association with solvent exposure, its appearance under these circumstances is not universal. Depression may occur in the absence of any exposure as well as in the absence of demonstrated neurological dysfunction. So, the documentation of depression in an individual patient will only tell us that the patient is depressed, together with other aspects of the nature of that disturbance. The presence of depression will tell us little about the underlying pathophysiology and perhaps even less about cause. Since so many of the behavioral symptoms reported for solvent exposure (e.g., poor concentration, memory impairment, and poor problem solving) can reflect multiple causes, accurate measurement and objective documentation of their presence will not be sufficient alone to determine cause.

It appears that solvent exposure sufficient to produce persistent neurological dysfunction is likely at some point to be demonstrated on conventional MRI brain imaging studies (Rosenberg, Grigsby, Dreisbach, Busenbark, & Grigsby, 2002). Also, toxic-induced dysfunction that is evident on MRI will likely be associated with areas of impairment noted on neuropsychological test results (Filley & Kleinschmidt-DeMasters, 2001). Some have postulated, however, individual situations where one or the other of these measures (MRI or psychometric examination) fails to show findings of abnormality while the other method does show abnormality (Filley & Kleinschmidt-DeMasters, 2001; Rosenberg et al.). Still, the most accurate determination of both diagnosis and causal determination in the area of solvent-induced pathology involves the employment of a combination of neuropsychological testing together with neuroimaging and other neurological evaluation methods. Positive findings on brain imaging studies, with functional neuroanatomical sensible findings on the psychometric examination, increase the evidence for valid examination results for both procedures while lessening the possibility of false positive results in either examination (Berent et al., 1999).

Theoretically, the way to improve neuropsychological specificity itself would be to look for patterns of strengths and weaknesses that are associated with a specific cause, e.g., TCE exposure. In fact, there has been some success in this approach in the area of solvent-induced disorder (see *toluene* in chapter 16 for further discussion). Filley et al. (2004) described neurobehavioral impairments that they associated with solvent-induced neurological dysfunction, which they conceived of as primarily a white matter disease. The impairments included sustained attention, speed of information processing, memory retrieval, and visual–spatial skills. Very importantly, they described relative sparing of language related abilities, including procedural memory. Still, this neurobehavioral profile neither represents a universal response to solvent exposure nor is it specific to solvent-induced white matter disease (Filley et al.). As mentioned earlier, the results of neuro-psychological examinations represent very accurate measurement of behavior, but these results can never be more specific than is the underlying pathology that produced them.

From a research perspective, the determination of adverse effects of some substance on the nervous system requires a persistent and rigorous approach. In the case of solvents, this will likely demand a combination of animal and human studies that focus on one substance, or factors that are common to multiple substances, with research designs that allow for control of important confounding variables, including psychosocial factors, that compete for or interact with primary variables to explain the results. Clinically, the problem must be approached with the same methods as employed elsewhere in these volumes, in the context of the differential diagnosis and independent verification of cause for the final diagnosis. Even with the commitment to pursue such a course, the topic of solvents will prove difficult when it comes to human epidemiological studies, simply because of the myriad potential confounders to consider.

When is it sufficient to conclude *solvent-induced* disorder, as opposed to a more specific causal attribution, e.g., xylene-induced? The answer to this question will to some extent depend on the context in which it is asked, including the intended applications that will follow the answer. While in the scientific laboratory setting compounds may be studied for their biological effects in relatively pure form, the same compounds almost never occur exclusively in real-world applications. Xylene, e.g., has broad applications as a solvent in printing, rubber and leather industries, paints, cleaning agents, and other industrial products (Agency for toxic substances and disease registry [ATSDR], 2004). Xylene is derived from petroleum and although it has been said to be one of the top 30 chemicals produced in the United States in terms of volume, it is seldom the exclusive ingredient in a given product. The combination of xylene with other chemicals can affect the metabolism of all, which in turn can lead to altered clinical manifestations that result from exposure (including the inhibition or potentiation of one or more of the constituent chemicals) (Feldman, 1998). A person who is said to have abused xylene through solvent ingestion is likely to actually have abused a number of ingredients contained in that solvent. This may not be a problem from a clinical diagnostic viewpoint, assuming an appropriate formulation of the differential diagnosis. It may become a problem in terms of causal attribution should xylene-induced disorder be concluded without proper consideration of the other ingredients contained in the solvent. These causal distinctions may not be possible in many instances. When that is the case, one may still be able to limit the cause to a more general class of substances, e.g., solvents, even though the specific substance, xylene, cannot be specified. This may, in fact, sometimes be sufficient.

NERVOUS SYSTEM LOCALIZATION

The symptoms, signs, and test findings in the *case presentation* implicate the supratentorial level of the central nervous system.

VERIFICATION OF THE INITIAL CLINICAL DIAGNOSIS

The actual diagnosis listed, *toxic-induced encephalopathy*, reflected both the medical condition and the presumed cause, and we have separated these two for purposes of verification. The diagnosis of *encephalopathy* explains the clinical findings at the time of hospitalization and the subsequent clinical course, parsimoniously and coherently. This diagnosis, however, does not address the presumed psychological state or psychiatric disturbance that contributed to the patient's acute medical condition.

VERIFICATION OF THE REVISED CLINICAL DIAGNOSIS

The psychological diagnosis of *adjustment disorder, with depressed mood* (American Psychiatric Association, 1994) is straightforward in this instance. It explains all of the patient's behaviors that led to his TCE exposure as well as his subsequent clinical course following treatment of his medical condition, including a lack of persistence of his emotional symptoms. He does not satisfy criteria for primary differential considerations, which include most importantly acute depression or anxiety or exacerbation of pre-existing personality disorder. Here, the response was an acute change in behavior and mood in the face of a specific and identifiable stressor (personal rejection by his girlfriend). Even though his behavioral response to this interpersonal stressor (suicide attempt) might seem extreme, excessiveness is an expected component in the diagnosis.

CAUSE/ETIOLOGY

The patient's signs at the time of his hospitalization, and later residual mild cognitive impairments, were attributed to exposure to TCE as result of suicidal attempt. The adjustment reaction was attributed to over-reaction to a specific life stress.

VERIFICATION OF CAUSE/ETIOLOGY

All objective criteria for verifying the specific toxic etiology are met in this *case presentation*. The timing of exposure and onset of clinical signs were appropriate. The timing of the subsequent course of improvement following removal from exposure also is consistent with expected outcome. The occurrence of transient seizures following removal from exposure in the patient also is consistent with animal studies that have associated increased seizuregenicity with solvent exposure (Bowen, Wiley, Evans, Tokarz, & Balster, 1996; Chan & Chen, 2003; Chen, Chan, & Fu, 2002). While differences in effect are notable, commonalities in the adverse effects of various solvents and their often transient nature also have been emphasized (Bowen et al., 1996).

One criterion not met entirely relates to the exact mechanism of neurological injury that occurred as a result of the exposure to TCE in this instance. As mentioned earlier, hypoxic injury can be expected to produce clinical findings that are the same as those observed in the *case presentation*. These include the observed clinical signs and course, predicted outcome, as well as the occurrence of seizure and findings on EEG, MRI, and neuropsychometric examination (see section on *hypoxic encephalopathy* in chapter 17). Our knowledge regarding the exact mechanism of action involved in producing the adverse effects of TCE remains incomplete (Feldman, 1998). TCE is known to affect neurotransmission directly and via its various metabolites (Feldman, 1998). Secondary effects, on the central nervous system itself or by indirect complications that result from dysfunction in other organ systems, also can be important in producing cellular damage in the central nervous system. The fact that the patient in the *case presentation* experienced an apparent cardiorespiratory arrest (or at least profound respiratory insufficiency) and a relatively prolonged coma, for instance, can interfere with cellular oxygenation and these occurrences raise the possibility of hypoxic injury to the brain, independent of the direct effects of solvent intoxication. Neither the MRI findings during his hospitalization nor the residual impairments noted on neuropsychological examination following his hospitalization differentiate between the various possible mechanisms of injury (Dixit et al., 1999; Rosenberg et al., 2002). Nevertheless, and regardless of the specific mechanism responsible, it is clear that the patient's exposure to TCE resulted in his subsequent acute and residual abnormalities. This is consistent with the statement we made at the beginning of this section that exposure to solvents in sufficient dose can result in central nervous system injury, through direct neurotoxicity, consequences secondary to direct mechanism of action (e.g., hypoxia), or by way of indirect effects that result from damage to other organ systems (e.g., heart or lung). An important question remaining and that cannot be answered completely by the present case is whether or not exposure to TCE results in prolonged neurotoxic injury without reaching hypoxic levels.

Conclusion

Our knowledge regarding the adverse effects of exposure to solvents remains incomplete. The exact physiological mechanism of injury is not yet completely understood. Nevertheless, the *case presentation* in this instance demonstrates that by pursuing a systematic, evidence-based approach, the clinician can arrive at both an accurate diagnosis and a causal determination. Also, this case illustrates the importance of the multidisciplinary approach to neurobehavioral toxicology, in research as well as in clinical practice.

It was pointed out earlier that the topic of solvent-induced neurological dysfunction, especially dysfunction that is attributed to the general class of solvents and at chronic, low doses (e.g., painters' encephalopathy) remains controversial. One aspect of this controversy rests in the question of whether or not acceptable scientific evidence has been developed sufficient to conclude that the disorder actually exists. Many would argue that it has not, and the clash of opinions between those that argue against versus those that believe it represents a verifiable disorder has been an important source of the controversy. Controversy can arise when conclusions have been based on erroneous methods. One source of error derives from the employment of circular reasoning to address a scientific question. With regard to the published literature on the neurobehavioral effects of solvent exposure, instances of circular reasoning have occurred when symptoms known to accompany acute exposure are used as a surrogate for exposure in the absence of direct measures of exposure (Albers & Berent, 2000). A flaw in such an approach, aside from the circularity of using symptoms to define those who were likely to have been exposed, is the nonspecific nature of such symptoms (see Table 15.11). Spurgeon, Gompertz, and Harrington (1997) have emphasized that the majority of such symptoms overlap with those associated with complaints that derive from psychosocial origins apparently independent of physical toxicological mechanisms. These psychosocial factors, even among those not formally diagnosable with a psychiatric condition, may in turn reflect individual attitudes and beliefs that are influenced by factors such as personal stress and satisfaction with life in general (Spurgeon et al.). The fallacy of defining the presence and extent of exposure to a particular substance based solely on complaints is readily apparent.

Table 15.11 Nonspecific symptoms often associated with suspected solvent-induced neurotoxicity.

Psychomotor slowing
Depression (or related feelings of irritability, fatigue, anxiety, or other mood changes)
Attention deficits (including inability to concentrate)
Cognitive complaints in general
Confusion
Incoordination or balance problems
Short-term memory loss (or memory complaints in general)
Headache
Dizziness
Sleep difficulties

Modified from "Solvents and neurotoxicity," by R. F. White and S. P. Proctor, 1997, Lancet, 349, p. 1239.

Summary

The various agents reviewed in this chapter were chosen because of their representativeness and the fact that they reflect the ambivalence with which we embrace the benefits that derive from their use and, at the same time, remain concerned about their potential for harm. The introduction to this chapter described briefly the 1845 expedition to complete the mapping to the Northwest Passage, headed by Sir John Franklin. This story, as well as any in modern times, symbolizes the dilemma faced by modern society. While the loss of all members of that expedition was a disaster, the fact that any chance they might have had to survive was probably negated by the then modern invention (the "tin can") that was intended to ensure their survival, made the outcome all the more tragic. The Franklin Expedition provides a microcosm of the potential benefits that modern society derives from the applications of environmental agents to everyday life and the potential harm that can result from such use.

There is a tendency to think linearly when considering the way in which a toxicant produces its adverse effects on the organism. In fact, the mechanisms of injury are more likely to be multifactorial, some primary and perhaps many more via diverse routes that include interactions with constitutional, developmental, and other predisposing factors, secondary effects from damage to target organs, metabolized by-products, and interactions with other primary agents. This is not new information. As stated in the introduction to this chapter, the Franklin expedition did not die from the direct toxic effects of lead but, rather, from the critical but less direct effects of lead on other psychological and physiological systems and disease.

Aside from those agents that are harvested from the environment, we are exposed to many others that are naturally occurring and to which we are constantly exposed, e.g., elemental mercury, which is abundant in the earth's crust, or carbon monoxide from forest fires and other natural phenomena. As our scientific understanding of the ways in which an organism can be harmed by such agents has increased, it also has become more obvious that a simple linear model most likely will not be sufficient to account for the complex mechanisms that are involved. This does not negate the importance of a dose–response model, but it does lend to the difficulties that face the clinician or researcher who must arrive at a clinical conclusion or test a novel hypothesis.

The review of *carbon monoxide*, e.g., emphasized that although carbon monoxide has relatively specific biological effects that are easily documented following acute exposures, the neurobehavioral effects of CO poisoning can vary greatly between individuals. This variability results from differences that are present from situation to situation in dose-related variables but also results from inconsistency between individuals in terms of physiology and susceptibility to damage. Specified regions of the central nervous system are particularly sensitive to damage from CO exposure and the resulting hypoxic damage can occur more widely and unpredictably in the nervous system. This widespread and irregular pattern of injury mirrors in an unpredictable neurobehavioral pattern of impairment as well, and this presents a challenge to causal determination that is based on neurobehavioral test findings. The section on CO concluded with some suggested approaches to diagnosis and causal specification in light of these challenges.

Lead was discussed in two sections of this chapter, one written by Roth emphasizing the effect of lead on adults and the other concerned with the effects on children, written by Trask. Both emphasized the important role played by behavioral factors related to human development in influencing the organism's vulnerability to exposure to lead (e.g., different habits and opportunities for exposure and physiological differences in susceptibility to central nervous system damage between adults and children). Also, both authors emphasized the successes achieved in efforts to reduce the amount of lead in the environment and the beneficial effects this reduction appears to have had on reducing the lead burden in adults and children. Among other things, Roth talked about the interest and need to develop biochemical and physiological markers that are more efficient than are tools presently available and that will allow for further study of what he termed, "subclinical toxicity." Trask presented a similar concern, the need to study further the potential and perhaps subtle effects of "very low levels" of lead on neurobehavioral functioning in children.

For the reasons already given, the task of studying the effects of low lead levels on humans is a complex one. Stewart and colleagues, for instance, published the results of several studies that looked at former "organolead" workers up to 18 years after their last occupational exposure to organic lead (Schwartz et al., 2000; Stewart et al., 1999, 2006). Using a novel approach that combined measurement of tibia bone lead with measures of neurobehavioral function and MRI, the authors addressed the general hypothesis that lead causes persistent effects on the central nervous system as evidenced by functional impairment and, more specifically, in white matter and general and regional specific brain volumes (Stewart et al., 2006). The authors used tibia lead levels to estimate past lead exposure. They first reported that these peak tibia lead levels were associated with a decline in neurobehavioral test scores, with longitudinal declines in verbal learning and memory (Schwartz, Stewart, & Hu, 2002; Schwartz et al., 2000; Stewart et al., 1999). A subsequent analysis was said to document that cumulative doses of lead were associated with progressive declines in neurobehavioral function even after blood and brain lead had declined (Schwartz et al., 2001; Stewart et al., 2006). In their most recent study using the same cohort of 532 former lead-exposed workers, the authors interpreted their data to suggest that cumulative lead dose was associated with "persistent" brain lesions (Stewart et al., 2006). More specifically, they reported finding a significant association between increasing tibia lead and increasing white matter lesions ($p = 0.004$); associations between higher tibia lead and "smaller" total brain volume, frontal and total gray matter volume, and parietal white matter volume. Also, of nine specific regions examined, tibia lead was associated with smaller volumes for the cingulated gyrus and insula. This work has received considerable attention from the professional media (Carroll, 2006), with perhaps the only published and possible controversy to date being the researchers' decision to not control for blood pressure, which they found to be correlated with total brain volume and number of white matter lesions (Rowland & McKinstry, 2006). To quote from Rowland (Rowland & McKinstry, 2006), "Statistically, this is complicated because lead also increases blood pressure and is therefore an intermediate variable on the hypothesized causal path between lead exposure and white matter lesions or reduced brain volumes." While Rowland acknowledged the authors' contribution to the published literature on the effects of lead, he also pointed out that there remain a number of unanswered questions regarding the mechanisms by which lead produces its effects and with regard to specific functional areas that are affected by exposure (Rowland & McKinstry, 2006). In addition, he called attention to other variables that are known to correlate with white matter lesions, e.g., cardiovascular risk factors such as hypertension and advancing age.

With regard to aging, Filley (2001) stated that while gray matter loss in the cortex is less extensive than thought previously, newer evidence suggests that white matter undergoes significant changes with aging and that these alterations are accompanied by functional changes as well. Filley attributes much of the cortical atrophy found to be associated with aging to white matter loss, which he states is greater than gray matter loss. Incomplete myelination is specified by Filley as one interpretation explaining the reported white matter changes in aging. These changes are considered by Filley to be a consequence of the "normal aging process," to be distinguished from pathological conditions such as Alzheimer's disease. Still, the behavioral dysfunctions he reported to be associated with white matter loss, even though they may remain within normal limits, are referable to frontal brain regions and include behaviors such as processing speed, immediate and delayed recall, complex problem solving (i.e., executive functions), and indices of general ability (Filley, 2001), the same areas essentially as reported to be involved in the Stewart et al. (2006) work. Despite Filley's emphasis on the normality of white matter loss and declines in specific and general neurobehavioral functions with aging, no specific mechanism underlying these changes has yet been identified. Rowland and McKinstry (2006) asked if in addition to lead, do other environmental exposures to such substances as mercury, pesticides, or solvents also contribute to progressive impairments that mimic the aging process? Clearly, the work by Stewart et al. represents an exciting and promising response to such questions, at least for organic lead. The number of variables competing as potential explanations, singly and in combination, will prove a challenging task that may take many years to address.

Other substances presented in this chapter included organic mercury, pesticides, and solvents. Organic mercury (Hg) is abundant in the environment, but it is mercury vapor (Hg^0) that is considered to be more hazardous to health than is the liquid form of Hg. Hg^0 occurs as a result of natural degassing of the earth's crust and also as a result of various industrial processes. It is abundant in the atmosphere. Normally found in negligent amounts, industrial accidents and other human actions can lead to increased exposure to Hg^0 and other potentially harmful forms of Hg, e.g., organic mercury (MeHg). As in CO poisoning, neurological damage from MeHg can have unpredictable neurological effects, making it difficult to identify a clear neurobehavioral pattern of strengths and weaknesses.

Pesticides are of a number of types, defined in general on the basis of their intended purpose, to control pests. They rely for the most part on some mechanism that disrupts normal biological function. The threat to humans from exposure to pesticides comes from the fact that these agents are not species specific, and they can cause damage in people as well as in the pests they are intended to control. There are numerous ways in which humans can become exposed to pesticides and exposure prevention is an important factor in reducing personal injuries from these products.

In discussing solvents, it was pointed out that the proposed adverse effects of exposure to these substances have often been accompanied by controversy. One reason for the controversy may relate to the overly inclusive way in which solvents are defined, i.e., a liquid in which another substance can be dissolved. Often, the word "solvents" is used in a general way when attributing a person's symptoms to exposure to a substance. The tendency to combine various substances into one generic classification presents difficulties to clinicians and to scientists since these various substances are quite different in their composition and in their toxicity. In part, as a result of lack of specificity in the published literature on solvents, the scientific understanding of these substances and their potentially harmful effects remain incomplete.

In all of the sections of this chapter, there has been an emphasis on the need for objective, systematic, and evidence-based approaches to scientific inquiry and clinical evaluation. Each specific agent discussed in this chapter was described in terms of the challenges they present to the researcher and clinician, and suggestions were provided on how best to address these challenges.

Notes

1   Sometimes expressed as HbCO (Goldman & Bennett, 2000).
2   Details of the history have been modified to preserve the anonymity of the patient and the patient's family.
3   Carbon monoxide is odorless and, therefore, would not have been detectable by smell. The source of natural gas, which the roommate reported, remains unclear although it may have been related to the faulty space heater. The presence of natural gas in the apartment was not reported by the gas company workers, however.
4   In addition to being an atmospheric pollutant, CO occurs endogenously, producing a background COHb of 1–2% in nonsmokers and 5–6% in smokers (Bleeker, 1994), or higher, i.e., up to 10% (Piantadosi, 2000). With a half-life of 3–5 hr (Bleeker, 1994), it is possible that the patient's COHb level had been higher before being measured in the ED.
5   Case material from Ahn et al. (2000).

6   Case material from Ziegler et al. (2002).
7   Case material from Hettmansberger and Mycyk (2002).
8   Case material from Tuzun et al. (2002).
9   The described case was adapted from an article by Nierenberg et al. (1998). While the article specifies dimethylmercury, contrasts this compound with MeHg, and labels dimethylmercury as "supertoxic" because of the very small dose needed to achieve a lethal effect; the authors also indicated that the neurotoxic effects are similar to those caused by MeHg compounds. In addition, dimethyl- and other McHg compounds are known to be found together in biological sources of MeHg (Merck Research Laboratories, 2001).
10 *Neurasthenia* is a nonspecific term that has been used in a variety of ways in the published literature. Neurasthenic syndrome, for instance, is a term that has been used to characterize a vague condition associated with solvent exposure that is more often referred to as "painters' encephalopathy" or "chronic toxic enceph- alopathy" (Brown, 2002). "Neurasthenic," also has been defined as, "...per- taining to a disorder characterized by excessive fatigue, insomnia, weakness, anxiety, and mental and physical irritability" (Anderson, 1994).

References

Abelsohn, A., Sanborn, M. D., Jessiman, B. J., & Weir, E. (2002). Identifying and managing adverse environmental health effects: 6. Carbon monoxide poisoning. *Canadian Medical Association Journal, 166*, 1685–1690.

Agency for toxic substances and disease registry (ATSDR). (1997a). *Toxicological profile for tetrachloroethylene (PERC)*. Retrieved from http://www.atsdr.cdc. gov/toxprofiles/tp18.html

Agency for toxic substances and disease registry (ATSDR). (1997b). *Toxicological profile for trichloroethylene (TCE)*. Retrieved from http://www.atsdr.cdc.gov/ toxprofiles/tp19.html

Agency for toxic substances and disease registry (ATSDR). (1998). *Public health statement for chlorpyrifos*. Retrieved from http://www.atsdr.cdc.gov/toxprofiles/ phs84.html

Agency for toxic substances and disease registry (ATSDR). (1999). *Toxicological profile for lead*. Atlanta, GA: U.S. Department of Health and Human Services.

Agency for toxic substances and disease registry (ATSDR). (2004). *ToxFAQs for xylene*. Retrieved from http://www.atsdr.cdc.gov/tfacts71.html

Agency for toxic substances and disease registry (ATSDR). (2005a). *ToxFAQs for mercury*. Retrieved from http://www.atsdr.cdc.gov/tfacts46.html

Agency for toxic substances and disease registry (ATSDR). (2005b). *ToxFAQs*. Retrieved from http://www.atsdr.cdc.gov/

Ahn, H. C., Hwang, K. Y., Hong, S. Y., Yand, D. H., Lee, B. K., & Todd, A. C. (2000). Case study: Chronic lead nephrology with excessive body lead burden. *Occupational Health, 42*, 260–262.

Albers, J. W., & Berent, S. (2000). Controversies in neurotoxicology: Current status. *Neurologic Clinics, 18*, 741–764.

Albers, J. W., Berent, S., Garabrant, D. H., Giordani, B., Schweitzer, S. J., Garrison, R. P., et al. (2004). The effects of occupational exposure to chlorpyrifos on the neurologic examination of central nervous system function: A prospective cohort study. *Journal of Occupational and Environmental Medicine, 46*, 367–378.

Al-Saleh, I., Khalil, M. A., & Taylor, A. (1995). Lead, erythrocyte protoporphyrin, and hematological parameters in normal maternal and umbilical cord blood from subjects of the Riyadh region, Saudi Arabia. *Archives of Environmental Health*, *50*, 66–73.

American Academy of Pediatrics Committee on Environmental Health (1998). Screening for elevated blood lead levels. *Pediatrics*, *101*, 1072–1078.

American Psychiatric Association. (1994). *Diagnostic and statistical manual of mental disorders* (4th ed.). Washington, DC: Author.

Amy, R., Bhatnagar, R., Damkjar, E., & Beattie, O. (1986). The last Franklin expedition: Report of a postmortem examination of a crew member. *Canadian Medical Association Journal*, *135*, 115–117.

Anderson, K. N. (1994). *Mosby's medical dictionary* (4th ed.). St. Louis: Mosby.

Asai, K., & Toru, M. (1969). Changes of brain focal symptoms in two cases of carbon monoxide intoxication (interval form). *Seishin Shinkeigaku Zasshi—Psychiatria et Neurologia Japonica*, *71*, 776–789.

Baker, E. L., & Fine, L. J. (1986). Solvent neurotoxicity: The current evidence. *Journal of Occupational Medicine*, *28*, 126–129.

Bakir, F., Damluji, S. F., Amin-Zaki, L., Murtadha, M., Khalidi, A., al Rawi, N. Y., et al. (1973). Methylmercury poisoning in Iraq. *Science*, *181*, 230–241.

Baldi, I., Filleul, L., Mohammed-Brahim, B., Fabrigoule, C., Dartigues, J. F., Schwall, S., et al. (2001). Neuropsychologic effects of long-term exposure to pesticides: Results from the French Phytoner study. *Environmental Health Perspectives*, *109*, 839–844.

Banks, E. D., Ferretti, L. E., & Shucard, D. W. (1997). Effects of low level lead exposure on cognitive function in children: A review of behavioral, neuropsychological and biological evidence. *NeuroToxicology*, *18*, 237–282.

Bayliss, R. (2002). Sir John Franklin's last arctic expedition: A medical disaster. *Journal of the Royal Society of Medicine*, *95*, 151–153.

Beattie, O., & Geiger, J. (1988). *Frozen in time: Unlocking the secrets of the Franklin expedition* (1st American ed.). New York: Dutton.

Bellinger, D., Leviton, A., & Sloman, J. (1990). Antecedents and correlates of improved cognitive performance in children exposed in utero to low levels of lead. *Environmental Health Perspectives*, *89*, 5–12.

Bellinger, D. C. (2004). Lead. *Pediatrics*, *113*, 1016–1022.

Bellinger, D. C., Sloman, J., Leviton, A., Rabinowitz, M., Needleman, H. L., & Waternaux, C. (1991). Low-level lead exposure and children's cognitive function in the preschool years. *Pediatrics*, *87*, 219–227.

Bellinger, D. C., Stiles, K. M., & Needleman, H. L. (1992). Low-level lead exposure, intelligence and academic achievement: A long-term follow-up study. *Pediatrics*, *90*, 855–861.

Berent, S., Giordani, B., Foster, N., Minoshima, S., Lajiness-O'Neill, R., Koeppe, R., et al. (1999). Neuropsychological function and cerebral glucose utilization in isolated memory impairment and Alzheimer's disease. *Journal of Psychiatric Research*, *33*, 7–16.

Blain, P. G. (2001). Effects of insecticides. *Lancet*, *357*, 1442.

Bleeker, M. L. (1994). *Occupational neurology and clinical neurotoxicology*. Baltimore: Williams & Wilkins.

Bowen, S. E., Wiley, J. L., Evans, E. B., Tokarz, M. E., & Balster, R. L. (1996). Functional observational battery comparing effects of ethanol, 1,1,1-trichloroethane, ether, and flurothyl. *Neurotoxicology and Teratology*, *18*, 577–585.

Brewster, U. C., & Perazella, M. A. (2004). A review of chronic lead intoxication: An unrecognized cause of chronic kidney disease. *American Journal of the Medical Sciences, 327,* 341–347.

Bromberg, M. B. (2000). Peripheral neurotoxic disorders. *Neurologic Clinics, 18,* 681–694.

Brown, J. S. (2002). *Environmental and chemical toxins and psychiatric illness.* Washington, DC: American Psychiatric Publishing.

Buchanan, G. (1999). The tragedy of iron deficiency during infancy and early childhood. *The Journal of Pediatrics, 135,* 413–415.

Byard, R. W., & Couper, R. (1998). Death after exposure to dimethylmercury. *New England Journal of Medicine, 339,* 1243.

Byers, R. K., & Lord, E. E. (1943). Late effects of lead poisoning on mental development. *American Journal of Disease of Children, 66,* 471–494.

Can Manufacturers Institute. (2000). *History of the can.* Retrieved from http://www.cancentral.com/index.htm

Canfield, R. L., Gendle, M. H., & Cory-Slechta, D. A. (2004). Impaired neuropsychological functioning in lead-exposed children. *Developmental Neuropsychology, 26,* 513–540.

Canfield, R. L., Henderson, C. R. J., Cory-Slechta, D. A., Cox, C., Jusko, T. A., & Lanphear, B. P. (2003). Intellectual impairment in children with blood lead concentrations below 10 µg per deciliter. *New England Journal of Medicine, 348,* 1517–1526.

Carmel, A. G. (1970). Trichloroethylene inhalant analgesia in office practice: Experience in 6,000 administrations. *Diseases of the Colon and Rectum, 13,* 138–142.

Carroll, L. (2006, June). Adult exposure to lead may damage brain. *Neurology Today, 6,* 8.

Centers for Disease Control. (2004). *Childhood lead poisoning prevention program.* Retrieved March 10, 2005 from www.cdc.gov/nceh/lead/research

Centers for Disease Control and Prevention. (1991). *Preventing lead poisoning in young children: A statement by the Centers for Disease Control, October 1991.* Atlanta, GA: U.S. Department of Health and Human Services.

Chan, M. H., & Chen, H. H. (2003). Toluene exposure increases aminophylline-induced seizure susceptibility in mice. *Toxicology and Applied Pharmacology, 193,* 303–308.

Chang, Y. C. (1990). Patients with *n*-hexane induced polyneuropathy: A clinical follow up. *British Journal of Industrial Medicine, 47,* 485–489.

Chen, H. H., Chan, M. H., & Fu, S. H. (2002). Behavioural effects of tetrachloroethylene exposure in rats: Acute and subchronic studies. *Toxicology, 170,* 201–209.

Chin, Y., & Charlton, V. (2004). An asymptomatic middle-school-age boy with a blood lead concentration of 173 mcg/dL. *Clinical Pediatrics, 43,* 189–192.

Chiodo, L. M., Jacobson, S. W., & Jacobson, J. L. (2004). Neurodevelopmental effects of postnatal lead exposure at very low levels. *Neurotoxicology and Teratology, 26,* 359–371.

Choi, I. S. (1983). Delayed neurologic sequelae in carbon monoxide intoxication. *Archives of Neurology, 40,* 433–435.

Choi, I. S. (2001). Carbon monoxide poisoning: Systemic manifestations and complications. *Journal of Korean Medical Science, 16,* 253–261.

Clarkson, T. W. (1987). Metal toxicity in the central nervous system. *Environmental Health Perspectives, 75,* 59–64.

Clarkson, T. W. (1997). The toxicology of mercury. *Critical Reviews in Clinical Laboratory Sciences, 34*, 369–403.

Clarkson, T. W., Magos, L., & Myers, G. J. (2003). The toxicology of mercury—current exposures and clinical manifestations. *New England Journal of Medicine, 349*, 1731–1737.

Clarkson, T. W., & Strain, J. J. (2003). Nutritional factors may modify the toxic action of methyl mercury in fish-eating populations. *Journal of Nutrition, 133*, 1539S–1543S.

Committee on Drugs. American Academy of Pediatrics. (1995). Treatment guidelines for lead exposure in children. *Pediatrics, 96*, 155–160.

Cook, J. D., & Lynch, S. R. (1986). The liabilities of iron deficiency. *Blood, 68*, 803–809.

Coscia, J. M., Ris, M. D., Succop, P. A., & Dietrich, K. N. (2003). Cognitive development of lead exposed children from ages 6 to 15 years: An application of growth curve analysis. *Child Neuropsychology, 9*, 10–21.

Crump, K. S., Kjellstrom, T., Shipp, A. M., Silvers, A., & Stewart, A. (1998). Influence of prenatal mercury exposure upon scholastic and psychological test performance: Benchmark analysis of a New Zealand cohort. *Risk Analysis, 18*, 701–713.

Curley, A., Sedlak, V. A., Girling, E. D., Hawk, R. E., Barthel, W. F., Pierce, P. E., et al. (1971). Organic mercury identified as the cause of poisoning in humans and hogs. *Science, 172*, 66–67.

Davidson, P. W., Kost, J., Myers, G. J., Cox, C., Clarkson, T. W., & Shamlaye, C. F. (2001). Methylmercury and neurodevelopment: Reanalysis of the Seychelles Child Development Study outcomes at 66 months of age. *The Journal of the American Medical Association, 285*(10):1291–1293.

Davidson, P. W., Myers, G. J., Cox, C., Axtell, C., Shamlaye, C., Sloane-Reeves, J., et al. (1998). Effects of prenatal and postnatal methylmercury exposure from fish consumption on neurodevelopment: Outcomes at 66 months of age in the Seychelles Child Development Study. *The Journal of the American Medical Association, 280*(8):701–707.

Davis, L. E., Kornfeld, M., Mooney, H. S., Fiedler, K. J., Haaland, K. Y., Orrison, W. W., et al. (1994). Methylmercury poisoning: Long-term clinical, radiological, toxicological, and pathological studies of an affected family. *Annals of Neurology, 35*, 680–688.

De Gennaro, L. D. (2002). Lead and the developing nervous system. *Growth, Development, and Aging, 66*, 43–50.

del Amo, M., Berenguer, J., Pujol, T., & Mercader, J. M. (1996). MR in trichloroethane poisoning. *American Journal of Neuroradiology, 17*, 1180–1182.

Dietrich, K. N. (2000). Environmental neurotoxicants and psychological development. In K. O. Yeates, M. D. Ris, & H. G. Taylor (Eds.), *Pediatric neuropsychology: Research, theory and practice* (pp. 206–234). New York: The Guilford Press.

Dietrich, K. N., Ware, J. H., Salganik, M., Radcliffe, J., Rogan, W. J., Rhoads, G. G., et al. (2004). Effect of chelation therapy on the neuropsychological and behavioral development of lead-exposed children after school entry. *Pediatrics, 114*, 19–26.

Dixit, P., Nadimpalli, S. R., & Cavallino, R. P. (1999). Toxic encephalopathy due to chronic toluene abuse: Report of a case with magnetic resonance imaging [letter to the editor]. *Indian Journal of Radiology and Imaging, 9*(2), 1–4.

Dunham, M. D., & Johnstone, B. (1999). Variability of neuropsychological deficits associated with carbon monoxide poisoning: Four case reports. *Brain Injury, 13*, 917–925.

Easley, R. (2000). Open air carbon monoxide poisoning in a child swimming behind a boat. *Southern Medical Journal 93*(4), 430–432.

Ecobichon, D. J. (2003). Toxic effects of pesticides. In C. D. Klaassen & J. B. Watkins (Eds.), *Casarett and Doull's essentials of toxicology* (pp. 333–347). New York: McGraw-Hill.

Edling, C., Ekberg, K., Ahlborg, G., Jr., Alexandersson, R., Barregard, L., Ekenvall, L., et al. (1990). Long-term follow up of workers exposed to solvents. *British Journal of Industrial Medicine*, *47*, 75–82.

Ekberg, K., Barregard, L., Hagberg, S., & Sallsten, G. (1986). Chronic and acute effects of solvents on central nervous system functions in floorlayers. *British Journal of Industrial Medicine*, *43*, 101–106.

Ernhart, C. B., & Greene, T. (1990). Low-level lead exposure in the prenatal and early preschool periods: Language development. *Archives of Environmental Health*, *45*, 342–355.

Errebo-Knudsen, E. O., & Olsen, F. (1986). Organic solvents and presenile dementia (the painters' syndrome). A critical review of the Danish literature. *Science of the Total Environment*, *48*, 45–67.

Espinoza, R., Hernandez-Avila, M., Narciso, J., Castanga, C., Moscoso, S., Ortiz, G., et al. (2003). Determinants of blood-lead levels in children in Callao and Lima metropolitan area. *Salud Publica de Mexico*, *45*(Suppl. 2), S209–S219.

Eto, K. (2000). Minamata disease. *Neuropathology*, *20*, S14–S19.

Eto, K., Takizawa, Y., Akagi, H., Haraguchi, K., Asano, S., Takahata, N., et al. (1999). Differential diagnosis between organic and inorganic mercury poisoning in human cases—the pathologic point of view. *Toxicologic Pathology*, *27*, 664–671.

Eto, K., Tokunaga, H., Nagashima, K., & Takeuchi, T. (2002). An autopsy case of minamata disease (methylmercury poisoning)—pathological viewpoints of peripheral nerves. *Toxicologic Pathology*, *30*, 714–722.

Factor-Litvak, P., Wasserman, G., Kline, J. K., & Graziano, J. (1999). The Yugoslavia prospective study of environmental lead exposure. *Environmental Health Perspectives*, *107*, 9–15.

Falk, H. (2003). International environmental health for the pediatrician: Case study of lead poisoning. *Pediatrics*, *112*, 259–264.

Farahat, T. M., Abdelrasoul, G. M., Amr, M. M., Shebl, M. M., Farahat, F. M., & Anger, W.K. (2003). Neurobehavioural effects among workers occupationally exposed to organophosphorous pesticides. *Occupational and Environmental Medicine*, *60*, 279–286.

Farman, J. V. (1981). Some long established agents—a contemporary review. *British Journal of Anaesthesia*, *53*(Suppl. 1), 3S–9S.

Federman, D. G., Kirsner, R. S., & Federman, G. S. (1997). Pica: Are you hungry for the facts? *Connecticut Medicine*, *61*, 207–209.

Feldman, R. G. (1987). Occupational neurology. *Yale Journal of Biology and Medicine*, *60*, 179–186.

Feldman, R. G. (1998). *Occupational and environmental neurotoxicology*. Philadelphia: Lippencott-Raven.

Feldman, R. G., White, R. F., Eriator, I. I., Jabre, J. F., Feldman, E. S., & Niles, C. A. (1994). Neurotoxic effects of trichloroethylene in drinking water: Approach to diagnosis. In R.L. Isaacson & R. F. Jensen (Eds.), *The vulnerable brain and environmental risks: Special hazards from air and water* (pp. 3–23). New York: Plenum Press.

Fewtrell, L. J., Pruss-Ustun, A., Landrigan, P., & Ayuso-Mateos, J. L. (2004). Estimating the global burden of disease of mild mental retardation and cardiovascular diseases from environmental lead exposure. *Environmental Research, 94*, 120–133.

Filley, C. M. (2001). *The behavioral neurology of white matter.* New York: Oxford University Press.

Filley, C. M., Halliday, W., & Kleinschmidt-DeMasters, B. K. (2004). The effects of toluene on the central nervous system. *Journal of Neuropathology and Experimental Neurology, 63*, 1–12.

Filley, C. M., & Kleinschmidt-DeMasters, B. K. (2001). Toxic leukoencephalopathy. *New England Journal of Medicine, 345*, 425–432.

Finkelstein, Y., Markowitz, M. E., & Rosen, J. F. (1998). Low-level lead-induced neurotoxicity in children: An update on central nervous system effects. *Brain Research Reviews, 27*, 168–176.

Fischbein, A. (1992). Occupational and environmental lead exposure. In W. N. Rom (Ed.), *Environmental and occupational medicine* (2nd ed., pp. 735–758). Boston: Little, Brown.

Gade, A., Mortensen, E. L., & Bruhn, P. (1988). "Chronic painter's syndrome." A reanalysis of psychological test data in a group of diagnosed cases, based on comparisons with matched controls. *Acta Neurologica Scandinavica, 77*, 293–306.

Gale, S. D., & Hopkins, R. O. (2004). Effects of hypoxia on the brain: Neuroimaging and neuropsychological findings following carbon monoxide poisoning and obstructive sleep apnea. *Journal of the International Neuropsychological Society, 10*(1), 60–71.

Gale, S. D., Hopkins, R. O., Weaver, L. K., Bigler, E. D., Booth, E. J., & Blatter, D. D. (1999). MRI, quantitative MRI, SPECT, and neuropsychological findings following carbon monoxide poisoning. *Brain Injury, 13*, 229–243.

Gao, W., Li, Z., Kaufmann, R. B., Jones, R. L., Wang, Z., Chen, Y., et al. (2001). Blood lead levels among children aged 1 to 5 years in Wuxi City, China. *Environmental Research, 87*, 11–19.

Geltman, P. L., Brown, M. J., & Cochran, J. (2001). Lead poisoning among refugee children resettled in Massachusetts, 1995 to 1999. *Pediatrics, 108*, 158–162.

Gibson, J. L., Love, W., Hardine, D., Bencroft, P., & Turner, D. (1892). Note on lead poisoning as observed amongst Queensland children. *Australian Medical Gazette, 23*, 149–153.

Gidlow, D. A. (2004). Lead toxicity. *Occupational Medicine (Oxford), 54*, 76–81.

Gilbert, M. E., Mack, C. M., & Lasley, S. M. (1999). The influence of developmental period of lead exposure on lead-term potentiation in the adult rat dentate gyrus in vivo. *Neurotoxicology, 20*, 57–69.

Ginsberg, M. D. (1979). Delayed neurological deterioration following hypoxia. *Advances in Neurology, 26*, 21–44.

Gochfeld, M. (2003). Cases of mercury exposure, bioavailability, and absorption. *Ecotoxicology and Environmental Safety, 56*, 174–179.

Gochfeld, M. (2005). Chronologic history of occupational medicine. *Journal of Occupational and Environmental Medicine, 47*, 96–114.

Golding, J., Smith, M., Delves, H. T., & Taylor, H. (1998). The ALSPAC study on lead in children. In D. Gompertz (Ed.), *Recent UK blood lead surveys* (Report R9, pp. 35–39). Leicester, UK: MRC Institute for Environment and Health.

Goldman, L., & Bennett, J. C. (2000). *Cecil textbook of medicine* (21 ed.). Philadelphia: W.B. Saunders.

Goyer, R. A. (1993). Lead toxicity: Current concerns. *Environmental Health Perspectives, 100,* 177–187.

Grandjean, P., Weihe, P., White, R. F., Debes, F., Araki, S., Yokoyama, K., et al. (1997). Cognitive deficit in 7-year-old children with prenatal exposure to methylmercury. *Neurotoxicology and Teratology, 19,* 417–428.

Graziano, J., Slavkovich, V., Liu, X., Factor-Litvak, P., & Todd, A. (2004). A prospective study of prenatal and childhood lead exposure and erythropoietin production. *Journal of Occupational and Environmental Medicine, 46,* 924–929.

Grosse, S. D., Matte, T. D., Schwartz, J., & Jackson, R. J. (2002). Economic gains resulting from the reduction in children's exposure to lead in the United States. *Environmental Health Perspective, 110,* 563–569.

Guilarte, T. R., Toscano, C. D., McGlothan, J. L., & Weaver, S. A. (2003). Environmental enrichment reverses cognitive and molecular deficits induced by lead exposure. *Annals of Neurology, 53,* 50–56.

Haley, V. B., & Talbot, T. O. (2004). Seasonality and trend in blood lead levels of New York State children. *BMC Pediatrics, 4,* 8.

Hanlon, D. P. (1998). Death after exposure to dimethylmercury. *New England Journal of Medicine, 339,* 1243–1244.

Hansen, O. N., Trillingsgaard, A., Beese, I., Lyngbye, T., & Grandjean, P. A. (1989). A neuropsychological study of children with elevated dentine lead level: Assessment of the effect of lead in different socio-economic groups. *Neurotoxicology and Teratology, 11,* 205–213.

Harr, J. (1995). *A civil action.* New York: Random House, Inc.

Herskowitz, A., Ishii, N., & Schaumburg, H. (1971). *N*-hexane neuropathy. A syndrome occurring as a result of industrial exposure. *New England Journal of Medicine, 285,* 82–85.

Hettmansberger, T. L., & Mycyk, M. B. (2002). Lead poisoning presents a difficult diagnosis. *American Family Physician, 66,* 1839–1840.

Hill, A. B. (1965). The environment and disease: Association or causation. *Proceedings of the Royal Society of medicine, 58,* 295–300.

Hogstedt, C., Anderson, K., & Hane, M. (1984). Questionnaire approach to the monitoring of early differences in central nervous function. In A. R. Rinaulski & H. Vanio (Eds.), *Biological monitoring and surveillance of workers exposed to chemicals* (pp. 275–287). Washington, DC: Hemisphere Publishing.

Igata, A. (1993). Epidemiological and clinical features of Minamata disease. *Environmental Research, 63,* 157–169.

Institute for Environment and Health. (1998). *Recent blood lead surveys* (Report R9). Leicester, UK: Author.

Jarosinska, D., Peddada, S., & Rogan, W. J. (2004). Assessment of lead exposure and associated risk factors in urban children in Silesia, Poland. *Environmental Research, 95,* 133–142.

Jin, C. F., Haut, M., & Ducatman, A. (2004). Industrial solvents and psychological effects. *Clinics in Occupational and Environmental Medicine, 4,* 597–620.

Kaiser, R., Henderson, A. K., Daley, W. R., Naughton, M., Khan, M. H., Rahman, M., et al. (2001). Blood lead levels of primary school children in Dhaka, Bangladesh. *Environmental Health Perspectives, 109,* 563–566.

Kaufman, A. S. (2001). How dangerous are low (not moderate or high) doses of lead for children's intellectual development? *Archives of Clinical Neuropsychology, 16,* 403–431.

Kaufman, J. D., Burt, J., & Silverstein, B. (1994). Occupational lead poisoning: Can it be eliminated? *American Journal of Industrial Medicine, 26*, 703–712.

Keogh, J. P. (1992). Lead. In J. B. Sullivan & G. R. Krieger (Eds.), *Hazardous materials toxicology: Clinical principles of environmental health* (pp. 834–844). Baltimore: Williams & Wilkins.

Khan, A. H., Khan, A., Ghani, F., & Khurshid, M. (2001). Low-level lead exposure and blood lead levels in children: A cross-sectional survey. *Archives of Environmental Health, 56*, 501–505.

Kim, J. H., Chang, K. H., Song, I. C., Kim, K. H., Kwon, B. J., Kim, H. C., et al. (2003). Delayed encephalopathy of acute carbon monoxide intoxication: Diffusivity of cerebral white matter lesions. *American Journal of Neuroradiology, 24*, 1592–1597.

Klaassen, C. D., & Watkins, J. B. (2003). *Casarett and Doull's essentials of toxicology*. New York: McGraw-Hill Medical Publishers.

Koger, S. M., Schettler, T., & Weiss, B. (2005). Environmental toxicants and developmental disabilities: A challenge for psychologists. *American Psychologist, 60*, 243–255.

Koller, K., Brown, T., Spurgeon, A., & Levy, L. (2004). Recent developments in low-level lead exposure and intellectual impairment in children. *Environmental Health Perspectives, 112*, 987–994.

Kordas, K., Lopez, P., Rosado, J. L., Garcia Vargas, G., Alatorre Rico, J., Ronquillo, D., et al. (2004). Blood lead, anemia, and short stature are independently associated with cognitive performance in Mexican school children. *Journal of Nutrition, 134*, 363–371.

Korogi, Y., Takahashi, M., Okajima, T., & Eto, K. (1998). MR findings of Minamata disease—organic mercury poisoning. *Journal of Magnetic Resonance Imaging, 8*(2), 308–316.

Kwong, W. T., Friello, P., & Semba, R. D. (2004). Interactions between iron deficiency and lead poisoning: Epidemiology and pathogenesis. *Science of the Total Environment, 330*, 21–37.

Landrigan, P. J. (1990). Current issues in the epidemiology and toxicology of occupational exposure to lead. *Environmental Health Perspectives, 89*, 61–66.

Landrigan, P. J. (1994). Lead. In L. Rosenstock & M. R. Cullen (Eds.), *Textbook of clinical occupational and environmental health* (pp. 745–754). Philadelphia: Saunders.

Landrigan, P. J., Silbergeld, E. K., Froines, J. R., & Pfeffer, R. M. (1990). Lead in the modern workplace. *American Journal of Public Health, 80*, 907–908.

Lanphear, B. P., Dietrich, K., Auinger, P., & Cox, C. (2000). Cognitive deficits associated with blood lead concentrations <10 microg/dL in US children and adolescents. *Public Health Reports, 115*, 521–529.

Lanphear, B. P., Hornung, R., Ho, M., Howard, C. R., Eberle, S., & Knauf, K. (2002). Environmental lead exposure during early childhood. *Journal of Paediatrics, 140*, 40–47.

Lee, R., Lee, H., Yoo, I., & Kim, S. R. (2002). Trend of blood lead levels in children in an industrial complex and its suburban area in Ulsan, Korea. *International Archives of Occupational and Environmental Health, 75*, 507–510.

Lewis, R. (1990). Metals. In J. LaDou (Ed.), *Occupational medicine* (pp. 306–310). Norwalk, CT: Appleton & Lange.

Li, S., Zhenyia, Z., Lon, L., & Hanyun, C. (2004). Preschool children's lead levels in rural communities of Zhejiang Province, China. *International Journal of Hygiene and Environmental Health, 207*, 437–440.

Lidsky, T. I., & Schneider, J. S. (2003). Lead neurotoxicity in children: Basic mechanisms and clinical correlates. *Brain, 126*, 5–19.

Life Sciences Research Office. (2004). *Review and analysis of the literature on the potential adverse health effects of dental amalgam: Report to the trans-agency working group on the health effects of dental amalgam.* U.S. Department of Health and Human Services Bethesda, MD: 1–231.

Lippmann, M. (1990). 1989 Alice Hamilton lecture. Lead and human health: Background and recent findings. *Environmental Research, 51*, 1–24.

Liu, X., Dietrich, K. N., Radcliffe, J., Ragan, N. B., Rhoads, G. G., & Rogan, W. J. (2002). Do children with falling blood lead levels have improved cognition? *Pediatrics, 110*, 787–791.

London, L., Flisher, A. J., Wesseling, C., Mergler, D., & Kromhout, H. (2005). Suicide and exposure to organophosphate insecticides: Cause or effect? *American Journal of Industrial Medicine, 47*, 308–321.

Lozoff, B., Wolf, A. W., & Jiminez, E. (1996). Iron-deficiency anemia and infant development: Effects of extended oral iron therapy. *The Journal of Pediatrics, 129*, 382–389.

Mahaffey, K. R. (2000). Recent advances in recognition of low-level methylmercury poisoning. *Current Opinion in Neurology, 13*, 699–707.

Maizlish, N. A., Fine, L. J., Albers, J. W., Whitehead, L., & Langolf, G. D. (1987). A neurological evaluation of workers exposed to mixtures of organic solvents. *British Journal of Industrial Medicine, 44*, 14–25.

Marchetti, C. (2003). Molecular targets of lead in brain neurotoxicity. *Neurotoxicity Research, 5*, 221–236.

Martin, C. J., Werntz, C. L., III, & Ducatman, A. M. (2004). The interpretation of zinc protoporphyrin changes in lead intoxication: A case report and review of the literature. *Occupational Medicine (Oxford), 54*, 587–591.

Mathee, A., von Schirnding, Y. E. R., Levin, J., Ismail, A., Huntley, R., & Cantrell, A. (2002). A survey of blood lead levels among young Johannesburg school children. *Environmental Research, 90*, 181–184.

Medlin, J. (2004). Sweet candy, bitter poison. *Environmental Health Perspectives, 112*, A803.

Merck Research Laboratories. (2001). *The Merck Index: An encyclopedia of chemicals, drugs, and biologicals* (13th ed.). Whitehouse Station, NJ: Merck & Co., Inc.

Meyer, P. A., Pivetz, T., Dignam, T. A., Homa, D. M., Schoonover, J., & Brody, D. (2003). Surveillance for elevated blood lead levels among children—United States, 1997–2001. *Summaries: Morbidity and Mortality Weekly Report, 52*, 1–21.

Mielke, H. W., & Reagan, P. L. (1998). Soil is an important pathway of human lead exposure. *Environmental Health Perspectives, 106*(Suppl. 1), 217–229.

Moreira, F. R., & Moreira, J. C. (2004). Effects of lead exposure on the human body and health implications. *Pan American Journal of Public Health, 15*, 119–129.

Morgan, B. W., Todd, K. H., & Moore, B. (2001). Elevated blood lead levels in urban moonshine drinkers. *Annals of Emergency Medicine, 37*, 51–54.

Morgan, R. E., Garavan, H., Smith, E. G., Driscoll, L. L., Levitsky, D. A., & Strupp, B. J. (2001). Early lead exposure produces lasting changes in sustained attention, response initiation, and reactivity to errors. *Neurotoxicology and Teratology, 23*, 519–531.

Morita, H., Yanagisawa, N., Nakajima, T., Shimizu, M., Hirabayashi, H., Okudera, H., et al. (1995). Sarin poisoning in Matsumoto, Japan. *Lancet, 346*, 290–293.

Munoz, C., Garbe, K., Lilienthal, H., & Winneke, G. (1989). Neuronal depletion of the amygdala resembles the learning deficits induced by low level lead exposure in rats. *Neurotoxicology and Teratology, 11*, 257–264.

Nagashima, K., Fujii, Y., Tsukamoto, T., Nukuzuma, S., Satoh, M., Fujita, M., et al. (1996). Apoptotic process of cerebellar degeneration in experimental methylmercury intoxication of rats [see comment]. *Acta Neuropathologica, 91*, 72–77.

National Research Council. (2000). *Toxicological effects of methylmercury.* Washington, DC: National Academy Press.

Needleman, H. (2004). Lead poisoning. *Annual Review of Medicine, 55*, 209–222.

Nierenberg, D. W., Nordgren, R. E., Chang, M. B., Siegler, R. W., Blayney, M. B., Hochberg, F., et al. (1998). Delayed cerebellar disease and death after accidental exposure to dimethylmercury. *New England Journal of Medicine, 338*, 1672–1676.

Nilson, L. N., Backman, L., Sallsten, G., Hagberg, S., & Barregard, L. (2003). Dose-related cognitive deficits among floor layers with previous heavy exposure to solvents. *Archives of Environmental Health, 58*, 208–217.

Nilson, L. N., Sallsten, G., Hagberg, S., Backman, L., & Barregard, L. (2002). Influence of solvent exposure and aging on cognitive functioning: An 18 year follow up of formerly exposed floor layers and their controls. *Occupational and Environmental Medicine, 59*, 49–57.

Ostlund, K. (1969). Studies on the metabolism of methyl mercury and dimethyl mercury in mice. *Acta Pharmacologica et Toxicologica, 27*, 1–132.

Peoples, R. W., & Weight, F. F. (1994). Trichloroethanol potentiation of gamma-aminobutyric acid-activated chloride current in mouse hippocampal neurones. *British Journal of Pharmacology, 113*, 555–563.

Peoples, R. W., & Weight, F. F. (1998). Inhibition of excitatory amino acid-activated currents by trichloroethanol and trifluoroethanol in mouse hippocampal neurones. *British Journal of Pharmacology, 124*, 1159–1164.

Perez-Bravo, F., Ruz, M., Moran-Jimenez, M. J., Olivares, M., Rebolledo, A., Codoceo, J., et al. (2004). Association between aminolevulinate dehydrase genotypes and blood lead levels in children from a lead-contaminated area in Antofagasta, Chile. *Archives of Environmental Contamination and Toxicology, 47*, 276–280.

Pershad, J., Palmisano, P., & Nichols, M. (1999). Chloral hydrate: The good and the bad. *Pediatric Emergency Care, 15*, 432–435.

Peterson, K. E., Salganik, M., Campbell, C., Rhoads, G. G., Rubin, J., Berger, O., et al. (2004). Effects of succimer on growth of preschool children with moderate blood lead levels. *Environmental Health Perspectives, 112*, 233–237.

Piantadosi, C. L. (2000). Physical, chemical, and aspiration injuries of the lung. In L. Goldman, & J. C. Bennett (Eds.), *Cecil textbook of medicine* (21 ed., pp. 425–442). Philadelphia: W.B. Saunders Company.

Pierce, P. E., Thompson, J. F., Likosky, W. H., Nickey, L. N., Barthel, W. F., & Hinman, A. R. (1972). Alkyl mercury poisoning in humans. Report of an outbreak. *The Journal of the American Medical Association, 220*, 1439–1442.

Pilkington, A. B. (2001). An epidemiological study of the relations between exposure to organophosphate pesticides and indices of chronic peripheral neuropathy and neuropsychological abnormalities in sheep farmers and dippers. *Occupational and Environmental Medicine, 58*, 702–710.

Pirkle, J. L., Kaufmann, R. B., Brody, D. J., Hickman, T., Gunter, E. W., & Paschal, D. C. (1998). Exposure of the U.S. population to lead, 1991–1994. *Environmental Health Perspectives, 106*, 745–750.

Pocock, S., Smith, M., & Baghurst, P. (1994). Environmental lead and children's intelligence: A systematic review of the epidemiological evidence. *British Medical Journal, 309,* 1189–1197.

Rabito, F. A., Shorter, C., & White, L. E. (2003). Lead levels among children who live in public housing. *Epidemiology, 14,* 263–268.

Rahman, A., Maqbool, E., & Zuberi, H. S. (2002). Lead-associated deficits in stature, mental ability, and behavior in children in Karachi. *Annals of Tropical Paediatrics, 22,* 301–311.

Raub, J. A., & Benignus, V. A. (2003). Carbon monoxide and the nervous system. *Neuroscience and Biobehavioral Reviews, 26,* 925–940.

Raub, J. A., Mathieunolf, M., Hampson, N. B., & Thom, S. R. (2000). Carbon monoxide poisoning: A public health perspective. *Toxicology, 145,* 1–14.

Rice, D. C. (1990). Lead-induced behavioral impairment on a spatial discrimination reversal task in monkeys exposed during different periods of development. *Toxicology and Applied Pharmacology, 106,* 327–333.

Rice, D. C. (1992a). Lead exposure during different developmental periods produces different effects on FI performance in monkeys tested as juveniles and adults. *Neurotoxicology, 13,* 757–770.

Rice, D. C. (1992b). Behavioral effects of lead in monkeys tested during infancy and childhood. *Neurotoxicology and Teratology, 14,* 235–245.

Richardson, R. J., Moore, T. B., Kayyali, U. S., & Randall, J. C. (1993). Chlorpyrifos: Assessment of potential for delayed neurotoxicity by repeated dosing in adult hens with monitoring of brain acetylcholinesterase, brain and lymphocyte neurotoxic esterase, and plasma butyrylcholinesterase activities. *Fundamental and Applied Toxicology, 21,* 89–96.

Richardson, W. S., Wilson, M. C., Williams, J. W., Jr., Moyer, V. A., & Naylor, C. D. (2000). Users' guides to the medical literature: XXIV. How to use an article on the clinical manifestations of disease. Evidence-Based Medicine Working Group. *The Journal of the American Medical Association, 284,* 869–875.

Ris, M. D., Dietrich, K. N., Succop, P. A., Berger, O. G., & Bornschein, R. L. (2004). Early exposure to lead and neuropsychological outcome in adolescence. *Journal of the International Neuropsychological Society, 10,* 261–270.

Rogan, W. J., Dietrich, K. N., Ware, J. H., Dockery, D.W, Salganik, M., Radcliffe, J., et al. (2001). The effect of chelation therapy with succimer on neuropsychological development in children exposed to lead. *The New England Journal of Medicine, 344,* 1421–1426.

Rosenberg, N. L., Grigsby, J., Dreisbach, J., Busenbark, D., & Grigsby, P. (2002). Neuropsychologic impairment and MRI abnormalities associated with chronic solvent abuse [see comment]. *Journal of Toxicology—Clinical Toxicology, 40,* 21–34.

Rosenstock, L., Keifer, M., Daniell, W. E., McConnell, R., & Claypoole, K. (1991). Chronic central nervous system effects of acute organophosphate pesticide intoxication. The Pesticide Health Effects Study Group. *Lancet, 338,* 223–227.

Rowland, A. S., & McKinstry, R. C. (2006). Lead toxicity, white matter lesions, and aging. *Neurology, 66,* 1464–1465.

Rowland, R. W. (1989). *Merritt's textbook of neurology* (8th ed.). Philadelphia: Lea & Febiger.

Ruangkanchanasetr, S., & Suepiantham, J. (2002). Risk factors of high lead level in Bangkok children. *Journal of the Medical Association of Thailand, 85*(Suppl. 4), S1049–S1058.

Ruff, H. A., Bijur, P. E., Markowitz, M., Ma, Y. C., & Rosen, J. F. (1993). Declining blood lead levels and cognitive changes in moderately lead-poisoned children. *The Journal of the American Medical Association, 269*, 1641–1646.

Ruff, H. A., Markowitz, M. E., Bijur, P., & Rosen, J. H. (1996). Relationships among blood lead levels, iron deficiency, and cognitive development in two-year-old children. *Environmental Health Perspectives, 104*, 180–185.

Sager, P. R., Aschner, M., & Rodier, P. M. (1984). Persistent, differential alterations in developing cerebellar cortex of male and female mice after methylmercury exposure. *Brain Research, 314*, 1–11.

Sanfeliu, C., Sebastia, J., Cristofol, R., & Rodriguez-Farre, E. (2003). Neurotoxicity of organomercurial compounds. *Neurotoxicity Research, 5*, 283–305.

Saryan, L. A., & Zenz, C. (1994). Lead and its compounds. In C. Zenz, O. B. Dickerson, & E. P. Horvath Jr. (Eds.), *Occupational medicine* (3 ed., pp. 506–541). St. Louis: Mosby.

Savage, E. P., Keefe, T. J., Mounce, L. M., Heaton, R. K., Lewis, J. A., & Burcar, P. J. (1988). Chronic neurological sequelae of acute organophosphate pesticide poisoning. *Archives of Environmental Health, 43*, 38–45.

Savours, A. (1990). The diary of assistant surgeon Henry Piers, HMS Investigator, 1850–54. *Journal of the Royal Naval Medical Service, 76*, 33–38.

Scheibler, P., Kronfeld, A., Illes, P., & Allgaier, C. (1999). Trichloroethanol impairs NMDA receptor function in rat mesencephalic and cortical neurones. *European Journal of Pharmacology, 366*, R1–R2.

Schnaas, L., Rothenberg, S. J., Flores, M. F., Martinez, S., Hernandez, C., Osorio, E., et al. (2004). Blood lead secular trend in a cohort of children in Mexico City. *Environmental Health Perspectives, 112*, 1110–1115.

Schnaas, L., Rothenberg, S. J., Perroni, E., Martinez, S., Hernandez, C., & Hernandez, R. M. (2000). Temporal pattern in the effect of postnatal blood lead level on intellectual development of young children. *Neurotoxicology and Teratology, 22*, 805–810.

Schneider, J. S., Lee, M. H., Anderson, D. W., Zuck, L., & Lidsky, T. I. (2001). Enriched environment during development is protective against lead-induced neurotoxicity. *Brain Research, 896*, 48–55.

Schwartz, B. S., Lee, B. K., Lee, G. S., Stewart, W. F., Lee, S. S., Hwang, K. Y., et al. (2001). Associations of blood lead, dimercaptosuccinic acid-chelatable lead, and tibia lead with neurobehavioral test scores in South Korean lead workers. *American Journal of Epidemiology, 153*, 453–464.

Schwartz, B. S., Stewart, W. F., Bolla, K. I., Simon, P. D., Bandeen-Roche, K., Gordon, P. B., et al. (2000). Past adult lead exposure is associated with longitudinal decline in cognitive function. *Neurology, 55*, 1144–1150.

Schwartz, B. S., Stewart, W., & Hu, H. (2002). Neurobehavioural testing in workers occupationally exposed to lead. *Occupational and Environmental Medicine, 59*, 648–649.

Sears, W., & Sears, M. (1993). *The baby book: Everything you need to know about your baby from birth to age two.* Boston: Little, Brown, and Company.

Shepherd, M. J. (1976). Learning disabled or slow learner? *School Psychology Digest, 5*, 32–35.

Silbergeld, E. K. (1992). Mechanisms of lead neurotoxicity, or looking beyond the lamppost. *The FASEB Journal, 6*, 3201–3206.

Singhi, S., Ravishaker, R., Singhi, R., & Nath, R. (2003). Low plasma zinc and iron in pica. *Indian Journal of Pediatrics, 70*, 139–143.

Spencer, P. S., & Schaumburg, H. H. (1985). Organic solvent neurotoxicity. Facts and research needs. *Scandinavian Journal of Work, Environment and Health, 11* (Suppl. 1), 53–60.

Spencer, P. S., Schaumburg, H. H., Raleigh, R. L., & Terhaar, C. J. (1975). Nervous system degeneration produced by the industrial solvent methyl n-butyl ketone. *Archives of Neurology, 32*, 219–222.

Spurgeon, A. (2002). Models of unexplained symptoms associated with occupational and environmental exposures. *Environmental Health Perspectives, 110*(Suppl. 4), 601–605.

Spurgeon, A., Gompertz, D., & Harrington, J. M. (1997). Non-specific symptoms in response to hazard exposure in the workplace. *Journal of Psychosomatic Research, 43*, 43–49.

Stanek, E. J., & Calabrese, E. J. (1995). Daily estimates of soil ingestion in children. *Environmental Health Perspectives, 103*, 276–285.

Staudinger, K. C., & Roth, V. S. (1998). Occupational lead poisoning. *American Family Physician, 57*, 719–726.

Stephens, R., Spurgeon, A., Calvert, I. A., Beach, J., Levy, L. S., Berry, H., et al. (1995). Neuropsychological effects of long-term exposure to organophosphates in sheep dip. *Lancet, 345*, 1135–1139.

Stewart, W. F., Schwartz, B. S., Davatzikos, C., Shen, D., Liu, D., Wu, X., et al. (2006). Past adult lead exposure is linked to neurodegeneration measured by brain MRI. *Neurology, 66*, 1476–1484.

Stewart, W. F., Schwartz, B. S., Simon, D., Bolla, K. I., Todd, A. C., Links, J., et al. (1999). Neurobehavioral function and tibial and chelatable lead levels in 543 former organolead workers. *Neurology, 52*, 1610–1617.

Suls, M. E. (2003). The importance of taking an occupational history. *American Family Physician, 67*, 1684.

Tamashiro, H., Arakaki, M., Akagi, H., Futatsuka, M., & Roht, L. H. (1985). Mortality and survival for Minamata disease. *International Journal of Epidemiology, 14*, 582–588.

Tamashiro, H., Arakaki, M., Futatsuka, M., & Lee, E. S. (1986). Methylmercury exposure and mortality in southern Japan: A close look at causes of death. *Journal of Epidemiology and Community Health, 40*, 181–185.

Tamashiro, H., Fukutomi, K., & Lee, E. S. (1987). Methylmercury exposure and mortality in Japan: A life table analysis. *Archives of Environmental Health, 42*, 100–107.

Tateyama, M., Takeda, R., Tokuno, M., Hashimoto, M., Fukukawa, Y., Osada, H., et al. (2003). Visual motor gestalt task indicates that "deficit schizophrenics" become severely disturbed with age. *Psychogeriatrics, 3*, 73–77.

Tong, S. (1998). Lead exposure and cognitive development: Persistence and a dynamic pattern. *Journal of Paediatric and Child Health, 34*, 114–118.

Tong, S., Baghurst, P., McMichael, A., Sawyer, M., & Mudge, J. (1996). Lifetime exposure to environmental lead and children's intelligence at 11–13 years: The Port Pirie cohort study. *British Medical Journal, 312*, 1569–1575.

Tong, S., Baghurst, P. A., Sawyer, M. G., Burns, J., & McMichael, A. J. (1998). Declining blood lead levels and changes in cognitive function during childhood. The Port Pirie cohort study. *Journal of the American Medical Association, 280*, 1915–1919.

Townsend, C. L., & Maynard, R. L. (2002). Effects on health of prolonged exposure to low concentrations of carbon monoxide. *Occupational and Environmental Medicine, 59*(10), 708–711.

Trimble, M. R., & Krishnamoorthy, E. S. (2000). The roles of toxins in disorders of mood and affect. In J. W. Albers, & S. Berent (Eds.), *Clinical neurobehavioral toxicology* (pp. 649–664). Philadelphia: W.B. Saunders.

Trope, I., Lopez-Villegas, D., Cecil, K. M., & Lenkinski, R. E. (2001). Exposure to lead appears to selective alter metabolism of cortical gray matter. *Pediatrics, 107*, 1437–1442.

Tsuzuki, Y. (1982). Effect of methylmercury exposure on different neurotransmitter systems in rat brain. *Toxicology Letters, 13*, 159–162.

Tuthill, R. W. (1996). Hair lead levels related to children's classroom attention-deficit behavior. *Archives of Environmental Health, 51*, 214–220.

Tuzun, M., Tuzun, D., Salan, A., & Lu, B. (2002). Lead encephalopathy: CT and MR findings. *Journal of Computer Assisted Tomography, 26*, 479–481.

U.S. Consumer Product Safety Commission. (2004). *Carbon monoxide questions and answers* (CPSC document # 466, Report No. 466). Washington, DC: U.S. Government.

U.S. Consumer Product Safety Commission. (2005). CPSC announces new policy addressing lead in children's metal jewelry. Retrieved March 16, 2005 from www.cpsc.gov/cpscpub/prerel/prhtml05/05097.html

U.S. Department of Human Services, PHS, ATSDR. (1992). *Case studies in environmental medicine: Lead toxicity.* Washington, DC: U.S. Government.

U.S. Department of Health and Human Services. (2005) *About head start.* Retrieved June 8, 2005 from www.acf.hhs.gov/programs/hsb/about/index.htm

U.S. Environmental Protection Agency (U.S. EPA). (2005) *Lead in paint, dust, and soil.* Retreived February 27, 2005 from www.epa.gov/lead/

U.S. Environmental Protection Agency Office of Air Quality Standards. (1997). *Mercury Report to Congress.* Retrieved from http://www.epa.gov/oar/mercover.html

Uchino, M., Tanaka, Y., Ando, Y., Yonehara, T., Hara, A., Mishima, I., et al. (1995). Neurologic features of chronic Minamata disease (organic mercury poisoning) and incidence of complications with aging. *Journal of Environmental Science and Health—Part B: Pesticides, Food Contaminants, and Agricultural Wastes, 30*, 699–715.

van Arsdale, J. L., Leiker, R. D., Kohn, M., Merritt, T. A., & Horowitz, B. Z. (2004). Lead poisoning from a toy necklace. *Pediatrics, 114*, 1096–1099.

von Schirnding, Y., Mathee, A., Kibel, M., Robertson, P., Strauss, N., & Blignaut, R. (2003). A study of pediatric blood lead levels in a lead mining area in South Africa. *Environmental Research, 93*, 259–263.

Walkowiak, J., Altmann, L., Kramer, U., Sveinsson, K., Turfeld, M., Weishoff-Houben, M., et al. (1998). Cognitive and sensorimotor functions in 6-year-old children in relation to lead and mercury levels: Adjustment for intelligence and contrast sensitivity in computerized testing. *Neurotoxicology and Teratology, 20*, 511–521.

Wang, J. D., Chang, Y. C., Kao, K. P., Huang, C. C., Lin, C. C., & Yeh, W. Y. (1986). An outbreak of *N*-hexane induced polyneuropathy among press proofing workers in Taipei. *American Journal of Industrial Medicine, 10*, 111–118.

Wasserman, G. A., Staghezza-Jaramillo, B., Shrout, P., Popovac, D., & Graziano, J. (1998). The effect of lead exposure on behavior problems in preschool children. *American Journal of Public Health, 88*, 481–486.

Wayne State University. College of Urban, Labor, & Metropolitan Affairs. *Lead poisoning research at the center for urban studies.* Retrieved February 27, 2005 from www.detroitleaddata.cus.wayne.edu/problem-facts_figures.asp

Weiss, B. (2000). Vulnerability of children and the developing brain to neurotoxic hazards. *Environmental Health Perspectives, 108*(Suppl. 3), 375–381.

Weiss, B., Clarkson, T. W., & Simon, W. (2002). Silent latency periods in methyl-mercury poisoning and in neurodegenerative disease. *Environmental Health Perspectives, 110*(Suppl. 5), 851–854.

Weitzman, M., & Glotzer, D. (1992). Lead poisoning. *Pediatric Review, 13*, 461–468.

White, R. F., & Proctor, S. P. (1997). Solvents and neurotoxicity. *Lancet, 349*, 1239–1243.

Wigg, N. R. (2001). Low-level lead exposure and children. *Journal of Pediatrics and Child Health, 37*, 423–425.

Winneke, G. (1995). Endpoints of developmental neurotoxicity in environmentally exposed children. *Toxicology Letters, 77*, 127–136.

Winneke, G., Brockhaus, A., Ewers, U., Kramer, U., & Neuf, M. (1990). Results from the European multicenter study on lead neurotoxicity in children: Implications for risk assessment. *Neurotoxicology and Teratology, 12*, 553–559.

Winneke, G., & Kramer, U. (1997). Neurobehavioral aspects of lead neurotoxicity in children. *Central European Journal of Public Health, 5*, 65–69.

Woods, H. F., & the Working Group on Organophosphates (1999). *Organophosphates. Committee on toxicity of chemicals in food, consumer products and the environment*. United Kingdom: Working Group on Organophosphates.

Wooltorton, E. (2002). Facts on mercury and fish consumption. *Canadian Medical Association Journal, 167*, 897.

World Health Organization. (1999). *Environmental health criteria: Carbon monoxide* (Report No. 213). Helsinki, Finland: Author.

World Health Organization, International Programme on Chemical Safety. (1995). *Environmental health criteria 165—inorganic lead*. Geneva: Author.

Ziegler, S., Wolf, C., Salzer-Muhar, U., Schaffer, A., Konnaris, C., Rudiger, H., et al. (2002). Acute lead intoxication from a mug with a ceramic inner surface. *American Journal of Medicine, 112*, 677–678.

16 Medications and substances of abuse

The statement that "depending on dose, all substances are toxic," has been considered factual at least since the time of Paracelsus (1493–1541) (Klaassen & Watkins, 2003). At the same time, we are influenced by intent and social convention to perceive some substances as inherently toxic (i.e., bad) and others as beneficial or, at the least, minimally harmful (i.e., good). Such perceptions vary over time as a function of changes in societal (or personal) experiences, sophistication, and values. The notion from the 1940s and 1950s, most often applied to industrial agents, "better living through chemistry," has given way to a growing suspicion of anything "chemical." As discussed in the previous chapter, caution regarding the use of substances, when based on scientifically based knowledge, is wise. For the professional, it is imperative. However, the magnitude of society's concerns, and likewise the exercise of caution, is greatly influenced by the perceived value of intent. Intent might be seen as appropriate (e.g., a substance used to relieve pain in a patient with a severe injury or medical illness) or inappropriate (e.g., abusing a substance solely to experience the euphoric feelings associated with intoxication). Paradoxically, the same substance might be used in either instance just mentioned (e.g., opioids). When the intent is medicinal, the general view is that it is appropriate. Along with this view is the tendency to forget, or at least to minimize, the potential for toxicity. Yet, as discussed in volume II, the adverse effects from medications are among the most common neurotoxic syndromes. The following presentations include examples of adverse effects on the central nervous system and behavior that can result from a variety of commonly used substances.

Selected presentations

Anticonvulsants

Henry A. Buchtel and Linas Bieliauskas

Seizure disorder has long been conceived as reflecting any number of underlying conditions, and considerable effort has been expended over the years to develop an accurate and comprehensive system of classification (Commission on Classification and Terminology of the International League Against Epilepsy, 1989; Dreifuss, 1987). The view of epilepsy as a collection of symptoms and signs that reflect a variety of underlying disorders, each being theoretically associated with indentifiable and distinguishable etiologies, implies that different treatments are needed depending on the type of epilepsy encountered. With the advent of a reliable and valid system of classification, drugs have been developed that are efficient in the treatment of one or another of these various types of epilepsy. The prevention of seizures is important due to their debilitating neurological effects, ranging from disturbances of consciousness and cognition, to affective disorder and thought disturbance. In most cases, there is a significant negative impact on daily life functions. Seizures can influence employability, driving privileges, and accidental injury (Yablon, Meythaler, & Englander, 1998).

The pharmacological management of seizures primarily targets the frequency and severity of associated abnormal neuronal activity. Such activity can be the result of many causes, including traumatic brain injury, brain tumors, cerebrovascular accidents, or idiopathic antecedents. Whatever the agent, there are generally resulting structural, metabolic, and neurophysiological changes associated with the abnormal neuronal activity.

In general, antiepileptic drugs (AEDs) either block the initiation of electrical discharges from a hyperirritable focus or, more commonly, prevent the spread of abnormal electrical discharges to adjacent brain areas (Winkelman, 1999). While AEDs represent the major treatment modality in epilepsy, they nevertheless carry with them a number of potential adverse side effects that in themselves can be debilitating. In fact, the first anticonvulsant medication (bromide) was discovered because of its side effects (Meador, 1996). A German paper published in the 1850s reported that potassium bromide caused temporary impotency in men. On hearing of this paper, Sir Charles Locock (1799–1875) proposed that bromide might be useful in treating "hysteria." Encouraged by the success of this treatment, he then prescribed the durg in cases of "hysterical epilepsy." That bromide had actual anticonvulsant effects became known once its treatment was broadened to include larger numbers of patients. Bromide became so popular that by the middle of the 1860s one of the London neurological hospitals was using 2.5 tons of the substance every year (Temkin, 1971).

Although seizures themselves can cause untoward cognitive and behavioral changes, it is unfortunate that treatment by AEDs also can independently cause such changes. When faced with adverse cognitive decline or behavioral disturbance, it becomes a challenge for the clinician to attempt to disentangle the potential original neuronal etiology of the disturbance from neuronal-associated change resulting from treatment, a situation well reflected in the following *case presentation.*

Case presentation[1]

A 22-year-old, right-handed college student developed seizures at the age of 15 years. She was the product of a full-term uncomplicated pregnancy and there was no history of febrile convulsions or central nervous system infections. She had no history of severe head injury but was hit on the head with a baseball bat as a child. Also, she reported being hit on the head with a telephone by a childhood friend. Neither of these instances resulted in loss of consciousness or other symptoms or signs of severe injury. Also, she had two falls from a horse as a child, suffering fractures of both arms but no apparent head injury. There were no family members with epilepsy. The vast majority (90%) of her typical seizures begin with an aura of flashing lights in the left upper quadrant, followed sequentially by a queasy and nauseated feeling, a metallic taste in back of her throat, a spacey feeling with partial to complete loss of awareness and reduced responsiveness. These seizures almost invariably clustered and increased in severity to partial complex seizures with or without generalized tonic–clonic seizure activity. She described always having a post-ictal headache. In the past, her seizures occurred once every 1–2 years, but recently she reported having a seizure every 1–4 months. She has had five atypical seizures in addition. These last mentioned phenomena consisted of drooling, especially from the right corner of the mouth, associated with slurred speech, loss of awareness, staring, and chewing automatisms. There has never been an episode of status epilepticus. Most recently, clinical phenomena associated with her seizures have come to include symptoms of sudden onset of left face and arm numbness followed by left arm pain (on occasion), followed by left lower facial twitching, drooling, and inability to speak and, finally, dysarthria and weakness in her left face and arm. Consciousness appears to be preserved during these episodes.

Her antiepileptic medication at the time of her evaluation was topiramate (Topamax), although several other medications had been tried in the past. These included Tegretol (carbamazepine), which she discontinued because of rash, and divalproex (Depakote), which she discontinued because of weight gain and excess hair growth, phenytoin (Dilantin), and levetiracetam (Keppra). Her neurological examination was normal, including formal visual field testing.

The results of a neuropsychological evaluation suggested a bilateral disturbance of cortical functions. The scores available from this baseline evaluation are contained in Table 16.1. Based on her educational level (college student working on her bachelor's degree) and single-word reading, her premorbid intellectual level was estimated to be in the average range (90–109). In contrast, her current abilities were in the low-average range. This patient's score on a confrontation naming test (Boston Naming Test) was more than 3 SDs below the mean for her age and educational level, and the Memory Quotient was in the low-average range, with poor delayed recall on both verbal and pictorial memory measures. The neuropsychological report concluded that she had undergone a moderate decline from presumed past levels of functioning, with disturbances currently of both verbal and visual-spatial abilities. Mood assessment did not suggest the presence of anxiety or depression, although history indicated periods of depressed mood.

The speech pathologist reported diminished "nonverbal agility skills," compromised auditory comprehension, reduced reading comprehension skills, impaired verbal fluency skills, and diminished written expressive skills. All of

Table 16.1 Neuropsychological test results before and after removal from exposure.

Test administered	Domain measured	Test results (time 0/time 2)
WAIS-III, VIQ	Verbal intellect	87/102
WAIS-III, PIQ	Performance intellect	89/99
WAIS-III, FSIQ	General intellectual ability	86/101
Boston Naming Test	Confrontation naming	46/54
WAIS, Similarities	Abstract conceptualization	19/53 (percentile)
WAIS, Block Design	Visual-motor problem solving	33/39 (percentile)
WAIS, Digit Symbol	Psychomotor problem solving	32/63 (percentile)
MMSE	General mental status	26 of 30/29 of 30
WMS, MQ	General memory and orientation	93/98
WMS, Passages	Verbal recall, percent retained	63/81 (percent retention)
WMS, Visual Reproductions	Visual recall, percent retained	69/71 (percent retention)
WRAT-3, Reading	Reading recognition	97/99
Depression Ratings	Clinical ratings of depression	Mild/euthymic

these impairments were considered to be mild in terms of severity. Visual confrontation naming skills were far below normal limits. Although she was working on a bachelor's degree at a state university at the time of the neuropsychological evaluation, she was encountering difficulties because of a decline in memory abilities. She had previously been achieving grades of "A" and "B" but was now getting "C"s in some classes and barely passing others that required demands for memorization. As a result, she reduced the number of classes she was taking. According to her mother, the patient had recently become irritable and intermittently tearful, possibly depressed and anxious about issues related to her epilepsy as well as her capacity to be independent. However, the patient denied depression when confronted with this issue.

An interictal Scalp EEG showed continuous right anterior/mid temporal rhythmic and semi-rhythmic delta slowing, sometimes sharply contoured, with occasional right temporal sharp waves maximum at F8/T4. An ictal EEG during one of her typical seizures showed a right temporal onset with a diffuse burst of delta–theta slowing followed by an organized theta discharge in the right temporal region and rapid spread to the adjacent parietal region.

MRI results were consistent with right mesial temporal sclerosis. The right hippocampus had an increased signal on FLAIR with a somewhat dysmorphic shape and enlargement of the right temporal horn. There was right mid-temporal sulcal thickening noted between the superior and mid-temporal gyri and possibly sulcal widening in the right basal temporo-occipital region.

Other imaging studies included two ictal SPECT scans, one of which showed an increase in activity within the right lateral temporal lobe and right inferior parietal lobe and the second a large intense focus of increased metabolic activity in the mid-lateral right frontal lobe. The surrounding cortex was hypometabolic, consistent with "surround cortical inhibition." Smaller, less intense hypermetabolic foci were seen in the right pericentral cortex and antero-inferior to this area. Ipsilateral increased hypermetabolism was also seen in the caudate and putamen.

INITIAL CLINICAL DIAGNOSIS

In addition to her medical diagnosis of epilepsy, the patient received a neurobehavioral diagnosis reflecting her cognitive impairment. This consisted of a *DSM-IV*-based diagnosis of cognitive disorder due to the direct physiological effect of a general medical condition (American Psychiatric Association, 1994), a diagnostic conclusion that combined the clinical diagnosis (cognitive disorder) with a presumed cause ("medical" condition).

NERVOUS SYSTEM LOCALIZATION

The symptoms, signs, and initial test findings in the *case presentation* are consistent in implicating the supratentorial level of the central nervous system. Within this part of the brain, the patient's seizure characteristics additionally pointed to fronto-temporal cortical areas, most pronounced in the right cerebral hemisphere.

ADDITIONAL INFORMATION

A Wada Test[2] revealed that language was lateralized to the left cerebral hemisphere and that memory abilities of the left hemisphere were relatively intact while memory abilities of the right cerebral hemisphere were present but relatively weak.

VERIFICATION OF THE CLINICAL DIAGNOSES

The diagnosis of cognitive disorder explains most of the clinical findings in the case presentation; however, the diagnosis is so general as to miss aspects of the case that could have implications important for treatment decisions. For instance, the general diagnosis fails to speak to the fact that the patient had shown a decline in academic performance that apparently represented a change from her usual baseline performance level. The overly general nature of the neurobehavioral diagnosis was not improved by attributing the impairment to her underlying medical condition as that specification, too, was relatively vague. The additional information led to a modification of the medical diagnostic and etiological conclusions in this *case presentation*. The neurobehavioral diagnosis and conclusions regarding nervous system localization were also refined in light of this additional information. With regard to the latter, a more specific statement regarding localization could be made. The pattern of neurobehavioral deficits present in the first neuropsychological assessment suggested bilateral dysfunction. The improvement in language abilities after modifying the patient's medication regimen (discussed below) removed any objection to the proposed lateralization of the patient's epileptogenic focus to the right hemisphere.

The revised clinical diagnosis was "Epilepsy arising from the non-dominant right hemisphere." Using verification criteria (Richardson, Williams, Moyer, & Naylor, 2000), the clinical diagnosis was verified in the following way. First, this diagnostic hypothesis adequately explains all the important clinical findings. Her seizures were found to be epileptic in origin based on interictal and ictal EEG recordings. After her change in medication, the conflicting evidence of a disturbance of left hemisphere functions (also discussed below in terms of causation), which had initially been attributed to the physiological changes associated with her seizure disorder, was no longer present, allowing a clear diagnosis of right-hemisphere seizure onset. Her depression was not concluded to be a direct effect of her damaged tissue, since it resolved when her language problems were reversed and prognosis for improvement or seizure elimination improved. Second, the diagnostic hypothesis fits the pathophysiologic state observed and inferred in this patient. Thus, the hypothesis is pathophysiologically coherent. Third, this diagnostic hypothesis provides the best fit to the pattern of the patient's illness and none of the alternative hypotheses fit the patient's illness better. Fourth, this diagnostic hypothesis is the simplest explanation of this patient's illness and there is no hypothesis that is simpler. Fifth, this diagnostic hypothesis appears to possess the characteristics that make it robust to attempts to falsify it. Alternative hypotheses were not successful in displacing the hypothesized etiology. Sixth, the diagnostic hypothesis best predicts the subsequent course of the patient's illness. In terms of the etiology of her seizures, the reduction of her seizure frequency after cortical resection on the right side confirms the hypothesis that this site contained epileptogenic tissue. No alternative hypothesis predicts the patient's course better.

Discussion

Anti-convulsants are among the most frequently prescribed medications that affect the central nervous system. Unlike many other medications, their effects at the molecular level are poorly understood and their effectiveness in the case of a particular patient cannot be predicted easily based simply on their mode of action. Several of the anticonvulsants appear to act by blocking voltage-dependent sodium channels (carbamazepine, felbamate, lamotrigine, oxcarbazepine, phenytoin, topiramate, and zonisamide). Blockade of calcium channel types is also implicated in the case of some of the same or other anticonvulsants (ethosuximide, gabapentin, lamotrigine, pregabalin, and zonisamide). The suppression of calcium channels in turn blocks high-frequency repetitive neuronal firing. Other anticonvulsant medications act by suppressing neuronal activity through the enhancement of the activity of inhibitory (GABA) neurons (benzodiazepines, felbamate, phenobarbital, tiagabine, topiramate, valproic acid, and vigabatrin). Anticonvulsants can have serious medical and behavioral side effects. Felbamate and vigabatrin are used only occasionally because of the frequency of their serious medical side effects (e.g., aplastic anemia and irreversible visual field defects, respectively). Anticonvulsants also have the potential to cause cognitive and other behavioral side effects. Some of the first-generation anticonvulsants, such as phenobarbital, are used less commonly today than before because of their sedating effects and, importantly, their potential negative effects on childrens' attention and other cognitive abilities needed for satisfactory educational progress (Bourgeois, 2004; Meador, 2002a).

To better estimate relative contributions of a disease process versus treatment effect, it is important to recognize the potential for AEDs to cause cognitive and behavioral side effects. All AEDs will cause significant transitive cognitive and behavioral effects if administered at levels that cause serum toxicity, though many also have significant effects at therapeutic levels. It has become recognized, as well, that in using AEDs, polydrug therapy carries greater potential for producing adverse effects than does monotherapy, including the potential for neurodevelopmental effects in utero (Meador, 2002b; Motamedi, & Meador, 2006).

CAUSE/ETIOLOGY

The diagnosis of cognitive disorder was attributed to the patient's medical condition, which included consequences that were related to her ictal events (seizures), the potential adverse effects of treatment (i.e., anticonvulsant medication), and to any underlying neurological or other systemic dysfunction that could potentially give rise to her seizures. In terms of the diagnosis of cognitive disorder, the patient in the current *case presentation* was taking topiramate. Topiramate is an efficatious anticonvulsant and, as will be discussed more fully in a moment, a drug that can negatively affect cognitive and other neurobehavioral functions. As an antiepileptic medication this drug is used to control seizures in patients with several types of epilepsy, in particular partial onset seizures with or without secondarily generalized seizures, seizures associated with Lennox–Gastaut syndrome, and primary generalized tonic–clonic seizures. (French et al., 2004a, 2004b). In a study of 224 patients of all ages with all types of epileptic seizures, Herranz (2000) found a reduction of seizures by over 50% in 78% of the patients; and seizures were abolished altogether in 25% of the total cases being treated with topiramate. The drug was generally well tolerated, and side effects leading to suspension of the drug occurred in only 5% of the cases.

Topiramate, in common with most antiepileptic drugs, has a variety of central nervous system and behavioral side effects in addition to those already mentioned. Several studies have shown that this medication has significant effects on cognitive abilities such as language and memory in adults (Lee et al., 2003; Kockelmann, Elger, & Helmstaedter, 2004; Martin et al., 1999; Mula, Trimble, Thompson, & Sander, 2003; Thompson et al., 2000; Wilding et al., 2004) and in children (Gross-Tsue & Shalev, 2004). In a comparison of new antiepileptic agents, topiramate was found to have the greatest overall incidence of adverse events, even at low doses (Cramer et al., 1999).

During the patient's evaluation, it was recognized that several patients who were being treated with topiramate had complained about a loss in verbal abilities such as name finding. This recognition led to a change in the patient's anticonvulsant medication. Shortly after the patient switched from topiramate, she improved in terms of her cognitive symptoms. In addition, repeat neuro-psychological testing showed that her name finding difficulties and several other test scores improved, including resolution of what had been false lateralizing cognitive deficits (see Table 16.1).

REVISED CAUSE/ETIOLOGY

The seizure etiology was modified to reflect the new knowledge regarding an underlying neurological disorder. The verbal cognitive dysfunction noted at the time of her initial evaluation was attributed to the anticonvulsant medication she was taking at that time, specifically topiramate. The specific neurological and neurobehavioral abnormalities identified, together with the possible etiologies initially proposed and the revised etiologies, are shown in Table 16.2. The attribution of the patient's neurobehavioral difficulties to her underlying medical condition was likely correct, essentially meeting objective criteria for verification of this as the cause. However, the attribution was much too general, to the extent that its usefulness was seriously limited. Referring in general to an underlying medical condition also makes it difficult to deal adequately with potential treatable causes of certain cognitive and emotional changes (name finding difficulties and possible depression). Treatment decisions in these cases require a more finely tuned analysis of the cause(s).

Table 16.2 Differential diagnoses in a patient with symptoms of bilateral brain dysfunction.

Neurological and behavioral abnormalities	Possible etiologies	Revised etiologies
Seizures	Psychogenic	Not confirmed
	Nonlocalized	Not confirmed
	Localized	Confirmed
Language deficits	Developmental delay	Not confirmed
	Interictal effects	Not confirmed
	Depressed mood	Not confirmed
	Damage to language areas	Not confirmed
	Medication side effect	Confirmed
Visual–spatial deficits	Developmental delay	Not confirmed
	Interictal effects	Not confirmed
	Depressed mood dysfunction within	Confirmed
	Nondominant hemisphere	Not confirmed
	Medication side effect	

VERIFICATION OF REVISED CAUSE/ETIOLOGY

The patient's cognitive deficits as described in the case presentation were attributed to the side-effects of topiramate. Alternative explanations were considered, but their likelihood was determined to be low for the following reasons. The propensity for topiramate to produce adverse verbal effects was eventually confirmed (Mula et al., 2003), and resolution of her name finding and several other cognitive deficits after discontinuing topiramate were supportive of a causal association between those cognitive difficulties and the medication. The possibility that she had reversed cerebral dominance, that is, language abilities in the right hemisphere rather than in the left hemisphere, was excluded on the basis of the Wada Test (Wada & Rasmussen, 1960), which showed that language abilities were lateralized to the left hemisphere with no evidence of language abilities in the right hemisphere. The possibility that her verbal problems reflected a long-standing history of weak verbal abilities was unlikely because of her status as a college student at a university with competitive admissions and who had been receiving grades of "A" and "B" in her courses. The decline in her grades occurred only relatively recently. It was possible that her continuing seizure disorder caused a deterioration of cognitive abilities, but this also seemed unlikely based on evidence that seizures by themselves are unlikely to cause persistent cognitive decline (Selwa et al., 1994, but see Andersson-Roswall et al., 2004).

This patient's seizure-related symptoms and signs, interictal and ictal EEG abnormalities, MRI and ictal SPECT data all pointed to a diffuse zone of epileptogenesis in the right hemisphere. In contrast, behavioral observations and her cognitive deficits suggested a disturbance of both verbal and non-verbal abilities, an occurrence usually indicating bilateral cortical disturbance. Low scores on language tests in a patient with a unilateral right hemisphere focus could reflect the presence of language areas in the right hemisphere, which were functioning inefficiently because of their proximity to or involvement in the focal seizure area. Also, if the patient had left-hemisphere language lateralization, low verbal scores could be explained if her verbal abilities had always been at this level (low-average). Alternatively, her uncontrolled seizures could have led to a deterioration of cognitive abilities in both hemispheres through repeated hypoxic episodes. Finally, she could have been exhibiting the effects of one or more of her anticonvulsants. Based on the findings discussed earlier, an adverse effect of medication (topiramate) was seen as the most likely explanation for the apparently inconsistent neurobehavioral test findings. She was tapered off topiramate and started on Lamictal. Her verbal deficits disappeared over a period of several months following this change in her treatment.

Comment

This case presentation emphasized the diagnostic confusion caused by the adverse cognitive and other behavioral effects that were eventually attributed to topiramate. Other anticonvulsant medications also produce adverse central nervous system (CNS) effects as summarized for reference in the following materials. For example, All AEDs produce some degree of sedation, thus affecting attention and other cognitive functions. Five of the most commonly encountered classes of AEDs include hydantoins, barbiturates, benzodiazepines, succinamides, and diones. In addition, five commonly encountered AEDs are carbamzepine, valproic acid, gabapentin, lamotrigine, and topiramate. Newer medications with varying cognitive and behavioral profiles are continually being introduced.

Barbiturates are sedatives and include phenobarbital. They act to increase the threshold for electrical stimulation of the motor cortex, making a seizure focus less irritable (Winkelman, 1999). Side effects include drowsiness and difficulties with memory and visuomotor performance (Metythaler & Yablon, 1999). In addition to the expected sedating effects, however, barbiturates may also produce a disinhibition syndrome chateracterized by impulsiveness, aggressive behavior, and hyperactivity (Ettinger, 2006).

Benzodiazepines are classed under hypnotics and sedatives and employed often as anxiolytic or anticonvulsant medications. Diazepam and lorazepam are most commonly used to treat status epilepticus, while Clonazepam is used for more chronic treatment. They act by augmenting chloride channels, leading to an inhibitory effect on cell firing at the presynaptic level (Winkelman, 1999). Side effects will include general nervous system depression, including decreased mental speed, sedation, and lethargy (Meythaler & Yablon, 1999; Trimble & Thompson, 1986). Similar to barbiturates, they may also produce a paradoxical disinhibition syndrome characterized by agitation and irritability (Ettinger, 2006).

Carbamazepine (Tegretol) is classified as an iminostilbene derivative and is chemically related to tricyclic antidepressants (Meythaler & Yablon, 1999). It blocks voltage and sodium channels, inhibiting the generation of post-synaptic activity (Winkelman, 1999). Cognitive side effects include decreased concentration, visual scanning, and visuomotor speed (Trimble & Thompson, 1986). Also, carbamazepine is used as a mood stabilizing agent, particularly for treatment of bipolar disorder (Ettinger, 2006).

Diones raise the threshold for repetitive activity in the thalamus, inhibiting relay transmission (Winkelman, 1999). This class of AEDs generally is not available in the United States of America and the behavioral profile is not well known.

Felbamate is believed to produce its anticonvulsant effects by blocking repetitive neuronal firing of sodium channels. It is associated clinically with headache, dizziness, and insomnia (Onat & Ozkara, 2004).

Gabapentin (Neurontin) is a GABA derivative, but does not interact with GABA receptors. Its mechanism of action is not well known. Among the most common side effects of gabapentin is somnolence (Meythaler & Yablon, 1999). Depression, aggression, and anxiety also have been reported (Onat & Ozkara, 2004). We have noted patients to fall asleep in the middle of psychomotor tasks after having taken an earlier does of this drug. Gabapentin has been noted to have anxiolytic properties (Ettinger, 2006). Oxcarbazepine is a structurally similar agent and also has been used as a mood stabilizer in patients with bipolar disorder (Ettinger, 2006). Pregabalin, also structurally simiiar to gabapentin, has been described as having anxiolytic properties (Ettinger, 2006).

Hydantoins include phenytoin (Dilantin) as the most commonly prescribed of this class of drug. Dilantin operates by stabilizing neuronal membrances, blocking sodium channels, thus blocking the initiation and spread of electrical discharge (Winkelman, 1999). Side effects of Dilantin include problems with memory, concentration, mental efficiency, and motor speed (Trimble & Thompson, 1986). Phenytoin also has been studied as a possible mood stabilizing agent (Ettinger, 2006).

Lamotrigine (Lamictal) is an ion channel modulator. It seems to stabilize neuronal membranes and inhibit the release of presynaptic neuotransmitters. Side effects include potential behavioral disturbance such as aggressive behavior and violence in some patients (Meythaler & Yablon, 1999; Winkelman, 1999), though favorable psychostimlant effects have also been reported (Onat & Ozkara, 2004). Lamotrigine is another medication used for mood enhancement and is approved for treatment of bipolar disorder (Ettinger, 2006).

Levetiracetam is unclear as to its mechanism of antiseizure effects and is generally indicated as adjunctive treatment for partial-onset seizures. Somnolence, dizziness, and headache are reported early in treatment (Onat & Ozkara, 2004). It has been demonstrated to promote depression or anxiety symptoms in some patients (Ettinger, 2006).

Succinamides include ethosuximide, methsuximide, and phensuximide. They are usually used to treat absence seizures with the mechanism of action poorly defined, but potentially raizing seizure threshold (Winkelman, 1999). Cognitive side effects are described as minimal though lethargy and drowsiness are reported.

Topiramate (Topamax) is classified as a sulfamate-substituted monosaccharide and seems to act by blocking the spread of seizure activity, perhaps by sustaining depolarization of neurons. Somnolence and fatigue are frequent side effects (Meythaler & Yablon, 1999; Winkelman, 1999) and irritability, depression, and acute psychotic symptoms have been reported (Onat & Ozkara, 2004). Topiramate can induce psychomotor slowing as well, including difficulty expressing words, and depression and has been used for treatment of anger and aggression (Ettinger, 2006).

Valproic acid (Depakote, Valproate) is a carbolic acid derivative and may involve increasing brain levels of gamma-aminobutyric acid (GABA) (Meythaler & Yablon, 1999). Side effects include decreased memory, concentration, and mental speed (Trimble & Thompson, 1986). Mood stabilization properties have also been noted for valproate (Ettinger, 2006) and it is not uncommonly used in the treatment of bipolar disorder.

Zonisamide is effective for both partial and generalized seizures and is proposed to mediate antiseizure effects by affecting neuronal sodium channels, calcium channels, and glutamate-mediated synaptic transmission. Somnolence, dizziness, nervousness, and fatigue are commonly reported side effects (Onat & Ozkara, 2004). Zonisamide has been associated with sporadic reports of psychosis, though improvement of mood state is often reported

(Ettinger, 2006). At high doses, Zonisamide also has been associated with transient memory impairment (Berent, Sackellares, Giordani, Wagner, Donofrio, & Abou-Khalil, 1987).

General consideration must also be given to two additional medication-related issues with AEDs. First, the occurrence of neuro-toxic side-effects is better correlated with concentration of the drug in serum rather than actual dosage (Trimble & Thompson, 1986). Second, patients are frequently on more than one anticonvulsant when seizures are not controlled with a single AED. Seizures are generally completely controlled in about 50% of patients, with meaningful improvement in an additional 25% (Winkelman, 1999).

Conclusion

Clinical symptoms and signs are not unexpected in seizure disorders. Often the clinical manifestations are primarily neurobehavioral, reflecting emotional, cognitive, or motor behaviors. These clinical disorders may reflect the medical conditions that underlie the seizure disorder or even the pre-ictal, ictal, or post-ictal characteristics of the seizures themselves. Sometimes, the neurobehavioral symptoms and signs that accompany seizure disorder reflect the treatments that are employed to treat the disorder (e.g., neurosurgical or other medical intervention). Very often, however, these neurobehavioral symptoms and signs represent specifically the adverse side effects of the medications used to treat that disorder.

Amphetamines

Stanley Berent

Amphetamine and related stimulants have proven to be very popular as street drugs in addition to having a number of therapeutic applications in children as well as in adults. Therapeutic applications have included treatment for narcolepsy, hyperactivity, attention deficit disorder, obesity, depression, and other medical disorders (Alberta Alcohol and Drug Abuse Commission [AADAC], 2004; Arnulf, 2005; Calello & Osterhoudt, 2004; Ioannides-Demos, 2005; Vickers, Rodrigues, & Brown, 2002). The relative severity of physiological dependence and withdrawal with amphetamine use, short-term use especially, may be disputed by some (Klaassen & Watkins, 2003; McGregor, 2005; Richter, 1989), but most agree that these substances can lead to functional and structural central nervous system changes and are accompanied by very strong reinforcing effects that leave them highly prone to abuse and habitual use (Badiani & Robinson, 2004; Office of National Drug Control Policy [ONDCP], 2006; Richter, 1989; Robinson & Berridge, 1993; Robinson & Kolb, 1997, 2004). Observations regarding the reinforcement value of amphetamine, together with the fact that these drugs have the potential for dangerous adverse side effects, especially in cases of overdose, have increasingly limited their practical therapeutic usefulness (Alberta Alcohol and Drug Abuse Commission [AADAC], 2004).

Acute use of amphetamine at high doses (sometimes termed, *binging*) can induce hallucinations and other manifestations of altered consciousness, and both acute and chronic amphetamine use can induce overt psychosis that may be behaviorally indistinguishable from schizophrenia (Flaum & Schultz, 1996; Jain, 1996; Richter, 1989). Amphetamine acts as a dopamine receptor agonist and has been shown to induce psychotic episodes, while neuroleptics also have been shown to have affinity for brain dopamine (D2) receptors (Kuhar, Couceyro, & Lambert, 1999). Such observations have led to what has been termed the dopamine hypothesis of psychosis, that is, that psychotic disorders result from over stimulation of D2 receptors (Kuhar et al., 1999). Poisoning among low-dose users of amphetamine is considered rare (Jain, 1996). Nevertheless, published descriptions of psychiatric and medical complications associated with amphetamine abuse are fairly common and include cardiac arrhythmias, convulsions, choreoathetoid dyskinesia, and the various manifestations of sympathomimetic stimulation; e.g., tremulousness, delusions, hyperreflexia, paranoia, hypertension, tachycardia, anxiety, mania, and dysrhythmias (Jain, 1996; Richter, 1989).

Amphetamine is usually taken orally but can be smoked, snorted, or injected. Some forms of amphetamine (e.g., methamphetamine) lend to intravenous (IV) use. Called "speed" on the street, IV use can lead easily to acute overdose, which, in turn, can produce hypertensive crisis precipitating cerebral or myocardial infarction or other vascular damage (Costa et al., 2001; Klys, Konopka, & Rojek, 2005; Petitti, Sidney, Quesenberry, & Bernstein, 1998; Richter, 1989; Waksman et al., 2001). Also, there are instances of "accidental exposures," some of which have occurred as a result of "stuffing" or "packing" substances within a body cavity in the course of smuggling or to conceal evidence in the perceived threat of imminent arrest (Kashani & Ruha, 2004). Malay (2001) reported another kind of accidental exposure where a 30-year-old man mistakenly used a filter to brew a pot of coffee that had previously been used in the home production of methamphetamine.

Some forms of amphetamine (and some of their street names) include methamphetamine (speed, meth, crank, crystal, and ice; the latter when in smokeable form), methylenedioxymethamphetamine (MDMA, ecstasy, or Adam), dextroamphetamine (dexies), methphenmetrazine, and methylphenidate (Alberta Alcohol and Drug Abuse Commission [AADAC], 2004; Merck, 2003; Office of National Drug Control Policy [ONDCP], 2006; Richter, 1989). Users report similar experiences regardless of the type of amphetamine taken (Alberta Alcohol and Drug Abuse Commission [AADAC], 2004). These subjective experiences have been said to include a sense of heightened alertness, activity, energy, and sense of well-being. Similar to cocaine, amphetamine at higher doses can lead the user to experience euphoria (Malay, 2001). The individual's response to amphetamine can escalate from elation to more intense feelings of power, superiority, and in some instances, hostile aggressiveness and loss of contact with reality (Alberta Alcohol and Drug Abuse Commission [AADAC], 2004; Office of National Drug Control Policy [ONDCP], 2006).

Case presentation[3]

Malay described a 30-year-old male who was brought by his wife to the emergency department (ED) 2 hr after "unintentionally" ingesting methamphetamine. The patient was said to have a 9-year history of methamphetamine abuse but that the present overdose occurred unintentionally when he drank coffee that had been made using the same filter he had used in the process of manufacturing methamphetamine. His behavior changed dramatically over an approximately 2 hr time period following his ingestion of the contaminated coffee. At the time he was seen at the ED, he was described as combative and in an altered state of consciousness, with rapid and incoherent speech. While he attempted to respond to some commands, his agitation led to his being placed in restraint. Physically, his pupils were dilated but reactive bilaterally. His skin was hot, and he was profusely diaphoretic. He was shaking, and his muscles were described as extremely rigid. No seizures were found, however. His pulse rate was irregular and high (180 bpm), with heightened respirations and rectal temperature. He was initially hypotensive (blood pressure, 74/28 mmHg) but developed mild hypertension (160/98 mmHg) after about 2 days of treatment. Cardiac monitoring revealed tachycardia and also metabolic acidosis was indicated by arterial blood gas results. Urine drug screen was positive for "high levels of amphetamine." The remainder of the physical examination findings was said to be negative.

The patient was treated symptomatically, and his physical condition improved rapidly over a 2 hr period in the ED and continued to improve over the next few days. Nevertheless, cardiac related symptoms necessitated a 24 hr intensive care unit (ICU) stay, followed by admission to a regular hospital bed. He received a psychiatric consultation during his hospitalization but refused the recommended inpatient psychiatric treatment. He was discharged on the seventh day of hospitalization with plans made for outpatient psychiatric "monitoring."

INITIAL CLINICAL DIAGNOSIS

These findings reflected a number of medical diagnoses, e.g., hypotension, converting to hypertension, diaphoresis, muscular rigidity, and tachycardia. The symptoms and signs that are most relevant to the neurobehavioral emphasis in the present discussion, however, included delirium, agitation, combativeness, altered consciousness, rapid and incoherent speech. Also, by history, descriptions were given regarding long-term amphetamine abuse as well as involvement in illicit drug manufacturing. The relevant, possible neurobehavioral diagnoses are presented and discussed later in this section.

CAUSE/ETIOLOGY

The multiple clinical findings in the *case presentation* were attributed to severe methamphetamine intoxication resulting from acute overdose.

NERVOUS SYSTEM LOCALIZATION

The diagnoses listed in the *case presentation* reflect involvement of multiple bodily systems and levels of the nervous system. The neurobehavioral diagnostic considerations implicate the supratentorial level of the central nervous system.

Discussion

Amphetamine and its various forms, e.g., methamphetamine, affect multiple bodily systems and all levels of the nervous system, directly and indirectly. The severity of its toxicity is to a great extent dose related, with relatively higher doses, as in the current *case presentation*, producing primary neuro-behavioral and cardiovascular effects as well as involvement of other systems, e.g., pulmonary (Chan, Chen, Lee, & Deng, 1994; Lan, Lin, Yu, Lin, & Chu, 1998; Lynch & House, 1992). The neurobehavioral effects of amphetamine are often psychiatric and may be associated with intoxication or withdrawal periods. These psychiatric effects at times include bizarre, self-injurious behaviors. There is considerable evidence that substance abuse can initiate psychotic episodes (Calello & Osterhoudt, 2004; Flaum & Schultz, 1996; Kratofil, Baberg, & Dimsdale, 1996); but, also, substance abuse is common in persons with psychiatric problems but no known substance-induced psychotic disorders (American Psychiatric Association, 1994). In fact, a primary consideration in the differential diagnosis of psychosis in the amphetamine user is substance-induced disorder versus a primary psychotic disorder, usually schizophrenia. Amphetamine has been described as an indirectly acting sympathomimetic that can displace catecholamines from nerve terminal storage vesicles and lead to an increase in deaminated metabolites, which, in turn, can have important affects on norepinephrine, serotonin, dopamine, and other brain catecholamines (Kuhar et al., 1999). Importantly, although not entirely free of debate, the dopaminergic system has been focused on as a key element in the development of schizophrenia (Salgado-Pineda, Delaveau, Blin, & Nieoullon, 2005). Evidence for this hypothesis comes from the observation that neuroleptics, which block dopaminergic D2 receptors, have antipsychotic effects in schizophrenia and that amphetamine, a dopamine agonist, can enhance psychotic symptoms in schizophrenic patients and induce psychotic symptoms in users (Salgado-Pineda et al., 2005). Direct and indirect dopamine agonists, including in addition to amphetamine, bromocriptine and lasuride, also have been reported to induce psychotic incidents (Kuhar et al.). Such observations have led to what has been termed the "dopamine hypothesis of schizophrenia," which among other things postulates a substrate of increased dopaminergic function in schizophrenia (Abi-Dargham, 2004; Abi-Dargham & Moore, 2003; Laruelle & Abi-Dargham, 1999; Laruelle, Abi-Dargham, Gil, Kegeles, & Innis, 1999; Salgado-Pineda et al.; Scatton & Sanger, 2000).

Amphetamine in its various forms has been shown to impact the central nervous system in multiple ways. There is evidence based on animal studies that amphetamine use alters chemistry in the brain. Robinson, Castaneda, and Whishaw (1993), for instance, reported reduced central nervous system serotonin levels in response to repeated administration of ecstasy, even though behavioral changes remained minimal. In addition to chemical changes, however, amphetamine appears to alter structure, especially with chronic or high-dose use (Robinson & Kolb, 1997; Segal & Kuczenski, 1997a, 1997b). The discoveries in the area of how amphetamine affects the nervous system have led to the creation of models that allow for the study of interactions between the various aspects of drug reactions. These approaches, in turn, have provided a theoretical basis for studies on psychoses, as well as direct inquiries on mechanisms of reward, habit, substance abuse, and addiction. Lipton, Zeigler, Wilkins, and Ellison (1991), for instance, implanted pellets in rats in order to study the effects of continuous amphetamine delivery. In comparing amphetamine with cocaine, Lipton et al. (1991) reported that the rats on amphetamine evidenced distinct stages in terms of behavioral changes, progressing from initial hyperactivity to motor stereotypies and to a hallucinogenic-like late stage. In another rat study, Segal and Kuczenski (1997a, 1997b) reported that "psychotic-like behaviors" were most frequently associated with amphetamine when the dosage was high, chronic, and included multiple daily (binge) exposure patterns. Segal and Kuczenski (1997a, 1997b) hypothesized that a shift in relative brain activation takes place in response to these high levels of amphetamine exposure, in mesolimbic and nigro-striatal dopamine pathways, and accompanying the changes in behavior. Borowski and Kokkinidis (1998) showed a potentialtion of startle and fear responses in animals' response to dopamine agonist drugs such as amphetamine and that treatment with amphetamine was accompanied by resistance to extinction of a conditioned fear response.

While learning theory has traditionally held the most promise for explaining the habitual use of chemical substances, advances in neuroscience have allowed for reexamination of learning within a chemical–biological context. It has been shown, e.g., that animals in "rewarding" or reinforcing situations release dopamine in the nucleus accumbens (Young, Moran, & Joseph, 2005). While some have thought this to represent a direct, rewarding aspect of dopamine, others have argued that the release of dopamine enhances attention and in this way strengthens conditioning. The biological situation is undoubtedly much more complex, involving such well-known drug-related phenomena as *tolerance* (the decrease in some aspect of a drug's effects with repeated exposures) and *sensitization* (the increase in some aspects of a drug's effects with repeated exposures). There appears not only to be a chemical analogue to experience but also dendritic changes accompanying conditioning (Badiani & Robinson, 2004; Robinson & Kolb, 1997, 2004). Most important, perhaps, these structural changes have been shown to vary as a consequence of environmental factors present at the time of experience (Badiani & Robinson, 2004; Robinson & Kolb, 2004). While these animal studies hold tremendous promise to increase our understanding of the complex drug-environment-experience effects and interactions on changes in drug-driven behaviors, including habitual use and addiction, they are not conclusive to date.

Do the psychotic reactions that sometimes accompany amphetamine overdose differ qualitatively from, or include more bizarre and self-injurious behaviors than, that usually expected in primary schizophrenia? Kratofil et al. (1996) described several cases that were seen in a general hospital setting and said to involve psychoses attributed to amphetamine abuse. The case descriptions presented by Kratofil included a 31-year-old, Caucasian, single, man who was taken to the ED on Christmas Eve. The patient had severed his right hand and stabbed himself in the eye with a serrated bread knife. He was covered with blood and clutching a Bible when he had been discovered by friends and family members in a bathroom. He was taken to the operating room immediately upon arriving at the ER, where his right hand was reattached and his right eye repaired. Unfortunately, neither procedure was entirely successful. Motivations associated with such instances of self-mutilation are said to be religious, sexual, or neurotic, and the biblical passage said to be most frequently associated with eye enuclecation is from Matthew, " ... if thy right eye offend thee, pluck it out, and cast it from thee ... " (Kratofil et al.). Despite the extreme nature of the behavioral aberrations in this case described by Kratofil, the patient's thinking was said to rapidly return to normal, with good subsequent insight into his disorder. Since discharge from the hospital, he was said to have been compliant with his treatment and had become active in a substance abuse support group. The documented relationship between drug intoxication and the manifestation of psychotic behavior is an important factor in differentiating between substance induced and primary psychosis (American Psychiatric Association, 1994).

A relationship between drug and behavior as in the Kratofil case just described, as well as in the *case presentation*, is not always clear, however. In the two other cases presented by Kratofil et al. (1996), for instance, the 29-year-old man in one case had a history of multiple (six) genital self-mutilations. He admitted using amphetamines intermittently, but he also reported experiencing intrusive ego-dystonic impulses that he hoped to prevent through his self-mutilations. Despite the deep-seated and complex emotional disturbance implied by these revelations, the patient did not comply with the recommended psychiatric treatment after hospital discharge. In Kratofil et al.'s third and final case, the authors described a 27-year-old with a history of multiple-substance abuse dating to adolescence, including abuse of not only amphetamines but also alcohol and other substances. On admission, a urine toxicology screen was positive only for opiates. For 6 months before his hospital admission, he had become preoccupied with religious thoughts, including the delusion that the world was about to end and that, as the messiah, he alone could save it. Also, however, his delusions included that his body was infested with worms and that he was receiving messages that were being broadcast from kitchen appliances. His visit to the hospital was precipitated by a serious self-inflicted knife wound to the chest. The intent appeared to be to save the world by sacrificing himself, that is, his motive was based in his own delusional, suicidal preoccupations. Unfortunately, in this final case, as in the other two cases presented by Kratofil, the specific relationship between the patient's psychotic behaviors and use of amphetamine, alone or in combination, remained unknown.

Is bizarre self-mutilation specific to stimulant intoxication? There are innumerable instances of self-injurious behaviors that are associated with psychotic illness. Some believe that the most bizarre of these instances occur in acute substance abuse, especially amphetamine or other stimulant abuse, and that this is especially likely when the patient presents with paranoia and agitation and responds quickly (within a few hours) to antipsychotic medications (Kratofil et al., 1996). A distinction is sometimes further made between psychosis that follows acute amphetamine intoxication and that which occurs following chronic amphetamine use. The latter has been said to involve fixed delusions, disordered thought processes, and hallucinations; and such illness has been said to be initially indistinguishable from schizophrenia (Kratofil et al.). Distinctions also have been drawn between psychoses that develop as a result of intoxication and those that occur after cessation of amphetamine use (American Psychiatric Association, 1994; Flaum & Schultz, 1996).

Even the cases presented by Kratofil et al. (1996) differed from one another in ways that present important implications for determining a common etiology. All had committed what most of us would consider bizarre self-mutilations, and all reflected some historical involvement with amphetamines. Also, each of the three had what appeared to be a relatively rapid recovery from their psychotic episodes. Beyond these similarities, there are some very important differences between these cases. Two cases reported histories that included alcohol and other substance abuse in addition to amphetamine, and objective evidence of amphetamine was apparently not available in these cases. One had a history of repeated self-mutilations that appeared to be associated with homophobia. He appeared to have been floridly psychotic in one of these instances for several days before harming himself, and one may have represented a suicide attempt. Beyond these specific cases, many professionals who have spent time working in facilities devoted to the treatment of severe mental illness know there are, thankfully small, percentage of cases who commit acts of self-mutilation. Because of the nature of psychosis, most of the patients are on some type of medication, many of which, similar to amphetamine, may have dopaminergic or serotonergic effects. Patients who suffer from schizophrenia are more prone than the average person to abuse a variety of substances, including amphetamine; however, substance abuse is not universal in this population, or in the subpopulation of self-mutilators (American Psychiatric Association, 1994).

Does amphetamine use cause schizophrenia? Flaum and Schultz (1996) raised the question of whether or not amphetamine-induced psychosis might be a cause of chronic schizophrenia. They described a 36-year-old man who had a 20-year history of mental illness. This history was divided into two 10-year phases, the first characterized by "heavy polysubstance abuse, primarily with amphetamines," and the second phase described as reflecting symptoms and signs "prototypical" for schizophrenia. Flaum and Schultz (1996) argued that their published case study reflected a clinical presentation and course that was similar to that seen in the early phases of developing schizophrenia. They used this case to raise questions regarding the role of stimulant drugs, especially amphetamines and other central dopamine agonists, in producing chronic psychotic conditions that are indistinguishable from schizophrenia. They listed the features or amphetamine-induced psychosis as including an onset of symptoms consistent with "up- or down-regulation of neurotransmitters," presumably those known to be involved in psychotic disorders and also affected by amphetamine (e.g., dopamine), rapid therapeutic response to neuroleptic medication, with a florid exacerbation of *positive symptoms* (i.e., symptoms that reflect an excess or distortion of normal function, like delusions or hallucinations) in response to decreased dopamine blocking medications. Also, the patient's premorbid functioning should be good, with no positive family history for psychotic disorders. Finally, according to Flaum and Schultz (1996), there should be evidence for prominent *negative symptoms* (i.e., symptoms that reflect lessening or loss of normal function like affective flattening or avolition) between psychotic episodes (Flaum & Schultz, 1996).

At this time, there is no single, proven association between amphetamine-induced psychosis and schizophrenia. Also, many people use, or abuse, amphetamine and related substances without developing psychosis. Why some people respond to amphetamine with psychotic symptoms and others do not remains unclear. However, Chen et al. (2005) tested the hypothesis that users of methamphetamine who develop psychosis have a stronger family history for psychotic disorder than do those who do not develop psychosis. In a study of 450 methamphetamine users, Chen et al. reported that first-degree relatives of amphetamine users with a lifetime diagnosis of psychosis had a significantly higher morbid risk for schizophrenia than did the relatives of those users who never became psychotic (OR $= 5.4$, 95% CI: 2.0–14.7, $p < .001$). Further, the morbid risk for schizophrenia in the relatives of those users with a prolonged amphetamine-induced psychosis was higher than it was for relatives of those with a shorter period of disorder (OR $= 2.8$, 95% CI: 1.0–8.0, $p < .04$). Chen et al. concluded that the higher the amphetamine user's familial loading on schizophrenia, the more likely he or she was to develop psychosis and the longer the psychosis was likely to last. It is difficult to control all relevant variables and potential counfounders in epidemiological studies involving psychosis. Because of this, the Chen et al. study results cannot be interpreted as conclusive. The study results appear consistent with familial influence on manifestation of psychosis, but the specific relationship to amphetamine remains unclear, that is, how can one be certain that amphetamine caused the psychoses observed in the users studied? Nevertheless, such observations do contribute to the circumstantial evidence for such an association and have led to complex and often philosophical discussions about differentiating between substance-induced versus primary psychoses (American Psychiatric Association, 1994;

Flaum & Schultz, 1996). Flaum and Schultz (1996), despite their arguments for amphetamine-induced psychosis, have suggested that the diagnosis, schizophrenia, should be used until enough scientific evidence has been accumulated to justify a causative role for amphetamine in the initiation and maintenance of a chronic disorder.

Schizophrenia is a type of psychotic disorder. As such, the diagnosis of schizophrenia occurs in two steps. First, a primary psychotic disorder must be established, that is, a disorder in which psychotic symptoms (e.g., delusions or hallucinations) are the defining feature (American Psychiatric Association, 1994). *DSM-IV* makes a distinction between disorders that might contain psychotic symptoms secondarily to the primary condition, e.g., Alzheimer's disease, and disorders in which the psychotic symptoms are the defining feature. Within these primary psychotic disorders, schizophrenia is defined, in general, as a disturbance that lasts at least 6 months, with at least 1 month of two or more "active-phase symptoms, (i.e., delusions, hallucinations, disorganized speech, grossly disorganized behavior, catatonic behavior, or negative symptoms)" (American Psychiatric Association, 1994). To diagnose schizophrenia, it must be shown that the disturbance is not due to the direct physiological effects of a substance, drug, medicine, or a general medical condition. A diagnosis of brief psychotic disorder is more appropriate to use than schizophrenia when describing a disorder that lasts for at least a day but not more than a month and includes delusions, hallucinations, disorganized speech, disorganized behavior, or catatonia (American Psychiatric Association, 1994). For further discussion on the diagnostic topics of substance abuse, schizophrenia, and psychosis more generally, see the sections on *toluene* and *chlorpromazine* in chapter 16, the section on *other psychological/ psychiatric considerations* in chapter 17, and elsewhere in this book.

How does one deal with a clinical diagnosis that combines the presumed cause or etiology with the clinical condition? We have repeatedly emphasized the need to separately approach the tasks of diagnosis and causal determination. In many instances, however, the published diagnostic possibilities will include a number that mix diagnosis with cause. One such diagnosis with relevance to this discussion is the *DSM-IV* diagnosis, substance-induced psychotic disorder, defined as, "...psychotic symptoms that have been judged to be a direct physiological consequence of a drug of abuse, a medication, or toxin exposure" (American Psychiatric Association, 1994). Despite the apparent contamination of cause and diagnosis reflected in the *DSM* classification, we recommend independent verification of each component before assigning a formal *DSM* diagnosis in situations where the manual requires a combined statement. With regard to the current *case presentation*, for instance, one would first establish the presence of the clinical condition(s) (e.g., psychosis, schizophrenia, substance abuse) and then approach the problem of etiology. If it were found through these independent approaches that the patient's symptoms met criteria for psychosis and that this disorder was the result of substance abuse, verified independently from the clinical diagnosis, then a final, revised diagnosis of substance-induced psychotic disorder could be specified.

VERIFICATION OF THE INITIAL CLINICAL DIAGNOSIS

The various clinical findings described in the *case presentation* were associated with amphetamine intoxication directly or secondarily, and these conditions met objective criteria for verifying the diagnoses. Although no specific psychiatric diagnosis was listed by the author of the *case presentation*, behavioral disturbance was described and several psychiatric diagnoses were implied by the author's descriptions. The neurobehavioral diagnoses would need to be added to make the diagnostic statement fully adequate in this case. Because of this, verification will address a revised diagnostic statement.

REVISED CLINICAL DIAGNOSIS

On the basis of the case description, the most likely neurobehavioral diagnoses include *brief psychotic disorder* and chronic *substance abuse*; or, if the patient's psychotic behavior is attributed to amphetamine exposure, *substance-induced psychotic disorder*. In addition, the reported involvement in the home manufacture of methamphetamine raises the possibility of antisocial personality disorder (at times referred to as psychopathy, sociopathy, or dissocial personality disorder) (American Psychiatric Association, 1994). Also, and by historical description, the patient would most likely be diagnosed with substance-abuse disorder, chronic.

VERIFICATION OF REVISED CLINICAL DIAGNOSIS

No well-formed hallucinations or delusions were noted in the *case presentation*. Nevertheless, the patient displayed altered consciousness, disorganized speech, and other abnormal behaviors sufficient to conclude that the patient was psychotic. In fact, the relatively brief and poorly formed behavioral alterations, symptoms that do not mimic well those seen in schizophrenia, are what would be expected for psychosis induced by acute amphetamine intoxication. Also, these changes improved fairly rapidly following removal from amphetamine and initiation of symptomatic treatment. Except for a reported history that included chronic use of amphetamine, the patient did not display a history of mental illness. In fact, his history was silent with regard to past, similar episodes. While the psychiatric symptoms were present relatively briefly, they did appear to last for at least a day, but not more than a month. Thus, these symptoms qualify for brief psychotic disorder.

The patient's substance abuse determination is based on a history of chronic use and is determined independently of conclusions about what caused the current episode. In this particular case, however, it is concluded that amphetamine was the cause of the patient's neurobehavioral and other problems. Because of this, substance-induced psychotic disorder is contained in the diagnostic list.

With the additions listed in the revised diagnosis, all criteria for objective verification of the diagnosis are met. Together, these diagnostic entities are adequate to explain the clinical findings coherently and parsimoniously.

The listed neurobehavioral diagnoses fit the pattern of illness as described in the *case presentation* and predict the symptom course.

VERIFICATION OF CAUSE/ETIOLOGY

While amphetamine, methamphetamine in this case, can be verified as the cause of the patient's difficulties and trip to the ED, not all of the patient's final diagnoses are the proximate result of amphetamine exposure, even though intimately related. The personality disorder, for instance, is most likely a disorder that predates the patient's use of amphetamine. And, although there is no objective evidence to substantiate the claim in this specific case, personality disorder could explain the patient's initial drug abuse.

For the remainder of the diagnoses, however, the findings are consistent with criteria to objectively establish that amphetamine was the cause. This includes the timing of exposure and other criteria. As is the case with any substance-induced disorder, however, the question of poly-substance abuse must be addressed. Arguing for amphetamine as the sole substance in this case is the laboratory findings that indicated high levels of amphetamine, with no other drugs identified. The medical, and behavioral, manifestations were biologically plausible on the basis of what is known about amphetamine and its effects (see *discussion*). These effects have been established by animal and human research. And, removal from exposure modified the clinical picture. These effects are known to be relatively specific to amphetamine and are approximated by the drug in its various forms as well as by other similar drugs, e.g., other stimulants.

Conclusion

As much or more as any other substance discussed in these volumes, amphetamine use emphasizes the importance of separating causal attribution from clinical diagnosis. This is so when exposure is treatment related, but it is even more the case when amphetamine has been taken as an illegal substance. In the latter circumstances, the history, whether provided by the patient or someone close to the patient always, will be viewed as suspect. The motivations for producing a history of questionable validity can be many. Perhaps the circumstances surrounding the exposure included acts that were incriminating. Perhaps, someone was hurt, robbed, or maybe the person was engaged in illegal manufacture or sale of controlled substances. Even in the present case, and although it could be seen as surprising that the patient's wife would be willing to reveal that illegal drug manufacturing was involved in the patient's overdoes, questions could remain about the exact circumstances surrounding the exposure. Nevertheless, the symptomatic effects of exposure were evident, diagnosable, and treatable, regardless of the exact circumstances of exposure. Also, it was possible to isolate amphetamine as the causal agent for most, if not all, of the clinical diagnoses. Some questions might remain. For instance, is the patient a poly-drug abuser? Was the exposure really an accident as described? Might there be a more extensive history of psychiatric disturbance than revealed here? Nevertheless, and despite the possibility of continuing questions, it was possible to effectively evaluate, diagnosis, and treat the patient in the present case.

Clioquinol[4]

James W. Albers

Relatively few neurotoxicants are known to produce a pure or a prominent involvement of sensory and motor axons confined to, or predominately involving, the central nervous system. Yet, those that do are of particular interest given the large number of central nervous system neurodegenerative disorders, such as hereditary spastic paraparesis, amyotrophic lateral sclerosis, and other forms of motor neuron disease that are thought to represent a combination of individual genetic susceptibility and possible environmental factors.

In the 1950s, reports appeared from Japan of patients who experienced a subacute-onset myelitis-like illness characterized by combinations of myelopathy, optic neuropathy, and possibly peripheral neuropathy (Nelson, 1972; Sobue et al., 1971). The onset usually began with painful dysesthesias and sensory loss involving the legs, often including the lower trunk (Toyokura & Takasu, 1975). Motor involvement, when present, consisted of a spastic paraparesis with hyperactive knee reflexes, absent ankle reflexes, and extensor plantar responses (Sobue et al.). Occasional patients developed flaccid leg paralysis; some experienced visual loss or blindness. Initially believed to be a benign encephalomyelitis or a type of multiple sclerosis or Devic's disease, this syndrome eventually was characterized as subacute myelo-optico neuropathy (SMON), a description based on the distribution of neurological involvement (Rose & Gawel, 1984; Tsubaki, Toyokura, & Tsukagoshi, 1964a, 1964b). The following *case presentation* is representative of adults diagnosed with this syndrome.

Case presentation[5]

A 66-year-old female developed painful lower extremity dysesthesias and paresthesias associated with progressive leg weakness. Within a month she was unable to stand. Her evaluation, which included myelography, was unremarkable and did not result in a specific diagnosis. Six months later, she experienced visual loss that progressed to blindness over 1 month. Her neurological impairments remained unchanged for several years until she was readmitted to the hospital with acute onset cardiorespiratory failure. Aside from her neurological problems, her past medical history was remarkable only for recurrent episodes of fever, abdominal pain, and diarrhea that began when she was 45 years old. At that time, she was prescribed a medication containing 200 mg of clioquinol, which she continued to take daily despite resolution of her abdominal symptoms. Neurological examination revealed bilateral blindness with optic atrophy; marked weakness and wasting of the distal lower extremities and, to a lesser extent, the distal upper extremities; and diminished vibration and joint position sensations in the distal legs. Muscle stretch reflexes were hyperactive in the arms and at the knees but absent at the ankles. There were bilateral Hoffmann and Babinski signs. On the basis of the neurological signs suggesting a myelopathy involving ascending and descending long tracts, optic atrophy, and peripheral neuropathy, a diagnosis of SMON was proposed. Laboratory examinations of blood, urine, and cerebrospinal fluid (CSF) were unremarkable, aside from a mild anemia. A vitamin B_{12} level was not measured. A cranial CT showed mild cerebral atrophy consistent with age. Despite intensive care, her medical condition deteriorated and she died of cardiorespiratory complications after a brief hospitalization.

CLINICAL DIAGNOSIS

Clioquinol-induced SMON

Discussion

The initial descriptive reports of SMON tabulated frequencies of symptoms and signs. Such descriptions make it difficult to determine the overall pattern(s) of impairment or the various combinations of impairments among sensory, motor, reflex, and cranial nerve signs (Rose & Gawel, 1984). Later reviews described the various patterns of involvement reflecting symptoms and signs referable to the spinal cord or peripheral nerves (or both), as well as the optic nerves and optic nerve tracts (Baumgartner et al., 1979). Included were cases of isolated optic atrophy, observed most frequently in children receiving clioquinol for acrodermatitis enteropathica, and combinations of myelopathy, visual disturbance, and peripheral neuropathy. Of these combinations, lesions localized to the spinal cord and optic nerves or optic nerve tracts were most consistently reported. Isolated cases of myelopathy or peripheral neuropathy, alone or occurring together, were infrequent. Regardless of the underlying cause, the combinations of symmetrical involvement could represent varying degrees of susceptibility, with mild involvement limited to one or more of the vulnerable tissues or nerve tracts (e.g., isolated optic neuropathy or myelopathy) and with more severe involvement encompassing all vulnerable tissues (complete SMON syndrome). Individual signs and their relevance to the main components of SMON are discussed in the following paragraphs.

NERVOUS SYSTEM LOCALIZATION

The distal symmetrical sensory loss described in the *case presentation* localizes to the peripheral nerves or the spinal cord, although the distal predilection favors a peripheral localization. Nevertheless, the presence of a sensory level on the trunk, usually around T-10, was frequently described among patients diagnosed with SMON. Evidence of a sensory level on the trunk strongly supports localization to the spinal cord. Only rarely does peripheral neuropathy produce sensory loss involving the entire leg or showing a level to the hip or iliac crest, let alone sensory loss that could be mistaken to represent a circumferential level on the trunk. Furthermore, sensory loss due to peripheral neuropathy that ascends above mid-calf usually is accompanied by sensory loss in the hands, something not reported for the patient in the *case presentation* and infrequently reported in SMON. Vibration sensation was the sensory modality most often impaired in SMON, with some cases showing abnormal joint position sensation. Impaired joint position sensation also favors spinal cord localization, as this is an insensitive clinical test that is abnormal only in relatively severe forms of neuropathy. Myelopathy is further supported by pyramidal distribution leg weakness, spasticity with hyperactive reflexes, and positive Babinski signs (Rose, 1986). Hyperactive reflexes reflect lateral corticospinal tract involvement, whereas large fiber peripheral neuropathies generally show hypoactive or absent ankle and knee reflexes. The relatively consistent presence of large fiber sensory loss and hyperactive knee reflexes with positive Babinski signs indicates involvement of the rostral posterior columns and the caudal lateral corticospinal tracts. Additional signs of a more complete myelopathy, such as bladder, bowel, or sexual dysfunction, were present in a minority of SMON cases. The combined signs suggest a selective myelopathy localized to specific portions of individual nerve tracts, not generally findings of the type seen in transverse myelitis, spinal cord infarction, or spinal cord compression due to trauma.

The combination of severe visual loss and ophthalmoscopy evidence of pale optic discs is characteristic of an optic neuropathy with loss of optic nerve axons. Numerous reports include descriptions of optic neuropathy either isolated or as a component of SMON, with descriptions of markedly reduced visual acuity or blindness presenting with bilateral central scotoma in the presence of pale optic discs (Billson, Reich, & Hopkins, 1972; Derakhshan & Forough, 1978; Garcia-Perez, Castro, Franco, & Escribano, 1974; Giraud, 1987; Pittman & Westphal, 1974; Selby, 1972). The ocular findings in SMON included evidence of optic atrophy, possible peripheral retinal pigment irregularities, visual field loss with a centrocecal scotoma, and dyschromatopsia (Bardelli & Biagini, 1986).

The combination of distal sensory loss and absent ankle reflexes, as in the *case presentation*, suggests peripheral nerve involvement, consistent with the initial descriptions of SMON and of "neuropathy" in the descriptor *myelo-optico-neuropathy*. Most reports of peripheral neuropathy in SMON are in the context of a myelopathy with or without optic neuropathy (Inoue, Nishibe, & Nakamura, 1971; Nakae, Yamamoto, & Igata, 1971; Olesen & Jensen, 1991; Tsubaki, Honma, & Hoshi, 1971). It remains unclear whether or not the full SMON syndrome included peripheral nervous system involvement. The most compelling evidence of peripheral nervous system involvement is loss of ankle reflexes, as ankle reflexes usually are unobtainable in large fiber peripheral neuropathies of more than mild severity. In contrast, corticospinal tract lesions produce hyperreflexia, not areflexia. Absent ankle reflexes reflect interruption of the reflex arc at any level, including selective degeneration of sensory axons within the central nervous system (Rose, 1986). In other words, loss of ankle reflexes could reflect involvement of the intramedullary portion of the afferent fibers subserving the monosynaptic reflex (Baumgartner et al., 1979; Thomas et al., 1984). Rose noted that peripheral nervous system involvement was supported in some SMON cases by the presence of significant wasting or weakness due to lower motor neuron involvement, although support by EMG evidence of denervation and nerve conduction evidence of peripheral neuropathy was usually lacking (Rose, 1986).

Reviews, such as those performed by Baumgartner et al. (1979), included peripheral nervous system involvement if one or more of the following were present: (a) bilateral distal sensory loss, (b) loss of ankle reflexes, (c) weakness or significant wasting due to lower motor neuron involvement, or (d) nerve conduction evidence of peripheral neuropathy. Without electrodiagnostic or pathological confirmation of sensory or motor nerve fiber degeneration or of segmental demyelination in the peripheral nerves, any statement about the existence of peripheral neuropathy remains tentative. None of the reported signs in SMON excludes the combination of a peripheral neuropathy superimposed on a myelopathy. A peripheral neuropathy that involves motor axons would have to be mild, however, relative to the myelopathy component because the peripheral motor axons represent the final common pathway. In the presence of a substantial peripheral neuropathy, the signs of myelopathy (e.g., hyperactive reflexes) would not be manifest.

There is another possible explanation for the symptoms and signs associated with SMON. Namely, it is possible that SMON represents a pure central nervous system disorder. Thomas (1997) summarized the reasoning that identified SMON as a selective *central* distal axonopathy syndrome. The term *selective* was used to highlight involvement of the central sensory projections, with relative sparing of the dorsal root ganglia neurons and their peripheral sensory projections (Thomas, 1997; Thomas et al., 1984). The neuropathology findings in SMON confirmed symmetrical axonal degeneration in the lateral columns of the lumbar cord and in the gracile columns at the cervicomedullary junction, SSEP studies showed normal peripheral but delay peripheral sensory conduction, and at least some studies showed normal sural nerve electrophysiological and histology (Thomas, 1997; Thomas et al.). In other words, the sensory neuron and its peripheral extension remained intact, but the distal segment of its rostral projection in the posterior columns degenerated. Sobue et al. (1971) reported that in SMON cases, recovery of weakness was fairly good, whereas sensory disturbances often persisted. Thomas et al. suggested that the poor prognosis for recovery of sensation in SMON was atypical of most sensory neuropathies, and supported the concept of a distal central axonopathy due to the reduced capacity for axonal regeneration in the central nervous system.

The evidence implicating SMON as a selective central distal axonopathy is compelling and explains the findings observed for a majority of cases diagnosed with SMON. The evidence supporting a superimposed peripheral component in some cases may represent the coincidental presence of an otherwise nondescript peripheral neuropathy (a syndrome common among the general population). The existing data does not exclude the possibility, however, that among cases with severe SMON are included some with a distal peripheral neuropathy superimposed on the otherwise typical selective central distal myelopathy.

ADDITIONAL INFORMATION

Postmortem examination of the patient described in the *case presentation* addressed several of the localization issues discussed above (Ricoy, Ortega, & Cabello, 1982). Neuropathological abnormalities included loss of neurons with gliosis affecting the spinal cord (most prominent the cervical posterior columns [ascending gracile tracts] and the descending lateral corticospinal tracts in the lumbosacral cord but also involving the dorsal spinal cerebellar tracts and the olivo- and pontocerebellar tracts); the optic nerves; and the peripheral nerves. Findings indicative of peripheral nervous system involvement included loss of axons in the dorsal and ventral nerve roots and mild loss of sensory ganglia. The sural and sciatic nerves showed loss of large myelinated fibers with demyelination and isolated axonal swellings (irregularities of the axons and myelin sheaths). The ocular pathology included severe loss of myelin in the optic nerves, optic chiasm, and optic tracks. The lateral geniculate bodies showed eccentric neuronal nuclei and atypical chromatolysis consistent with trans-synaptic degeneration. The geniculocalcarine radiations to the visual cortex were described as pale, but the cortical neurons in the occipital lobes were unremarkable (Ricoy et al., 1982). The neuropathology findings are those of a myelo-optico-neuropathy and are consistent with the neurological symptoms and signs.

Additional postmortem investigations of SMON reported in the literature are in general agreement in terms of spinal cord findings of degenerative changes in portions of the bilateral posterior columns (fasciculus gracilis) and the lateral corticospinal tracts (Cavanagh, 1971; Shiraki, 1975; Sobue et al., 1971; Sobue, Mukoyama, Takayanagi, Nishigaki, & Matsuoka, 1972; Tatetsu, Miyakawa, Fujita, Takaki, & Harada, 1971; Tsubaki et al., 1964a, 1964b). Axons in the fasciculus gracilis conduct sensory impulses from the legs and are among the longest ascending central nervous system axons. The lateral corticospinal tracts are descending myelinated axons that conduct motor impulses from the brain to lower motor neurons in the anterior horns of the cord. Axons in the corticospinal tracts conduct motor impulses to motor neurons innervating the legs and represent the longest descending central nervous system axons. Additional degenerative changes also are found in the optic nerves and optic nerve tracts. Questions remain about the presence of peripheral nerve and involvement of dorsal root ganglia. Kono (1978) reviewed and summarized the SMON studies in Japan based on the review of the Pathology Section of the Commission of pathological specimens collected from 62 institutions and involving 132 autopsy cases diagnosed with definite or probable SMON. An accompanying summary figure, adapted from others, included selective involvement of the optic nerves, posterior columns, and the peripheral component of the sensory nerves (dorsal root, dorsal root ganglia, and peripheral sensory projections). Some cases, including the thorough neuropathological studies of Shiraki (1991), also show abnormality of nerve roots, dorsal root ganglia, and peripheral nerves. Considering all reports, peripheral nervous system involvement is not found as consistently as is central nervous system involvement. This may reflect greater attention to the central nervous system tissues relative to the peripheral nervous system, or it could reflect the spectrum of SMON severity, with central involvement exceeding peripheral involvement.

VERIFICATION OF THE CLINICAL DIAGNOSIS

SMON is defined here as a clinical diagnosis applied to cases with features of subacute onset, paresthesias and lower leg numbness with diminished sensation extending at times onto the trunk, spastic paraparesis with unsteady gait or flaccid paralysis when severe, hyperactive knee reflexes but hypoactive or absent ankle reflexes, positive Babinski reflexes, and visual loss ranging from mildly decreased acuity to blindness with severe optic atrophy (Thomas et al., 1984). Despite the characterization as a SMON, no emphasis is applied to be peripheral neuropathy component, as many of the symptoms and signs suggestive of peripheral neuropathy may reflect involvement within the spinal cord (myelopathy).

Using objective questions such as those outlined by Richardson et al. (2000), SMON explains all of the clinical findings among cases presenting with various combinations of bilateral selective myelopathy and optic atrophy (*adequacy*). The presence of a superimposed distal sensory or sensorimotor peripheral neuropathy would also be explained. The diagnosis of SMON would not explain neurologic conditions characterized by substantial asymmetry, cranial nerve involvement other than the optic nerves, isolated mononeuropathies, upper extremity predominance, or protracted clinical course. SMON also fits the illness pattern described for most cases in terms of subacute onset, symmetry, and a pattern of symptoms and signs referable to selected areas of the spinal cord, the optic nerves, and possibly the peripheral nerves (*primacy or dominance*). Involvement of the peripheral nerves is not required to establish the diagnosis and, if a predominant feature, may argue against the diagnosis. SMON would not explain a neurological syndrome showing progression without ongoing exposure to a neurotoxicant or other causative factor. In most cases, the symptoms and signs attributed to classical SMON fulfill the observed neuropathology (*primacy or dominance*). However, a dying-back axonopathy cannot be distinguished from "longest fiber" disease due to selective degeneration of the cell bodies giving rise to the longest fibers (Baumann & Hauw, 1980). The diagnosis of SMON is the simplest explanation for the characteristic combination of symptoms and signs typically attributed to this condition (*parsimony*). Alternative explanations, aside from individuals with isolated myelopathy or optic neuropathy, are unlikely. The diagnosis of SMON, or at least a diagnosis of clioquinol-associated SMON, anticipated the subsequent clinical course in most cases (*prediction*). The typical course was monophasic and consisted of progression, plateau, and improvement, although residual paresthesias and sensory loss were common. Greater severity was associated with greater residual deficits. Initial SMON descriptions included a high relapse rate that may have reflected additional clioquinol exposures. Subsequent reports described a favorable prognosis once removed from additional exposure. For several competing explanations, such as vitamin B_{12} deficiency, it would not be anticipated that removal from clioquinol exposure alone would be associated with recovery.

To this point, all questions used to verify the diagnosis of SMON can be answered in the affirmative. The remaining question involves that possibility of alternative diagnoses; e.g., can the diagnosis of SMON escape disproof (*robustness*)? Disapproval requires identification of a more likely diagnosis and can be addressed in the context of a complete differential diagnosis. SMON in its classic form is relatively distinct and there are only a few neurological disorders that present with the same combination of findings. That is not to say that individual cases were not misdiagnosed in the large surveys, especially those who had nonspecific symptoms and possible few objective signs, and who were diagnosed by clinicians unfamiliar with neurological conditions. Confirmation of a diagnosis of SMON requires examination of all items included in the differential diagnosis of a SMON.

CAUSE/ETIOLOGY

By 1970, SMON had reached epidemic proportions, with nearly 10,000 Japanese cases identified and 11,127 cases eventually confirmed (Iwashita, 2001; Shigematsu, Yanagawa, Yamamoto, & Nakae, 1975; Sobue, 1991; Sobue et al., 1971). The etiology remained unknown despite suspicion for infectious or environmental causes until an iron chelate of clioquinol (clioquinol) was identified as the source of green tongue, urine, and feces observed in some SMON cases (Tamura, Yoshioka, Imanari, Fukaya, & Kusaka, 1973). Ultimately, an epidemiological link was established between clioquinol and SMON. Clioquinol, an over-the-counter (OTC) medication frequently used in Japan but also elsewhere for a variety of gastrointestinal conditions, readily binds metal and especially iron, explaining the green pigmentation associated with high dosage (Schaumburg, 2000). The results of epidemiological surveys implicated clioquinol with SMON (Kono, 1975; Nakae et al., 1971; Nakae, Yamamoto, Shigematsu, & Kono, 1973; Tateishi, Kuroda, Saito, & Otsuki, 1972), but not all cases of SMON had known exposure to clioquinol prior to developing neurological symptoms or signs (Inoue et al., 1971). The suspected causal linkage between SMON and clioquinol resulted in the Japanese Ministry of Health banning the sale of clioquinol as of September 1970 (Spillane, 1972; Tsubaki et al., 1971). At the time of the ban, about 1,000–2,000 cases of SMON were being diagnosed per year in Japan (Spillane, 1972). Following the ban, the number of new SMON cases gradually declined and eventually disappeared (Hanakago & Uono, 1981; Nelson, 1972).

Despite the generally accepted causal linkage between SMON and clioquinol, some controversy surrounds the current understanding of SMON, both as an entity and in terms of the association with clioquinol. The controversy reflects the specificity of diagnostic criteria, the localization of the clinical features, unanswered questions about the high incidence in Japan compared to other countries, the paucity of electrodiagnostic information, and the strength of the causal association between clioquinol and SMON.

The first step in addressing the cause of SMON in terms of clioquinol is to recognize that numerous conditions are capable of producing SMON, just as there are numerous conditions capable of producing a sensorimotor polyneuropathy. For example, consider the items listed in Table 16.3. All are capable of producing, to varying degrees, components of a SMON. The diagnosis of SMON cannot be applied without developing an appropriate differential diagnosis and excluding (by appropriate imaging or measures of CSF and blood) problems that produce similar symptoms and signs. Some nutritional disorders (e.g., vitamin B_{12}, vitamin E, or copper deficiency) produce a distal axonopathy with clinical and neuropathological findings similar to SMON. Vitamin B_{12} and vitamin E deficiencies have been implicated

Table 16.3 The differential diagnosis of a subacute-onset myelo-optico-neuropathy (SMON).

Inflammatory conditions
  Devic's disease
  Encephalomyelitis
  Guillain–Barré syndrome
  Multiple sclerosis
  Primary central nervous system vasculitis
  Rare combinations of central and peripheral nervous system demyelinating disorders (variants of chronic inflammatory demyelinating neuropathy)
  Systemic lupus erythematosus
  Tropical spastic paraparesis (TSP, HTLV-1 associated myelopathy)

Neurodegenerative disorders
  Hereditary spastic paraplegia (HSP)

Neurotoxic conditions
  Cuban opticoneuropathy
  Organophosphate-induced delayed neurotoxicity (jake leg palsy)
  Nigerian tropical ataxic neuropathy

Nutritional disorders
  Celiac disease
  Pancreatitis
  Postbariatric surgery with copper deficiency
  Vitamin B_{12} deficiency
  Vitamin E deficiency
  Whipple's disease

at times in connection with SMON, and they are reviewed separately in the following paragraphs, along with conditions causing mixed vitamin deficiencies.

Numerous conditions, including encephalomyelitis, multiple sclerosis, Devic's disease (neuromyelitis optica), and numerous conditions caused by neurotoxicants or deficiency states, resemble SMON. Tropical peripheral neuropathy (Nigerian tropical ataxic neuropathy) is a disorder characterized by burning dysesthesias, ataxia, optic neuropathy, and neurogenic deafness often in the presence of malnutrition. Although the etiology of tropical peripheral neuropathy appears to be multifactorial, it is postulated that this condition is caused by several neurotoxins acting separately; the likelihood of developing disease depends on individual genetic susceptibility and adverse environmental factors including malnutrition and infections (Bahemuka, 1981). The epidemiology of tropical spastic paraparesis (TSP, HTLV-1 associated myelopathy) suggests that environmental factors contribute to the etiology. Glutamate-mediated excitotoxicity, central distal axonopathies, and exposure to a variety of neurotoxicants may explain most cases of tropical spastic paraparesis (Zaninovic', 2004). Another disorder, referred to as Cuban epidemic neuropathy, superficially resembles SMON. In the early 1990s, an epidemic of neuropathy and optic neuropathy occurred in Cuba. The "epidemic neuropathy" was initially thought to represent an exposure to some unrecognized neurotoxicant. However, the epidemic appeared in association with acute worsening of Cuba's economic situation, and the syndrome was eventually attributed to acute nutritional deficiencies caused by malnutrition, possibly in combination with alcohol consumption (tobacco–alcohol amblyopia) and exposure to other unidentified substances (Ordunez-Garcia, Nieto, Espinosa-Brito, & Caballero, 1996). Support for a deficiency syndrome hypothesis was provided by disappearance of additional cases after widespread vitamin supplementation, similar to the disappearance of SMON cases after the ban of clioquinol. The Cuban epidemic neuropathy syndrome did not include signs of myelopathy, avoiding confusion with SMON.

Clinically evident nutritional neuropathies produce combined deficiencies related to dietary insufficiency or malabsorption. A common presentation of nutritional neuropathy occurs in the setting of gastric resection or diversion, with about 5% of patients undergoing gastric restriction surgery for morbid obesity developing some neurologic complication (Abarbanel, Berginer, Osimani, Solomon, & Charuzi, 1987). Although the situation in which this disorder arises prevents confusion with SMON, the resultant abnormalities serve as a model for other nutrition-deficiency disorders. Symptoms associated with postgastrectomy neuropathy include distal dysesthesias and weakness, most severe in the lower limbs. Examination shows distal sensory loss, weakness, and hypoactive or absent reflexes without signs of corticospinal tract dysfunction (Banerji & Hurwitz, 1971; Koike et al., 2001). Most of the patients demonstrated multiple vitamin deficiencies including low serum levels of thiamine, pyridoxine folate, and vitamin B_{12}. Sural nerve histology shows reduced fiber density, perineural edema, and rare segmental demyelination

(Koike et al.). Acquired copper deficiency (hypocupremia), as occasionally develops after bariatric surgery, also causes a myelopathy that resembles vitamin B_{12} deficiency (Kumar, Ahlskog, & Gross, 2004). Anesthesia paresthetica is a syndrome associated with nitrous oxide-induced vitamin B_{12} deficiency. It is characterized by sensory ataxia, spastic paraparesis with positive Babinski signs, a sensory level on the trunk, and brisk knee but absent ankle reflexes, signs reflecting posterior column and lateral corticospinal tract involvement and peripheral neuropathy resembling SMON (Gutmann & Johnsen, 1981; Kinsella & Green, 1995; Layzer, Fishman, & Schaefer, 1978). Organophosphate-induced delayed neuropathy (OPIDN) is a clinical syndrome closely resembling the myeloneuropathy of SMON. Forms of OPIDN include "jake leg palsy," a dying-back motor axonopathy characterized by spastic paraparesis, ataxia, and distal weakness and atrophy following exposure to tri-ortho-cresyl phosphate (TOCP), an organophosphate adulterant found in Jamaican Ginger, an alcohol-containing tonic used during prohibition (Morgan & Penovich, 1978). Numerous medications (e.g., amiodarone, chloramphenicol, chloroquine, disulfiram, ethambutol, isoniazid, penicillamine, and vincristine) are capable of producing optic neuropathy and peripheral neuropathy (opticoneuropathy) among their adverse effects (Herskovitz, 2006).

Many aspects of SMON resemble combined system degeneration of the spinal cord and peripheral nerves due to vitamin B_{12} (cobalamin) deficiency. Vitamin B_{12} deficiency is associated with various combinations of shooting leg pain, visual loss, ataxia, sensory loss with positive Romberg sign, altered reflexes, and extensor plantar reflexes, symptoms, and signs suggesting involvement of the optic nerves or tracts and posterior or lateral columns of the spinal cord (Nolan & Albers, 2005). The signs of variably depressed reflexes and peripheral neuropathology showing axonal loss and occasional demyelination suggest a component of neuropathy (Albers, Nostrant, & Riggs, 1989; McCombe & McLeod, 1984; Windebank, 1993). Early neurological features of vitamin B_{12} deficiency include painful, tingling paresthesias involving the hands and the feet equally or the hands more severely than the feet, findings atypical of SMON (Hemmer, Glocker, Schumacher, Deuschl, & Lucking, 1998; Victor, 1989). Optic neuropathy occurs more frequently in SMON than in vitamin B_{12} deficiency. A review of the literature prior to 1960, as summarized by Bron, Korten, Pinckers, and Majoor (1972), identified only 28 cases of vitamin B_{12} deficiency (pernicious anemia) and optic neuropathy. Most cases of vitamin B_{12} deficiency occur in the setting of pernicious anemia, but not all vitamin B_{12} deficient patients show a megaloblastic anemia (Healton, Savage, Brust, Garrett, & Lindenbaum, 1991; Hemmer et al., 1998; Klee, 2000).

Vitamin E deficiency is an additional item in the differential diagnosis of SMON. The tocopherols (α, β, γ, and δ) are fat-soluble antioxidants thought to prevent peroxidation of fatty acids in cell membranes (Kayden, 1993). Vitamin E or α-tocopherol is the most common and potent antioxidant in this group of compounds. The ubiquitous nature of the tocopherols makes dietary insufficiency nearly impossible. However, functional deficiencies related to vitamin metabolism and absorption exist, with malabsorption and steatorrhea associated with celiac disease, Whipple's disease, and pancreatitis representing the most common causes of vitamin E deficiency (Jackson, Amato, & Barohn, 1996). Because patients with gastrointestinal disorders were most likely to be treated with SMON, it could be hypothesized that vitamin E deficiency, rather than clioquinol, was causally related to SMON.

Much of our understanding of vitamin E deficiency results from study of abetalipoproteinemia (Bassen-Kornzweig syndrome), a well-defined auto-somal recessive disorder resulting in α-tocopherol deficiency. The congenital absence of apoprotein B produces deficiencies in vitamins E and A, with progressive ataxia, areflexia, steatorrhea, and retinitis pigmentosa (Albers et al., 1989; Brin et al., 1986). A second autosomal recessive defect in the α-tocopherol transporter protein results in inadequate incorporation of α-tocopherol in very-low-density lipoproteins and an isolated α-tocopherol deficiency (Hentati et al., 1996). The neuropathy of vitamin E deficiency begins insidiously and is usually not painful, features atypical for SMON. Like vitamin B_{12} deficiency, vitamin E deficiency usually presents with combined evidence of neuropathy and myelopathy, with unsteady gait and lower extremity numbness. Proprioception and vibration sensations are impaired with preserved pinprick, temperature, and light touch. Diminished proprioception, when severe, results in pseudoathetosis. The reflexes are depressed or absent, but the response to plantar stimulation is variable. Truncal and extremity ataxia, plus tremor and dysarthria attributable to cerebellar dysfunction, may develop. The combined findings are those of a sensory neuropathy of the axonal type. Dorsal root ganglia neurons are sensitive to vitamin E deficiency, resulting in a central and peripheral sensory axonopathy. Sural nerve biopsies can be normal or show retrograde degeneration of large-caliber myelinated axons (Jackson et al., 1996; Nelson, 1983; Traber et al., 1987). Patients with abetalipoprotei-nemia show a marked loss of large diameter fibers (Wichman, Buchthal, Pezeshkpour, & Regg, 1985). The distal projection of the central afferents of the dorsal root neuron shows marked degeneration in the fasciculi gracilis and cuneatus (Landrieu, Selva, Alvarez, Ropert, & Metral, 1985; Windebank, 1993).

On the basis of the clinical and pathological descriptions, it is unlikely that vitamin E deficiency could be confused with SMON or contribute causally to SMON, other than as part of a multifactorial disorder. The neuropathy associated with vitamin E deficiency resembles a sensory ganglionopathy or neuronopathy with painless loss of large fiber modalities. However, when considering the combined syndrome of neuropathy, myelopathy, and ataxia, some of the additional features resemble those of vitamin B_{12} deficiency and some components of SMON. Vitamin E could contribute to SMON in ways separate from a deficiency neuropathy, and vitamin E is known to promote the development of axonal degeneration and neuronal axonal dystrophy in animals and in humans (Schmidt, Coleman, & Nelson, 1991).

Recognition that the green pigment appearing in some SMON cases was a ferric chelate of clioquinol suggested a causal association between clioquinol and SMON (Tamura et al., 1973). Initial findings supporting a causal association included evidence that most SMON cases had taken clioquinol prior to the onset of the syndrome and an apparent relationship between the amount of clioquinol ingested and the onset of SMON (Igata & Toyokura, 1970). The SMON Research Commission concluded that the majority of SMON cases resulted from clioquinol (SMON Research Committee, 1975). The hypothesis causally associating clioquinol and SMON was not unopposed, however. Kono (1971) proposed several potential causes. These included intoxication, noting that extensive use of agricultural pesticides, environmental contamination with industrial wastes, and excessive use of medications have been common in Japan since the 1950s. Clinical and neuropathological conditions similar to SMON included subacute combine degeneration due to vitamin B_{12} deficiency, tropical neuropathy in Jamaica and Nigeria, nontropical sprue, celiac disease, paraneoplastic disorders, and diabetic peripheral neuropathy. It also was generally accepted that SMON occurred in the absence of clioquinol exposure (Baumgartner, Elmqvist, & Shigematsu, 1984). This conclusion is not unexpected, as many neurotoxicants produce conditions similar or identical to conditions having other cause (e.g., arsenical peripheral neuropathy and Guillain–Barré syndrome). Finally, an infectious agent, such as a virus, the leading explanation following early descriptions of SMON, remained a possible consideration (Kono, 1971).

Results of the national surveys supported a causal association of clioquinol and SMON. In Japan, 85% of SMON cases had onset within 6 months of starting clioquinol (temporality) (Toyokura & Takasu, 1975). SMON showed an increased incidence from around 1963 to 1969 (Sobue et al., 1971), with almost no new cases after 1970, a decline coincident with the ban on the use and sale of clioquinol (Shigematsu et al., 1975; Sobue, 1991). The dramatic decrease in SMON incidence after January 1970 was evident in most parts of Japan (Kusui, 1975). Although the number of new SMON cases was noted to decline before the ban, clioquinol consumption also decreased prior to the ban, likely in response to negative publicity (Sobue, 1991).

Despite the large number of articles describing SMON, many reflect reports of individuals or a small number of cases. Although the SMON Commission conducted several descriptive national surveys, relatively few case-control studies or cohort studies are available to establish the relative risk of developing SMON in association with clioquinol. After SMON became linked to clioquinol, evaluation of causation became difficult, as focus switched to describing the presumed harmful effects of clioquinol (Sonoda, 1978). The resultant reports reflected the need to rapidly report the results of the surveys, with many reports published in the letter form or in summaries with little information about methodology.

Several cross-sectional studies compared groups of patients who had received clioquinol with those patients who had not. Tsubaki et al. (1971) compared the records of 263 patients who had been prescribed clioquinol to treat various gastrointestinal disorders and who had received clioquinol with those of 706 patients who also had gastrointestinal disorders but had not received clioquinol. The comparison showed that none of the 706 referents displayed neurological symptoms suggestive of SMON, whereas 44 of the 263 patients receiving clioquinol did display such symptoms. Of the 110 patients who received clioquinol for more than 2 weeks, 40 (35%) developed symptoms. In 29 cases, the main symptoms consisted of bilateral sensory loss and paresthesias in the legs, most severe in the feet. Sixteen cases (6% of those receiving clioquinol) had SMON, consisting of myelopathy, evidence of peripheral neuropathy, and occasional optic neuropathy. They described the results in terms of an association between clioquinol and SMON, without further causal conclusions (Tsubaki et al.). In one of the few studies providing information on the frequency of clioquinol use among clinic patients, Aoki, Ohtani, Sobue, and Ando (1972) reviewed the medical records of 4,318 patients receiving care from one hospital during 1969. Among these patients, 12% had been prescribed clioquinol. The frequency of SMON was 2.2% among patients who had been prescribed clioquinol compared to 0.1% among patients who had not been prescribed clioquinol ($p = .001$). Four SMON cases had no history of clioquinol intake before developing SMON.

Much of the epidemiological information related to SMON is the result of surveys (survey research or epidemiological studies) conducted by the SMON Research Commission; a report authored by the chair of the SMON Research Commission detailed the survey research evidence linking SMON to clioquinol (Kono, 1971). The SMON Research Commission conducted four national SMON surveys (Shigematsu et al., 1975). The results represent the primary data used to establish the changing trends of SMON over time in Japan. The initial survey consisted of two parts: (a) retrospective identification of SMON cases at participating medical institutions during 1967 and 1968 to establish SMON prevalence and (b) review of evaluations that occurred between January 1969 and June 1970 to determine SMON incidence, with separate review of evaluations collected after June 1970, to evaluate for change in SMON incidence after introduction of the clioquinol causation hypothesis. The third survey involved retrospective study of prescription medications used by 890 definite SMON cases evaluated at the 18 hospitals participating in the Clinical Section of the SMON Commission. The fourth SMON survey involved follow-up evaluations conducted in 1973 on all SMON cases who visited the study hospitals during 1972, a survey designed to clarify the clinical course of previously identified SMON cases. The results of the individual SMON surveys were reported in a variety of forms in Japan, but all of the summary information appears to have been summarized in English publications, such as reported by Shigematsu et al. (1975). The initial nation-wide SMON survey identified 4,355 SMON cases (4.5 per 100,000). This figure represents the number of SMON cases diagnosed during 1967 and 1968. The age-specific prevalence peaked in the seventh decade of life; few children under 10 years of age were identified. The male/female ratio was 1/1.9, suggesting a possibly increased susceptibility among females.

Shimada and Tsuji (1971) described an epidemiological investigation of SMON from an area of Japan where SMON was most endemic. In addition to their study of SMON incidence discussed earlier, they examined 113 SMON cases, 79% of whom had taken clioquinol before SMON onset. Among those who had taken clioquinol, they found a relationship between the dose and the interval between administration and onset of neurological symptoms. Igata (1971) reported that all 34 SMON cases diagnosed in one clinic had received clioquinol before onset of neurological symptoms; no instance of SMON was found among cases who had not used clioquinol. In the same letter, they reported that among 70 SMON cases identified in one city, most cases (80%) have been receiving treatment for abdominal complaints at one of the two clinics when the neurological symptoms began. They confirmed that larger amounts of clioquinol (not further described) were prescribed at these two clinics than at other clinics in the area (Igata, 1971). Similarly, Tsubaki et al. (1971) reported that among 171 SMON cases, 166 (96%) had taken clioquinol. An additional survey of SMON cases made in two cities found that, in one institution, 17 of 21 confirmed SMON cases (81%) received clioquinol before onset (Nakae et al., 1971). The SMON Commission identified 1,839 SMON cases, of which 1,381 (75%) had used clioquinol before onset of neurological symptoms (Nakae et al., 1973). Despite the high percentage of cases that had used clioquinol prior to SMON onset, the authors felt that the existence of SMON cases that had never used clioquinol argued against a causal association. They acknowledged that some cases could have purchased clioquinol in one of its different forms without knowing clioquinol was an ingredient. If 14% of cases did not result from clioquinol, as initially proposed, it remained unexplained why the number of new SMON cases eventually declined so dramatically after the ban of clioquinol. Lacking a control group, they were unable to clarify the relationship between clioquinol and SMON (Nakae et al.). Clioquinol use among SMON cases reported in the initial nationwide survey was similar to that reported by the SMON Research Commission Clinical Section investigation, based on questionnaires sent to all 20 SMON Research Commission members. The larger national survey identified 890 SMON cases; medication information was available on 742 cases. Among those 742 SMON cases, 632 cases (85%) used clioquinol within 6 months before onset of neurological symptoms (Kusui, 1975). That study did not provide any additional information as to the timing of use of clioquinol and development of neurological symptoms.

There is less survey information relating clioquinol to SMON available from other countries. Wadia reviewed medical records during 1970–1971 from among hospital admissions in India to identify SMON cases; only two cases were detected among a review of 3,503 patient records. Both the patients had have taken clioquinol over a prolonged period (Wadia, 1973). A third patient later was identified who had subacute myelopathy probably due to clioquinol (Wadia, 1973). Baumgartner et al. (1984) reviewed 137 additional SMON cases of suspected clioquinol toxicity reported between 1977 and 1983. They concluded there was a probable relationship of clioquinol with

SMON in 27 and a possible relationship in 28. Of 359 reported cases, they found 69 probable and 97 possible associations with clioquinol. Although many of the initial cases were excluded for insufficient information, the remainder suggested an association between clioquinol and SMON. Taken together, the survey results reported from Japan indicated that a substantial proportion of SMON cases (80–85%) had clioquinol exposure. Despite the seemingly high proportion of SMON cases receiving clioquinol, none of these reports included a control group or information about the frequency of clioquinol usage among the general population. The causal relationship between clioquinol and SMON remained uncertain.

A summary of the results from descriptive surveys and case-control studies performed by the SMON Commission, as reported by Shigematsu et al. (1975), identified a past history of pulmonary tuberculosis or abdominal surgery, onset in a hospital setting, and use of clioquinol within 6 months before SMON onset as potential risk factors. Records of 1,035 patients hospitalized with pulmonary tuberculosis were reviewed to identify SMON cases and to determine the use of clioquinol and other drugs in the same period (Kuratsune et al., 1974). The 114 patients who received clioquinol for at least 1 day showed a significantly higher incidence of SMON compared to those with similar abdominal symptoms but treated with other drugs. All five SMON cases had received clioquinol in amounts larger than those received by patients who had been given clioquinol but did not develop SMON.

Several cohort studies exist that include adverse effects of clioquinol relevant to SMON. McEwen (1971) reported a prospective study in which 35 patients received clioquinol at 750 mg per day for 3 months in an investigation of use of clioquinol to modify the gut flora of patients with allergies. Three subjects developed extremity numbness and tingling during clioquinol treatment that resolved when clioquinol was stopped (McEwen, 1971). One patient who experienced transient encephalitis continued to receive clioquinol beyond the 3-month trial and subsequently developed distal leg paresthesias and weakness with foot drop after taking clioquinol continuously for 10 months. A sixth patient developed probable optic neuritis while taking clioquinol and symptoms disappeared in a day after discontinuing clioquinol. Three of the six cases described were among the 35 subjects enrolled in the prospective study, leading McEwen to suggest that the risk of clioquinol-induced "peripheral neuropathy" was a little below 10% (McEwen, 1971). The details of this study are limited and the definition of neuropathy seemed to be based only on subjective symptoms of paresthesias.

Ritchie et al. (2003) performed a randomized controlled study, in which the effect of clioquinol ($n = 18$) was compared to placebo ($n = 18$) among patients with moderately severe Alzheimer disease. After 36 weeks, the effect of clioquinol treatment (125 mg twice daily for 12 weeks, 250 mg twice daily for 12 weeks, and 375 mg twice daily for 12 weeks) was significantly better in the more severely affected group due to a substantial worsening of those taking placebo compared with minimal deterioration for the clioquinol group. Clioquinol was well tolerated and the presence of adverse symptom and signs or results of nerve conduction studies, visual evoked responses, or ophthalmoscopy examination did not differ significantly between groups at baseline, week 16, and before the final visit. One subject, a 66-year-old woman with hypertension, hyperlipidemia, glaucoma, and visual migraine developed impaired visual acuity and impaired color vision without other neurological symptoms or signs while receiving clioquinol, 750 mg per day. Clioquinol-associated optic neuropathy was suspected. The adverse visual symptoms and signs resolved on clioquinol cessation. In summary, the overall scientific peer-reviewed literature, while not conclusive, supports a causal association between clioquinol and SMON.

The hypothesis that clioquinol produces a dying-back axonopathy is compelling. The clinical signs, electrophysiology, and neuropathology reflect involvement of the most distal portions of the longest motor and sensory axons. Spinal cord abnormalities consisted of symmetrical degeneration of distal ascending sensory axons in the posterior columns (fasciculus gracilis) at the cervicomedullary level and of distal descending motor axons in the lateral columns (corticospinal tracts) in the lumbar and sacral regions. Our understanding of distal axonopathies is derived primarily from studies of neurotoxicants. Most iatrogenic peripheral neuropathies are manifested by distal symmetrical axonal degeneration involving the longest axons (dying-back axonal degeneration with secondary loss of myelin) (Spencer & Schaumburg, 1978). Paradoxically, the lesion in most dying-back neuropathies is due to abnormal metabolism in the neuron, not the axon (Spencer, Sabri, Schaumburg, & Moore, 1979). The neuron is responsible for maintaining the axon, and many synthetic processes that reside in the neuron are lacking in the axon. The products of neuronal synthesis are transported to the axon via axonal flow, rendering the axon vulnerable to a variety of problems. The transport systems include slow anterograde axonal transport of microtubules and neurofilaments to the cytoskeleton and fast anterograde transport of membrane-associated materials including neurotransmitters, metabolic enzymes, and other proteins, and retrograde transport of proteins back to the neuron (Masson, Boulu, & Henin, 1992). Defects in basic nutritive processes in the neuron or abnormalities of anterograde or retrograde axonal flow typically produce an axonopathy involving the distal, most vulnerable, portion of the axon. It is not surprising that the majority of exogenous substances that cause neuropathies produce a distal axonal degeneration (distal axonopathy).

An unusual feature of the proposed clioquinol-induced axonopathy is the exclusive or predominate central nervous system localization. Most dying-back neuropathies involving sensory nerves display simultaneous distal degeneration of the central and peripheral axons of the dorsal root ganglia (sensory neurons). Clinical evaluations are used to identify peripheral abnormalities (e.g., sensory NCSs and sural nerve biopsy), and the term sensory peripheral neuropathy is used almost exclusively despite the related involvement of central sensory projections. Recognition of central abnormalities occurs only occasionally, usually as an incidental finding of posterior column atrophy on neuroimaging (e.g., MRI of the cervical spinal cord). It is clear that some toxins, possibly including clioquinol, evoke severe tract-oriented central degeneration with only minor changes in the peripheral nervous system (Schaumburg, 1979b).

Thomas and Schaumburg and colleagues addressed the idea of a central distal axonopathy (Schaumburg, 1979a; Schaumburg, Arezzo, & Spencer, 1989; Schaumburg & Spencer, 1979; Spencer & Thomas, 1974; Thomas, 1997; Thomas et al., 1984). Thomas (1997) proposed that clioquinol produced a selective central nervous system distal axonopathy in which degeneration was confined to, or predominately affected, the longest central nervous system fiber tracts. Such a proposal is not without precedent, as many familial disorders such as hereditary spastic paraparesis show similar abnormalities and may reflect a particular metabolic defect or selective vulnerability. Thomas et al. (1984) proposed mechanisms that could explain selective vulnerability of central axons of the dorsal root sensory neurons. It is known that the central and peripheral sensory axons have different environments, including the association of central nervous system axons with oligodendrocytes and peripheral nervous system axons with Schwann cells. The axons also have different functional capabilities; slow axonal transport is faster in peripheral axons relative to central axons. Transport of structural proteins to the distal axon likely is less efficient in the central nervous system compared to the periphery, a factor possibly explaining the poor regeneration of central dorsal root ganglia axons. The explanation for the apparent vulnerability of central sensory projections in clioquinol-induced axonopathy remains unclear, as it is not certain that any of these biological mechanisms are relevant. Much of this discussion would be moot if it were determined that the dorsal root ganglia definitely degenerated in response to clioquinol exposure as suggested by the neuropathology, or if peripheral sensory axons were, in fact, involved in SMON. The neuropathology evidence of degeneration of dorsal root ganglia and the electrophysiology descriptions of intact sural nerve action potentials are in conflict. Alternatively, involvement of central and peripheral sensory axons may display relative differences in their vulnerability, with peripheral sensory axons degenerating only as the axonopathy progresses and sensory neurons degenerating only in the most severe cases.

The selective vulnerability of the central nervous system motor system also is unexplained. However, many degenerative motor system disorders include central (corticobulbar and corticospinal) and peripheral components. Peripheral motor neurons (lower motor neurons) reside within the central nervous system, but send their axons into the periphery. Central motor neurons (upper motor neurons) originate in the cortex, and their axons remain within the central nervous system, as part of the corticobulbar and corticospinal tracts. Like sensory neurons, the environments of motor axons in the central nervous system and peripheral nervous system differ. Disorders exist that involve the upper motor neurons (hereditary spastic paraparesis and primary lateral sclerosis), the lower motor neurons (forms of progressive muscular atrophy), or combinations of the two (motor neuron disease of the amyotrophic lateral sclerosis type). An example of a central distal axonopathy suggested by Thomas et al. (1984) is lathyrism due to excessive consumption of the neurotoxic species of *Lathyrus* peas (Spencer, Schaumburg, Cohn, & Seth, 1984). Lathyrism is characterized by spastic paraparesis and lower extremity hyper-reflexia, sparing the arms, suggesting an abnormality involving the thoracolumbar corticospinal tracts, similar to the motor abnormalities in SMON.

Dying-back neuropathies are associated with several pathological features including *axonal dystrophy*, a pathological condition characterized by focal axonal swellings due to localized accumulation of cytoskeleton components, particularly neurofilaments. The axon caliber distal to the swollen portion of the axon is smaller than normal, with evidence of distal axonal degeneration (Dyck, Gianni, & Lais, 1993). The mechanism underlying axonal dystrophy is thought to reflect an abnormality of anterograde axonal transport of neurofilament proteins, resulting in accumulation of neurofilaments along the axon (Dyck et al., 1993). Focal axonal swellings indicative of axonal dystrophy are found in a variety of situations, including the neuropathies associated with excessive exposure to *n*-hexane, methyl butyl ketone, acrylamide, and 2,5-hexanedione (Allen, Mendell, Billmaier, Fontaine, & O'Neill, 1975; Schaumburg & Berger, 1993; Smith & Albers, 1997). In general, the distribution of the axonal swellings relates to the dosage and potency of the neurotoxicant. Disorders associated with axonal swellings and axonal dystrophy, such as *n*-hexane neuropathy, are remarkable for coexisting evidence of substantial conduction slowing and profuse denervation. The profuse denervation potentials indicate the presence of severe axonal degeneration producing muscle fiber denervation. There is experimental support for the concept the axonal atrophy leads to secondary demyelination, explaining the conduction slowing, and eventual axonal degeneration. The NCS findings are sufficiently impressive in conditions like *n*-hexane neuropathy that it seems unlikely they would have been overlooked if the peripheral nervous system is involved in SMON. On the other hand, a few studies exist of SMON cases that had prominent conduction slowing, and the question remains unanswered.

The descriptive term *neuroaxonal dystrophy* is another possible pathological consequence of clioquinol exposure. Neuroaxonal dystrophy is thought to reflect a molecular abnormality that differs from that of axonal dystrophy, but the two conditions may represent different aspects along a continuum of axonal degeneration. While axonal dystrophy is associated with accumulation of neurofilaments along the axon, neuroaxonal dystrophy may reflect abnormal transport of membrane-associated materials with accumulation of axonal or nerve terminal proteins most prominent in the distal axon. Neuroaxonal dystrophy also is characterized by swollen and degenerating preterminal axons and degenerating synapses (Dyck et al., 1993). In humans, evidence of neuroaxonal dystrophy in association with aging is particularly abundant in the gracile nuclei and is described in the dorsal root and autonomic ganglia (Schmidt, 2002). The swellings contain a variety of subcellular elements (not just neurofilaments as described in axonal dystrophy) thought to reflect deterioration of the cellular processes important for replacement and remodeling of synaptic and preterminal axonal proteins (Schmidt, 2002). Any condition interfering with the transportation of structural proteins between the terminal axon and the neuron represents an ideal model of a distal dying-back axonopathy, such as SMON.

Most investigators agreed that extremely acute clioquinol intoxications associated with gastrointestinal and neurological symptoms reflected ingestion of clioquinol in amounts exceeding therapeutic doses; symptoms generally rapidly resolved when exposure ceased (Malizia, Macchiarelli, Ambrosini, Smeriglio, & Andreucci, 1979). Further, the occurrence of SMON following clioquinol administration appeared to be dose dependent (Igata & Toyokura, 1971). Evidence of dose response was inferred by the occurrence of natural experiments, in which some regions or individual clinics prescribed greater among of clioquinol than did others (Igata, 1971). Institutions reporting large outbreaks of SMON reportedly prescribed clioquinol in high dosage; prescribing less than 1,000 mg per day was not profitable relative to prescribing more than 2,000 mg per day (Pallis, 1984). A difficult problem to resolve is the high prevalence of SMON in Japan relative to other parts of the world (Wadia, 1973). Outside of Japan, despite extensive sales and use of clioquinol, Rose and others identified only 220 reports of clioquinol neurotoxicity (de Pinto & Burley, 1977; Rose & Gawel, 1984; Rose, 1986). Throughout the literature, there was question that the Japanese may have a specific sensitivity to clioquinol in terms of developing SMON (Chevaleraud & Hamard, 1985). In fact, the apparent striking susceptibility of the Japanese to develop clioquinol-associated SMON was used by some as an example of a genetic susceptibility to an adverse medication effect (Igata & Toyokura, 1971; Naranjo, Fornazzari, & Sellers, 1981). Despite numerous attempts to explain the Japanese outbreak by racial differences, however, no differences in enzymes status have been found that would explain the increased susceptibility (Rose, 1986).

Whether there was over-diagnosis of SMON in Japan or racial susceptibility is unknown, but clioquinol was an extraordinarily popular drug given to many million Japanese who had vague intestinal ailments. Hansson and Herxheimer (1980) were among those who believed that sufficient dose was the only factor required to explain enhanced toxicity of clioquinol in some individuals. Clioquinol use in other countries, such as Australia, was much less, representing as little as 1% of the more than 10 million Japanese who received clioquinol (Selby, 1972). In addition, the clioquinol dosage used in Japan was much higher than those in other countries (Igata, 1974). In Europe and the United States, clioquinol dosage usually did not exceed 600 mg per day for 2 weeks, whereas in Japan a 1,200 mg per day clioquinol dose was customary (Degos & Thomas-Lamotte, 1977).

Toyokura and Takasu (1975) reported that 85% of SMON cases in Japan had onset within 6 months of starting clioquinol, and that 75% of cases had used between 1,000 and 2,000 mg per day, usually for more than 2 weeks. The relative importance of the daily clioquinol dose versus the duration or cumulative exposure is unresolved. Not all investigators agree that a dose response had been identified. Selby reported the details of five SMON cases observed in Australia and reviewed and critiqued the literature, concluding that the those who developed SMON taking small doses of clioquinol suggests an idiosyncrasy to the drug or one of its metabolites, not a predictable effect (Selby, 1973). He also argued that the occurrence in Australia makes it unlikely that such an idiosyncrasy is restricted to specific ethnic groups (Selby, 1973). However, the low incidence of SMON in Europe and America may have reflected lower clioquinol doses prescribed, with few prescriptions exceeding 600 mg per day for several weeks, compared to Japan where clioquinol doses of 1,200 mg per day were customary (Degos & Thomas-Lamotte, 1977). The interval between initial use of clioquinol and onset and severity of neurological symptoms was variable but was said to reflect the cumulative dose (Schaumburg, 2000).

The numerous studies purporting a relationship between clioquinol and SMON consistently identified a similar pattern of neurological symptoms and signs and a full spectrum of neurological impairments, from mild-to-severe involvement. Excluding cases with vague or nonspecific symptoms and few neurological signs from consideration, who could nonetheless reflect mild cases of SMON, the manifest SMON syndrome included relatively characteristic features. The resultant SMON syndrome in humans is not unique, but it is unusual in terms of the combination of symmetrical spinal cord, ocular, and peripheral abnormalities compared to most neurological disorders. Unlike conditions such as distal symmetric sensory or sensorimotor peripheral neuropathy for which there are hundreds of possible causes, the differential diagnosis of an individual SMON patient is relatively limited. Further, among the few competing explanations in addition to clioquinol (e.g., vitamin B_{12} deficiency, symmetrical monophasic multiple sclerosis, transverse myelitis; myeloneuropathy associated with systemic lupus erythematosus, other neurotoxicants, or Jamaican neuropathy), none occurs commonly among the general population or even among patients seen by neurologists.

There is evidence that some groups show particular vulnerability to clioquinol. For example, most surveys found that females were more likely to develop SMON than males at about a 2:1 ratio. Further, in follow-up studies 30 years after the clioquinol ban, there were more severely affected females than males (Hsu et al., 2002). The female to male discrepancy has not been explained. It is possible that clioquinol exposure differed among females and males. It is unknown, however, whether more female were prescribed clioquinol for gastrointestinal disorders or whether they received a higher mg/kg dose. Also, children appeared to be more susceptible to clioquinol-associated optic neuropathy and less susceptible to clioquinol-induced SMON than adults, as the incidence of SMON was higher in older persons between 65 and 70 years of age (Chevaleraud & Hamard, 1985). The explanation for both observations is unknown. In terms of increased risk with increasing age, most peripheral neurotoxicants show an increasing detrimental effect with increasing age. The mechanisms underlying axonal dystrophy or neuroaxonal dystrophy with their resultant dying-back axonal degeneration of nerve terminal and preterminal axons most prominent in the longest axons likely are age dependent and would explain the paucity of clioquinol-induced myeloneuropathy among the very young. There are many explanations for this observation, including decreased rates of metabolism and clearance, thereby resulting in increased drug exposure, as well as declining regenerative processes in older adults compared with those who are younger. The high frequency of isolated optic neuropathy among the very young may reflect relative protection from the other components of SMON, not an increased risk of developing optic neuropathy.

Patients with impaired renal function may have been more likely to develop clioquinol-associated SMON, presumable in association with decreased clioquinol clearance and increasing clioquinol exposure (Gendre, Barbanel, Degos, & Le Quintrec, 1974; Zeraidi, Zeggwagh, Abouqal, Zekraoui, & Kerkeb, 1995). Also, because of its high iodine content, clioquinol should not be administered to patients with iodine sensitivity or to patients with serious hepatic or renal disorders (Malizia et al., 1979). Finally, clinical human and animal observations indicate that the absorption rate of clioquinol is increased in inflammatory bowel disease, suggesting that patients with certain gastrointestinal disorders may have been most likely to have used clioquinol in relatively large amounts and also more likely to have received a larger dose than others because of increased absorption (Hansson & Herxheimer, 1980).

There is general agreement that SMON was a monophasic disease, not a progressive disorder. Further, relapses of SMON, common early in the course of the Japanese epidemic, appeared to reflect recurrent or continued use of clioquinol. In terms of the overall occurrence of SMON, one factor suggesting a causal relationship between clioquinol and SMON is the sudden decline in new SMON cases after clioquinol was banned. The observational information reported after the clioquinol ban represents a pseudo-experiment that is capable, to some extent, of breaching the information void created by the limited number of randomized, hypothesis-testing studies (Guzelian, Victoroff, Halmes, James, & Guzelian, 2005). The ban of clioquinol also represents an opportunity to test prediction, as the ban was established in anticipation that the frequency of SMON would decline. When clioquinol was available in Japan as an OTC medication, 1,000 to 2,000 cases of SMON occurred per year; after clioquinol was withdrawn from the market in September 1970, the incidence of SMON fell to 15 cases in 1971 (Spillane, 1972). In five hospitals where SMON had been continually reported, no new cases were reported after the 1970 ban (Igata, 1974). This remarkable decrease in subsequent disappearance of new cases after clioquinol was removed from the market is a strong evidence of a causal association. After the suggestion that clioquinol was casually related to SMON, numerous case reports documented partial or complete recovery of SMON after removal from additional clioquinol exposure among adults and children (Charasz et al., 1979; Chevaleraud & Hamard, 1985; Derakhshan & Forough, 1978; Garcia-Perez et al., 1974; Mackiewicz & Wendorff, 1980; Osterman, 1971; Otte, De Coster, Thiery, De Reuck, & Vander, 1976; Selby, 1972, 1973). There also were cases in which visual symptoms developed during exposure to clioquinol, resolved after clioquinol was discontinued, reappeared when clioquinol was restarted, and again improved after discontinuing clioquinol (Billson et al., 1972; Reich & Billson, 1973).

A myeloneuropathy clinically and pathologically identical with human SMON and characterized by dying-back axonal degeneration has been established in dogs and baboons following repeated administration of clioquinol (Krinke, Schaumburg, Spencer, Thomann, & Hess, 1979; Schaumburg, 2000; Thomas et al., 1984). The myelo-optico-neuropathy demonstrated in mongrel dogs, beagles, cats, and monkeys is in accord with the changes observed in SMON in humans (Chevaleraud & Hamard, 1985; Tateishi, Kuroda, Saito, & Otsuki, 1973). The central nervous system abnormalities demonstrated in animal models are seen only at very high clioquinol doses, and not all of the signs of the lesions attributed to SMON are found. For example, no evidence of any adverse effect on peripheral nerves or spinal ganglia developed in beagle dog SMON models (Worden & Heywood, 1978). Similarly, neurophysiological studies in chronically clioquinol-dosed cats confirmed dorsal column abnormalities, whereas peripheral sensory axons of the sural nerve showed no significant functional abnormalities as described by Schaumburg (2000). The overall findings support the hypothesis that clioquinol usually produces a central axonopathy. Alternatively, peripheral nervous system involvement may develop as part of a spectrum of abnormality, occurring in only the most severe cases.

VERIFICATION OF CAUSE/ETIOLOGY

Although there is no universal agreement that the Japanese SMON epidemic was due to clioquinol, none of the other proposed causes or associations described seems more likely than clioquinol to have been responsible for most of the cases. It is true that outside Japan there was more limited evidence for an association between clioquinol and SMON (de Pinto & Burley, 1977), at least in terms of the number of cases observed. However, in terms of the question proposed by Hill to establish causation, the casual link between clioquinol and SMON, as a condition producing various combinations of myelopathy, optic neuritis, and occasionally peripheral neuropathy, appears well established (Critchley, 1979).

Conclusion

SMON was initially defined in terms of the subacute onset of neurological symptoms and signs preceded by abdominal complaints that were thought to be cardinal features of the syndrome (Nakae et al., 1971; Sobue et al., 1971). The neurological features included varying combinations of myelopathy, optic neuropathy, and possibly peripheral neuropathy. The myelopathy associated with SMON was characterized by a spastic paraparesis, sensory loss frequently showing a sensory level on the lower trunk, hyperactive knee reflexes, absent ankle reflexes, and extensor plantar responses. This combination of signs reflects involvement of the rostral posterior columns in the cervical region and the caudal lateral corticospinal tracts in the lumbosacral region, the terminal portions of the ascending sensory axons and the descending motor axons in the spinal cord, findings confirmed by postmortem examinations. Taken together with optic neuropathy, neurological involvement in SMON represents a predominant dying-back axonopathy limited to, or predominantly involving, the central nervous system. Dying-back neuropathies are associated with several pathological features that may represent a continuum of axonal degeneration. These pathological features include axonal dystrophy, a condition characterized by focal axonal swellings due to localized accumulation of cytoskeleton components, and neuroaxonal dystrophy, a condition thought to reflect abnormal transport of membrane-associated materials with accumulation of axonal or nerve terminal proteins most prominent in the distal axon.

Recognition that the green tongue, urine, and feces in some SMON cases represented a chelate of clioquinol linked this medication to SMON. It became apparent that abdominal symptoms might have resulted in the use of clioquinol and that clioquinol, in turn, contributed to the neurological condition (Rose & Gawel, 1984). The epidemiology evidence associating clioquinol to SMON is convincing, as are the animal models. Perhaps the most robust causal support linking clioquinol and SMON is the near complete disappearance of this syndrome after clioquinol was removed from the market. Clioquinol-induced SMON appears to represent a disorder that shows predominant involvement of sensory and motor axons confined to, or predominately involving, the central nervous system.

Corticosteroids

James W. Albers

Corticosteroids (also known as glucocorticoids) are medications that closely resemble cortisol, a "stress" hormone secreted from the adrenal cortex during the "fight or flight" response, which is involved in maintenance and regulation of glucose, blood pressure, and immune function. Corticosteroids are among the most commonly prescribed medications because they possess potent anti-inflammatory and immunosuppressant effects. Disease applications include the treatment of the inflammatory disorders, such as rheumatoid arthritis and related connective tissue diseases (as in the following *case presentation*), asthma and related allergic conditions (Bolanos et al., 2004; Brown, Khan, & Nejtek, 1999), and nephrotic syndrome (Hall, Thorley, & Houtman, 2003) Like the immunosuppressant medication *cyclosporine* discussed in the following section, corticosteroids also are used to control the progression of several autoimmune nervous system disorders commonly treated by neurologists, including chronic inflammatory demyelinating polyradiculoneuropathy (Albers & Kelly, 1989; Mehndiratta & Hughes, 2002) and myasthenia gravis (Bromberg, Wald, Forshew, Feldman, & Albers, 1997; Seybold & Drachman, 1974). In addition to treatment of many connective tissue diseases such as rheumatoid arthritis, corticosteroids also are used in disorders such as systemic lupus erythematosus (SLE) and many forms of vasculitis, conditions that frequently present with central nervous system manifestations.

The major adverse systemic side effects attributed to chronic corticosteroid use are weight gain with redistribution of body fat, hursitism, acne, hypertension, hypertriglyceridemia, hypercholesterolemia, impaired glucose tolerance, thinning of the skin, capillary fragility, peripheral edema, cataract formation, and osteoporosis (Lucasey, 2001; Nashel, 1986; Pecora & Kaplan, 1996). Patients with a history of peptic ulcer disease who are administered the combination of corticosteroids with nonsteroidal anti-inflammatory drugs (NSAIDs) are at high risk to develop corticosteroid-induced ulcers (Pecora & Kaplan, 1996). Atherosclerotic heart disease is another consequence of long-term corticosteroid treatment, perhaps in response to corticosteroid-induced hyperlipidemia and accelerated atherosclerosis (Lucasey, 2001; Nashel, 1986). Neurological adverse effects include accentuated postural tremor, generalized muscle atrophy, and corticosteroid-myopathy producing proximal weakness, which may be profound (Bird & Rich, 2002), as discussed in volume II. Other behavioral effects attributed to corticosteroids include altered mood characterized by combinations of agitation, anxiety, mania, and depression during treatment (Brown, Suppes, Khan, & Carmody, 2002). Less common adverse behavioral effects include encephalopathy, psychosis, and possibly memory loss; effects typically observed shortly after initiating high-dose corticosteroid treatment. When central nervous system toxicity in the form of encephalopathy or psychosis develops in the setting of a central nervous system vasculitis or cerebritis, the distinction between a central nervous system vasculitic encephalopathy and a corticosteroid psychosis is difficult to determine in the absence of distinguishing features. The following *case presentation* is representative of patients who develop central nervous system manifestations due to corticosteroids.

Case presentation[1]

A 40-year-old woman with a history of connective tissue disease characterized by migratory arthralgias, generalized fatigue, and an erythematosus malar "butterfly" rash experienced the insidious onset of symmetrical proximal muscle weakness associated with mild muscle tenderness. Despite progression, she did not seek evaluation until an episode of exertional shortness of breath prompted an emergency department visit. She denied other symptoms such as active joint pain, diplopia, chest pain, sensory loss, or dark colored urine suggestive of rhabdomyolysis, but she did experience occasional dysphagia. There was no history of photosensitivity, oral or nasopharyngeal ulcers, pluritis or pericarditis, or seizure. She was not taking any medications.

The general physical examination showed normal vital signs including a normal respiratory rate and a strong, forceful cough. Her joints were unremarkable and there was no skin rash. Neurological examination was normal aside from the motor examination. Manual muscle testing showed symmetrical weakness involving her neck flexors, arm abductors, and hip flexors, Medical Research Council (MRC) grade 3+ or 4−. She was unable to arise from chair without using her arms, and her gait was mildly wide based, consistent with the degree of proximal weakness. Examination of facial and of more distal muscles was normal. The remainder of her examination, including evaluation of mental status, cranial nerves, sensation, and reflexes was normal. Laboratory evaluations performed prior to admission to the hospital included normal arterial blood gases, a normal chest x-ray, and normal routine evaluations of blood and urine. There specifically was no evidence of lymphopenia or thrombocytopenia.

The differential diagnosis on admission was connective tissue disease possibly representing SLE, although she was not thought to fulfill clinical or laboratory criteria for a diagnosis of SLE. The proximal weakness was felt to represent an inflammatory myopathy (e.g., polymyositis) or defective neuro-muscular transmission as seen in myasthenia gravis. The possibility of a metabolic myopathy, as seen in association with hypothyroidism, was included in the differential diagnosis. Additional laboratory evaluations per-formed shortly after admission included an EMG showing normal nerve conduction studies, including repetitive motor nerve stimulation to evaluate neuromuscular transmission. The needle EMG examination showed profuse fibrillation potentials and positive waves in proximal muscles, including the paraspinal muscles. Motor unit recruitment was increased in weak muscles and motor units were described as highly polyphasic and of brief duration. The combined findings were interpreted as those of an inflammatory myopathy producing muscle fiber necrosis. A serum creatinine kinase level was moder-ately increased (>4,000 IU). Other laboratory abnormalities included an increased Westermann erythrocyte sedimentation rate (WESR) (>40 mm/hr), an elevated total hemolytic complement (CH50), and elevated titers of several auto-antibodies, including antinuclear antibody (ANA) (1:320) and rheumatoid factor (RF), but not anti-DNA antibody or antineutrophil cytoplasmic antibody (ANCA) titers. A serum acetylcholine receptor antibody titer was negative, as were thyroid function studies. Evaluation of the urine was negative for myoglobin. A muscle biopsy ultimately documented the presence of an inflam-matory myopathy. Prior to receiving the biopsy results, treatment was started with an NSAID medication and a corticosteroid medication (prednisone 100 mg per day in divided dosage).

Within 2 days of starting prednisone, the patient appeared anxious and became agitated. She was noted to be sleeping poorly, often out of bed during the night, complaining that she was unable to sleep because of hospital noise. Evaluation in the morning showed tachypnea with a respiratory rate of 20/min but otherwise normal vital signs, including a normal temperature. She was markedly agitated and impatient with the examiner, refusing to answer most questions and complaining that "a party on the roof" the previous evening had kept her awake. In response to direct questions, she frequently responded, "I don't remember." She exhibited persistent, purposeless hand movements and a prominent postural tremor of her hands. Although oriented, she appeared to be responding in a bizarre manner to events unrelated to her, such as nurses speaking in the hallway. On occasion, she appeared to be responding to visual hallucinations that she would not describe. Although she readily followed simple one-step commands (show me your tongue), she did not respond to more complicated commands or requests for a more detailed history. Language function was intact, aside from intermittent perseveration. During the evaluation, she abruptly became tearful, appearing confused but unable to explain what was bothering her. The remainder of her neurological examination was unchanged, although her reflexes, grade as normal on admission, were now brisk (3+) without clonus or pathological reflexes. Her neck was supple, without evidence of nuchal rigidity.

The family was contacted to obtain additional information, and they confirmed that there was no prior emotional or psychiatric history.

DIFFERENTIAL DIAGNOSIS

This patient was thought to have an acute encephalopathy, although the cause, in the context of her medical condition, was unclear. The initial concern was that she had become transiently hypoxic during the night, either due to respiratory insufficiency or due to aspiration or a pulmonary embolus. Other considerations included inflammatory, infections, or metabolic conditions producing encephalopathy. Specific conditions included central nervous system vasculitis, meningitis, encephalitis, hypoglycemia, or corticosteroid-induced hyperglycemia producing hyperosmolarity with resultant cerebral symptoms. The only medication she was receiving was prednisone and an antacid, and a corticosteroid psychosis was included in the differential diagnosis, as was the syndrome of corticosteroid-induced benign intracranial hypertension. There was no history of alcohol overuse or abuse, and no eye-movement abnormalities, but an acute Wernicke's encephalopathy also was considered.

Additional Information

After obtaining serum for laboratory testing, thiamine and glucose were administered without improvement. A digital pulse oximeter showed normal oxygenation. Arterial blood gases were normal, as were the forced vital capacity (>3.0 L) and negative inspiratory force, making the possibility of a hypoxic encephalopathy unlikely in the absence of any additional information suggesting an episode of respiratory insufficiency. Chest x-ray was normal. The serum glucose was slightly elevated, consistent with a nonfasting examination. The remainder of the laboratory tests, including electrolytes, creatinine, blood urea nitrogen, thyroid function, and liver function, was normal, eliminating concern for these forms of metabolic encephalopathy. Examination of the CSF was normal, including opening pressure, cell count, total protein, and immunoglobulin indices, there being no indication of inflammation or infection. A cranial CT scan was normal, without evidence of cerebral atrophy or ventricular dilatation. A brain MRI showed no white matter abnormalities suggestive of vasculitis or leukoencephalopathy.

Prednisone was initially withheld and later administered at a reduced dosage in combination with another immunosuppressant medication, mycophenolate mofetil. Over several days, she slowly improved, and within 1 week all central nervous system abnormalities had resolved, aside from the accentuated postural tremor. Specifically, her behavior was considered normal by all examiners and by her family, and there were no residual signs of impaired cognition or memory. Over several weeks, her strength began to improve and the creatine kinase level fell toward the normal range. After 6 weeks, a further prednisone taper was initiated, and she eventually was maintained on a prednisone dose of 10 mg every other day in combination with mycopheno-late mofetil. Her postural tremor improved on the lower maintenance dose of prednisone. Over the next several years, mild exacerbations of weakness were treated with slight increases in prednisone or, on one occasion, intravenous SoluMedrol (another form of corticosteroid medication suitable for intraven-ous administration). None of the treatments resulted in recurrence of the behavioral abnormalities.

Discussion

The nervous system localization of the patient's acute neurobehavioral dis-order, and the likelihood that the problem was caused by corticosteroids or her underlying systemic connective tissue disease resembling SLE, is examined in the following paragraphs.

NERVOUS SYSTEM LOCALIZATION

In addition to the established diagnosis of myopathy, a disorder of the peripheral nervous system, the primary neurobehavioral clinical diagnosis was "encephalopathy" or delirium, a state of hypomania with hyperarousal and increased anxiety in combination with confusion and often accompanied by hallucinations or illusions. In the absence of any additional localizing signs, the behavioral symptoms and signs localize to the bilateral supratentorial level of the central nervous system, as do the symmetrical postural tremor, diffuse hyper-reflexia, and the possible visual hallucinations. The absence of asymmetry or focal sings argues against a multifocal localization and supports a diffuse distribution. Conditions producing visual hallucinations that could be considered in the differential are listed in Table 16.4 (including localization and potential causes). Included among the possible conditions producing visual hallucinations are connective tissue disease, central nervous system vasculitis, and drug intoxication (or withdrawal). These conditions also potentially explain all of the other central nervous system symptoms and signs.

VERIFICATION OF THE CLINICAL DIAGNOSIS

The clinical diagnosis of encephalopathy was established by the symptoms and signs, although there were no supportive electrodiagnostic or imaging abnormalities. Although suggestive, the clinical symptoms and signs in the

Table 16.4 Differential diagnosis of visual hallucinations.

Ocular
  Cataracts
  Enucleation
  Macular degeneration
  Sensory deprivation

Optic nerve and tract; midbrain; geniculocalcarine radiation
  Compression
  Ischemia
  Multiple sclerosis
  Stroke
  Tumors

Occipital or temporal cortex
  Seizure
  Stroke
  Tumor

Others
  Alzheimer's disease
  Central nervous system connective tissue disease
  Depression or mania
  Diffuse Lewy body disease
  Drug intoxication or withdrawal
  Metabolic encephalopathy (delirium)
  Migraine
  Narcolepsy
  Parkinson's disease with dopaminergic treatment
  Schizophrenia
  Vasculitis

From *A Concise Guide to Behavioral Neurology and Neuropsychiatry*, by J. Cummings and M. R. Trimble, 1995, Washington: American Psychiatric Association Press.

absence of objective EEG or imaging abnormalities are insufficient to establish a diagnosis more precise than "encephalopathy" or "delirium." Despite the nonspecific nature of the clinical symptoms and signs, the clinical diagnosis of encephalopathy in this case satisfies most of the questions required to verify the diagnosis, although a diagnosis of acute delirium or acute psychosis could have been applied, as well (Richardson et al., 2000).

CAUSE/ETIOLOGY

The primary diagnostic considerations for the cause of the transient encephalopathy and behavioral changes included a central nervous system vasculitis, a cerebritis related to her underlying connective tissue disease (as frequently associated with diseases such as systemic lupus erythematosus), or a corticosteroid-induced psychosis. In terms of attributing causation to an underlying vasculitis or cerebritis, the ultimate "cause" of the underlying autoimmune connective tissue disorder remains unknown. In contrast, identifying an iatrogenic cause such as a corticosteroid-induced psychosis can be formally addressed using the Hill criteria. A distinction between these different entities is clinically important because, ironically, corticosteroids are effective treatment for vasculitis and other forms of connective tissue disease, including SLE. Further, the patient with SLE who is treated with corticosteroids and who develops an acute or subacute neurobehavioral change poses a special diagnostic problem, not dissimilar to the problem addressed by the neurologist treating the patient in the current *case presentation.*

Without addressing the distinction between a diffuse cerebritis and a multifocal cerebral vasculitis, there are several reasons why neither is a likely consideration in the current *case presentation.* First, although there were laboratory abnormalities consistent with a connective tissue disease, firm criteria for a specific disorder like SLE were lacking. Also, the subacute onset immediately following initiation of high-dose prednisone is atypical of a lupus-induced psychosis and more characteristic of an adverse medication effect. Had the presentation included complaint of headache or had the onset been associated with a seizure, vasculitis or angiitis would have been a more likely consideration. The absence of CSF abnormalities does not exclude the possibility of either a vasculitis or a cerebritis, although an abnormally high total protein, hypoglycorrachia, a slightly elevated cell count, or abnormal immunoglobulin indices would have supported the diagnosis of an autoimmune disorder. Similarly, the normal MRI does not exclude a cerebral vasculitis or cerebritis, whereas evidence of numerous white matter hyperintensities would be consistent with a vasculitis and diffuse white matter abnormalities suggestive of a leukoencephalopathy (despite the prominent brain gray matter abnormalities in lupus).

The evidence associating corticosteroids with a subacute-onset psychosis is incomplete, but there is a large body of evidence associating the onset of changes in mood with corticosteroid therapy (Bolanos et al., 2004; Brown et al., 2002). Psychiatric symptoms in the form of hypomania or depression develop in a substantial percentage of patients treated with high doses of corticosteroids, with about 5% of patients experiencing severe psychiatric reactions (Lewis & Smith, 1983). Effects typically emerge within days to a few weeks of starting treatment (Brown et al., 1999), and the descriptor *corticosteroid psychosis* refers to combined effects involving cognition, mood, anxiety, and psychotic symptoms (Cerullo, 2006). The most prominent symptom constellation to appear sometime during the course of the corticosteroid treatment includes a combination of emotional lability, anxiety, distractibility, insomnia, depression, agitation, hallucinations, intermittent memory impairment, delusions, and hypomania (Hall, Popkin, Stickney, & Gardner, 1979). Among the corticosteroid-induced psychiatric conditions, mood disturbances, in the form of mania or depression, are the most prevalent (35% and 28%, respectively), followed by mixed mood episodes (12%), delirium (13%), and psychotic thought disturbance (11%) (Sirois, 2003). The influence of corticosteroid-induced psychiatric dysfunction in terms of the number of patients is substantial, and corticosteroid-induced mania is said to account for over 50% of hospital psychiatric consults for evaluation of mania (Rundell & Wise, 1989). Although usually not life threatening, mania occasionally can be detrimental to the underlying condition requiring corticosteroid treatment. Travlos and Hirsch (1993) described the advent of high-dose methylprednisolone among acute spinal cord injured patients, a treatment protocol that puts this population at potentially increased risk for acute psychotic reactions. They conservatively estimated that about 5% of acute spinal cord injured patients so treated develop corticosteroid-induced psychiatric dysfunction. Despite the ready reversibility of corticosteroid-induced psychosis, they noted that these reactions place the patient at increased risk of further spinal cord injury and worsening permanent neurologic deficit.

In terms of prospective studies better able to address causation, Bolanos et al. (2004) used standard clinician ratings and patient self-report measures in a cross-sectional study to evaluate mood changes among 20 patients receiving long-term, relatively low-dose corticosteroid therapy and compared the results to those of 11 control subjects. Depressive symptom severity, global psychiatric symptom severity, and manic symptom severity were greater among patients receiving prednisone than controls, and 12 of 20 (60%) corticosteroid-treated patients met diagnostic criteria for a prednisone-induced mood disorder. The investigators concluded that mood symptoms and disorders were common among corticosteroid-dependent patients. Unlike short-term prednisone therapy, long-term therapy may be more associated with depressive than manic symptoms based on the clinician-rated assessments. In a cross-sectional study, the frequency of self-reported depressive symptoms was tabulated following exposure to three classes of medications (angiotensin converting enzyme [ACE] inhibitors, calcium-channel blockers, and corticosteroids) (Patten, Williams, & Love, 1995). No associations were observed between depressive symptoms and exposure to ACE inhibitors or calcium-channel blockers. In contrast, corticosteroid administration was associated with new onset of depressive symptoms. The association was strongest among subjects with a personal or family history of depression. The authors concluded that corticosteroids pose a risk factor for depressive symptoms (Patten et al., 1995).

Brown et al. (2002) quantified psychiatric changes during brief courses of prednisone (>40 mg per day) among 32 patients with asthma. Asthma patients receiving prednisone bursts were evaluated before, during, and after corticosteroid therapy using the Hamilton Rating Scale for Depression, the Young Mania Scale, the Brief Psychiatric Rating Scale, the Internal State Scale, and a structured clinical interview to examine past psychiatric history. Significant increases were found in measures of mania during the first 3–7 days of therapy. Mood changes were not related to improvement in airway obstruction, indicating that improved mood elevations likely did not reflect improvement in asthma symptoms. Paradoxically, patients with past or current symptoms of depression had a significant decrease in depressive symptoms during prednisone therapy compared with those without depression. Some patients with post-traumatic stress disorder reported increases in depression and memories of the traumatic event during prednisone therapy (Brown et al.).

In another prospective study, Naber, Sand, and Heigl (1996) evaluated 50 ophthalmologic patients treated with corticosteroids, examining psychopathology and neuropsychological function before and after initial therapy. Although none of the patients developed psychosis, dementia, or delirious states, a substantial proportion of patients experienced an organic mood disorder, with about 30% experiencing hypomania and about 11% depression. In contrast, most neuropsychological tests showed no significant effects of corticosteroid treatment (Naber et al., 1996).

Similar results identifying corticosteroid-induced behavior abnormalities have been reported for children. Hall et al. (2003) performed a prospective assessment of the behavior of 12 children with nephritic syndrome initiating treatment with high-dose oral corticosteroids and control children using a standardized psychological questionnaire at the time of diagnosis and again after 4 weeks. They identified a significant increase in the total behavior score ($P = .03$) and specifically in aggressive and poor attention behavior items in the corticosteroid-treated group compared with the control group, and four corticosteroid-treated children developed abnormal behavior in the clinical range compared with none of the controls (Hall et al.). Regardless of the severity of the corticosteroid-induced psychosis, most patients recover within several weeks of the onset of symptoms if corticosteroids are tapered (Lewis & Smith, 1983). Delirium usually resolves within a few days, whereas depressive symptoms or mania may persist for several weeks. About 50% of patients with corticosteroid psychosis improve in 4 days and the remainder within 2 weeks (Cerullo, 2006; Lewis & Smith, 1983).

A question related to the development of encephalopathy involves the possibility that transient corticosteroid-induced central nervous system dysfunction results in residual cognitive or memory impairments. A potential association was described in terms of a reversible corticosteroid dementia that developed in six patients (Varney, Alexander, & MacIndoe, 1984). The six patients developed dementia-like cognitive changes following administration of corticosteroids. Two of the patients developed a transient corticosteroid psychosis but continued to show evidence of dementia well after the corticosteroid psychoses had resolved. Four other patients never showed symptoms of corticosteroid psychosis but did show persistent signs of dementia, characterized by deficits in memory retention, attention, concentration, mental speed and efficiency, and occupational performance. All six patients eventually recovered normal mental status following discontinuation or reduction of corticosteroids. The authors were unable to conclude a causal association of transient dementia due to corticosteroids, indicating that prospective studies would be required to identify the prevalence and nature of the purported syndrome (Varney et al.).

On the basis of the case report and cross-sectional studies described above, confirmation of a corticosteroid-induced dementia remains speculative, as other factors, such as increased anxiety or sleep deprivation, provide alternative explanations. As is almost always the case, the medical condition necessitating the use of high-dose corticosteroids is typically associated with increased level of stress, anxiety, and emotion. Also, specific individual corticosteroid-induced adverse effects, such as insomnia, are alone capable of producing many of the adverse behavioral effects (including agitation, depression, psychosis, and impaired memory) attributed to corticosteroids. Further, corticosteroids are often administered to treat central nervous system vasculitis or cerebritis, disorders which themselves produce neurological impairments including encephalopathy or psychosis. Nevertheless, the existing prospective cohort studies do support the hypothesis that corticosteroids, either directly or indirectly, contribute to the condition of corticosteroid-induced psychosis.

Evidence of recurrence of a corticosteroid-induced mood disorder following re-exposure to corticosteroids is an important consideration in terms of causation. A recent retrospective study focused specifically on recurrent corticosteroid-induced mood disorders in terms of long-term outcome (Wada, Yamada, Suzuki, Lee, & Kuroda, 2000). Nine patients whose initial clinical presentations met criteria for a substance-induced mood disorder were identified by a medical record review. All nine corticosteroid-treated patients demonstrated a clinical course of bipolar disorder; seven patients initially developed mania or hypomania of subacute onset and of 1–3 months duration. Four of five patients who had received corticosteroid pulse therapy rapidly became manic or hypomanic. Six of the patients experienced manic episodes in association with psychotic features. Seven patients also had abnormal mood episodes preceded by various psychosocial stressors that were independent of corticosteroid therapy. This small group of patients with recurrent episode of abnormal mood characterized by subacute onset, manic predominance, and frequent accompanying psychotic features highlight the similarities between and importance of precipitant psychosocial stressors and corticosteroid use (Wada et al., 2000).

The presence of a dose–response gradient appears well established for corticosteroid-induced psychosis, which is infrequent with short-term low-dose corticosteroid treatment but of relatively high incidence during high-dose treatment or long-term treatment, particularly when milder subjectively discernible symptoms are assessed (Wolkowitz, Reus, Canick, Levin, & Lupien, 1997). For example, about 1–2% of patients receiving less than 40 mg of prednisone per day experience psychiatric symptoms, compared to about 5% taking 41–80 mg per day, and almost 20% of patients taking more than 80 mg per day (Cerullo, 2006). Most other studies have reached similar conclusions. For example, Hall and associates reported that, among their patients, those receiving daily doses of at least 40 mg of prednisone or its equivalent were at greater risk for developing corticosteroid psychosis than were patients receiving small doses, with psychotic reactions being twice as likely to occur during the first 5 days of treatment as compared to later (Hall, 2006; Hall et al., 1979). In contrast, one prospective study in which 5% of 92 patients with SLE developed a corticosteroid-induced psychosis, reported that the onset of psychosis was not predictable by the corticosteroid dosage. Factors predictive of psychosis included low serum levels of albumin, complement, and creatinine; history of anxiety disorders; and a family history of psychiatric illnesses. After multivariate adjustment, however, only hypoalbuminemia remained a significant predictor (Chau & Mok, 2003). The discrepancy between these studies may reflect the timing of administration, with a dose–response relationship best established for acute corticosteroid administration.

In summary, in terms of causation, the diagnosis of corticosteroid psychosis for the *case presentation*, a "diagnosis" that includes the nature of the behavioral disorder and the cause of the disorder, was based on several considerations. First, there was documented systemic exposure to corticosteroids that was closely related to the onset of symptoms and signs. Second, all features of the patient's encephalopathy such as tremor, sleep disturbance, hyperreflexia, excessive anxiety, mania, and visual disturbance are known to occur in association with initiation of high-dose corticosteroid treatment. Third, removal from excessive corticosteroid exposure produced resolution of all neurobehavioral abnormalities. Fourth, major competing explanations such as metabolic dysfunction, infection, or vasculitis were eliminated from consideration, with two exceptions, by the investigation and the follow-up clinical course. The first exception involved the possibility that the acute stress associated with the progressive medical condition and the resultant evaluation and diagnosis were sufficient to precipitate an acute, transient reactive psychosis. While possible, this seems unlikely in the absence of any pre-existing or subsequent psychological or psychiatric problems. The second exception was that of a possible cerebritis due either to SLE or a related connective tissue disease. This consideration seems highly unlikely for several reasons, the most important of which is that the anti-inflammatory and immunosuppressive effects of corticosteroids are the primary treatment for cerebritis, and clinical improvement (and resolution) coincident with their withdrawal argues strongly against a diagnosis of cerebritis. Further, the subsequent course of sustained neurobehavioral improvement is not coherent with the course of the underlying systemic condition, had it been the cause of the central nervous system abnormalities. Regardless, the distinction is important and reviewed further in the following paragraphs.

Corticosteroid-induced psychosis in the setting of established SLE or other connective tissue disease is rare but clinically important and difficult to distinguish from an inflammatory cerebritis (Kohen, Asherson, Gharavi, & Lahita, 1993; Lim, Kraus, & Giles, 2004). In lupus cerebritis, the differentiation between cognitive difficulties secondary to the underlying illness, which might warrant more aggressive treatment with corticosteroids, versus those secondary to corticosteroids treatment alone, which might warrant dosage reduction, can be problematic (Wolkowitz et al., 1997). As an example of this dilemma, Denko (1977) described a 34-year-old woman with an organic psychosis presumably attributed corticosteroid psychosis because of prednisone treatment for urticaria. A diagnosis of SLE was subsequently established as the cause of the urticaria and the psychosis, and the lupus psychosis was reversed when sufficiently high doses of corticosteroids in combination with immunosuppressant agents were given. Similarly, Hirohata et al. (1988)

described a patient with established SLE who presented at different times with either corticosteroid-induced psychosis or central nervous system lupus. This patient was found to have abnormal CSF immunoglobulin indexes and an abnormal EEG, both of which reliably identified exacerbations of central nervous system lupus. The authors concluded that normal test results in the appropriate clinical setting of recently increased corticosteroids would have supported a diagnosis of corticosteroid-induced psychosis. Their observational report provided substantial evidence that both conditions, corticosteroid-induced psychosis and SLE-induced psychosis, can occur in the same individual at different times.

In contrast, Kohen et al. (1993) reported a patient with SLE who became depressed following an increase in her corticosteroid dosage. Despite the temporal association of deterioration following increase in the corticosteroid dose, a diagnosis of lupus cerebritis was based on her clinical presentation and high levels of antibodies in both cerebrospinal fluid and serum. Subsequently, Hirohata (2004) reported that among patients with central nervous system lupus, cerebrospinal fluid IgM, IgA, and IgG indexes, all indicators of intrathecal immunoglobulin synthesis, were significantly elevated relative to control levels. Further, among patients with lupus psychosis, but not in those with focal central nervous system lesions, sera antiribosomal P antibody (anti-P) and CSF antineuronal antibody titers reflected their central nervous system disease activities. The immune system activation within the central nervous system plays an important role in the pathogenesis of lupus psychosis, and evidence of such activation is a strong evidence against diagnosis of corticosteroid-induced psychosis in a patient with established SLE.

A case of corticosteroid withdrawal psychosis occurred in a patient with closed head injury who had been treated with high-dose corticosteroids in an attempt to reverse her neurological impairment and for the reduction of cerebral edema (Alpert & Seigerman, 1986). The idea that the introduction of high-dose corticosteroid treatment or the abrupt withdrawal of corticosteroids could result in a similar syndrome of corticosteroid psychosis is of interest, but not without precedent. Consider, e.g., development of increased intracranial pressure after initiating or discontinuing corticosteroids. This 18-year-old patient had sustained a basilar skull fracture during a car–pedestrian accident. After a 2-week course of corticosteroids, the medication was abruptly discontinued. Later that day, she became severely depressed and exhibited an organic psychosis that persisted for 10 weeks and necessitated psychiatric hospitalization and psychopharmacologic therapy. Following discharge, she participated in cognitive retraining for closed head injury patients and soon returned to her studies. One explanation for the organic psychosis was the abrupt withdrawal of corticosteroids, although alternate explanations exist, including the closed head injury and a reactive psychosis (Alpert & Seigerman, 1986). Isolated case reports exist of new-onset psychosis, including schizophrenia, developing after withdrawal of corticosteroid therapy (Judd, Burrows, & Norman, 1983). In all, the specific role of corticosteroid withdrawal in terms of causation of these illnesses is unclear, and any implication related to etiology of a persistent psychosis is only speculative (Judd et al., 1983).

The link between neuroendocrine regulation and depression has been the source of substantial investigation, including study of differences in response to cortisol suppression between clinically depressed and normal individuals, an observation made many years ago (Carroll, Curtis, & Mendels, 1976). Namely, an overnight dexamethasone test of hypothalamopituitary-adrenal (HPA) suppression was said to suggest that patients who were classified in the Carroll et al. (1976) studies as "endogenomorphic depression" had significantly greater HPA activity before dexamethasone challenge and less complete HPA suppression after dexamethasone relative to patients with depressive neuroses and most patients with other nondepressive psychiatric disorders. The mechanisms of corticosteroid toxicity in terms of neurobehavioral or psychiatric effects are uncertain, but the roles of the dysregulation of the limbic-hypothalamic-pituitary-adrenocortical axis and especially excess cortisol in major depression have become prime candidates for a contributory role in depression (Hatzinger, Seifritz, Hemmeter, & Holsboer-Trachsler; 1994; Sonino, Fava, Raffi, Boscaro, & Fallo, 1998). Several lines of research have supported these hypothesized relationships, including the commonality of psychiatric disturbances in endocrine disorders generally (Barchas & Altemus, 1999), the association between hypercortisolism in Cushing syndrome and especially the apparent reversibility of depressive symptoms following successful treatment of Cushing's disease (Starkman, Gebarski, Berent, & Schteingart, 1992) and the rise in excess cortisol during active depression and fall in cortisol following successful treatment (Young et al., 1994) (Also, see chapter 18).

Corticosteroids have established effects on central nervous system biochemistry and electrophysiology, and existing evidence indicates that they increase the vulnerability of hippocampal neurons to a variety of metabolic influences (Wolkowitz et al., 1997). The experimental literature supports the hypothesis that disruption of hippocampus-dependent memory function contributes to the observed clinical effects, although in most cases the disruption is relatively mild and, in the vast majority of cases, reversible (Wolkowitz et al.).

In terms of depression, exogenous corticosteroid exposures are associated with increased recollection of traumatic life events. Animal studies suggesting that corticosteroids enhanced conditioning in stressful learning paradigms lead to the hypothesis that enhance recall of stressful experiences may contribute to corticosteroid-induced depression in humans (Patten, 1999). As a part of the Canadian National Population Health Survey, 17,626 subjects were interviewed to obtain information on drug and medication exposure and psychosocial stressors. Overall, a significantly higher percentage of subjects treated with corticosteroids in the month prior to the interview reported one or more of the major psychosocial stressors during their lifetime compared to those who had not received corticosteroids (52% versus 41%, $p < .05$). Although statistically significant and consistent with the proposed mechanism underlying associations between corticosteroids and depression, the magnitude of difference between groups was relatively small. Further, this cross-sectional survey of trauma recollections cannot establish a causal connection between exposure to corticosteroids and enhanced recollection of stressful life events and traumatic experiences.

Animal studies support the hypothesis that corticosteroids influence memory retrieval. For example, Sprague-Dawley rats receiving corticosteroids immediately before and after memory retention testing demonstrated significantly impaired retention performance compared to control rats receiving vehicle treatment (Roozendaal, de Quervain, Schelling, & McGaugh, 2004). Coadministration of propranolol, a centrally acting β-adrenoceptor antagonist, blocked the corticosteroid-induced impairment in contextual memory retrieval induced, supporting the view that corticosteroids interact with noradrenergic mechanisms in influencing memory retrieval (Roozendaal et al., 2004).

VERIFICATION OF CAUSE/ETIOLOGY

The syndrome of corticosteroid-psychosis fulfills most of the Hill criteria for causation. This medication-induced behavioral disorder is well established despite the relative limited number of characteristic features, aside from the strong temporal association of relative abrupt onset following the introduction of corticosteroids, resolution following withdrawal, and recurrence when they are reintroduced. Ironically, a typical corticosteroid psychosis may be present after abrupt withdrawal of corticosteroids.

Conclusion

Corticosteroids are among the most commonly prescribed medications, primarily because of their potent anti-inflammatory and immunosuppressant effects. Aside from their striking anti-inflammatory effects, they frequently produce undesirable adverse neurobehavioral effects, in addition to numerous adverse systemic effects including hyperglycemia, hypertension, and electrolyte imbalance. The most troublesome adverse behavioral effects associated with short-term high-dose corticosteroid administration include abnormalities of neurological function and mood consisting of combinations of agitation, anxiety, mania, depression, insomnia, hyperreflexia, and postural tremor. Less commonly observed central nervous system effects include encephalopathy, psychosis, and, possibly, memory loss, collectively referred to as corticosteroid-induced psychosis. Establishing the cause of the behavioral abnormalities that appear after initiation of corticosteroids is difficult. The difficulty reflects, at least in part, the fact that the medical situation necessitating the use of high-dose corticosteroids is typically associated with increased level of stress, anxiety, and emotion. Also, some adverse effects produced by corticosteroids, such as insomnia, are in and of themselves capable of producing many of the adverse behavioral effects, including agitation, depression, psychosis, and impaired memory. Further, corticosteroids are often administered to treat conditions such as central nervous system vasculitis or cerebritis, disorders that themselves produce neurological impairments including encephalopathy or psychosis. Regardless, corticosteroid-induced behavioral abnormalities likely reflect an interaction with or dysregulation of the limbic-hypothalamic-pituitary-adrenocortical axis, an important neuroanatomical substrate in depression. As such, the adverse neurobehavioral effects associated with corticosteroids serve as a model of chemical-induced encephalopathy or psychosis. Like other forms of chemical-induced encephalopathy or psychosis, corticosteroid-induced psychosis appears to be completely reversible after removal from excessive corticosteroid exposure.

Cyclosporine

James W. Albers

Cyclosporine is a potent immunosuppressant medication that interferes with humoral and cellular immunity possibly by blocking the action of calcineurin, an enzyme important in T-cell activation (Mascarell & Truffa-Bachi, 2003). Cyclosporine is most frequently used to reduce the rate and severity of allograft rejection following organ transplantation (Cohen & Raps, 1995; Kahan, 1989). It also is used to control the progression of several autoimmune nervous system disorders, including myasthenia gravis and chronic inflammatory demyelinating polyneuropathy (Barnett, Pollard, Davies, & McLeod, 1998; Tindall, Rollins, Phillips, & Greenlee, 1987). The major adverse side effects attributed to cyclosporine are hypertension and nephrotoxicity. Less commonly observed are central nervous system effects, including encephalopathy, tremor, and seizure. When central nervous system toxicity develops in the setting of impaired liver function, the distinction between hepatic encephalopathy, cyclosporine encephalopathy, and other forms of encephalopathy is difficult in the absence of distinguishing features. The following *case presentation* is representative of patients who develop neurological effects due to cyclosporine intoxication. The *case presentation* also is characteristic of patients who present with a toxic leukoencephalopathy due to any of numerous possible causes (Filley & Kleinschmidt-DeMasters, 2001).

Case presentation[1]

A 41-year-old man was admitted to the hospital because of "confusion." He had undergone a successful orthotopic liver transplant 3 months earlier for end-stage primary biliary cirrhosis. Following the liver transplant, he was immunosuppressed with cyclosporine and corticosteroids without complications, other than a mild elevation in blood pressure and transient elevations of serum creatinine and fasting serum glucose levels. Two weeks prior to admission, he developed a recurrent urinary tract infection and was prescribed antibiotic treatment with an oral aminoglycoside. Urinary tract symptoms resolved, but several days later he became nauseated and complained of generalized malaise. The following day, he complained of a headache and said he had been unable to sleep. His wife and daughter commented that his speech was "slurred." He was nauseated and refused to eat or take his medications. He made several bizarre and inappropriate comments to his daughter, and he became agitated when she questioned him about the comments. He became increasingly confrontational and confused, and his family took him to the hospital for evaluation and treatment.

In the ED, his vital signs were normal, including temperature and blood pressure, as was a general physical examination. His neck was supple. He was confused and oriented only to person. He persistently picked at his hospital gown and rearranged his sheets (akathesia). He was easily distractible and his comments were inappropriate for the surroundings. He was dysarthric and made frequent paraphasic errors. In addition, he was thought to have a possible receptive aphasia. At times, he appeared to be responding to visual hallucinations, but he refused to describe what he was seeing. He responded only to simple, one-step commands (show me your teeth), and ignored more complicated multiple-step commands. He refused formal visual testing, but he did respond by withdrawing from gross visual threat. Nevertheless, his vision seemed abnormal, as he bumped into objects in his path and he could not find objects within his grasp. Ophthalmoscopy examination was normal. Extraocular eye movements showed impaired pursuit, and he had course, saccadic eye movements, but no evidence of ophthalmoparesis. Motor examination showed normal strength. He was tremulous and exhibited an accentuated postural tremor and asterixis. He also had frequent, multifocal myoclonic movements. Coordination seemed intact, but his gait was unsteady. He would not cooperate for Romberg testing. Sensation was grossly normal. Reflexes were diffusely hyperactive, including the jaw reflex. He had bilateral Hoffmann reflexes and unsustained ankle clonus but no pathological reflexes.

Shortly after his initial neurological examination, he had a major motor seizure lasting minutes. The seizure was followed by profound and prolonged postictal lethargy. There were no new focal abnormalities.

DIFFERENTIAL DIAGNOSIS

This patient was thought to have an acute encephalopathy attributed to cyclosporine neurotoxicity. Other considerations for the acute encephalopathy included possible liver failure or other metabolic abnormality (renal toxicity or hyperosmolar state), central nervous system infection, cerebral hemorrhage, generalized sepsis, vasculitis, nonconvulsive status, or Wernicke's syndrome.

ADDITIONAL INFORMATION

Thiamine and glucose were given without improvement. A cranial CT scan, obtained urgently to rule-out cerebral hemorrhage or hydrocephalus, showed diffuse white matter hypodensities in the cerebral hemispheres bilaterally, maximal posteriorly. There was no cerebral atrophy and the ventricles were not dilated. The imaging abnormalities showed a diffuse leukoencephalopathy, consistent with the clinical impression. The CSF was unremarkable, other than showing a borderline-elevated total protein level. Routine laboratory evaluations of serum were normal, including electrolytes, glucose, liver-function studies, and renal function. Urinalysis was unremarkable. Urine culture subsequently returned normal results. A cyclosporine trough level, measured about 12 hr after his last dosage, was elevated. An EEG examination, performed about 24 hr after the major motor seizure to evaluate for the possibility of nonepileptogenic status, showed a moderately severe dysrhythmia characterized by persistent generalized slowing of the background rhythm into the theta range. This nonspecific EEG abnormality was symmetrical, without localizing features and without evidence of an epileptogenic focus. There were no cortical manifestations of the clinically evident myoclonus. A head MRI, performed several days after admission, showed diffuse hyperintensity of the cerebral white matter, confirming the white matter abnormalities typical of leukoencephalopathy (Filley & Kleinschmidt-DeMasters, 2001).

Cyclosporine was initially withheld and later administered at a reduced dosage. He was not started on anticonvulsant medications. Over several days, his neurological condition slowly improved. Three weeks after remission, all central nervous system signs had resolved, including the mental status changes, visual problems, tremor, myoclonus, and hyper-reflexia. He had no further seizures. He had no memory of the events leading up to or including the initial part of the hospitalization. A repeat MRI study was improved, but it continued to show scattered residual white matter abnormalities, maximal posteriorly. A repeat awake EEG was normal.

Approximately 5 months later, an almost identical episode of neurobehavioral abnormalities recurred in this patient over about 24 hr in association with an elevated cyclosporine trough level. As before, reduction in the cyclosporine dosage resulted in gradual but complete recovery.

Discussion

The nervous system localization of the patient's neurologic disorder, and the likelihood that the problem was caused by cyclosporine, is examined in the following paragraphs.

NERVOUS SYSTEM LOCALIZATION

The primary neuroanatomical clinical diagnosis was "encephalopathy." The neurologic problem was readily localized to the supratentorial level of the central nervous system bilaterally. The symptoms and signs referable to this localization included abnormalities of behavior, receptive and expressive language function, and vision. The seizure also localizes to the cerebral cortex. Other signs consistent with this localization, although nonspecific, included diffuse hyperreflexia, presumed visual hallucinations, and myoclonus. The differential diagnosis for visual hallucinations (including localization and potential causes) is listed in Table 16.4 (p. 884). There were no lateralizing signs, and involvement appeared symmetric, although possibly multifocal as opposed to diffuse. The only symptoms and signs that were not entirely explained by supratentorial localization were "slurred speech," "dysarthria," and unsteady gait, each of which could reflect a posterior fossa (cerebellar) localization. Alternatively, these signs may be explained by his altered level of consciousness. The absence of other symptoms or signs referable to the posterior fossa such as diplopia, dysphagia, dizziness, ataxia, dysmetria, nystagmus, or weakness of facial, palatal, or tongue muscles made involvement of the posterior fossa structures unlikely. The presence of myoclonus also localized to the central nervous system. Myoclonus consists of a sudden brief, shock-like, involuntary movement. Given the characteristic features of myoclonus, this clinical sign might seem to have important diagnostic implications. Unfortunately, the differential diagnosis associated with myoclonus is likely broader than for any of the other movement disorders (Table 16.5) (Lang, 1996).

Table 16.5 Etiological classification of myoclonus.

Physiological myoclonus (normal subjects)
  Sleep jerks (hypnic or hypnagogic jerks)
  Anxiety-induced
  Exercise-induced
  Hiccough (singultus)

Essential myoclonus
  Hereditary
  Sporadic
  Epileptic myoclonus (seizures dominate)
  Fragments of epilepsy
    Isolated epileptic myoclonic jerks
    Epilepsia partialis continua
    Idiopathic stimulus-sensitive myoclonus
    Photosensitive myoclonus
    Myoclonic absences in petit mal
  Benign familial myoclonic epilepsy
  Progressive myoclonus epilepsy

Symptomatic myoclonus (progressive or static encephalopathy dominate)
  Storage disease
    Lafora body disease
    Lipidoses, such as GM2 gangliosidosis, Tay-Sachs, Krabbe
    Ceroid-lipofuscinosis (Batten, Kuff)
    Sialidosis (cherry-red spot)
  Spinocerebellar degeneration
    Ramsay Hunt syndrome (many causes)
    Friedreich's ataxia
    Ataxia telangiectasia
  Basal ganglia degenerations
    Wilson's disease
    Torsion dystonia
    Hallervorden–Spatz's disease

Table 16.5 (continued) Etiological classification of myoclonus.

Progressive supranuclear palsy
Huntington's disease
Parkinson's disease
Cortical–basal ganglionic degeneration
Pallidal degenerations
Multiple system atrophy

Mitochondrial encephalopathies

Dementias
Creutzfeldt–Jakob disease
Alzheimer's disease

Viral encephalopathies
Subacute sclerosing panencephalitis
Encephalitis lethargica
Arbovirus encephalitis
Herpes simplex encephalitis
Postinfectious encephalitis
Metabolic
Hepatic failure
Renal failure
Dialysis syndrome
Hyponatremia
Hypoglycemia
Nonketotic hyperglycemia
Toxic encephalopathies
Bismuth
Heavy metal poisons
Methyl bromide, DDT
Drugs, including levodopa, tricyclics, cyclosporine

Physical encephalopathies
Post hypoxia (Lance-Adam)
Posttraumatic
Heat stroke
Electric shock
Decompression injury
Focal central nervous system damage
Post stroke
Post thalamotomy
Tumor
Trauma
Olivodentate lesions (palatal myoclonus)
Spinal cord lesions (segmental or spinal myoclonus)

From "Definition and Classification of Myoclonus," by S. Fahn, C. D. Marsden, and M. H. van Woert, 1986, *Advances in Neurology, 43*, p. 1.

VERIFICATION OF THE CLINICAL DIAGNOSIS

The clinical diagnosis of encephalopathy was established by the clinical neurological signs, and the diagnosis was supported by the EEG and imaging abnormalities. As discussed in volume I, the clinical and EEG findings are not specific for a diagnosis more precise than "encephalopathy." Further, there were no EEG features suggesting a cause for the cortical disturbance (e.g., triphasic waves implicating hepatic encephalopathy). The brain imaging studies (CT and MRI) provided documentation of diffuse, symmetric white matter abnormalities characteristic of leukoencephalopathy. Taken together, the clinical diagnosis of encephalopathy satisfies all explicit questions required to verify the diagnosis (Richardson et al., 2000). This impression included electrophysiological and imaging confirmation.

CAUSE/ETIOLOGY

What evidence associates cyclosporine with a subacute leukoencephalopathy? The number of causes of leukoencephalopathy is extensive (Table 16.6), and the potential causes include several neurotoxicants (Table 16.7). Almost all of the original evidence for a cyclosporine-induced encephalopathy reflected information derived from anecdotal case reports and cross-sectional studies. However, many of the individual case reports include information about reintroduction of cyclosporine, as in the *case presentation*, with documented elevation of serum levels and recurrence of objective neurological signs and electrophysiological abnormalities. Such information, while inconclusive for definitive causation, provides strong evidence of a dose–response abnormality related to cyclosporine.

Table 16.6 Differential diagnosis for conditions other than toxins producing a cerebral white matter myelinopathy (leukoencephalopathy).

Cause	Condition
Autoimmune/inflammatory	Acute disseminated encephalomyelitis, isolated angiitis of the central nervous system[a], multiple sclerosis, systemic lupus erythematosus (SLE)[a], Sjogren's[a], Wegener's granulomatosis[a]
Hereditary-genetic	Adrenoleukodystrophy, aminoacidurias, Krabbe's, metachromatic leukodystrophy, myotonic dystrophy, Plizeus–Merzbacker, neurofibromatosis
Hydrocephalus	Early obstructive, normal-pressure
Infectious	Acquired immunodeficiency (HIV), progressive multifocal leukoencephalopathy (paraneoplastic), sarcoidosis[a], subacute sclerosing panencephalitis (SSPE), varicella-zoster, Lyme, cytomegalovirus
Metabolic	Cobalamin deficiency, folate, hypoxia, hypertensive encephalopathy, eclampsia, high-altitude cerebral edema
Neoplastic	Diffuse glioma, gliomatosis cerebri, primary central nervous system lymphoma (PCNSL)
Trauma	Traumatic brain injury
Vascular	Binswanger's, autosomal dominant arteriopathy, amyloid angiopathy

[a] Most prominent neuropathological abnormalities are in the brain gray matter. Adapted from Filley & Kleinschmidt-DeMasters (2001).

Table 16.7 Spectrum of clinical, neuropsychological, imaging and neuropathological findings associated with toxic leukoencephalopathy.

Class	Agent
Antineoplastic	Cranial radiation
	Medications: carmustine, cisplatin, cytarabine, fludarabine, fluorouracil, interferon alfa, interleukin-2, methotrexate, thiotepa
Antimicrobial	Amphotericin B, hexachlorophene
Environmental	Arsenic, carbon monoxide, carbon tetrachloride
Drugs of abuse	Ethanol, cocaine, intravenous heroin, inhaled "heroin" pyrolysate, 3,4-methylenedioxyamphetamine, psilocybin, toluene
Immunosuppression	Cyclosporine, tacrolimus

Adapted from Filley & Kleinschmidt-DeMasters (2001).

The diagnosis of cyclosporine encephalopathy for this patient was based on several considerations. First, there was documented systemic exposure, with an elevated serum cyclosporine level. Second, some features of the encephalopathy such as visual disturbance, seizure, and CT and MRI findings occur frequently in association with cyclosporine toxicity. Third and fourth, major competing explanations such as hepatic or renal dysfunction, infection, malignant hypertension, or vasculitis were eliminated from consideration by the investigation and the follow-up clinical course. Namely, removal from excessive cyclosporine exposure produced resolution of all neurobehavioral abnormalities. Fifth, the objective clinical and electrophysiological features were reproduced when the cyclosporine level inadvertently increased later.

The introduction of cyclosporine immunosuppression in the 1980s was associated with an increased number of orthotopic liver transplants by reducing the rate and severity of allograft rejection. Cyclosporine was associated with reversible nephrotoxicity, but the clinical benefit of this potent immunosuppressant outweighed its toxicity (Fathman & Myers, 1992). With increased use of cyclosporine, case reports began to appear describing neurologic side effects, despite the belief that cyclosporine did not cross the intact blood–brain barrier (Hughes, 1990; Steg & Garcia, 1991; Stein, Lederman, & Vogt, 1992). Reported neurological symptoms and signs included tremor, burning distal dysesthesias, headache, depression, and confusion (Kahan, 1989). Additional features of encephalopathy, seizure, cortical blindness, and reversible white-matter abnormalities on head MRI were seen in association with elevated plasma cyclosporine levels (Hughes, 1990; Kahan, 1989). Myoclonus, as described earlier in this section, has been reported in association with cyclosporine toxicity. The broad differential diagnosis for myoclonus limits the diagnostic usefulness of this nonspecific sign, other than being "consistent with" encephalopathy. Another neurological complication associated with cyclosporine toxicity, but one not experienced by the patient described in the *case presentation,* is rhabdomyolysis. This peripheral nervous system disorder often occurs in association with use of cholesterol lowering medications, as described in volume II of this book (van Puijenbroek, Du Buf-Vereijken, Spooren, & van Doormaal, 1996). Importantly, reduction of excessive cyclosporine levels results in recovery of all of the adverse neurologic complications (Gijtenbeek, van den Bent, & Vecht, 1999; Stein et al., 1992).

Why did the patient described in the *case presentation* suddenly develop signs of cyclosporine toxicity? Cyclosporine is metabolized by the hepatic cytochrome P-450 enzyme superfamily (Kahan, 1989). Drugs that interact with the cytochrome P-450 enzyme system, of which there are many, can affect cyclosporine metabolism and produce elevated (or reduced) serum levels. Even ingestion of grapefruit juice, e.g., is capable of increasing systemic exposure to cyclosporine (Hermann et al., 2002). The introduction of an aminoglycoside antibiotic may have resulted in the elevated cyclosporine level, as part of a drug interaction (Zylber-Katz, 1995). Drugs reported to increase cyclosporine levels include ketoconazole, oral contraceptives, androgens, methylprednisolone, and calcium-channel antagonists, although most reports are anecdotal (Duell, Connor, & Illingworth, 1998; Kahan, 1989; Tal, Rajeshawari, & Isley, 1997).

The mechanisms of cyclosporine toxicity are uncertain and controversial. Among some patients, toxicity was associated with decreased serum cholesterol levels. For example, de Groen, Aksamit, and Rakela (1987) reported a retrospective evaluation of 54 liver transplantations performed in 48 patients, which included 13 patients who had symptoms of central nervous system toxicity. These symptomatic patients had significantly lower serum cholesterol levels than did remaining patients, suggesting a mechanistic role between cyclosporine and cholesterol. Possible mechanisms attributable to low cholesterol levels include enhanced passage of unbound cyclosporine through the blood–brain barrier and reduced unesterified cholesterol and phospholipid brain levels (de Groen et al., 1987; Montpied et al., 2003). Among other patients, however, serum cholesterol levels were elevated at the time when symptoms were most marked, indicating that factors other than cholesterol explain the toxic effects (Hughes, 1990). Cyclosporine-induced neurological signs do not appear to be the result of hypertension-related renal disease, and among patients with cyclosporine-induced hypertension, the elevations are not of the magnitude typically associated with malignant hypertension (de Groen et al.).

The imaging abnormalities associated with cyclosporine encephalopathy appear to preferentially involve the cerebral cortex, and the MRI features resemble changes resulting from many causes, including hypoxic injury or cortical vasculitis (Filley & Kleinschmidt-DeMasters, 2001; Jansen, Krieger, Krieger, & Sartor, 1996). The latter observation suggests a potential mechanism whereby a vascular injury produces cortical hypoperfusion, perhaps as part of a cyclosporine-induced vasculopathy (Schwartz et al., 1995). A patient who had cyclosporine-induced encephalopathy was reported to have findings of unusually prolonged vasospasm, perhaps contributing to slow neurological recovery (Lin et al., 2003). Autopsy findings from a patient who died shortly after developing cyclosporine-induced encephalopathy showed diffuse patchy white matter edema and astrocytic injury, but no evidence of axonopathy, demyelination, microvascular injury, or infectious or inflammatory process (Gopal, Thorning, & Back, 1999). Importantly, the white matter abnormalities represent a sensitive indication of a cerebral abnormality. They are not, however, diagnostic of a specific disorder.

The mechanisms mediating cyclosporine-evoked convulsions have been investigated experimentally, and cyclosporine appears to increase neuronal excitability at dosages that are clinically relevant (Gorji, Scheld, & Speckmann, 2002; Shuto et al., 1999). Cyclosporine significantly increased the intensity of convulsions induced by bicuculline, a GABA receptor antagonist. Convulsions induced by the combination of bicuculline and cyclosporine were significantly suppressed by an activation of GABA-ergic transmission with Diazepam, Phenobarbital, and Valproate. Rat cerebellar granule cell cultures exposed to cyclosporine showed decreased binding to intact granule cells compared to control cell cultures, suggesting that cyclosporine inhibits GABA-ergic neural activity and binding properties of the GABA receptor. These events appear to be causally related to the occurrence of cyclosporine-induced tremors, convulsions, coma, and encephalopathy (Shuto et al., 1999). Cyclosporine also has a direct cytotoxic effect on the brain capillary endothelial cells, and inhibition of P-glycoprotein may be partly involved in the occurrence of cyclosporine-induced encephalopathy (Kochi et al., 1999). In rats, cyclosporine inhibited acetylcholinesterase activity in certain portions of the brain (Herink et al., 2003), although it is unclear how this might be related to the clinical manifestations of neurotoxicity.

VERIFICATION OF CAUSE/ETIOLOGY

The syndrome of cyclosporine-induced encephalopathy fulfills all criteria for causation. This form of encephalopathy is a well-established disorder with relatively characteristic features. When these features are present, the diagnosis of cyclosporine encephalopathy is established with a high degree of confidence, and the diagnosis supported by resolution of the neurobehavioral abnormalities with removal from excessive cyclosporine exposure.

Conclusion

The importance of cyclosporine encephalopathy in terms of its prevalence is not substantial, yet the importance of this toxic encephalopathy relates to its role as a model of toxic encephalopathy or leukoencephalopathy in general. Toxic leukoencephalopathy of any cause has an impressive spectrum of clinical, electrophysiological, imaging, and neuropathological features (Table 16.8). Like other forms of encephalopathy, most or all of the abnormalities associated with cyclosporine-induced toxic leukoencephalopathy are reversible after removal from excessive cyclosporine exposure, unless the disorder is sufficiently severe to produce cellular necrosis. Cyclosporine is one of a select group of central nervous system neurotoxicants producing reversible white matter changes in the central nervous system, perhaps as part of a toxic vasculopathy producing ischemia and diffuse but transient cerebral edema.

Table 16.8 Spectrum of clinical, neuropsychological, imaging and neuropathological findings associated with toxic leukoencephalopathy.

Measure	Mild	Moderate	Severe
Mental status	Confusion	Drowsy, somnolent	Abulia
	Short attention span	Apathy	Akinetic mutism
	Forgetfulness	Memory impairment	Stupor
	Fatigued, altered sleep	Disorientation	Coma
	Personality change	Delirium	Death
Other signs	Postural tremor	Asterixis	Babinski/Chaddock signs
	Slowed coordination	Dysarthria	Rapid respiration
		Akathisia	Nystagmus
		Primitive reflexes	Myoclonus
		Gross ataxia/ paratonia	Decerebrate posturing
		Hyperreflexia	Dilated pupils
Neuropsychological	Attention and memory deficits	Marked attention, memory, visuospatial, and executive deficits	Global impairments (too impaired to test)
	Depression and anxiety		
	Language normal	Language relatively normal	
Imaging CT	Usually normal	Possible mild hypo-density white matter	Diffuse hypodensity white matter, necrotic areas
MRI	Hyperintensity Periventricular white matter	Diffuse hyperintensity of white matter	Severe hyperintensity of white matter Necrotic areas
Neuropathology	Patchy intramyelinic edema; myelin preserved	Widespread edema	Oligodendrocytes destroyed
		Demyelination; axons preserved	Axonal loss Necrosis

From Filley et al. (2001).

Ethyl Alcohol

Kenneth M. Adams

Ethyl alcohol (ethanol) is a type of alcohol, a term that includes any organic compound in which a hydroxyl group (–OH) is bound to a carbon atom. Ethanol (CH_3CH_2OH) can be consumed in beverages that have been produced in myriad forms (e.g., distilled spirits, wine, and beer). This substance has been consumed for all of the recorded history of mankind and also with evidence of prehistoric use (McGovern, 2003). It has been used for reasons of a formal or societal nature (e.g., medical, dietary, religious, cultural); as well as for individual motivations involving recreational, inspirational, mood-altering, or aphrodisiacal effects. Expectancies about reward from drinking are reinforcing, and account for future drinking on both a biological and a social basis (Goldman, 2002). Dependence can accompany ethanol use and, following the establishment of alcohol dependence, the avoidance of withdrawal effects constitutes a different kind of mechanism of reinforcement for drinking behavior (Koob & Le Moal, 1997).

In the United States, ethanol consumption has occurred since colonial times (Levine, 1978). Concerns about chronic drunkenness were expressed during this historical period by individual observers and clergy that comprise some of the origins of the modern view of individual models of disease and addiction in chronic alcohol dependence (National Institute on Alcohol Abuse and Alcoholism, 2000).

Approximately 15 million Americans meet the diagnostic criteria for alcohol abuse or alcoholism at the present time (Grant et al., 1994), while about 3 million residents of the United Kingdom meet the same criteria. Earlier onset of excessive drinking in adolescence and persistence of alcohol abuse in older age are associated with more problematic health, behavioral, and social adjustment than are other aspects of alcohol use (National Institute on Alcohol Abuse and Alcoholism, 2003). The estimated combined social costs of alcoholism in the United States on an annualized basis were estimated at almost $200 billion in the year 2000 (Harwood, 2000). More recent literature on the methodology for the evaluation of treatment costs (Bray & Zarkin, 2006) suggests that this is actually an underestimate, the current projection of which would be significantly higher considering all impacts and treatment costs.

The *case presentation* that follows reflects a clinical scenario seen unfortunately more or less typically in clinical practice. While the patient's symptoms and signs may be documented relatively easily, determining their etiology may be more difficult.

Case presentation[1]

A 54-year-old male was referred to a neurology outpatient clinic by his primary care physician for evaluation of memory impairment and possible decreased sensation in his lower extremities. The memory impairment was most apparent to the patient's current girlfriend and children, who all had been concerned about repeated instances of memory lapses over the year preceding the physician's evaluation. These "memory lapses" included the patient forgetting that conversations had taken place, leaving things half-finished or undone, and forgetting scheduled appointments or other commitments he quite clearly and confidently had made. Also, it was reported that he found it more difficult than in the past to keep his financial affairs in order, and he had made some substantial and obvious banking errors of a kind he had never done before. The family expressed concern about his drinking, which had been occurring on a daily basis until 6 weeks before the present appointment. The patient has been abstinent since that time and in an outpatient alcohol treatment program. He has been monitored continuously while living at his son's home. He has not worked since entering treatment.

When working, the patient was a horse trainer (to break and train trotting horses, usually those that are used at race tracks around the region), an occupation he has practiced for 25 years. His family reported that his reputation is that he is very good at this work. He has a high school education with one semester of community college. He served in the United States Navy from age 18 through 26 years as a gunner's mate and began drinking while in the peacetime Navy. His first drink was at age 17 years, but his first extensive use of alcohol occurred during binge weekends in which he estimated that he would consume 24 to 30 cans of beer or more. After discharge from the service, he began working as a truck driver and, if not driving, drank 3 to 6 beers per evening, more on weekends. Also, he had come to drinking daily on the farm where he worked out with horses as his drinking increased.

The patient married at age 20 years, and this marriage lasted 13 years. He has been married three times. Two of these marriages ended in divorce. He has been separated from his third wife for 10 years. His alcohol use was a precipitating factor in the breakup of all three marriages. He has two sons aged 47 and 44 years, who are in good health.

When he first divorced at age 32 years, he began increasing his beer consumption to 6 to 8 cans of beer per day; usually beginning around noon and continuing into the evening. On weekends, he sometimes would go on a 2 to 3 day binge consuming a case—that is 24 cans of beer—per day during these times. During these periods, he would go without food for 2 to 3 days at a time. This binging occurred irregularly but occurred to the extent of drinking described on many weekends. As he grew older, into his early 40s, he reported that he became more careful to eat regularly, even if he did not particularly want to do so. Also, he attempted to stop drinking and had dry spells (periods when he did not drink) that occurred irregularly but lasted 4 to 6 months at a time. His wives all attempted to get him to quit drinking. He never consumed wine and took almost no hard liquor. His weekends of bingeing without food would occur on an average of six times per year. Otherwise, he regularly had three small meals per day.

There was no history of medical illness other than for peptic ulcer, for which he was prescribed Ranitidine (150 mg daily). He did require one surgical intervention which was a cervical fusion. Also, he reported a fall that occurred at work 9 months previously but with no loss of consciousness he could recall. He reported there were no significant injuries from this incident, but he did sustain bruises and soreness. He was deemed to have had a possible brief loss of consciousness but no obvious injury to the head and was taken to the hospital after that fall, examined, treated for his superficial injuries, and released. He had no seizure episodes either while drinking or shortly after becoming abstinent and no diagnosis of Wernicke–Korsakoff syndrome or other alcohol-related formal medical diagnoses. The patient had been encouraged on several occasions to take a multivitamin–mineral supplement, a recommendation he reported complying with over approximately the past 6 months (Centrum Silver). He denied having *delirium tremens* ever, but he reported two episodes of *alcoholic blackouts*, a phenomenon associated with severe alcohol dependence wherein the patient cannot recall events of the previous day when they have been drinking. His first such blackout occurred at age 50 years, and he reported that he could recall nothing that occurred the previous day after he had started drinking. More recently, he had another alcoholic blackout with no memory of the evening before. He seldom was a morning drinker and usually started consuming alcohol at noon. He did experience *morning shakes* a few times, which are characterized as a mild but visible resting tremor and are a common symptom of alcohol withdrawal. The patient has been counseled by many to get help with his drinking but to no avail. He eventually became a member of *Alcoholics Anonymous* and had been in this program for 14 months at the time of his current evaluation. He has been arrested twice for driving under the influence of alcohol in the past year, and it was an arrest (while driving under the influence) that led to his joining *Alcoholics Anonymous*. He usually drinks alone.

In terms of other past medical history, the patient has smoked one package of cigarettes per day for 38 years but denied taking other drugs, other than alcohol. He has had four surgical interventions, including a fractured right leg with a plate placed at age 28 years after he slipped off a curb while "drunk," and a cervical fusion about 10 years previous to this evaluation. He denied any exposure to industrial toxic materials, and he emphasized that he has been able to work in a relatively healthy and semirural outdoors environment for most of all his working career.

Review of systems and medical examination found head, eyes, ears, nose, and throat to be normal. With regard to the cardiorespiratory system, his long history of smoking was mentioned, and he reported having a chronic cough. Abdominal pain had been diagnosed as a peptic ulcer, currently treated with Zantac. A review of all other systems, including orthopedic and sexual history, was negative for active disease.

Physical examination showed the patient to be of roughly average height and weight (68 in., 201 lb.) and in no acute distress, with a chronic cough, and smelling of tobacco. His blood pressure was 120/74 mmHg, with a pulse rate of 64 bpm and regular. Respirations were 20/min. The chest was barrel shaped, with coarse rhonchi at the bases but no rales. There were no murmurs or thrills. Carotid pulses were normal, and there were no bruits. Radial pulses were normal.

The patient's mental status was not tested formally, but he was deemed by observation to have a normal general mental status and to be an accurate historian. Visual fields were full to moving objects, and the fundi showed no abnormalities. The pupils were 3 mm, round, regular, equal, and reactive to light and accommodation. Extraocular movements were full, with no nystagmus. There was good up-gaze and good down-gaze. Facial sensations were intact, and facial musculature was symmetrical. His speech was normal by observation. The palate elevated symmetrically. The tongue protruded in the midline and moved normally. An upper dental plate was present, and only the front teeth were present on the lower.

There was normal stance but a somewhat wide-based gait. There was no tremor present. He displayed a slight head tilt with somewhat limited neck mobility secondary to cervical fusion performed about 10 years previously and which produced relief from neck pain. Finger–nose–finger testing was normal but heel-to-shin testing was abnormal and difficult for the patient to control. There was good strength throughout with normal bulk. There was normal resistance to passive manipulation. He was able to walk on his toes and on his heels and but his tandem gait was abnormal and he was unsteady throughout this maneuver. His Romberg test was normal; he could stand on either leg without falling over and could hop on either leg. Muscle bulk was full throughout, with no fasciculations or atrophy. He had decreased vibration sensation though the stimulus could be perceived at the big toe bilaterally. Vibration sense was better at the ankles than at the toes, bilaterally. Pin prick sensation was decreased at the toes but intact at the ankles and did not change above that level on both legs. Cold sensation was intact throughout. Joint position sense was intact. There did not appear to be any significant optic atrophy. Deep tendon reflexes were 2+ in the upper extremities, 2+ at the knees, and 1+ at the ankles. No pathological reflexes were present.

With regard to family history, the patient's mother died at age 54 years of suffocation from ingestion of a portion of food that was caught in her trachea. His father died at age 59 years with colon cancer. Both parents were alcoholic. He has three brothers and two sisters. One sister has ovarian carcinoma. The others are in good health. None of his siblings are alcoholic.

INITIAL CLINICAL DIAGNOSIS

The diagnosis on referral was possible mild memory impairment and possible *mild peripheral neuropathy*. A neuropsychological assessment was requested to help in characterizing his suspected memory impairment. No other working diagnoses were being entertained at that time based upon physical examination and available laboratory studies.

VERIFICATION OF INITIAL CLINICAL DIAGNOSIS

The diagnosis of memory impairment made initially was based primarily on subjective symptoms, with no objective test or other examination findings to substantiate the working diagnosis. Alcohol and other substance-induced disorders of the peripheral nervous system, including peripheral neuropathy, were presented in volume II of the present book (see volume II, pages 455ff and Table 11.1, page 433). Therefore, the diagnosis of *peripheral neuropathy* in the current case presentation will not be discussed, except as this might become relevant to concerns regarding the patient's possible memory impairment. Discussion regarding a revised diagnosis and its verification is presented later in this section.

ADDITIONAL INFORMATION

Laboratory test and imaging results. The patient's laboratory tests of blood and urine taken 1 week before the current examination proved to be essentially within normal limits. In particular AST (aspartate aminotransferase), ALT (alanine aminotransferase), and their ratio were not suggestive of alcohol-induced liver disease or damage. In conjunction with the patient's fall 9 months previously (he tripped and fell out of a barn loft), he apparently had a noncontrast CT scan which showed no focal abnormality, but mild brain volume loss for age and with slightly larger ventricular size than was expected for age. There were no focal features or asymmetry noted in the CT study. The patient's military record showed that he served in job capacities and on naval vessels where no systematic exposure to toxic substances was likely. He saw no combat duty.

Findings from neuropsychological examination. Neuropsychological examination was conducted to evaluate the patient's memory complaint and his current cognitive, perceptual, and psychomotor status more generally. Measures of validity and completeness of effort were satisfactory. Neuropsychological testing revealed a normal full scale IQ (102) with no evidence of significant disparities in his intellectual abilities. He demonstrated normal everyday academic skills in reading, spelling, and arithmetic; all at lower high school grade levels. There was no evidence now for learning difficulties or problems that may have affected his academic development. On aphasia screening, he made two errors in repetition reflecting mild dysarthria. His verbal fluency performance was mildly impaired, but his categorical fluency was normal. He demonstrated mild bilateral impairment on finger agnosia and dysgraphesthesia testing, worse on the dominant right hand. He performed with normal limits on tests of strength, alternating movements, and fine coordination in the hands. He performed just within normal limits on a problem-solving task requiring use of touch alone. His performance on tests of memory function was borderline for immediate memory, but impaired on delayed recall for both verbal and nonverbal stimuli (worse for verbal material). His performance on simple perceptual-motor tasks was within normal limits, but more complex tasks requiring "multitasking" or shifting attention between things proved very difficult for the patient. Tests of concept formation, abstraction, and ability to shift between organizing principles were impaired. It appears that he had a mild degree of impairment in executive functions, with specific difficulties in concept formation and the ability to shift between organizing principles. For example, in the Halstead Category Test, he could use the concept of the number of objects being displayed to get a correct answer, but he showed no ability to use oddity or spatial position as ideas to guide his choices despite continuous feedback that he needed to use a new concept. He also completed testing for psychological adjustment and psychopathology and was within normal limits with no evidence of clinically significant anxiety, depression, mood, or thought disorder (see Table 16.9, which contains selected scores from the patient's neuropsychological examination).

Table 16.9 Selected neuropsychological performances for patient in the *clinical presentation*.

Test	Score	Normal reference value
Verbal IQ	108	100
Performance IQ	95	100
Full Scale IQ	102	100
Wide Range Reading	High school (10)	NA
Wide Range Spelling	High school (10)	NA
Wide Range Arithmetic	High school (9)	NA
Speech Perception errors	6	5
Rhythm Test errors	3	3
Tapping dominant	46	50
Tapping nondominant	42	46
Trail Making A	45 s	<30 s
Trail Making B	176 s	<90 s
Tactual Performance Test	14.9 min	<15.0 min
Category Test	108 errors	<75 errors
Wisconsin Cart Sorting Categories	3	6
Wechsler Logical Memory Immediate/Delay	6/1.5	NA
Wechsler Visual Reproduction Immediate/Delay	10/2.0	NA

Requests for all available laboratory and other test results were made and authorized by written patient consent. The patient, his primary care physician, and his family were briefed on the nature of the findings and neurological implications of further alcohol use. Considering the examination results in light of (a) the clinical history provided by the referring physician, (b) the self-report of the patient, and (c) the history and observations provided independently by the family; the patient was thought to have impairments in neurological and neurobehavioral functioning secondary to his chronic alcohol abuse. The length of time that the patient had been positively abstinent probably allowed for a clear evaluation of what deficits might be persisting in the absence of recent alcohol intoxication.

Discussion

Ethyl alcohol is made by fermentation or distillation, and it is present in alcoholic beverages in different concentrations by volume. The amount of alcohol ranges from 4% to 6% for beer, 8% to 14% for wine, and from 40% to 75% for distilled spirits such as whiskey, gin, vodka, or rum. Alcohol ingestion by volume can be converted from a quantity–frequency history to a reasonable estimate of grams of ethanol consumed within a particular time epoch by computing absolute pure ethanol volume to milliliters, and multiplying this datum by the specific gravity of ethanol (0.79). Thus, for a patient who indicates that they drink a "six pack" of beer every evening, the six 12 oz containers amount to 72 oz a day or 504 oz per week. At an alcohol content of 5%, the amount described would result in 25.2 oz of pure ethanol, or 756 ml. The final step of applying the specific gravity of 0.79 would result in an estimate of 597 g pure ethanol ingestion, substantially over the 500 g per week, which is associated with the highest level of health risk (Rehm et al., 2001).

Blood alcohol concentration (BAC) can increase significantly within 20 min of having an alcoholic beverage, and an average person can eliminate approximately 0.5 oz or 15 ml of alcohol per hour. While minor amounts of alcohol are eliminated through the kidneys and lungs (about 5% of the total volume for each of these organs), oxidation of alcohol occurs primarily in the liver. Acute effects of alcohol consumption include heightened mood, agitation or excitement, altered sensations and consciousness, confusion, stupor, and eventual coma or even death; all of which occur in a dose-dependent manner, in relation to increasing BAC (National Institute on Alcohol Abuse and Alcoholism, 2001). Chronic use of alcohol creates tolerance to increasing amounts of alcohol and also increases the effects of withdrawal in a balance that strongly implies neuroadaptive processes that are ongoing after acute alcohol use. Tolerance and actual sensitization to the effects of alcohol are characteristic of continuous use and relatively intermittent use of alcohol, respectively (Stewart & Badiani, 1993). Differing patterns of alcohol abuse involving frequency of use, length of alcohol abuse history, maximal amount of alcohol consumed per drinking occasion, nutritional health, and other substance abuse will affect mood, sleep, and cognitive functioning to various degrees.

Alcoholism as a medical disorder has its origins in physiological, genetic, and social realms (National Institute on Alcohol Abuse and Alcoholism, 2000). Earlier initial onset of drinking alcohol in conjunction with other risk factors, in social environment and for learning disorder, is associated with greater risk for alcohol dependence and a sustained abuse of alcohol (Zucker et al., 2000). Neurological and neuropsychological impairments are not predominant in alcoholic patients even in their 30s who have been detoxified after long abuse. Follow-up of severely alcoholic patients at one year after treatment shows that only 1 in 3 show persisting deficits and these occur almost uniformly in those patients who have relapsed (Adams, Grant, & Reed, 1980). However, after age 40, continued alcohol abuse—in conjunction with other risk factors for impairment such as birth or early development anomalies, learning disorder, head injury, and other illness—results in a greater probability of neuropsychological impairment which will persist even after detoxification (Adams & Grant, 1986). This scenario of emergent mild neurological and neuropsychological impairments in middle age is consistent with this clinical course and with available data on the epidemiology of drinking behavior and its consequences (cf, Office of Applied Statistics, Substance Abuse and Mental Health Services Administration, United States Department of Health and Human Services, http://www.samhsa.gov/). Accordingly, the timing of the exposure and onset of signs are appropriate here along with the risk.

A substantial number of studies have reported numerous adverse health effects associated with alcohol use. There is evidence, for instance, that long-term exposure to alcohol in sufficient amounts can become associated with (a) gradual onset of hepatitis, necrosis, and hardening in the liver (cirrhosis) (Lieber, 1998), (b) hypertension with associated cardiovascular risk (Stranges et al, 2004), (c) irritation of the esophagus and gastric membranes (Franke, Teyssen, & Singer, 2005), (d) pancreatitis (Lerch et al., 2003), (e) poor nutrition (National Institute on Alcohol Abuse and Alcoholism, 1993), (f) immune deficiency (Brown et al., 2006; Kovacs & Messingham, 2002), (g) reduction in brain volume with age (Harper & Matsumoto, 2005; Oscar-Berman & Marinkovic, 2003), (h) impairment in cognitive, perceptual, and motor functioning (Grant, Adams, & Reed, 1984), and (i) bruises, broken bones, and other injuries associated with falls and accidents (Cawthon et al., 2006). Of course, even acute exposure to alcohol can lead to any number of adverse consequences for the individual (e.g., injuries from improper use of motor vehicles or other machines, acute injuries from falls, potential adverse consequences of risky sexual practices, and poor decision making in general).

The diagnosis of alcohol-induced neuropsychological impairment in the present case is based upon the neurotoxcity of prolonged alcohol abuse, which in the central nervous system is held to be due to the interaction between glutamate, an amino acid that is the major excitatory neurotransmitter in the brain, and a specific glutamate receptor, the N-methyl-D-aspartate (NMDA) receptor. The NMDA receptor is rendered supersensitive to glutamate stimulation during alcohol exposure and becomes an excitotoxic agent in the NMDA killing of neurons. While this mechanism is still controversial and not specific to alcoholism, a second pathway to neurotoxicity from alcohol is thought to lie in oxidative stress (National Institute on Alcohol Abuse and Alcoholism, 2000). It should be noted that oxidative stress is also broadly implicated in carcinogenesis (Upham & Wagner, 2001). Extreme occurrences of these neurotoxic events, in conjunction with nutritional (thiamine) deficiency, probably account for the most severe Wernicke–Korsakoff syndrome cases that are not at all frequent in clinical practice, but quite dramatic (Victor, Adams, & Collins, 1971).

Nutritional practices involving binge drinking, as was present in this case, place patients at greater risk for the more severe manifestations of alcohol-induced neurological and neuropsychological impairment than might otherwise be the case (Martin, Singleton, & Hiller-Sturmhöfel, 2003; National Institute on Alcohol Abuse and Alcoholism, 2003). Nutritional disorders such as dry beriberi seen in southeastern Asia where diets are limited to white rice can reproduce the thiamine deficiency symptoms seen in advanced cases of alcohol dependence including cognitive dysfunction, peripheral sensory loss/tingling, nystagmus, and gait difficulties. These symptoms in dry beriberi can be very rapidly treated and reversed by nutritional intervention with thiamine. The role of thiamine in the emergence of neurological and neuropsychological impairments from alcohol has been carefully investigated (Martin et al., 2003). People differ in their susceptibility to thiamine deficiency, and there is established evidence of differential thiamine deficiency sensitivity of certain brain regions, such as the cerebellar vermis (Baker, Harding, Halliday, Kruill, & Harper, 1999). Still there remains a controversy not only about the primacy of thiamine deficiency in the structural brain changes observed in alcohol abuse cases but also in the role of thiamine deficiency in more profound dementia that is alcohol related (Oslin, Atkinson, Smith, & Hendrie, 1998).

Behaviors that result from the use or abuse of a substance such as alcohol also occur as a consequence of various medical conditions that are unrelated to exposure to alcohol. Even disorders that have been seen traditionally as having a strong association with alcohol use (e.g., *Wernicke's encephalopathy*) result from factors (e.g., metabolic or nutritional) that may or may not be influenced by exposure to alcohol (Gui, Zhao, & Wang, 2006; Reuler, Girard, & Cooney, 1985; Wilson, Kuncl, & Corse, 1958). Improvement in acute Wernicke's encephalopathy often is followed by *Korsakoff's syndrome* and, although clinically distinct, the two are at times referred to as Wernicke–Korsakoff syndrome (Reed et al., 2003; Rowland, 1989). Dementia can accompany either Wernicke's encephalopathy or Korsakoff's syndrome, although pronounced amnestic disturbance is more likely in the latter; while disorientation, indifference, and inattentiveness characterize Wernicke's encephalopathy. Because of the importance of these clinical diagnoses to the differential diagnosis in dementia, they both are discussed as well in the section on *dementia* in chapter 17 of the present volume.

Concluding, in the given case, that alcohol has caused dementia (or other cognitive disorder or other disorders that involve the nervous system) should be approached cautiously and with the objective evidence needed to exclude what may be a multitude of potentially competing explanations. For instance, many conditions (e.g., congenital defects such as cystic fibrosis, malabsorption syndromes such as short-bowel syndrome, adverse effects of medicines or drug interactions, and consequences of other treatments such as bariatric surgery) lead to nutritional deficiencies, which, in turn, can produce neurological disorders (Goldman & Bennett, 2000; Koffman, Greenfield, Ali, & Pirzada, 2006; Rowland, 1989; So & Simon, 1996). Severe dietary restriction as result of starvation, although reduced in much of the modern world, produces deficient nutrition with adverse neurological consequence as a result as well as persisting neuropsychological impairment, which has been documented in cases where prisoners of war, e.g., have been extensively malnourished (Sulway et al., 1996; Sutker, Vasterling, Brailey, & Allain, 1995). So and Simon (1996) reviewed the neurological consequences of deficient nutrition due to inadequate diet. Some of these include *Beriberi* and *Wernicke–Korsakoff syndrome* resulting from thiamine deficiency; encephalopathy and seizures from pyridoxine deficiency, peripheral neuropathy and dementia from folate deficiency, and *cretinism* from iodine deficiency (Table 16.10).

Alcoholism itself can lead to deficient nutrition, with reduced thiamine and other essential nutrients. While alcohol is known to directly inhibit gastric emptying and absorption of nutrients in the intestine (Goetz, 1985; So &

Table 16.10 Nutritional deficiencies that occur often as a consequence of, or coincident to, alcoholism and their potential adverse clinical affects on central nervous system mediated functions.

Nutrient	Potential adverse effects
Folate	Cognitive impairments and dementia, myelin degeneration, mental retardation
Iodine	Cretinism, mental retardation
Nicotinic acid	Pellagra, dementia, encephalopathy
Pyridoxine	Seizures, encephalopathy
Thiamine	Beriberi, Wernicke–Korsakoff syndrome, dementia, optic neuropathy
Vitamin B_{12}	Systemic degeneration, dementia
Vitamin D	Myelin degeneration
Vitamin E	Myelin degeneration

Simon, 1996), lifestyle characteristics associated with alcoholism may be the most important factor contributing to general malnutrition in the alcoholic. Aside from Wernicke–Korsakoff syndrome, other nutritional-related neurological disorders can accompany alcoholism, including *Marchiafava–Bignami disease* (MBD). While the exact cause of MBD is unknown, it has been associated with nutritional deficiencies and probable hereditary factors (patients of Italian descent appear to be at higher risk than others for the disease), but a direct toxic (alcohol) etiology has not been excluded (So & Simon, 1996). Since many patients with MBD present with coma or other signs of advanced disease, information regarding the neurobehavioral symptoms that manifest in earlier stages of the disease remains incomplete. On the other hand, patients with relatively less severe MBD have been observed. Such patients have been described as manifesting symptoms and signs of frontal lobe dementia, at times with sucking, grasping, and other atavistic reflexes. To the extent known, behavioral findings included slowed mental processing, changes in personality, dysarthria, incontinence, seizures, and impaired motor function (So & Simon, 1996). While the patients with milder symptoms and signs might represent individuals at an earlier point in the disease course, some investigators hold that there may be more than one type of MBD, with one type evidencing less neurological involvement and a better outcome than the other (Heinrich, Runge, & Khaw, 2004; Menegon, Sibon, Pachai, Orgogozo, & Dousset, 2005).

Abnormalities have been reported in MBD for behaviors associated with frontal regions and the corpus callosum (e.g., interhemispheric disconnection) (Heinrich et al., 2004; Sair et al., 2006). MRI and related imaging techniques have clarified the neuroanatomical regions affected in MBD, and imaging technology has proven to be important to the diagnosis and scientific study of MBD (Heinrich et al.). These studies have shown MBD to be accompanied by pathophysiology that includes abnormal signal intensities throughout the corpus callosum (Nardone et al., 2006); demyelination, necrosis, and disruption of axonal fiber bundles in the corpus callosum; and symmetrical involvement of white matter tracks beyond the corpus callosum (So & Simon, 1996). There is evidence of reversibility of both symptoms and abnormal neuroradiological findings, one in tandem with the other, following successful treatment interventions (e.g., nutritional supplements and high-dose corticosteroids) (Hlaihel et al., 2005; Nardone et al., 2006).

While MBD is a rare disorder, the findings regarding white matter lesions in MBD and its potential relationship to nutritional factors are important theoretically because white matter disease and disruptions in behaviors associated with frontal, interhemispheric connection, and cortical–subcortical connection regions in the brain are reported for a number of toxicants, in addition to alcohol (Ersche et al., 2005; Filley, 2001; Filley, Halliday, & Kleinschmidt-DeMasters, 2004). (Also, see relevant sections for related discussion, e.g., sections on *solvents* in chapter 15, *toluene* in chapter 16.)

With regard to alcoholism specifically, abnormalities in frontal regions of the cerebral cortex are a prominent finding, with or without cerebellar degeneration (Chen et al., 2007; Ende et al., 2006; Gilman et al., 1990) (Figure 16.1), and often such findings are associated with corresponding behavioral abnormalities (e.g., disinhibition) (Chen et al.). Other neuropsychological dysfunction has been associated with white matter damage in alcoholism, especially in frontal brain regions, and includes executive dysfunction, attention, and working memory (Filley, 2001). Some investigators have reported finding atrophy of the corpus callosum, as demonstrated on MRI in alcoholics with no known nutritional disorder or overt dementia. For instance, in one cross-sectional and correlational study using MRI and diffusion tensor imaging (DTI) to examine alcoholic men and women, Pfefferbaum, Adalsteinsson, and Sullivan (2006) reported finding "shrinkage" of the corpus callosum in relation to a history of alcohol use that was most pronounced in the genu and body and less evident in the splenium. They reported that correlational analyses of their data showed an interaction between alcohol and age, with the older subjects having a smaller genu and splenium than did younger subjects. Also, they reported finding significant correlations between their imaging findings and various performance measures (e.g., working memory, visual–spatial ability, and gait). However, evidence for involvement of frontal brain regions (as well as structures of the corpus callosum) is not specific for alcohol and has been reported to occur in association with a number of conditions that include psychiatric disorders, as well as aging itself (Avants, Grossman, & Gee, 2005; Boxer & Miller, 2005; Filley, 2000, 2001; Sullivan & Pfefferbaum, 2003). It has been shown in some preliminary data, however, that those alcoholic patients with Korsakoff's amnestic syndrome are more likely to show greater abnormalities of frontal system functioning than non-Korsakoff alcoholic patients of similar severity (Oscar-Berman, Kirkley, Gansler, & Couture, 2004). These rather focal functional deficits match quite closely with what is found in carefully documented postmortem neuropathological studies on large numbers of

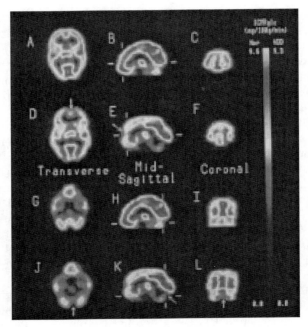

Figure 16.1 PET scan measured with [18]FDG and comparing cerebral glucose utilization between a 46-year-old alcoholic male with diagnosed cerebellar degeneration and a normal 57-year-old control.
From "Cerebellar and Frontal Hypometabolism in Alcoholic Cerebellar Degeneration Studied with Positron Emission Tomography," by S. Gilman, K. Adams, R. A. Koeppe, S. Berent, K. J. Kluin, J. G. Modell, et al., 1990, *Annals of Neurology, 28,* 775. With permission.
The scan shows hypometabolism in medial frontal regions of the cerebral cortex and in anterior superior cerebellar vermis (arrows).

patients with Wernicke's encephalopathy who expire in urban areas (Harper, Dixon, Sheedy, & Garrick, 2003).

As discussed earlier, nutritional variables can have profound implications in the development of pathology, and it is well known that poor nutrition accompanies alcoholism and substance abuse more generally. Also, it is well known that "real-life" exposures to various substances, including alcohol, rarely occur in isolation, polysubstance abuse being more the rule than the exception. Alcohol abuse, in addition, can adversely affect the nervous system indirectly by damage to a number of organ systems, e.g., hepatic encephalopathy. There is some evidence that alcohol may disrupt normal GABA-ergic function in the central nervous system, but again such alterations are not specific to alcohol (Olsen & DeLorey, 1999). In short, a specific mechanism of alcohol neurotoxicity remains incompletely understood. As a result, determining the exact substance-exposure variable or variables that lead to pathology due to a single substance such as alcohol will continue to be a challenge to the clinician.

NERVOUS SYSTEM LOCALIZATION

Leaving out the previously diagnosed peripheral nervous system disorder, the symptoms, signs, and test findings associated with the current *case presentation* implicate involvement of the medial temporal lobe (periventicular nuclei) and the frontal cingulate regions of the central nervous system. Short-term memory impairment has been shown in clinical case studies to be associated with neuropathology in temporal regions of the brain, regions that are anatomically adjacent to the ventricular system (Torvik, Lindboe, & Rodge, 1982). Impairment in the anterior superior cingulate area of the frontal lobe has been shown to relate actual neuropsychological test performance to selectively reduced metabolism in patients with known cerebellar degeneration and, similarly, specific reduction in metabolic activity (Gilman et al., 1990).

FINAL CLINICAL NEUROBEHAVIORAL DIAGNOSIS

The neurobehavioral diagnosis, based upon the *DSM-IV*-TR nosology (American Psychiatric Association, 2000), was substance-induced persisting dementia disorder due to alcohol. The cognitive deficits (memory, language, executive function) observed in the neuropsychological testing were clearly established in a reliable and valid fashion. The diagnostic practice of the *DSM* is to link a suspected cause to a particular set of findings and presentation, although additional external sources of evidence are needed in almost all cases to establish causality. In other words, the presumptive link between the neurobehavioral impairments in the present *case presentation* and the etiology for these impairments will need further explication.

Comment

The present volumes have emphasized consistently the need to arrive independently at clinical diagnosis and cause. As is the case here, some formal, but at times personal preference-based, diagnostic systems incorporate cause into the nomenclature of a clinical diagnosis, e.g., *toxicant-induced encephalopathy*. The *DSM* (American Psychiatric Association, 1994, 2000), for instance, classifies most disorders associated with exposure to a chemical or other substance under the category, termed, "substance-related disorders." This category includes toxicant exposure as well as adverse effects from medication. Also included are disorders that result from drug use or abuse, including alcohol. The *DSM* divides substances in this category into classes based on some common feature such as drug type (e.g., alcohol versus amphetamine), some other commonality within a particular class such as intended use (e.g., a medication versus a pesticide), some elemental characteristic (e.g., metal versus gas), or with consideration to the exposed person's behavior (e.g., classifying a volatile substance as an "inhalant" when used for purposes of intoxication versus a "toxin" when the exposure is accidental). In descriptive or public health applications, substances of abuse are also organized around broad descriptions of drug effects (e.g., stimulants versus hallucinogens) or particular drug sources (e.g., opiates), which have additional forensic context.

The *DSM* divides substance-related disorders into two groups. These include substance-use disorders (e.g., dependence) and substance-abuse disorders associated with intoxication and withdrawal; and which include the various abnormalities that can result from exposure to a given substance (e.g., delirium, amnestic disorder, dementia, disturbed mood [e.g., depression], or thought disorder [i.e., psychosis]). Even though the *DSM* organizes various substances in classes and groups, there is considerable overlap across substances in terms of their behavioral effects and accompanying substance-use or -abuse characteristics. Alcohol, for instance, shares many features in common with other substances discussed in the present book, e.g., hypnotics and sedatives, opioids, various solvents like toluene, and some psychotropic medications such as anxiolytics.

Regardless of the nosological characteristics of a given diagnostic system, the clinical condition and its cause should be arrived at objectively and independently. Once verified separately, the two can be formally joined diagnostically, e.g., substance-induced persisting dementia disorder due to alcohol. Until then, the designation might best be viewed as a yet to be verified proposition.

VERIFICATION OF FINAL CLINICAL NEUROBEHAVIORAL DIAGNOSIS

The final diagnosis (substance-induced persisting dementia) best explains the clinical findings in the *case presentation* and meets objective criteria for verification. The patient's physical symptoms and persisting consumption of alcohol over most of his adult life—particularly in the face of failed attempts to cease drinking and social and behavioral consequences—place this case firmly in the realm of abuse. The historical course and clinical course presented in this case are classic instances of a lifelong pattern of continued and extensive consumption of alcohol that has now produced the dementia documented in the formal neuropsychological testing, even when the patient had been abstinent from alcohol for some 6 weeks prior to the assessment.

This formulation of diagnosis fits the pattern of illness expected, in that it develops slowly and manifests itself in middle age when there is a long, documented history of excessive alcohol consumption with increasing consequences in behavior and physical health. The diagnosis explains virtually all of the most important clinical data with respect to cognitive/behavioral functioning and deficits, physical and neuroimaging findings, and the consequences to health usually observed at this stage in the disease. The diagnosis is coherent in the sense that it is consistent with our current knowledge regarding the pathophysiology that underlies such disorder, and the diagnosis represents the simplest and most probable explanation for the patient's complaints and findings from evaluation. There are no alternative diagnoses that better fit the patient's history, symptoms, clinical examination, and laboratory results. The diagnosis is robust and manifests from a number of independent evidential domains that are resistant to falsification or impression management. While alcoholic patients may under-report or even deny problems with alcohol abuse and dependence earlier in their careers, patients with disease severity that results in consequences of a public and undeniable nature such as accidents, arrests, and frank impairment in cognition can no longer manipulate or hide their disease. Usually, the forecast of future health for patients with severe and chronic alcoholism is unfortunately not an optimistic one (Beaglehole & Jackson, 1992; Rehm, Gmel, Sempos, & Trevision, 2003).

INITIAL CAUSE/ETIOLOGY

The cause for the patient's clinical diagnosis at referral was reported to be chronic alcohol abuse.

VERIFICATION OF INITIAL CAUSE/ETIOLOGY

While alcohol abuse might have been the causal factor in the patient's symptoms of memory impairment, the findings available at the time of referral were too sparse to allow for meaningful comparison to objective criteria for causal determination (see chapter 8, volume I of this book).

FINAL CAUSE/ETIOLOGY

The patient in the current *case presentation* has neurobehavioral impairment that is attributed to alcohol abuse.

VERIFICATION OF FINAL CAUSE/ETIOLOGY

The proposed cause–effect relationship between alcohol and neurological and neuropsychological impairment here is both biologically plausible, and certainly dose related. That is, the degree to which the cessation of alcoholic drinking ameliorates deficits is quite dependent on individual health factors involving age, physical condition, activity levels, and other health behaviors. Cessation of alcoholic drinking stops the progression of neurological and neuropsychological impairments, but the effect of cessation in the restorative sense is uncertain in the long term, although there are data suggesting continued improvement in neuropsychological functioning as much as 5 years following cessation of drinking (Grant, Reed, & Adams, 1987). Animal models of intoxication have been foundational in the study of chronic alcohol exposure and brain functioning (National Institute on Alcohol Abuse and Alcoholism, 1994). Most animal studies of alcoholism are aimed at understanding antecedents of drinking, maintenance of drinking behavior and its effects, and end-organ damage that occurs as a function of alcoholism. With respect to consistency of findings, there is a robust international generalizability of methods and findings with respect to the neurological and neuropsychological effects of alcohol. The International Society for Biomedical Research on

Alcoholism (ISBRA) includes a working section that sponsors research communications at the Society's biennial meetings. Findings in this area have been reproduced across geographic and ethnic boundaries.

Mild impairment in neuropsychological functioning can occur for a variety of reasons, both endogenous and exogenous. In the current *case presentation*, the patient has not been exposed to any extreme or toxic environmental or occupational situations, which could serve to explain his neurological and neuropsychological results. He did not recall any adverse exposure in the military such as due to repeated breathing solvent or jet/helicopter fuel (JP4/JP8) or exposure to nerve gases or other toxicants. He might be considered to be vulnerable to dementia, but his relatively young age and the absence of other diseases (e.g., cerebrovascular) that often are associated with diffuse white matter changes and seen in entities such as vascular dementia argue against such a formulation. Frank dementia due to alcohol abuse is usually emergent in the sixth or seventh decades of life and is often difficult to distinguish from more primary dementing illnesses. The current patient did not appear to have any indicators of significant cardiopulmonary or hepatic disease or dysfunction. The evidence for very mild peripheral neuropathy in his lower extremities in the absence of other indicators or causes of peripheral nerve disease argues for alcoholism as its proximal cause; although it is important to note that peripheral neuropathy alone is not causally specific.

Other potential causes for the patient's clinical examination findings were explored and excluded as being less likely than alcohol to explain the patient's symptoms. Alcoholic liver disease, for instance, has been associated with subacute hepatic encephalopathy (Collie, 2005; Ferenci et al., 2002), which would be consistent with the patient's presenting difficulties in cognitive function. While the patient has been in the care of a primary care physician alert to the possibility, it is also worth noting that changes in cognitive functioning are associated with prolonged type 2 diabetes mellitus (Biessels, ter Braak, Erkelens, & Hijman, 2001). This diagnostic entity would also serve to correlate with the findings of very mild peripheral neuropathy; although the likelihood of such neuropathy would be greatly increased in the presence of hypertension (Jarmuzewska, Ghidoni, & Mangoni, 2007). It is also possible that prolonged environmental or occupational exposures to toxic substances might have the effect of producing results such as these independent or additionally in relation to the alcohol consumption history. Other drug use—licit or illicit—could also be at work to produce the present findings in the absence of a candid and complete history. Polydrug abuse has long been known to be associated with subtle cognitive impairments, even in younger patients (Grant et al., 1978).

Mild neurological and neuropsychological impairment from chronic alcohol abuse represents the simplest explanation most consonant with the temporal course and longitudinal presentation of the patient's problems. These diagnostic and causal conclusions account for the most important clinical problems and issues identified in the *case presentation*. The patient's prognosis derives from this diagnosis and depends quite strongly on continued abstinence from alcohol and maintenance of positive health behaviors (e.g., cessation of tobacco use and improved nutrition). The patient appeared to cooperate fully with the clinical examinations. There was no evidence for lateralized impairment or focal neurological impairment, as might be associated with nonalcohol-related injury or disease. Although his observed executive functioning limitations and short-term memory impairment are selective in terms of functional neuroanatomical involvement, these are brain regions known to be particularly vulnerable to the damaging effects of alcohol exposures (Harper et al., 2003; Rourke & Løberg, 1996).

The additional information from the neuroimaging study (CT) done in conjunction with the patient's fall at work 9 months earlier provided information that is consistent with a "premature aging" model of how chronic alcohol intoxication affects the brain (Oscar-Berman & Marinkovic, 2003). Briefly, this model holds that chronic alcohol abuse accelerates the aging process of the brain; making deficits in cognition appear in a patient at a younger age than would have been the case without alcohol abuse. With respect to neuroimaging studies, the premature aging hypothesis would suggest that findings often seen in the brains of older patients (reduction in brain volume, cortical atrophy, and ventricular enlargement) similar to those found in the patient in the current *case presentation* would occur at an earlier age in alcohol abuse.

Comment and additional case presentation

The importance of interview and history is discussed in several places in these volumes (see, e.g., in volume I, especially chapters 4, 5, and 6; and *the importance of the patient history and interview* in chapter 19 of the present volume). Nowhere is this more important than in the area of substance abuse, wherein patients may be inaccurate historians for a variety of reasons (e.g., periods of altered consciousness, denial, or embarrassment regarding their actions) and significant others may be unaware of important aspects of the patient's abuse. The *case presentation* that follows illustrates some of these points as well as highlighting central nervous system effects associated with excessive exposure to ethyl alcohol, alone or in combination with vitamin deficiency states.

Case presentation[1,6]

A 36-year-old clinical psychologist had been hospitalized for evaluation of peripheral neuropathy. His complaints included burning pain and sensory loss in his hands and feet. He also described poor balance, a symptom attributed by his physicians to sensory loss. His symptoms and signs were those of a moderately severe sensory neuropathy or neuronopathy, and his evaluation focused on nutritional factors because the problems had developed in the context of substantial weight loss attributed to depressed mood and poor eating habits. Regardless, the differential diagnosis for this neuropathy was extensive (listed in Table 11.1, see chapter 11, volume II). Included were numerous conditions in which the weight loss was a secondary consideration (e.g., a paraneoplastic syndrome due to an occult malignancy independently producing neuropathy and weight loss). Ethyl alcohol was included among the potential causes of the sensory neuropathy, but he described himself as only a social drinker, occasionally enjoying a glass of wine or beer with dinner, a description supported by his wife and parents. In fact, his parents later indicated that they could not recall ever observing him to have more than a glass of beer or wine at a family gathering. His history also was noteworthy for intermittent depression and an anxiety disorder that included panic attacks. These were remote problems that seemed inactive at present, as he only demonstrated what appeared to be appropriate concern surrounding the uncertainty of his progressive neuropathy.

The laboratory evaluation identified few abnormalities, aside from a mild macrocytic anemia with an elevated platelet count and a low reticulocyte count and mild, nonspecific liver-function abnormalities, all of which could be explained by his poor nutrition. Numerous normal findings included evaluations of vitamin B_{12}, folate, vitamin E, pyridoxine, thyroid function, ANA, sedimentation rate, anti-DNA, rheumatoid factor, complement, SPEP, anti-Hu, anti-Yo, ENA, HIV and syphilis serology, and urine heavy metal evaluation. The paraneoplastic evaluation for an occult malignancy included imaging studies of the chest, abdomen, and pelvis. The only abnormality identified was evidence of a fatty liver on the abdominal CT study, a finding that was unexplained but felt not to warrant additional evaluation at that time. The mild anemia was treated with folate and vitamin B_{12}, and the reticulocyte count increased. The evaluation was considered complete, although unrewarding, and discharge to an outpatient physical rehabilitation facility for gait training and reconditioning was planned, along with follow-up in the neurology outpatient clinic.

That night prior to transfer, the nurses found the patient acutely disoriented and confused, although, in retrospect, other attendants said he had been acting "strangely" earlier in the day. On entering the room that evening, he attempted to get out of bed, insisting he had to attend a meeting. When questioned, he said his wife was waiting for him in their car. The resident who was called to evaluate the patient believed that the patient was responding to hallucinations and confabulating. During questioning, the patient repeatedly looked toward the door or the closet and asked "What did you say," although no one was there. The resident had not seen the patient previously, but the patient responded "of course" when asked if they knew each other. When challenged, he insisted he knew the resident and told the nurse that they worked together in the past in his clinical psychology practice. Neurological examination, which primarily had shown only peripheral nervous system abnormalities previously, now showed marked cognition and attention deficits. Expressive and receptive language functions were intact by clinical observation, with the exception of instances of abnormal content and periods of disorientation. But, he could neither explain why he was in the hospital nor was it clear that he knew he was in the hospital. He could not correctly identify the time of day, day of the week, month, or year. He did not hesitate to answers the questions, but he appeared unaware that most of his answers were incorrect. Nor did he appear concerned when corrected. He showed impaired short-term memory (0 of 3 items) and was markedly distracted and able to follow only the simplest, one-step commands. He could not perform serial subtractions due to inattention. Examination of the cranial nerves showed impaired eye movements (ophthalmoparesis) with continuous course nystagmus in all directions of gaze, a new finding since earlier in the day. He showed dramatic limb ataxia and could not walk unassisted, findings in excess of his previous ataxia and unsteadiness. Strength appeared unchanged and normal, as did the reflex examination, showing 2+ reflexes in the arms but absent reflexes in the legs. No pathologic reflexes were demonstrated.

DIFFERENTIAL DIAGNOSIS

The combination of signs was recognized as being consistent with Wernicke's encephalopathy (triad of dementia with or without confabulation, ophthalmoplegia, and ataxia).

ADDITIONAL INFORMATION

Thiamine, the established treatment of Wernicke syndrome, was administered 100 mg intravenously and continued daily during the hospitalization, although there is little consensus on the appropriate dosage and duration of treatment in this condition. Laboratory studies included a normal glucose level. The CSF was examined and found to be normal, aside from a slightly elevated total protein. That evening, MRI of the brain was obtained and that was normal. By morning, the neurological abnormalities remained unchanged. However, the ophthalmoparesis and nystagmus resolved over several days, and the patient's mental status steadily improved and returned to normal over several weeks.

The initial decision to defer evaluation of the fatty liver (as shown on the abdominal CT) was reconsidered, and a gastroenterologist specializing in diseases of the liver was consulted who recommended liver biopsy. The biopsy demonstrated hepatic fibrosis, micronodular regeneration, and fatty infiltration consistent with a pathological diagnosis of chronic cirrhosis, results strongly suggestive of alcohol toxicity. Despite this finding, the patient and his family expressed disbelief and maintained firm denial of excessive alcohol use. It was felt that it was unlikely that starvation–malnutrition could produce the biopsy abnormalities. The gastroenterologist also noted that impaired nutrition invariably accompanies Wernicke's encephalopathy in alcoholic patients.

Three months after discharge, the patient contacted one of his physicians and confessed to drinking up to a fifth of alcohol every 1–2 days after losing his job. He was increasingly embarrassed at his behavior and unable to tell anyone of this problem because everyone was supportive of his denial. He reported abstinence from alcohol following discharge from the hospital, eventually enrolled in an alcohol treatment program, and experienced no further episodes of confusion.

CLINICAL DIAGNOSIS

Acute (transient) Wernicke's encephalopathy, with systemic manifestations of chronic alcohol abuse, including hepatic cirrhosis.

Discussion

The combination of alcohol abuse and malnutrition is known to affect the nervous system at almost all levels. While the acute medical conditions associated with the patient's need for hospitalization in this additional *case presentation* could be diagnosed and treated, an accurate history proved to be necessary in order to fully identify, understand, and more effectively treat the factors underlying these conditions. The case not only underscores the importance of interview and history but also provides a basis for understanding both the potential for a patient to conceal clinically important details of their history as well as the reasons such concealment might occur.

NERVOUS SYSTEM LOCALIZATION

The acute onset of confusion, impaired attention, memory problems, impaired eye movements, and gait ataxia localized to the cerebrum and brain stem.

VERIFICATION OF THE CLINICAL DIAGNOSIS

The final diagnosis of acute (transient) Wernicke's encephalopathy, with systemic manifestations of chronic alcohol abuse, including hepatic cirrhosis satisfies all objective criteria to verify the clinical diagnosis (see appendix).

CAUSE/ETIOLOGY

This case illustrates the observation made at several points in the present book, that a specific cause for a problem is often not required in order to arrive at a correct clinical diagnosis and to effectively treat the patient's immediate medical problems. Information concerning exposure to a particular substance like alcohol, however, may be needed to establish causality in a given case. In the present instance, the lack of such information led to some initial diagnostic confusion. Also, the later addition of this information was critical in identifying psychosocial and other neurobehavioral factors needing specialized treatment as well as in unambiguously establishing the cause for the patient's condition—chronic and substantial alcohol abuse.

VERIFICATION OF CAUSE/ETIOLOGY

As discussed for instances of neuropathy in chapter 11 of volume II, it is likewise difficult to separate the effects of alcohol from nutritional factors in objectively establishing cause in cases involving the central nervous system.

The two factors, alcohol and nutrition, co-occur often (Charness, Simon, & Greenberg, 1989; Victor, Adams, & Collins, 1989) and when considered together in the present case, all objective criteria for verifying the combined causal attribution are met (see appendix).

Conclusion

Alcohol dependence and abuse is a significant public health problem in many countries. Early initiation of drinking and its prolonged and abusive continuance past midlife is associated in research findings consistently with dysfunction and disease in most of the body's major systems. However, the emergence of effects in any particular organ system in an individual is variable and a challenge for clinical medicine. The social–emotional context of alcoholism and its maintenance are important to understand, as are family history and relative risk for neuropsychological impairment that results from alcohol as well as other factors (e.g., genetic, nutritional, aging, and other interactive illnesses).

Chronic alcohol abuse affects the central nervous system across a continuum, ranging from mild and isolated memory effects, through more serious impairments in executive and perceptual-motor skills, to more profound and obvious psychomotor, intellectual, language, amnestic, communication, and other cognitive dysfunction that reflects cortical and subcortical regions of the central nervous system. Although the specific agent or mechanism remains incompletely understood there is increasing and convincing evidence that the primary adverse effects of alcohol use producing this spectrum are neurotoxic in nature. Patients with distinctive syndromes from chronic alcoholism (e.g., Wernicke–Korsakoff), with frank psychiatric features, and with focal neurological tissue necrosis are very often additionally associated with malnutrition, homelessness, and extreme levels of alcohol abuse. Resolving the differential diagnosis of the various adverse effects of alcoholism most often requires specific expertise in multiple areas (e.g., medical and nonmedical specialty areas) and available diagnostic resources.

Hypnotics and Sedatives

Stanley Berent

Hypnotics and sedatives are a loosely associated group of drugs that can be classified under prescription drugs or pharmaceuticals. But, also, they represent illicit street drugs, many times with a corresponding street name that differs from the prescription counterpart (Table 16.11). Barbiturates and benzodiazepines comprise two major types of hypnotics and sedatives, but other types of drugs are included as well. Whether hypnotics and sedatives are seen as medications or as agents of abuse seems to rest to an important degree on intent, that is, if its use is for therapy of a diagnosed medical or psychiatric condition versus for recreation. Some forms of these drugs (e.g., flunitrazepam)

Table 16.11 Selected hypnotics and sedative prescription drugs, showing commercial and street names.

Drug type	Commercial name(s)	Commercial, medical use(s)	Street name(s)	Street use(s)
Barbiturates	Amytal Nembutal Seconal Phenobarbital	Sedation Insomnia Antianxiety Anesthesia	Barbs Downers Reds Red birds Phennies Toolies Yellows Yellow jackets	Intoxication "downers"
Benzodiazepines	Ativan Halcion Librium Valium Xanax	Sedation Insomnia Antianxiety Anesthesia	Candy Downers Sleeping pills Tranks	Intoxication "downers"
Zolpiderm	Ambien	Insomnia Sedation	Sleeping pill	Intoxication

Flunitrazepam (benzodiazepine derivative)	Rohypnol	Restricted use in some parts of the world. Not approved for medical use in USA. Insomnia, severe. short acting anticonvulsant.	Forget-me pill Mexican valium R2 Roche Roofies Roofnol Rope Rophies	Has been used as "knock-out" drug for "date rape" robberies.
Ketamine	Ketalar	Short-acting analgesic, anesthesic.	Cat valium K Special K Vitamin K	"Downers" intoxication.
Some other sedatives and hyponotics	Methaqualone (Quaalude, Sopor) Placidyl Chloral hydrate (Noctec). mebromate	Hyponotics, anxiolytic, sedative, insomnia, (alcohol withdrawl)	Quaalude Ludes quad Quay "knock-out drops"	Euphoria Sexual stimulation Intoxication Date rape Robbery

Modified in part from NIDA Web site tabular and other information (*Information on Drugs of Abuse—Prescription Drug Abuse Chart*, by National Institute on Drug Abuse, 2005, Retrieved from http://www.drugabuse.gov/DrugPages/PrescripDrugsChart.html).

also have been used in the commission of criminal activities, e.g., to render someone unconscious for purposes of sexual assault or robbery. Such abuse has given rise to terms as "date-rape" and "date-rape drugs" (National Institute on Drug Abuse, 2005). Also referred to as "sedative-hypnotics" or "depressants," these substances include chemicals that are tranquilizing, sedating, anesthetizing, or produce other similar physical and psychological effects. Depending on dose, the same drug can be used for one or more of the purposes just listed. A characteristic of most hypnotics and sedatives is the capacity to exert inhibitory effects on neuronal systems of the central nervous system. As a result, they are sometimes referred to collectively as "CNS depressants" (National Institute on Drug Abuse, 2005).

Many drugs have the capacity to depress the central nervous system, and they may do so via different biochemical mechanisms (e.g., one drug activating an inhibitory receptor site while another deactivates an excitatory site). The fact that various drugs act in different ways to achieve a common end (e.g., neuronal inhibition) is important because polypharmacy is common. Drugs that are additive in their effects, that potentiate or synergize one another, that duplicate neuronal actions, or that are otherwise contraindicated for simultaneous use can easily be administered to the same person. While polypharmacy can reflect a purposeful therapeutic plan, it can occur inadvertently and, often, without the involvement of medical supervision. Polypharmacy can result also as a by-product of substance abuse. Prescription drug abuse has been described both as an emerging and an increasing trend in the United States, where one U.S. government survey concluded that about 20% of the U.S. population aged 12 years or older had at some time used prescription drugs for nonmedical reasons (Volkow, 2005). One can only speculate about the reasons for these increases, which could reflect a rise in prescribed medications as well as commercial advertising for specific drugs and the advent of online drug sales. Also, these situations might occur because of the availability of nonprescription drugs, the increasing ease of web-based pharmaceutical purchases, and the availability and abuse of drugs "on the street." A variety of "naturalistic" health aids and dietary supplements are easily obtained, as well, and many of these substances contain chemicals that duplicate those used in prescription medicines or that may otherwise reflect an element of toxicity (Leung & Foster, 2003; Taylor, 2005).

The potential for abuse for most sedatives is relatively low in comparison to other substances (e.g., opioids, stimulants, marijuana); nevertheless, drug tolerance and physiological dependence leading to habit and perhaps addiction can be observed with these drugs (Goldman & Bennett, 2000; Siegel, Agranoff, Albers, Fisher, & Uhler, 1999; The National Institute on Drug Abuse (NIDA), 2005). These facts have implications for substance abuse; however, it can also be a problem for those using these drugs for legitimate medical reasons. Such concerns are especially true not only for the very young or the elderly but also for those with chronic medical conditions who must use these drugs for prolonged periods. Among those with multiple medical conditions and taking a number of different medications, the possibility for adverse drug interactions is compounded.

The following case contains elements that occur in treatment situations involving hypnotics and sedatives.

Case presentation[7]

Stewart (2004) described a 78-year-old man with a diagnosis of generalized anxiety disorder (GAD). This patient's psychiatric condition was long standing, and he had been successfully treated with Diazepam for 30 years without any apparent drug-related incident. Six months before the present evaluation, he developed a fixed notion that his sister-in-law was masquerading as his wife, replacing his wife in the home, a type of delusion that is sometimes referred to generically as "delusional misidentification" (Feinberg & Roane, 2005) or more specifically as "Capgras syndrome" (Bourget & Whitehurst, 2004; Capgras & Rebaul-Lachoux, 1923). There was no change in the nature of his anxiety symptoms otherwise and detailed testing reflected no cognitive impairment. The need for hospitalization became apparent when his symptoms escalated to his trying to remove the wife from the home. His delusion was limited to this one subject and occurred only on physically seeing her. For instance, he recognized her as his wife and not an impersonator when he talked to her on the telephone. There were no hallucinations or other psychotic manifestations.

The patient's past medical history included "senile macular degeneration," laryngeal carcinoma (remote and with no indication of recurrence), essential hypertension, well-controlled hypothyroidism, and benign prostatic hypertrophy. There was no history of alcohol use. Current medications included diazepam (5 mg, bid), paroxetine (40 mg per day), levothyroxine, rabeprazole, ranitidine, and finasteride. A brain MRI was reported as unremarkable.

The hospital course included tapering and discontinuation of diazepam with replacement by risperidone (0.5 mg, qid). The patient's "Capgras" delusion resolved within 10 days, with complete and accurate recognition of his wife when she visited him in the hospital. At 18-month follow-up evaluation, the patient's anxiety was well controlled by resperidone, with no indication of delusions or dementia.

INITIAL CLINICAL DIAGNOSIS

The patient was described diagnostically as having delusions (Capgras syndrome), with pre-existing and controlled anxiety and in the absence of dementia, schizophrenia, or other severe psychiatric disorder (Stewart, 2004).

CAUSE/ETIOLOGY

The patient's delusional disorder was attributed to diazepam.

NERVOUS SYSTEM LOCALIZATION

The patient's cognitive (i.e., delusions) and emotional (i.e., anxiety) signs and symptoms implicated the supratentorial level of the central nervous system.

Discussion

Hypnotics and sedatives can lead to a number of behavioral symptoms. Some are seen as desirable, even the reason for their use (e.g., reducing pain or anxiety, as well as for sedation), while others are considered to be adverse (e.g., difficulties with concentration, memory, judgment, and other cognitive impairments; dizziness and incoordination; addiction; and depression) (National Institute on Drug Abuse, 2005). Drugs in this category depress the central nervous system. From a mechanistic viewpoint, drugs that cause central nervous system depression can do so in multiple ways. For instance, a substance can act as an agonist for inhibitory neuron receptor sites (e.g., $GABA_A$ receptor sites) or as an antagonist for excitatory sites (e.g., glutamate receptors). Like ethanol and some general anesthetics (e.g., halothane), barbiturates and benzodiazepines induce sedation via neuronal inhibition by activating $GABA_A$ receptors in central nervous system neurons (Gregus & Klaassen, 2003). Ketamine, in contrast, acts as a glutamatergic receptor antagonist, also achieving sedative and anesthetic results but by way of this alternative route to neuronal inhibition (Gregus & Klaassen, 2003).

There are a variety of inhibitory pathways in the central nervous system, with any number of substances that have the capacity to influence these pathways. Some, like ethanol, act as $GABA_A$ receptor agonists; while others like morphine and related substances, e.g., heroin, meperidone (opioids), activate selective opioid receptors (Gregus & Klaassen, 2003; Klaassen & Watkins, 2003). Yet other substances provide an inhibitory function by disrupting normal sodium (Na^+), calcium (Ca^+), or other ionic channels, or their related "pumps." Phenytoin, like tetrodotoxin, for the most part, achieves its "desired" neuronal inhibition and, in the case of phenytoin, anticonvulsant properties through antagonism of voltage-gated Na^+ channels (Gregus & Klaassen, 2003; Klaassen & Watkins, 2003). Bromide, which can replace Cl^- ions and activate Cl^- receptors, was once used as a sedative and anticonvulsant but was found to have severe side effects that included psychosis, tremor, ataxia, dysarthria, and other signs; often sufficiently severe to mimic Creutzfeldt–Jakob disease, differing only in reversibility (*bromism*) (Schaumburg & Spencer, 2000). Schaumburg and Spencer (2000) wrote that any agent is a potential neurotoxin if it possesses the capacity to regulate the release of presynaptic neurotransmitters, perturb the concentration or duration of the neurotransmitter in the synaptic gap, or act as agonist or antagonist on the postsynaptic receptor site. Many drugs classified as hypnotics and sedatives can at various times perform one or more of the functions just listed. The results of such toxicity can have far-reaching effects, including adverse effects on neurobehavioral functions (e.g., cognitive, emotional, motor, and psychiatric).

Since neuronal activation of glutamatergic receptors can lead to convulsions and neuronal injury—excitotoxicity—some antagonists such as ketamine and some other general anesthetics are believed to protect against excitotoxicity (Gregus & Klaassen, 2003; Klaassen & Watkins, 2003). As a result some investigators have looked to central nervous system depressant drugs, such as the barbiturates, e.g., to protect neurons against the excitotoxic ischemic injury that occur in stroke or other acute injury (Kawaguchi, Furuya, & Patel, 2005). Benzodiazepine, also, can adversely affect the central nervous system. A dose-dependent relationship exists between benzodiazepine use and declines in mental status, memory, and psychomotor test scores (Bush & Martin, 2005; Gonzales, Mustelier, & Rey, 2005; Greenblatt et al., 1991). Long-term use of benzodiazepines can result in reversible cognitive decline (Barker, Greenwood, Jackson, & Crowe, 2004a, 2004b; Foy et al., 1995). And, the elderly exhibit special vulnerabilities to these medicaitons not only because of the greater likelihood for long-term use but also because of age-related changes in physiology that, in turn, adversely influence absorption, metabolism, and elimination (Bush & Martin, 2005; Johnson-Green & Inscore, 2005). The presence of polypharmacy complicates the relationships between aging and potential adverse drug reactions even further.

The patient in the *case presentation* used diazepam for 30 years without incident of adverse reaction. Why now? While there was apparently no change in the patient's clinical symptoms or treatment, what had changed was his age. Along with advancing age went a host of physiological changes that impacted his responses to pharmaceutical treatment (Bush & Martin, 2005). The benzodiazepines, in general, have been associated with many adverse reactions in the elderly, including heightened risks for injuries from falls and other accidents (Johnson-Green & Inscore, 2005). More specific to the present case, the benzodiazepines have been associated with heightened risk for delirium, as have other substances that are generally seen as belonging to the group of sedatives and hypnotics. This includes some medications that are classed as "atypical antipsychotics" or even anticonvulsants (Francis & Kapoor, 1990; Francis, Martin, & Kapoor, 1990; Johnson-Green & Inscore, 2005; Lim, Trevino, & Tampi, 2006; Santana, Wahlund, Varli, Tadeu, & Eriksdotter, 2005). Aspects of cognitive function other than delirium have been shown to be adversely affected, at least in the short term, by benzodiazepines as well (Nakazono et al., 2005). As to the question of a more pervasive picture of cognitive impairment following long-term benzodiazepine, the issue appears to be unresolved. Verdoux, Lagnaoui, and Begaud (2005) reviewed prospective epidemiological population based studies and found substantial differences between published findings. Seven papers met their fairly stringent criteria for review. Of these, two reported a lower risk of cognitive decline, two found no association between use and cognitive decline, and three found an increased risk of cognitive decline in benzodiazepine users. Verdoux et al. (2005) concluded that methodological differences between the various studies most likely explained the discrepant findings and called for further and more carefully designed research on this question. A continuing challenge for studies of hypnotic-sedative adverse effects in neurobehavioral functioning in the elderly will be the changes that occur with aging independent of any known drug contributions.

VERIFICATION OF THE INITIAL CLINICAL DIAGNOSIS

While the patient described in the *case presentation* carried a number of diagnoses, appropriately listed by the author in the published case report (Stewart, 2004), the published description left it clear that onset, persistence, and escalating severity of delusional symptoms were the reasons for hospitalization in this specific instance. The delusional behavior was referred to as "Capgras syndrome," a relatively fixed idea that someone has taken over the identity of a person known to the patient, invading this person, and misrepresenting their true identity. This is not a wrong diagnosis; however, it could be argued that it is not complete either. For instance, "Capgras" may describe the type or content of a delusion, but the more basic diagnosis would focus on the delusional behavior itself, provided that all clinical criteria for this disorder are met.

REVISED CLINICAL DIAGNOSIS

It is likely that the formal psychiatric diagnosis would be psychotic disorder due to adverse reaction to a medication (believed to be diazepam), with delusions (American Psychiatric Association, 1994).

VERIFICATION OF REVISED CLINICAL DIAGNOSIS

DSM-IV (American Psychiatric Association, 1994) does not index the term, "Capgras." Delusions of various types are relatively common in the elderly, sometimes as a result of misinterpretation of sensory input but also because of age- or illness-related changes in physiology. The content of delusions can be esoteric, but many appear to reflect themes that are reported regularly by different individuals. Some delusional themes are fairly common (e.g., the paranoid delusion that a secret government agency has been monitoring the patient's activities). *Delusory parasitosis*, to give another example, is the belief that small bugs have invaded some part of the patient's body (e.g., rectum, vagina, under the skin). The patient with this delusion is usually female, elderly, and can present with skin lesions from excoriation (Schlossberg, 2000). Somatic disease, including true parasitosis, is excluded clinically, and the patient is then evaluated psychiatrically (Schlossberg, 2000).

Delusional disorder is a diagnosable type of psychotic disorder (American Psychiatric Association, 1994). The type of delusional disorder can be specified according to the delusional theme, e.g., grandiosity, persecutory, or as in the current *case presentation*, misidentification of another individual (i.e., Capgras syndrome). Using the *DSM* approach to diagnosis, however, it is likely that the type of delusion would be described as persecutory, based on the patient's escalating aggression toward moving the misidentified wife from the home, that is, responding to her as if she were a threat. Importantly in the present case, the diagnosis of delusional disorder requires exclusion of competing explanations for the delusional behavior. One of these exclusions is that the behavior is not due to the direct physiological effects of a substance (e.g., medication) or general medical condition. Since it was concluded in this instance that the observed delusional symptoms were due to medication the patient was taking, the correct diagnosis would specify that the delusional behavior was substance induced.

The revised diagnosis, psychotic disorder due to adverse reaction to a medication (believed to be diazepam), with delusions, accounts for these additional considerations and meets objective criteria for verification of a clinical diagnosis (Richardson et al., 2000).

VERIFICATION OF CAUSE/ETIOLOGY

The author of the *case presentation* was appropriately cautious in attributing the patient's delusional disorder to diazepam (Stewart, 2004). He described the situation as one in which the patient "seemed to develop Capgras syndrome as an adverse reaction to diazepam." Later, he pointed out that the patient's rapid and continuing resolution of his delusions also was suggestive of a causal relationship between the medication and the delusional behavior. At the same time, however, he expressed his disappointment in not being able to rechallenge the patient with diazepam or to take other actions in order to confirm the causal relationship.

There is no doubt that several factors that were present in this case compete to explain the patient's diagnosis. For example, other medications the patient was taking could arguably produce adverse reactions that include psychotic-like behaviors. Ranitidine (Zantac), e.g., is an H_2 blocker that has on occasion been associated with confusion and other psychiatric symptoms (Epocrates, 2006; Fennelly, Earnshaw, & Soni, 1987; Mandal, 1986; Picotte-Prillmayer, DiMaggio, & Baile, 1995). In terms of drug interactions, both paroxetine and levothyroxine carry cautions regarding their use with central nervous system depressants. On the other hand, the patient's delusional behavior ceased following discontinuation of his diazepam, despite the continuation of these other drugs. While this does not rule out the possibility of adverse reaction due to drug interaction, the patient's diazepam was replaced with risperidone, another medicine with cautions similar to diazepam (Epocrates, 2006). The patient's long-standing psychiatric condition itself, GAD, could manifest in delusional behavior theoretically on its own. Several things argue against this, including the fact that such behavior had not been observed previously in this patient, is not an expected symptom of GAD, and the cessation of his delusions was timed to discontinuation of his medication. Of course, the patient also had been on diazepam for many years and without incident. As there had been no change in his dosage, there is no evidence for a dose–response relationship related to the onset of his psychiatric symptoms. The patient was getting older, however, leaving it possible that age-related changes in metabolism or other physiology relevant to drug absorption were effectively altering the dose impact if not the actual amount of drug received. The proposed relationship between drug and symptoms is biologically plausible, and the cessation of symptoms following drug removal remains perhaps the strongest evidence for a causal relationship. The patient's pre-existing illnesses, e.g., hypothyroidism, were appropriately included in the differential diagnosis and were found not to be contributory to the patient's psychiatric symptoms (Stewart, 2004). While some doubt about the causal conclusion might remain in this particular case, most objective criteria for establishing causality appear to be met (Hill, 1965).

Conclusion

It should be readily apparent that it is difficult to assign hypnotics and sedatives to one drug category. While barbiturates and benzodiazepines may be most associated with what we think of as hypnotics and sedatives, the foregoing presentation should leave it readily apparent that the situation is actually much more complex. It appears that one cannot define hypnotics and sedatives on the basis of a specific class of drugs, e.g., benzodiazepines. Rather, the classification derives from the effect of a given substance on the central nervous system. Hypnotics and sedatives, then, would include those substances that depress the central nervous system, through neuronal inhibition or some other mechanism of action. Viewed in this way, a specific drug can be seen as a sedative or hypnotic, but it might fall on some other occasion into another class as well.

This topic not only sensitizes us to the challenges of classification but also highlights other as yet to be resolved issues in neurobehavioral toxicology. These include topics of polypharmacy (with prescription and with OTC drugs), when a substance is viewed as therapeutic versus a substance of abuse, the influences of aging and other demographic variables on drug reactions, and the long-known fact that it is the dose that makes the poison. One might add the observation that any and all of the factors just listed might interact (synergistically or otherwise) to create a situation that is totally different from that associated with any one of these factors alone. An accurate clinical conclusion in cases when hypnotics and sedatives are causally suspected, therefore, will depend on the adequacy of the differential diagnosis.

Lithium

Stanley Berent

The metallic, lithium (Li), exists naturally in the environment, its 1817 discovery in the mineral, petalite, credited to Johan August Arfredson (Web-Elements, 2006). Derived from the Greek word for stone, *lithos*, lithium occurs naturally in trace amounts in animals and plants but has no known biological role. At the same time, lithium does affect the organism and, if ingested, this substance can impact kidney and other organ systems, including the nervous system. The central nervous system is included especially, with lithium having potential adverse affects on supratentorial functions like learning, memory, and problem solving as well as mood (Bartha, Marksteiner, Bauer, & Benke, 2002; Ilagan, Carlson, & Madden, 2002; Klaassen & Watkins, 2003;

Pachet & Wisniewski, 2003). Except in the form of lithium hydride, which can burn the skin, lithium is not considered hazardous particularly from an industrial viewpoint and has a number of industrial applications. To give some examples, lithium has been used as an alloy in aircraft and ball bearings, chemical reagent, catalyst, a glass strengthener, as a lubricant, and in the manufacturing of ceramics, batteries, and electronic tubes (Klaassen & Watkins, 2003; WebElements, 2006).

In addition to its industrial applications, lithium has been used to treat a variety of medical and psychiatric illnesses (Ilagan et al., 2002; Klaassen & Watkins, 2003; Vestergaard & Licht, 2001). While it is used at times in the treatment of acute mania or schizoaffective disorder, the primary psychiatric application of lithium is in the treatment of bipolar disorder, including, especially, the prevention of recurrent manic episodes (American Psychiatric Association, 1994; Goldman & Bennett, 2000; WebElements, 2006). The lithium-based compound, lithium carbonate (Li_2Co_3) is commonly used in medications to treat psychiatric conditions and marketed generically as lithium and under brand names such as Eskalith and Lithobid (Epocrates, 2006; WebElements, 2006). As a medication, lithium has many and varied side effects, including direct adverse reactions as well as the adverse consequences of unintended drug interactions. Reflecting the potential for lithium to affect multiple biological systems, some of the serious adverse reactions include arrhythmia, bradycardia, syncope, goiter, hypothyroidism, hyperparathyroidism, diabetes insipidus, seizure, coma, and death (Adityanjee, Munshi, & Thampy, 2005; Bilanakis & Gibiriti, 2004; Chakrabarti & Chand, 2002; Dang & Hershman, 2002; Epocrates, 2006; Suraya & Yoong, 2001). Bilanakis and Gibiriti (2004), for instance, reported a 54-year-old bipolar patient with a 15-year history of successful treatment with lithium who developed lithium intoxication. The patient displayed aversion to water and food, hypercalcemia (presumably because of parathyroid hypersecretion), and renal insufficiency. Hemodialysis (said to be the "most useful" treatment in severe cases that result from insufficient drug clearance by the kidney [Ilagan et al.]), was employed with dramatic improvement in the patient's condition, medically and behaviorally, e.g., amelioration of aversion to water and food. Relatively less serious adverse neurobehavioral reactions to lithium include tremor, blurred vision, drowsiness, muscle weakness, anorexia, and fatigue (Epocrates, 2006). Also, lithium can affect and be affected by other chemicals. The interactions that occur in the context of polypharmacy, therefore, carry the capacity for potentiation of toxicity in one or another of the drugs employed (Abraham & Owen, 2004; Abraham & Voutsilakos, 2004; Meyer, Dollarhide, & Tuan, 2005; Tuglu, Erdogan, & Abay, 2005). Over time, polypharmacy (combining lithium with traditional antidepressants as well as with anticonvulsants) has become more common in the treatment of bipolar disorder (Shulman et al., 2005; Siegel et al., 1999; Tuglu et al., 2005). This has occurred in some part as clinicians have tried to deal both with the prevention of recurrent hypomanic or manic episodes in bipolar disorder and, at the same time, to treat the depressive component of the illness. Avoiding lithium intoxication during treatment is challenging because of a very narrow therapeutic window. The task becomes even more difficult with the addition of other drugs to the treatment regimen.

Case presentation[7]

Tuglu et al. (2005) reported a 62-year-old female with an approximate 20-year history of bipolar disorder and a 7-year history of lithium treatment for that condition. She had been referred to the ED because of subacute onset of altered mental status and changes in psychomotor function (i.e., difficulties walking, motor slowness, and tremor). The history was provided by a family member, who reported that although the patient's bipolar illness started about 20 years earlier, with several hospitalizations for symptoms associated with the disorder, she had been started on lithium only 7 years previously. She had been on lithium continuously since. Information from her physician indicated that she was receiving a combination of lithium (900 mg per day) and olanzapine (5 mg per day). There had been no "positive" symptoms of bipolar disorder nor symptoms or signs of lithium toxicity in the last 12 months. A plasma lithium level taken during the last month was within the therapeutic range (0.81 mM/L; therapeutic range: 0.8–1.2 mM/L; toxic: >2.0 mM/L) (Goldman & Bennett, 2000). Her general physical examination on admission was essentially normal. She responded well to verbal commands, but she was disoriented to place and time. She was judged to exhibit "loosened associations and rhyming." The neurological examination revealed some abnormalities, including bradykinesia and severe rigidity of the forelimbs with positive cogwheel, and rest and postural tremor. On admission, her initial lithium plasma level was 3.0 mM/L, with mild increase in white blood cell count. A urine toxicology screen was negative, and CT of the head was negative except for age-related cortical atrophy.

Other history indicated that this patient had been hospitalized for deteriorating mental status about 1 year earlier and 10 days after the addition of 200 mg per day chlorpromazine to her lithium treatment in response to an abrupt onset of insomnia. She was lethargic and confused at that time, but her lithium level had been within normal limits. Brain MRI at the time revealed multiple microlacunar infarcts, but these were judged inconsistent with her clinical presentation. All of her medications were discontinued, and she developed complete remission within 3 days. She was restarted on lithium thereafter, with no adverse clinical symptoms developing until 3 weeks before the present hospitalization, when olanzipine (Zyprexa) (5 mg per day) was added to the lithium she was already receiving. The new drug was added because of an increase in psychotic symptoms that included heightened suspiciousness and possible auditory hallucinations.

The patient became more alert about 24 hr after discontinuing lithium during her current admission. Psychomotor hyperactivity continued, however. Her serum lithium level decreased over the next 2 days, to 1.8 mM/L, and this decrease was accompanied by lessoned confusion. Her lithium level after

4 days was 0.3 mM/L, with concomitant improvement in dysarthria, rigidity, and involuntary limb movements. The patient was ambulatory, with absence of most clinical symptoms and signs except "perioral dyskinesia" by the end of the fifth day. She was started on carbamazepine to prevent recurrence of bipolar symptoms and was completely oriented with no indication of disordered thought at time of discharge. She was seen 3 months later and found to be euthymic with no evidence of psychosis. Her "perioral dyskinesia" continued, however.

INITIAL CLINICAL DIAGNOSIS

The patient was described diagnostically with delirium and extrapyramidal signs.

CAUSE/ETIOLOGY

While the patient's clinical findings were attributed to lithium intoxication, the authors of this case appropriately discussed the complexities involved in establishing cause with multiple drug treatment.

NERVOUS SYSTEM LOCALIZATION

The patient's signs and symptoms implicated cortical and subcortical regions of the central nervous system, including involvement of bilateral cerebellum and basal ganglia.

Discussion

Lithium has been used for over 50 years in the treatment of psychiatric disorders (Vestergaard & Licht, 2001). The discovery that lithium might be effective in treating mania has been described as serendipitous (Barchas & Altemus, 1999). According to Barchas and Altemus (1999), John Cade in 1949, while attempting to identify toxins, injected an animal model, guinea pigs, with urine taken from manic psychiatric patients. Cade observed that the guinea pigs often reacted to the injection with sedation. He showed through further study that it was the lithium that was the sedative agent. This was followed by clinical experiments and formal clinical trials, and lithium was found to have a positive effect on manic patients, both in terms of direct treatment of mania and in preventing the recurrence of mania in patients with cyclical illness. Lithium, as a result of the work just described, became a common treatment in Europe by the mid-1960s and in the United States by 1969 (Barchas & Altemus, 1999).

While lithium is effective in the treatment of both mania and depression, it is known also to have a number of biological affects. Lithium, e.g., has been shown to perturb normal enzymatic functions, ion channels and pumps, membrane transport mechanisms, monoamine receptors, and other mechanistic aspects of monoamine function that can lead to increased uptake of neurotransmitters (e.g., norepinephrine at synapses) (Barchas & Altemus, 1999). Excretion is primarily through the kidneys, with 95% excreted unchanged in urine (Epocrates, 2006). Lithium impacts sodium and potassium in the body, readily interacts with other chemical agents, and can disrupt normal neurotransmission (Klaassen & Watkins, 2003; Mendhekar, 2005; Siegel et al., 1999; Tuglu et al., 2005). The half-life of lithium is 24–36 hr, and it takes a minimum of 4 days to reach the maintenance therapeutic serum levels of 0.8–1.2 mM/L, and with a toxic threshold of >2.0 mM/L, serum levels must be carefully monitored during treatment (Goldman & Bennett, 2000). A toxic level of lithium is considered a medical emergency, requiring immediate hospitalization and possible hemodialysis (Goldman & Bennett, 2000).

In addition to the common side effects of lithium, side effects associated with long-term use of this drug can also emerge. These effects include development of psychotic symptoms, hypothyroidism, renal tubular damage, diabetes insipidus, tardive dyskinesia, and tremor (Goldman & Bennett, 2000). The lack of control comparison in published case reports, however, makes it often difficult to specify lithium as the cause, or sole cause, of the adverse events observed in such studies. Dallocchio and Mazzarello (2002) reported a case of a 77-year-old woman who had been treated successfully for over a year with lithium but then abruptly developed parkinsonism, characterized by severe bradykinesia, severe rigidity of the upper limbs, positive cogwheel phenomenon, rest, and postural tremor with mild amplitude and frequency of 4–5 Hz in all limbs. Her plasma lithium level was found to be in the toxic range (3.7 mmol/L), although a subsequent decrease to therapeutic level was not accompanied by improvement in her extrapyramidal signs. She responded dramatically to pramipexole, with resolution of all neurological symptoms and signs. In comparison to the sudden onset of parkinsonism in the Dallocchio and Mazzarello case, Lang and Davis (2002) reported what they termed "insidious" development of lithium toxicity. Their patient developed cerebellar and pyramidal dysfunction while on maintenance lithium treatment for bipolar disorder and in the face of only moderate changes in measured lithium plasma levels and evidenced partial recovery of his symptoms and signs following discontinuation of lithium, the only residual being cerebellar ataxia. As mentioned earlier, the addition of other drugs, such as anticonvulsants (e.g., topiramate) or antipsychotics (e.g., olanzapine), can potentiate the effects of lithium (Abraham & Owen, 2004; Abraham & Voutsilakos, 2004; Barchas & Altemus, 1999; Mendhekar, 2005; Meyer, Dollahide, & Tuan, 2005; Siegel et al., 1999; Tuglu et al., 2005).

Importantly, the effects of lithium can vary as a function of age and other demographic or physical aspects of the patient (Berry, Pradhan, Sagar, & Gupta, 2003; Juurlink et al., 2004; Pinelli, Symington, Cunningham, & Paes, 2002; Stemper, Thurauf, Neundorfer, & Heckmann, 2003). Oakley, Whyte, and Carter (2001) analyzed retrospectively 97 presumed cases of lithium toxicity treated at a community clinic over a 13-year period. Looking at a variety of demographic and risk factors in a logistic regression model, Oakley et al. (2001) identified four factors that independently contributed to the risk of chronic lithium toxicity. These factors were nephrogenic diabetes insipidus, age over 50 years, thyroid dysfunction, and impaired renal function. Aging and poor renal function have been identified as special risk factors by others as well, e.g., see Meyer et al. (2005). Presumably, the presence of renal dysfunction from any cause leaves the patient at risk for lithium toxicity; however, the possible specific contribution of lithium to impaired renal function in patients included in the studies just described is unknown.

On the basis of their findings, Oakley et al. (2001) concluded that severe lithium neurotoxicity almost always occurred in their sample within a context of chronic lithium treatment, resulting rarely from acute ingestion of lithium. Ilagan et al. (2002) described three types of lithium poisoning by adding "acute on chronic" to the acute versus chronic dichotomy. Acute on chronic intoxication is said to occur in patients who take an overdose while already receiving lithium treatment. Such patients were said to have a more severe clinical course because of a longer half-life for lithium associated with this scenario (Ilagan et al.). Also, Ilagan et al. described a common system used for grading lithium toxicity into "mild" (1.5–2.5 mM/L), "moderate" (2.5–3.5 mM/L), and "severe" (>3.5 mM/L). And, they concluded that while mild levels of toxicity for either acute or chronic exposure could be managed conservatively, severe elevations require hemodialysis.

Of course, bipolar disorder itself produces a number of symptoms that can mimic the effects of medications (see also section on *mood disorders* in chapter 17 of the present volume). Cognitive impairments, for instance, are known to manifest in major depression, at times to the point of reflecting a pseudodementia, with special vulnerability in memory acquisition, delayed recall, attention, and concentration, and other cognitive functions (Zakzanis, Leach, & Kaplan, 1999). Also, disturbances in mood, overly elevated or depressed, can signal a number of underlying medical disorders, e.g., thyroid dysfunction, adrenal disorders, hypersecretion of cortisol, etc. (Siegel et al., 1999). It has been said that age of onset of bipolar disorder, that is after age 40 years, should automatically alert the clinician to consider the presence of an underlying medical condition, potentially interacting medications, or substance abuse (American Psychiatric Association, 1994; Hoblyn, 2004; Juurlink et al., 2004). Age is not the sole consideration; however, whether or not the various factors that potentially affect the patient's mood represent interacting or independent contributions to the patient's clinical condition, they should always be considered in the differential diagnosis (Castillo et al., 2006; Mouaffak, Gourevitch, Baup, Loo, & Olie, 2006).

In the case of lithium treatment and its potential effects on the patient, the disorder being treated (e.g., bipolar disorder) becomes an important factor to consider. This is because the symptoms of the disorder can mimic many of the side effects known to be associated with lithium (Pachet & Wisniewski, 2003). As mentioned earlier, cognitive and other neuropsychological impairments are recognized to occur in depression (Zakzanis et al., 1999). These impairments may be associated with structural brain changes as well (Brambilla, Glahn, Balestrieri, & Soares, 2005). Bipolar disease, as well, has been observed to occur at a higher than normally expected rate in demyelinating diseases, such as multiple sclerosis (Filley, 2001). Also, bipolar illness can have many different presentations, which, in turn, can produce unique clinical profiles in terms of symptoms and signs that might differ from one patient to another (American Psychiatric Association, 1994; Papakostas et al., 2003; Voderholzer et al., 2002). This includes neuro-psychological symptoms that can persist during periods when the primary mood disorder is judged to be in remission (Martinez-Aran et al., 2004). Unfortunately, the etiology of the behavioral manifestations in bipolar and similar disorders is not yet fully known. Differentiating those signs and symptoms that derive from disease pathophysiology from the effects of treatment will remain a clinical challenge.

VERIFICATION OF THE INITIAL CLINICAL DIAGNOSIS

The neurological conditions presented in the description of this case serve to explain the important clinical findings (Richardson et al., 2000). An exception to this conclusion is the lack of emphasis on bipolar disorder and its role or lack of contribution to the patient's clinical presentation. However, this was a published case report, and the authors wished to emphasize the medication aspects. As a result, the primary disorder was described historically and relatively briefly. The diagnoses concluded are otherwise coherent. A diagnostic challenge in this particular case, aside from the extent to which findings could reflect bipolar illness itself, is the accuracy of the delirium designation. Delirium represents a disturbance of consciousness, accompanied by cognitive changes that are not better explained by another illness, such as dementia (American Psychiatric Association, 1994). The patient's rapid return to normal mental status is inconsistent with progressive dementia or ongoing intoxication. The differential diagnosis of delirium includes dementia, but other conditions that are relevant in the present instance include schizophrenia, a brief psychotic disorder, or some other manifestation of psychosis that could include the patient's preexisting mood disorder if that disorder had become associated with psychotic features. In this instance, and by the descriptions made in the *case presentation*, the patient had what appeared to be a clear and relatively rapid change in consciousness. The change was accompanied by poorly formed and transient psychotic-like symptoms (e.g., "loosened associations"), unlike the more, well-formed, and persistent symptoms in a psychosis-like schizophrenia (see chapter 17, section on *other psychological/psychiatric considerations*). Her disturbance developed over a relatively brief time period and improved quickly as well. Like other psychiatric diagnoses we have discussed, delirium can be classed as being due to a general medical condition or as substance induced (American Psychiatric Association, 1994). Relevant here, the classification of "substance-induced" includes those instances when the delirium is related to medication use. Consistent with the approach used in the present volumes, the cause for the patient's illness will need to be determined independent of causal attribution. Then, depending on the causal findings, the original diagnosis would be modified as appropriate.

In the present instance, the initial diagnoses of delirium and extrapyramidal signs provide the simplest explanation for the patient's illness. Also, the subsequent hospital course that included improved functioning (concomitant with reduced lithium levels) was consistent with predictions that could be derived from these diagnoses more so than with regard to the various alternative diagnoses discussed earlier.

REVISED CLINICAL DIAGNOSIS

The only revision to the initial clinical diagnosis in the *case presentation* would be the addition of bipolar illness, but this diagnosis was implied based upon the history.

VERIFICATION OF REVISED CLINICAL DIAGNOSIS

There is insufficient information provided in the *case presentation* to make other than a generic diagnosis of bipolar disorder (perhaps formally as bipolar disorder, not otherwise specified). The reason for the lack of specificity is that bipolar disorder is most often divided into type I, where there is occurrence of one or more manic episodes, or type II, in which there are recurrent depressive episodes, with at least one hypomanic (but no manic) episode (American Psychiatric Association, 1994). In addition, the potential diagnoses in the area of mood disturbance can become quite complicated, with clinical distinctions that call for careful analyses (e.g., differentiation of depression from dysthymia and bipolar from cyclothymic disorders).

VERIFICATION OF CAUSE/ETIOLOGY

Lithium is known for its narrow therapeutic index and risk for toxicity in treatment (Goldman & Bennett, 2000; Ilagan et al., 2002). Ilagan et al., in fact, indicated that among patients chronically treated with lithium, 75–90% will develop toxicity at some point during the course of treatment. The potential for adverse reactions can be increased in the case of polypharmacy. In the current *case presentation*, olanzipine was added to the patient's lithium treatment for bipolar disorder, a combination known to carry some cautions because of possible additive effects, especially perhaps on the monoamine system (Epocrates, 2006). Regardless of mechanism of action, which is poorly understood for both drugs involved in the present case, it is known that combining lithium with antipsychotic medications can increase the risk of lithium toxicity, perhaps through lowered excretion (Epocrates, 2006; Ilagan et al., 2002; Tuglu et al., 2005). As indicated earlier, Tuglu et al., the authors of the patient discussed in the current *case presentation*, appropriately acknowledged the possible role played by the interaction of lithium and the added antipsychotic medication to the patient's clinical symptoms and signs, especially perhaps in regard to the persistence of dyskinesia for a prolonged period after other symptoms had dissipated. At the same time, they were comprehensive in excluding a host of factors, including, e.g., medication overdose (intentional or accidental), hyperglycemia, hyperosmolar nonketotic coma, diabetic ketoacidosis, and cerebral vascular disease.

The onset of symptoms and signs in the patient was appropriate to a rise in levels of lithium in the body as was the measured plasma level at time of hospitalization. The serum lithium level (3.0 mM/L) was of a magnitude known to represent a risk for toxicity, and the advent of her extrapyramidal symptoms and mental changes was consistent with biological expectations. The course of symptoms during her hospitalization and treatment was biologically plausible, fitting with dose–response expectations and measured changes in lithium levels as well. While it remains possible that her one persisting problem, perioral dyskinesia, could be related to something other than lithium, it also could be lithium related. Most importantly, all of the remaining and most dramatic of her symptoms and signs dissipated in association with removal from lithium exposure.

Conclusion

As much as any substance discussed in these volumes, lithium highlights the challenges associated with determination of cause in a given clinical case. Making such a determination in the context of the central nervous system is especially difficult, not only because of the complexity of the central nervous system itself but also because of the fact that central nervous system functions are most often multiply determined, influenced by biology–environment interactions, and include compensatory alternatives. Aside from biological and psychopathological variability, it has been shown that the signs and symptoms of lithium intoxication vary as a function of multiple factors, including the nature of drug ingestion (e.g., chronic versus acute) (Ilagan et al., 2002). Especially in the case of chronic therapy, Ilagan et al. pointed out that initial symptoms of lithium intoxication can be nonspecific, even vague. Because of this, their advice is to consider lithium toxicity in any patient taking this medication.

Sometimes, most often in cases of severe lithium toxicity, there may be little question regarding the responsible agent. One such case was reported by Gill, Singh, and Nugent (2003), which involved intentional overdose in a 45-year-old man. The patient ingested ninety 450 mg sustained release lithium tablets, developing multiple symptoms and signs of lithium intoxication and neuroleptic malignant syndrome. Despite extensive treatment that included multiple sessions of hemodialysis, the patient died after developing acute renal failure and respiratory distress. Most clinical cases, however, are likely to involve intoxication in the context of polypharmacy. In the case reported by Ilagan et al. (2002), for instance, the 57-year-old man was brought to the ED with complaints of lethargy, ataxia, weakness, and confusion. His medications, in addition to lithium (reported serum level: 3.1 mM/L), included atenol, doxazosin, lisinopril, atorvastain, glipizide, metformin, ciprofloxacin, sertraline, risperidone, olanzapine, and lorazepine. Because some of these medications can affect the potency of lithium, or produce their own adverse effects, the poly-pharmacy introduces obvious complications to clinical tasks of diagnosis, causal identification, and treatment determination.

Pain Medications (Opioids)

Stanley Berent

While a number of prescription and OTC medications are used to treat pain (e.g., acetaminophen and nonsteroidal anti-inflammatory drugs [NSAIDS]), the *opioids* represent a major class of analgesics used commonly in the treatment of acute and chronic, moderate to severe pain. Opioid medications are derived from alkaloids of the poppy plant (*papaver somniferum*) and the plant's exudate, *opium*; but synthetics and chemically altered alkaloid compounds are included in this class, as well (Samet, 2000). Drugs that contain or that are derived directly from opium are termed *opiates*, while those with a secondary connection to opium (hydrocodone, e.g., which is derived from codeine) represent the *opioids* (Merck Research Laboratories, 2001; Merck Source, 2005; Merriam-Webster, 1993). In practice, the term *opioid* often is used generically when referring to the various preparations in this class of medications. Also at times referred to as *narcotics*, the most familiar of the opium-derived drugs include morphine, codeine, and oxycodone (the last an opioid agonist sold under the trade names Oxycontin, Percodan, and Percocet). In addition to their analgesic and in some cases euphoric effects, some drugs in this class are used to suppress cough (e.g., codeine) and diarrhea (diphenoxylate [Lomotil]).

Drugs derived from opium have a long history of use for treatment of a vast number of medical and psychiatric disorders. Heroin (diacetylmorphine, a derivative of morphine) was commercially available in the United States into at least the early 1900s (see Figure 16.2); and it was used, often in combination with aspirin, to treat a variety of common complaints, e.g., minor lacerations, inflammations, and headaches (Bloodworth, 2005). Heroin is no longer legal in the United States but continues to be used therapeutically in some parts of the world.

As with stimulants (e.g., amphetamine) and the hypnotic and sedative medications (e.g., benzodiazepine) discussed earlier in the present chapter, opioids lend themselves to abuse. Aside from purposeful use of illicit substances (e.g., heroin), prescription and OTC compounds frequently are intentionally misused. It has been estimated that approximately 20% of the population aged 12 years and older in the United States has at some time in their lives used a prescription drug for nonmedical reasons (Volkow, 2005). As this statistic suggests, the risk for opioid misuse extends to children as well as adults, and this is before considering the many children (and other individuals who are dependent on others for care) who become exposed to opioid medications through neglect (e.g., improper storage and handling of prescription and OTC medications that contain opioid compounds) or abuse

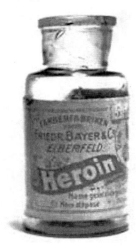

Figure 16.2 Photograph of a commercial bottle that originally contained 5 g of heroin. The exact date of the picture is unknown and is available in the public domain (from wikipedia.org).

(Katz & Hays, 2004). Individuals from any walk of life can fall victim to opioid addiction, as illustrated in the following *case presentation.*

Case presentation[8]

The patient is a 35-year-old physician (exact specialty not reported), married to a physician and with two young children. He had been well until several years before the present evaluation when he experienced grief following a "stressful life event" (not specified). He began to self-medicate from office cabinet supplies of antidepressants and continued this practice for several months. He reported experiencing no relief of his symptoms and stopped taking the medications. His feelings of grief gradually resolved spontaneously. At a later time, he experienced an upper respiratory illness. Again, he self-medicated from supplies in the office cabinet, this time with a cough syrup that contained hydrocodone. While the medication suppressed his cough, he also experienced improvement in his mood and a sense of increased energy and productivity. He continued to take the medication regularly even after his cough subsided, obtaining hydrocodone from his office medication cabinet and consuming numerous bottles each week. He began to write prescriptions for tablet and liquid forms of the medication to ensure he would have an ample supply for his needs. He eventually confided in his wife about what he was doing, and this led to discontinuing his use of the medication. Thereafter, he experienced withdrawal symptoms after about 36 hr of nonuse, including fatigue, anxiety, and depression. As a result, he resumed taking hydrocodone, reporting that he took about 200 mg per day of the medication over the next 18 months.

While he later indicated that he knew he had a problem, he did not tell his wife about the resumed use of hydrocodone. Also, he did not confide in or seek help from anyone else. His behavior, especially fluctuations in mood, raised the suspicions of a colleague who confronted him about potential drug use. While the patient at first strongly denied that anything was amiss, eventually, he relented and was referred to a physician health program, where he was required to seek inpatient addiction treatment, which he did.

There was no history of previous addiction to any substance, and no past alcohol- or tobacco-related problems. He denied a history of psychiatric illness, and there was no family history of addiction. On admission to the addiction treatment program, he had not used hydrocodone for several days. His physical examination, including neurological examination, was normal, and laboratory tests showed normal blood cell count, chemistry, and thyroid function. A urine drug screen was unexpectedly positive for tetrahydrocannabinol (THC, 91 ng/dl) and negative for all other substances, including opiates.

ADDITIONAL INFORMATION

During clinical interview, the patient reported that he took mostly a cough syrup form of hydrocodone, which seemed to energize him and leave him feeling better in general than he did before he took the medication. Admitting that he might have had some symptoms of depression before he started taking hydrocodone, he said those symptoms dissipated within 10–15 min of his taking hydrocodone. While he had to increase the dose he was taking over time, he continued to experience the positive feelings when on the medication. When he did not take the medication, however, he would experience negative feelings of anxiety and, especially, depression; and he would become unable to function. He emphatically denied that there were any negative consequences in terms of his job performance. He saw the only consequence being the missing drug samples and his colleagues discovering that he had taken them. Also, he talked about the susceptibility of physicians generally to addiction, the ease of obtaining drugs; the lack of meaningful training about what addiction is while in school; and how one needs to realize they have a problem, admit it, and ask for help. He commented on some of the physical and genetic aspects of addiction and the important role of stress in leading to addiction, the need to find some means of experiencing pleasure when it is missing otherwise from one's life, and how a chemical can satisfy that need. He emphasized the inadequacy of training in this area and asked if things were being done to improve that aspect of professional training as well as to improve drug addiction treatment itself.

INITIAL CLINICAL DIAGNOSIS

The patient in the current *case presentation* had been referred for inpatient treatment with the diagnostic statement, substance-abuse disorder, and opioid dependence. In addition, a diagnosis of underlying depression appeared to be implied although not formally stated (Knight, 2004).

CAUSE/ETIOLOGY

Opioid dependence and presumably underlying depression were the stated reasons for the patient's symptoms (e.g., lack of functionality) that led to his need for inpatient drug addiction treatment.

NERVOUS SYSTEM LOCALIZATION

The patient's symptoms are referable to the supratentorial level of the central nervous system.

Discussion

Opioids achieve their various physiological effects through exposure to the exogenous substance's capacity to target nervous system opioid receptor sites. These receptor sites are located at numerous places within and outside of the central nervous system, with large numbers found in the limbic system and in pathways associated with the perception of pain (Dykstra, 1992). These receptors use endogenous opioid peptides—endomorphin, enkephalin, and dynorphin—for neurotransmission and neuromodulation (Siegel et al., 1999; Uhl, 1999). Of the various potential binding sites for exogenous opioids, the mu (μ) receptor site, which has an important role in mediating activation of "G proteins" that, in turn, play a role in K^+ and Ca^{2+} channel activation, is a primary site involved in morphine reward, e.g., as measured by extent of electrical self-stimulation in rodents (Uhl, 1999). Knowledge regarding the mechanisms of action is increasingly well-established. There is growing evidence for neuroanatomical relationships between opioid receptor sites and the neurotransmitter circuitry (e.g., μ-related neurotransmission) that mediates the rewarding aspects associated with a number of abused substances (opioids and other substances), memory formation (Agranoff, Cotman, & Uhler, 1999; Grant et al., 1996; Uhl, 1999), and emotion (Zubieta et al., 2003). Studies on this topic suggest that the neuroanatomical areas associated especially with the *craving* aspects of drug addiction include prefrontal and temporal lobe (limbic and para-limbic) structures and perhaps the cerebellum (Grant et al., 1996; Zubieta et al., 2001). Activation of these memory- and affective-associated areas may be independent of drug type, e.g., stimulant, sedative, or analgesic. It is well accepted, for instance, that tobacco addiction is associated with nicotine-induced activation of brain regions rich in nicotinic receptors, e.g., thalamus (Zubieta et al., 2001). Consistent with the proposition that common neuroanatomical areas are involved in aspects of dependence regardless of drug type, Zubieta et al. (2005) used positron emission tomography to show that smoking led to changes not only in brain areas rich in nicotinic receptors but also in regions that mediate learned relationships between drugs in general and the environmental cues associated with drug use (the right hippocampus), drug craving behavior, and relapse to addictive behavior (the left dorsal anterior cingulate).

While research to date has led to increased sophistication in terms of our knowledge about the neural mechanisms that seems clearly to provide a neuro-chemical and neurophysiological basis for substance abuse and addiction to specific substances, including the opioids, it is likewise well recognized that abuse and addiction are multidetermined (Zacny & Galinkin, 1999). Individual differences characterize substance abuse, with genetic and experiential factors contributing importantly to abuse (Siegel et al., 1999). In a case-control study by Prasant, Mattoo, and Basu (2006), for instance, the authors assessed the preva-lence of psychiatric and substance-abuse disorders in first-degree relatives of 100 opiate-dependent males. They found that the first-degree relatives of the opiate-dependent males were in general more likely to have a psychiatric disorder in comparison to control relatives (adjusted odds ratio [OR] 4.47, 95% CI 1.97–10.11, $p < .001$) and, more specifically, for opioid use disorders in brothers (adjusted OR 6.55, 95% CI 1.44–29.88, $p < 0.001$) and alcohol use disorders in fathers (adjusted OR 5.64, 95% CI 2.39–13.24, $p < 0.001$).

Aside from individual psychological factors (e.g., discovering that a par-ticular drug reduces a negative feeling like anxiety or depression), social, economic, and other group factors also contribute to substance abuse and also help in a given case to determine a drug of choice. *Availability* is one such factor. The fact that the patient in the current *case presentation* had easy access to narcotic-containing substances almost certainly played a role in hydrocodone becoming his drug of choice. *Culture* influences drug choice as well. Abuse of prescription medications has been on the rise for a number of years (National Institute on Drug Abuse, 2005). A 2004 study of drug preferences in an addiction treatment program revealed that 27% of the patients surveyed (N = 534) were dependent on prescription opiate medica-tions, with 53% of these addicted to hydrocodone (Miller & Greenfeld, 2004). Cough medicine has reportedly been touted as a "smart drug of choice" by some adolescent users because of its relatively low cost, easy availability (some, like those containing dextromethorphan are sold OTC), quality con-trol, and lack of the stigma associated with abuse of street drugs, such as heroin (Miller, 2005). Dextromethorphan is a synthetic opioid derivative of levorphanol, a codeine analogue. An 8-oz bottle of dextromethorphan cough suppressant contains about 720 mg dextromethorphan (one teaspoon = 15 mg). In prescribed doses, dextromethorphan is an effective cough suppressant, without some of the severe adverse effects associated with other opioid prepar-ations (e.g., central nervous system depression and respiratory suppression). More than 4 oz of dextromethorphan, however, can produce *dissociation* and perhaps other effects being sought by its user (Miller, 2005). Miller (2005) described a 16-year-old adolescent who was introduced to dextromethorphan by his peers. He began by stealing the family's supply of cough medicine and progressed to using dextromethorphan in tablet form (better tasting, more easily concealed, and stronger [30 mg/dose as opposed to 15 mg/dose for cough syrup]). Physical tolerance developed relatively quickly, with with-drawal symptoms (e.g., restlessness, insomnia, and dysphoria) on termination of dextromethorphan use.

The case of dextromethorphan abuse just described as presented by Miller (2005) was relatively uncomplicated, involving no polysubstance abuse and occurring within a supportive family environment. Such situations are most likely rare, and any number of factors can complicate evaluation, causal attribution, and treatment. Katz and Hays (2004), e.g., described several cases that involved adolescent abuse of OxyContin (a controlled release form of oxycodone hydrochloride that is designed to provide delivery of the drug over a 12-hr period for the relief of moderate-to-severe pain. OxyContin was introduced in 1995, and its misuse surged in a geographic specific manner, underscoring perhaps the social and cultural influences on drug use. On the street, OxyContin became referred to as "poor man's heroin" or "hillbilly heroin," and its illicit users often disable the sustained release covering by crushing the tablet and then ingesting it orally, "snorting" the powder, or injecting it dissolved in water (Katz & Hays, 2004). Taking OxyContin in one of these manners produces an instant euphoria. Addiction to OxyContin is rapid, and once addicted, experience suggests that the person will do almost anything to maintain their habit. Katz and Hays (2004) described a 16-year-old with no prior history of drug abuse who was introduced to the drug at age 14 years. She began stealing the narcotic from her mother who was being treated for chronic pain. On one occasion, she intercepted a mail order package containing the drug that was intended for her mother. Fearful that her mother would try to retrieve the package, the young woman stayed awake all night armed with a skillet, which she admitted later she intended to use to kill her mother should she try to take the drug package away.

Drug abuse most often involves polysubstance use within a context of other psychological or psychiatric disturbances. Although the patient in the current *case presentation*, for instance, denied using drugs other than hydrocodone, he tested positive for cannabis. Also, he claimed that the depressive feelings he experienced when he first began to self-medicate had resolved and, presumably, were no longer relevant to his drug use. In contradiction, his interview contained statements that suggested a continuance of depressed feelings, e.g., feeling better when taking the drug, feeling low when the drug effects wore off. Psychoactive properties are associated with opioid use (including euphoria and possible reduction of negative mood) and believed to supplement the positive effects associated with analgesia alone (Zautra & Smith, 2005). Conversely, negative mood can be a consequence of withdrawal (Siegel et al., 1999). With regard to the current *case presentation*, this leaves the patient's (denied) depression an important factor in his clinical presentation. Katz and Hays (2004) suggested that 25% of opioid-dependent individuals reflect a history of childhood stress, including sexual abuse or exposure to violence, and they cautioned that attempts to treat addiction in these individuals must attend to issues of comorbidity, e.g., anxiety, depression, conduct, and other disorders; including those that might derive from aspects of drug use itself, e.g., HIV infection and other transmittable diseases (Chawarski, Mazlan, & Schottenfeld, 2006; Maxwell et al., 2006; Tang, Zhao, Zhao, & Cubells, 2006).

What about cognitive and other neuropsychological aspects of opioid use? As discussed earlier, it is well documented that opioid exposure (including overexposure and withdrawal) impacts neural circuitry and is capable of producing relatively profound physiological reactions, e.g., seizure, respiratory depression, hypoxia, and cerebral infarction (Goldman & Bennett, 2000). Other complications occur by way of infection from injection of drugs, e.g., hepatitis, endocarditis, and HIV-related disease. Some neural changes can be long lasting or perhaps even permanent (Dykstra, 1992; Uhl, 1999). Also, the brain regions that appear to be most affected by opioid exposure (e.g., frontal and temporal) are those that mediate affective and cognitive functioning (Agranoff et al., 1999; Uhl, 1999; Zubieta et al., 2003). It would not be surprising, therefore, to find that opioid abuse is accompanied by cognitive or affective impairment; and a number of studies have shown that to be the case (Mintzer, Copersino, & Stitzer, 2005). On the other hand, many of the studies that associated opioid use with cognitive, psychomotor, and affective disturbances suffered from multiple methodological problems (e.g., small sample sizes, lack of relevant control populations, cross-sectional designs, paucity of quantitative behavioral measures, and inadequate historical subject information) (Mintzer et al., 2005). One problem facing the researcher who is interested in studying the effects of opioids on neuro-behavioral functioning is the presence of polysubstance abuse in many of the study subjects, making it difficult to causally isolate the substance of immediate interest. Some further complications can arise from the fact that the effects of opioid exposure are dose dependent, can vary from one opioid type to another, one individual to another, and the opioid often is combined with other substances that in themselves may be psychoactive (Zacny, Gutierrez, & Bolbolan, 2005).

One way to control some of the nuisance variables just mentioned is to administer a known quantity of a specified substance to normal subjects (Zacny, 2003; Zacny & Gutierrez, 2003) or to subjects with a known drug use history and to examine the effects of exposure under controlled laboratory conditions (Zacny et al., 2003, 2005). Zacny et al. (2005) used such an approach to profile the subjective, psychomotor, and physiological effects of a hydrocodone/acetaminophen product among a group of recreational drug users. They found that subjective ratings by subjects showed hydrocodone had a "desirability rating" for some subjects that was comparable to ratings for morphine (seen as the "gold standard" in terms of desirability, that is, "wanting to take the drug again"), but other subjects found the experience to be "dysphoric." These subjective effects were dose dependent, with no significant effects noted at the lowest, customary therapeutic dose of 5 mg. "Abuse liability-related subjective effects" were limited to the highest doses administered (20 mg orally). At a dose of 20 mg, a significant increase in subjective feelings of confusion, difficulty concentrating, dizziness, nausea, and (for females only) "unpleasant bodily sensations" was observed. Both hydrocodone and morphine at 20 mg doses produced impairments in psychomotor functions, statements answered correctly on a computer-administered logical reasoning test, and digit symbol substitution; but only subtle changes were observed in reaction time and eye–hand coordination. The authors commented that while hydrocodone produced some effects in this instance, the study involved acute dosing only, and the usual treatment with hydro-codone for pain involves taking the drug several times a day for several days (Zacny et al., 2005). The investigators concluded that the results they observed were similar to those found to result from other μ-opioid agonists (Zacny et al., 2003; Zacny et al., 2005).

Comparing current and former primarily chronic abusers of amphetamine and opiates, Ersche Clark, London, Robbins, and Sahakian (2006) found that all substance-abuse groups were impaired in executive and memory functions in comparison to healthy, non-drug-using controls. Also, the researchers found a sex difference, as female substance users performed better than their male counterparts. No explanation was given for this finding. No differences were observed between current and former drug users. Neither years of drug abuse nor years of drug abstinence were correlated significantly with test perform-ance, and the researchers concluded that the memory and executive function impairments they observed were consistent with underlying neurological dysfunction in frontal and temporal brain regions (Ersche et al., 2006). In an earlier study, Ersche et al. (2005) found abnormal frontal lobe activation on functional neuroimaging (using a decision-making and risk-taking task adminis-tered during H_2O^{15} positron emission tomography) in both current and former (at least 1 year of abstinence) amphetamine- or opiate-dependent individuals. Rapeli et al. (2006) in a study of newly abstinent opioid-dependent individuals indicated that while "executive function" (e.g., planning, problem solving, reasoning, and control over impulsivity) was the primary long-term residual impairment of past opiate abuse, newly abstinent users continued to evidence more general cognitive deficits beyond executive functions alone. The deficits are similar to those reported for current, long-term users (including attention, memory, and executive function), and were found by Rapeli to correlate significantly with days of withdrawal (Rapeli et al.). They suggested that the deficits during early periods of abstinence were a transient product of withdrawal-induced neural deregulation in prefrontal cortical regions. Finally, in a functional magnetic resonance imaging (fMRI) study of cognitive behavioral regulation among heroin users, Lee et al. (2005) found that in comparison to controls, the heroin users performed a complex dual-task-demand test more quickly while making significantly more errors. This pattern of test results is consistent with disinhibition and impulsivity. The test-taking behavior by the heroin users was associated with fMRI findings that also differed from controls, reflecting attenuation of activity in the anterior cingulate and recruitment of the right inferior parietal region of the brain.

Together, the various cognitive and other neurobehavioral findings reviewed here are remarkably consistent in terms of cognitive domains and corollary brain regions that are adversely affected by exposure to opioid drugs. Critically, these findings also are consistent with what is known about the neural circuitry associated with opioid exposure. But, as alluded earlier, the differences in response to opioid medications between individuals is remarkable as well. These differences underscore the importance of societal, cultural, psychological, genetic, and other individual difference variables to the understanding of medication effects in the individual case. One of these individual difference variables is the person's unique preexposure history, a variable that could influence individual susceptibility to drug dependence. For instance, the studies reviewed report impairments in executive function as a consequence of addiction, and impairments in this area of functioning appear to persist even after other cognitive impairments have dissipated. Since studies in this area rarely include measures of predrug, baseline neurocognitive function, the question of whether or not impaired judgment may be independent of drug exposure remains incompletely answered. In other words, might poor judgment be a factor in an individual's propensity for addiction? This question has relevance for all drugs of abuse, e.g., alcohol (Gilman et al., 1990), in addition to the opioids. Regardless of the answer with regard to the predrug user, it does appear that impaired executive function continues to be a factor following successful treatment for drug-dependence and may be an important consideration for predicting relapse.

VERIFICATION OF THE INITIAL CLINICAL DIAGNOSIS

The initial diagnosis of substance-abuse disorder, opioid dependence was coherent, robust, and adequate in explaining the patient's immediate need for inpatient treatment for his opioid addiction. It is not clear, however, that this diagnosis alone would predict the patient's clinical course following successful treatment of his opioid dependence (see *comment*).

Comment

The nature of the article from which the *case presentation* was drawn led its author to focus on aspects of drug addiction. At the same time, that author left it clear that there was more to the patient's condition than could be detailed in the relatively brief published report. The patient's clinical evaluation and treatment was to continue following his inpatient treatment. His continuing evaluation most likely would lead to additional clinical diagnoses. For instance, the positive THC urine finding suggested at least the presence of polysubstance use, a common occurrence among substance users, and raises the probability of a more general substance abuse problem beyond opioid dependence. Also, the patient's history and presentation in clinical interview suggested the presence of mood disorder and, possibly, other behavioral diagnoses.

REVISED CLINICAL DIAGNOSIS

Verified: substance-abuse disorder, opioid dependence.

Probable:
1. Mood disorder (major depressive disorder versus dysthymic disorder (see *mood disorders*, chapter 17).
2. Polysubstance abuse

Possible
Personality disorder

VERIFICATION OF REVISED CLINICAL DIAGNOSIS

While the initial diagnosis was seen as adequate for his immediate treatment setting, this diagnosis may not have fit the entirety of the patient's illness pattern. As mentioned, the positive THC urine finding suggested polysubstance abuse. Also, the likelihood of multiple-substance abuses was raised by the patient's history of self-medication with antidepressants before he began using opioids. That he concealed this activity in addition raises the possibility of personality disorder.

No formal neurobehavioral examination results were reported, but the patient's behavior in interview belied several probable neurobehavioral abnormalities, nevertheless. For instance, the patient claimed that his depression had remitted before he began taking hydrocodone. However, his report in clinical interview revealed that his depressed mood likely continued throughout his relatively prolonged period of narcotic use. Upon questioning, e.g., the patient admitted that he might have had some symptoms of depression before taking his daily dose of hydrocodone and that these symptoms dissipated within 10–15 min of taking the drug. He felt energized and "better" during periods of exposure than when he was off the drug. He developed tolerance and had to adjust the dose of hydrocodone he was taking, but he continued to experience the positive feelings when on the drug. At times that he did not take the medication; he described experiencing negative feelings that included anxiety and, especially, depression. He stated that during these periods, he was unable to function. At the same time, he was emphatic in stating that his hydrocodone never interfered with his job performance. When asked, he stated that the only negatives about his narcotic use were related to the missing samples and the fact that his colleagues learned that it was he who was taking them (another expression that raises the possibility of personality disorder in addition to poor judgment).

In interview, the patient reflected probable lack of insight, to the point of denial with regard to his underlying mood disorder. The content was often illogical, e.g., denying depression, while describing depressive symptoms in another sentence, or even directly admitting to being depressed. These logically inconsistent utterances also could reflect difficulties with memory if, in fact, he "forgot" that he had earlier said something inconsistent with a later expressed idea. Denial, illogical thinking, and lack of insight were apparent in his insistence that he was able to perform his job well, while at the same time claiming that he was depressed to the point of becoming dysfunctional when not taking the medication.

The patient's coping style in general appeared to be repressive like. He avoided personal confrontation or acceptance of responsibility for his actions through externalization and intellectualization. Examples of this style were reflected in his concerns regarding the adequacy of training, in general, but also implying that his own training had not prepared him to deal with issues of drug addiction or how to avoid becoming addicted. This style may have included some passive-dependence (e.g., he did not seek help until discovered) and passive–aggressive tendencies (e.g., questioning the adequacy of his current treatment).

VERIFICATION OF CAUSE/ETIOLOGY

Opioid dependence and depression were the reasons given for the patient's symptoms that led to his need for inpatient drug addiction treatment. Within this context, the conclusions meet all criteria for formal verification. The patient's historical report reflects appropriate timing between exposure and onset signs and symptoms, with evidence for an expected dose–response relationship. The negative urine drug screen results for hydrocodone are not surprising since approximately 70% of this drug is excreted in the first 24 hr following exposure, with the remainder of the drug excreted by 72 hr (Cone, Darwin, Gorodetzky, & Tan, 1978). The effects described are those known to be associated with opioids, and this substance is known to carry a high relative risk for dependence. Removal from exposure was accompanied by symptoms of withdrawal, and was accompanied by manifestation of the patient's underlying depression.

As mentioned earlier, it is likely that further evaluation will lead to additional diagnoses. Incompletely explained at the moment is the basis for the patient's depression. This "missing information" may become apparent with further evaluation. For instance, mention was made of a "stressful life event" that was said to have led to the patient's first self-medication (Knight, 2004). The nature of that event remains unspecified. Given the known association between life stresses and substance abuse discussed earlier, learning more about this event, and other as yet unknown stresses in the patient's history, might help to explain this patient's depression and its contribution to his drug abuse. To quote from the patient's own words, as reported by Knight (2004), "... stress plays a huge role in creating addiction." "If you don't experience pleasure, then you need something to create that pleasure. And, it is very easy for physicians to have access to chemicals that will do that."

Conclusion

Issues related to substance abuse reflect commonalities across drug classifications, and substance abuse can be seen as a diagnostic entity with its own implications for the affected patient, regardless of the drug involved. There is evidence that the rewarding and craving sensations associated with various drugs depend upon common biological mechanisms. At the same time, differences exist in likelihood of use, abuse, and dependence liability between various drug classifications and even within a specified drug class. While some of these differences result from the biological attractiveness (i.e., mechanism of action characteristics) of a given substance (e.g., opioids versus benzodiazepines, morphine versus codeine), environmental, personal, and other extra-drug considerations play important roles in drug selection, continuation, and other aspects of drug abuse.

The misuse of drugs intended for the treatment of medical conditions has been on the rise for several decades. As exemplified by the primary *case presentation* in the current section, drug abuse often transcends age and other demographic boundaries. While professional education and training may reduce instances of illicit drug use in comparison to the general population to some extent, no one is guaranteed immunity to drug abuse and dependence. The rate for substance-use disorders for U.S. physicians (8–15% lifetime prevalence), e.g., is comparable to that for the general population (Knight, 2004).

Psychotropic Medications (Chlorpromazine)

James W. Albers

Chlorpromazine (used generically or under a number of brands, e.g., Thorazine) was introduced in the 1950s to treat a variety of psychiatric conditions. It is one of the oldest neuroleptic medications currently in use. Neuroleptic medications are very effective in treating psychosis, but chlorpromazine, like most medications, is associated with various adverse side effects, including a delayed-onset movement disorder termed *tardive dyskinesia* that typically develops after long-term administration of the medication. The neurotoxicity of chlorpromazine vis-à-vis neuroleptic-induced tardive dyskinesia is atypical of some of the other central nervous system disorders discussed in this volume in terms of its onset, which typically is delayed following a period of chronic use, and frequent tendency to persist after removal from exposure. In contrast, delayed onset associated with organophosphorus-induced delay neurotoxicity (OPIDN) denotes the emergence of a toxic neuropathy shortly (weeks) after an acute, massive exposure and after the initial organophosphorus toxicity has subsided. Further, some forms of parkinsonisms appear to have delayed onset long after (months or years) the initiating event, which produced a subclinical injury to neurons and receptors in the basal ganglia. Nevertheless, some of the adverse features attributed to chlorpromazine are shared with other neurotoxicants that target neurons and receptors in the basal ganglia, particularly those associated with parkinsonism. The following *case presentation* is representative of patients who develop this involuntary movement disorder in association with use of neuroleptic medications.

Case presentation[1]

A 32-year-old male developed uncontrollable involuntary movements described as "restlessness," and which included frequent blinking, licking and pursing of his lips, and rapid jerking movements of his limbs. His history was remarkable only for a well-controlled psychiatric disorder described as a "mild form of schizophrenia." That disorder was diagnosed 5 years earlier but, in retrospect, had developed many years before the diagnosis was considered. Such history is relatively common in schizophrenia, which is considered to have a prodromal phase that can precede onset of a blatant psychotic disorder by years (see *other psychological/psychiatric considerations* in chapter 17). His symptoms included episodes of confusion and disordered thinking more generally, with paranoid features and occasional auditory hallucinations that interfered with his social and work activities. All of these behavioral symptoms resolved after a psychiatrist prescribed treatment with chlorpromazine, a neuroleptic medication used to control a variety of psychotic symptoms.

The uncontrollable, involuntary movements first appeared about 48 months after beginning chlorpromazine. He ignored them for a time, in part because those around him seemed bothered by the movements more than they bothered him, and because he suspected they reflected a side effect of his medication, something he did not wish to discontinue or change. However, the movements increased in magnitude and extent over time, resulting in his current evaluation. On neurological examination, he displayed no mental status abnormalities and no evidence of a thought disorder. Abnormal signs included frequent blinking of his eyelids, arching of his brow, and facial grimacing with lip smacking. He showed a combination of choreiform limb movements and slower, writhing athetoid movements of his fingers, hands, and wrists. He appeared restless, with intermittent foot tapping, rocking, twisting of his neck and trunk, and shrugging of his shoulders. Aside from the involuntary movements, there were no neurological abnormalities. As part of his neurodiagnostic evaluation, he underwent a cranial CT scan and MRI brain imaging, both of which were normal.

DIFFERENTIAL DIAGNOSIS

This patient's hyperkinetic movement disorder was attributed to tardive dyskinesia, a diagnosis that includes reference to the characteristics of the abnormal movements (dyskinesia) and implication to the cause (tardive, meaning "late" or "delayed onset" due to prior use of the antipsychotic medication, chlorpromazine). The abnormal motor activity represented a combination of choreiform movements (rapid, jerky, nonrepetitive, purposeless), athetoid movements (slow, sinuous, continual), and stereotypical rhythmic facial (grimacing, protruding of the tongue, lip smacking, sucking, and chewing), neck and trunk (twisting, torticollis), and limb movements (jerking, hand clenching) with superimposed irregular, tic-like movements. An example of involuntary facial grimacing associated with neuroleptic-induced tardive dyskinesia is shown in Figure 16.3. In the absence of exposure to a neuroleptic medication, a variety of neurological conditions could be considered to explain some of his abnormal signs, including Huntington's chorea (a hereditary neurodegenerative condition), Tourette's syndrome, Wilson's disease, parkinsonism, restless leg syndrome, vasculitis, basal ganglia infarction, and specific behavioral conditions, including excessive anxiety,

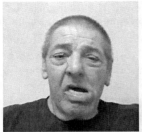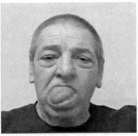

Figure 16.3 Involuntary facial grimacing associated with neuroleptic-induced tardive dyskinesia. Reprinted with permission from a video made by Joseph H. Friedman, MD, Brown Medical School, whose support is gratefully acknowledged.

obsessive-compulsive disorder, autism, manic-depressive illness, agitated depression, and schizophrenia.

Discussion

The nervous system localization of the patient's neurologic disorder and the likelihood that chlorpromazine caused the problem are examined in the following paragraphs.

NERVOUS SYSTEM LOCALIZATION

The primary neuroanatomical clinical diagnosis was "dyskinesia," a hyperkinetic movement disorder localized to the bilateral supratentorial level of the central nervous system. Within this level, the abnormal involuntary movements appear to originate within the basal ganglia. Whether or not the other areas of the central nervous system are potential targets as part of this condition is unknown, but available evidence does not provide strong support for additional sites of involvement. Importantly, neurological testing of typical patients with tardive dyskinesia does not identify consistent clinical abnormalities of the posterior fossa (brain stem and cerebellum) or spinal cord. It is unknown whether there are any cerebral manifestations of tardive dyskinesia. An association between tardive dyskinesia and dementia among patients chronically receiving neuroleptic medications has been identified in most epidemiological studies, but tardive dyskinesia and cognitive impairment both increase with age and tardive dyskinesia alone cannot account for the severity of cognitive impairment found in this population of subjects (Byne et al., 1998). Further, neuroimaging studies and neuropathological investigations similarly have not documented other sites of abnormality in tardive dyskinesia (discussed in more detail below), although these same studies, particularly imaging studies, do not identify abnormalities within the basal ganglia, either. Cognitive impairments have been associated with schizophrenia, with or without tardive dyskinesia (Zakzanis et al., 1999).

VERIFICATION OF THE CLINICAL DIAGNOSIS

The relatively characteristic clinical neurological signs established the clinical diagnosis of dyskinesia, a diagnosis supported by the absence of abnormalities suggesting other diagnoses. This included other possible psychiatric conditions, mentioned in the differential diagnosis as capable of producing signs of abnormal movement. The brain imaging studies (CT and MRI) provided no evidence of any structural or vascular problems. Taken together, the clinical diagnosis of dyskinesia is highly descriptive, yet it satisfies all explicit questions required to verify the diagnosis (Richardson et al., 2000), including the ability to predict the subsequent clinical course, as described below.

Additional Information

Chlorpromazine was withheld, and the abnormal movements began to improve within approximately 6 months, eventually disappearing. Unfortunately, signs of the preexisting thought disorder began to reappear. Psychiatric evaluation resulted in the recommendation of one of the newer, atypical neuroleptic medications. Initiation of the new medication resulted in resolution of his psychiatric symptoms. There was no recurrence of his movement disorder, even several years after starting the new medication.

CAUSE/ETIOLOGY

By definition, tardive dyskinesia is a specific, purposeless, involuntary, hyperkinetic, potentially persistent disorder of voluntary movement that is drug induced (Chouinard, 2004). This hyperkinetic movement disorder is strongly associated with neuroleptic (dopamine receptor blocking) medications, including chlorpromazine. The early description of neuroleptic-induced tardive dyskinesia appeared in the 1950s, shortly after the introduction of neuroleptic drugs (Crane, 1973; Wickman & Cold, 2000). Soon thereafter, neuroleptic medication package inserts included information and warnings about this potential adverse side effect (Slovenko, 2000). Tardive dyskinesia is one of the most common neurotoxic diseases in North America, and recognition of this well-described syndrome and identification of the causative pharmaceutical agent are seldom difficult (Schaumburg & Spencer, 1987). Among individual patients, several factors increase the likelihood of developing tardive dyskinesia after initial neuroleptic therapy. For example, the patient's age is an important contributing factor, and tardive dyskinesia is about five times more prevalent among elderly patients than in younger patients (Jeste, 2000). Cumulative neuroleptic dose and duration of neuroleptic treatment are additional risk factors for this condition (Jeste, 2000). Other risk factors include the specific neuroleptic medication prescribed, use of other medications, gender, race, alcohol intake, and genetic predisposition (Wickman & Cold, 2000).

The impression that chlorpromazine caused this patient's movement disorder was based on several considerations. First, there was documented exposure. Second, the movement disorder did not develop until well after his first exposure to chlorpromazine, a characteristic finding and the basis for the designation tardive dyskinesia. Somewhat paradoxically, however, some patients treated with neuroleptic medications first develop tardive dyskinesia when the neuroleptic dosage is reduced or the medication discontinued (withdrawal dyskinesia) (Escobar & Tuason, 1979; Gunne, Haggstrom, Johansson, Levin, & Terenius, 1988).

Epidemiological data vary on the type and frequency of neuroleptic-induced adverse medication effects. Early descriptions of neuroleptic-induced movement disorders are confusing, in part because they were based on identifiable conditions such as parkinsonism, dystonia deformans, Huntington's chorea, and dopamine-induced dyskinesia resulting in complicated and confusing nomenclature that limited the communication about these conditions (Chouinard, 2004). Nevertheless, a substantial number of patients started on the older neuroleptic medications develop characteristic signs of tardive dyskinesia, particularly among elderly patients. Despite differences in study methodologies, it is estimated that among young adults initiating typical neuroleptics, the annual incidence of tardive dyskinesia is 5% at 1 year, 10% at 2 years, and 15% at 3 years (Jeste, 2000). In contrast, the prevalence of tardive dyskinesia among chronically hospitalized geriatric inpatients with schizophrenia is reported at 60% (Byne et al., 1998). In addition to tardive dyskinesia, other adverse neurological conditions associated with the neuroleptic medications include acute dyskinesia, parkinsonism, catatonic neuroleptic syndrome, and neuroleptic malignant syndrome (Stubner et al., 2004). Acute drug-induced parkinsonism is a known predictor of subsequent tardive dyskinesia, and acute and tardive extrapyramidal syndromes may share vulnerabilities (Sachdev, 2004), information potentially important in identifying the underlying pathophysiology.

Neuroleptic-induced tardive dyskinesia and dopamine-induced dyskinesia, the two most common types of drug-induced movement disorders, share a number of similarities in terms of epidemiology, risk factors, and pathophysiology mechanisms (Rascol & Fabre, 2001). For both conditions, long-lasting dysregulation of striatal dopaminergic receptors and related nondopaminergic neurotransmitter systems are thought to contribute to the development and persistence of the mechanisms causing dyskinesia (Rascol & Fabre, 2001). Proposed pathophysiology mechanisms used to explain tardive dyskinesia include dopamine receptor supersensitivity, catecholamine hyperactivity, and GABA hypoactivity (Wickman & Cold, 2000). The dopamine receptor supersensitivity model has substantial appeal, because of the role of dopamine in schizophrenia and the dopamine receptor blocking action of the older (i.e., typical, or conventional) neuroleptic agents. In addition, dopamine-induced dyskinesias are well established among patients with chronic Parkinson's disease. This dopamine receptor supersensitivity hypothesis suggests that blockade of postsynaptic dopamine receptors by neuroleptics increases either the number or sensitivity of the dopamine receptors (Wickman & Cold, 2000). This mechanism is similar to acetylcholine hypersensitivity induced fibrillation potentials recorded from denervated skeletal muscle fibers after upregulation of postsynaptic acetylcholine receptors. The dopamine receptor supersensitivity hypothesis cannot entirely explain the pathogenesis of tardive dyskinesia, however, as neuroleptic-induced dopamine receptor supersensitivity appears long before development of tardive dyskinesia (Casey, 2000; Wickman & Cold, 2000). Further, supersensitivity resolves rapidly after neuroleptics are withdrawn, while tardive dyskinesia may persist for months, years, or indefinitely (Casey, 2000; Richelson, 1999). The specific mechanism of neuroleptic-induced neurotoxicity is unknown, but it has been proposed that damage to basal ganglia neurons could be caused by free radicals (Casey, 2000). It is known that dopamine is metabolized by monoamine oxidase to dihydroxyphenylacetic acid, and hydrogen peroxide, a potent oxidant, is a by-product of this reaction (Wickman & Cold, 2000). The hypothesize proposes that hydrogen peroxide generates free radicals that react with proteins, lipids, and other cellular components, eventually resulting in neuronal dysfunction (Wickman & Cold, 2000).

An additional mechanism for neuroleptic-induced tardive dyskinesias involves the GABA system and GABA hypoactivity. GABA-ergic neurons are located throughout the subcortical regions of the brain, and they play an important role in control of normal movement and generation of abnormal movements. Tardive dyskinesia induced by conventional neuroleptics is associated with loss of basal ganglia GABA-ergic markers, although the underlying cause of the GABA-ergic depletion is unclear (Mitchell, Cooper, Griffiths, & Cooper, 2002). It has been proposed that tardive dyskinesia could be associated with decreased glutamic acid decarboxylase, the GABA-synthesizing enzyme, resulting in decreased GABA levels (Wickman & Cold, 2000). Nevertheless, GABA-agonist medications do not seem to produce sustained improvement in tardive dyskinesia (Casey, 2000). The frequency by which different neuroleptic medications produce tardive dyskinesia offers some insight to possible inciting pathophysiological mechanisms. For example, neuroleptics that block serotonin-2A (5-HT(2A)) receptors seem to produce fewer drug-induced extrapyramidal movement disorders than conventional agents that block dopamine-2 (D(2)) receptors (Bai, Yu, & Lin, 2003). Whether this difference reflects the location or duration of blockade, or other factors, such as selective increased sensitivity to dopamine within the nigrostriatal dopamine receptors following dopamine blockade but not serotonin blockade or even genetic factors involving the dopamine D(3) allele, is unknown (Bai et al., 2003).

There is some experimental evidence that haloperidol (Haldol), another typical neuroleptic similar to chlorpromazine, is toxic in vitro, and in vivo administration results in an increased number of apoptotic neurons in the striatum and in the substantia nigra (Mitchell et al., 2002). The toxicity of haloperidol is possibly a consequence of its conversion to pyridinium-based metabolites and potentially by raising glutamate-mediated transmission (Mitchell et al.).

Recognition that tardive dyskinesia frequently persists after neuroleptic withdrawal suggests a form of permanent neurological damage, as opposed to a short-term pharmacological effect. Nevertheless, tardive dyskinesia has not been associated with specific neuropathological alterations (Eyles, Pond, Van der Schyf, & Halliday, 2000). Neuroleptics are thought to interfere with *normal* mitochondrial function, possibly in association with tardive dyskinesia, by altering mitochondrial ultrastructure in basal ganglia neurons of patients and animals, including the baboon (Eyles et al., 2000). Despite this observation, neuropathological examination showed no consistent difference either in size or number of mitochondria between animals displaying persistent tardive dyskinesia after withdrawal of neuroleptics and control animals, suggesting that even if striatal neuronal mitochondria undergo ultrastructural alterations during neuroleptic treatment, these changes do not persist after drug withdrawal (Eyles et al.).

Imaging studies have limited utility in establishing the diagnosis of tardive dyskinesia. The patient described in the *case presentation* had normal CT and MRI studies, a finding important in excluding structural or vascular causes for the hyperkinetic movement disorder. A meta-analysis review of reports describing cranial CT results obtained from patients with tardive dyskinesia and referents suggested some possible neuroanatomical group differences, and a trend for patients with tardive dyskinesia to have slightly larger lateral ventricles than unaffected patients (Hoffman & Casey, 1991). The same reviewers concluded, however, that several well-conducted studies found no significant abnormalities (Hoffman & Casey, 1991). PET imaging may have greater application than conventional neuroimaging studies in identifying mechanisms important to dyskinesia in general, and tardive dyskinesia, in particular. Patients with Parkinson's disease who exhibit dose-related dopamine-induced dyskinesias have been studied using PET with [11C]raclopride (Fuente-Fernandez et al., 2004). Results suggest that the same dose of levodopa induced increasingly larger increases in dopamine at the synaptic level as Parkinson's disease progressed. Such increase in synaptic dopamine can lead to dramatic changes in receptor occupancy, possibly explaining the appearance of peak-dose dyskinesias as Parkinson's disease progresses (Fuente-Fernandez et al., 2004). These results have implications into the mechanism of neuroleptic-induced tardive dyskinesia. Possibly more relevant, striatal dopamine transporter (DAT) binding potential has been compared between schizophrenic subjects with and without tardive dyskinesia and controls. Subjects with tardive dyskinesia had lower DAT density than schizophrenic subjects without tardive dyskinesia, although the groups did not differ in terms of striatal binding potential (Yoder et al., 2004).

On occasion, response to treatment has important implications in establishing pathogenesis. Unfortunately, the treatment of tardive dyskinesia is relatively limited. The most obvious treatment is discontinuation of the neuroleptic medication, a treatment that results in gradual resolution of abnormal movement in some patients. This response is not uniformly effective, however, as tardive dyskinesia often persists despite discontinuation of the presumably offending agent. Antioxidants have been recommended by some to treat tardive dyskinesia, based on the hypothesis that dysfunction of basal ganglia neurons results from oxidative stress caused by hydrogen peroxide-generated free radicals (Wickman

& Cold, 2000). Prophylactic use of anticholinergic medications in association with neuroleptic medications is thought to reduce some of the associated motor system side effects, although it is unclear whether the use or the withdrawal of these anticholinergic drugs plays any role in the treatment of neuroleptic-induced tardive dyskinesia (Soares & McGrath, 2000). A recent Cochrane review of studies describing treatment of neuroleptic-induced tardive dyskinesia concluded that the currently available information is insufficient to evaluate the effectiveness of anticholinergic medications or the effectiveness of anticholinergic withdrawal (Soares & McGrath, 2000). There is some evidence that dopamine depleting agents are possibly useful for tardive dyskinesia (Rascol & Fabre, 2001). In a controlled study, risperidone, a dopamine receptor and serotonin receptor agonist, was more effective than neuroleptic discontinuation in the treatment of severe tardive dyskinesia (Bai et al., 2003). There also is some evidence that dopamine depleting agents are possibly useful treatments for tardive dyskinesia (Rascol & Fabre, 2001).

VERIFICATION OF CAUSE/ETIOLOGY

The syndrome of chlorpromazine-induced tardive dyskinesia fulfills all major criteria for causation. In terms of objective criteria for establishing a toxic etiology (see appendix) and as reflected in the preceding discussion, there is a known and relatively high risk of developing fairly consistent signs of the disorder, criteria that were met in the *case presentation* with appropriate timing between initiation of the medication and onset of these signs. Despite the fact that questions persist about the specific biology underlying tardive dyskinesia, the cause–effect plausibility is well established. The disorder is relatively specific and coherent, and as was the case here, removal from exposure most often modifies the adverse effects of the medication. Through the use of an appropriate differential diagnosis, other potential explanations for the patient's condition were excluded. This movement disorder is a well-established condition with relatively characteristic features, limiting confusion with other conditions producing abnormal movement. When these abnormal dyskinetic movements appear in the setting of chlorpromazine use, the diagnosis of chlorpromazine-induced tardive dyskinesia is established with a high degree of confidence, and the diagnosis is supported by resolution of the neurobehavioral abnormalities (dyskinesia) with removal from exposure in some patients. This was the case here, despite the continued presence of schizophrenia that was ultimately and successfully controlled with alternative medications. Unfortunately, the abnormal movements persist for some patients, although progression ceases.

Summary

Chlorpromazine is one of the older, typical neuroleptic medications. It is of interest in the context of neurobehavioral toxicology because of its association with neuroleptic-induced tardive dyskinesia. This disorder, in turn, is important in terms of its high prevalence, delayed onset, and frequent permanency, features relatively uncommon among the numerous neurotoxicants discussed in these volumes. Since chlorpromazine and similar neuroleptic medications are used often for prolonged periods of time, for a variety of conditions (including signs of agitation), and sometimes beginning in childhood (e.g., in treatment of Tourette's syndrome) or young adulthood (e.g., schizophrenia), there are important philosophical issues that should be carefully considered in such treatment. Despite strong clinical and experimental evidence linking tardive dyskinesia to neuroleptic medications and to specific motor circuits in the basal ganglia, there is little certainty about the underlying pathophysiology. Neurotoxicological models of tardive dyskinesia implicate long-lasting dysregulation of striatal dopaminergic receptors and related nondopaminergic neurotransmitter systems in the development and persistence of this disorder. At present, neuroleptic blockade of postsynaptic dopamine receptors is thought to result in an increased number of dopamine receptors or increased dopamine receptor sensitivity. The common persistence after removal from neuroleptic exposure is not fully explained, but the paucity of neuroimaging or neuropathological alteration supports a process involving neuronal receptors, or even mitochondria, without substantial loss of neurons or support tissues.

Toluene

Stanley Berent

Toluene is a clear, flammable, refractive liquid with distinctive odor that is found mainly as a natural component of crude oil and is produced during the process of making gasoline and other fuels from crude oil or coke (Agency for toxic substances and disease registry [ATSDR], 2005). Also, toluene is present in the Tolu (or balsam) tree (*Myroxylon balsamum*) (Agency for toxic substances and disease registry [ATSDR], 2005). This last observation is potentially important primarily because of the relatively wide use of Tolu-derived products in some nail polishes and OTC health aids (Leung & Foster, 2003; Taylor, 2005). Toluene has applications as a solvent in the manufacture of a wide variety of products, including paints and paint thinners, lacquers, adhesives, rubber, inks, perfumes, dyes, explosives, and other organic compounds (Agency for toxic substances and disease registry [ATSDR], 2005; Merck Research Laboratories, 2001).

Readily absorbed by ingestion or inhalation and to a lesser extent through contact with the skin, exposure to toluene can adversely affect multiple organ systems. However, it is toluene's affinity for the central nervous system (Benignus, 1981; Benignus, Muller, Barton, & Bittikofer, 1981; Filley et al., 2004; Greenberg, 1997), its adverse effects on the nervous system, as well as its potential to disrupt normal fetal development that have become the predominant public health concerns (Agency for toxic substances and disease registry [ATSDR], 2005). Although everyone can be expected to be exposed to toluene in some amount (e.g., from the use of home products containing this substance), those in certain occupations like printers who use toluene as a solvent in some settings and gas station attendants who inhale toluene fumes at work remain at increased risk for higher than usual levels of exposure. Also, exposure to toluene by way of purposeful inhalation of fumes from gasoline, glues, or other solvents containing this substance has been labeled as a troubling and urgent health problem (Agency for toxic substances and disease registry [ATSDR], 2005). While the prevalence of specific toluene substance abuse is not known, estimates suggest that 10–15% of young people in the United States have used inhalants at some time (Filley & Kleinschmidt-DeMasters, 2001). According to Filley et al., the use of inhalants may serve as the initial substance of abuse for young people, and the use of inhalants is likely to occur earlier than is abuse of ethanol, marijuana, or other substances. These investigators reported 1994 data indicating that approximately 20% of eighth graders claimed to have used inhalants at some time, with almost 6% admitting to such use within the past month (Filley et al.). Also, they pointed out that while the use of inhalants may start at a young age, its use may continue for many years and often well into adulthood.

Case presentation[9]

Dixit, Nadimpalli, and Cavallino (1999) reported a 29-year-old male with complaints of a worsening 8-month history of incoordination, unsteady and staggering gait, and tremor. The tremor was intermittent but appeared to be associated with his incoordination and involved all extremities. The patient admitted to a history of toluene inhalation abuse that he dated from age 16 years onward, but claimed he had stopped using toluene about 5 months before his appointment. The reported symptoms continued with slight improvement in ability to walk despite the termination of his substance abuse. The patient denied history of pain, memory difficulties, or sensory impairments.

NEUROLOGICAL EXAMINATION

The neurological examination, as described by Dixit et al. (1999) "... revealed dysarthric speech with intact cranial nerves, except for saccadic eye movement. Muscle strength was 5/5 in all four limbs and the deep tendon reflexes were well preserved. Sensory examination was completely normal. The patient's gait was ataxic and broad based with a positive finger-nose test and an equivocal Romberg test. Significant tremors were present at rest, which increased on intention. There was lack of coordination of rapid alternating movements. The rest of the physical exam was non-contributory."

NEUROPSYCHOLOGICAL EVALUATION

No neuropsychological evaluation was reported. While the neurological examination failed to document any difficulties in cognition or other neuropsychological impairments, Dixit et al. (1999) pointed out in discussion that neurobehavioral impairments are a frequent aspect in toluene intoxication, representing the most disabling feature of disorder and at times indicating irreversible central nervous system dysfunction. Along with cognitive dysfunction, other persistent problems can include ataxia, due to cerebellar degeneration, optic neuropathy, sensory-neural hearing loss, and disorders of equilibrium (Dixit et al.).

OTHER TEST RESULTS

Although toluene was not specifically included, a serum screening test for toxic substances and other laboratory tests all were within normal ranges. MRI of the brain, with and without contrast, showed diffuse atrophy of the cerebrum, cerebellum, and brainstem; hyperintensities on T2-weighted images in the internal capsule; hypointensities on T2-weighted images in thalamus bilaterally and symmetrically; and diffuse abnormal signal on T2-weighted images in white matter with indistinct gray–white matter differentiation (Dixit et al., 1999).

COMMENT

The half-life for toluene in tissue is relatively short, 0.5–2.7 days, with retention times varying as a result of amount of body fat (Feldman, 1998). Toluene can be directly detected in blood and by urine concentrations of hippuric acid, a metabolite of toluene. Neither of these tests is readily available, however, existing only at some specialized centers (Filley et al., 2004). Since the patient in the *case presentation* reported that he had stopped using toluene some time before his clinical evaluation, it is likely that laboratory testing would have been of little help in documenting his remote use even if such testing had been done. Moreover, and because such testing is not routinely available, the determination of toxicity is often made on the basis of history, behavioral observation, and clinical symptoms (Filley et al.).

DIFFERENTIAL DIAGNOSIS

The investigators established a diagnosis of "toxic encephalopathy," which they attributed specifically to toluene exposure. Other possible diagnoses they listed, and ruled out on the basis of history, examination, and laboratory test results included "neurodegenerative disease," leukodystrophy, HIV-infection, and multisubstance abuse.

Comment

Although "multisubstance abuse" was included in the differential diagnosis, Dixit et al. (1999) did not conclude a diagnosis of substance abuse. The absence of this diagnosis was likely more a matter of the authors' emphasis on radiological findings for publication purposes than outright oversight. Also, the authors appeared to be more focused on excluding multisubstance abuse than on substance abuse itself, perhaps considering the idea of substance abuse in this particular case to be self-evident and believing it was important to exclude possible exposures to substances other than toluene, the substance of their immediate interest. With the publication of *DSM-IV* (American Psychiatric Association, 1994), diagnoses became available to the clinician, e.g., "inhalant related disorders" that were specific to disorders brought on by aliphatic and aromatic hydrocarbons. The application of this diagnosis carries implications for behaviors that can be important to consider in cases of toxic encephalopathy, e.g., a knowledge base that includes research showing that substance abusers are likely to experiment with more than one chemical (American Psychiatric Association, 1994; Feldman, 1998; Filley et al., 2004; Goldman & Bennett, 2000) (also, see *other psychological/ psychiatric considerations* in chapter 17, for further discussion regarding substance abuse).

It is unclear from the Dixit et al. (1999) publication that individual components of a diagnosis of "encephalopathy" were documented in the clinical examination. That is, while no specific conclusion is listed in the publication, the investigators did describe neurobehavioral abnormalities, including cerebellar and pyramidal tract abnormalities, as being features of toluene-induced disorder, with neurobehavioral impairments representing the most frequent and disabling feature (Dixit et al.). Such neurobehavioral manifestations are essential to the clinical diagnosis of encephalopathy (Albers et al., 2004). Specific neuropsychological functions that would be expected to occur in toluene-induced dysfunction include inattention, apathy, memory disturbance, visuospatial impairment, but preserved language functions (Filley et al., 2004). These neurobehavioral impairments are said to correlate with the extent of MRI detected white matter abnormalities, especially with hyperintensities as observed on T2-weighted images, and subtle neurobehavioral manifestations are believed to be detectable early in the disorder before the development of clinical dementia (Filley et al.). The specific neuropsychological functional areas listed by Filley should be included under the general heading of dementia and other cognitive disorders. Worth noting is the necessity to include measurement of functions that are expected to be normal (language in this specific case) in the neurobehavioral examination, as well as those for which abnormal findings are expected. Strengths and weaknesses in various behavioral domains constitute a pattern that can be critical in concluding a neurobehavioral diagnosis.

NERVOUS SYSTEM LOCALIZATION

Symptoms, signs, and test findings in the *case presentation* consistently implicate the supratentorial and posterior fossa levels of the central nervous system.

CAUSE/ETIOLOGY

The cause for the patient's encephalopathy in the *case presentation* was said to be chronic exposure to toluene.

Discussion

The effects of toluene that have been reported in the scientific literature range from reversible neurobehavioral symptoms in acute exposures (including fatigue, headaches, impaired manual dexterity, sensory changes, and intoxication) (Berenguer, Soulage, Perrin, Pequignot, & Abraini, 2003; Boey, Foo, & Jeyaratnam, 1997; Byrne, Kirby, Zibin, & Ensminger, 1991; Campagna et al., 2001; Cavalleri, Gobba, Nicali, & Fiocchi, 2000; Klaassen & Watkins, 2003; Merck Research Laboratories, 2001) to permanent dysfunction or death in prolonged exposures, e.g., chronic abuse of toluene via purposeful inhalation, sometimes referred to as "snorting," "sniffing," "bagging," or "huffing" (Aydin et al., 2002; Bale, Tu, Carpenter-Hyland, Chandler, & Woodward, 2005; Byrne et al., 1991; Dixit et al., 1999; Filley et al., 2004; Filley, Heaton, & Rosenberg, 1990; Klaassen & Watkins, 2003). Central nervous system mediated cognitive and motor dysfunctions have been observed at toluene levels less than 150 ppm (Boey et al., 1997). Chronic exposures in workers at ambient levels below 130 ppm have been associated with impaired hearing and color vision (Abbate, Giorgianni, Munao, & Brecciaroli, 1993; Zavalic et al., 1998). Central nervous system changes in monoamine biosynthesis in response to long-term toluene exposure at levels as low as 40 ppm have been reported in animal studies (Soulage, Perrin, Berenguer, & Pequignot, 2004). These levels can be contrasted to those reported for solvent abusers, who might be exposed repeatedly to toluene at levels of 4,000–12,000 ppm (Agency for toxic substances and disease registry [ATSDR], 2005). Chronic toluene exposure can be associated with MRI with loss of brain gray–white matter differentiation, atrophy of the cerebrum, cerebellum, and brain stem in addition to other regions of the central nervous system (e.g., corpus callosum) (Caldemeyer, Armstrong, George, Moran, & Pascuzzi, 1996; Filley et al., 1990; Kamran & Bakshi, 1998; Rosenberg et al., 1988). Kamran and Bakshi (1998) documented low signal on T2-weighted signals in the cerebral cortex on MRI images over a 3-year period in a male toluene abuser with progressive neurological decline (Figure 16.4). These authors found that cerebral atrophy involved the corpus callosum and cerebellar vermis most prominently, with reduction in contrast between gray and white matter, low signal in the basal ganglia and midbrain, and diffuse supratentorial white matter high signal lesions (Kamran & Bakshi, 1998).

Filley and colleagues (Filley et al., 2004, 1990, 2001) have associated toluene exposure with leukoencephalopathy, a change in cerebral white matter in which myelin reflects the most pronounced abnormality. Geschwind (Geschwind, 1965; Geschwind & Kaplan, 1962) has been credited with advancing the idea that white matter is importantly involved in reciprocal connections between brain structures and that lesions that disrupt these interconnections are associated with a host of neurobehavioral dysfunctions, referred to collectively by Geschwind as representing a "disconnection syndrome." More recently, Filley (1998) continued to emphasize the importance of this aspect of the brain, providing a theoretical basis for predicting the clinical signs associated with white matter lesions. Filley pointed out, for instance, that in addition to white matter pathways that serve functions such as sensory-motor and interhemispheric communications and connections between cortical areas, there is asymmetry in white to gray matter

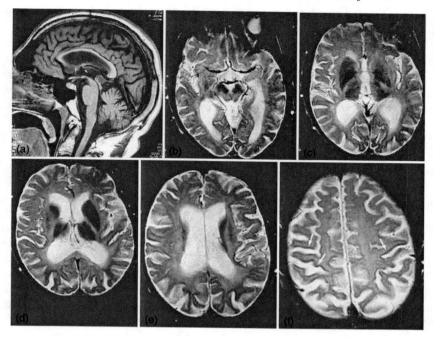

Figure 16.4 Conventional spin–echo images of a toluene abuser. **a.** Sagital view (non-contrast T1-weighted [500/16]) showing cerebral atrophy most prominent in corpus callosum and cerebellar vermis. **b–e.** Axial T2-weighted (2,000/100) views indicating generalized atrophy as reflected in enlarged ventricals and sulci, loss of gray–white matter distinction, and diffuse paraventricular white matter high signal. Bilateral low signal foci are present in caudate, putamen, globus pallidas, red nucleus, substantia nigra, and thanlamus. **c and f.** Low signal in lobar gray matter, prominent in medial occipital (see arrow in **c**), posterior frontal (see arrows in **f**), and peri-Rolandic parietal cortex.
From "MRI in Chronic Toluene Abuse: Low Signal in the Cerebral Cortex on T2-Weighted Images," by S. Kamran and R. Bakshi, 1998, *Neuroradiology*, 40, 519. With permission.

ratios between hemispheres, especially in the frontal lobes. On the basis of such observations, Filley (1998) advanced the idea that diffuse white matter pathology, as would be expected to result from toxic exposure, would lead to dysfunctions in attention, visuospatial ability, frontal lobe mediated behaviors, and emotional status. Admitting the incompleteness of our understanding with regard to the specific roles played by white matter in brain–behavior relationships, Filley et al. (1990) first advanced the notion of "white matter dementia" to summarize their findings. More recently, and in regard to toluene more specifically, Filley and colleagues (Filley et al., 2004; Filley et al., 2001) have referred to the clinical syndrome as "toxic (when specific, 'toluene') leukoencephalopathy" (see Table 16.7, and *cyclosporine* for a summary of the spectrum of neuropsychological, imaging, and neuropathological findings associated with toxic leukoencephalopathy).

Abnormalities evidenced on MRI in cases of leukoencephalopathy possibly reflect increased water in white matter or metabolic changes in myelin induced by toluene (Dixit et al., 1999). The disorders resulting from toluene abuse have been said by Dixit et al. to reflect multifocal central nervous system involvement, reflecting most likely variations in region-specific lipid content. While MRI and CT images usually reveal cerebral, cerebellar, and brainstem atrophy (Dixit et al.; Poungvarin, 1991; Valk & van der Knaap, 1992), other central nervous system neuroanatomical regions have been reported to be involved in individual cases (Dixit et al.) and have included the thalamus (Caldemeyer et al., 1996; Dixit et al.; Thuomas, Moller, Odkvist, Flodin, & Dige, 1996) and, in at least one case, the corpus callosum (Ikeda & Tsukagoshi, 1990).

While toxic leukoencephalopathy can be caused by exposure to a variety of substances including a number of therapeutic agents, toluene has the capacity to produce severe neurobehavioral impairments via its selective adverse effects on white matter (Filley et al., 2001). Filley et al. (2004) described "toluene leukoencephalopathy" as a syndrome that includes dementia, cerebellar ataxia, corticospinal tract dysfunction, brainstem impairment, and cranial neuropathies. He further described dementia as being the most pronounced clinical feature, with the dementia reflecting a pattern of inattention, apathy, memory and visuospatial impairments, but, importantly, preserved language functions.

These findings attributed to humans have been supported by data from animal studies, where changes in behavior, sensory impairments, and changes in brain structure and neurotransmitter levels in response to toluene exposure have been reported (Bale et al., 2005; Filley et al., 2004; Gerasimov et al., 2003; Miyagawa, Ohtani, & Suda, 1998; Paez-Martinez, Cruz, & Lopez-Rubalcava, 2003; Rogers, Miller, & Bunegin, 1999). Animals exposed to inhaled or orally administered toluene, for instance, show greater distributions of toluene in lipid rich regions of the central nervous system (i.e., brain stem) than in regions with less myelin (e.g., cerebral cortex grey matter), with a distribution similar to that found in the single human autopsy data reported in the same study (Ameno et al., 1992). These animal data have been seen as compatible with the hypothesis that toluene preferentially targets white matter in the central nervous system, serving as a basis for the development of toxic leukoencephalopathy (Filley et al.). At the same time, no animal model exists that explains completely the specific adverse effects of toluene exposure on myelin or other cellular aspects of the central nervous system nor the mechanism for white matter injury (Filley et al.).

With respect to the teratogenic effects of toluene, exposure to high levels of toluene during pregnancy has been associated with toxic effects on the developing fetus, with adverse consequences for fetal growth and development (Agency for toxic substances and disease registry [ATSDR], 2005; Bukowski, 2001; Chen, Wei, & Chan, 2004; Gospe & Zhou, 2000). The resultant condition has been referred to as *fetal solvent syndrome* and likened to *fetal alcohol syndrome* in terms of its clinical manifestations (Costa, Guizzetti, Burry, & Oberdoerster, 2002; Toutant & Lippmann, 1979). These manifestations include both morphological anomalies (e.g., growth retardation, cleft palate, microcephaly) and neurobehavioral impairments that can include developmental delays, cerebellar dysfunction, and behavioral disturbances such as hyperactivity (Filley et al., 2004). Looking at infants born to 56 mothers who abused solvents during pregnancy, Scheeres and Chudley (2002) reported that 21% were born preterm, with medical complications that ranged from adverse neurological sequelae (3.6%) to major physical anomalies (16.1%). Seven (12.5%) infants in the Scheeres and Chudley study had fetal alcohol syndrome-like facial features, and six (10.7%) evidenced hearing loss. They concluded that maternal substance abuse in pregnancy is associated with severe neonatal consequences. Embryopathy resulting from toluene exposure specifically has been shown to occur in animal models (Gospe & Zhou, 1998, 2000).

The occurrence of a toluene-induced disorder as a result of low-level exposures in occupational settings or in the conductance of routine household maintenance has not yet been determined (Filley et al., 2004). In addition, considerable variability exits in extent of myelin and axonal loss in autopsied cases for which exposure to toluene has been established (Filley et al.). This variability has been hypothesized to reflect one or more of a number of possible though difficult to establish individual differences, including duration and extent of exposure, polysubstance abuse, and genetic differences in enzymatic (e.g., aldehyde dehydrogenase) metabolism (Dixit et al., 1999; Filley et al.). Leukoencephalopathy detected by MRI was said by Filley et al. to represent severe white matter injury detectable only after many years of heavy toluene exposure, even though myelinotoxic injury may be occurring earlier.

Comment

Filley's proposition that myelinotoxic injury may be occurring although changes in white matter are detectable on imaging studies only after some years of exposure likely is characteristic of a number of human illnesses, e.g., progressive dementia (Berent et al., 1999). While some process like this most likely represents a reality about the nature of disease (e.g., that injury begins before the process is detectable with existing technology), attempts to reach clinical conclusions based on unproven hypotheses are likely to be wrong and, at best, lead to controversy. No matter how reasonable a hypothesis seems, until scientifically proven, it cannot be used in a manner other than speculative. Unfortunately, it is not uncommon to hear someone attribute clinical findings to a presumed, yet still unproven, underlying disease mechanism. One such instance involved a patient whose impaired neuropsychological examination results were interpreted as being suggestive of underlying neurological dysfunction due to toxicant exposure. Brain imaging and other neurological studies of this patient had been unrevealing, however. The clinician, nevertheless, described the patient's examination results as abnormal and attributed the impairments to underlying neuropathology that was at a still early stage in disease progression. While the clinician was correct in his descriptions of the patient's neurobehavioral strengths and weaknesses and in the conclusion that the pattern represented an abnormal neuropsychological condition, he was in error in attributing the findings to the hypothesized presence of a specific kind of neuropathology. Why? The neurobehavioral examination is a sensitive and powerful method for measuring a patient's behavioral functions as well as in identifying the presence and nature of behavioral abnormalities. In isolation, however, these behavioral measures are nonspecific, with a number of physical and psychological variables that can potentially explain the findings in a given case. The same can be said with regard to examination findings other than neuropsychological, e.g., a brain imaging finding in isolation. Since such measures cannot serve as their own criteria in establishing construct validity (Boll, 2000), there is no actual variable to compare the findings when a hypothetical concept is the only potential extra-test, clinical criterion. Once the hypothesized concept has been shown scientifically to be fact, additional studies become possible that can produce a valid understanding of the brain–behavior relationships in a given realm. At that point, a particular pattern of results on neuropsychological, or other, tests can become critical as a component in establishing both diagnosis and cause. Fortunately, such understanding does exist for many of the diagnostic problems seen in research and clinical practice.

VERIFICATION OF THE INITIAL CLINICAL DIAGNOSIS

The authors attached both a diagnosis (i.e., encephalopathy) and an etiology (i.e., toluene exposure) to their diagnostic statement. Here, we will discuss separately these two considerations. From the radiographic viewpoint of the authors who reported their findings on the patient in the *case presentation*, their diagnosis of "encephalopathy" can be verified. The MRI results they presented show unequivocal abnormalities in multiple locations in the central nervous system. From a neurobehavioral viewpoint, however, the lack of findings with regard to the presence of dementia or other cognitive impairment or emotional disturbance is concerning and excludes verification of "clinical encephalopathy" (Albers et al., 2004). Nevertheless, the authors did list the neurobehavioral consequences that are usually associated with the nature of their MRI results. Taking into account the fact that this case was drawn from a published article that sought to focus on the radiographic aspects of the case, we could consider that such findings were present even though not specifically mentioned. At the same time, these authors did rule out dementia, or even memory impairment. Given the literature reviewed earlier, this last observation, together with the fact that by history the patient had experienced symptomatic improvement after terminating his abuse of a toxic substance, it is likely that the patient was in a relatively early stage in terms of manifesting signs of toluene neurotoxicity, although a stage sufficient to produce positive findings on imaging studies.

Earlier, we discussed the relevance of substance abuse as an additional diagnosis that would be appropriate in this instance. While the authors excluded what they termed, "multisubstance abuse," they did not list *substance abuse* itself in their final conclusion. While we will not discuss this omission further here, this diagnosis should be added to the final diagnostic statement (see *other psychological/psychiatric considerations*, chapter 17 for further discussion of this topic).

VERIFICATION OF THE INITIAL CAUSE/ETIOLOGY

The primary clinical neurological findings in the *case presentation* were attributed to toluene exposure. The strongest evidence supporting this conclusion is represented by MRI findings that show the nature and location of pathology that is consistent with findings reported in the scientific literature as being associated with such exposure. The patient's symptoms of incoordination worsening over time and tremor, together with the signs observed during the neurological examination (e.g., ataxic gait, tremor worsening with intention, and lack of coordination on rapid alternating movements) also were consistent with findings associated with toluene exposure. Also consistent with toluene exposure was the approximately 13-year history of toluene abuse, as well as the slight improvement in his symptoms following discontinuation of substance abuse.

The absence of findings of cognitive impairment, outright dementia, or behavioral disturbances represents a significant weakness in documenting toluene as the cause of this patient's complaints. The presence of neuropsychological impairments has been well established as a hallmark of toluene-induced central nervous system dysfunction. Given that the authors who first described this patient discussed the topic of neurobehavioral disturbance in their publication, it may well be that neuropsychological impairments were present but not specifically described in the publication. If that was the case, the findings would meet the majority of objective criteria for establishing a toxic etiology related to the patient's substance abuse as the cause for his clinical condition. The following caveat should be mentioned, however. That is, attributing toxic effects to one substance, toluene, is difficult. Inhalant abusers, in general, are known to experiment with, and often abuse, a variety of substances on a continuing basis (American Psychiatric Association, 1994; Feldman, 1998; Goldman & Bennett, 2000). Multiple-substance abuse was ruled out in this case; however, this was based on patient report only, and no laboratory results or other information were available to document the presence of toluene or other substances. Even when the substance user might intend to limit their use to toluene, most often substances thought to be toluene contain other chemicals that in themselves can be harmful. In the now classic case presented by Grabski (1961) and later by Knox and Nelson (1966), the patient, who was described as going to unusual lengths to obtain and use only pure toluene, was found to have used other substances as well (see *other psychological/*

psychiatric considerations, chapter 17 for further details related to the case presented by Grabski and Knox).

In terms of specific criteria for establishing a toxic etiology in general (Hill, 1965), the timing of exposure and onset of signs are consistent with the causal conclusion. Also, the conclusion fits with what is known about the risk associated with such use. The reported findings are biologically plausible, and the slight improvement in symptoms following abstinence implies both a temporal relation and a biological gradient. Other potential explanations in the differential diagnosis were investigated and excluded. As mentioned, however, some weaknesses in terms of causality persist, especially with regard to identifying toluene as the specific toxicant causing the patient's dysfunction. So, while it is likely based on the radiographic and differential diagnostic findings that toluene exposure was causal to the diagnosis in this *case presentation*, a number of assumptions are necessary to make this conclusion.

Conclusion

As is the case with many of the substances reviewed in these volumes, this presentation underscores the importance of the differential diagnosis as well as the important distinction between diagnosis and causal determination. Behavioral factors need to be considered in reaching final diagnostic conclusions. Especially in terms of what is known about the effects of toluene on the central nervous system, behavioral strengths and weaknesses fit a predictable pattern that corresponds to radiographic findings and should always be included in the clinical evaluation.

This case illustrates how a substance that is abundant in our environment can have the capacity to harm, especially when exposure to a substance such as toluene is purposely abused. The social and psychological consequences of substance abuse can be devastating to the individual, their families, and friends, and costly to society. At the same time, such abuse presents a serendipitous model that affords an opportunity to study the effects on the nervous system from high and prolonged chemical exposures.

Summary

The cases chosen for this chapter reflect toxicant-induced neurobehavioral disorders that may be encountered in clinical practice. The *case presentations* all implicate involvement of the central nervous system. The symptoms and signs associated with the various medications and substances reviewed can at times be relatively specific (e.g., chlorpromazine-induced tardive dyskinesia). More often, however, the clinical findings are nonspecific, reflecting the complexity of the central nervous system. Behavior and underlying physiology are multiply determined. And, while a given substance can adversely affect normal brain–behavior functions, a host of other variables compete to explain findings in a given case. For each presentation in this chapter, a systematic approach was used to identify objectively and simplify a differential diagnosis independent of causal attribution. The cause of the patient's pathology was then approached using a criteria- and evidence-based model designed to account for what is scientifically known about each potential causal factor and to account for or exclude potentially explanatory alternatives.

Among other things, the presentations in this chapter underscore the futility of arriving at diagnostic and causal conclusions that are based on oversimplified models that rely on partial or nonvalidated methods, e.g., determination of cause and effect solely on the basis of temporal correlation, a specified symptom pattern, or in the absence of a complete differential diagnosis.

Notes

1 Details of the history have been modified to protect the anonymity of the patient and family.
2 The Wada Test is a procedure in which the neural activity of one cerebral hemisphere is blocked by injecting an anesthetic through a catheter in the internal carotid artery. While one hemisphere is inactivated, language and memory functions of the other hemisphere are assessed (Wada, 1997; Wada & Rasmussen, 1960).
3 The patient described in this *clinical presentation* was adapted from Malay (2001).
4 Preparation of this section was supported in part by funding from Prana Biotechnology Ltd.
5 This *case presentation* is modified from Ricoy, Ortega, and Cabello (1982).
6 The patient described has been reported previously by Albers (2003), as well as in chapter 11 of volume II of the present book.
7 Adapted from Tuglu et al. (2005).
8 Adapted from Knight (2004).
9 Adapted from Dixit et al. (1999).

References

Alberta Alcohol and Drug Abuse Commission (AADAC). (2004). *Amphetamines: The ABCs.* Retrieved from http://corp.aadac.com/other_drugs/the_basics_about_other_drugs/amphetamines_abcs.asp

Abarbanel, J. M., Berginer, V. M., Osimani, A., Solomon, H., & Charuzi, I. (1987). Neurologic complications after gastric restriction surgery for morbid obesity. *Neurology, 37*, 196–200.

Abbate, C., Giorgianni, C., Munao, F., & Brecciaroli, R. (1993). Neurotoxicity induced by exposure to toluene. An electrophysiologic study. *International Archives of Occupational and Environmental Health, 64*, 389–392.

Abi-Dargham, A. (2004). Do we still believe in the dopamine hypothesis? New data bring new evidence. *International Journal of Neuropsychopharmacology, 7*(Suppl. 1), S1–S5.

Abi-Dargham, A., & Moore, H. (2003). Prefrontal DA transmission at D1 receptors and the pathology of schizophrenia. *Neuroscientist, 9*, 404–416.

Abraham, G., & Owen, J. (2004). Topiramate can cause lithium toxicity. *Journal of Clinical Psychopharmacology, 24*, 565–567.

Abraham, G., & Voutsilakos, F. (2004). Norwalk precipitates severe lithium toxicity. *Canadian Journal of Psychiatry—Revue Canadienne de Psychiatrie, 49,* 215–216.

Adams, K. M., & Grant, I. (1986). The influence of premorbid risk factors on neuro-psychological performance in alcoholics. *Journal of Clinical and Experimental Neuropsychology, 8,* 362–370.

Adams, K. M., Grant, I., & Reed, R. (1980). Neuropsychology in alcoholic men in their late thirties: One year follow-up. *American Journal of Psychiatry, 137,* 928–931.

Adityanjee, Munshi, K. R., & Thampy, A. (2005). The syndrome of irreversible lithium-effectuated neurotoxicity. *Clinical Neuropharmacology, 28,* 38–49.

Agency for toxic substances and disease registry (ATSDR). (2005). *ToxFAQs for toluene.* Retrieved from http://www.atsdr.cdc.gov/tfacts56.html

Agranoff, B. W., Cotman, C. W., & Uhler, M. D. (1999). Learning and memory. In G. J. Siegel, B. W. Agranoff, R. W. Albers, J. W. Fisher, & M. D. Uhler (Eds.), *Basic neurochemistry: Molecular, cellular and medical aspects* (6th ed., pp. 1027–1052). Philadelphia: Lippincott-Raven.

Albers, J. W. (2003). Toxic neuropathies. In M. B. Bromberg (Ed.), *AAN 55th Annual Meeting Education Program Syllabus: Peripheral Neuropathy* (pp. 7FC.006-149–7FC.006-168). Hawaii: American Academy of Neurology.

Albers, J. W., Berent, S., Garabrant, D. H., Giordani, B., Schweitzer, S. J., Garrison, R. P., et al. (2004). The effects of occupational exposure to chlorpyrifos on the neurologic examination of central nervous system function: A prospective cohort study. *Journal of Occupational and Environmental Medicine, 46,* 367–378.

Albers, J. W., & Kelly, J. J., Jr. (1989). Acquired inflammatory demyelinating poly-neuropathies; clinical and electrodiagnostic features. *Muscle and Nerve, 12,* 435–451.

Albers, J. W., Nostrant, T. T., & Riggs, J. E. (1989). Neurologic manifestations of gastrointestinal disease. In J. E. Riggs (Ed.), *Neurology clinics. Neurologic manifestations of systemic disease* (Vol. 7, pp. 509–548). Philadelphia: W. B. Saunders Company.

Allen, N., Mendell, J. R., Billmaier, D. J., Fontaine, R. E., & O'Neill, J. (1975). Toxic polyneuropathy due to methyl *n*-butyl ketone: An industrial outbreak. *Archives of Neurology, 32,* 209–218.

Alpert, E., & Seigerman, C. (1986). Steroid withdrawal psychosis in a patient with closed head injury. *Archives of Physical Medicine and Rehabilitation, 67,* 766–769.

Ameno, K., Kiriu, T., Fuke, C., Ameno, S., Shinohara, T., & Ijiri, I. (1992). Regional brain distribution of toluene in rats and in a human autopsy. *Archives of Toxicology, 66,* 153–156.

American Psychiatric Association. (1994). *Diagnostic and Statistical Manual of Mental Disorders* (4th ed.). Washington, DC: Author.

American Psychiatric Association. (2000). *Diagnostic and Statistical Manual of Mental Disorders (DSM-IV-TR).* Washington, DC: Author.

Andersson-Roswall, L., Engman, E., Samuelsson, H., Sjoberg-Larsson, C., & Malmgren, K. (2004). Verbal memory decline and adverse effects on cognition in adult patients with pharmacoresistant partial epilepsy: A longitudinal controlled study of 36 patients. *Epilepsy and Behavior, 5,* 677–686.

Aoki, K., Ohtani, M., Sobue, I., & Ando, K. (1972). Clinico-epidemiological study on the occurrence of subacute-myelo-optico-neuropathy (SMON) in relation to clio-quinol. *Japanese Journal of Public Health, 19,* 305–310.

Arnulf, I. (2005). Kleine-Levin syndrome: A systematic review of 186 cases in the literature. *Brain, 128,* 2763–2776.

Avants, B., Grossman, M., & Gee, J. C. (2005). The correlation of cognitive decline with frontotemporal dementia induced annualized gray matter loss using diffeomorphic morphometry. *Alzheimer Disease and Associated Disorders, 19*(Suppl. 8), S25–S28.

Aydin, K., Sencer, S., Demir, T., Ogel, K., Tunaci, A., & Minareci, O. (2002). Cranial MR findings in chronic toluene abuse by inhalation. *AJNR: American Journal of Neuroradiology, 23*, 1173–1179.

Badiani, A., & Robinson, T. E. (2004). Drug-induced neurobehavioral plasticity: The role of environmental context. *Behavioural Pharmacology, 15*, 327–339.

Bahemuka, M. (1981). Neurotoxicity in relation to tropical peripheral neuropathy: A re-appraisal. *East African Medical Journal, 58*, 478–483.

Bai, Y. M., Yu, S. C., & Lin, C. C. (2003). Risperidone for severe tardive dyskinesia: A 12-week randomized, double-blind, placebo-controlled study. *Journal of Clinical Psychiatry, 64*, 1342–1348.

Baker, K. G., Harding, A. J., Halliday, G. M., Kruill, J. J., & Harper, C. (1999). Neuronal loss in functional zones of the cerebellum of chronic alcoholics with and without Wernicke's encephalopathy. *Neuroscience, 91*, 429–438.

Bale, A. S., Tu, Y., Carpenter-Hyland, E. P., Chandler, L. J., & Woodward, J. J. (2005). Alterations in glutamatergic and gabaergic ion channel activity in hippocampal neurons following exposure to the abused inhalant toluene. *Neuroscience, 130*, 197–206.

Banerji, N. K., & Hurwitz, L. J. (1971). Nervous system manifestations after gastric surgery. *Acta Neurologica Scandinavia, 47*, 485–513.

Barchas, J. D., & Altemus, M. (1999). Biochemical hypotheses of mood and anxiety disorders. In G. J. Siegel, B. W. Agranoff, S. K. Fisher, R. W. Albers, & M. D. Uhler (Eds.), *Basic neurochemistry: Molecular, cellular and medical aspects* (6th ed., pp. 1074–1093). Philadelphia: Lippincott-Raven.

Bardelli, A. M., & Biagini, L. (1986). Hydroxyquinolines and SMON (subacute-myelo-optic-neuropathy). Presentation and discussion of two cases of optic atrophy. *Bollettino di Oculistica, 65*, 705–718.

Barker, M. J., Greenwood, K. M., Jackson, M., & Crowe, S. F. (2004a). Cognitive effects of long-term benzodiazepine use: A meta-analysis. *CNS Drugs, 18*, 37–48.

Barker, M. J., Greenwood, K. M., Jackson, M., & Crowe, S. F. (2004b). Persistence of cognitive effects after withdrawal from long-term benzodiazepine use: A meta-analysis. *Archives of Clinical Neuropsychology, 19*, 437–454.

Barnett, M. H., Pollard, J. D., Davies, L., & McLeod, J. G. (1998). Cyclosporin A in resistant chronic inflammatory demyelinating polyradiculoneuropathy. *Muscle and Nerve, 21*, 454–460.

Bartha, L., Marksteiner, J., Bauer, G., & Benke, T. (2002). Persistent cognitive deficits associated with lithium intoxication: A neuropsychological case description. *Cortex, 38*, 743–752.

Baumann, N., & Hauw, J. J. (1980). Iatrogenic neurological diseases of the peripheral nervous system. *Progress in Clinical and Biological Research, 39*, 327–336.

Baumgartner, G., Elmqvist, D., & Shigematsu, I. (1984). SMON in Japan. *Acta Neurologica Scandinavia, 100*, 171–174.

Baumgartner, G., Gawel, M. J., Kaeser, H. E., Pallis, C. A., Rose, F. C., Schaumburg, H. H. et al. (1979). Neurotoxicity of halogenated hydroxyquinolines: Clinical analysis of cases reported outside Japan. *Journal of Neurology, Neurosurgery and Psychiatry, 42*, 1073–1083.

Baumgartner, G., Gilland, O., Kaeser, H. E., Pallis, C. A., Rose, F. C., Schaumburg, H. H. et al. (1984). Neurotoxicity of halogenated hydroxyquinolines. *Journal of Neurology, Neurosurgery and Psychiatry, 47*, 100.

Beaglehole, R., & Jackson, R. (1992). Alcohol, cardiovascular disease and all causes of death: A review of the epidemiological evidence. *Drug Alcohol Review, 11*, 275–290.

Benignus, V. A. (1981). Health effects of toluene: A review. *Neurotoxicology, 2*, 567–588.

Benignus, V. A., Muller, K. E., Barton, C. N., & Bittikofer, J. A. (1981). Toluene levels in blood and brain of rats during and after respiratory exposure. *Toxicology and Applied Pharmacology, 61*, 326–334.

Berenguer, P., Soulage, C., Perrin, D., Pequignot, J. M., & Abraini, J. H. (2003). Behavioral and neurochemical effects induced by subchronic exposure to 40 ppm toluene in rats. *Pharmacology, Biochemistry & Behavior, 74*, 997–1003.

Berent, S., Giordani, B., Foster, N., Minoshima, S., Lajiness-O'Neill, R., Koeppe, R., et al. (1999). Neuropsychological function and cerebral glucose utilization in isolated memory impairment and Alzheimer's disease. *Journal of Psychiatric Research, 33*, 7–16.

Berent, S., Sackellares, J. C., Giordani, B., Wagner, J. G., Donofrio, P. D., & Abou-Khalil, B. (1987). Zonisamide (CI-912) and cognition: Results from preliminary study. *Epilepsia, 28*, 61–67.

Berry, N., Pradhan, S., Sagar, R., & Gupta, S. K. (2003). Neuroleptic malignant syndrome in an adolescent receiving olanzapine–lithium combination therapy. *Pharmacotherapy, 23*, 255–259.

Biessels, G. -J., ter Braak, E., Erkelens, D. W., & Hijman, R. (2001). Cognitive function in patients with Type 2 diabetes mellitus. *Neuroscience Research Communications, 28*, 11–22.

Bilanakis, N., & Gibiriti, M. (2004). Lithium intoxication, hypercalcemia and "accidentally" induced food and water aversion: A case report. *Progress in Neuro-Psychopharmacology and Biological Psychiatry, 28*, 201–203.

Billson, F. H., Reich, J., & Hopkins, I. J. (1972). Visual failure in a patient with ulcerative colitis treated by clioquinol. *Lancet, 1*, 1015–1016.

Bird, S. J., & Rich, M. M. (2002). Critical illness myopathy and polyneuropathy. *Current Neurology & Neuroscience Reports, 2*, 527–533.

Bloodworth, D. (2005). Issues in opioid management. *American Journal of Physical Medicine and Rehabilitation, 84*(Suppl. 55), S42–S55.

Boey, K. W., Foo, S. C., & Jeyaratnam, J. (1997). Effects of occupational exposure to toluene: A neuropsychological study on workers in Singapore. *Annals of the Academy of Medicine, Singapore, 26*, 184–187.

Bolanos, S. H., Khan, D. A., Hanczyc, M., Bauer, M. S., Dhanani, N., & Brown, E. S. (2004). Assessment of mood states in patients receiving long-term corticosteroid therapy and in controls with patient-rated and clinician-rated scales. *Annals of Allergy, Asthma, and Immunology, 92*, 500–505.

Boll, T. J. (2000). Measuring behavior. In J. W. Albers & S. Berent (Eds.), *Clinical neurobehavioral toxicology* (pp. 579–599). Philadelphia: W. B. Saunders Company.

Borowski, T. B., & Kokkinidis, L. (1998). The effects of cocaine, amphetamine, and the dopamine D1 receptor agonist SKF 38393 on fear extinction as measured with potentiated startle: Implications for psychomotor stimulant psychosis. *Behavioral Neuroscience, 112*, 952–965.

Bourgeois, B. F. (2004). Determining the effects of antiepileptic drugs on cognitive function in pediatric patients with epilepsy. *Journal of Child Neurology, 19*(Suppl. 24), S15–S24.

Bourget, D., & Whitehurst, L. (2004). Capgras syndrome: A review of the neurophysiological correlates and presenting clinical features in cases involving physical violence. *Canadian Journal of Psychiatry—Revue Canadienne de Psychiatrie, 49*, 719–725.

Boxer, A. L., & Miller, B. L. (2005). Clinical features of frontotemporal dementia. *Alzheimer Disease and Associated Disorders, 19*(Suppl. 6), S3–S6.

Brambilla, P., Glahn, D. C., Balestrieri, M., & Soares, J. C. (2005). Magnetic resonance findings in bipolar disorder. *Psychiatric Clinics of North America, 28*, 443–467.

Bray, J. W., & Zarkin, G. A. (2006). Economic evaluation of alcoholism treatment. *Alcohol Research and Health, 29*, 27–33.

Brin, M. F., Pedley, T. A., Lovelace, R. E., Emerson, R. G., Gouras, P., MacKay, C. et al. (1986). Electrophysiologic features of abetalipoproteinemia: Functional consequences of vitamin E deficiency. *Neurology, 36*, 669–673.

Bromberg, M. B., Wald, J. J., Forshew, D. A., Feldman, E. L., & Albers, J. W. (1997). Randomized trial of azathioprine or prednisone for initial immunosuppressive treatment of myasthenia gravis. *Journal of the Neurological Sciences, 150*, 59–62.

Bron, H. L., Korten, J. J., Pinckers, A. J., & Majoor, C. L. (1972). Subacute myelo-optico-neuropathy following use of large amounts of iodochlorhydroxyquinoline (Enterovioform). [Dutch]. *Nederlands Tijdschrift voor Geneeskunde, 116*, 1615–1618.

Brown, E. S., Khan, D. A., & Nejtek, V. A. (1999). The psychiatric side effects of corticosteroids. *Annals of Allergy, Asthma, and Immunology, 83*, 495–503.

Brown, E. S., Suppes, T., Khan, D. A., & Carmody, T. J., III. (2002). Mood changes during prednisone bursts in outpatients with asthma. *Journal of Clinical Psychopharmacology, 22*, 55–61.

Brown, L. A., Kolls, J. K., Wands, J. R., Nagy, L. E., Cook, R. T., Jerrells, T. R., et al. (2006). Acute and chronic alcohol abuse modulate immunity. *Alcohol: Clinical and Experimental Research 30*, 1624–1631.

Bukowski, J. A. (2001). Review of the epidemiological evidence relating toluene to reproductive outcomes. *Regulatory Toxicology and Pharmacology, 33*, 147–156.

Bush, S. S., & Martin, T. A. (2005). *Geriatric neuropsychology: Practice essentials.* London and New York: Taylor & Francis.

Byne, W., White, L., Parella, M., Adams, R., Harvey, P. D., & Davis, K. L. (1998). Tardive dyskinesia in a chronically institutionalized population of elderly schizophrenic patients: Prevalence and association with cognitive impairment. *International Journal of Geriatric Psychiatry, 13*, 473–479.

Byrne, A., Kirby, B., Zibin, T., & Ensminger, S. (1991). Psychiatric and neurological effects of chronic solvent abuse. *Canadian Journal of Psychiatry—Revue Canadienne de Psychiatrie, 36*, 735–738.

Caldemeyer, K. S., Armstrong, S. W., George, K. K., Moran, C. C., & Pascuzzi, R. M. (1996). The spectrum of neuroimaging abnormalities in solvent abuse and their clinical correlation. *Journal of Neuroimaging, 6*, 167–173.

Calello, D. P., & Osterhoudt, K. C. (2004). Acute psychosis associated with therapeutic use of dextroamphetamine. *Pediatrics, 113*, 1466.

Campagna, D., Stengel, B., Mergler, D., Limasset, J. C., Diebold, F., Michard, D., et al. (2001). Color vision and occupational toluene exposure. *Neurotoxicology and Teratology, 23*, 473–480.

Capgras, J., & Rebaul-Lachoux, J. (1923). L'illusion des sosies dans un delire systematise. *Bulletin de la societe clinique de medicine mentale, 11,* 6–16.

Carroll, B. J., Curtis, G. C., & Mendels, J. (1976). Neuroendocrine regulation in depression. II. Discrimination of depressed from nondepressed patients. *Archives of General Psychiatry, 33,* 1051–1058.

Casey, D. E. (2000). Tardive dyskinesia: Pathophysiology and animal models. *Journal of Clinical Psychiatry, 61*(Suppl. 4), 5–9.

Castillo, P., Woodruff, B., Caselli, R., Vernino, S., Lucchinetti, C., Swanson, J., et al. (2006). Steroid-responsive encephalopathy associated with autoimmune thyroiditis. *Archives of Neurology, 63,* 197–202.

Cavalleri, A., Gobba, F., Nicali, E., & Fiocchi, V. (2000). Dose-related color vision impairment in toluene-exposed workers. *Archives of Environmental Health, 55,* 399–404.

Cavanagh, J. B. (1971). The aetiology of S.M.O.N. *Lancet, 2,* 868–869.

Cawthon, P. M., Harrison, S. L., Barrett-Connor, E., Fink, H. A., Cauley, J. A., Lewis, C. E., et al. (2006). Alcohol intake and its relationship to bone mineral density, falls, and fracture risk in older men. *Journal of the American Geriatric Society 54*(11), 1649–1657.

Cerullo, M. A. (2006). Corticosteroid-induced mania: Prepare for the unpredictable. Retrieved from www.currentpsychiatry.com/article_pages.asp?AID=4147&UID

Chakrabarti, S., & Chand, P. K. (2002). Lithium-induced tardive dystonia. *Neurology India, 50,* 473–475.

Chan, P., Chen, J. H., Lee, M. H., & Deng, J. F. (1994). Fatal and nonfatal methamphetamine intoxication in the intensive care unit. *Journal of Toxicology—Clinical Toxicology, 32,* 147–155.

Charasz, N., Vacherot, B., Dougados, M., Bousser, M. G., Belaiche, J., & Cattan, D. (1979). Subacute myelo-optic-neuropathy during treatment with chloro-iodo-hydroxyquinoleine. [French]. *Gastroenterologie Clinique et Biologique, 3,* 371–374.

Charness, M. E., Simon, R. P., & Greenberg, D. A. (1989). Medical progress: Ethanol and the nervous system. *New England Journal of Medicine, 321,* 442–454.

Chau, S. Y., & Mok, C. C. (2003). Factors predictive of corticosteroid psychosis in patients with systemic lupus erythematosus. *Neurology, 61,* 104–107.

Chawarski, M. C., Mazlan, M., & Schottenfeld, R. S. (2006). Heroin dependence and HIV infection in Malaysia. *Drug and Alcohol Dependence, 82*(Suppl. 42), S39–S42.

Chen, A. C., Porjesz, B., Rangaswamy, M., Kamarajan, C., Tang, Y., Jones, K. A., et al. (2007). Reduced frontal lobe activity in subjects with high impulsivity and alcoholism. *Alcoholism: Clinical and Experimental Research, 31,* 156–165.

Chen, C. K., Lin, S. K., Sham, P. C., Ball, D., Loh, E., & Murray, R. M. (2005). Morbid risk for psychiatric disorder among the relatives of methamphetamine users with and without psychosis. *American Journal of Medical Genetics, Part B, Neuropsychiatric Genetics, 136B,* 87–91.

Chen, H. H., Wei, C. T., & Chan, M. H. (2004). Neonatal toluene exposure alters glutamate-induced calcium signaling in developing cerebellar granule neurons. *Annals of the New York Academy of Sciences, 1025,* 556–560.

Chevaleraud, J. P., & Hamard, H. (1985). Optic neuropathies. [French]. *Bulletin des Societes d Ophtalmologie de France, Spec No,* 167–180, 185–192.

Chouinard, G. (2004). New nomenclature for drug-induced movement disorders including tardive dyskinesia. *Journal of Clinical Psychiatry, 65,* 9–15.

Cohen, J. A., & Raps, E. C. (1995). Critical neurologic illness in the immunocompromised patient. *Neurologic Clinics, 13*, 659–677.

Collie, A. (2005). Cognition in liver disease. *Liver International, 25*, 1–8.

Commission on Classification and Terminology of the International League against Epilepsy. (1989). Proposal for revised classification of epilepsies and epileptic syndromes. *Epilepsia, 30*, 389–399.

Cone, E. J., Darwin, W. D., Gorodetzky, C. W., & Tan, T. (1978). Comparative metabolism of hydrocodone in man, rat, guinea pig, rabbit, and dog. *Drug Metabolism and Disposition, 6*, 488–493.

Costa, G. M., Pizzi, C., Bresciani, B., Tumscitz, C., Gentile, M., & Bugiardini, R. (2001). Acute myocardial infarction caused by amphetamines: A case report and review of the literature. *Italian Heart Journal: Official Journal of the Italian Federation of Cardiology, 2*, 478–480.

Costa, L. G., Guizzetti, M., Burry, M., & Oberdoerster, J. (2002). Developmental neurotoxicity: Do similar phenotypes indicate a common mode of action? A comparison of fetal alcohol syndrome, toluene embryopathy and maternal phenylketonuria. *Toxicology Letters, 127*, 197–205.

Cramer, J. A., Ben-Menachem, E., French, J., & Mattsson, R. H. (1999). New antiepileptic drugs: Comparison of key clinical trials. *Epileptia, 40*, 590–600.

Crane, G. E. (1973). Persistent dyskinesia. *British Journal of Psychiatry, 122*, 395–405.

Critchley, E. M. (1979). Drug-induced neurological disease. *British Medical Journal, 1*, 862–865.

Cummings, J., & Trimble, M. R. (1995). *A concise guide to behavioral neurology and neuropsychiatry*. Washington: American Psychiatric Association Press.

Dallocchio, C., & Mazzarello, P. (2002). A case of Parkinsonism due to lithium intoxication: Treatment with pramipexole. *Journal of Clinical Neuroscience, 9*, 310–311.

Dang, A. H., & Hershman, J. M. (2002). Lithium-associated thyroiditis. *Endocrine Practice, 8*, 232–236.

de Groen, P. C., Aksamit, A. J., & Rakela, J. (1987). Central nervous system toxicity after liver transplantation. *New England Journal of Medicine, 317*, 861–866.

de Pinto, O., & Burley, D. (1977). Clioquinol: Time to act. *Lancet, 1*, 1256.

Degos, C. F., & Thomas-Lamotte, P. J. (1977). A iatrogenic disease … subacute myelo-optico-neuropathy. [French]. *Revue du Praticien, 27*, 2277–2285.

Denko, J. D. (1977). Problems in diagnosis and treatment of lupus psychosis. Report of a patient with systemic lupus erythematosus, Hashimoto's thyroiditis, and Sjogren's syndrome. *American Journal of Psychotherapy, 31*, 125–137.

Derakhshan, I., & Forough, M. (1978). Progressive visual loss after eight years on clioquinol. *Lancet, 1*, 715.

Dixit, P., Nadimpalli, S. R., & Cavallino, R. P. (1999). Toxic encephalopathy due to chronic toluene abuse: Report of a case with magnetic resonance imaging (letter to the editor). *Indian Journal of Radiology and Imaging 9*(2), 1–4.

Dreifuss, F. E. (1987). Classification of the epilepsies: Influence on management. *Revue Neurologique, 143*, 375–380.

Duell, P. B., Connor, W. E., & Illingworth, D. R. (1998). Rhabdomyolysis after taking atorvastatin with gemfibrozil. *American Journal of Cardiology, 81*, 368–369.

Dyck, P. J., Gianni, C., & Lais, A. (1993). Pathological alteration of nerves. In P. J. Dyck, P. K. Thomas, J. W. Griffen, P. A. Low, & J. F. Poduslo (Eds.), *Periphral neuropathy* (3rd ed., pp. 514–595). Philadelphia: W.B. Saunders Co.

Dykstra, L. (1992). Drug action. In J. Grabowski & G. R. VandenBos (Eds.), *Psychopharmacology: Basic mechanisms and applied interventions* (pp. 59–96). Washington, DC: American Psychological Association.

Ende, G., Walter, S., Welzel, H., Demirakca, T., Wokrina, T., Ruf, M., et al. (2006). Alcohol consumption significantly influences the MR signal of frontal choline-containing compounds. *Neuroimage, 32*, 740–746.

Epocrates, I. (2006). *Epocrates Rx Online*. Retreived from http://www.rxonline.epocrates.com/rxmain.jsp

Ersche, K. D., Clark, L., London, M., Robbins, T. W., & Sahakian, B. J. (2006). Profile of executive and memory function associated with amphetamine and opiate dependence. *Neuropsychopharmacology, 31*, 1036–1047.

Ersche, K. D., Fletcher, P. C., Lewis, S. J., Clark, L., Stocks-Gee, G., London, M., et al. (2005). Abnormal frontal activations related to decision-making in current and former amphetamine and opiate dependent individuals. *Psychopharmacology, 180*, 612–623.

Escobar, J. I., & Tuason, V. B. (1979). Neuroleptic withdrawal dyskinesia. *Psychopharmacology Bulletin, 15*, 71–74.

Ettinger, A. B. (2006). Psychotropic effects of antiepileptic drugs. *Neurology, 67*, 1916–1925.

Eyles, D. W., Pond, S. M., Van der Schyf, C. J., & Halliday, G. M. (2000). Mitochondrial ultrastructure and density in a primate model of persistent tardive dyskinesia. *Life Sciences, 66*, 1345–1350.

Fahn, S., Marsden, C. D., & van Woert, M. H. (1986). Definition and classification of myoclonus. *Advances in Neurology, 43*, 1.

Fathman, C. G., & Myers, B. D. (1992). Cyclosporine therapy for autoimmune disease. *New England Journal of Medicine, 326*, 1693–1695.

Feinberg, T. E., & Roane, D. M. (2005). Delusional misidentification. *Psychiatric Clinics of North America, 28*, 665–683.

Feldman, R. G. (1998). *Occupational and environmental neurotoxicology*. Philadelphia: Lippencott-Raven.

Fennelly, M. E., Earnshaw, G., & Soni, N. (1987). Ranitidine-induced mental confusion. *Critical Care Medicine, 15*, 1165–1166.

Ferenci, P., Lockwood, A., Mullen, K., Tarter, R., Weissenborn, K., & Blei A. T. (2002). Hepatic encephalopathy—definition, nomenclature, diagnosis, and quantification: Final report of the working party at the 11th World Congresses of Gastroenterology, Vienna, 1998. *Hepatology, 35*, 716–721.

Filley, C. M. (1998). The behavioral neurology of cerebral white matter. *Neurology, 50*, 1535–1540.

Filley, C. M. (2000). Clinical neurology and executive dysfunction. *Seminars in Speech and Language, 21*, 95–108.

Filley, C. M. (2001). *The behavioral neurology of white matter*. New York: Oxford University Press.

Filley, C. M., Halliday, W., & Kleinschmidt-DeMasters, B. K. (2004). The effects of toluene on the central nervous system. *Journal of Neuropathology and Experimental Neurology, 63*, 1–12.

Filley, C. M., Heaton, R. K., & Rosenberg, N. L. (1990). White matter dementia in chronic toluene abuse. *Neurology, 40*, 532–534.

Filley, C. M., & Kleinschmidt-DeMasters, B. K. (2001). Toxic leukoencephalopathy. *The New England Journal of Medicine, 345*, 425–432.

Flaum, M., & Schultz, S. K. (1996). When does amphetamine-induced psychosis become schizophrenia? *American Journal of Psychiatry, 153,* 812–815.

Foy, A., O'Connell, D., Henry, D., Kelly, J., Cocking, S., & Halliday, J. (1995). Benzodiazepine use as a cause of cognitive impairment in elderly hospital inpatients. *Journals of Gerontology Series A—Biological Sciences and Medical Sciences, 50,* M99–M106.

Francis, J., & Kapoor, W. N. (1990). Delirium in hospitalized elderly. *Journal of General Internal Medicine, 5,* 65–79.

Francis, J., Martin, D., & Kapoor, W. N. (1990). A prospective study of delirium in hospitalized elderly. *The Journal of the American Medical Association, 263,* 1097–1101.

Franke, A., Teyssen, S., & Singer, M. V. (2005). Alcohol-related diseases of the esophagus and stomach. *Digestive Diseases, 23,* 204–213.

French, J. A., Kanner, A. M., Bautista, J., Abou-Khalil, B., Browne, T., Harden, C. L., et al. (2004a). Therapeutics and Technology Assessment Subcommittee of the American Academy of Neurology; Quality Standards Subcommittee of the American Academy of Neurology; American Epilepsy Society. Efficacy and tolerability of the new antiepileptic drugs I: Treatment of new onset epilepsy: Report of the Therapeutics and Technology Assessment Subcommittee and Quality Standards Subcommittee of the American Academy of Neurology and the American Epilepsy Society. *Neurology, 62,* 1252–1260.

French, J. A., Kanner, A. M., Bautista, J., Abou-Khalil, B., Browne, T., Harden, C. L., et al. (2004b). Therapeutics and Technology Assessment Subcommittee of the American Academy of Neurology; Quality Standards Subcommittee of the American Academy of Neurology; American Epilepsy Society. Efficacy and tolerability of the new antiepileptic drugs II: Treatment of refractory epilepsy: Report of the Therapeutics and Technology Assessment Subcommittee and Quality Standards Subcommittee of the American Academy of Neurology and the American Epilepsy Society. *Neurology, 62,* 1261–1273.

Fuente-Fernandez, R., Sossi, V., Huang, Z., Furtado, S., Lu, J. Q., Calne, D. B., et al. (2004). Levodopa-induced changes in synaptic dopamine levels increase with progression of Parkinson's disease: Implications for dyskinesias. *Brain, 127,* 2747–2754.

Garcia-Perez, A., Castro, C., Franco, A., & Escribano, R. (1974). A case of optic atrophy possibly induced by quinoline in acrodermatitis enteropathica. *British Journal of Dermatology, 90,* 453–455.

Gendre, J. P., Barbanel, C., Degos, J. D., & Le Quintrec, Y. (1974). Serious sensory-motor neuropathy. A case of renal failure following clioquinol absorption. [French]. *Nouvelle Presse Medicale, 3,* 2395–2398.

Gerasimov, M. R., Collier, L., Ferrieri, A., Alexoff, D., Lee, D., Gifford, A. N., et al. (2003). Toluene inhalation produces a conditioned place preference in rats. *European Journal of Pharmacology, 477,* 45–52.

Geschwind, N. (1965). Disconnexion syndromes in animals and man. I. *Brain, 88,* 237–294.

Geschwind, N., & Kaplan, E. (1962). A human cerebral deconnection syndrome. A preliminary report. *Neurology, 12,* 675–685.

Gijtenbeek, J. M., van den Bent, M. J., & Vecht, C. J. (1999). Cyclosporine neurotoxicity: A review. *Journal of Neurology, 246,* 339–346.

Gill, J., Singh, H., & Nugent, K. (2003). Acute lithium intoxication and neuroleptic malignant syndrome. *Pharmacotherapy, 23,* 811–815.

Gilman, S., Adams, K., Koeppe, R. A., Berent, S., Kluin, K. J., Modell, J. G., et al. (1990). Cerebellar and frontal hypometabolism in alcoholic cerebellar degeneration studied with positron emission tomography. *Annals of Neurology, 28,* 775–785.

Giraud, D. (1987). Toxic, metabolic and hereditary optic neuropathies. [French]. *Revue du Praticien, 37,* 42–48.

Goetz, C. G. (1985). *Neurotoxins in clinical practice.* New York: Spectrum Publications.

Goldman, L., & Bennett, J. C. (2000). *Cecil textbook of medicine* (21 ed.). Philadelphia: W.B. Saunders.

Goldman, M. S. (2002). Expectancy and risk for alcoholism: The unfortunate exploitation of a fundamental characteristic of neurobehavioral adaptation. *Alcoholism: Clinical and Experimental Research 26,* 737–746.

Gonzales, E. A., Mustelier, M. M., & Rey, J. A. (2005). Geriatric psychopharmacology. In S. S. Bush & T. A. Martin (Eds.), *Geriatric neuropsychology: Practice essentials* (pp. 401–428). London and New York: Taylor & Francis.

Gopal, A. K., Thorning, D. R., & Back, A. L. (1999). Fatal outcome due to cyclosporine neurotoxicity with associated pathological findings. *Bone Marrow Transplantation, 23,* 191–193.

Gorji, A., Scheld, H. H., & Speckmann, E. J. (2002). Epileptogenic effect of cyclosporine in guinea-pig hippocampal slices. *Neuroscience, 115,* 993–997.

Gospe, S. M., Jr., & Zhou, S. S. (1998). Toluene abuse embryopathy: Longitudinal neurodevelopmental effects of prenatal exposure to toluene in rats. *Reproductive Toxicology, 12,* 119–126.

Gospe, S. M., Jr., & Zhou, S. S. (2000). Prenatal exposure to toluene results in abnormal neurogenesis and migration in rat somatosensory cortex. *Pediatric Research, 47,* 362–368.

Grabski, D. A. (1961). Toluene sniffing producing cerebellar degeneration. *American Journal of Psychiatry, 118,* 461–462.

Grant, B. F., Harford, T. C., Dawson, D. A., Chou, P., DuFour, M., & Pickering, R. (1994). Prevalence of *DSM-IV* alcohol abuse and dependence: United States, 1992. Epidemiologic Bulletin No. 35. *Alcohol Health and Research World 18*(3), 243–248.

Grant, I., Adams, K. M., Carlin, A., Rennick, P., Judd, L. L., & Schooff, K. (1978). Thecollaborative neuropsychological study of polydrug users. *Archives of General Psychiatry 35,* 1063–1074.

Grant, I., Adams, K. M., & Reed, R. (1984). Aging, abstinence and medical risk factorsin the prediction of neuropsychological deficit amongst chronic alcoholics. *Archives of General Psychiatry 41,* 710–718.

Grant, I., Reed, R., & Adams, K. M. (1987). Diagnosis of intermediate-duration and subacute organic mental disorder in abstinent alcoholics. *Journal of Clinical Psychiatry 48,* 319–323.

Grant, S., London, E. D., Newlin, D. B., Villemagne, V. L., Liu, X., Contoreggi, C., et al. (1996). Activation of memory circuits during cue-elicited cocaine craving. *Proceedings of the National Academy of Sciences of the United States of America, 93,* 12040–12045.

Greenberg, M. M. (1997). The central nervous system and exposure to toluene: A risk characterization. *Environmental Research, 72,* 1–7.

Greenblatt, D. J., Harmatz, J. S., Shapiro, L., Engelhardt, N., Gouthro, T. A., & Shader, R. I. (1991). Sensitivity to triazolam in the elderly. *New England Journal of Medicine, 324,* 1691–1698.

Gregus, Z., & Klaassen, C. D. (2003). Mechanisms of toxicology. In C. D. Klaassen & J. B. Watkins (Eds.), *Casarett and Doull's essentials of toxicology* (pp. 21–45). New York: McGraw-Hill.

Gross-Tsur, V., & Shalev, R. S. (2004). Reversible language regression as an adverse effect of topiramate treatment in children. *Neurology, 62*, 299–300.

Gui, Q. P., Zhao, W. Q., & Wang, L. N. (2006). Wernicke's encephalopathy in nonalcoholic patients: Clinical and pathologic features of three cases and literature reviewed. *Neuropathology, 26*, 231–235.

Gunne, L. M., Haggstrom, J. E., Johansson, P., Levin, E. D., & Terenius, L. (1988). Neurobiochemical changes in tardive dyskinesia. *Encephale, 14*, 167–173.

Gutmann, L., & Johnsen, D. (1981). Nitrous oxide-induced myeloneuropathy: Report of cases. *Journal of the American Dental Association, 103*, 239–241.

Guzelian, P. S., Victoroff, M. S., Halmes, N. C., James, R. C., & Guzelian, C. P. (2005). Evidence-based toxicology: A comprehensive framework for causation. *Human and Experimental Toxicology, 24*, 161–201.

Hall, A. S., Thorley, G., & Houtman, P. N. (2003). The effects of corticosteroids on behavior in children with nephrotic syndrome. *Pediatric Nephrology, 18*, 1220–1223.

Hall, R. C. (2006). Psychiatric adverse drug reactions: Steroid psychosis. Retreived from www.drrichardhall.com/steroid.htm

Hall, R. C., Popkin, M. K., Stickney, S. K., & Gardner, E. R. (1979). Presentation of the steroid psychoses. *Journal of Nervous and Mental Disease, 167*, 229–236.

Hanakago, R., & Uono, M. (1981). Clioquinol intoxication occurring in the treatment of acrodermatitis enteropathica with reference to SMON outside of Japan. *Clinical Toxicology, 18*, 1427–1434.

Hansson, O., & Herxheimer, A. (1980). Neurotoxicity of oxyquinolines. *Lancet, 1*, 1253–1254.

Harper, C., Dixon, G., Sheedy, D., & Garrick, T. (2003). Neuropathological alterations in alcoholic brains. Studies arising from the New South Wales Tissue Resource Centre. *Progress in Neuro-Psychopharmacology and Biological Psychiatry, 27*, 951–961.

Harper, C., & Matsumoto, I. (2005). Ethanol and brain damage. *Current Opinion in Pharmacology 5*, 73–78.

Harwood, H. (2000). Updating Estimates of the Economic Costs of Alcohol Abuse in the United States: Estimates, Update Methods and Data. Report prepared by the The Lewin Group for the National Institute on Alcohol Abuse and Alcoholism.

Hatzinger, M., Seifritz, E., Hemmeter, U., & Holsboer-Trachsler, E. (1994). Cortisone-induced delusional depression in systemic lupus erythematosus. [German]. *Psychiatrische Praxis, 21*, 199–203.

Healton, E. B., Savage, D. G., Brust, J. C., Garrett, T. J., & Lindenbaum, J. (1991). Neurologic aspects of cobalamin deficiency. *Medicine, 70*, 229–245.

Heinrich, A., Runge, U., & Khaw, A. V. (2004). Clinicoradiologic subtypes of Marchiafava-Bignami disease. *Journal of Neurology, 251*, 1050–1059.

Hemmer, B., Glocker, F. X., Schumacher, M., Deuschl, G., & Lucking, C. H. (1998). Subacute combined degeneration: Clinical, electrophysiological, and magnetic resonance imaging findings. *Journal of Neurology, Neurosurgery and Psychiatry, 65*, 822–827.

Hentati, A., Deng, H. X., Hung, W. Y., Nayer, M., Ahmed, M. S., He, X., et al. (1996). Human alpha-tocopherol transfer protein: Gene structure and mutations in familial vitamin E deficiency. *Annals of Neurology, 39*, 295–300.

Herink, J., Krejcova, G., Bajgar, J., Svoboda, Z., Kvetina, J., Zivnu, P., et al. (2003). Cyclosporine A inhibits acetylcholinesterase activity in selected parts of the rat brain. *Neuroscience Letters, 339*, 251–253.

Hermann, M., Asberg, A., Reubsaet, J. L., Sather, S., Berg, K. J., & Christensen, H. (2002). Intake of grapefruit juice alters the metabolic pattern of cyclosporin A in renal transplant recipients. *International Journal of Clinical Pharmacology and Therapeutics, 40*, 451–456.

Herranz, J. L. (2000). Datos actuales sobre el topiramato [current data on topiramate]. *Revista de Neurologia, 30*(Suppl. 1), S132–S136.

Herskovitz, S. (2006). Pharmaceutical neurotoxins. In H. H. Schaumburg (Ed.), *Neurotoxicology. Education Program Syllabus, 2PC.005, AAN 58th Annual Meeting*, San Diego, CA: American Academy of Neurology.

Hill, A. B. (1965). The environment and disease: Association or causation. *Proceedings of the Royal Society of Medicine, 58*, 295–300.

Hirohata, S. (2004). Central nervous system involvement in connective tissue diseases. [Japanese]. *Nihon Rinsho Meneki Gakkai Kaishi, 27*, 109–117.

Hirohata, S., Iwamoto, S., Miyamoto, T., Sugiyama, H., Nakano, K., & Inokuma, S. (1988). A patient with systemic lupus erythematosus presenting both central nervous system lupus and steroid induced psychosis. *Journal of Rheumatology, 15*, 706–710.

Hlaihel, C., Gonnaud, P. M., Champin, S., Rousset, H., Tran-Minh, V. A., & Cotton, F. (2005). Diffusion-weighted magnetic resonance imaging in Marchiafava-Bignami disease: Follow-up studies. *Neuroradiology, 47*, 520–524.

Hoblyn, J. (2004). Bipolar disorder in later life. Older adults presenting with new onset manic symptoms usually have underlying medical or neurologic disorder. *Geriatrics, 59*, 41–44.

Hoffman, W. F., & Casey, D. E. (1991). Computed tomographic evaluation of patients with tardive dyskinesia. *Schizophrenia Research, 5*, 1–12.

Hsu, Z. -N., Nakae, K., Iwashita, H., Matsuoka, Y., Iida, M., & Ando, K. (2002). Study of validity of the severity criteria and SMON patients. Changes of severity in 30 years. *Dokkyo Journal of Medical Science, 29*, 43–48.

Hughes, R. L. (1990). Cyclosporine-related central nervous system toxicity in cardiac transplantation. *New England Journal of Medicine, 323*, 420–421.

Igata, A. (1971). Halogenated oxyquinoline derivatives and neurological syndromes. *Lancet, 7714*, 42.

Igata, A. (1974). The clioquinol poisoning theory of SMON. *Jikeikai Medical Journal, 21*, 107–111.

Igata, A., & Toyokura, Y. (1970). Subacute myelo optico neuropathy and chinoform. *Proceedings of the Symposium on Chemical Physiology and Pathology, 10*, 74–77.

Igata, A., & Toyokura, Y. (1971). Subacute myelo-optico-neuropathy (SMON) in Japan. The question of chinoform poisoning. [German]. *Munchener Medizinische Wochenschrift, 113*, 1062–1066.

Ikeda, M., & Tsukagoshi, H. (1990). Encephalopathy due to toluene sniffing. Report of a case with magnetic resonance imaging. *European Neurology, 30*, 347–349.

Ilagan, M. C., Carlson, D., & Madden, J. F. (2002). Lithium toxicity: Two case reports. *Delaware Medical Journal, 74*, 263–270.

Inoue, Y. K., Nishibe, Y., & Nakamura, Y. (1971). Virus associated with S.M.O.N. in Japan. *Lancet, 1*, 853–854.

Ioannides-Demos, L. L. (2005). Pharmacotherapy for obesity. *Drugs, 65*, 1391–1418.

Iwashita, H. (2001). The history and present of SMON research in Japan. *Japanese Journal of National Medical Services, 55,* 510–515.

Jackson, C. E., Amato, A. A., & Barohn, R. J. (1996). Isolated vitamin E deficiency. *Muscle and Nerve, 19,* 1161–1165.

Jain, K. K. (1996). *Drug-induced neurological disorders.* Seattle, WA: Hogrefe & Huber.

Jansen, O., Krieger, D., Krieger, S., & Sartor, K. (1996). Cortical hyperintensity on proton density-weighted images: An MR sign of cyclosporine-related encephalopathy. *American Journal of Neuroradiology, 17,* 337–344.

Jarmuzewska, E. A., Ghidoni, A., & Mangoni, A. A. (2007). Hypertension and sensorimotor peripheral neuropathy in Type 2 diabetes. *European Neurology, 57,* 91–95.

Jeste, D. V. (2000). Tardive dyskinesia in older patients. *Journal of Clinical Psychiatry, 61,* 27–32.

Johnson-Green, D., & Inscore, A. B. (2005). Substance abuse in older patients. In S. S. Bush & T. A. Martin (Eds.), *Geriatric neuropsychology: Practice essentials* (pp. 429–451). London and New York: Taylor & Francis.

Judd, F. K., Burrows, G. D., & Norman, T. R. (1983). Psychosis after withdrawal of steroid therapy. *Medical Journal of Australia, 2,* 350–351.

Juurlink, D. N., Mamdani, M. M., Kopp, A., Rochon, P. A., Shulman, K. I., & Redelmeier, D. A. (2004). Drug-induced lithium toxicity in the elderly: A population-based study. *Journal of the American Geriatrics Society, 52,* 794–798.

Kahan, B. D. (1989). Cyclosporine. *New England Journal of Medicine, 321,* 1725–1738.

Kamran, S., & Bakshi, R. (1998). MRI in chronic toluene abuse: Low signal in the cerebral cortex on T2-weighted images. *Neuroradiology, 40,* 519–521.

Kashani, J., & Ruha, A. M. (2004). Methamphetamine toxicity secondary to intravaginal body stuffing. *Journal of Toxicology—Clinical Toxicology, 42,* 987–989.

Katz, D. A., & Hays, L. R. (2004). Adolescent OxyContin abuse. *Journal of the American Academy of Child and Adolescent Psychiatry, 43,* 231–234.

Kawaguchi, M., Furuya, H., & Patel, P. M. (2005). Neuroprotective effects of anesthetic agents. *Journal of Anesthesia, 19,* 150–156.

Kayden, H. J. (1993). The neurologic syndrome of vitamin E deficiency: A significant cause of ataxia. *Neurology, 43,* 2167–2169.

Kinsella, L. J., & Green, R. (1995). 'Anesthesia paresthetica': Nitrous oxide-induced cobalamin deficiency. *Neurology, 45,* 1608–1610.

Klaassen, C. D., & Watkins, J. B. (2003). *Casarett and Doull's essentials of toxicology.* New York: McGraw-Hill Medical Publishers.

Klee, G. G. (2000). Cobalamin and folate evaluation: Measurement of methylmalonic acid and homocysteine vs vitamin B(12) and folate. *Clinical Chemistry, 46,* 1277–1283.

Klys, M., Konopka, T., & Rojek, S. (2005). Intracerebral hemorrhage associated with amphetamine. *Journal of Analytical Toxicology, 29,* 577–581.

Knight, J. R. (2004). A 35-year-old physician with opioid dependence. *Journal of the American Medical Association, 292,* 1351–1357.

Knox, J. W., & Nelson, J. R. (1966). Permanent encephalopathy from toluene inhalation. *New England Journal of Medicine, 275,* 1494–1496.

Kochi, S., Takanaga, H., Matsuo, H., Naito, M., Tsuruo, T., & Sawada, Y. (1999). Effect of cyclosporin A or tacrolimus on the function of blood–brain barrier cells. *European Journal of Pharmacology, 372,* 287–295.

Kockelmann, E., Elger, C. E., & Helmstaedter, C. (2004). Cognitive profile of topiramate as compared with lamotrigine in epilepsy patients on antiepileptic drug polytherapy: Relationships to blood serum levels and comedication. *Epilepsy and Behavior, 5*, 716–721.

Koffman, B. M., Greenfield, L. J., Ali, I. I., & Pirzada, N. A. (2006). Neurologic complications after surgery for obesity. *Muscle and Nerve, 33*, 166–176.

Kohen, M., Asherson, R. A., Gharavi, A. E., & Lahita, R. G. (1993). Lupus psychosis: Differentiation from the steroid-induced state. *Clinical and Experimental Rheumatology, 11*, 323–326.

Koike, H., Misu, K., Hattori, N., Ito, H., Hirayama, M., Nagamatsu, M., et al. (2001). Postgastrectomy polyneuropathy with thiamine deficiency. *Journal of Neurology, Neurosurgery and Psychiatry, 71*, 357–362.

Kono, R. (1971). Subacute myelo-optico-neuropathy, a new neurological disease prevailing in Japan. *Japanese Journal of Medical Science and Biology, 24*, 195–216.

Kono, R. (1975). Introductory review of subacute myelo-optico-neuropathy (SMON) and its studies done by the SMON Research Commission. *Japanese Journal of Medical Science and Biology, 28*(Suppl.), 1–21.

Kono, R. (1978). A review of SMON studies in Japan. In M. Gent & I. Shigematsu (Eds.), *Epidemiological issues in reported drug-induced illnesses. SMON and other examples* (pp. 121–136). Hamilton, Canada: McMaster University Library Press.

Koob, G. F., & Le Moal, M. (1997). Drug abuse: Hedonic homeostatic dysregulation. *Science 278*(5353), 52–58.

Kovacs, E. J., & Messingham, K. A. (2002). Influence of alcohol and gender on immune response. *Alcohol Research and Health, 26*(4), 257–263.

Kratofil, P. H., Baberg, H. T., & Dimsdale, J. E. (1996). Self-mutilation and severe self-injurious behavior associated with amphetamine psychosis. *General Hospital Psychiatry, 18*, 117–120.

Krinke, G., Schaumburg, H. H., Spencer, P. S., Thomann, P., & Hess, R. (1979). Clioquinol and 2,5-hexanedione induce different types of distal axonopathy in the dog. *Acta Neuropathologica, 47*, 213–221.

Kuhar, M. J., Couceyro, P. R., & Lambert, P. D. (1999). Catecholamines. In G. J. Siegel, B. W. Agranoff, R. W. Albers, S. K. Fisher, & M. D. Uhler (Eds.), *Basic neurochemistry: Molecular, cellular, and medical aspects* (6th ed., pp. 243–262). Philadelphia: Lippincott-Raven.

Kumar, N., Ahlskog, J. E., & Gross, J. B., Jr. (2004). Acquired hypocupremia after gastric surgery. *Clinical Gastroenterology and Hepatology, 2*, 1074–1079.

Kuratsune, M., Yoshimura, T., Tokudome, S., Kouchi, S., Matsuzaka, J., & Mishizumi, M. (1974). An epidemiologic study on the association between subacute myelo-optic neuropathy (SMON) and quinoform. *Japanese Journal of Hygiene, 28*, 450–455.

Kusui, K. (1975). Outline of the joint SMON investigation by the clinical section. *Japanese Journal of Medical Science and Biology, 28*(Suppl.), 57–62.

Lan, K. C., Lin, Y. F., Yu, F. C., Lin, C. S., & Chu, P. (1998). Clinical manifestations and prognostic features of acute methamphetamine intoxication. *Journal of the Formosan Medical Association, 97*, 528–533.

Landrieu, P., Selva, J., Alvarez, F., Ropert, A., & Metral, S. (1985). Peripheral nerve involvement in children with chronic cholestasis and vitamin E deficiency. A clinical, electrophysiological and morphological study. *Neuropediatrics, 16*, 194–201.

Lang, A. E. (1996). Movement disorder symptomatology. In W. G. Bradley, R. B. Daroff, G. M. Fenichel, & C. D. Marsden (Eds.), *Neurology in clinical practice. Principles of diagnosis and Management* (pp. 110–117). Boston: Butterworth-Heinemann.

Lang, E. J., & Davis, S. M. (2002). Lithium neurotoxicity: The development of irreversible neurological impairment despite standard monitoring of serum lithium levels. *Journal of Clinical Neuroscience, 9,* 308–309.

Laruelle, M., & Abi-Dargham, A. (1999). Dopamine as the wind of the psychotic fire: New evidence from brain imaging studies. *Journal of Psychopharmacology, 13,* 358–371.

Laruelle, M., Abi-Dargham, A., Gil, R., Kegeles, L., & Innis, R. (1999). Increased dopamine transmission in schizophrenia: Relationship to illness phases. *Biological Psychiatry, 46,* 56–72.

Layzer, R. B., Fishman, R. A., & Schaefer, J. A. (1978). Neuropathy following abuse of nitrous oxide. *Neurology, 28,* 504.

Lee, S., Sziklas, V., Andermann, F., Farnham, S., Risse, G., Gustafson, M., et al. (2003). The effects of adjunctive topiramate on cognitive function in patients with epilepsy. *Epilepsia, 44,* 339–347.

Lee, T. M., Zhou, W. H., Luo, X. J., Yuen, K. S., Ruan, X. Z., & Weng, X. C. (2005). Neural activity associated with cognitive regulation in heroin users: A fMRI study. *Neuroscience Letters, 382,* 211–216.

Lerch, M. M., Albrecht, E., Ruthernberger, M., Mayerle, J., Halangk, W., & Kruger, B. (2003). Pathophysiology of alcohol-induced pancreatitis. *Pancreas, 27*(4), 291–296.

Leung, A. Y., & Foster, S. (2003). *Encyclopedia of common natural ingredients used in food, drugs, and cosmetics* (2 ed.). New York: John Wiley & Sons.

Levine, H. G. (1978). Discovery of addiction—changing conceptions of habitual drunkenness in America. *Journal of Studies on Alcohol, 39*(1), 143–174.

Lewis, D. A., & Smith, R. E. (1983). Steroid-induced psychiatric syndromes. A report of 14 cases and a review of the literature. *Journal of Affective Disorders, 5,* 319–332.

Lieber, C. S. (1998). Hepatic and other medical disorders of alcoholism: From pathogenesis to treatment. *Journal of Studies on Alcohol 59,* 9–25.

Lim, C. J., Trevino, C., & Tampi, R. R. (2006). Can olanzapine cause delirium in the elderly? *Annals of Pharmacotherapy, 40,* 135–138.

Lim, J. K., Kraus, M. L., & Giles, S. S. (2004). Lupus cerebritis and steroid psychosis in mixed connective tissue disorder. *Yale Journal of Biology and Medicine, 77,* 63–69.

Lin, J. T., Wang, S. J., Fuh, J. L., Hsiao, L. T., Lirng, J. F., & Chen, P. M. (2003). Prolonged reversible vasospasm in cyclosporin A-induced encephalopathy. *AJNR: American Journal of Neuroradiology, 24,* 102–104.

Lipton, J., Zeigler, S., Wilkins, J., & Ellison, G. (1991). A silicone pellet for continuous cocaine: Comparison with continuous amphetamine. *Pharmacology, Biochemistry and Behavior, 38,* 927–930.

Lucasey, B. (2001). Corticosteroid-induced osteoporosis. *Nursing Clinics of North America, 36,* 455–466.

Lynch, J., & House, M. A. (1992). Cardiovascular effects of methamphetamine. *Journal of Cardiovascular Nursing, 6,* 12–18.

Mackiewicz, J., & Wendorff, J. (1980). Case of subacute myelo-optico-neuropathy. [Polish]. *Neurologia i Neurochirurgia Polska, 14,* 121–123.

Malay, M. E. (2001). Unintentional methamphetamine intoxication. *Journal of Emergency Nursing, 27*, 13–16.

Malizia, E., Macchiarelli, L., Ambrosini, M., Smeriglio, G., & Andreucci, G. (1979). Acute and chronic toxicity of clioquinol and its derivatives. *Rivista di Tossicologia Sperimentale e Clinica, 9*, 121–140.

Mandal, S. K. (1986). Psychiatric side effects of ranitidine. *British Journal of Clinical Practice, 40*, 260.

Martin, R., Kuzniecky, R., Ho, S., Hetherington, H., Pan, J., Sinclair, K., et al. (1999). Cognitive effects of topiramate, gabapentin, and lamotrigine in healthy young adults. *Neurology, 52*, 321–327.

Martin, R. R., Singleton, C. K., & Hiller-Sturmhöfel, S. (2003). The role of thiamine deficiency in alcoholic brain disease. *Alcohol Reasearch and Health, 27*(2), 134–142.

Martinez-Aran, A., Vieta, E., Colom, F., Torrent, C., Sanchez-Moreno, J., Reinares, M., et al. (2004). Cognitive impairment in euthymic bipolar patients: Implications for clinical and functional outcome. *Bipolar Disorders, 6*, 224–232.

Mascarell, L., & Truffa-Bachi, P. (2003). New aspects of cyclosporin a mode of action: From gene silencing to gene up-regulation. *Mini-Reviews in Medicinal Chemistry, 3*, 205–214.

Masson, C., Boulu, P., & Henin, D. (1992). Iatrogenic neuropathies. [French]. *Revue de Medecine Interne, 13*, 225–232.

Maxwell, J. C., Cravioto, P., Galvan, F., Ramirez, M. C., Wallisch, L. S., & Spence, R. T. (2006). Drug use and risk of HIV/AIDS on the Mexico-USA border: A comparison of treatment admissions in both countries. *Drug and Alcohol Dependence, 82*(Suppl. 93), S85–S93.

McCombe, P. A., & McLeod, J. G. (1984). The peripheral neuropathy of vitamin B12 deficiency. *Journal of the Neurological Sciences, 66*, 117–126.

McEwen, L. M. (1971). Neuropathy after clioquinol. *British Medical Journal, 4*, 169–170.

McGovern, P. E. (2003). *Ancient Wine: The Search for the Origins of Viniculture.* Princeton, NJ.: Princeton University Press.

McGregor, C. (2005). The nature, time course and severity of methamphetamine withdrawal. *Addiction, 100*, 1320–1329.

Meador, K. J. (1996). Effects of antiepileptic drugs on cognition. In J. C. Sackellares & S. Berent (Eds.), *Psychological disturbances in epilepsy* (pp. 223–232). Boston: Butterworth-Heinemann.

Meador, K. J. (2002a). Cognitive outcomes and predictive factors in epilepsy. *Neurology, 58*(Suppl. 6), S21–S26.

Meador, K. J. (2002b). Neurodevelopmental effects of antiepileptic drugs. *Current Neurology and Neuroscience Reports, 2*, 373–378.

Mehndiratta, M. M., & Hughes, R. A. (2002). Corticosteroids for chronic inflammatory demyelinating polyradiculoneuropathy. [Update of Cochrane Database Syst Rev. 2001;(3):CD002062; PMID: 11687011]. *Cochrane Database of Systematic Reviews,* CD002062.

Mendhekar, D. N. (2005). Rabbit syndrome induced by combined lithium and risperidone. *Canadian Journal of Psychiatry—Revue Canadienne de Psychiatrie, 50*, 369.

Menegon, P., Sibon, I., Pachai, C., Orgogozo, J. M., & Dousset, V. (2005). Marchiafava-Bignami disease: Diffusion-weighted MRI in corpus callosum and cortical lesions. *Neurology, 65*, 475–477.

Merck. (2003). *Amphetamines*. Retrieved from http://www.merck.com/mmhe/print/sec07/ch108/ch108g.html

Merck Research Laboratories. (2001). *The Merck index: An encyclopedia of chemicals, drugs, and biologicals* (13 ed.). Whitehouse Station, NJ: Merck & Co., Inc.

Merck Source. (2005). *Dorlands medical dictionary online*. Retrieved from http://www.mercksource.com

Merriam-Webster, A. (1993). *Merriam-Webster's collegiate dictionary* (10th ed.). Springfield, MA: G & C Merriam Company.

Meyer, J. M., Dollarhide, A., & Tuan, I. L. (2005). Lithium toxicity after switch from fosinopril to lisinopril. *International Clinical Psychopharmacology, 20,* 115–118.

Meythaler, J. M., & Yablon, S. A. (1999). Antiepileptic drugs. *Rehabilitation Pharmacotherapy, 10,* 275–300.

Miller, N. S., & Greenfeld, A. (2004). Patient characteristics and risk factors for development of dependence on hydrocodone and oxycodone. *American Journal of Therapeutics, 11,* 26–32.

Miller, S. C. (2005). Coricidin HBP cough and cold addiction. *Journal of the American Academy of Child and Adolescent Psychiatry, 44,* 509–510.

Mintzer, M. Z., Copersino, M. L., & Stitzer, M. L. (2005). Opioid abuse and cognitive performance. *Drug and Alcohol Dependence, 78,* 225–230.

Mitchell, I. J., Cooper, A. C., Griffiths, M. R., & Cooper, A. J. (2002). Acute administration of haloperidol induces apoptosis of neurones in the striatum and substantia nigra in the rat. *Neuroscience, 109,* 89–99.

Miyagawa, M., Ohtani, K., & Suda, M. (1998). Effects of acute exposure to toluene on mixed schedule controlled behavior as a memory measure in rats. *Journal of Toxicological Science, 23,* 352.

Montpied, P., Batxelli, I., Andre, M., Portugal, H., Lairon, D., Bockaert, J., et al. (2003). Effects of cyclosporine-A on brain lipids and apolipoprotein E, J gene expression in rats. *Neuroreport, 14,* 573–576.

Morgan, J. P., & Penovich, P. (1978). Jamaica ginger paralysis. Forty-seven-year follow-up. *Archives of Neurology, 35,* 530–532.

Motamedi, G. K., & Meador, K. J. (2006). Antiepileptic drugs and neurodevelopment. *Current Neurology and Neuroscience Reports, 6,* 341–346.

Mouaffak, F., Gourevitch, R., Baup, N., Loo, H., & Olie, J. P. (2006). Interrelations between lithium therapy, auto-immune thyroiditis and TSH—a case report. *Pharmacopsychiatry, 39,* 77–78.

Mula, M., Trimble, M. R., Thompson, P., & Sander, J. W. A. S. (2003). Topiramate and word-finding difficulties in patients with epilepsy. *Neurology, 60,* 1104–1107.

Naber, D., Sand, P., & Heigl, B. (1996). Psychopathological and neuropsychological effects of 8-days' corticosteroid treatment. A prospective study. *Psychoneuroendocrinology, 21,* 25–31.

Nakae, K., Yamamoto, S., & Igata, A. (1971). Subacute myelo-optico-neuropathy (S.M.O.N.) in Japan. A community survey. *Lancet, 2,* 510–512.

Nakae, K., Yamamoto, S., Shigematsu, I., & Kono, R. (1973). Relation between subacute myelo-optic neuropathy (S.M.O.N.) and clioquinol: Nationwide survey. *Lancet, 1,* 171–173.

Nakazono, K., Watanabe, Y., Nakaya, S., Asami, Y., Masuhara, K., Itoh, F., et al. (2005). Impairment state of cognitive performance and the affecting factors in outpatients following gastrointestinal endoscopy after single-dose diazepam. *Yakugaku Zasshi—Journal of the Pharmaceutical Society of Japan, 125,* 307–314.

Naranjo, C. A., Fornazzari, L., & Sellers, E. M. (1981). Clinical detection and assessment of drug induced neurotoxicity. *Progress in Neuro-Psychopharmacology, 5*, 427–434.

Nardone, R., Venturi, A., Buffone, E., Covi, M., Florio, I., Lochner, P., et al. (2006). Transcranial magnetic stimulation shows impaired transcallosal inhibition in Marchiafava-Bignami syndrome. *European Journal of Neurology, 13*, 749–753.

Nashel, D. J. (1986). Is atherosclerosis a complication of long-term corticosteroid treatment? *American Journal of Medicine, 80*, 925–929.

National Institute on Alcohol Abuse and Alcoholism. (1993). *Alcohol Alert*. No. 22 PH 346: Alcohol and Nutrition, October 1993.

National Institute on Alcohol Abuse and Alcoholism. (1994). Alcohol Alert No. 24 PH 350: Animal Models in Alcohol Research, April 1994.

National Institute on Alcohol Abuse and Alcoholism. (2000). 10th Special Report to the U.S. Congress on Alcohol and Health. Washington, DC: Public Health Service.

National Institute on Alcohol Abuse and Alcoholism. (2001). Alcohol Alert No. 52, April 2001.

National Institute on Alcohol Abuse and Alcoholism. (2003). Alcohol Alert No. 59: Underage Drinking: A Major Public Health Challenge, April 1993.

National Institute on Drug Abuse. (2005). *Information on drugs of abuse—prescription drug abuse chart*. Retrieved from http://www.drugabuse.gov/DrugPages/PrescripDrugsChart.html

Nelson, E. (1972). Subacute myelo-optico-neuropathy (SMON). *Annals of Internal Medicine, 77*, 468–470.

Nelson, J. S. (1983). Neuropathological studies of chronic vitamin E deficiency in mammals including humans. *Ciba Foundation Symposium, 101*, 92–105.

Nolan, P. C., & Albers, J. W. (2005). Nutritional neuropathies. In M. B. Bromberg & A. G. Smith (Eds.), *Handbook of peripheral neuropathy* (pp. 325–350). New York: Taylor & Francis.

Oakley, P. W., Whyte, I. M., & Carter, G. L. (2001). Lithium toxicity: An iatrogenic problem in susceptible individuals. *Australian and New Zealand Journal of Psychiatry, 35*, 833–840.

Office of Applied Statistics, Substance Abuse and Mental Health Services. (2008). http://www.samhsa.gov.

Office of National Drug Control Policy (ONDCP). (2006). *Methamphetamine*. Retrieved from http://www.whitehousedrugpolicy.gov/drugfact/methamphetamine/index.html

Olesen, L. L., & Jensen, T. S. (1991). Prevention and management of drug-induced peripheral neuropathy. *Drug Safety, 6*, 302–314.

Olsen, R. W., & DeLorey, T. M. (1999). GABA and glycine. In G. J. Siegel, B. W. Agranoff, R. W. Albers, S. K. Fisher, & M. D. Uhler (Eds.), *Basic neurochemistry: Molecular, cellular and medical aspects* (6th ed., pp. 335–346). Philadelphia: Lippincott-Raven.

Onat, F., & Ozkara, C. (2004). Adverse effects of new antiepileptic drugs. *Drugs of Today, 40*, 325–342.

Ordunez-Garcia, P. O., Nieto, F. J., Espinosa-Brito, A. D., & Caballero, B. (1996). Cuban epidemic neuropathy, 1991 to 1994: History repeats itself a century after the "amblyopia of the blockade." *American Journal of Public Health, 86*, 738–743.

Oscar-Berman, M., Kirkley, S. M., Gansler, D. A., & Couture, A. (2004). Comparisons of Korskaoff and non-Korsakoff alcoholics on neuropsychological tests of prefrontal functioning. *Alcoholism: Clinical and Experimental Research, 28*(4), 667–675.

Oscar-Berman, M., & Marinkovic, K. (2003). Alcoholism and the brain: An overview. *Alcohol Research and Health, 27*(2), 125–133.

Oslin, D., Atkinson, R. M., Smith, D. M., & Hendrie, H. (1998). Alcohol related dementia: Proposed clinical criteria. *International Journal of Geriatric Psychiatry, 13*, 203–212.

Osterman, P. O. (1971). Myelopathy after clioquinol treatment. *Lancet, 2*, 544.

Otte, G., De Coster, W., Thiery, E., De Reuck, J., & Vander, E. H. (1976). Subacute myelo-optic neuropathy. A toxic or a viral etiology? *Acta Neurologica Belgica, 76*, 331–334.

Pachet, A. K., & Wisniewski, A. M. (2003). The effects of lithium on cognition: An updated review. *Psychopharmacology, 170*, 225–234.

Paez-Martinez, N., Cruz, S. L., & Lopez-Rubalcava, C. (2003). Comparative study of the effects of toluene, benzene, 1,1,1-trichloroethane, diethyl ether, and flurothyl on anxiety and nociception in mice. *Toxicology and Applied Pharmacology, 193*, 9–16.

Pallis, C. (1984). Some thoughts on 'SMON.' *Acta Neurologica Scandinavica, Supplementum, 100*, 147–153.

Papakostas, G. I., Petersen, T., Pava, J., Masson, E., Worthington, J. J., III, Alpert, J. E., et al. (2003). Hopelessness and suicidal ideation in outpatients with treatment-resistant depression: Prevalence and impact on treatment outcome. *Journal of Nervous and Mental Disease, 191*, 444–449.

Patten, S. B. (1999). Exogenous corticosteroid exposures are associated with increased recollection of traumatic life events. *Journal of Affective Disorders, 53*, 123–128.

Patten, S. B., Williams, J. V., & Love, E. J. (1995). Self-reported depressive symptoms in association with medication exposures among medical inpatients: A cross-sectional study. *Canadian Journal of Psychiatry—Revue Canadienne de Psychiatrie, 40*, 264–269.

Pecora, P. G., & Kaplan, B. (1996). Corticosteroids and ulcers: Is there an association? *Annals of Pharmacotherapy, 30*, 870–872.

Petitti, D. B., Sidney, S., Quesenberry, C., & Bernstein, A. (1998). Stroke and cocaine or amphetamine use. *Epidemiology, 9*, 596–600.

Pfefferbaum, A., Adalsteinsson, E., & Sullivan, E. V. (2006). Dysmorphology and microstructural degradation of the corpus callosum: Interaction of age and alcoholism. *Neurobiology of Aging, 27*, 994–1009.

Picotte-Prillmayer, D., DiMaggio, J. R., & Baile, W. F. (1995). H2 blocker delirium. *Psychosomatics, 36*, 74–77.

Pinelli, J. M., Symington, A. J., Cunningham, K. A., & Paes, B. A. (2002). Case report and review of the perinatal implications of maternal lithium use. *American Journal of Obstetrics and Gynecology, 187*, 245–249.

Pittman, F. E., & Westphal, M. C. (1974). Optic atrophy following treatment with diiodohydroxyquin. *Pediatrics, 54*, 81–83.

Prasant, M. P., Mattoo, S. K., & Basu, D. (2006). Substance use and other psychiatric disorders in first-degree relatives of opioid-dependent males: A case-controlled study from India. *Addiction, 101*, 413–419.

Poungvarin, N. (1991). Multifocal brain damage due to lacquer sniffing: The first case report of Thailand. *Journal of the Medical Association of Thailand, 74*, 296–300.

Rapeli, P., Kivisaari, R., Autti, T., Kahkonen, S., Puuskari, V., Jokela, O., et al. (2006). Cognitive function during early abstinence from opioid dependence: A comparison to age, gender, and verbal intelligence matched controls. *BMC Psychiatry, 6*, 9.

Rascol, O., & Fabre, N. (2001). Dyskinesia: L-dopa-induced and tardive dyskinesia. *Clinical Neuropharmacology, 24*, 313–323.

Reed, L. J., Lasserson, D., Marsden, P., Stanhope, N., Stevens, T., Bello, F., et al. (2003). FDG-PET findings in the Wernicke–Korsakoff syndrome. *Cortex, 39,* 1027–1045.

Rehm, J., Gmel, G., Sempos, T., & Trevision, M. (2003). Alcohol-related morbidity and mortality. *Alcohol Research and Health 27,* 39–51.

Rehm, J., Montiero, M., Room, R., Gmel, G., Jernigan, D., Frick, U., & Graham, F. (2001). Steps toward constructing a global risk analysis for alcohol consumption: Determining indicators and empirical weights for patterns of drinking, deciding about theoretical minimum, and dealing with different consequences. *European Addiction Research 7,* 138–147.

Reich, J. A., & Billson, F. A. (1973). Toxic optic neuritis. Clioquinol ingestion in a child. *Medical Journal of Australia, 2,* 593–595.

Reuler, J. B., Girard, D. E., & Cooney, T. G. (1985). Current concepts. Wernicke's encephalopathy. *New England Journal of Medicine, 312,* 1035–1039.

Richardson, W. S., Wilson, M. C., Williams, J. W. J., Moyer, V. A., & Naylor, C. D. (2000). Users' guides to the medical literature: XXIV. How to use an article on the clinical manifestations of disease. *Journal of the American Medical Association, 284,* 869–875.

Richelson, E. (1999). Receptor pharmacology of neuroleptics: Relation to clinical effects. *Journal of Clinical Psychiatry, 60*(Suppl. 10), 5–14.

Richter, R. W. (1989). Drug abuse. In L. P. Rowland (Ed.), *Merritt's textbook of neurology* (8th ed., pp. 909–917). Philadelphia: Lea & Febiger.

Ricoy, J. R., Ortega, A., & Cabello, A. (1982). Subacute myelo-optic neuropathy (SMON). First neuro-pathological report outside Japan. *Journal of the Neurological Sciences, 53,* 241–251.

Ritchie, C. W., Bush, A. I., Mackinnon, A., Macfarlane, S., Mastwyk, M., MacGregor, L., et al. (2003). Metal–protein attenuation with iodochlorhydroxyquin (clioquinol) targeting Abeta amyloid deposition and toxicity in Alzheimer disease: A pilot phase 2 clinical trial. *Archives of Neurology, 60,* 1685–1691.

Robinson, T. E., & Berridge, K. C. (1993). The neural basis of drug craving: An incentive-sensitization theory of addiction. *Brain Research—Brain Research Reviews, 18,* 247–291.

Robinson, T. E., Castaneda, E., & Whishaw, I. Q. (1993). Effects of cortical serotonin depletion induced by 3,4-methylenedioxymethamphetamine (MDMA) on behavior, before and after additional cholinergic blockade. *Neuropsychopharmacology, 8,* 77–85.

Robinson, T. E., & Kolb, B. (1997). Persistent structural modifications in nucleus accumbens and prefrontal cortex neurons produced by previous experience with amphetamine. *Journal of Neuroscience, 17,* 8491–8497.

Robinson, T. E., & Kolb, B. (2004). Structural plasticity associated with exposure to drugs of abuse. *Neuropharmacology, 47*(Suppl. 1), 33–46.

Rogers, W. R., Miller, C. S., & Bunegin, L. (1999). A rat model of neurobehavioral sensitization to toluene. *Toxicology and Industrial Health, 15,* 356–369.

Roozendaal, B., de Quervain, D. J., Schelling, G., & McGaugh, J. L. (2004). A systemically administered beta-adrenoceptor antagonist blocks corticosterone-induced impairment of contextual memory retrieval in rats. *Neurobiology of Learning and Memory, 81,* 150–154.

Rose, F. C. (1986). Clioquinol. *Progress in Clinical and Biological Research, 214,* 323–330.

Rose, F. C., & Gawel, M. (1984). Clioquinol neurotoxicity: An overview. *Acta Neurologica Scandinavica, Supplementum, 100,* 137–145.

Rosenberg, N. L., Kleinschmidt-DeMasters, B. K., Davis, K. A., Dreisbach, J. N., Hormes, J. T., & Filley, C. M. (1988). Toluene abuse causes diffuse central nervous system white matter changes. *Annals of Neurology, 23*, 611–614.

Rourke, S. B., & Løberg, T. (1996). The neurobehavioral correlates of alcoholism. In I. Grant, & K. M. Adams (Eds.), *Neuropsychological assessment of neuropsychiatric disorders* (2nd ed., pp. 423–485). New York: Oxford University Press.

Rowland, R. W. (1989). *Merritt's textbook of neurology* (8 ed.). Philadelphia: Lea & Febiger.

Rundell, J. R., & Wise, M. G. (1989). Causes of organic mood disorder. *Journal of Neuropsychiatry and Clinical Neurosciences, 1*, 398–400.

Sachdev, P. (2004). Early extrapyramidal side-effects as risk factors for later tardive dyskinesia: A prospective study. *Australian and New Zealand Journal of Psychiatry, 38*, 445–449.

Sair, H. I., Mohamed, F. B., Patel, S., Kanamalla, U. S., Hershey, B., Hakma, Z., et al. (2006). Diffusion tensor imaging and fiber-tracking in Marchiafava-Bignami disease. *Journal of Neuroimaging, 16*, 281–285.

Salgado-Pineda, P., Delaveau, P., Blin, O., & Nieoullon, A. (2005). Dopaminergic contribution to the regulation of emotional perception. *Clinical Neuropharmacology, 28*, 228–237.

Samet, J. H. (2000). Drug abuse and dependence. In L. Goldman & J. C. Bennett (Eds.), *Cecil textbook of medicine* (21st ed., pp. 54–59). Philadelphia: W.B. Saunders.

Santana, S. F., Wahlund, L. O., Varli, F., Tadeu, V. I., & Eriksdotter, J. M. (2005). Incidence, clinical features and subtypes of delirium in elderly patients treated for hip fractures. *Dementia and Geriatric Cognitive Disorders, 20*, 231–237.

Scatton, B., & Sanger, D. J. (2000). Pharmacological and molecular targets in the search for novel antipsychotics. *Behavioural Pharmacology, 11*, 243–256.

Schaumburg, H. H. (1979a). Morphological studies of toxic distal axonopathy. *Neurobehavioral Toxicology, 1*(Suppl. 1), 187–188.

Schaumburg, H. H. (1979b). Neurology of toxic neuropathies. 6th International Congress of Electromyography. *Acta Neurologica.Scandinavica, 60*, 50–51.

Schaumburg, H. H. (2000). Clioquinol. In P. S. Spencer, H. H. Schaumburg, & A. C. Ludolph (Eds.), *Experimental and clinical neurotoxicology* (2nd ed., pp. 396–401). New York: Oxford University Press.

Schaumburg, H. H., Arezzo, J. C., & Spencer, P. S. (1989). Delayed onset of distal axonal neuropathy in primates after prolonged low-level administration of a neurotoxin. *Annals of Neurology, 26*, 576–579.

Schaumburg, H. H., & Berger, A. R. (1993). Human toxic neuropathy due to industrial agents. In *Peripheral neuropathy* (3rd ed., pp. 1533–1547). Philadelphia: W.B. Saunders Company.

Schaumburg, H. H., & Spencer, P. S. (1979). Clinical and experimental studies of distal axonopathy—a frequent form of brain and nerve damage produced by environmental chemical hazards. *Annals of the New York Academy of Sciences, 329*, 14–29.

Schaumburg, H. H., & Spencer, P. S. (1987). Recognizing neurotoxic disease. *Neurology, 37*, 276–278.

Schaumburg, H. H., & Spencer, P. S. (2000). Classification of neurotoxic responses based on vulnerability of cellular sites. *Neurologic Clinics, 18*, 517–524.

Scheeres, J. J., & Chudley, A. E. (2002). Solvent abuse in pregnancy: A perinatal perspective. *Journal of Obstetrics and Gynaecology Canada: JOGC, 24*, 22–26.

Schlossberg, D. (2000). Arthropods and leeches. In L. Goldman & J. C. Bennett (Eds.), *Cecil textbook of medicine* (21st ed., pp. 1995–2000). Philadelphia: W.B. Saunders Company.

Schmidt, R. E. (2002). Age-related sympathetic ganglionic neuropathology: Human pathology and animal models. *Autonomic Neuroscience-Basic and Clinical, 96,* 63–72.

Schmidt, R. E., Coleman, B. D., & Nelson, J. S. (1991). Differential effect of chronic vitamin E deficiency on the development of neuroaxonal dystrophy in rat gracile/ cuneate nuclei and prevertebral sympathetic ganglia. *Neuroscience Letters, 123,* 102–106.

Schwartz, R. B., Bravo, S. M., Klufas, R. A., Hsu, L., Barnes, P. D., Robson, C. D., et al. (1995). Cyclosporine neurotoxicity and its relationship to hypertensive encephalopathy: CT and MR findings in 16 cases. *American Journal of Roentgenology, 165,* 627–631.

Segal, D. S., & Kuczenski, R. (1997a). An escalating dose "binge" model of amphetamine psychosis: Behavioral and neurochemical characteristics. *Journal of Neuroscience, 17,* 2551–2566.

Segal, D. S., & Kuczenski, R. (1997b). Repeated binge exposures to amphetamine and methamphetamine: Behavioral and neurochemical characterization [comment]. *Journal of Pharmacology and Experimental Therapeutics, 282,* 561–573.

Selby, G. (1972). Subacute myelo-optic neuropathy in Australia. *Lancet, 1,* 123–125.

Selby, G. (1973). Subacute myelo-optico-neuropathy (SMON)—neurotoxicity of clioquinols. *Proceedings of the Australian Association of Neurologists, 9,* 23–30.

Selwa, L. M., Berent, S., Giordani, B., Henry, T. R., Buchtel, H. A., & Ross, D. A. (1994). Serial cognitive testing in anterior temporal lobe epilepsy: Longitudinal changes with medical and surgical therapies. *Epilepsia, 35,* 743–749.

Seybold, M. E., & Drachman, D. B. (1974). Gradually increasing doses of prednisone in myasthenia gravis. Reducing the hazards of treatment. *New England Journal of Medicine, 290,* 81–84.

Shigematsu, I., Yanagawa, H., Yamamoto, S., & Nakae, K. (1975). Epidemiological approach to SMON (subacute myelo-optico-neuropathy). *Japanese Journal of Medical Science and Biology, 28*(Suppl.), 23–33.

Shimada, Y., & Tsuji, T. (1971). Halogenated oxyquinoline derivatives and neurological syndromes. *Lancet, 2,* 41–43.

Shiraki, H. (1975). The neuropathology of subacute myelo-optico-neuropathy, "SMON," in the humans: With special reference to the quinoform intoxication. *Japanese Journal of Medical Science and Biology, 28*(Suppl.), 101–164.

Shiraki, H. (1991). Neuropathological aspects of the etiopathogenesis of subacute myelo-optico-neuropathy (SMON). In *Handbook of clinical neurology: Intoxications of the nervous system, Part 2* (pp. 141–198). Amsterdam: Elsevier/North Holland Biomedical Press.

Shulman, K. I., Sykora, K., Gill, S., Mamdani, M., Bronskill, S., Wodchis, W. P., et al. (2005). Incidence of delirium in older adults newly prescribed lithium or valproate: A population-based cohort study. *Journal of Clinical Psychiatry, 66,* 424–427.

Shuto, H., Kataoka, Y., Fujisaki, K., Nakao, T., Sueyasu, M., Miura, I., et al. (1999). Inhibition of GABA system involved in cyclosporine-induced convulsions. *Life Sciences, 65,* 879–887.

Siegel, G. J., Agranoff, B. W., Albers, R. W., Fisher, S. K., & Uhler, M. D. (1999). *Basic neurochemistry: Molecular, cellular and medical aspects* (6 ed.). Philadelphia: Lippincott-Raven.

Sirois, F. (2003). Steroid psychosis: A review. *General Hospital Psychiatry, 25,* 27–33.

Slovenko, R. (2000). Update on legal issues associated with tardive dyskinesia. *Journal of Clinical Psychiatry, 61*(Suppl. 4), 45–57.

Smith, A. G., & Albers, J. W. (1997). *n*-Hexane neuropathy due to rubber cement sniffing. *Muscle and Nerve, 20,* 1445–1450.

SMON Research Committee. (1975). Summary of research findings in 1972–1975 and future problems. *Japanese Journal of Medical Science and Biology, 28,* 287–293.

So, Y. T., & Simon, R. P. (1996). Deficiency diseases of the nervous system. In W. G. Bradley, R. B. Daroff, G. M. Finichel, & C. D. Marsden (Eds.), *Neurology in clinical practice* (2nd ed., pp. 1373–1388). Boston: Butterworth-Heinemann.

Soares, K. V., & McGrath, J. J. (2000). Anticholinergic medication for neuroleptic-induced tardive dyskinesia. *Cochrane Database of Systematic Reviews (2):CD000204.*

Sobue, I. (1991). Clinical aspects of subacute myel-optico-neuropathy (SMON). In P. J. Vinken & G. W. Bruyn (Eds.), *Handbook of clinical neurology: Intoxications of the nervous system, Part 2* (pp. 115–139). Amsterdam: Elsevier North-Holland, Inc.

Sobue, I., Ando, K., Iida, M., Takayanagi, T., Yamamura, Y., & Matsuoka, Y. (1971). Myeloneuropathy with abdominal disorders in Japan. A clinical study of 752 cases. *Neurology, 21,* 168–173.

Sobue, I., Mukoyama, M., Takayanagi, T., Nishigaki, S., & Matsuoka, Y. (1972). Myeloneuropathy with abdominal disorders in Japan. Neuropathologic findings in seven autopsied cases. *Neurology, 22,* 1034–1039.

Sonino, N., Fava, G. A., Raffi, A. R., Boscaro, M., & Fallo, F. (1998). Clinical correlates of major depression in Cushing's disease. *Psychopathology, 31,* 302–306.

Sonoda, K. (1978). SMON and other socially induced diseases in Japan. *Social Science and Medicine, 12,* 497–506.

Soulage, C., Perrin, D., Berenguer, P., & Pequignot, J. M. (2004). Sub-chronic exposure to toluene at 40 ppm alters the monoamine biosynthesis rate in discrete brain areas. *Toxicology, 196,* 21–30.

Spencer, P. S., Sabri, M. I., Schaumburg, H. H., & Moore, C. L. (1979). Does a defect of energy metabolism in the nerve fiber underlie axonal degeneration in polyneuro-pathies? *Annals of Neurology, 5,* 501–507.

Spencer, P. S., & Schaumburg, H. H. (1978). Distal axonopathy: One common type of neurotoxic lesion. *Environmental Health Perspectives, 26,* 97–105.

Spencer, P. S., Schaumburg, H. H., Cohn, D. F., & Seth, P. K. (1984). Latherism: A useful model of primary lateral sclerosis. In F. C. Rose (Ed.), *Progress in motor neurone disease* (pp. 312–327). London: Pitman Books.

Spencer, P. S., & Thomas, P. K. (1974). Ultrastructural studies of the dying-back process. II. The sequestration and removal by Schwann cells and oligodendrocytes of organelles from normal and diseases axons. *Journal of Neurocytology, 3,* 763–783.

Spillane, J. D. (1972). S.M.O.N. *Lancet, 1,* 154.

Starkman, M. N., Gebarski, S. S., Berent, S., & Schteingart, D. E. (1992). Hippo-campal formation volume, memory dysfunction, and cortisol levels in patients with Cushing's syndrome. *Biological Psychiatry, 32,* 756–765.

Steg, R. E., & Garcia, E. G. (1991). Complex visual hallucinations and cyclosporine neurotoxicity. *Neurology, 41,* 1156.

Stein, D. P., Lederman, R. J., & Vogt, D. P. (1992). Neurological complications following liver transplantation. *Annals of Neurology, 31,* 644–649.

Stemper, B., Thurauf, N., Neundorfer, B., & Heckmann, J. G. (2003). Choreoathetosis related to lithium intoxication. *European Journal of Neurology, 10,* 743–744.

Stewart, J., & Badiani, A. (1993). Tolerance and sensitization to the behavioral effects of drugs. *Behavioral Pharmacology, 4*(4), 289–312.

Stewart, J. T. (2004). Capgras syndrome related to diazepam treatment. *Southern Medical Journal, 97*, 65–66.

Stranges, S., Tiejan, W., Dorn, J. M., Freudenheim, J. L., Muti, P., Fariano, E., et al. (2004). Relationship of alcohol drinking pattern to risk of hypertension: A population-based study. *Hypertension, 44*, 813–819.

Stubner, S., Rustenbeck, E., Grohmann, R., Wagner, G., Engel, R., Neundorfer, G., et al. (2004). Severe and uncommon involuntary movement disorders due to psychotropic drugs. *Pharmacopsychiatry, 37*, S54–S64.

Sullivan, E. V., & Pfefferbaum, A. (2003). Diffusion tensor imaging in normal aging and neuropsychiatric disorders. *European Journal of Radiology, 45*, 244–255.

Sulway, M. R., Broe, G. A., Creasey, H., Dent, O. F., Jorm, A. F., Kos, S. C., et al. (1996). Are malnutrition and stress risk factors for accelerated cognitive decline? A prisoner of war study. *Neurology, 46*, 650–655.

Suraya, Y., & Yoong, K. Y. (2001). Lithium neurotoxicity. *Medical Journal of Malaysia, 56*, 378–381.

Sutker, P. B., Vasterling, J. J., Brailey, K, & Allain, A. N. (1995). Memory, attention, and executive deficits in POW survivors: Contributing biological and psychosocial factors. *Neuropsychology, 9*, 118–125.

Tal, A., Rajeshawari, M., & Isley, W. (1997). Rhabdomyolysis associated with simvastatin–gemfibrozil therapy. *Southern Medical Journal, 90*, 546–547.

Tamura, Z., Yoshioka, M., Imanari, T., Fukaya, J., & Kusaka, J. (1973). Identification of green pigment and analysis of clioquinol in specimens from patients with subacute myelo-optico-neuropathy. *Clinica Chimica Acta, 47*, 13–20.

Tang, Y. L., Zhao, D., Zhao, C., & Cubells, J. F. (2006). Opiate addiction in China: Current situation and treatments. *Addiction, 101*, 657–665.

Tateishi, J., Kuroda, S., Saito, A., & Otsuki, S. (1972). Neurotoxicity of clioquinol. 1. Oral administration of clioquinol to several species of animals. [Japanese]. *Seishin Shinkeigaku Zasshi—Psychiatria et Neurologia Japonica, 74*, 739–755.

Tateishi, J., Kuroda, S., Saito, A., & Otsuki, S. (1973). Experimental myelo-optic neuropathy induced by clioquinol. *Acta Neuropathologica, 24*, 304–320.

Tatetsu, S., Miyakawa, T., Fujita, E., Takaki, M., & Harada, M. (1971). A clinical and pathological study of myeloneuropathy following abdominal disorders. *Folia Psychiatrica et Neurologica Japonica, 25*, 225–233.

Taylor, L. (2005). *The Healing Power of Rainforest Herbs*. Garden City Park, New York: Square One Publishers.

Temkin, O. (1971). *The Falling Sickness* (pp. 298–299). Baltimore: The Johns Hopkins Press.

The National Institute on Drug Abuse (NIDA). (2005). Diagnosis and treatment of drug abuse in family practice. Retrieved from http://www.drugabuse.gov/diagnosis-treatment/diagnosis1.html

Thomas, P. K. (1997). Tropical neuropathies. *Journal of Neurology, 244*, 475–482.

Thomas, P. K., Schaumburg, H. H., Spencer, P. S., Kaeser, H. E., Pallis, C. A., Rose, F. C., et al. (1984). Central distal axonopathy syndromes: Newly recognized models of naturally occurring human degenerative disease. *Annals of Neurology, 15*, 313–315.

Thompson, P. J., Baxendale, S. A., Duncan, J. S., & Sander, J. W. (2000). Effects of topiramate on cognitive function. *Journal of Neurology, Neurosurgery and Psychiatry, 69*, 636–641.

Thuomas, K. A., Moller, C., Odkvist, L. M., Flodin, U., & Dige, N. (1996). MR imaging in solvent-induced chronic toxic encephalopathy. *Acta Radiologica, 37*, 177–179.

Tindall, R. S. A., Rollins, J. A., Phillips, J. T., & Greenlee, R. G. (1987). Preliminary results of a double-blind, randomized, placebo-controlled trial of cyclosporine in myasthenia gravis. *New England Journal of Medicine, 316*, 719–724.

Torvik, A., Lindboe, C. F., & Rodge, S. (1982). Brain lesions in alcoholics: Neuropathological study with clinical correlations. *Journal of Neurological Science, 56*, 233–248.

Toutant, C., & Lippmann, S. (1979). Fetal solvents syndrome. *Lancet, 1*, 1356.

Toyokura, Y., & Takasu, T. (1975). Clinical features of SMON. *Japanese Journal of Medical Science and Biology, 28*(Suppl.), 87–99.

Traber, M. G., & et al. (1987). Lack of tocopherol in peripheral nerves of vitamin E-deficient patients with peripheral neuropathy. *New England Journal of Medicine, 317*, 262–264.

Travlos, A., & Hirsch, G. (1993). Steroid psychosis: A cause of confusion on the acute spinal cord injury unit. *Archives of Physical Medicine and Rehabilitation, 74*, 312–315.

Trimble, M. R., & Thompson, P. J. (1986). Neuropsychological aspects of epilepsy. In I. Grant & K. M. Adams (Eds.), *Neuropsychological assessment of neuropsychiatric disorders* (pp. 321–346). New York: Oxford.

Tsubaki, T., Honma, Y., & Hoshi, M. (1971). Neurological syndrome associated with clioquinol. *Lancet, 1*, 696–697.

Tsubaki, T., Toyokura, Y., & Tsukagoshi, H. (1964a). Symposium on nonspecific encephalomyelitis. (1) A clinical and pathological study of subacute myelo-optico neuropathy following abdominal symptoms. 61st Japanese Internal Medicine Society conference (1964). *Nippn Naika Gakkai Zasshi, 53*, 779–784.

Tsubaki, T., Toyokura, Y., & Tsukagoshi, H. (1964b). Symposium on non specific encephalomyelitis. (1) Subacute myelo-optico-neuropathy following abdominal symptoms: A clinical and pathological study. [Japanese]. *Nippon Naika Gakkai Zasshi—Journal of Japanese Society of Internal Medicine, 53*, 779–784.

Tuglu, C., Erdogan, E., & Abay, E. (2005). Delirium and extrapyramidal symptoms due to a lithium–olanzapine combination therapy: A case report. *Journal of Korean Medical Science, 20*, 691–694.

Uhl, G. R. (1999). Neurochemical bases of drug abuse. In G. J. Siegel, B. W. Agranoff, S. K. Fisher, R. W. Albers, & M. D. Uhler (Eds.), *Basic neurochemistry: Molecular, cellular and medical aspects* (6th ed., pp. 1095–1108). Philadelphia: Lippincott-Raven.

Upham, B. L., & Wagner, J. G. (2001). Toxicant-induced oxidative stress in cancer. *Toxicological Sciences, 64*, 1–3.

Valk, J., & van der Knaap, M. S. (1992). Toxic encephalopathy. *AJNR: American Journal of Neuroradiology, 13*, 747–760.

van Puijenbroek, E. P., Du Buf-Vereijken, P. W., Spooren, P. F., & van Doormaal, J. J. (1996). Possible increased risk of rhabdomyolysis during concomitant use of simvastatin and gemfibrozil. *Journal of Internal Medicine, 240*, 403–404.

Varney, N. R., Alexander, B., & MacIndoe, J. H. (1984). Reversible steroid dementia in patients without steroid psychosis. *American Journal of Psychiatry, 141*, 369–372.

Verdoux, H., Lagnaoui, R., & Begaud, B. (2005). Is benzodiazepine use a risk factor for cognitive decline and dementia? A literature review of epidemiological studies. *Psychological Medicine, 35*, 307–315.

Vestergaard, P., & Licht, R. W. (2001). 50 Years with lithium treatment in affective disorders: Present problems and priorities. *World Journal of Biological Psychiatry, 2*, 18–26.

Vickers, J. N., Rodrigues, S. T., & Brown, L. N. (2002). Gaze pursuit and arm control of adolescent males diagnosed with attention deficit hyperactivity disorder (ADHD) and normal controls: Evidence of a dissociation in processing visual information of short and long duration. *Journal of Sports Sciences, 20*, 201–216.

Victor, M. (1989). Neurologic disorders due to alcoholism and malnutrition. In R. J. Joynt (Ed.), *Clinical neurology* (pp. 1–94). Philadelphia: J.B. Lippincott.

Victor, M., Adams, R. D., & Collins, G. H. (1971). *The Wernicke–Korsakoff syndrome*. Philadelphia: F.A. Davis.

Victor, M., Adams, R. D., & Collins, G. H. (1989). *The Wernicke–Korsakoff syndrome and related neurologic disorders due to alcoholism and malnutrition. Contemporary neurology series, Vol. 3*. Philadelphia: F.A. Davis.

Voderholzer, U., Weske, G., Ecker, S., Riemann, D., Gann, H., & Berger, M. (2002). Neurobiological findings before and during successful lithium therapy of a patient with 48-hour rapid-cycling bipolar disorder. *Neuropsychobiology, 45*(Suppl. 1), 13–19.

Volkow, N. D. (2005). NIDA community drug alert bulletin—prescription drugs. Retrieved from http://www.drugabuse.gov/PrescripAlert/index.html

Wada, J. (1997). Clinical experimental observations of carotid artery injections of Sodium Amytal. *Brain and Cognition, 33*, 11–13.

Wada, J., & Rasmussen, T. (1960). Intracarotid injection of sodium Amytal for the lateralization of cerebral speech dominance: Experimental and clinical observations. *Journal of Neurosurgery, 17*, 266–282.

Wada, K., Yamada, N., Suzuki, H., Lee, Y., & Kuroda, S. (2000). Recurrent cases of corticosteroid-induced mood disorder: Clinical characteristics and treatment. *Journal of Clinical Psychiatry, 61*, 261–267.

Wadia, N. H. (1973). Is there SMON in India? *Neurology India, 21*, 95–103.

Waksman, J., Taylor, R. N., Jr., Bodor, G. S., Daly, F. F., Jolliff, H. A., & Dart, R. C. (2001). Acute myocardial infarction associated with amphetamine use. *Mayo Clinic Proceedings, 76*, 323–326.

WebElements. (2006). *WebElements periodic table*. Retrieved from http://www.webelements.com/

Wichman, A., Buchthal, F., Pezeshkpour, G. H., & Regg, R. E. (1985). Peripheral neuropathy in abetalipoproteinemia. *Neurology, 35*, 1289.

Wickman, J. M., & Cold, J. (2000). *Recognizing and treating tardive dyskinesia. US Pharmacist. A Jobson Publication*. Retrieved from http://www.uspharmacist.com/oldformat.asp?url=newlook/files/feat/may00tar.htm

Wilding, J., Van Gaal, L., Rissanen, A., Vercruysse, F., Fitchet, M., & OBES-002 Study Group. (2004). A randomized double-blind placebo-controlled study of the long-term efficacy and safety of topiramate in the treatment of obese subjects. *International Journal of Obesity and Related Metabolic Disorders: Journal of the International Association for the Study of Obesity, 28*, 1399–1410.

Wilson, R. K., Kuncl, R. W., & Corse, A. M. (1958). Wernicke's encephalopathy: Beyond alcoholism. *Nature Clinical Practice Neurology, 2*, 54–58.

Windebank, A. J. (1993). Polyneuropathy due to nutritional deficincy and alcoholism. In P. J. Dyck, R. K. Thomas, J. W. Griffen, P. A. Low, & J. F. Poduslo (Eds.), *Peripheral neuropathy* (3rd ed., pp. 1310–1321). Philadelphia: W.B. Suausnders Co.

Winkelman, C. (1999). A review of pharmacodynamics and pharmacokinetics in seizure management. *Journal of Neuroscience Nursing, 31*, 50–53.

Wolkowitz, O. M., Reus, V. I., Canick, J., Levin, B., & Lupien, S. (1997). Glucocorticoid medication, memory and steroid psychosis in medical illness. *Annals of the New York Academy of Sciences, 823,* 81–96.

Worden, A. N., & Heywood, R. (1978). Clioquinol toxicity. *Lancet, 1,* 212.

Yablon, S. A., Meythaler, J. M., & Englander, J. G. (1998). Practice parameter: Antiepileptic drug prophylaxis of posttraumatic seizures. *Archives of Physical Medicine and Rehabilitation, 79,* 594–597.

Yoder, K. K., Hutchins, G. D., Morris, E. D., Brashear, A., Wang, C., & Shekhar, A. (2004). Dopamine transporter density in schizophrenic subjects with and without tardive dyskinesia. *Schizophrenia Research, 71,* 371–375.

Young, A. M., Moran, P. M., & Joseph, M. H. (2005). The role of dopamine in conditioning and latent inhibition: What, when, where and how? *Neuroscience and Biobehavioral Reviews, 29,* 963–976.

Young, E. A., Haskett, R. F., Grunhaus, L., Pande, A., Weinberg, V. M., Watson, S. J., et al. (1994). Increased evening activation of the hypothalamic-pituitary-adrenal axis in depressed patients. *Archives of General Psychiatry, 51,* 701–707.

Zacny, J. P. (2003). Characterizing the subjective, psychomotor, and physiological effects of a hydrocodone combination product (Hycodan) in non-drug-abusing volunteers. *Psychopharmacology, 165,* 146–156.

Zacny, J. P., & Galinkin, J. L. (1999). Psychotropic drugs used in anesthesia practice: Abuse liability and epidemiology of abuse. *Anesthesiology, 90,* 269–288.

Zacny, J. P., & Gutierrez, S. (2003). Characterizing the subjective, psychomotor, and physiological effects of oral oxycodone in non-drug-abusing volunteers. *Psychopharmacology, 170,* 242–254.

Zacny, J. P., Gutierrez, S., & Bolbolan, S. A. (2005). Profiling the subjective, psychomotor, and physiological effects of a hydrocodone/acetaminophen product in recreational drug users. *Drug and Alcohol Dependence, 78,* 243–252.

Zakzanis, K. K., Leach, L., & Kaplan, E. (1999). *Neuropsychological differential diagnosis.* Lisse: Swets & Zeitlinger.

Zaninovic', V. (2004). Possible etiologies for tropical spastic paraparesis and human T lymphotropic virus I-associated myelopathy. *Brazilian Journal of Medical and Biological Research, 37,* 1–12.

Zautra, A. J., & Smith, B. W. (2005). Impact of controlled-release oxycodone on efficacy beliefs and coping efforts among osteoarthritis patients with moderate to severe pain. *Clinical Journal of Pain, 21,* 471–477.

Zavalic, M., Mandic, Z., Turk, R., Bogadi-Sare, A., Plavec, D., Gomzi, M., et al. (1998). Assessment of colour vision impairment in male workers exposed to toluene generally above occupational exposure limits. *Occupational Medicine (Oxford) 48,* 175–180.

Zeraidi, N., Zeggwagh, A. A., Abouqal, R., Zekraoui, A., & Kerkeb, O. (1995). Kidney insufficiency: toxicity factor of methyl-bromo-hydroxyquinoline. [French]. *Annales de Medecine Interne, 146,* 593–595.

Zubieta, J. K., Heitzeg, M. M., Xu, Y., Koeppe, R. A., Ni, L., Guthrie, S., et al. (2005). Regional cerebral blood flow responses to smoking in tobacco smokers after overnight abstinence. *American Journal of Psychiatry, 162,* 567–577.

Zubieta, J. K., Ketter, T. A., Bueller, J. A., Xu, Y., Kilbourn, M. R., Young, E. A., et al. (2003). Regulation of human affective responses by anterior cingulate and limbic mu-opioid neurotransmission. *Archives of General Psychiatry, 60,* 1145–1153.

Zubieta, J., Lombardi, U., Minoshima, S., Guthrie, S., Ni, L., Ohl, L. E., et al. (2001). Regional cerebral blood flow effects of nicotine in overnight abstinent smokers. *Biological Psychiatry, 49,* 906–913.

Zucker, R. A., Fitzgerald, H. E., Refior, S. K., Puttler, L. I., Pallas, D. M., & Ellis, D. A. (2000). The clinical and social ecology of childhood for children of alcoholics: Description of a study and implications for a differentiated social policy. In H. E. Fitzgerald, B. M. Lester, & B. S. Zuckerman (Eds.), *Children of addiction: Research, health and policy issues* (Chap. 4, pp. 109–141). New York: Routledge Falmer.

Zylber-Katz, E. (1995). Multiple drug interactions with cyclosporine in a heart transplant patient. *Annals of Pharmacotherapy, 29,* 127–131.

17 Conditions associated with or sometimes mimic toxic-induced central nervous system disease

Aging and other demographic factors, medical and psychiatric illnesses, and even normal variations in behavior compete in many instances to explain signs and symptoms that also may accompany toxic-induced disorders. As mentioned previously, the central nervous system is complex and the same neural pathways implicated in toxic-induced disease can be affected by injury, illness, or other conditions that may seem unrelated to neuropathology as well. A complete differential diagnosis in a given case will require recognition and inclusion of these potential explanations for the patient's complaints and clinical findings. A correct diagnosis depends on such consideration and is a requisite for accurate causal determination. In this chapter we present several demographic, behavioral, psychiatric, and medical conditions that are representative of these types of factors.

The influence of aging on clinical and psychometric examinations

Stanley Berent

The issue of aging has become increasingly important to clinicians and researchers, a major reason being because people are living longer. As pointed out by Bennett (2000) and others, someone born in 1900 could be expected to live to be 50 years old while the life expectancy for someone born in the year 2000 is close to 80 years. One factor in a longer life span is a healthier youth (Crimmins & Finch, 2006; Whalley, Dick, & McNeill, 2006). Nevertheless, along with the increase in longevity have come increased opportunities for illness and injury and the adverse consequences of these occurrences for the central nervous system. The signs and symptoms associated with these various illnesses and, indeed, with aging itself, overlap with and at times mirror those we expect to see in neurotoxic-induced illnesses. Because of this, the professional interested in neurobehavioral toxicology must be familiar with how aging affects the organism. Age should always be considered in clinical evaluation, if not formally listed in the differential diagnosis, and seen as a potential confounder in a research plan.

Some individuals live long lives, even exceptionally long lives, with little or no serious medical problems (Bernstein et al., 2004). Such a benign experience, however, does not appear to be the norm (Amella, 2004; Bennett, 2000; Boyes, Evans, Eklund, Janssen, & Simmons, 2005; Geller & Zenick, 2005; van Boxtel et al., 1998). Living longer provides the opportunity for diseases that are associated more with the elderly than with youth. In addition, and while many diseases have been reduced or perhaps eradicated (e.g., polio, smallpox), a longer life combined with less than complete cures for other diseases affords the opportunity for a longer time course of illness and injuries that do occur. In short, a longer life can paradoxically mean having to deal with illnesses that in the past might have been avoided by death. Diabetes mellitus, many cancers, hypertension and other vascular problems, cardiac and pulmonary illnesses, obesity, sleep disorders, nutritional deficiencies; all have relationships to aging and all have potential consequences for the central nervous system. Whether the problem reflects a direct effect of the illness or some secondary factor (e.g., adverse consequences of treatments or secondary injury to an organ system, depression or other psychiatric condition or psychological reaction), all can have a negative impact on the patient's neurobehavioral functioning. These factors will need to be considered, and they will influence our approach to research and to the clinical evaluation of patients.

Change characterizes aging. Change in the organ systems can alter disease susceptibility and even the nature of clinical presentations. Janssens and Krause (2004), for instance, discussed how changes in respiratory, immune, and digestive systems can interact with comorbidities brought about by age-associated diseases to increase the frequency and severity of (nonterminal) pneumonia in the elderly. Change characterizes every aspect of the aging person and many if not all of these changes have implications for health and the individual's quality of life. Many of the changes go unrecognized, at times even by health service providers. As mentioned earlier, pneumonia may become more frequent and severe in the elderly in comparison to younger people. At the same time, however, classic symptoms of pneumonia may be absent in the elderly, with mental confusion or physical falls taking their place (Janssens & Krause 2004). Most important here, the nature of symptoms associated with diseases other than pneumonia might be expected to change with advancing age. Individual sleep patterns, too, change with age, with insomnia being the most common sleep-related problem reported by people over 60 years of age (Maher, 2004). Age-related changes, in turn, can have their own secondary consequences. Insomnia can, for instance, lead to treatment with sleep-inducing medication, which might then produce other problems for the individual or serve to confound some otherwise sensible clinical diagnosis. Treatment issues become increasingly important in the elderly. Confusion, and the more serious condition of delirium, for instance, is relatively common in older patients, especially if ill or hospitalized (Francis & Kapoor, 1990; Francis, Martin, & Kapoor, 1990). Issues of treatment compliance can, therefore, become increasingly important in an elderly population. It should be easy to see how factors associated with age-related changes could impact on treatment with some medication, say the sleep medication mentioned earlier, and lead to an adverse consequence. The patient's behavior during interview, psychometric examination, or some other aspect of the clinical evaluation could well be a reflection of such a factor (e.g., lack of sleep or adverse reaction to sleep medications). It is the clinician's responsibility to uncover these possibilities and to exclude, or include, them in final diagnoses and causal determinations.

While considerable attention has been given to the potential relationships between cognitive decline and cumulative incidents of physical stresses (e.g., illnesses, injuries, and various surgical and medical treatments, including medications and other drugs) that occur with aging, the issue of cognitive decline in normal aging has been addressed to some extent as well. van Boxtel et al. (1998), for instance, studied 1,360 community dwelling individuals, aged 21–81 years. Using a regression model, stratified for age, sex, and general ability, they found that while some specific diseases (e.g., diabetes) did appear to aggravate age-related decline in cognitive ability, morbidity as a whole contributed only modestly to total variance in cognitive ability (van Boxtel et al.). Somewhat in contrast, Swan et al. (2000) studied nondemented older adults and found a relationship between indices of subclinical brain atrophy (including decreased total brain volume [TBV] and increased white matter hyperintensities [WMH] as measured by MRI) and what the authors termed "accelerated aging." They reported further that their indices of atrophy were related to several historical health characteristics of the individuals in their sample (those variables still significant after multivariate analysis included decline in diastolic blood pressure over time, low ankle/arm systolic blood pressure ratio [<0.9], and number of years smoked) as well as to measurable functional neurobehavioral consequences (e.g., executive functions like sequencing and planning, working memory, psychomotor speed, and selective attention). They reported finding functional differences between individuals with lower TBV and greater WMH in comparison to others with indications of less brain atrophy. Subjects with relatively greater atrophy showed greater cognitive decline over a 10 year period than those with less atrophy (Swan et al.). Although the studies reported by van Boxtel et al. and Swan et al. purportedly were to study normal individuals or those without diagnosable illness, they only partially addressed the issue of decline in ability with age. One can easily interpret these results as being consistent with a pathological model of functional decline, examined in a sample of individuals who were still at an early stage in terms of disease progression.

Issues of specific causality aside, cognitive abilities such as attention, memory, information processing speed, sensations, visual perception, and motor speed appear to be especially sensitive to factors producing change in the central nervous system and tend to decline with age (Bush & Martin, 2005; Mattay et al., 2006; van Boxtel et al., 1998). Whether or not all or even the majority of these age-related changes represent normal or pathological conditions has been the subject of debate for decades (Berent et al., 1999). Cognitive problems, including progressive loss of memory, are common problems among the elderly (Bennett, 2000). A number of medical conditions are known to have negative implications for memory and other cognitive impairments, and many medical conditions that are rare in younger people may be common in older age (e.g., cardiac disease). Certainly, some proportion of the cognitive declines associated with aging is likely due to various chronic illnesses or the treatments associated with them.

Issues of accommodation in evaluating the elderly

While the scientific debate over the normality of neurobehavioral decline with aging continues, there are some practical issues that cannot be ignored. For instance, we know that sensory ability declines with age, e.g., people do not hear or see as well as they did when young. Clinical evaluations (and much research) occur within the context of interpersonal interactions. We need to communicate with the patient in order to accomplish the neurobehavioral evaluation. This produces a paradox. In order to perform an effective evaluation, the clinician needs to accommodate to the patient's weaknesses (e.g., reduced hearing). But, also, there is the need to evaluate what the patient can and cannot do. So, how can the first be accomplished without interfering with the primary objective of evaluation? The answer is that the clinician needs to do both. Although it may lead to both personal and interpersonal stress in the clinical situation, the examiner will likely need to confront the patient's weaknesses before compensating for those weaknesses, e.g., gradually raising one's voice until the patient is able to hear what is being said. Of course, there may be times when the patient's condition will prevent this. Aside from extreme situations, the clinician is likely to meet with resistance on the part of the patient, his or her caregivers, or even the clinician's own sense of aversion at "pushing" a person who has obvious limitations. There are a variety of motives for not wanting to confront an area of lessened ability. For example, a given patient's hesitancy might prove to be based on a desire to avoid the embarrassment of being personally confronted with their own areas of weakness. It is not uncommon to see a patient become tearful when confronted with a neurobehavioral task they cannot perform successfully. Sometimes, the patient might be aware that he or she is unable to perform but wishes to avoid allowing someone else witness what they perceive as a personal weakness. At other times, the patient might appear to be legitimately ignorant of their weaknesses. In the authors' experiences, such confrontations, while stressful, most often prove to be therapeutic. One typical scenario is represented by a patient who following such confrontation agreed to stop using the stove for cooking when alone in the kitchen, something he had until that point insisted he could do well. Further, he agreed to accompany his wife to a support group that was sponsored by a geriatric center in their community and to work with his treating clinicians to complete all of his diagnostic procedures and to consider various treatment options. When asked later why he had been so reluctant to admit to having difficulty remembering to cut off the stove, he said he had always been a "take charge kind of guy" and feared his wife might think less of him if she knew his memory was declining.

At some point, most clinician's working with the elderly find that they must supplement information derived in interview with the patient with that obtained from others, e.g., spouse, children, other caregivers. Obtaining information regarding the patient's functioning from others is important, but it is critical to evaluate the patient's functioning directly during some portion of the evaluation, when the patient is alone and without the support of others. By gradually adding such supports to the evaluative process, one can learn not only what the patient can and cannot do and how they do it, but also how much benefit is derived from the provision of additional resources. In short, we are first interested in measuring the patient's functioning, not solely his or her functioning under conditions of accommodation. The same rules apply for psychometric examination as for clinical observation. One of the more difficult things to teach a person in training is to either formally document the patient's limitations (e.g., a psychometrically determined reading level too low to take a given test) or, when appropriate, allow the elderly patient to try to complete a task on their own before providing assistance or deciding prematurely that the patient is unable to accomplish the task at hand. On one occasion, for instance, a trainee indicated that the *sentence completion* task (a task that in this instance required the patient to read a partial sentence and then complete the sentence in their own writing) had been administered orally and that the sentences were completed in the trainee's writing. When asked why the standard procedure for the task had been changed, the trainee said that the patient indicated that she was unable to do the written part of the task. The trainee was encouraged to return and properly complete the examination, i.e., having the patient complete the task on her own. Although there may be times when a person is truly unable to perform a specified function, the only way to know is to engage the patient in direct examination. This is no different than the evaluation of any symptom presented by a patient. Further an objective evaluation is indicated in every such instance. All that was learned by the patient's claim that she could not write is that she said she could not write. Although one does not need to (nor should they) carry a procedure to the extreme, it is necessary to learn something more than just the patient's complaint. Is she completely unable to write? Is she able to write but does so poorly? What is the nature of her writing difficulty—mechanical, conceptual? Is she also unable to spell, write in cursive, maintain orientation on the page, or conceptualize the task? Does she have performance anxiety or some other personal or emotional reason for not participating in the task? Even in extreme instances where the patient might produce illegible scribbles, something is learned. The patient in such an extreme instance can be allowed at the least to complete enough of the task to provide data for meaningful clinical analysis. The aim of this approach is to obtain information regarding the patient's actual abilities in comparison to their potential abilities. Analogous to determining a patient's temperature before administering a fever reducing medication, the neurobehavioral clinician would first wish to determine what the patient's abilities are in comparison to others. A premature introduction of accommodations could obscure an accurate measurement of these abilities. Once this determination has been made, however, the clinician can evaluate what the patient can do under various levels of accommodation. The same should hold for all accommodations that might be made in the clinical evaluation, e.g., using larger than usual print, using a hearing aid, sign language, etc. In the psychometric examination, it is important to remember that any departures from standardized procedures need to be described and also considered in analyzing test results (Wechsler, 1997).

It is worth mentioning before leaving this section that people develop their own methods of accommodation in everyday life. A person whose memory (or hearing, vision, or other ability) is declining, for instance, may become dependent on a spouse or close acquaintance to compensate for their loss. The process of developing such compensation may be gradual, occurring over many years. As a result, the parities involved may remain unaware that such a process is taking place. Often, the affected person's symptoms come to light only after the loss of someone who was providing the compensation. When this happens, others at times believe the person is reflecting onset of new symptoms when, in fact, they are seeing something that has been there for some time, hidden from view by the interpersonal accommodation.

Issues of bias

Why was the trainee in the example given earlier resistant to having the patient complete the writing task? Although motivations will differ from person to person, the trainee discovered through supervision that he assumed the patient would not be able to do the task and simply did not want to confront the patient with the experience of failure. There are biases at work in such resistance, and it is important for professionals to discover their own biases in working with all their patients. Other phrases for "bias," as we are using it here, is "mental set" or "basic assumption." Regardless of the words or phrases used, it is important to recognize that such proclivities exist in everyone. Such biases may be outside of the person's immediate awareness, yet still can adversely affect motivation and work. Also, the patient will have his or her own biases, and these will affect the patient's behavior during an evaluation, his or her view of the clinician, and even their performance on tests (Cohen, Silverman, & Shmavonian, 1961). Certainly in western culture, and maybe in every culture, strong biases exist in views toward the elderly. These biases are part of our personal and cultural development, and until we come to recognize and control them, they can interfere with our objectivity. Some biases relevant here include the idea that an older person should be respected and not embarrassed by requiring him or her to do something he or she is unable to do, or unable to do well. Another, and perhaps more insidious bias, is the idea that people become less able in general as they age, and that this decline in ability is normal and most likely minimally reversible. A number of consequent beliefs can derive from the last mentioned basic assumption.

For instance, if it is one's destiny to progressively decline with advancing age, do we expend the same clinical effort in evaluating (or treating) an older person as we would for a younger person? While it would be the extremely rare person who would answer "no," to such a question, the thought can still occur even if unconsciously. Such thoughts, in fact, exist in our cultural mentality, finding expression in folklore, literature, and cinema (e.g., *Soylent Green*, a futuristic novel [and movie] that reflects the theme of state supported euthanasia [Fleischer, Greenberg, & Harrison, 1973], and *Logan's Run*, another futuristic novel [and movie] reflecting a similar theme [Anderson, 1976]).

Normative data in the context of age

The psychometric process itself was discussed in some detail in volume I of this book and, of course, in numerous other publications. For the present discussion, it can be said that a patient's productions on a neuropsychological test yield raw scores that are often transformed to standard scores by comparison to some (specified for a given test on the basis of age or some other demographic variable) normative reference group. While the raw scores reflect how the patient performed on a given test (responded correctly, etc.), the normalized scores speak to what the patient's performance means in comparison to some reference (normative) data. These later standard scores allow one to compare the patient's performance to others or even to their own performance on different examinations or within a given examination. It is the standard score that is most often used for clinical interpretations. The norms that are used to develop the standard scores are continually being evaluated, and often changed, in attempts to make them more objective and clinically meaningful. The changes are usually empirical, but will also reflect professional judgments that are based on scientific knowledge. Recent articles, for instance, have explored the idea of anchoring normative comparisons to measures of general ability as a change from earlier bases in education level (Steinberg, Bieliauskas, Smith, & Ivnik, 2005a, 2005b; Steinberg, Bieliauskas, Smith, Ivnik, & Malec, 2005c). The rationale given by the authors for making this change was that additions to the scientific literature on the subject suggested that the then current use of score adjustments based on years of formal education might be less closely related to performance on the tests they specified than was level of general ability (Steinberg et al., 2005b).

With the introduction of the current edition of the Wechsler Adult Intelligence Scale-III (WAIS-II) (Wechsler, 1997), a change was made from earlier versions in how normative scores are determined. It is still possible to use a general reference comparison to establish a scaled score on the WAIS-III, but earlier versions used only the reference group approach (ages 20–34 years). Noting that using the general reference group approach led to greater discrepancies between scores for older age groups in comparison to younger age groups than was the case with earlier versions of the WAIS, the developers moved to converting raw scores to scaled scores relative to the examinee's own age group. There is nothing wrong with either the general reference group or the age group approach to transforming scores. These approaches, and perhaps especially the age group approach, appear to accept uncritically the idea that decline in level of performance is to be expected (normally) as one gets older. In a way, this could be seen as a kind of accommodation for the older test taker. This *psychometric accommodation* is similar in some respects to, and could be viewed as a quantitative analogy to, a brain imaging interpretation of "age-consistent atrophy." In fact, we accept the idea that decline with age, if not normal, is to be expected to such an extent that sometimes one hears the term, "super normal" applied to an elderly person who is functioning at a high level of ability or a level comparable to that expected of a younger person.

As illustrated in Table 17.1, raw scores on many psychometric tests decline with age and this occurrence appears to be stable enough to consider it a factual characterization of life. However, questions of its inevitability and related theoretical issues of progression and irreversibility remain incompletely answered. That we reflect the situation in our test norms suggests a certain level of acceptance of the situation as fact, and this invites another kind of bias. It remains important, however, that clinicians and researchers recognize the bias and avoid even stronger biases that can derive from these observations. Consider the following. Table 17.1 contains a theoretical case example, with the same neurobehavioral test raw scores converted to scaled scores across four age-based normative comparison groups. While little change is apparent across the various age-related normative groupings in some domains of neuropsychological functioning, other areas reflect substantial differences. These changes appear to be most pronounced in performance areas. While verbal IQ (VIQ) shows almost no change across age, performance IQ (PIQ) reflects a dramatic change (i.e., a raw score earning a PIQ $= 122$) at age 75 years in comparison to the same level of performance at age 25 years (PIQ $= 87$). The same score that would be classed as "superior" at age 75 would be seen as "low average" at age 25, according to qualitative descriptions provided by the *WAIS-III Manual* (Wechsler, 1997). The difference between these two IQ scores is greater than 2 SD from approximately >1 SD above the mean (100) to approximately 1 SD below the mean. This corresponds to a percentile difference of more than 70 points, from >90th percentile to approximately the 20th percentile (Wechsler, 1997). A comparable change observed in an actual patient within a one to several year time frame would be viewed clinically as highly significant. If, as is reflected in Table 17.1, the change was accompanied by no comparable change in VIQ, the clinical significance might well be interpreted as implying a focal neurological pattern (Berent & Trask, 2000). However, many, if not most, people accept that slowed and in some cases less efficient performance is an expected outcome of the aging process, considered perhaps by most to be normal. One very real risk of such a bias is that some clinically relevant pattern in the elderly person's test results will be dismissed on the basis of age and the expected decline that comes with aging. Even though decline may be inevitable, it remains critical that every patient be evaluated as

Table 17.1 Raw test scores and their correspondence to normative scores across four age categories.

Test	Raw score	25 years old	45 years old	65 years old	75 years old
WAIS-III					
FSIQ		102	102	113	122
VIQ		114	107	114	118
PIQ		87	95	110	122
VCI		118	110	116	118
POI		88	93	105	114
WMI		102	102	108	117
PSI		86	93	108	122
Verbal Subtests					
Vocabulary	54	14	12	13	13
Similarities	26	12	11	13	13
Arithmetic	16	12	11	12	14
Digit Span	17	10	10	11	14
Information	23	14	13	13	14
Comprehension	24	12	11	12	12
Letter-Number Sequencing	10	9	10	11	13
Performance Subtests					
Picture Completion	19	8	9	11	12
Coding	65	7	9	12	14
Block Design	29	7	8	10	11
Matrix Reasoning	14	9	10	12	14
Picture Arrangement	15	10	11	13	15
Symbol Search	27	8	9	11	14
WRAT-3					
Reading	45	96	93	101	No norms available
Spelling	41	98	95	103	
Arithmetic	39	93	92	105	
PPVT-III (Form A)					
Correct	178	99	90	91	92
Trail Making[a]					
A	41″	77	87	98	104
B	101″	82	88	102	109
Verbal Fluency					
FAS[b]	33	84	83	91	93[c]
Animals[d]	19	97	94	104	111
WCST					
Categories	5	11–16%	11–16%	>16%	>16%
Errors	50	79	77	89	98
PR	36	70	74	89	96
PE	32	68	73	88	95
Booklet Category[e]					
Errors	57	84	93	105	111

(*continued*)

Table 17.1 (continued) Raw test scores and their correspondence to normative scores across four age categories.

Test	Raw score	25 years old	45 years old	65 years old	75 years old
CVLT-II					
Total Correct	57	111	120	129	132
WMS-III					
Auditory Immediate		102	102	111	117
Visual Immediate		91	94	106	112
Immediate Memory		96	98	110	118
Auditory Delayed		102	102	114	120
Visual Delayed		88	100	109	115
Auditory Recognition Delayed		90	90	100	105
General Memory		92	98	111	118
Working Memory		91	102	108	115
Subtests					
LM I	38	10	10	11	12
LM II	26	11	11	13	14
Faces I	35	9	9	10	11
Faces II	35	8	9	10	12
VPA II	6	10	10	12	13
Family Pict I	42	8	9	12	13
Family Pict II	44	8	11	13	13
Spatial Span	15	8	11	12	12
Visual Repro I	81	7	9	12	13
Visual Repro II	77	11	13	16	17
Tapping[f]					
Dominant	46	74	85	95	98
Nondominant	40	74	83	91	94
Pegs[g]					
Dominant	61	111	111	133	No norms
Nondominant	70	106	109	125	

The scores used in the construction of this table are theoretical and intended for illustrative purposes only. The normative data were derived from standard reference materials used in clinical practice. These materials included the standard test manuals for specific tests as well as other published normative data, cited in the table where relevant. The table was initially constructed by Steven T. Michael, MA, modified and included here with his permission.

[a] Drane, Yuspeh, Huthwaite, & Klinger, 2002.
[b] Mitrushina, Boone, Razani, & D'Elia, 2005.
[c] Norms presented for 74 year old.
[d] Tombaugh, Kozak, & Rees, 1999.
[e] Defilippis & McCampbell, 1997.
[f] Mitrushina et al., 2005.
[g] Ruff & Parker, 1993.

a unique individual and as objectively as possible. The most accurate characterization of human behavior rests on the concept of individual differences. While knowledge of such differences is important in clinical tasks such as separating pathology from normality, using knowledge of a group's mean performance alone to predetermine the importance of complaints on an individual level should be avoided. It may be, for instance, that an elderly person with symptoms, or even signs, of memory decline may be evidencing a clinical picture that characterizes many in his or her age group. In the individual case, however, it also could be that these signs and symptoms reflect some underlying and potentially treatable medical or psychological condition.

We mentioned that Table 17.1 reflects what appears to be a differential decline with age in some performance items (e.g., BD, Coding, PIQ, PSI, Trails, Pegs, tapping), and perhaps some visual/perceptual areas (e.g., Picture Arrangement, POI), in comparison to scores in verbal areas (e.g., VIQ, Vocab, SIM,). There are some exceptions (e.g., complex solving tasks [Category test] and tasks that demand good short-term memory [Digit Span]). Although there is little question that lessened efficiency as measured by standard neuropsychological tests occurs with aging, it is important, nevertheless, to note that these changes may not always reflect normal destiny. In addition to psychological explanations, disease and injury, even the cumulative effects of multiple traumas over the years, may be contributing to these changes. The clinician should look at the test results in terms of normalized values but also in terms of actual performance levels and, to the fullest extent possible, to consider the individual's performance against the person's own baseline. Previously obtained test results, school records, job performance records, and the like all can be used to estimate the person's base-rate performance. While objective, contemporaneously made measures of historical performance represent most often the preferable indication of past performance levels, a baseline can be estimated from within current test data as well, looking at those areas that do not change as easily (e.g., vocabulary) in comparison to those that do change (e.g., memory). Questions about decline in neurobehavioral functioning in normal individuals aside, we know that numerous diseases, such as Alzheimer's disease (AD), are associated with functional decline. Accurate measurements of neurobehavioral functioning, together with information from recorded and reported history and interview, can allow for reasonable baseline estimates, which, in turn, can allow for conclusions regarding presence, pattern, rate, severity, and other aspects of changed functioning. Putting this together with the objective, criteria-based approach to the differential diagnosis will allow for accurate clinical diagnosis and causal determination.

While the question of "normal cognitive decline with aging" is incompletely resolved, we do know that some measurable changes in memory and other cognitive functions can be associated with progressive neurodegenerative diseases, and also that sometimes these changes are reversible. In a study of *isolated memory impairment* (IMI), for instance (Berent et al., 1999), 10 of 20 of the IMI categorized subjects had progressed over a 3 year period to diagnosable AD. Of the remaining 10 subjects who did not meet National Institute of Neurologic, Communicative Disorders and Stroke—AD and Related Disorders Association (NINCDS–ADRDA) criteria for AD

(McKhann et al., 1984), three improved in their neuropsychological functioning and were reclassified as having *pseudodementia*. This was despite the fact that none of these subjects met criteria for depression at the time of initial evaluation and none had a known medical or neurological condition that would explain the reverse in their test findings. It was observed later that those persons with cognitive problems beyond memory alone were more likely than the strictly IMI patients to progress to dementia, at least in the short-time periods studied (e.g., as little as 2 years in some instances). Although it is now fairly widely accepted that memory impairment is necessary to predict progressive dementia, it may not be sufficient to do so in the absence of involvement of cognitive impairments other than memory. The patients who fall in this later category, i.e., those with extramemory impairments, are increasingly classified as having *mild cognitive impairment* (MCI) (Bozoki, Giordami, Heidebrink, Berent, & Foster, 2001; Petersen et al., 2001; Sacuiu, Sjogren, Johansson, Gustafson, & Skoog, 2005). It remains possible, of course, that the finding of multiple cognitive impairments as opposed to relatively fewer impairments or impaired memory alone results from the point in time that the individual is evaluated (Berent et al., 1999). That is, a later point in the progression of neurodegenerative disease might be expected to be accompanied by greater functional impairment than would be present earlier in the course of disease. Also, the interval between evaluation and clinically diagnosable dementia would logically be shorter in the case of a later as opposed to an earlier examination-based prediction. Since presently there is no reliable way to gauge the exact time of onset in progressive dementia, the issue remains incompletely resolved. IMI and MCI appear to be used in practice increasingly, but neither classification reflects a formal clinical diagnosis at this time, and neither implies any specific cause for the classified condition. These classifications are descriptive, and both offer classification schemes that may have positive research and clinical applications. Also, both provide additional tools that allow for objective and quantified evaluation and monitoring with respect to the cognitive changes that often accompany the aging process.

Models of cognitive change in aging

There is no single model at this time that can explain the differences between or resolve the issues regarding normal versus pathological neurobehavioral changes in aging, nor is there a comprehensive causal model to explain the neurobiology of dementia (Whalley et al., 2006). One reason for the lack of a model may have to do with the complexity of the central nervous system. The issue of functional compensation, for instance, is quite complex. Not only might a given individual compensate psychologically for impaired or lost function (e.g., relying on a spouse or other to provide information the patient can no longer spontaneously retrieve), but the central nervous system contains mechanisms of redundancy that allow compensation for lost capacity. Fera et al. (2005) postulated that changes in brain organization that have been observed to occur in aging enable the person to use alternative neural substrates to accomplish tasks that were handled differently in the past. Others have reported similar findings with regard to changes in neural mechanisms associated with age-related changes in behavior (Mattay et al., 2006; Tisserand, McIntosh, van der Veen, Backes, & Jolles, 2005). These issues are important for neurobehavioral toxicology. One reason for this importance is that many of the functional changes that occur with age are similar to or even mirror those seen in toxicant-induced injuries. Also, central nervous system mechanisms of pathophysiology that are similar to those seen in aging appear at times to be involved in neurotoxicant-induced injuries, and nontoxicant-induced illnesses producing cognitive impairment (e.g., white and gray matter degeneration in brain [Filley, 2001]). As a result, aging will very often be included in the differential diagnosis and causal determinations for a given clinical case.

Even in conditions that on the surface appear to reflect underlying pathology, the situation is not clear-cut. As mentioned, there is a lack of homogeneity in IMI, MCI, and other categories used to describe potentially early or "prodromal" phases of progressive dementias (Berent et al., 1999; Bozoki et al., 2001; Nordlund et al., 2005; Petersen, Smith, Ivnik, Kokmen, & Tangalos, 1994). Complicating matters further is the observation that not all changes associated with aging are primarily based on physical mechanisms. Whether the compensation is primarily physiological or experiential (i.e., learning-based), people change in the strategic approach to a task as well as in their ability to perform the task (Birren & Botwinick, 1955; Birren & Fisher, 1995; Cohen et al., 1961; Duverne & Lemaire, 2005). For instance, Cohen et al. demonstrated that older and younger subjects viewed a task differently and that these differences in viewpoint influenced the nature of their task performance, regardless of the level of arousal. Although arousal was found to be important to task attention and, therefore, task performance, the subjects' motivation to perform also was affected by their understanding of the task demands, e.g., whether the task was perceived as positive or negative. The tendency to view the task as positive or negative was found to be dependent on age. Cohen et al. concluded that the aged subjects tended to view a task demand as requiring retention, recall, and report of what was presented to them and a desire to perform the task well. Younger subjects, in contrast, tended to view the task with more suspicion, suspecting that the task would in some way reveal to the examiner some personal attribute. These differences in mental set in the approach to task performance led to differences in performance, with the elderly being more accurate than the younger, but the younger being quicker and more brief in their responses to a task. The role of cultural differences in producing these different "mind sets" is not clear. What is clear from the work of Cohen et al., however, is the importance of interpretation of task demand to performance, the observation that such interpretations can be personally determined independent of another's intent, and that age can play a role in influencing the nature of such interpretations.

The changes that occur over the life span are not limited to perceptual and cognition-related variables. Motor-related variables like muscle bulk, strength, speed, and endurance show changes with aging (sarcopenia) that can some-times interact with, effect and confound cognitive function (for example, a person's accuracy on a cognitive task can depend on the speed with which the task is performed) (Cohen et al., 1961; Metter, Schrager, Ferrucci, & Talbot, 2005; Stephens, 2006). The same can be said of mood, which also shows different presentations with advancing age (Boyd & Amsterdam, 2004).

Emotion and other psychological/psychiatric considerations in the elderly represent a special challenge for the clinician. At times, depression, anxiety, and even bizarre symptoms are not easily recognized because the symptoms of these conditions may be expressed differently in the aged person than in the younger patient. The older person may be resistant, or even unable to express their symptoms well. This is especially likely if the patient suffers from dementia. Angry outbursts, aggressive acts against others, damage to pro-perty, or accidental injuries may substitute for more direct statements about "feeling blue" in response to life stresses such as the loss of a friend or if facing physical abuse in the home. Exceptions aside, the elderly have had time to experience more losses and other potential stressors than has someone more junior to them. Many events that younger people see as relatively benign can be experienced by the elderly as very stressful; e.g., moving from a house to an apartment or to assisted living, a room change in a nursing home, learning that the person's regular physician is on vacation or no longer in practice, or having to undergo neurobehavioral evaluation. The elderly person may even have strong reactions to events that others have assumed are outside their conscious awareness. For instance, a psychologist was asked to see an elderly nursing home resident because of a dramatic change in the resident's usually calm demeanor. The resident was in a relatively advanced stage of dementia, and it was reported that he had become increasingly agitated and aggressive over the preceding 2 weeks; breaking objects in his room, throwing food, and striking out at others. When the staff at the home were asked about alterations to his routine schedule or unusual events that might have preceded the resident's changed behavior, one aid replied, "nothing of major importance or that he would even be aware of." Following up on the aid's remark, the psychologist clarified that he wished to know about any changes, regardless of its apparent importance to the resident. It was learned that because of the resident's worsening dementia, he had been moved to a room where the staff could observe him more easily. In so doing, the resident also had been moved to a single room from a room that he shared for some time with another resident. Hypothesizing that the resident's behavioral changes were in response to his move, his former roommate was asked to spend some time in the new room with him each day. Within a few days, the resident's "acting out" ceased. His demeanor remained calm even though the former room-mate's visits became increasingly less over time. The less familiar the clin-ician is with evaluating the elderly, the more likely he or she is to miss these often subtle or indirect communications. The lack of familiarity with this special patient group is not surprising. As mentioned earlier in this section, dealing with the elderly (especially the very old and in more than specialized settings) is in many ways relatively new to the helping professions. Professionals, including scientists and clinicians, are likely to have a much richer history with children and other specialized groups than with the elderly.

Again, issues of bias may come into the clinical enterprise. Such biases, or perhaps more properly here, "counter transferences," can lead the clinician to miss what is being communicated, as in the nursing home example given in the last paragraph. In addition, the clinician should exercise caution least he or she (perhaps unconsciously) excuse the patient's behavior or rationalize it as "normal." Such rationalization will most likely rest on some aspect of the patient's age or medical condition. In reference to the nursing home example again, the actual meaning of the resident's behavior easily could be missed, attributing the outbursts solely to disease progression. Even when a patient's behavior is perceived accurately, there is a risk that the clinical response might differ from that provided to a younger individual. One might, e.g., think: "Well, this patient has a right to be depressed. I would be if I were in their situation." Maybe, the rationalizing person is thinking about a given patient's impotence, his or her incontinence, loneliness, physical deconditioning, financial difficulties, grief in response to the loss of loved ones, or any of a number of other experiences that can be associated with old age, and which many of us fear will happen to us. Certainly, the items just listed seem to tie the patient's depression to a certain reality, but it is not the clinician's job to use the understandability of a situation to explain away the diagnosis. Most certainly, it is not the clinician's job to assume what precisely the patient is experiencing and how he or she is reacting to such experiences. Just as with a person of any age, the clinician's job is to arrive at an accurate diagnosis, a cause, a treatment plan, and other clinical objectives described in volume I. For example, one might ask, "Is the patient depressed?" Once the diagnosis of depression has been established, a systematic approach to causal determination might reveal that the depression is not related to the various experiential issues as listed earlier but may be explained by additional diagnoses related perhaps to disease progression, medication, other toxic induced affectual disturbance, or some other medical or neurological condition.

Conclusion

Aging has implications for a person's functioning on every level. In many instances, age will be explanatory to a given patient's complaints. At other times, age will be a factor that influences the clinical presentation or the data obtained in clinical examination or research. Age should always be considered in clinical evaluations and, often, listed in the differential diagnosis. Age, also, is almost always a potential confounder in research and should be accounted for appropriately in research designs. An understanding of the issues involved in normal and abnormal aging—issues that include changes in neurological and neuropsychological functions, individual accommodations to such changes, recognition of societal and personal biases in thinking about the elderly, and the impact of these issues on the symptoms and signs of illnesses—will enable the professional to deal effectively with clinical and research demands that are inherent in evaluating the elderly.

Psychological and emotional considerations in central nervous system disease

Stanley Berent

Whether normal or abnormal, behavior influences the nature and expression of study variables in research designs and the symptoms and signs of disease in the clinical setting. There are similarities between normal and abnormal behavior, leaving it easy to mislabel something as being abnormal when, in fact, it is a normal variation in behavior. At the same time, behavior disorders are encountered frequently in clinical practice. More than a quarter of the population in the United States has been estimated to have had some form of clinically diagnosable anxiety disorder at some time in their lives (Mineka & Zinbarg, 2006). Major depression has been reported to occur in up to 25% of cases diagnosed with medical conditions and higher in some specified diseases, up to 40% in Parkinson's disease or AD and greater than 50% in Cushing's disease (American Psychiatric Association, 1994). The emotional and other psychological conditions, therefore, occupy a prominent role in neurobehavioral toxicology. Depression, anxiety, and other emotion-related factors are potential *confounders* in toxicant related research, or they may reflect an area of primary interest to the researcher. In clinical practice, these same factors will often be listed in the differential diagnosis, and frequently one of these will emerge as the primary, final diagnosis. Because the symptoms (anxious feelings, depressed mood, difficulties with concentration, memory impairment) and signs (e.g., unsteady gait, physiological tremor, agitation) that accompany some behavioral disorders can overlap with those associated with toxicant-induced disorders or other medical illnesses, they lend themselves to misdiagnosis or mistaken causal attribution. Consider, e.g., the following *case presentation* that was abstracted from the published literature.

Case presentation[1]

This case involved a 44-year-old woman who reported having been exposed to natural gas fumes at her place of employment 2 years before the present evaluation. She said that at the time of exposure, which occurred over a 2 week period, she had experienced an unsteady gait, light-headedness, and a tingling sensation in her lips. Her symptoms ceased when she was moved to an alternate work area, but she reexperienced the same symptoms when she was moved back to her original site a few weeks later. At this later time, her symptoms also increased to include headache, muscle weakness, nausea, and "cloudy vision." She was flown on an emergency basis to a medical care center 80 miles away, where an evaluation was reported to be "unremarkable." She was discharged the following day. Over a period of some months, the patient developed what were termed, "reactions" to "strong odors." Also, she became very fearful of strong chemical odors. In response, she stopped working, attending church, and shopping. Someone diagnosed the patient with multiple chemical sensitivity syndrome (MCS), and she began to receive workers' compensation.

Approximately 2 years after her period of "exposure," the patient was referred for a psychiatric evaluation. She was found to be mildly depressed but did not meet formal criteria for major depressive disorder. Her descriptions of continuing fear and reactions to chemical odors were said to be identical to panic attacks, and she was diagnosed with "panic disorder with agoraphobia." She was subsequently treated with paroxetine and Trazodone. The patient's symptoms of depression and anxiety, as well as her reactions to chemical odors, resolved within 3 months after beginning treatment. She became more active, again shopping and attending church and, by 5 months later, had returned to work. She continued to receive "maintenance treatment" with antidepressants, and a 4 year follow-up showed her to be "symptom free." Interestingly, the patient continued to hold to the idea that she had MCS that was induced by chemical odors, despite the successful treatment of her emotional disorder.

Discussion

The author of the *case presentation* just described expressed the opinion that at least some patients who have been diagnosed with MCS actually suffer from an underlying psychiatric disorder such as anxiety (panic attacks) or depression that will respond positively to appropriate treatment. The observation that the patient in the *case presentation* just described continued to believe in the accuracy of her previously diagnosed MCS, even after successful treatment for psychiatric disorder, can be viewed as an example of the interaction between normal behavioral coping strategies and behavioral disorder. From this viewpoint, her reaction is not surprising. We described a similar situation in volume I (see pages 84–85), wherein a young woman came to her physician with complaints that she attributed to exposure to toxicants. She became angry when her clinician wanted to consider factors other than toxicant exposure as explanatory to her symptoms, chiefly, a long-standing anxiety disorder whose onset predated the reported exposure. The reasons for resistance as exhibited by the patient in the *case presentation*, as well as the case described in volume I and many others seen in practice, are rooted in the psychology of normal behavior, in personal dynamics and, sometimes, in psychopathology.

Many have been interested in these topics and have studied, theorized, and written about such phenomena for well over a 100 years in terms of the modern era, and longer in terms of antiquity. Sigmund Freud attended to such concerns in his writings, as did his students and colleagues (Fenichel, 1945; Freud, 1966, 1997; Munroe, 1955).

The importance of understanding normal behavior

Within the context of psychological conditions that produce symptoms that are similar to those seen in central nervous system disease, one must consider normal behaviors in addition to those behaviors that characterize abnormality. There are several reasons for this. First, the distinction between normal and abnormal is not always easy to discern, for the professional or for the patient. Most physicians would likely admit readily to having seen patients who presented with a physical complaint that was based entirely on a misinterpretation of a normally occurring event, e.g., concern that a myoclonic contraction the patient experienced during a hypnogogic state indicated a seizure disorder. Although the professional is obligated to evaluate the patient's symptoms, the most likely clinical response in such a situation ultimately will be reassurance and perhaps some brief education about normal physiology. Emotions and other behavioral phenomena, too, can be mislabeled as abnormal when they might be normal. In fact, abnormal psychological symptoms most often have analogous counterparts that are more accurately viewed as being normal. A good example of this is grief over the loss of a loved one, which can be severe and protracted over some period of time. Such a condition can very well meet many of the qualitative criteria of abnormality to be reviewed a little later in this section (e.g., disruption of efficient role performance, substantial personal pain, even extreme behaviors that are otherwise uncharacteristic for the individual). Contrast the expression of grief, considered by most to be normal if not overly protracted or extreme for the cultural context in which it appears (Volkan, 1970), to the abnormal grief reaction described by Mineka and Zinbarg (2006), wherein a patient had personally witnessed as a young man the death of his grandmother. The event proved to be traumatic for the patient, and he was plagued his entire life with thoughts associated with that experience, to the point that he considered suicide in his later years. Second, some knowledge of what is normal enhances one's understanding of what is not normal, leading to a clearer concept of the signs and symptoms of psychological abnormality than might otherwise be the case. Third, psychological phenomena impact physical signs and symptoms. A person's attitudes and beliefs, for instance, can affect their physical presentation (Spurgeon, 2002; Spurgeon, Gompertz, & Harrington, 1997), even to the point that perceived decline in "personal safety" in response to witnessing a traumatic event has been said to be associated with altered health behaviors and increased use of health care services (Fullerton et al., 2006). Fourth, a good understanding of normal behavior enhances communication between doctor and patient, which, in turn, is important to accurate diagnosis and treatment. For instance, a patient who has identified with a particular explanation for their complaints has an investment in the correctness of that explanation, whether or not the explanation is accurate. As such, they will be motivated to maintain that view and to resist alternative explanations. This is a predictable and normal occurrence in itself even though the consequences of such behavior can at times be disruptive to the clinical process (e.g., failure to disclose aspects of the personal history or noncompliance with prescribed treatments). The bases for the motivation to maintain a particular belief may be multiple, although it often reflects simple anxiety reduction, and the anxiety need not be abnormal in order to provoke the motivational response.

Even when no psychopathology is involved, an individual is inclined to guard strongly any internalized beliefs. As advanced by Festinger (1957, 1962), the simple act of identifying with a particular viewpoint motivates a person to defend that position, regardless of other potential, personal dynamics, or emotional investment (a concept Festinger termed, *cognitive dissonance*). Cognitive dissonance is a normal behavioral mechanism that, among other functions, serves to provide stability in a person's approach to the environment. Nevertheless, and depending on how strongly a view is held, considerable emotion can be expressed in response to what the person perceives as a challenge to that view. Whether or not such emotional expression remains within normal limits will depend to a large extent on the presence and nature of the individual's psychopathology. As with most adaptive functions, there is both benefit and cost associated with cognitive dissonance even when no psychopathology is present. Cognitive dissonance, for instance, can underlie an active resistance to the clinician's attempts at interpretive intervention or other aspects of diagnosis and treatment, but it also can manifest subtly and still adversely affect the clinical process (e.g., a passive–aggressive approach to treatment compliance).

When is behavior abnormal?

While it is important to recognize normal variations in behavior and also to understand the ways in which normal psychological mechanisms can affect a patient's clinical presentation, it is likewise important to recognize behavioral abnormalities and to include these in a differential diagnosis as indicated in a particular case. A professor of introductory psychology once said to his students, "Before I can teach you what psychology is, I have to convince you that you do not now know what it is." The reason behind such a remark most likely had to do with the fact that many of the basic issues in psychology (perhaps especially when it comes to emotions) are seemingly familiar to people. Who has not experienced fear, anxiety, even depression? Who has not on some one occasion or more "felt too sick" when it was time to go to school or work? Who has not misplaced a personal item, missed taking the proper exit from a highway, or forgotten something they believed they should be able to recall; a name or an item on a grocery list? The most likely answer, if one is honest with themselves, is no one! These and similar behavioral complaints are reported often by patients who are concerned that they have been injured by a toxicant. But, are these complaints the same as those observed in psychopathology? Attention can vary normally within and between individuals, to the extent that failures in adequate attention are common place. There will be no one reading this who has not heard it said, "Can you repeat that? I was not paying attention." However, disordered attention also can be a symptom of mental disorder (American Psychiatric Association, 1994), toxicant-induced illness (Filley, 2001), or other neurological and medical illnesses (Goldman & Bennett, 2000). What makes something pathological as opposed to simply a variation of normality? The answer to this last question relates to issues that are basic to psychology and, in this instance, they are of critical importance to those engaged in neurobehavioral toxicology.

Models of abnormality

In volume I (see, e.g., chapter 4), we discussed in some detail the need to objectively determine neurobehavioral abnormality. Such objectivity is enhanced by the application of a model for determining abnormality. Briefly here, there are two primary models that can be employed for this purpose—a statistical model and a qualitative one. The statistical model is based on observations of how most people perform with regard to some specific behavior. While this model can be employed with data that are generated subjectively, e.g., recognizing that a particular individual's gait is awkward in comparison to a subjective concept of normal gait, the statistical model is most powerful when quantitative data are employed, such as those derived from neuropsychological tests or other functional indices such as brain imaging or electrophysiological studies. In these instances, quantified data can be applied to measurements that were made on normal individuals (i.e., reference groups). A predetermined cutoff for normal can be determined based on the reference measurements (usually, and depending on the specific measure employed, greater than a 1.5–2.0 SD difference from the mean score for the comparison group). There are deficiencies inherent in a purely statistical approach to abnormality that should be obvious to all. For instance, there is the demand for an appropriately representative reference group. A number of technical demands must be met as well, such as properly determining that the test employed is *valid*, i.e., that it does, in fact, provide an accurate reflection of the construct of interest (e.g., depression). Despite drawbacks to the use of a statistical model, this model does allow for objective scaling of individual or group levels of functioning, and this alone is extremely valuable.

   In contrast to the statistical model, a qualitative model is one that is criterion-based, listing attributes that must be met in order to determine abnormality or, for that matter, normality. Criteria can be symptom-based or they may reflect what have been defined as characteristics of ideal health. Diagnostic manuals, such as the *DSM-IV* (American Psychiatric Association, 1994), often are based on a qualitative model. In practice, the two models, statistical and qualitative, are frequently combined. For instance, the *DSM-IV* defines *mental retardation* (MR) for the most part on the basis of test scores that fall below a specified level (usually 70 or below, representing ≥ 2 SD difference from the reference group mean) and that have been derived from standardized and individually administered tests of intelligence (e.g., Wechsler, 1997). However, to be diagnosed with MR also requires that the individual evidence impairments in adaptive functioning in two or more specified areas (e.g., self-care, work) and a specified age of onset (American Psychiatric Association, 1994).

In many respects both models, statistical and qualitative, are inherently attractive, used by professionals in making decisions about pathology and also seemingly intuitively by individuals in deciding if they themselves may have a problem or not. In addition to formal diagnostic manuals, a useful subjective guide in interpreting the clinical significance of observed or reported behavior is to determine how the patient's complaints impact on his or her efficiency, comfort, and conformity. Is the person efficient in work and family role or has there been a change in efficiency over time? Is the person complaining of emotional or physical pain that is beyond that explainable on the basis of reasonable or known circumstances, e.g., loss of a loved one? Does the person's behavior appear to be extremely unusual or bizarre for the circumstances in which they occur, e.g., seeing small animals in the waiting room that others do not see? While the answers to these questions will not provide a clinical diagnosis, they do often suggest the presence or absence of disorder. Especially since human behavior is so variable, between individuals and within a given individual over time, the list of subjective ratings can be a clinically useful supplement to formal statistical and qualitative models.

The formal diagnosis of psychopathology

Once determined, behavioral abnormalities can be classified using one or another formal diagnostic approach (American Psychiatric Association, 1994; World Health Organization, 2001). What can be termed the modern approach to classification of psychopathology began with the work of Kraepelin (1909). Traditional classification schemes included neuroses, psychoses, psychosomatic disorders, conduct disorders, developmental disorders, and behavioral disorders that resulted from neurological or other medical disease (Berent, 1986). While the specific categories (i.e., diagnoses) of mental disorders have been modified a number of times between Kraepelin's era and the present, most recently with the advent of the *DSM-IV* (American Psychiatric Association, 1994) and related publications (e.g., American Psychiatric Association, 2000), the traditional classes continue to be reflected in clinical diagnoses. Changes in diagnostic groupings and their names result largely from advances in knowledge and current theoretical orientations. The term, "neurosis," e.g., which had both descriptive and etiological implications (Trimble, 1988) was dropped in favor of more empirically derived categories with the publication in the early 1980s of *DSM-III* (American Psychiatric Association, 1987), and this orientation has persisted to the present time.

In the following paragraphs, some psychopathological diagnoses that appear regularly in the practice of neurobehavioral toxicology are discussed. These include the related diagnostic categories of anxiety, mood, and somatoform disorders, followed in the next section by a discussion of other psychological and psychiatric considerations of special relevance for neurobehavioral toxicology. Also, and because of their importance to clinical neurobehavioral toxicology, we will include some comment on approaches to the clinical interview and some of the consequences that can result from a failure to include psychological and emotional factors in the differential diagnosis of potential toxicant-induced or other central nervous system disorders.

Anxiety

Anxiety can be viewed from a number of perspectives. First, it is important to recognize that anxiety has both normal and pathological expressions. Second, the presence of anxiety has implications for what the individual subjectively experiences and how he or she is perceived by others because of its affects on the person's mental state and actions (e.g., attention, energy, and effort). Third, anxiety has physiological consequences for the organism, many of these reflecting the autonomic nervous system's response to perceived threat. This response includes parasympathetic suppression concomitant with sympathetic arousal. The resultant responses include increased sweating, heart-rate, and respiration; diversion of blood from the gastrointestinal system to muscles, and pupillary dilation. The (normal) functional purpose of these autonomic responses is to prepare the organism for fight or flight in the face of perceived danger. When no physical action ensues, the individual may experience symptoms such as dizziness or light-headedness, which depending on factors such as frequency of such responses may or may not be of psychopathological significance (also see volume II, pages 549–550). And, fourth, anxiety can be defined as a disorder. In fact, anxiety-based disorders have been said to comprise the most often diagnosed psychiatric disorder, with estimates of about 29% of the population in the United States having experienced an anxiety disorder at some point in their lives (Mineka & Zinbarg, 2006). It is important in neurobehavioral toxicology to understand the distinctions between these various aspects of anxiety, because the symptoms of anxiety can be associated with, obscure, or even mimic those seen in toxicant-induced disorders.

Normal versus abnormal anxiety

Anxiety, as opposed to anxiety disorder, also is a normal human attribute. The experience of anxiety should be familiar to everyone, although the subjective feeling might differ from one individual to another. Likewise, the term, *anxiety*, is used freely in everyday parlance to refer to a person's response to any number of situations, usually those that contain some element of trepidation. From a professional viewpoint, it is almost regrettable that the term anxiety is used in referring both to normal and abnormal behavioral states. It is for this reason that we began this paragraph by separating "anxiety" from *anxiety disorder*. The freedom with which the term anxiety is used in the general population most likely reflects the acceptance that the feeling of anxiety is a normal aspect of behavior, which, in fact, it can be. Of course, there are individual circumstances when a person might show reluctance to admit to anxiety, e.g., someone who believes it a sign of weakness or cowardliness to admit publicly to such a feeling or someone who mislabels or even fails to recognize the feeling for what it is. Also, there is considerable evidence indicating that individuals differ in sensitivity to anxiety and, perhaps as a result, in the perception of threat (Bale et al., 2000; Chaouloff, 2000; Gershenfeld & Paul, 1998). In fact, and although the relationship is most likely multifactorial, insensitivity to anxiety has been postulated as a risk factor for the development of character based risk-taking, sensation-seeking, and, even *psychopathy* (Frick, Lilienfeld, Ellis, Loney, & Silverthorn 1999; Levenson, Kiehl, & Fitzpatrick, 1995). Still, most seem to accept anxiety as an aspect of normal human behavior, at least when it is used to refer to a sense of apprehension in the face of an identifiable but common-place threat (e.g., speaking before an audience or going on a trip).

Anxiety is motivating, and even when normal (e.g., at a level expected for a given situation), the individual will be driven to reduce that anxiety in order to restore homeostasis. For example, a patient, as well as family members who had accompanied the patient to a clinical evaluation, became angry when the doctor asked that they consider other than a toxicant-induced disorder as being explanatory to the patient's symptoms. In this instance, the cause specified by the patient was toxicant exposure, but any self-identified cause could well have elicited the same reaction. Why? Such a patient might well have experienced some anxiety reduction when he or she initially embraced the toxicant hypothesis. It is the extremely rare person who is not (normally) anxious when experiencing symptoms of a magnitude sufficient to lead them to seek professional attention. When a person arrives at an insight that seems to explain their complaints it provides them with an answer to the important question, "What's wrong with me?" Knowing what's wrong can lead to knowing what to do about it, and this expectation, too, can lessen the patient's worries, especially if reinforced by an authority figure. To challenge that belief can have the effect of opening the patient, and individuals close to the patient, to renewed feelings of anxiety that had to some extent been put aside once "the cause" had been identified.

From a functional viewpoint, the capacity to experience anxiety is an important element in an organism's ability to survive. Analogous to the threat of physical pain, anxiety allows the person to avoid placing themselves in a dangerous situation. Just as a person "learns" quickly to take proper precautions before approaching a hot stove, in so doing avoiding what could be serious injury, the individual learns to predict and avoid other dangerous situations as well. Viewed in this way, anxiety can be seen as an early warning system, one that signals forthcoming danger.

The sense of anxiety is tied to fear and from a learning perspective, it can be argued that it is most likely derived from the experience of fear, personally or vicariously (Mineka & Zinbarg, 2006). In fact, it might be correct to say that anxiety is the anticipation of fear. Living organisms other than humans also act in an avoidant manner when confronted with a stimulus they have learned to associate with physical pain or other noxious stimulation, and with behaviors that approximate what can be described as fear (Gershenfeld & Paul, 1998; Knapp, Saiers, & Pohorecky, 1993; Weiss, Lightowler, Stanhope, Kennett, & Dourish, 2000). So, too, human anxiety is not completely language dependent. Rather, it can be viewed as an adoptive mechanism that evolved most likely before language added to the human capacity to survive in a hostile environment.

The addition of language enhanced the human ability to recognize a fearful situation as a dangerous one. Undoubtedly, the addition of language also introduced a multitude of abstract (language mediated) situations that in themselves possess the capacity to produce feelings of anxiety (i.e., apprehensions that are sufficient to encourage avoidant, or even perhaps thoughts of avoidant, behaviors, or that motivate superstitious behaviors that are designed to ward off or neutralize danger). Such apprehension can be in response to a primary association with a previously experienced stimulus that produced fear (e.g., going skiing following a serious fall or even after witnessing someone else fall [vicarious learning]). Or, a feeling of apprehension might result from secondarily generalized responses (e.g., talking to someone about skiing). Also, there is evidence that earlier experiences can sensitize (or sometimes desensitize) the person to later ones, interacting with genetic or other biological propensities to physiological arousal, to eventuate in increased anxiety, or anxiety disorder, as a function of repeated stresses (Bennet & Stirling, 1998; De Masi, 2004; Forsell, 2000). Why do some individuals develop an anxiety disorder, while others with similar, or worse, historical experiences do not? Mineka and Zinbarg (2006) evoked a multifactor theory in attempting to answer this question. They described differing vulnerabilities (presumably including congenital variability as well as early and repeated adverse experiences) between individuals and referred to these as the *diatheses* that leave some individuals more susceptible to the experience of stress and, therefore, more likely than others to develop an anxiety disorder (Mineka & Zinbarg, 2006).

Anxiety as an adaptive response: benefits and costs

As is the case for most living organisms, there are two methods a person has for dealing with danger (i.e., fear or the threat of fear, anxiety). These methods, or strategies, are fighting to control or contain the threat or fleeing from the threat. Traditionally, the two approaches are referred to collectively as, "fight or flight." These defenses can both be thought of as adaptive mechanisms of control. By controlling the danger (and therefore the fear the danger generates), the threat can be lessened or even eliminated. There are costs associated with each maneuver, fight or flight, even when the chosen action may be successful. On a basic level, entering into a fight places the individual at risk for injury or death in its own rite. Even when successful, the injuries that are sustained may lead ultimately to disease or even death. Or, the injuries sustained may slow the individual, leaving him or her less able to deal with the next threat that might arise. To choose to run, also, is not without risk. For example, the person could fall and suffer an injury that increases their vulnerability to the pursuing threat.

Limited still to fight or flight, language introduces a wide range of alternative expressions for dealing with danger. Language opens the door to knowledge, and the increased sophistication that results allows one to prepare before being confronted with danger (e.g., wearing protective clothing when handling hazardous materials or learning how to practice good hygiene), but also it provides a basis for additional fears about events that species with lesser ability to imagine than humans remain ignorant. In terms of benefit, language (and, therefore, language-based intelligence) enables the person to employ higher order methods for control in addition to basic physical running or combat (e.g., inventing and using insecticides to control disease transmitting mosquitoes [fight] or cutting a vacation short because of an outbreak of cholera [flight]). But, there are costs associated with these intellectually based maneuvers as well.

What are some of the costs for increased knowledge? For one thing, costs are related to increases in what is defined as fearful, because the person becomes aware of dangers that previously were unknown (e.g., the potential consequences of global warming), because of incomplete knowledge about what makes something dangerous (e.g., killing harmless snakes that might, in fact, prey on other snakes that pose a more serious threat), or because language permits imagined fears (e.g., to quote from an article by Sullivan [2002], "While we never actually saw the Boogie Man, we instinctively knew that he lurked in the dark recesses of our room and meant to do us harm"). Also, costs can relate to how one responds to perceived danger. In addition to those that are experienced directly (e.g., the fear experienced by a soldier in combat who is facing the employment of nerve gas by an enemy), for instance, language provides the capacity to anticipate being in danger (e.g., the anxiety when using public transportation associated with the likelihood of a toxic chemical attack by terrorists). Language allows for the capacity to anticipate, and this ability can lead a person (or a group) to develop a sense of control (another aspect of "fight") over the perception of what is to come, and a sense of safety as a result. At times, of course, this ability to foresee danger can be life-saving, but responses to the anxieties generated by this ability also can be ill-advised or even counter productive. Under the perceived threat of nuclear war, e.g., families in the United States were encouraged during the 1950s to build home bomb shelters and to stock them with provisions. Children in schools at the time were taught to "duck and cover" in response to mock air raid warnings. The intent was to provide people with some sense that there was something they could do to protect themselves from what must have seemed the insurmountable threat of nuclear holocaust. With hindsight, this appearance of knowledge may seem now to be naïve, but it may have reduced anxiety at the time. The nature of perceived threat changes over time. More recently, rather than the anxiety of all out war, it has been the threat of terrorist attack, and with it, attempts to arrive at some sense that something can be done to prevent (i.e., to control) such an event (e.g., "the war on terror" [The University of Michigan, 2006]). However, these anticipatory actions, while providing the semblance of control and safety, come often with a high personal price (e.g., the time and effort diverted from other economically productive work, sustained apprehension in attending to threat, and the costs and destruction from combat based solutions, to name a few).

Aside from societal examples, people experience personal fears and anxieties, and developing a belief that there is something that one can do about the threat leads to a sense of safety (Clark, 1999). Every clinician has experienced the patient who appears to be anxious in the face of symptoms for which they do not yet have an explanation. That anxiety, of course, may dissipate when a benign conclusion is presented to the patient. What may be surprising, however, is that some will express relief even when a more serious diagnosis is rendered. It is as if the knowledge of what has been concerning them is in itself reassuring, perhaps because that knowledge allows them to develop a plan of action. In other words, the knowledge generates hopefulness and restores their sense of control. But, what if the answer is wrong? From the point of view of anxiety reduction, a wrong answer, if "accepted" by the person as explanatory, appears to make little difference in terms of anxiety reduction. Their sense of control is the key to the reduction of their apprehension, and they will be motivated to defend the explanation once it has been adopted. The "answer" can be self-generated, or it can derive from what they have read or have been told by someone, especially by someone they recognize as an authority on the subject.

Abnormal anxiety

Anxiety is a normal expression of human adaptability. It is important, however, to distinguish between normal anxiety and anxiety that is pathological (the latter perhaps because it is overly intense, reflects a noticeable change from the patient's usual demeanor, because it occurs within a context that is not usually considered to be anxiety provoking, or because its expression contains an element of apparent irrationality). The hallmark of abnormal anxiety can be seen as the lack of functionality in terms of the organism's survival or well-being and its interference in attaining such aims. The experience of anxiety is universal, and with some variations of expression due to cultural and other demographic considerations (Hepple, 2004; Interian et al., 2005; Yeung et al., 2004), anxiety disorder is universal as well (Barchas & Altemus, 1999). The prevalence rate for clinically significant anxiety has been estimated at 3% to 8% of the population, across cultures at any given time (Barchas & Altemus, 1999). As is true of all of the disorders discussed in this section, lack of functionality can be defined statistically (e.g., extremeness) or qualitatively (its interference with comfort, efficiency, or reasonable conformity). Consider the following *case presentation*.

Case presentation[2]

A young mother approached her dentist with the request that her child's dental amalgams be removed. When asked why, she replied that she had read a newspaper account of the dangers of mercury from dental amalgams and realized that her child's difficulties in school fit perfectly with the account of symptoms reported in the news account. The dentist examined the child and presented the mother with the finding that her child's fillings contained no mercury. In response, the mother insisted angrily that the dentist was wrong and that her child did indeed have mercury in his restorations. She left saying she would seek another dentist to remove the fillings. The second dentist confirmed that the child had no mercury in his fillings, to which the mother finally acquiesced. However, perhaps in response to the mother's reluctant acceptance of the dentist's conclusions, the second dentist added the following question (understandable though perhaps ill-advised in this particular instance); "Has your child been around lead-based paint?"

The mother, as it turned out, was in the midst of a custody evaluation and had been ordered by the court to enter counseling. The mother and father had recently divorced, and it was around this time that the child started having difficulties in school. Even though the mother was able to verbalize that the event of the marital breakup had been troubling to her child (she neglected to say that it was troubling to her), she still insisted that a toxicant was to blame for her child's problems. Having given up on mercury in the face of the obtained second opinion, she reported that she had the child evaluated for lead exposure. Even though the child was found to have a urine lead level within the normal range, she reported that a "friend" had told her of an "expert" who used the results of chelation therapy to "arrive at a more accurate diagnosis of lead poisoning." The psychologist's report among other things concluded that by proxy, this mother was using her child in an attempt to reduce her own, yet to be fully understood, anxieties. No longer a normal anxiety response as might be expected in her situation, e.g., having to assume all responsibility for her child's well-being and to "make it on her own" in light of her divorce, her behavior met all criteria for an abnormal condition. Statistically, her behavior in terms of its persistence, resistance to alternative factual explanations, and other factors was far removed from normal expectations. Qualitatively, her insistence on a toxicant explanation in the face of evidence to the contrary was illogical. The energy and money she was spending on evaluations of her child were interfering with the efficiency with which she performed her other roles in life, e.g., she was unable to seek employment, now necessary as a result of the divorce, and because of the demand she perceived to "help her child." She was experiencing sleep disturbance, difficulties in concentration, irritability, and the psychological pain of "worrying about what toxicants were doing to her child." In addition, the child was missing school in order to go for various examinations. Of course, one might describe her behavior as highly unusual, if not bizarre.

CLINICAL DIAGNOSIS

The psychologist in this *case presentation* diagnosed the mother with a generalized anxiety disorder with obsessive-compulsive symptoms and an element of separation anxiety related to her marital breakup, with a note regarding the "proxy component" in relation to her son.

Discussion

The current and most often used formal system for diagnosing anxiety (American Psychiatric Association, 1994, 2000) divides anxiety disorders into six primary types, in various combinations (Table 17.2). All have anxiety as a defining characteristic. While not the only way to view the diagnostic classifications listed in Table 17.2, they can be seen as differing from one another as a function of their immediacy, current or delayed, and cognitive component, or lack thereof (e.g., panic and stress disorders); stimulus specificity (e.g., phobia); level of awareness and response strategies, usually "uncontrollable" despite awareness of their inappropriateness (e.g., obsessive-compulsive disorder); and persistence and recurrence (e.g., generalized anxiety disorder).

As can be seen from perusing the list in Table 17.2, the symptoms and signs that can manifest in the anxiety disorders are nonspecific and overlap with those that might arise from toxicant-induced illness. Anxiety disorders in general can coexist with other medical and psychiatric disorders, and often do, even when the co-occurrence is not believed to be due to a direct physiologically based causal connection (O'Donohue & Cucciare, 2005). When it is determined that the anxiety disorder is due directly to a medical condition, the diagnosis should specify that fact, i.e., anxiety disorder due to a general medical condition, or in the case of toxicant-induced anxiety, as in a response to a stimulant such as amphetamine, substance-induced anxiety. Also, the prolonged nature of most anxiety disorders, e.g., generalized anxiety disorder, is often associated with headache, depression, and other symptoms of chronic stress (American Psychiatric Association, 1994). It occurs often with major depression. As with most psychiatric disorders, the symptoms or signs must cause significant distress and impaired role performance in order to be diagnosed.

The DSM system of diagnosis often calls for a causal determination in reaching a final clinical diagnosis (e.g., substance-induced anxiety disorder). Also, the diagnostic process will include a number of competing conditions in the differential diagnosis. As a result of these considerations, the likely steps in reaching a final diagnosis when causal specification is required would be to determine that an anxiety disorder best fits the clinical findings, determine the cause if possible, and then arrive at a final diagnosis. If no cause can be identified, or when the findings do not fit the criteria for a specific anxiety disorder, then the correct diagnosis is "anxiety disorder not otherwise specified."

Table 17.2 The diagnostic classification of anxiety disorders.

Diagnosis	Associated signs and symptoms	Comments
Panic attack	During an attack: shortness of breath, choking sensation or feeling as if being "smothered," cardiac palpitations, chest discomfort or pain, feelings of loss of control or of "going crazy." Also, fear of dying, sweating, tremor, nausea and abdominal distress, dizziness or light-headedness or feeling faint, unsteadiness, derealization or depersonalization, paresthesia, chills or hot flashes.	A panic attack is defined as a sudden onset of intense apprehension, fear, or terror. There may be a sense of impending doom. Panic attacks often are associated with agoraphobia and so qualified when indicated.
Agoraphobia	Anxiety about being in places or at times when it would be difficult or embarrassing to escape, or in which help might not be available if a panic attack occurred.	Agoraphobia may or may not be associated with panic attacks. The correct diagnoses when unexpected panic attacks are recurrent, with persistent concern, is panic disorder without agoraphobia; "panic disorder with agoraphobia," when both are present. Agoraphobia without history of panic disorder is used when both agoraphobia and symptoms of panic are present in the absence of a history of unexpected panic attacks.
Phobia	Intense anxiety brought on by a feared object or situation, often associated with avoidance behaviors.	When the phobic response is to a specific object or situation, the diagnosis is "specific phobia"; "social phobia" when some type of performance or social situation is the feared stimulus.
Obsessive-compulsive disorder	Recurrent obsessions (persistent thoughts, impulses, or images) that cause anxiety, e.g., worries about being contaminated or doubts about having done something like turn off a stove, with impulses to do something about it. Compulsions are represented by actions, repeated behaviors (e.g., hand washing), or repetitive thoughts (e.g., counting, reciting a phrase). While children may not yet be aware of the significance of these symptoms, the adult is usually aware that the obsessions and compulsions are unreasonable and inappropriate. Avoidant behaviors at time,	The thoughts and impulses in obsessive-compulsive disorder are not excessive worries about real-life concerns. The symptoms cause marked anxiety in the affected person, and the person may try to suppress these thoughts, impulses, or images, sometimes with alternate thoughts or actions. He or she recognizes that the symptoms are of their own making, not inserted by some external person or machine. While most anyone might experience phenomena that is similar in some respects to obsessions and compulsions, for the person affected

(continued)

Table 17.2 (continued) The diagnostic classification of anxiety disorders.

	usually to avoid situations that provoke obsessive and compulsive symptoms. Hypochondriacal concerns. Signs and symptoms of other disorders can coexist with the primary obsessive-compulsive disorder, e.g., depression, substance abuse, personality disorder. Guilt, sleep disturbance, tics or other motor abnormalities.	with this disorder, the symptoms cause significant distress, occupy considerable time (more than an hour a day), and interfere significantly with work or other role performance.
Stress disorders	The experience of an extremely traumatic event that is accompanied by symptoms of arousal and avoidance. These can include a sense of despair, hopelessness, guilt (especially if the person was partially or wholly responsible for the event) or survivor guilt (that they remained intact when others were injured), phobias, other secondary manifestations (marriage or other interpersonal difficulties, vocational difficulties, loss of prior beliefs or feelings of reasonable safety, depression).	When the response occurs immediately after experiencing the traumatic event, the diagnosis is "acute stress disorder." When, the response involves reexperiencing a traumatic event, with arousal and avoidance of stimuli associated with the past event, the diagnosis is "posttraumatic stress disorder."
Generalized anxiety disorder	Restlessness, fatigue, irritability, concentration difficulties, disturbed sleep, muscle tension or soreness, trembling or twitching, dry mouth, sweating, nausea, diarrhea, and other somatic complaints, enhanced startle response.	Characterized by 6 months or more of persistent, excessive anxiety (a sense of "apprehensive expectation"). Worries are about a number of things and the person has difficulty controlling these worries. Co-occurrence with major depression is common. A few anxiety related conditions are diagnosed on the basis of their association with specified topics and are included in the *DSM* system under topics other than anxiety disorder (e.g., "separation anxiety" is grouped with other childhood disorders; phobic avoidance of genital sexual contact, "sexual aversion disorder," is included under "sexual and gender identity disorders").

Some of the contents in this table reprinted with permission from the *Diagnostic and Statistical Manual of Mental Disorders*, Fourth Edition, 1994 and Text Revision, Copyright 2000, American Psychiatric Association.

VERIFICATION OF THE CLINICAL DIAGNOSIS

The diagnostic conclusions reached in the *case presentation* meet all formal criteria for verification. In addition to objective criteria as presented in Appendix A, the diagnoses listed essentially fit DSM-based criteria for the specified disorders (see Table 17.2). The fact that the mother in the *case presentation* was believed by the counselor to be expressing her emotions through her son serves to obscure the picture somewhat. In choosing to see these complaints as relating to her directly, the clinician was correct in his diagnoses. An alternative would have been to diagnose anxiety disorder, not otherwise specified. While this latter diagnostic category might have called for slightly less "uncovering" in interview, or even speculation, the clinician is most likely correct in his analysis, and the end result or either diagnosis would likely be the same in terms of treatment. Note that some disorders that contain an anxiety component are classified under topics other than anxiety in the *DSM-IV*, e.g., separation anxiety (American Psychiatric Association, 1994). These are anxiety disorders, nevertheless. Also, separation disorder implies that as a child the person most likely suffered some trauma that was associated with separation from parents, even though a secondary and more recent stimulus may have served as the trigger for a current episode. That trigger in the current case presentation most likely was the marital breakup and perhaps even fears about losing the child in a custody battle. As a practical matter, the general practitioner may not be in a position to know such details about the patient. They can be surmised, however, and the hypothesis that such detail can be discerned can be referred to a specialist who can verify these dynamics.

Comment

The *case presentation* just described contains some details that might not be familiar to all clinicians. The particular dentists in this case, for instance, although most likely very familiar with anxiety in general, might not have recognized the mother's somewhat complex presentation of an anxiety disorder. Eventually, the mother did come to the attention of a clinician who was in a position to redirect clinical attention to the correct emotional problems underlying her overt behavior. In terms of the initial concerns regarding dental amalgams voiced by the mother, any need for determination of cause was resolved easily because of lack of any possible exposure. But, what if amalgam had been present in the child's fillings? Without knowledge of the entirety of the mother's and the family's dynamics, one can envision a persisting concern about dental amalgam even though it is likely that other factors were causing the complaints.

One final note regarding the diagnosis in the current *case presentation*, the mother's behavior in relation to her child could raise suspicion regarding a diagnosis of "Munchausen's syndrome by proxy" (*DSM-IV* diagnosis, "factitious disorder by proxy" [American Psychiatric Association, 1994]), an "abnormal illness behavior" in which a principle (usually a mother) uses another (usually her child) to purposely feign physical or mental symptoms of disorder (Folks, 1995). A diagnosis of factitious disorder by proxy requires that the behavior be simulated or made up for the purpose of deception, presumably for the purpose of assuming a "sick role" by proxy but not in an attempt to gain some external incentive such as economic or other advantage, as in malingering (American Psychiatric Association, 1994). While no one can read another's mind, evidence was lacking in the current *case presentation* that the mother was purposely seeking external gain through such a mechanism. Rather, the "proxy" behaviors appeared to be an unconscious extension of her own anxieties. She did evidence many of the characteristics described in the *DSM-IV* for factitious disorder by proxy. Since many of the criteria presented in the *DSM-IV* for factitious disorder by proxy are considered to be in need of further study (American Psychiatric Association, 1994), the designation "by proxy" in the present instance was descriptive and sufficient without further specification.

The observations made during the present discussion again underscore the importance of psychological factors in cases of suspected toxicant exposure. This does not imply that every professional needs to obtain a level of psychological sophistication that is possessed by specialists in these areas. It does indicate, however, that one should aspire to gain a level of understanding that allows him or her to be sensitive to the possible role of these factors in a given case and that provides a basis for determining when to refer the patient for more detailed evaluation.

It was mentioned earlier that one is unable to read another's mind. Anxiety is a personal experience, and while often the signs of anxiety (e.g., sweating, hyperventilation, or tremor) may provide clues that the person is anxious, these do not confirm it without the person choosing to acknowledge the experience. True of anxiety in general, this especially may be the case when the person's thought content is an important part of the clinical picture, as in *obsessive-compulsive disorder*. Consider the case that follows, for example.

Case presentation[2]

A 38-year-old male was seen in brief counseling. He held a relatively high management position with a government agency, and he emphasized the need for confidentiality. His home and work were at some distance from where the clinician was located. The patient arrived punctually for his first interview, by way of a hired car and driver, and he described arriving early and having the driver "ride around" for 2 hr so as not to be late for the appointment. Following a substantial monologue about the importance that no one know that he was being seen by a "mental health professional," to which the clinician responded with appropriate reassurances and without colluding with some of the patient's more extreme demands for secrecy, the patient revealed his concerns. He revealed that he was plagued persistently by thoughts over which he felt he had very little control. Sometimes, these "thoughts" would follow being introduced to someone for the first time, the person's name repeating in his mind, sometimes for days. At times, the intrusive thought would be a rhythmic sound or a portion of a musical piece or song. At other times, he would say something that afterwards he would think was "stupid," or he would experience a fear that something bad was about to happen. These episodes occurred regularly, despite his trying to suppress the thoughts. One method he used in an attempt to control his unwanted thoughts was to perform an action of some sort, like counting backwards from 100 aloud. If something interrupted him or if he lost his place, he would need to start again from 100 and continue the subtraction, until the process was completed successfully. On occasion, the thought itself directed him to an action, e.g., a dictate to walk down a hallway stepping only on the black tiles. When asked why he now felt the need to seek consultation about these complaints, he responded that he had experienced these symptoms for as long as he could remember, but lately he found himself engaged in these activities more and more, to the point that they were interfering with his productivity. Also, he said, colleagues were asking more frequently about his unusual behaviors. He concluded by stating that although he knew these thoughts and his responses to them were not appropriate, he felt unable to control them.

Since the patient had traveled from some distance (in order to avoid having anyone discover that he was seeing a mental health professional, likely another reflection of his symptoms), a goal became to successfully reduce the stigma he seemed to associate with seeing a mental health professional and then to encourage him to enter treatment with someone closer to his home. These aims were achieved.

CLINICAL DIAGNOSIS

The diagnosis for this *case presentation* was obsessive-compulsive disorder.

Comment

The patient in the *case presentation* presented with a classic picture of obsessive-compulsive disorder. There was no indication of psychosis in his clinical presentation, e.g., thoughts directing him to specified actions were recognized by the patient to be his own. The thoughts he described represented obsessions (i.e., persistent thoughts, impulses, or images that cause anxiety). His actions can be defined as compulsions (repetitious behaviors over which the person has minimal control). The patient was aware of the inappropriateness of his thoughts and actions but unable to control their occurrence. The presence of these symptoms was interfering with the efficiency with which the patient could perform his roles in life, they were of a nature that most people would recognize as being highly unusual, and the symptoms were subjectively painful to the patient. The clinical picture meets all objective criteria for verifying the stated diagnosis. The *case presentation*, very importantly, illustrates the subjective nature of anxiety symptoms, perhaps especially when the presence and content of a person's thoughts are critical in arriving at a clinical diagnosis (in this case, obsessive-compulsive disorder).

While the current *case presentation* did not involve a toxicant, it is not unusual for toxicants to become involved in the expression of an anxiety disorder. Fear of contamination of one sort or another, for instance, often is the subject matter of obsessions (e.g., fear that one has been contaminated by exposure to germs or poisons) or compulsions (e.g., needing to wash one's hands repeatedly or in a specified manner to eradicate the contamination). When possible exposure to a toxicant has been listed in a differential diagnosis, the presence of a psychological condition will need to be evaluated, included, or dismissed, and the contributions to the patient's symptoms and signs from each diagnosed condition carefully determined.

Mood disorders

The mood disorders have particular relevance to neurobehavioral toxicology because often the symptoms (e.g., change in energy level, dizziness, and problems with memory) and signs (e.g., a test finding of impaired concentration) of these disorders mimic those reported to occur in many toxicant-induced disorders (Ahmed, Yaffe, Thornton, & Kinney, 2006; Albers & Berent, 2000b; Albers, Wald, Garabrant, Trask, & Berent, 2000; Baelum, 1999; Brown, 2002; Feldman, 1998). Also, many environmental and endogenous toxicants affect mood directly or secondarily (Barchas & Altemus, 1999). Mood disorders can co-occur with a toxicant-induced disorder independent of that exposure or as a psychological reaction to the primary illness, and the presence of a mood disorder can alter or obscure an otherwise sensible clinical presentation of the primary illness (Amella, 2004; Barchas & Altemus, 1999; Filley, 1998; Stowell & Barnhill, 2005).

As in the case of anxiety, mood also has both normal and pathological expressions. One might describe their mood as "up" or "down." Individuals even may casually use terms like "depressed" or "manic" to describe how they are feeling on a given day. Whether or not mood can be formally diagnosed as abnormal, however, depends largely on the degree or severity of its expression. From this perspective, mood can be viewed as a continuous variable between excitement and severe depression, as opposed to discretely occurring conditions that differ qualitatively from normal mood. This idea of continuity has some appeal, at least for some aspects of depression, as it likely fits with most people's experiences with regard to their personal moods. Most recognize that there are atypical expressions of mood that can disrupt a person's usual behavioral efficiency or require professional attention even though the mood might not meet formal criteria for a clinical diagnosis (Ahmed et al., 2006). And, it is difficult to know the extent to which alcohol and other drugs are used by individuals for the purpose of self-treatment of undiagnosed depression or other mental health problems (Comeau, Stewart, & Loba, 2001; Goswami, Singh, Mattoo, & Basu, 2003; Harris & Edlund, 2005).

Without discounting the personal discomfort that results from normal and atypical variations in mood, most people do not experience the severely incapacitating consequences of a clinically diagnosed mood disorder. Mood disorders are among the most serious of emotional disturbances. The reasons for this conclusion include the pain they can produce in the affected person and those close to the person; and the adverse economic consequences for the affected person, family, and society. The exact economic burden that results to society from depression and other mood disorders is difficult to determine, but published estimates have been in the billions of dollars, with specific estimates ranging from approximately 40 to 80 billion or more dollars a year in the United States alone, with most (>60%) of that cost impacting on the workplace (Brown, Brown, & Sharma, 2004; Greenberg et al., 2003; Kessler et al., 1999). Of primary importance, mood disorders are among the most serious of the emotional disturbances because they can be life-threatening; with a suicide rate up to 15% in major depressive disorder (American Psychiatric Association, 1994). Mood disorders often coexist with other medical illnesses, at times contributing to added health care costs, confounding the clinical diagnosis, or even going unrecognized and, therefore, untreated (Ahmed et al., 2006; Franco et al., 1995; Kessler, 2004; Kessler et al., 2001). Consider, for example, the following *case presentation* abstracted from a published report by Ahmed et al.

Case presentation[3]

An 82-year-old female was seen at a geriatric heart failure clinic with complaints of shortness of breath, dizziness, chest tightness, fatigue, short-term memory loss, and generally not feeling well. She did have a history of "dizzy spells" for a period of time during her childhood but with no clear etiology. During the year preceding her present visit, she had been hospitalized on three occasions with similar complaints but comprehensive evaluations that included MRI of the brain and heart catheterization were unrevealing. She denied suicidal thinking or depression but did report that her husband had died within the past year and that she had subsequently moved to a new city to be near her daughter. It was reported that she remained independent in her daily activities and was active socially.

The physical examination was unremarkable, with no indication of abnormal mental status (MMSE: 29 of 30). Screening for depression with a geriatric rating scale (GDS) was elevated but within normal limits (GDS: 3 of 15). Nevertheless, and despite the absence of clear objective findings of mood disorder, she was given a "presumptive diagnosis" of depression and started on an antidepressive medication. The patient was seen again 6 months later and found to be completely free of her initial symptoms. She was maintained on the antidepressant medication and at the time of publication of the case had been symptom free for 1 year.

INITIAL CLINICAL DIAGNOSIS

Geriatric depression

INITIAL CAUSE/ETIOLOGY

No specific cause was formally specified, but adverse life events in an elderly person were offered as the explanation for her presumed depression.

Discussion

FORMAL CATEGORIES OF MOOD DISORDER

In terms of formal diagnosis, *DSM-IV* divides the categories between those disorders in which mania occurs, those that are characterized by depression, and those that reflect a mixed picture of mania and depression (Table 17.3 for a listing of the primary DSM diagnoses of mood disorder). Further distinctions are made between conditions that are recurrent, cyclical, or chronic and those that reflect a single episode. Finally, a distinction is made that rests importantly on degree of severity (e.g., dysthymia in comparison to major depression). Mood episodes involve symptoms that are new to the person or represent a clear worsening from the individual's baseline behavior. The type of episode is determined by the nature of the specific mood involved, e.g., mania, depression, or a mixture of the two. The symptoms of mood episodes can mimic those observed in progressive neurological disease but characteristically lack the chronic and usually slowly progressive decline seen in neuro-degenerative disorders like AD (Berent et al., 1999; Trimble, 1988). In many instances, these symptoms can reflect adverse effects from medication (e.g., corticosteroids or antidepressants (Brown, Rush, & McEwen, 1999; McAllister-Williams, Ferrier, & Young, 1998). Especially, the appearance of bipolar disorder after the age of 40 can actually result from medical illness (e.g., thyroid dysfunction, substance abuse, the adverse effects of medication, or other toxicant exposure). When substance exposure (e.g., a medicine or other chemical) is responsible for the depression, the patient's clinical symptoms usually can be expected to resolve following removal from exposure (American Psychiatric Association, 1994). These various possible medical causes for the patient who presents with a depressive episode need to be excluded in order to make an accurate diagnosis. *Dysthymia*, a chronic disorder that is less severe than major depression, can coexist with other psychiatric conditions (e.g., personality disorders, major depressive episode), but establishing that a toxicant is etiologically related to the mood disturbance rules out dysthymia as a diagnosis. In such a case, the correct diagnosis would be "Substance-Induced Mood Disorder" (American Psychiatric Association, 1994).

VERIFICATION OF THE CLINICAL DIAGNOSIS

The authors (Ahmed et al., 2006) of the publication upon which the current *case presentation* was based were correct in acknowledging that the patient

Table 17.3 Mood disorders: Major diagnostic categories.

Diagnosis	Associated signs and symptoms	Comments
Mood episodes Major depressive episode	New or worsened symptoms that include loss of interest or pleasure in most activities. Irritability might substitute for sadness in children and adolescents. In making a formal diagnosis, there is a specified number of additional symptoms that might include changes in appetite or weight, sleep (generally insomnia), energy level, psychomotor activity, and difficulties with thinking, learning, memory, making decisions, and other cognitive functions. Changes in feelings are present as well, e.g., feelings of guilt or worthlessness, as are dysphoric thoughts, e.g., thoughts about suicide, death, and dying.	Mood episodes can involve periods of depression, mania, hypomania, or a mixture of these features and is diagnosed on the basis of the predominant theme, e.g., depression. The symptoms need to be present most of the day, on most days, for some specified period of time (e.g., at least two consecutive weeks in the case of depression). Also, the condition must cause significant stress and disrupt work, social, or other important aspects of usual functioning.
Manic episode	A period (a week, or less if hospitalization is required) of abnormally elevated, expansive, or irritable mood. This may include grandiosity or inflated self-esteem, pressured speech, decreased need for sleep, increases in goal directed behaviors, excessive increases in pleasurable and often risky activities, psychomotor agitation, euphoria, and other reflections of increased and excessive excitement. For instance, the person may exhibit pressured, loud, rapid, and persistent speech (i.e., termed, "manic speech") or may exhibit grandiose schemes, or even delusions.	
Mixed episode	At least 1 week, most every day, in which the patient meets criteria for both major depressive episode and manic episode. Rapidly alternating mood between highs (euphoria) and lows (sadness). Other specific symptoms during this period include agitation, changes in appetite, insomnia, suicidal thinking, and other psychotic features.	

(continued)

Table 17.3 (continued) Mood disorders: Major diagnostic categories.

Diagnosis	Associated signs and symptoms	Comments
Hypomanic episode	A period (at least 4 days, but can last longer) of persistent and elevated mood and other symptoms. These can include grandiosity, decreased need for sleep, pressure of speech, psychomotor agitation, "flight of ideas," excessive involvement in pleasurable activities, distractibility, and other symptoms seen in the manic episode. However, these symptoms are not severe enough in the hypomanic episode to cause significant impairment to the individuals usual role performance (although there may be some disruption), and there is an absence of delusions and other psychotic features (e.g., hallucinations).	
Major depressive disorder	Major depression is at times preceded by other depressive conditions, such as dysthymia, and also may co-occur with other disorders, e.g., especially anxiety disorders. In addition to the symptoms associated with depressive episodes, the symptoms of the co-occurring disorders may be present as well.	Characterized by one or more depressive episodes, with no history of mania or hypomania, and must be distinguished from other conditions for which there is a recognizable cause (e.g., disorders due to a major medical condition, drug, or exposure to chemicals) as well as other primary psychiatric conditions that may have similar symptoms (e.g., schizoaffective disorder). Mortality is high in major depression, suicide in up to 15% of individuals who suffer from this condition. Also, major depression has been found to increase morbidity and mortality in other conditions, especially in the elderly. Also, the presence of major depression in medical illnesses (up to 25% in diabetes, myocardial infarction, stroke, and carcinoma) adversely affects the complexity and prognoses of these disorders.

	The disorder occurs more frequently in women (lifetime prevalence 10% to 25%) than in men (lifetime prevalence 5% to 12%). The average age of onset is in the mid-twenties but can begin at any age. A single episode can recur, at varying rates and with varying clinical pictures during periods of remission. The fact that many of the symptoms of depression involve cognitive functions (e.g., concentration and memory), it is at times difficult to differentiate depression from dementia, especially in the elderly.
Dysthymic disorder	Many of the same symptoms as those seen in major depressive disorder but usually less severe and chronic as opposed to episodic.	The two disorders, dysthymia and major depression, can be difficult to distinguish from one another. Distinguishing features include more severe and disruptive symptoms in the latter and a chronic, insidious onset in the former. Also, onset and duration differ between the two types of disorders.
Bipolar I disorder	The features of bipolar I disorder can be similar to, and difficult to distinguish from, psychotic disorders (e.g., Schizophrenia or Schizoaffective disorder). Symptoms can include delusions (relating especially to grandiosity or persecutory ideas), agitation, irritability, catatonia, and, or course, depression and mania. The nature of this illness leads to a number of consequences for the affected person; e.g., difficulties at work or school, marital discord, child abuse, or antisocial behavior more generally. Suicidal thinking and actions are a significant risk, with a completion rate of 10–15%.	The bipolar disorders are divided into types I and II, depending on the presence and nature of mania (excitement). For this reason, the two types have been listed separately in this table. Both types I and II can be classified further, depending on the presentation in a given case, e.g., if the most recent episode was manic, hypomanic, etc. Type I is characterized by multiple, or at least one, manic or mixed episodes that usually are accompanied by major depressive episodes. The disorder appears to be equally common in men and women, with a lifetime prevalence of less than 2%. This is a recurrent disorder, with >90% who have one episode going on to future episodes. While there is evidence for a genetic influence, there also is considerable variability in the expression of dysfunction between individuals.

(continued)

Table 17.3 (continued) Mood disorders: Major diagnostic categories.

Diagnosis	Associated signs and symptoms	Comments
Bipolar II disorder	The symptoms of type II bipolar disorder are similar to those seen in type I and, or course, in major depression, with the more serious symptoms occurring mostly as a result of the episodes of depression. These can be debilitating, causing significant work, school, family, and personal failures. Successful suicide occurs in 10–15% of patients.	Type II bipolar disorder involves the occurrence of one or more major depressive episodes with at least one hypomanic episode. The disorder occurs more often in women than in men and puts the affected woman at increased risk for postpartum episodes. The overall prevalence is about 0.5%. A possible genetic contribution has not been firmly established.
Cyclothymic disorder	The symptoms of cyclothymia are similar to those seen in depression or hypomania, depending on the nature of the current episode. The severity of symptoms is less than that seen in major depression or mania. Nevertheless, the disorder is accompanied by significant stress and subsequent impairments in work, school, interpersonal, and personal efficiency. The frequent cyclical changes in mood can leave the affected person appearing unpredictable, inconsistent, or unreliable. These perceptions by others can lead to social isolation, perhaps deepening the individual's feelings of depression.	A fluctuating but chronic disturbance of mood that involves multiple periods of hypomanic symptoms and numerous periods of depressive symptoms. The episodes do not reach a level that is sufficient to diagnose major depression or mania. These episodes must be present for at least a 2 year period (1 year in children), with no period during that time of being symptom free that lasted more than two months. The disorder usually begins in adolescence or young adulthood and may reflect a "temperamental predisposition" to other mood disorders (15% to 50% go on to develop a type I or II bipolar disorder). Estimates of prevalence range from less than 1% in the general public to up to 5% in clinic populations.

did not meet formal criteria for major depression. They concluded what was termed a "presumptive diagnosis of depression," and commented that the presentation of depression can be atypical in elderly patients. In sensitively recognizing the major changes that had occurred in the patient's life and the likelihood that her complaints represented an emotional response to those events, they likely saved the patient from additional and prolonged clinical investigations to discover the "physical" cause for her symptoms. In terms of a formal diagnosis of depression, however, the information provided does not fit the required criteria presented in Table 17.2.

Comment

In addition to pointing out correctly that depression in the elderly can manifest atypically, with indirect complaints that may be predominantly somatic, the authors who described the patient in the case presentation also made the important observation that elderly persons may not complain directly about depression and even may deny that they are depressed (Ahmed et al., 2006). Instead, the elderly patient may complain of sleep difficulties, fatigue, changes in appetite, irritability, or even memory problems. Perhaps as a result, it is often the patient's primary care physician who is confronted first with the patient's indirect expressions of emotional disturbance, even direct complaints of depression for that matter (Tesar, 2002). In fact, it has been estimated that 70% of all antidepressant prescriptions are written by primary care physicians (Tesar, 2002). As discuss elsewhere in the present volumes (see, for example volume I, pages 19ff. and *depression in a chronic medical condition* in chapter 18 in the present volume), there is growing evidence of an intimate relationship between stress and depression, especially perhaps, significant and repeated stresses (Barchas & Altemus, 1999; Sonino, Fava, Raffi, Boscaro, & Fallo, 1998; Young et al., 1994) and stressful encounters that serve as a basis for "Learned helplessness" (Barchas & Altemus, 1999). In this way, depression and anxiety, which at the time of formal diagnosis also often reflects earlier repeated stresses (McEwen, 2004; Mineka & Zinbarg, 2006), have much in common, and it is not unusual for the two emotional disorders to co-occur in a given patient (Barbee, 1998; Maier & Falkai, 1999).

Somatoform disorder

As the name implies, *somatoform disorder* shares the common features of symptoms and signs that suggest a medical condition, but is not explained entirely by the medical condition (American Psychiatric Association, 1994; Marjama, Troster, & Koller, 1995). The somatoform disorders are among the most interesting and clinically challenging of the mental disorders. Observations on the dynamic relationship between psychology and somatic symptoms are not new. Freud (1966, 1997) commented on the interactions between a current precipitating event and past trauma, stress, apprehension, and personality in the development of *hysteria* (now termed, *somatization disorder* [American Psychiatric Association, 1994]). Also, Freud allowed that trauma did not necessarily need to refer to one event of great magnitude but might be represented by a series of events, each contributing to the overall experience of trauma. Freud's ideas are strikingly similar to the current understanding of anxiety and the individual's pathological responses to that anxiety, including psychosomatic responses (Barchas & Altemus, 1999; Maaranen et al., 2005; Mineka & Zinbarg, 2006; Tull, Gratz, Salters, & Roemer, 2004). The major distinction between today's understanding of these psychological manifestations and that understanding in Freud's time relates to advances in the neuroscience of psychopathology, which have allowed for the study of biochemical and animal studies as well as the development of pharmacological treatments for these disorders (Barchas & Altemus, 1999). Seven formal types of somatoform disorders are described in the *DSM-IV* (American Psychiatric Association, 1994), presented in Table 17.4. According to the *DSM-IV*, the particular grouping of these disorders is not based on etiological considerations, which remain only partially understood and which might vary between the specific disorders listed. Rather, the common feature used in the DSM approach to diagnosis has been the presence of symptoms or nonvolitional signs suggesting a medical condition that is not explained by that condition or not better explained by another mental disorder. The presence of a medical disorder does not rule out the possibility that the person also suffers from somatoform disorder, or vice versa (Marjama et al., 1995).

Anxiety is a prominent aspect of almost all mental disorders, the somatoform disorders included. From a functional viewpoint, anxiety can be viewed as the anticipation of a fearful event, with depression representing one possible consequence of the physical and psychological stresses associated with such anticipation, especially when attempts to deal with these stresses have been wholly or partially unsuccessful. From this perspective of functionality, the somatoform disorders can be seen as resulting from the individual's (failed perhaps) attempts to cope with these stresses or the adverse consequences of prolonged, repeated, or overly intense stresses, e.g., depression. As was described earlier with regard to anxiety and depression, the symptoms seen in the somatoform disorders have counterparts in normal behavior as well. A primary difference between the formal disorders and the normal variant is the severity and disruptiveness of symptoms in the former. Even when these somatoform-like behaviors fail to reach diagnostic proportions, however, they can interfere with the clinical diagnostic examination as well as to adversely affect the prognosis and treatment of a primary illness. Also, an aggressive, even hostile, or resistive style, or the opposite expression of overdependence and passivity, can be a component of *somatization* and other somatoform types of coping strategies (Waller, Scheidt, & Hartmann, 2004; Henningsen, Jakobsen, Schiltenwolf, & Weiss, 2005). These behavioral styles can cause difficulties in the individual's personal life and interfere with the development of an effective doctor–patient relationship (Stone, Carson, & Sharpe, 2005; Waller et al., 2004).

Table 17.4 The diagnostic classification of somatoform disorders.

Diagnosis	Associated signs and symptoms	Comments
Somatization disorder	Primary symptoms are multiple and include a combination of pain, gastrointestinal, sexual, and pseudoneurological manifestations. More specifically, complaints include pain, in terms of anatomy (e.g., head, abdomen, back, joints, extremities, etc.) or functions (e.g., during sexual intercourse, urination, menstruation, etc.). Gastrointestinal symptoms (e.g., nausea, diarrhea, vomiting, bloating, etc.). Sexual symptoms (e.g., erectile dysfunction, sexual indifference, etc.). Pseudoneurological symptoms (conversion symptoms such as impaired coordination or balance, difficulty swallowing, hallucinations, double vision, blindness, seizures, dissociative symptoms like amnesia, loss of consciousness other than fainting, etc.)	In the past, this disorder was referred to as "hysteria" or "Briquet's syndrome." The onset of this disorder is before age 30 and extends for a period of years. The symptoms cannot be fully explained by medical illness or as the direct effect of medication or other chemical exposure, or if present, the symptoms or their functional consequences are excessive for the illness.
Undifferentiated somatoform disorder	Symptoms are as those seen in somatization disorder, but below the diagnostic threshold.	The medically unexplained symptoms are generally less severe than in somatization disorder, may be less in number, and may last for a briefer period of time, at least 6 months. As in all formally diagnosed mental disorders, the symptoms must cause significant disruption to important areas of the person's role performance.
Conversion disorder	Deficits or symptoms reflecting voluntary motor or sensory systems or that implicate neurological or other medical disorders.	The symptoms are unexplained medically, but psychological factors appear to be associated with the patient's symptoms. The onset or change in the patient's symptoms is preceded by conflict or other psychological stresses. The symptoms are not intentionally produced (as in malingering).

(*continued*)

Table 17.4 (continued) The diagnostic classification of somatoform disorders.

Diagnosis	Associated signs and symptoms	Comments
Pain disorder	Pain as a primary complaint.	Psychological factors appear to be associated with the patient's complaints—in terms of onset of symptoms, complaints of severity, worsening, or continuation. This disorder can co-occur with a medical disorder producing pain, the primary consideration being the presence of psychological factors in the pain. This may include complaints of pain that exceeds that apparently justified by the medical condition.
Hypochodriasis	Fear of or preoccupation with having a serious disease or persistent ideas about having such disease.	The basis for the patient's preoccupation or fear is based upon a misinterpretation or overinterpretation of physical symptoms or variations in normal bodily functions. Insight may be lacking, with the person failing to see that the concerns are excessive or not reasonable.
Body dysmorphic disorder	Preoccupation with an imagined physical deficit in terms of the patient's appearance or exaggeration of the deficit.	The concern must cause significant disruption to important areas of the person's role performance. The concern cannot be better explained by another disorder, e.g., anorexia nervosa.
Somatoform disorder not otherwise specified	Any of the symptoms of somatoform disorder.	The presence of somatoform symptoms, but the clinical picture is insufficient to diagnose a somatoform disorder, or the symptoms do not meet those seen usually in somatoform disorder. These might include a false belief that one is pregnant, which can reflect signs and symptoms usually seen in actual pregnancy (e.g., abdominal enlargement, nausea, amenorrhea, etc.). The symptoms can be for less than 6 months but should not reflect a psychotic disorder.

Some of the contents of this table reprinted with permission from the *Diagnostic and Statistical Manual of Mental Disorders*, Fourth Edition, 1994 and Text Revision, Copyright 2000. American Psychiatric Association.

As in the anxiety disorders, culture can influence the nature of symptoms and other characteristics of the somatoform disorders (e.g., differences between cultures in sex ratio of men to women with these disorders), but the basic defining characteristics remain across cultures (American Psychiatric Association, 1994). Also, the coexistence of personality disorder (e.g., histrionic personality disorder) is not uncommon. It is likely, in fact, that personal style, or personality, plays an important predisposing role in the development of a somatoform disorder, as well as the manifest nature of the disorder, e.g., whether the affected person behaves in a hostel or more passive-dependent manner (Hepple, 2004; Maaranen et al., 2005; Tull et al., 2004). Demographic (e.g., age) and existential (e.g., losing a loved one) factors also influence the expression of a somatoform disorder. And at times, a recent, traumatic event, or series of events, can trigger formal disorder in someone with a predisposing nature who had apparently until that time functioned normally. The change in behavior can be dramatic and often the symptoms of a somatoform disorder are difficult to distinguish from those of other mental disorders. Consider the following *case presentation*, abstracted from a publication by Vorhees (2003), and, as will be seen, titled appropriately, "I can't move."

Case presentation[4]

A 78-year-old widow, described as having a very large and gregarious family, was seen in the emergency department following a fall in her home and found to have "two minimally fractured ribs," treated, and discharged to home. Four days later, she again fell, was unable to get up but "scooted" from the bathroom where she fell to her bedroom. She lay there for about one half hour, describing feeling very "weird," and was then able to get to her bed where she phoned her son. The son came to her home and found her to be "OK." Later that day, the daughter brought her to see the physician. Her primary complaint on this occasion was "feeling weird." In talking to the patient and her daughter, the physician concluded that she was ambivalent in relating to her children, concerned that they might ignore her but also not wanting them to "control her life." The patient wanted the daughter to move into her house with her, and at the same time, the daughter wanted her mother to move to the daughter's home. The physician talked more with the patient about her life, losing friends and other losses. The patient had well-controlled diabetes.

The patient returned 1 week later, complaining that she had awakened the day before with uncontrollable movements of the left leg. Also, she complained that the right leg, both arms, and the rest of her body were "numb," and that she could neither feel nor move any part of her body. These sensations stopped abruptly after what seemed to her to be a long time, and she was able to get up. She had been frightened by the experience. On examination, she was able to move her leg normally and the physician informed her that the findings did not fit any pattern of disease and suggested that anxiety about losing her independence could explain her complaints.

She requested to see another doctor for a second opinion because the current physician was not finding a cause for her problems. She was referred to a neurologist. One week later, the patient experienced another episode in which she awoke unable to move her "head, either arm, her upper body, or one leg but could move the other leg quite well." After an hour and a half, she was able to get up and go to the bathroom. As her outside door was locked, she believed it was no use to call 911. She had not yet called the neurologist and an appointment was made for her to see this specialist.

She returned with her daughter 1 day before her scheduled neurology stating that she had experienced the "worst one ever." This time, on awakening, she could move only her head. Her entire body was uncontrollably trembling and shaking. Eventually, she was able to reach a phone and call one of her children. Her daughter arrived to find the patient sitting on the couch and apparently normal. The physician asked her to describe the one thing that had characterized each of her episodes, in response to which her speech seemed first to block, and then she hesitatingly replied, "I can't move!" The physician suggested that "moving" can have more than one meaning, that it can mean moving her body parts but also can mean moving in with her daughter.

She returned about 10 days later, having seen the neurologist. Her manner on this occasion was described as "upbeat, pleasant, and relaxed (and, as always, talkative)." She reported that the neurologist had told her the same things as the treating physician, telling her it was her "nerves" and prescribing Paxil and Ativan in case she had any more spells. She praised the primary physician's care, emphasizing that the neurologist had told her the physician's diagnosis had been correct. After leaving, the patient returned to the reception desk, leaving a message to tell the physician that she had moved in with her daughter and had experienced no further spells.

ADDITIONAL INFORMATION

Two cranial CT scans had been done over a 4 year period before the patient was currently seen. These were reviewed and found to reflect mild cerebral atrophy but nothing else.

CLINICAL DIAGNOSIS

The physician in the current *case presentation* diagnosed "abnormal involuntary movements, probably psychophysiologic, in a person living alone, in an anxiety state caused by aging and loss of independence."

Comment

The physician's clinical diagnosis was descriptive and undoubtedly captures the patient's condition. From a formal diagnostic viewpoint, however, the patient in the current *case presentation* meets criteria, and provides an excellent example of *conversion disorder* (American Psychiatric Association, 1994). Her symptoms involved voluntary motor (e.g., shaking, unable to move body parts) and sensory (e.g., numbness) none of which could be explained by a medical disorder. The clinical diagnosis did not include *seizure disorder or pseudoseizure* and such disorders will likely need to be excluded on the basis of further examination (e.g., EEG). The presence of an underlying medical disorder, however, does not preclude a diagnosis of *conversion disorder*.

Pseudoseizures are often an indication of *conversion disorder*, even when EEG documented seizures may be present, but the description of symptoms in the *case presentation* did not give the appearance of seizure (Haines, 2005; Sackellares & Berent, 1996). For example, her spell varied in terms of the involved neuroanatomical location from incident to incident and did not reflect a seizure sensible pattern (e.g., stereotyped or clonic movements). This leaves it unlikely but does not rule out completely the possibility of actual or pseudoseizure. As mentioned earlier, the discovery of such a condition does not rule out conversion unless it completely explains the patient's symptoms, a very unlikely eventuality in the present instance.

With regard to other criteria associated with conversion disorder, the patient's symptoms provided a good example of psychological involvement, especially in light of the almost classic nature of her motor and sensory symptoms representing symbolically her psychological conflicts, and epitomized by her complaint, "I can't move." She did not appear to be intentionally producing her symptoms. Her symptoms appeared to cause significant impairment, although conclusion may be difficult to discern in an older person with already limited responsibilities in everyday life. There was an absence of depression or other mental disorders that would compete to explain her symptoms, e.g., the report that she had remained socially oriented and relatively active despite her symptoms.

Before leaving this *case presentation*, it should be noted that *la belle indifference* (an inappropriate complacency or lack of concern regarding one's symptoms of medical disorder) is present at times in conversion disorder. While the patient in the current *case presentation* did not display frank indifference to her symptoms in presenting to the physician, there may have been occasions when complacency was present, e.g., on the occasion when her daughter found her sitting normally on the couch following an episode or on the occasion when she felt it not necessary to phone 911. Regardless, *la belle indifference* is not required to diagnose conversion disorder.

There are other psychological disorders that can be accompanied by symptoms that are similar in nature to those characterized as "somatoform," a grouping of convenience to some extent (American Psychiatric Association, 1994). The concept of "pseudodementia," for instance is classified in *DSM-IV* as a *dissociative disorder* (disruption in the normally integrated functions of attention, perception, memory, or other aspects of consciousness). When apparent cognitive impairment, including what can be termed "pseudodementia" occurs as a result of a primary disorder other than dissociation or one of the other somatoform disorders, the primary disorder is diagnosed (e.g., *dysthymia*). These two disorders, dissociation and conversion, are at times both diagnosed in the same person. An important distinction to be made in the differential diagnosis of dissociation or conversion is between these disorders and malingering or factitious disorders, the latter two involving intentionally produced or feigned symptoms (see volume I, chapter 4). Consider the following case abstracted from a publication by Hepple (2004).

Case presentation[5]

A former military pilot was retired early because his position was described as "redundant." He presented for evaluation with complaints of increasing memory loss, accompanied by increasing dependence on his wife. His behavior had changed in other ways as well, with occasional binge drinking, abusive verbal behavior toward his wife, and periodic "passive aggressive" acts (e.g., placing the couples' passports in a mailbox while on a trip). While he claimed amnesia for such events, his wife was convinced that he acted purposefully. His behavior in general was seen as inconsistent. While he was "unable" to take responsibility for financial and other activities of daily living, it was reported that he was able to continue his hobby of constructing complex airplane models as well as to drive alone on trips outside the home. Attempts at cognitive and couples therapy were unsuccessful because of his apparent memory problems and dissociation. While he was said to evidence some insight during sessions, such gains failed to extend to the home. Also, he performed erratically on neuropsychological examinations, with "erratic" performance on intelligence tests, below average scores on memory tests, but average or above on assessment of working memory. Many inconsistencies were noted on the psychological tests, and no meaningful clinical pattern could be discerned.

The patient was seen over a period of 16 years before being reported in Hepple's publication. During that time, the patient underwent numerous tests and examinations, none of which was clinically revealing. He had a normal cranial CT scan 10 years after the onset of his symptoms, and repeated blood tests during that period also were normal. His premorbid personality was described as containing traits of narcissism and perfectionism.

CLINICAL DIAGNOSIS

The patient was diagnosed as having "dissociative amnesia."

Comment

The patient in the *case presentation* meets criteria for the diagnosis provided. At the same time, however, this patient meets criteria for conversion disorder. Both diagnoses include pseudoneurological symptoms (pseudodementia) in this instance. Many of the classic findings for conversion disorder are exemplified in this *case presentation*. The patient's symptoms suggested a neurological illness, i.e., progressive dementia. While one might need to know more than was presented in the brief published description of this case, e.g., the presence and nature of stressors that may have preceded his symptoms, his reported premature retirement could have served as the precipitating stress. Appropriate clinical investigations failed to explain his symptoms, and the findings from these investigations proved to be inconsistent with a neurological illness, e.g., no progression of his dementia over a 16 year period, normal imaging and blood studies, and inconsistent findings on neuropsychological examination that included findings of intact working memory in the face of poor scores on other memory tests.

While a *factitious disorder*, with the purpose of assuming a "sick role" remains a possibility, no evidence was presented that suggested this patient was intentionally feigning his symptoms. And, there was no evidence that the patient stood to gain financially or otherwise as might indicate *malingering*. The very long course of his illness (16 years) also argues against intentional feigning. There is no doubt that the patient may have experienced "secondary gain" as a result of his "illness" (e.g., getting attention and being cared for by others), but secondary gain is an expected consequence of any illness and does not serve to negate the diagnostic conclusions in this case.

As mentioned earlier, culture and other demographic characteristics can influence the expression of symptoms in *somatoform disorder*. Living in a very rural geographic area, coming from a background of limited educational opportunities, or low socioeconomic status all influence the individual's persistent behavioral patterns (i.e., personality); and personality impacts on symptoms of disorder as well as contributing to the propensity for disorder. Also, limitations in intellect and other cognitive functions can negatively affect ability to cope with stress, including the stresses of everyday life (Berent, 1986).

Case presentation[2]

One of the authors had occasion to accept a referral from an ophthalmologist who had been treating a 32-year-old man for a sudden loss of vision in the right eye. The patient had been referred to the ophthalmologist, in turn, by an orthopedist who was evaluating the young man for a severely cramped right hand. Neither physician had been able to find physical explanations for the patient's condition despite extensive evaluations, although both suspected that a psychological component was involved or even explanatory. One evaluative interview with the patient eventuated in a brief neuropsychological examination and three one hour interview sessions. On each of these occasions, the patient was prompt and consistently polite. He was found to have a normal mental status but limited general ability (WAIS IQ = 76) vocabulary (WAIS Vocabulary = 6), and fund of general information (WAIS INFO = 6). He was born and raised on his family's small farm in a very rural mountain area, where he attended a one room school for grades 1–7. His performance in school was described as "standing around a lot, and doing errands for the teacher." In the middle of the 6th grade, he quit school, apparently with the teacher's encouragement, in order to help out his father on the farm. His current reading recognition was about 3rd grade level, too low for administration of a formal personality test like the MMPI.

The patient's manner in interview was quiet and polite, with a subdued, if not depressed deportment. He appeared to be genuinely interested, but with absence of expressed concern, in discovering the cause of his disabilities. When asked to state his primary complaints, he answered, "I can't shoot." In amplifying this statement, he raised his clenched fist for the clinician to see and asked, "How could I pull a trigger with this?"; going on to say that he used to hunt squirrels but now would not be able to "hit" anything even as large as a bear. He gestured while talking by holding his left arm up to his left eye, as if to demonstrate how awkward it would be to shoot a rifle in such a position. The patient reported that his mother died when he was very young, while giving birth, along with the infant, and that his father died from a massive heart attack about 2 years ago. He had two brothers who were 10 and 12 years older than the patient and who left the home while the patient was still in school. One was killed in "the war," and he was unaware of the second's whereabouts. Thereafter, he and his father were the only ones living in the home, where he has continued to live alone since his father's death.

The patient described an ambivalent relationship with the father, a somber sounding man already in his late 40s when the patient was born. While his father was still alive, most days on the farm consisted of the same routine, which included getting up around five o'clock in the morning, having breakfast, and working about 10 hr with a break for lunch. After dinner, he and his father would "read the scriptures," and go to bed. They did not attend a church, his father referring to them as "temples of false worship." Once or twice a month, he and his father would "squirrel hunt for meat," and once a month the two of them would drive into town to buy other necessary supplies. He said he continues to follow a similar lifestyle, absent the hunting.

When asked to describe his feelings about life on the farm and his relationship to his father, the patient's first response was, "One should honor their mother and father." With further inquiry and by midway into the second interview session, the patient described having been angry with his father, admitting that he blamed his father for the mother's death (because the father, he believed, insisted on her having the baby at home). The father, he continued, was a strict disciplinarian, private in his manner, and absent of any display of affection or emotions other than anger. The patient said he felt it was his duty to stay with his father to help him on the farm. On one occasion, he said, he brought up the idea of leaving, to which his father told him, "you'll get killed like your brother." By session three, the patient described occasions when he wished his father would die, adding that he sometimes would see his father at a distance in the field and imagine "sight'n in on him" and "shoot'n him like a squirrel." He indicated that he felt shame and guilt following such thoughts. At one point in the session, he asked the clinician, "Can a person wish a person dead?"

First, probing further to insure that the patient's statements did not represent the admission of an actual act, the clinician intervened with some comments and questions aimed at interpretation. The patient was told that the thoughts he had were perhaps his way of expressing feelings that he believed he could not express openly. Also, the clinician offered that despite his ambivalent feelings about his father, the father's death was a loss and that he most likely had strong feelings about that loss. The clinician commented in an open ended manner that it would most likely be impossible for the patient to kill his father now that he could no longer shoot.

ADDITIONAL INFORMATION

The patient did not return for a scheduled fourth session. The patient was encountered in the hospital a few weeks later, however, when he was waiting to be seen by the ophthalmologist. He greeted the clinician with his usual politeness and seemed very pleased to report that "the doctors" had "cured" his problems and that he could now hunt again. He thanked the clinician for the time spent with him.

FINAL CLINICAL NEUROBEHAVIORAL DIAGNOSIS

Conversion disorder, in a person with limited coping skills and a depressive and somewhat dependent personality.

Comment

Personality refers in general to a person's long-term and enduring traits, formed most importantly in childhood, and that characterize the person's style of behavior in approaching the environment (Lazarus, 1991). While *DSM-IV* (American Psychiatric Association, 1994) lists a number of types of *personality disorder*, the patient in the current case presentation did not meet the formal criteria for any of these clinical conditions. Rather, his personality, although perhaps foreign to many and with a combination of circumstances that most do not have to face (e.g., limited intellect), was consistent with others from a similar cultural, societal, and personal background. Certainly, the patient's clinical complaints were dramatic, and they did cause significant impairment in his ability to function. However, these symptoms could be completely and best accounted for by the diagnosed conversion disorder. In the absence of those symptoms, the evidence was that the patient was able to function sufficiently (e.g., to operate his household and farming responsibilities) despite the peculiarities of personal style.

SOME ADDITIONAL COMMENTS REGARDING PSYCHOLOGICAL AND EMOTIONAL
CONSIDERATIONS IN CENTRAL NERVOUS SYSTEM DISEASE

Intervention to understand. Psychological variables can potentially affect, or obscure, the patient's clinical presentation. Because of this, important psychological factors may be discoverable only through the professional's active clinical intervention. How, for instance, does one respond to a patient whose anxieties adversely affect their disclosure of important historical information in interview or otherwise obscure a full and accurate clinical picture? With regard to a patient who becomes angry in response to the suggestion that something other than a toxicant might be responsible for their complaints, the clinician in such a situation might perceive correctly that the patient's expression of emotion is overly intense and an inappropriate response in the current context, especially in the instance of lack of receptiveness despite factually based explanations. One might wonder if there is something the patient is not revealing. Such suspicions can be illuminated further by letting the observation serve as a hypothesis, which then needs to be tested through further historical inquiry. Consider, e.g., the young woman mentioned earlier who became angry at her doctor for suggesting other than a toxicant-induced cause for her complaints. As a result of further inquiry, it was learned that this patient had been sexually abused as a child and had carried around considerable feelings that had remained unresolved for many years. The opportunity to explain her difficulties as the result of exposure to a toxicant might have seemed to her to be more ego-syntonic, at the least less threatening and easier for her to talk about, than it would be to openly consider that her symptoms represented a continuation of difficulties related to unresolved earlier and tragic experiences. Without the active inquiry suggested here, it is entirely possible that this important history would have remained obscure, and this might have left a distorted view of what was causing the patient's refusal to accept reasonable alternatives to her insistence on a toxic explanation for the complaints.

One must be sensitive to the patient's view in order to achieve the rapport required for the patient to disclose the often personal and private items needed to fully understand the clinical presentation. This does not mean that one should accept uncritically the entirety of the patient's assertions, which often may be contrary to the professional's sophisticated understanding of the topic. Rather, it suggests that the clinician should convey an acceptance of the patient's right to have an opinion and to share that opinion. One way to accomplish this is to lessen the patient's anxiety, and this calls for a non-threatening and tolerant approach to topics that might elicit considerable emotion. Often, the patient's growing anticipation around certain topics can be fairly easily recognized. At such times, for instance, the patient may increase their grip on the arm rests of a chair, there may be a change in the intonation of their voice, or he or she might sigh or even become tearful. With a simple, empathetic comment by the clinician that notes the patient's change in behavior, one can often elicit more information regarding what about a given topic seems threatening to the patient. A phrase such as, "I notice that whenever I asked you about your family, you became tearful," is often all that is required to elicit the thoughts and feelings that reside behind the patient's reluctance to reveal those thoughts and emotions. Note that the hypothetical phrase reflected only the clinician's observations and not an inference, nor even a direct question, as to what the patient might be thinking or feeling.

Such phraseology is important for several reasons. For one, it avoids the sense of intrusion of privacy that might appear to the patient to be aggressive, threatening their sense of control and raising the anxiety even further. It allows the patient to maintain control of their privacy and for them to decide whether or not, when, and how much to reveal. Also, in revealing his or her own thoughts, one can serve as a model for the patient, essentially implying that it is acceptable in this situation to talk about private matters. Even when the patient's response to such an interpretation is one of simply acknowledging that the topic is troubling furthers meaningful interaction that can lead at some point to a more direct discussion of the topic. Here is an area where patience on the part of the clinician is critical.

While some things can be elicited fairly easily, others require time to be expressed. Also, an interpretive comment will at times elicit some stronger emotion than was seen initially, often before such feelings are translated into words. Nevertheless, the clinician is obligated to arrive objectively at a complete and accurate diagnosis and, when appropriate, an effective treatment plan. With an approach that is sensitive to the patient's concerns and acknowledges the reasonable aspects in their thinking and prior conclusions, rapport can usually be easily established. Such rapport enhances communication and enables one to view a greater number of symptoms that are unclouded by the patient's resistances than might be the case without such intervention. In addition, rapport-building intervention allows the patient to more easily consider alternative explanations for their complaints. Of course, one needs to avoid any inadvertent collusion with the patient that might lead to erroneous clinical conclusions. One final comment here, the patient's right to privacy should at all times be respected. He or she should not be forced or coerced into revealing, before wishing to do so, facts the patient believes are private or that involve revelations about others. While such information may potentially be critical to a full understanding of the case at hand (e.g., knowing that the patient was sexually abused as a child can change completely how one views their current anxiety and depression), it can be a mistake to pressure the patient into revealing such information before they are willing to do so. Premature disclosure also can be accompanied by pathological behavioral responses. The ideas discussed in this section have been aimed only at how to create an atmosphere that optimizes patient–doctor communication. When the patient's resistance is overly strong or revelations appear to elicit overt pathological behaviors, the best course may be to refer the patient for a more comprehensive psychiatric or psychological evaluation.

Some causal considerations in relation to behavior. The clinical determination of any specific disorder is independent of specific causal attribution. This is true for physiological as well as psychological abnormalities. Distinctions made between entities that are *psychological* and those that are physiological are to a certain degree arbitrary, and it is important to recognize that both are mediated by the nervous system and can involve common neural pathways. As a result, the symptoms of toxicant-induced disorders are often indistinguishable initially from manifestations of emotional or other psycho-logical disorders or even from variations in normal physiology or emotion. There are few signs pathognomonic for a given neurotoxic illness. The clinical findings in a given case, therefore, can be a direct, or a secondary, conse-quence of a toxicant. But also, the symptoms and signs may be independent of the exposure (see, e.g., the section *patient with cognitive symptoms attributed to dental amalgams* in chapter 18). The complaints associated with exposure to various organic solvents, for instance, can include memory and other disturbances in cognition, altered mood, difficulties in attention and concen-tration, imbalance, and other nonspecific symptoms (Albers & Berent, 2000b; Spurgeon et al., 1997; Spurgeon, Gompertz, & Harrington, 1996); also, see *solvents* in chapter 15. Hallucinations and other aspects of altered mental status also can be observed in toxicant-induced disorders. But, hallucinations and impaired mental status can reflect primary psychiatric disturbance as well (Pao, Lohamn, Gracey, & Greenberg, 2004; Zakzanis, Leach, & Kaplan, 1999), and the nature of these clinical manifestations may be initially indis-tinguishable from toxicant-induced illness.

Symptoms (e.g., complaints of numbness or tingling in the extremities) and signs (e.g., loss of consciousness) that often reflect involvement of some underlying neurological or systemic medical condition can have their bases in anxiety or other psychological mechanism. The combination of acral paresthesia and lightheadedness, for instance, can be consequences of hyper-ventilation, which is known to have an intimate relationship with panic and other aspects of anxiety (Nardi et al., 2004a, 2004b; Nixon, Resick, & Griffin, 2004; Roth, 2005). The most common form of syncope is vasovagal, in which vagally-mediated hypotension combines with bradycardia to produce cerebral hypoperfusion, leading to loss of consciousness (Simon, 2000). Hyperventilation in situations of stress, trauma, and other experien-tial based phenomena such as fatigue can lead to syncope, and the finding can be all to easily attributed to a toxicant etiology when that may not be the case.

Apparent pathophysiology, like apparent psychopathology, can reflect vari-ations of normal phenomena. In addition to distinguishing between potentially competing pathological conditions in the differential diagnosis, the clinician also must distinguish pathology from some variation of normality, or condi-tions that perhaps while not usually expected in the general population also are not unexpected for a given age or other demographic classification. Clinical symptoms and signs can reflect variations in normal physiology and individuals who experience, or witness, such phenomena can easily misinter-pret these as indicants of disease, especially when there exists a close temporal relationship between those clinical phenomena and an incident of toxicant exposure (e.g., working with solvents when the incident occurs). Similarly, the underlying pathophysiology in a given case might reflect a medical or a neurological disorder that did not result from toxicant exposure. Syncope, for instance, resulting from orthostatic hypotension, can be recurrent and can reflect a number of disorders, including those associated with dehydration and medications (e.g., antihypertensive agents) or conditions producing dys-autonomia (e.g., diabetes mellitus) (Simon, 2000). Especially in the elderly, antihypertensive, sedative, antidepressant, and other medications can lead to hypotension and syncope, even at standard doses.

Loss of consciousness has been stressed as an important historical consideration in neurobehavioral toxicology, because it can be used as an indication that the person has been exposed to a toxicant in an amount sufficient to alter consciousness. Other aspects of the reported loss of consciousness—e.g., precipitating events, duration, associated amnesia, and the like—are sometimes thought to help gauge the severity of exposure. Complaints of dizziness, feelings of faintness, and feeling lightheaded are common in persons suspected of having been injured by exposure to a toxicant. Also, it is not unusual for a patient to describe in interview some episode of feeling faint or of having had actual loss of consciousness associated with working or being around toxicants. In fact, the patient who reports such an association may already have concluded, or been told, that the history "proves" they were exposed to a toxicant. Such a belief may (reasonably) be accompanied by anxiety. It is a mistake, however, to assume that loss of consciousness in itself is the result of a reported exposure before all of the clinical findings are obtained. A reported history of episodes of altered consciousness does not verify its accuracy, nor does it establish a connection to a suspected causal event, e.g., toxic-induced loss of consciousness. Even when a history of unconsciousness is verifiable, it will not in itself determine its cause. Episodic loss of consciousness can reflect numerous conditions including vasovagal syncope and orthostatic hypotension, physical or emotional stress, neurological conditions (e.g., seizure disorder), decreased cardiac output, or psychiatric disorders. Also, sensations of lightheadedness, dissociation, and disequilibrium are common among the elderly (Baloh, 2000; Simon, 2000). Finally, the historical report of loss of consciousness for a substantial number of patients can remain unknown (Simon, 2000). Without a proper and complete evaluation of the patient's history of unconsciousness, one cannot assume it as an indication of exposure.

Once abnormality is clinically established, the cause of the abnormality should not be determined on the basis of symptoms alone since many different disorders can manifest in similar symptoms. Dizziness, a sense of unsteadiness, things moving in the visual field, or loss of balance, and similar symptoms have been associated with toxicant exposure (Albers & Berent, 2000a; Bleeker, 1994; Feldman, 1998). The nonspecific symptoms just listed are similar to symptoms observed in some psychogenic disorders. The final diagnosis(es) and established cause(s) for the diagnosis(es) should be determined through the application of objective diagnostic and causal criteria. A simple temporal relationship between events is not sufficient to conclude a causal relationship (see volume I, chapter 8, for an extensive discussion on causal determination).

Errors that can result from an incomplete differential diagnosis. A differential diagnosis that fails to consider psychological and emotional factors in the evaluation of potential toxicant-induced or other central nervous system disorders is incomplete. About 100 years ago, in a talk to the faculty of Harvard Medical School, Pierre Janet lectured on the topic of psychiatric and psychological considerations in medicine and the importance of arriving at an accurate diagnosis, and he warned against medical blunders that can result from treating a clinical condition for "what it is not" (Janet, 1920). Not only might an inaccurate diagnosis lead to clinical interventions that are not indicated, therefore increasing the risk of iatrogenic injury, it also results in failure to treat the correct, actual diagnosis. Understanding the behavioral aspects of disease can increase the likelihood of arriving at an accurate and complete diagnosis. The author has observed a number of erroneous conclusions wherein a toxicant was misidentified as the cause of symptoms and signs in a given case when it was not. At times these errors resulted from misinterpretation (or overinterpretation) of historical events, e.g., concluding that a reported but unsubstantiated history of loss of consciousness indicated an exposure event. Frequently, however, these errors resulted because of failure to consider some historically important extratoxicant explanation for the patient's complaints, either because the clinician was unaware of their potential significance or simply failed to consider them as potentially explanatory. Often, the actual explanation involves behavior, or physical events that affect behavior. Five of the more regularly occurring types of such instances include the following:

1   A history of significant personal stresses—traumatic loss of a loved one, or a series of losses within a relatively short time, marital discord, the stress associated with serious or chronic medical illness or treatment, work-related stress, military-related combat experiences (e.g., PTSD) or the effects of being in litigation.

2   Nontoxicant injuries adversely affecting behavior—a history of head injury or other traumatic injury resulting in cognitive or emotional impairments.

3   A history of low intellectual ability, low education, or specific learning disorder—while mental retardation is included, a low intellectual level short of mental retardation in the absence of a proper baseline estimate can at times be misconstrued as reflecting a decline from a presumed higher level.

4   Unrecognized, motivated lack of effort, or poor effort resulting from unrecognized adverse effects on motivation to perform—sufficient effort is required in many aspects of neuropsychological and neurological examinations. There is an important aspect of volition in the tasks associated with these examinations, and while fatigue and general malaise can result from medical illness, including toxicant-induced illness, it also can be driven by psychological factors that include various types of psychopathology (e.g., depression), quasi-normal conditions such as performance anxiety, or even malingering.

5   Unacknowledged physical agents or conditions other than the toxicant of immediate interest—substance abuse, medications (taken properly or improperly or in wrong combinations), sleep problems, obesity, hypertension, and other systemic illnesses or associated treatments that can have adverse behavioral consequences.

Other psychological/psychiatric considerations

Stanley Berent

The term, *neurobehavioral toxicology*, connotes a bias to viewing the human organism in a holistic manner. Physiology and psychology as well as the interactions between these and other environmental and biological factors need to be considered in order to achieve an acceptable level of understanding in a given clinical case or research effort. O'Donohue and Cucciare (2005) have written about the various ways in which psychological factors can influence a medical disorder. A psychiatric condition, for instance, may represent the primary clinical problem in a given patient. On the other hand, psychological factors could be secondary, influencing a primary medical or other psychiatric condition. The psychological considerations also might occur within the context of multiple diagnoses. The consideration of psychological factors should not be limited to psychopathology alone, as often such phenomena will include individual differences in character or personality, either of which may reflect normal individual variations or disorders. In short, whether normal or not, the presence of psychological factors influences the individual clinical presentation. Because of this, we have emphasized the importance of these factors in these volumes. As the following *case presentation* illustrates, no where is this more true than in attempting to develop an accurate clinical diagnosis.

Case presentation[6]

Over the course of several hospitalizations (from 1954 to 1958), Grabski (1961) described a 21-year-old male patient who starting in 1952 regularly inhaled toluene for its euphoric effects. Working in an aircraft factory, the patient had used toluene on the job and had come to "like" the smell and the "dizzy" sensation that accompanied these exposures. He began to experiment with other substances at home, including isopropyl alcohol, trichloroethylene, and methylethylketone but rejected all in favor of toluene. He began purchasing "chemically pure" toluene from a paint store, and he would use a rag soaked in the substance as a vehicle for inhalation. His eventual hospitalization resulted when his family became increasingly concerned about his symptoms that included, "mental confusion, dizziness, inappropriate laughter, staring into space, and threatening suicide" (Grabski, 1961).

The same patient was reported in more detail by Knox and Nelson (1966) when he was again hospitalized. Knox and Nelson described a typical day for the patient as involving inhalation of several whiffs of toluene upon awakening, followed by brief inhalations every 1–3 min throughout the day. He was said to use this substance even at mealtimes. He carried a supply of toluene with him throughout the day and preferred toluene over alcohol even at social functions where alcohol was served. In response to his mother's pleading for him to stop this practice, he justified his behavior by likening his substance use to people who smoke. During interview, the patient reported that his use of toluene relieved a state of "chronic anxiety." Following a number of warnings at work, he was discharged because of his continued use of toluene. Knox and Nelson reported that the patient performed slightly above-average when in high school.

Although the patient verbalized that this substance was injurious to his body, he also said that he was unable to stop the practice. Between the time of his initial hospitalization and when seen by Knox and Nelson, he was hospitalized multiple times. Not all of these hospital admissions were for medical complications of his substance abuse. Following the emergence of bizarre and inappropriate behavior, for instance, he was hospitalized for psychiatric reasons in 1954.

His hospitalization in 1965 served as the basis for the analysis published by Knox and Nelson (1966). This hospitalization was prompted by the patient's inhalation of carbon tetrachloride, a known hepatotoxin (Klaassen & Watkins, 2003), which he used reportedly this one period when he was unable to obtain toluene, even though he was aware that carbon tetrachloride was toxic. This use reportedly resulted in acute hepatic toxicity. His condition improved in a matter of days following hospitalization. He returned to normal gradually. The patient's neurological functioning was described as having returned to his "previous state." Presumably, this included the staggering, slowed movements, and difficulty remembering recent events that were said to have been present in the year before his 1965 hospitalization.

The results of examinations over the next 4 months were said to be similar to one another, the patient being described as fully oriented and alert although "overly cooperative and anxious to a moderate degree" (Knox & Nelson, 1966). Verbal responses were described as often inappropriate. His emotional expression was described as "explosive on occasion." He was said to minimize the severity of his difficulties. For example, he responded to information that his brain scan (using pneumoencephalography, the technology available at the time) had shown loss of brain substance with the response, "well, I guess that isn't too bad."

ADDITIONAL INFORMATION

As the patient was hospitalized multiple times over an approximate 10 year period, he underwent numerous examinations. Relevant findings from these examinations are reviewed in the following paragraphs.

Neurological examination. His neurological examination at the time of the patient's hospitalization in 1958 was positive for abnormalities that included "slight" nonpersistent nystagmus on lateral gaze (a normal finding), Babinski signs that were equivocal, and "classical titubating gait with redundant movements characteristic of cerebellar disease." Other cerebellar signs were listed as bilateral intention tremor that was more pronounced in the arms than in legs, mild upper extremity adiadochokinesis, and rebound phenomena in all extremities.

Psychological evaluation. Although actual scores were not available, the results of psychological evaluation at the time of the patient's 1958 hospitalization were said to be " . . . more compatible with a schizophrenic disorder than of organic brain disease, although the overall clinical impression was that of a *primary personality disorder* with secondary toxic symptoms produced by toluene inhalation" (Grabski, 1961).

Neuropsychological evaluation. The patient received at least a brief neuropsychological examination at the time of his 1965 hospitalization; however, the scores from the examination were not published. The results of this examination were described, however, and the patient was said to have performed erratically but at the upper end of the average range on the Wechsler Adult Intelligence Scale. His comprehension was good. Block design was normal, but he showed some impairment on digit-symbol, the latter difficulty presumed to be primarily due to tremor. The similarities subtest was performed normally. A Rorschach test was administered and was said to suggest, " . . . a chronic schizophrenic process with loose associations and frequent bizarre responses accompanied by little affect." Overall, the results of the psychometric examination were said to not conclusively indicate "organic mental deterioration." The results were said to be similar to those reported in 1954 and 1959 (Knox & Nelson, 1966).

Other test results. Electroencephalography (EEG) in a fully awake state was described as showing scattered and irregular theta activity at 4–6 Hz most pronounced in the left hemisphere. A recording made when the patient was asleep indicated "sleep spindles" that were slowed to 10 Hz.

The results of pneumoencephalography were said to reflect symmetric dilation of all ventricles except the fourth ventricle. Cortical sulci were described as widened, especially in frontal regions. No definite atrophy of the cerebellum was noted.

DIFFERENTIAL DIAGNOSIS

Grabski (1961) considered and excluded the possibility of multiple sclerosis as well as familial cerebellar disease on the basis of absence of family history by examination of family members and the absence of eye difficulties. Despite the negative findings on pneumoencephalography, Grabski's final impression was "degenerative lesion of the lateral cerebellar lobes due to prolonged inhalation of toluene vapors." In addition to the diagnosis based on clinical evidence of cerebellar disease, he was given a diagnosis of "chronic undifferentiated schizophrenia."

In contrast to Grabski's impression, Knox and Nelson (1966) concluded that the signs they observed (i.e., ataxia, tremor, limb incoordination, snout reflex, Babinski, and emotional explosiveness) were most consistent with the abnormality of the corticobulbar and corticospinal systems rather than degeneration of the cerebellum. Further, they concluded that the findings from pneumoencephalography and EEG were suggestive of damage to the cerebral hemispheres, and not limited to the cerebellum. They conceded, however, that the tremor they observed could have reflected changes in the cerebellum that were not severe enough to be shown by pneumoencephalography. They ruled out hepatic-induced illness on the basis of normal liver-function tests and concluded a diagnosis of *encephalopathy*, which they attributed to toluene exposure.

REVISED CLINICAL DIAGNOSES

A complete clinical diagnosis for the *case presentation* requires recognition of the role played by psychopathology in the patient's signs and symptoms. Chief among the psychopathological considerations listed in Table 17.5 is *substance-use disorder*. The descriptions provided in publications related to the *case presentation* are sufficient to conclude such a disorder. *Substance*

Table 17.5 Relevant behavioral diagnostic considerations in the case presentation.

Reported behavioral observation[a]	Disorder
Patient's claim that his substance use relieved his chronic anxiety. Moderate anxiety noted on clinical examination.	Anxiety disorder
Minimized severity of disabilities. Possible inappropriate affect.	Dissociative disorder
Poor judgment. Memory loss for recent events. Erratic subtest performance on the Wechsler scales of intelligence.	Cognitive disorder
Diagnosis on first admission of "primary personality disorder." Substance use. Reportedly stealing chemicals from work. Misrepresentation (lying) to purchase chemicals.	Personality disorder
Psychological test results read as consistent with schizophrenia. Bizarre and inappropriate behavior (e.g., laughter, mental confusion). Possible inappropriate affect. Suicidal threats. Diagnosis on two occasions of chronic undifferentiated schizophrenia. Repeat psychiatric hospitalizations. Age of likely onset of mental symptoms consistent with schizophrenia. Duration of symptoms, with little change in psychiatric picture over course of time that other symptoms worsened. Occupational and social dysfunction.	Schizophrenia
Enjoyment of feelings associated with toluene inhalation. Habitual use of substance regularly over multiple years. Increased symptom severity over time, with intermittent periods of improvement following abstinence. Increased "craving" following periods of abstinence. Fired from his job because of his substance abuse. Tremor other signs consistent with prolonged substance abuse. Indications of addiction ("need" to have the substance). Poor modulation of emotions ("explosive emotional expression").	Substance use disorder

[a] Descriptions based on publications by Grabski (1961) and Knox and Nelson (1966).

dependence also can be established as the essential feature of such use because the patient continued to use the substance despite the presence, and his awareness of, significant problems related to his use (American Psychiatric Association, 1994). *Inhalant abuse* can be added to the diagnostic statement as this mode of self-exposure was consistently preferred by the patient, descriptions of his practice meeting most of those published in *DSM-IV*, e.g., type and method of inhalation (American Psychiatric Association, 1994).

Although implied, neither Grabski nor Knox and Nelson listed a diagnosis of substance abuse. The absence of this diagnosis was likely more a matter of available classification schemes than outright oversight. Both groups would have relied upon the *Diagnostic and Statistical Manual of Mental Disorders* (*DSM-II*) (American Psychiatric Association, 1968). While it was possible to use the diagnostic criteria contained in the then current version of DSM to include a diagnosis related to substance abuse, it was likely neither the specific nor the prominent diagnosis it became in later editions of *DSM*. For example, with *DSM-II* one could have included a diagnosis of "drug dependence" with a specifier like "other psycho-stimulants." By the time *DSM-IV* (American Psychiatric Association, 1994) was published, however, more specific diagnoses became available to the clinician, e.g., "inhalant related disorders" that were specific to disorders brought on by aliphatic and aromatic hydrocarbons.

The complete revised clinical diagnosis includes the initial neurological and psychiatric diagnoses that were concluded by Grabski (1961) and Knox and Nelson (1966) as well as the substance-use disorders listed earlier.

Discussion

NERVOUS SYSTEM LOCALIZATION

Symptoms, signs, and test findings in the *case presentation* consistently implicate the supratentorial and posterior fossa levels of the central nervous system.

VERIFICATION OF THE INITIAL CLINICAL DIAGNOSIS

As described earlier, both groups of investigators (Grabski [1961] and Knox & Nelson [1966]) concluded diagnoses that implicated the posterior fossa level of the central nervous system. There was some disagreement, however, as to the primary involvement of the cerebellum in the patient's symptoms and signs, with Knox and Nelson attributing the clinical findings to abnormalities of the corticobulbar and corticospinal tracts rather than degeneration of the cerebellum itself. Knox and Nelson conceded, however, that the tremor they observed could have been due to cerebellar abnormality and that the pneumo-encephalography they relied upon could have missed this involvement because of limitations in image resolution at that time. In addition, Grabski attributed the patient's substance abuse to a *primary personality disorder*

(Grabski). Knox and Nelson included *encephalopathy* as a diagnosis (Knox & Nelson).

Clinical signs were mentioned in the descriptions given by both investigative groups that are consistent with cerebellar involvement in the patient's problems. In addition to the tremor just mentioned, these included persistent lateral gaze nystagmus, balance problems, titubating gait, slowed movements, incoordination, rebound in all extremities, balance problems, and difficulty writing. At the same time, other signs the authors mentioned are not explainable on the basis of posterior fossa abnormalities alone. These included inappropriate utterances, poor emotional modulation, lack of insight, poor judgment, difficulties with memory; as well as test findings (e.g., neuropsychological test results) that suggested relatively severe mental disorder, brain imaging findings of dilation of ventricles and widened sulci (pneumoencephalograpathy), and abnormal findings on EEG.

When objective criteria are applied to the authors' diagnostic conclusions, the diagnosis of cerebellar disease, or even dysfunction of posterior fossa more generally, is not adequate to explain all of the clinical findings. In addition, cerebellar disease by itself is not coherent in that it does not explain the symptoms and signs that are more clearly associated with supratentorial structures (e.g., patient complaints, EEG and other test findings, clinical neurological and neuropsychological signs of memory impairment and psychiatric disturbance). The diagnosis also is not predictive of the clinical course that eventuated in worsening psychopathology. The additional diagnosis of encephalopathy accounts for most of the reported clinical findings and satisfies the majority of objective criteria needed to verify the diagnosis (see Appendix, Table A). The different diagnostic emphases between the two groups of investigators also could have reflected changes in the patient's condition over time, i.e., disease progression, as a result of continued substance abuse. With the additional diagnosis of psychopathology, mentioned but not emphasized by both investigative groups, all criteria for diagnostic verification appear to have been met.

Comment

Progress in knowledge and technology has a profound impact on our understanding of disease. The information presented in the original articles we used in formulating the *case presentation* had been obtained in the 1950s and early 1960s, and the original authors' interpretations of their data were appropriate to the state of knowledge at that time. Today, the initial diagnostic conclusion of *encephalopathy* would very likely be leukoencephalopathy and the white matter lesions needed to verify this diagnosis could be documented with current imaging techniques (e.g., MRI) (Filley, Halliday, & Kleinschmidt-DeMasters, 2004; Filley, Heaton, & Rosenberg, 1990) (also see section on *toluene* in chapter 16).

The nature of the work from which the *case presentation* was taken emphasized the neurological abnormalities of a condition thought to reflect toluene exposure. As such, the writings did not emphasize the psychosocial and psychopathological aspects that were relevant to this case, even though these were appropriately mentioned. Our analysis of the various descriptions that were provided in those publications led to the behavioral differential diagnosis reflected in Table 17.5.

VERIFICATION OF THE REVISED CLINICAL DIAGNOSES

The various behavioral disorders other than *substance-use disorder* listed in Table 17.5 were addressed in the following ways. There does seem to be sufficient information to conclude the presence of anxiety as a disorder in the patient described in the *case presentation*. However, anxiety is known to be associated with substance use. Therefore, the observed anxiety would likely best be conceptualized as secondary to the primary substance abuse. The same can be concluded for dissociative disorder, as minimizing the adverse effects of substance abuse can be characteristic of such abuse (Voyer et al., 2004). While a diagnosis of schizophrenia could be considered in this case based upon the historical presence of this as a formal diagnose, the information available is simply not sufficient to independently verify the presence of schizophrenia (see further discussion below). Also, many of the psychotic-like behaviors attributed to the patient are behaviors seen in substance use and intoxication as well (American Psychiatric Association, 1994). This same argument holds for instances of cognitive impairments that were described, since memory impairment, poor judgment, and erratic performance are parsimoniously explained on the basis of the diagnosed encephalopathy and substance abuse.

Grabski (1961) described a primary personality disorder and attributed the initiation of substance use to that condition. Also, Knox and Nelson (1966) indicated that self-medication for anxiety served as a motivation for initiation of substance use by the patient. While both of these observations are sensible, they provide too little information to verify their accuracy. The diagnostic conclusion of a personality disorder, for instance, was made earlier than was the diagnosis of schizophrenia. Schizophrenia is known to have a prodromal phase, and the historical observations attributed to a disordered personality could well have been behaviors associated with onset of schizophrenia. Also, it is known that anxiety-like symptoms accompany early phases of schizophrenia (Berent, 1986), and the patient's self-medication could well have been conceptualized as attempts to treat his psychotic symptoms. Finally, there is a "chicken and egg" quality to speculations regarding the patient's motivations to begin his substance use. That is, which came first? The most parsimonious approach is to conclude the primary disorders for which there is clear documentation, listing other relevant observations as modifiers. In this case, these modifying variables would include anxiety, cognitive disorder, and, by history, schizophrenia. The alternative diagnoses meet all objective criteria for verification.

CAUSE/ETIOLOGY

Grabski (1961) and Knox and Nelson (1966) attributed the findings in the *case presentation* to toluene inhalation. The authors mentioned but did not focus on the various psychological and psychiatric manifestations that lead to a more complete understanding of this case.

VERIFICATION OF CAUSE/ETIOLOGY

The primary clinical neurological findings in the *case presentation* were attributed to toluene exposure. All objective criteria for establishing a toxic etiology for the patient's neurological diagnoses were met in this instance; however, attributing toxic effects to one substance, toluene, is difficult in this case (see Table B in Appendix). Inhalant abusers, in general, are known to experiment with and often use a variety of substances on a continuing basis (American Psychiatric Association, 1994; Feldman, 1998; Goldman & Bennett, 2000). In the current *case presentation,* the use of solvents other than toluene was, in fact, documented. In one instance, the use of carbon tetrachloride resulted in hospitalization and severe medical consequences, including a chemical hepatitis. The clinical findings in that instance did appear to be carefully accounted for, with some effort to document how those differed from the effects attributed previously to toluene (Knox & Nelson, 1966). Nevertheless, consideration of psychological factors such as behaviors known to be associated with substance abuse leaves identification of a single substance, e.g., toluene, uncertain.

What are some of the relevant psychological considerations in this case? While the specific topic of schizophrenia is most relevant to the *case presentation*, a variety of psychological or psychiatric considerations accompany every clinical case. With regard to the current *case presentation*, for instance, the patient was said to have used toluene in an attempt to treat his anxiety. Self-medication using a variety of substances is common though nonspecific in a variety of medical and psychiatric conditions—including both normal variations in mood and clinical mood disorders (Knight, 2004), social and more severe anxiety (Carrigan & Randall, 2003), in psychoses (Goswami, Mattoo, Basu, & Singh, 2004; Goswami, et al., 2003), and in mental health problems generally (Harris & Edlund, 2005). Again, in terms of the *case presentation*, the patient was described as tending to minimize his difficulties, showing a response to what most would consider very concerning news (i.e., loss of brain substance) with a kind of indifference. This type of behavior has sometimes been referred to as *la belle indifference* (Gould, Miller, Goldberg, & Benson, 1986). *La belle indifference* can reflect a somatoform or dissociative disorder (American Psychiatric Association, 1994) that in itself is problematic, and independently diagnostic. Care needs to be taken, however, not to discount any of the patient's clinical findings upon observing a behavior like *la belle indifference,* or other behaviors that at times have been termed *hysterical* (e.g., hypochondriasis) (Gould et al., 1986). Apathy, which has been described as a symptom in leukoencephalopathy (Filley & Kleinschmidt-DeMasters,

2001), also can be psychosocial in origin. Aside from diagnostic implications, it is equally important to recognize that behaviors such as indifference or apathy can interfere with the clinical examination, leading, e.g., to an understatement or distortion as to the nature of complaints made by the patient. Further, as in the present case, symptoms that are associated with a primary psychiatric disorder, e.g., substance abuse, can have implications for conclusions based on other medical considerations. Here, for instance, knowledge of behaviors that are generally associated with substance abuse made it difficult to conclusively limit the patient's use to a single agent, i.e., toluene.

What about the diagnosis of schizophrenia? Bizarre behaviors, confusion, inappropriate laughter, as well as psychological test results that were described as compatible with schizophrenic disorder were described in the history of the *case presentation* (Grabski, 1961). Indeed, the patient's 1954 admission to a psychiatric hospital resulted in a diagnosis of chronic undifferentiated schizophrenia (Knox & Nelson, 1966). While the acute effects of intoxication in substance abuse may include bizarre or otherwise psychotic-like behaviors, many clinicians may not be accustomed to including psychoses in a differential diagnosis in other than specialized settings like prisons and psychiatric hospitals. For this reason, a few words about psychosis as well as the more specific category of schizophrenia are warranted.

Schizophrenia is categorized in the *DSM-IV* as a *Psychotic Disorder* (American Psychiatric Association, 1994). *Psychotic disorders* have been historically defined by behavioral symptoms that are judged by the clinician, using either a statistical or qualitative approach, to reflect a substantial loss of contact with reality, usually represented by the presence of hallucinations or delusions in the face of lack of insight into the pathological nature of these phenomena (American Psychiatric Association, 1994; Berent, 1986) (also see volume I, chapter 4 for discussion on statistical and qualitative approaches to determining abnormality). Important for the present *case presentation*, these criteria have varied over time, with less restrictive diagnostic criteria being used in the past, e.g., in *DSM-II* (American Psychiatric Association, 1968) than is usually employed today (American Psychiatric Association, 1994). Behavior could be considered *psychotic* using the *DSM-II*, for instance, if it substantially interfered with adjustment to every day life (American Psychiatric Association, 1968, 1994). The term *psychotic* denotes no specific underlying condition.

Schizophrenia represents one type of disorder that is accompanied by psychosis. While neuropsychological impairments are common in schizophrenia, often severe, about half of the patients diagnosed with the disorder reflect average level scores in their neuropsychological test results (Heinrichs & Zakzanis, 1998; Zakzanis et al., 1999). It has been argued that even when average level neuropsychological test performance is observed, the scores still represent some abnormality in comparison to control populations (Allen, Goldstein, & Warnick, 2003). More importantly, however, even when most agree that cognitive impairments are common in this disorder, there appears to be no one neuropsychological pattern that distinguishes patients with schizophrenia from normal healthy individuals (Heinrichs & Zakzanis, 1998; Zakzanis et al.).

Similar to findings in the neuropsychological realm, neurological abnormalities are common but mostly nonspecific in schizophrenia (Zakzanis et al., 1999). Davidson and Heinrichs (2003) performed a meta-analysis on 155 brain imaging studies (MRI and PET), representing the results of 4,043 patients and 3,977 normal control subjects. They concluded that deficiencies in frontal metabolism and blood flow associated with cognitive activation tasks were the best supported findings in these studies, distinguishing about half of the patients from normal. It appears, however, that behavioral activation tasks are required to produce deficits that are visible to brain imaging (Arnold et al., 1998; Zakzanis & Heinrichs, 1999). The finding of frontal lobe involvement in many schizophrenic patients may not surprise those clinicians who are well acquainted with patients who reflect disinhibition and lack of impulse control, problem-solving deficits, and poor judgment in decision-making. In those cases where these observations are relevant, this knowledge may be helpful in distinguishing between items in the differential diagnosis.

Schizophrenia is diagnosed behaviorally, and *DSM-IV* presents a set of criteria for defining schizophrenia (i.e., delusions, hallucinations, disorganized speech, grossly disorganized or catatonic behavior, and negative symptoms [e.g., flattened affect, alogia, avolition]). Two or more of these behaviors must be present, and there are other specific criteria that must be met in order to more specifically diagnose the disturbance in terms of one or its five subtypes (American Psychiatric Association, 1994).

The five subtypes of schizophrenia include *paranoid, disorganized, catatonic, undifferentiated,* and *residual* (American Psychiatric Association, 1994). The most important of these for the current *case presentation* is *undifferentiated schizophrenia* since this diagnosis was mentioned in relation to the patient in 1954 (2 years after he reportedly began his abuse of toluene), diagnosed again in 1958, and in 1965. The average age for onset in first episode of schizophrenia in males is early to mid-20s (American Psychiatric Association, 1994; Schurhoff et al., 2004). Individual onset age varies, however, and different ages of onset may reflect distinct illness variations that have predictive consequences for factors such as illness course, nature of symptoms, and severity (McClellan, Prezbindowski, Breiger, & McCurry, 2004; Schurhoff et al.).

The patient in the *case presentation* had been diagnosed with *chronic undifferentiated* schizophrenia. If diagnosed with *DSM-IV* criteria, the patient would need to have shown two or more of the criteria listed earlier for a diagnosis of schizophrenia. Also, the patient would have shown dysfunction in occupation or social activities for some significant portion of time following onset of his disorder and a duration of disturbance for 6 months or more. In addition, other mental disorders with signs and symptoms similar to schizophrenia (e.g., major depressive episode) would have to have been ruled out. To be excluded as well would have been the other subtypes of schizophrenia, e.g., paranoid, catatonic, etc. (American Psychiatric Association, 1994).

In terms of comorbidity of schizophrenia and substance abuse, Kessler (2004) reviewed the literature on alcohol and drug use and concluded that most people with a dual diagnosis of mental disorder and substance abuse report that their first mental disorder occurred before their substance abuse. Reporting on only 22 cases, however, Goswami (2003) concluded that two-thirds of his sample of schizophrenic patients indicated that their substance abuse preceded their diagnosis of schizophrenia. The question of which disorder came first, schizophrenia or substance abuse, is likely to be complicated by the fact that schizophrenia is believed to have a prodromal phase that includes a number of aberrant behaviors for some period of time before an actual diagnosis of schizophrenia is made (American Psychiatric Association, 1994).

While, as mentioned earlier, a diagnosis of schizophrenia cannot be concluded based solely of the limited descriptions given in the published reports underlying the *case presentation*, it can be concluded that the patient met many of the criteria needed for such a diagnosis. These included gender-congruent age of onset of symptoms as well as other observations that are consistent with schizophrenia and summarized in Table 17.5. At the same time, many or all of these observations could have been directly due to the physiological effects of the substances he was abusing, an exclusionary criterion for schizophrenia (American Psychiatric Association, 1994).

Conclusion

This presentation underscores the importance of the differential diagnosis as well as the important distinction between diagnosis and causal determination. As in other cases presented in these volumes, we emphasized the importance of considering behavior in reaching final diagnostic and causal conclusions as well as the need to approach the tasks of diagnosis and causality objectively and separately.

We discussed the clinical approach in neurobehavioral toxicology in volume I, especially in chapters 4–6. There we emphasized that the clinical evaluation rests on a number of activities, including such components as taking a history, performing an examination, and consideration of test results and historical records. In other words, a complete evaluation of a given case will reflect more than its component parts. Put another way, conclusions that can be drawn from a given case will be limited by the type and amount of data available. In the present instance, the available data was confined to those that were obtainable from historical records and analyzed in relation to relevant published literature. This approach allowed us to develop a differential diagnosis. The list of diagnostic possibilities included in the differential diagnosis, when viewed from a scientific perspective, suggests questions from which hypotheses could be generated and defines the data needed to test those hypotheses. Much of the needed data, however, would require components of the clinical evaluation that were not available in the present instance. We were able to identify many of the behavioral factors relevant to the case. These data did not allow us to test all of the hypotheses relevant to the *case presentation* even though we could discuss what would be needed to accomplish that task. Implied is the rule of science to never go beyond the data in making conclusions, in research or in clinical practice.

Neurological or medical conditions associated with or mimicking toxic-induced central nervous system disease

Dementia

Stanley Berent

Dementia is discussed frequently in the present book because its symptoms are nonspecific to underlying disease and may appear to be identical to those seen often in cases of toxicant-induced disorders. The cardinal features of dementia include impairment in multiple cognitive functions, one of which must be some aspect of *memory* (short- and long-term). The cognitive deficits reflect a change from past levels of functioning, do not occur solely in the context of *delirium*, and they must be severe enough to disrupt the individual's normal activities of daily living (American Psychiatric Association, 1994; Knopman et al., 2001; McKhann et al., 1984). The behavioral symptoms of dementia reflect areas that are fundamental to the individual's ability to recognize, process, analyze, and interact effectively with the environment. As a result, the affected individual in some instances may remain unaware of their impairments. Psychological factors (e.g., embarrassment or outright denial) also may distort self-awareness, obscuring the presence of cognitive impairment. Perhaps as a result of such dynamics, it is common for concerns to be brought to professional attention by someone other than the patient; such as a spouse or other person with a close relationship to the patient. Also, self-complaint of memory impairment can reflect misinterpretation of normal behavioral variations or other phenomena (e.g., performance anxiety). In isolation, therefore, self-complaint of memory impairment may be a poor predictor of progressive dementia (Jorm et al., 1997). While subjective memory impairment can reflect underlying neurological changes (Jessen et al., 2006; Morris, 2005b), self-report of cognitive symptoms is of limited value in the process of identifying specific areas of impairment, gauging levels of severity, discerning patterns of cognitive strengths and weaknesses, interpreting subsequent changes over time, or in arriving at a specific clinical diagnosis. The subjective complaint serves as a starting point for the application of clinical or scientific methods to address the questions generated by the reported information (see volume I for further discussion on clinical and scientific methods).

The following *case presentation* reflects problems seen often in clinical practice; a case in which there are known risk factors (in this instance, advancing age, family concerns about changes in the patient's memory, the presence of a medication known to have adverse amnestic effects, and uncertain treatment compliance). As in most cases of this sort, the presence and behavioral nature of cognitive impairment can be relatively easily established through application of appropriate professional methods and criteria. Once documented, the neurobehavioral abnormalities serve as an entrée to diagnostic and causal analyses that are aimed at identification of conditions that explain the patient's symptoms and help to determine the ways in which these can be managed, controlled, or possibly even reversed with appropriate treatment.

Case presentation[2]

A 72-year-old retired male was referred by his physician for neuropsychological evaluation. The patient had a 2–3 years history of apparently nonprogressive, mild memory difficulties, but more recently he had experienced increasing difficulty in sleep initiation. Physical examination, including neurological examination, was normal, as were laboratory test results (e.g., thyroid function, serum B_{12} level, and drug screen). Exceptions to the patient's normal examination results included mildly impaired mental status (difficulty in recall of three objects over time) and a mildly, "flat affect." His history was negative for hypertension, stroke, depression, or other mental illness.

The physician had prescribed Ambien (zolpidem, 5 mg) initially for a period of 2 weeks as a temporary sleep aid. The patient and his wife reported that his sleep was much improved, and the physician renewed the Ambien prescription, with the instruction that he take the medication only when he felt he could not get to sleep. A formal sleep study also had been ordered, the results of which found no instances of polysomnographic abnormalities, electroencephalographic abnormalities, or abnormally prolonged apnea. A few months after the initial examination, the patient's wife phoned the physician and complained that while her husband seemed currently to be sleeping well, he appeared to be having increased difficulty in remembering things. Suspecting that the patient's increased memory problems might represent an adverse reaction to the sleep medication, the patient was asked to discontinue using Ambien. He did appear to comply with the physician's request (corroborated by his wife). Nevertheless, his memory problems persisted over the next few weeks, and the patient was referred by his physician for formal neuropsychological evaluation.

ADDITIONAL INFORMATION

Historical records indicated that the patient had completed high school with slightly above-average grades and had an Otis IQ of 108 in the 9th grade (an IQ estimate comparable to the AMNART score [SS = 102] obtained in the patient's current examination and reported in Table 17.6). The scholastic achievement test scores reported in school records were consistently grade level or better. He completed 2 years at a community college following his graduation from high school, receiving an associate arts degree in business management. He went to work following graduation as a management trainee for a large retail chain, where he remained for the entirety of his career.

Table 17.6 Results of serial testing (18 months apart) in a patient with symptoms of memory and other cognitive impairment.

Test administered	Domain measured	Test results (time 1)	Test results (time 2)
MMSE	General mental status	22/30	17/30
WRAT-3, Reading	Reading recognition	92	85
American National Adult Reading Test (AMNART)	Reading test used to predict premorbid ability level	102	98
WAIS-III, VIQ	Verbal intellect	84	65
WAIS-III, Information	Fund of general information, long-term memory	10	7
WAIS-III, Similarities	Abstract conceptualization	6	3
WAIS-III, Comprehension	Comprehension of societal morés and expectations	7	3
WAIS-III, Letter-Number Sequencing	Attention, logical reasoning and problem solving	7	4
WAIS-III, Block Design	Timed, visual-motor problem solving	6	4
WMS-III, Logical Memory I	Verbal, immediate learning	8	4
WMS-III, Logical Memory II	Delayed verbal recall	6	4
WMS-III, Visual Reproductions I	Visual, immediate learning	7	2
WMS-III, Visual Reproductions II	Delayed visual recall	6	2
Hopkins Verbal Learning Test—Revised	Verbal learning	Total Recall = 14th percentile Trial 4 (delay) = 10th percentile	Total Recall = 4th percentile Trial 4 (delay) = 1st percentile
Wisconsin Card Sorting Test (WCST)	Problem solving (executive functions)	Categories = 26th percentile	Categories = 18th percentile
Controlled Oral Word Association (COWA)	Verbal fluency (CFL)	36th percentile	22nd percentile
Hamilton Depression Scale	Clinical rating of depression	8 (Normal < 14)	4 (Normal < 14)

Selected tests were chosen that were repeated across examinations and that reflected a range of neuropsychological domains sufficient to discern a meaningful clinical pattern.

Work-related records indicated successful completion of numerous company sponsored training courses and regular promotions, eventually becoming the sales manager at one of the company's larger stores. He did not serve in the military and had no history of work-related exposures to toxic substances. There was no history of smoking or illicit drug use. He used alcohol occasionally in moderation (i.e., 2 to 3 glasses of wine a week, with dinner). The patient retired at age 65, after 40 years with the same company. A performance evaluation report from his last year of employment stated, "...an extremely well-organized and conscientious employee. His retirement will be a significant loss, and he will be sorely missed."

Results of a brain MRI showed cortical atrophy slightly greater than expected for age, most pronounced in temporal-parietal regions of cortex, bilaterally.

INITIAL CLINICAL DIAGNOSTIC STATEMENT AT TIME OF REFERRAL

While no formal diagnosis was listed, the referring physician described the patient's problems as including *subjective memory complaint*, with *history of sleep initiation difficulties, resolved*. The physician requested neuropsychological evaluation to determine presence of an organic dementia versus a psychological problem (such as depression) or medication-induced dysfunction.

Results of clinical neurobehavioral evaluation. The emphasis here will be on the evaluation that was completed in response to the initial referral. The patient was seen twice, however, first at the time of the initial referral and a second time 18 months later. Scores for selected tests administered in both examinations are contained in Table 17.6. While the initial examination is most often sufficient to establish a clinical diagnosis in a given case, change in scores over time is important as well. Such change can serve to verify issues related to disease progression, for instance.

Some information from the initial interview with the patient. The patient seemed uncomfortable in interview, did not remove his windbreaker or sports cap, and volunteered little information except in direct response to the interviewer's questions. When asked about his primary complaints, he said, "none, except that I have trouble getting to sleep. But, that seems to be okay now." He was asked his perception of why he was referred for the present examination. Again, initially, he said he did not know. With mild challenge to this last response, he said he was here for his wife. Asked what he meant, he said that "she" believes he has a problem with his memory. He was then asked what he thought about his wife's concerns, and he said he believed his memory was fine, that he was here to "go through these tests to get her off his back about it." The patient became more relaxed over the course of the evaluation, as adequate rapport was established. It might be noted that the patient's attitude was substantially different at the time of his second examination, 18 months later, than in the first interview. Rapport during the latter evaluation was established quickly and easily. In response to questions regarding his symptoms on this second occasion, the patient responded without hesitation, "I am having difficulty remembering things." Changes in a patient's attitude (e.g., apparent self-insight or defensiveness) over time is seen often in cases of progressive dementia, likely mirror the extent and nature of underlying neurological dysfunction, and emphasize the relative lack of importance with regard to self-complaint in the clinical evaluation of cognitive impairment.

Some information from the interview with the patient's wife. The patient was accompanied to the evaluation by his wife. In interview, the wife described the patient as having always been physically and mentally active. He had been retired from his job as sales manager for a large retail chain for about 7 years. They were financially comfortable and faced no extraordinary stresses that she could identify. Their social life was relatively active, going out to dinner about twice a month, usually with long-time friends or alone. Both she and her husband liked to travel, and they usually went on vacation trips about twice a year. Two grown children lived in the area, and they saw them and their three grandchildren on a regular basis. Her primary concern about her husband, she reported, was his memory. She said she first noticed this problem about 5 years previously when her husband seemed not to be able to recall a friend's name, someone they both had known for 20 years. Other similar instances followed. She at first said the problems were mild and that he was always able to recall eventually, reporting also that his memory had not seemed to worsen over time. On mild confrontation, however, she admitted that these instances had become more frequent, especially over the past year, and that occasionally they involved what she felt were more severe lapses in memory. By way of example, she said often he would forget to lock up or cutoff lights when coming to bed, forget to take out the trash, or perform some other duty like getting something from the store, and, on one occasion, he forgot to turn off the spigot to the sink after washing his hands. She said she was reluctant to say anything to him about these episodes because, " . . . he did not want to hear about it." She was asked about his medications and responded that he had only the prescription for Ambien, to help him with his sleep, adding that he rarely took them and that at least half of the most recent prescription for 20 pills remained unused.

Neuropsychological Examination. Table 17.6 contains selected scores from the patient's two psychometric examinations. These scores reflected an individual who met criteria for a dementia classification at the time of his initial evaluation. Importantly, and although the diagnosis concluded in this case was made on the basis of the initial evaluation, the results from follow-up examination 18 months later showed clearly progressive worsening of performance in a pattern consistent with a neurodegenerative process (Berent et al., 1999; Bozoki et al., 2001; Morris, 2005a; Turner, 2006). In the first examination, the Mini-mental Status Examination (MMSE) results reflected impaired general mental status, a score below the usual cutoff for normal functioning (in this instance, a score $\leq 23/30$) (Berent et al.; Folstein, Folstein, & McHugh, 1975). Typical for progressive dementia, the patient showed maintenance relative to apparent baseline functioning in areas reflecting previously learned and well-rehearsed behaviors, i.e., reading recognition and fund of general information. The patient's low normal verbal intelligence was lower than predicted on the basis of the 2 tests just mentioned as well as on the *American National Adult Reading Test* (AMNART). The verbal intellect score is consistent with the apparent decline in mental status suggested by the MMSE results and, together, the scores in this area of his functioning suggest a general decline from a previously normal and likely average or above level of neurobehavioral function. Delayed recall of both verbal and visual test materials was impaired and worse than his scores on initial learning, reflecting clinically significant memory impairments. Tests of problem solving, verbal and visual, were impaired as well. However, 2 tests related to frontal lobe functions (i.e., abstract organizational ability [WCST] and verbal fluency [COWA]) remained within normal limits and were performed relatively better than some other tests in the examination, better especially in relation to memory test results. Some decline in the patient's performance on these two tests between the first and second examinations is noted. Test-taking motivation was judged to be adequate during the examination and attention, although likely reduced from optimal levels, was normal as reflected in his likely reduced but normal scores on initial learning portions of the examination. There were no indications of depression or other psychiatric disorder based on medical history, self- and spousal-report, patient observation, and test results.

Although the results from the patient's initial examination were consistent with dementia and a clinically significant decline from estimated prior levels of functioning, the second examination administered 18 months later showed clearly that he was suffering from a progressive condition. The changed scores evidenced continuing decline in essentially all areas of neurobehavioral functioning, most pronounced in those behavioral domains reflecting compromised ability in the initial examination but also now involving areas that are seen as more resistant to impairment in the early stages of progressively worsening dementia, e.g., verbal intellect, information, reading recognition, and comprehension (Berent & Trask, 2000; Matarazzo, 1972; Steinberg et al., 2005b).

FINAL CLINICAL DIAGNOSIS

A final diagnosis, *Dementia of the Alzheimer's type, uncomplicated, probable,* was determined on the basis of the clinical neurobehavioral evaluation, taking into account results from all examinations and test findings, behavioral observations in interview, and historical reports.

Discussion

The presence of memory and other cognitive impairments in a given individual are documented ideally through objective psychometric examination (McKhann et al., 1984). Analyzing the results of the examination within the context of standard, formal clinical diagnostic criteria (American Psychiatric Association, 1994; American Academy of Neurology, 2001) allow for a diagnosis of dementia (Bush & Martin, 2005; Pasquier, 1999; Zakzanis et al., 1999). Going beyond a simple diagnostic statement about the presence or absence of dementia, however, the situation quickly becomes complex (also see, *patient with progressive dementia*, pages 12 ff in chapter 1, volume I). One major reason for the complexity is that dementia is not specific for underlying disease, or even for identifiable, underlying neurological dysfunction. Dementia, for instance, can reflect psychiatric disorder (e.g., emotional disturbance or psychotic disorder). Often, the disturbances in memory and cognition that manifest from psychiatric disorders vary with fluctuations in the underlying psychiatric condition (e.g., *major depressive disorder*), leading to the label, pseudodementia, to refer to the total or partial reversibility of cognitive impairments in some cases. Adverse reactions to various substances (medications, abused substances, or other toxicants) likewise, can lead to transient dementias (or more permanent impairments when the substance is of sufficient dose and exposure duration). The concept of reversible dementia must be considered with recognition that many disorders are coexistent. Depression, e.g., occurs in approximately 12% of persons with progressive dementia, and many patients who reflect symptoms of depression and memory impairment are found on follow-up evaluations to have underlying, neurologically-based dementia (Knopman et al., 2001).

It has long been recognized that aging is accompanied by decline in neurobehavioral function. Declines in white and gray matter and other potentially adverse changes in brain also are known to accompany aging whether or not dementia is present (Bush & Martin, 2005; Filley, 2001). Onset of clinically diagnosable dementia has been observed to follow these changes in brain and behavior in many individual instances. Increasingly, it is believed that the period of decline preceding a formal diagnosis of dementia most likely reflects prodromal illness (Katzman et al., 1989; Hanninen et al., 1994; Masur, Sliwinski, Lipton, Blau, & Crystal, 1994; Morris, 1994, 2005b). It remains incompletely resolved, however, if all such decline reflects disease, and substantial effort has been spent in attempting to create models that predict effectively who will or will not develop a progressive illness (Berent et al., 1999; Bush & Martin, 2005; Morris, 2005a).

THE DIFFERENTIAL DIAGNOSIS OF DEMENTIA

While the presence of dementia can be determined with relative ease, the *differential diagnosis* in terms of the specific classification and the list of potential causes is extensive. Potential types of dementia and their causes include neurodegenerative (e.g., Alzheimer's disease [AD]), hereditary (e.g., Huntington's disease), infectious (e.g., Creutzfeldt-Jacob disease), inflammatory (e.g., multiple sclerosis), metabolic (e.g., hypothyroidism), neoplasm (e.g., paraneoplastic vasculitis), seizure (e.g., prolonged subclinical status epilepticus), toxic (e.g., substances causing primary or secondary hypoxia), vascular conditions (e.g., multi-infarct dementia), and psychiatric (e.g., depression). While these various disorders can be accurately diagnosed, the exact mechanisms of action that explain the accompanying dementia are not known in all instances.

Alzheimer's disease. The most common form of dementia in older adults is AD, a progressive neurological disorder first described in a 1906 lecture and in a subsequent publication by Alois Alzheimer (Alzheimer, 1907). Alzheimer noted changes in brain tissue in a woman who died following what Alzheimer referred to as a strange (mental) illness. Although it was recognized fairly quickly that the disorder described by Alzheimer was relatively common in the elderly, Kraepelin named the affliction after Alzheimer in recognition of the uniqueness and importance of the findings (Hardy, 2006; Kraepelin, 1910). As described by Hardy (2006), the findings led quickly to the discovery that most cases of dementia that had before been termed "senile dementia" actually reflected the pathology described by Alzheimer and, therefore, could be viewed as the beginning of the modern era of dementia research. It is recognized currently that while AD can occur in both young and old, the majority of those affected are elderly, with an estimated 5% incidence of AD in those between the ages of 65 and 74 years old and a prevalence of 50% in those individuals over the age of 84 (National Institute on aging [NIH-NIA], 2006).

Alzheimer described the pathological changes he observed as including "clumps" (later termed *amyloid plaques*) and "tangled bundles of fibers" (now referred to as *neurofibrillary tangles*). These plaques and tangles are considered to be signs of AD, even though they are not entirely specific to AD. The same pathological findings also are known to occur in other neurological diseases (e.g., Parkinson's disease) and in some apparently asymptomatic, normal individuals (Turner, 2006). Aside from the recent classical findings of plaques and tangles, other aspects of neuropathology have been found to occur in AD; including depletion of some chemicals used in neurotransmission (e.g., acetylcholine), cell damage, and cell death in specified regions of the brain (e.g., progressive deterioration in entorhinal cortex, hippocampus, limbic structures, and neocortex) (Braak & Braak, 1991). The neuropathological signs of AD can be determined only through direct examination of brain tissue, requiring autopsy confirmation for a definitive diagnosis (McKhann et al., 1984). The primary pathological diagnosis in AD involves silver staining of brain sections and light microscopic examination to determine the distribution and density of *amyloid plaques and neurofibrillary tangles* (Turner, 2006). Although the pathology examination can be accomplished conceivably on tissue obtained from biopsy, it is practically almost always accomplished by autopsy. A variety of potential minimally-invasive biomarkers for AD (e.g., analysis of cerebral spinal fluid and specialized neuroimaging) are currently under study, although none has been shown to be specifically diagnostic at this time (Knopman et al., 2001; Morris, 2005a).

In the absence of pathological confirmation of AD, clinical criteria have been shown to be reasonably effective in correctly establishing the diagnosis (i.e., those criteria advocated by the American Academy of Neurology

[AAN], the American Psychiatric Association [APA], and the National Institutes of Health (i.e., NINCDS—ADRDA) (American Academy of Neurology, 2001; American Psychiatric Association, 1994, 2000; McKhann et al., 1984). The criteria presented in these various publications are compatible with one another. The APA *Diagnostic and statistical manual of mental disorders-IV* (*DSM-IV*) diagnosis of dementia specifies the type of dementia when known, e.g., *Alzheimer's type, Vascular Dementia, etc.* (American Psychiatric Association, 1994). In the case of AD, the formal DSM diagnosis is *dementia of the Alzheimer's type*. A "specifier" also may be used to indicate if the dementia is of early (before age 65 years) or late onset (after age 65 years) as well as to identify other clinical features that might be present at the time of diagnosis (i.e., delirium, delusions, depression, or uncomplicated). Note that for a diagnosis of AD to be made, delirium can be present but must not be explanatory to the patient's dementia. NINCDS-ADRDA criteria (McKhann et al.) allow for additional descriptors when diagnosing AD, i.e., classifying the AD diagnosis as being *possible* (meaning that AD is likely but another disorder may be affecting the patient's symptoms) or *probable* (meaning that other relevant disorders have been excluded, and AD is the most likely, primary explanation for the patient's symptoms) (Knopman et al., 2001; Turner, 2006). Both *possible* and *probable* AD reflect good predictive validity, with higher sensitivity (*possible*: average across studies about 93%; *probable*: 80%) than specificity (*possible*: average across studies about 48%; *probable*: average across studies about 70%) (Knopman et al.).

A number of laboratory tests have been studied in attempts to identify biological markers that can indicate AD or related dementias. To date, only a few such tests have been found to have the predictive validity needed to contribute meaningfully to this goal, i.e., to improve specificity substantially beyond that which is obtainable with clinical diagnosis alone. Even though several biological markers have been associated with AD, they lack specificity. Values for CSF tau and CSF amyloid beta, for instance, have been shown to be elevated in AD, but these CSF findings may be elevated in some other neurodegenerative conditions as well (Andreasen et al., 1999; Blasko et al., 2006; Sunderland et al., 1999). The genetic marker, apolipoprotein E4 (APOE E4), also has been shown to increase the diagnostic sensitivity of AD over a strictly clinical diagnosis but with variable specificity (Mayeux et al., 1998). Aside from those tests used to establish the presence of dementia (i.e., psychometric examination) or to rule out competing diagnoses (e.g., B_{12} deficiency, thyroid function, and depression), AAN guidelines at the present time limit recommended diagnostic tests for the routine diagnosis of AD to structural imaging using CT or MRI (American Academy of Neurology, 2001). Imaging studies serve to exclude competing pathological explanations for the patient's symptoms, such as neoplasm, subdural hematoma, and normal pressure hydrocephalus. In terms of findings from imaging studies that are considered positive for AD, the pattern or distribution of expected abnormality on structural imaging with CT or MRI includes maximal atrophy in medial temporal lobes (especially in the region of the hippocampus) (de Leon et al., 1997a, 1997b; Xu et al., 2000). Findings from PET glucose scans in AD show generally a pattern of hypometabolism that is maximal in posterior cortical regions (i.e., parietal cortex) (Kuhl, Metter, & Riege, 1985; Vander et al., 1997). While similar patterns of reduced cerebral activity in AD are reported for SPECT, PET maintains the advantage over SPECT because of its superior resolution (American Academy of Neurology, 2001). Functional neuroimaging using PET also is seen as potentially valuable because of its potential to identify AD early in the course of progression as well as to differentiate AD from other types of dementia (e.g., frontal dementia and multi-infarct dementia). However, and primarily because of lack of prospective studies, AAN guidelines do not at this time recommend PET for routine diagnosis of AD (American Academy of Neurology, 2001).

Vascular dementia. In concluding that a patient has AD, other forms of dementia need to be excluded, and this can be a challenging task. Signs of vascular dementia, for instance, often overlap with those for AD, and autopsy data suggest that vascular pathology exists in up to 40% of dementia cases that undergo postmortem examination (Knopman et al., 2001). The National Institute of Neurologic Disorders and Stroke (NINDS) and *Association Internationale pour la Recherche et l'Enseignment en Neurosciences* (AIREN) criteria are used often to determine vascular involvement in dementia, but these criteria have been said to have low sensitivity (Gold et al., 1997; Moroney et al., 1997; Roman et al., 1993). Perhaps as a result, AAN practice guidelines have suggested using the Hachinski ischemic score in diagnosing vascular dementia and as an alternative to the NINDS-AIREN criteria (Table 17.7) (Knopman et al.).

Dementia with Lewy bodies and frontotemperal dementia. Two additional dementia classifications include *dementia with Lewy bodies* (DLB) and *frontotemporal dementia* (FTD). Both DLB and FTD occur less frequently than AD, and the signs and symptoms of each overlap with AD. The clinical manifestations in DLB include disordered gait and balance, hallucinations, delusions, poor response to antipsychotic medications, and fluctuating alertness (McKeith et al., 1996, 2004). Memory may be relatively less affected in DLB than in AD, but patients with DLB also may evidence more visual-spatial and motor impairment than those with AD (Ballard et al., 1999; Heyman et al., 1999). FTD appears to occur less frequently than either DLB or AD (American Academy of Neurology, 2001). The early manifestations of FTD may be dramatic, however, and may include lessened self-awareness, increased oral and aggressive behaviors, perseveration, and reduced verbal fluency (Miller, Darby, Benson, Cummings, & Miller, 1997a; Miller et al., 1997b). Neuropsychological test results in FTD are likely to reflect underlying fronto-temporal neurological dysfunction (e.g., poor abstract conceptualization, verbal fluency, and other executive task performance). However, impairment in frontal system tasks is not specific to FTD as they can be seen in other dementias as well, including AD (American Academy of Neurology, 2001).

Table 17.7 The Hachinski ischemia scoring system.

Criteria	Score
Abrupt onset	2
Stepwise deterioration	1
Fluctuating course	2
Nocturnal confusion	1
Personality relatively unchanged	1
Depression	1
Somatic complaints	1
Emotional incontinence	1
History of hypertension	1
History of strokes	2
Evidence of associated atherosclerosis	1
Focal neurological symptoms	2
Focal neurological signs	2

Good discrimination between AD and multiple infarct dementia (MID), the instrument's intended purpose, has been reported using the cutoffs scores, ≤4 for AD and ≥7 for MID (Moroney et al., 1997). Adopted from "Cerebral Blood Flow in Dementia," by V. C. Hachinski, L. D. Iliff, E. Zilhka, G. H. Du Boulay, V. L. McAllister, and J. Marshall, 1975, *Archives of Neurology, 32*, p. 632.

Prion disease. The symptoms and signs of prion disease, such as *Creutzfeldt-Jacob disease* (CJD), also overlap with AD and other dementia etiologies. The clinical course in CJD in most cases is rapidly progressive, with 90% mortality within 1 year of illness-onset reported in one study (Brown, Cathala, Castaigne, & Gajdusek, 1986). In comparison, longevity in *probable* AD has been reported to be 4 to 6 years from time of clinical diagnosis (Morris, 2005a), although the preclinical stage in AD may extend for some years before a clinical diagnosis is made (Berent et al., 1999; Morris, 2005b; Turner, 2006). Familial CJD accounts for less than 10% of cases. Peak age of onset of CJD is generally earlier than AD (mean around 60 years old, in contrast to about 65 years in AD), early symptoms tend to be nonspecific and often solely neurological (e.g., reflecting cerebellar, visual, or extrapyramidal systems), and myoclonus with periodic EEG abnormalities may be present (Brown et al.). Unlike AD, wherein women appear to be slightly more likely to develop the disorder, CJD appears to be equally distributed in men and women (American Psychiatric Association, 1994; Brown et al.). Brain tissue examination is the only method available for confirming CJD, and many cases that had been diagnosed clinically as CJD are found on autopsy to have had another explanation for their symptoms (e.g., chronic inflammatory disease or rapidly progressive AD) (Brown et al.; Poser et al., 1999). In comparison to other clinical criteria (e.g., EEG or MRI), CSF 14-3-3 protein assay has been found to improve substantially the accuracy of a clinical diagnosis of CJD (American Academy of Neurology, 2001; Poser et al.). False positive and false negative results persist even with this diagnostic test.

Toxicant-induced dementia. Dementia can occur as a consequence of exposure to, or abuse of, toxic substances, including prolonged and extensive abuse of ethyl alcohol (see also section on ethyl alcohol in chapter 16). The most widely recognized dementia-related illnesses associated with ethyl alcohol abuse are *Wernicke's encephalopathy* and *Korsakoff's syndrome* (Dietemann et al., 2004; Reed et al., 2003; Rowland, 1989). These two syndromes are clinically distinct, with Korsakoff's syndrome often appearing after improvement in acute Wernicke's encephalopathy. While both syndromes can involve dementia, the cognitive impairments in Korsakoff's syndrome often are primarily amnestic, involving both short- and long-term memory. Although these syndromes have historically been associated with alcohol abuse, they likely are not the specific result of alcohol (Gui, Zhao, & Wang, 2006; Wilson, Kuncl, & Corse, 1958). Causal attribution in the case of alcohol-related dementia is complex, but thiamine deficiency, resulting usually from poor nutrition, is the factor believed to be primarily responsible for these clinical syndromes rather than alcohol itself (Brockington, 2006; Rowland, 1989; Thomson & Marshall, 2006). Although alcohol may play a contributory role in the development of nutritional deficiency, through poor eating habits or direct physiological effects on the gastrointestinal or other organ systems (e.g., the liver), conditions other than alcoholism when accompanied by thiamine deficiency (e.g., complications during pregnancy [hyperemesis gravidarum] or following bariatric surgery) also have been associated with these clinical syndromes (Attard et al., 2006; Reuler, Girard, & Cooney, 1985; Wilson et al., 1958).

Preexisting disorders compete in the diagnosis of dementia. Long-standing learning disabilities and general mental deficiency are important considerations in the differential diagnosis of dementia. While the pattern of results from neuropsychological examination can most often be used to identify long-standing cognitive and intellectual weaknesses and differentiate these from more recent alterations in behavior, change may be initially obvious only when one is familiar with the patient's history. For example, a middle-aged mother requested neurobehavioral evaluation of her 22-year-old son, stating that there seemed to be a change in his ability to learn and to remember things. The formal neuropsychological examination revealed impairments that were relatively substantial in comparison to normative data. The results were low generally, and included an FSIQ in the low 70s. The evaluation had been recommended by the patient's long-time family physician. In discussing the examination findings with this practitioner, he reported that the patient had likely never functioned at a level higher than that indicated by the current test results. The physician went on to disclose a lifelong history of mental retardation, describing the patient as a normally well-mannered young man with a caring but somewhat over-protective mother. The physician believed the mother's current concerns about her son arose because of the patient's reaction, and likely her own, to the recent death of the patient's maternal grandfather. He made the referral because of the mother's adamant concern that her son's change in behavior reflected an active neurological disease, even though his physical and neurological examinations had been normal. The patient's diagnosis of *mild mental retardation* was reaffirmed on the basis of psychometric results and formal diagnostic criteria (American Psychiatric Association, 1994), and these findings were discussed with the patient and his mother. The family was referred for brief family counseling, with beneficial results.

NERVOUS SYSTEM LOCALIZATION

The neurobehavioral symptoms and test findings in the current *case presentation* reflected involvement of the supratentorial level of the central nervous system, most pronounced in posterior, temporal regions bilaterally.

VERIFICATION OF THE INITIAL CLINICAL DIAGNOSTIC STATEMENT
AT THE TIME OF REFERRAL

The initial clinical diagnosis consisted primarily of a description of the patient's complaints, and this served as a basis for the revised, final diagnosis of *dementia of the Alzheimer's type, uncomplicated, probable.* The sleep problems listed in the original diagnostic statement were in remission, and this conclusion appeared to be accurate on the basis of historical report of examinations as well as patient and spousal report.

VERIFICATION OF THE FINAL CLINICAL DIAGNOSIS

The revised diagnosis of dementia, probable Alzheimer's type is adequate to explain most, if not all, of the important findings in the clinical presentation, including the patient's subsequent course of progressive behavioral deterioration. The diagnosis is parsimonious and best fits the implied physiology. Competing diagnoses that included depression or other psychological or psychiatric illnesses and adverse effects of medication were excluded.

AD is a diagnosis of exclusion, in that direct pathological verification is usually impractical at the time of clinical evaluation. Other potential causes for a patient's dementia must, therefore, be excluded in order to conclude the primary AD diagnosis and, therefore, the explanation for his symptoms. Documentation of dementia, clinically and before considering its cause or etiology, was based on psychometric examination, which considered and excluded the possibility that mood-related factors or extreme variations in normal behavior accounted for the findings. The various potential explanations were excluded in the present case, and the resulting diagnosis meets objective criteria for verification. The diagnostic and causal conclusions drawn here are biologically plausible, coherent, and compatible with extensive published scientific findings. *Age* has been said to be the greatest risk factor for developing AD (American Academy of Neurology, 2001; Morris, 2005a; Turner, 2006). The patient in the current *case presentation* is at the proper age for increased risk for the disorder, and the timing and course of his symptoms fit with the diagnosis. The behaviors found to be impaired were those known to be associated with the disorder, across studies using animal and human models, as was the pattern of behavioral deterioration over time (Turner, 2006).

The patient's dementia was documented clearly in the initial neuropsychometric examination, including verification of impairment in multiple cognitive domains aside from memory (e.g., visual-motor problem solving, reasoning, and other executive functions). General mental status was mildly impaired, both at the time of the referring physician's clinical neurological examination and in the neuropsychological examination that occurred subsequently. Also, comparisons made between historical and psychometric derived estimates of the patient's past levels of ability documented a decline from baseline in behavioral functioning. The level of severity of cognitive disturbance was too high to be explainable on the basis of normal behavioral variation or one of the milder conditions that are thought to be preclinical manifestations of progressive dementia (i.e., mild cognitive impairment [MCI], or isolated memory impairment [IMI]) (Berent et al., 1999; Morris, 2005b). The history provided by the patient's wife suggested gradual onset and decline in ability, beginning sometime between the patient's 66th and 68th year of life. Physical and neurological examinations and laboratory studies served to exclude potentially competing explanations for the patient's symptoms. The brain imaging study (MRI) findings (e.g., cortical atrophy that was most pronounced in temporal regions bilaterally) were consistent with the diagnosis of AD, and these findings helped also to rule out competing explanations for the dementia (e.g., a vascular etiology or frontal lobe disease). The absence of psychiatric disturbance, gait, or other motor disturbance was incompatible with Lewy-body disease. There was no history of infectious (e.g., HIV or other STD) or hereditary diseases, and the patient was in good general health except for his cognitive status.

Although the patient was irritable during the initial interview and appeared by history to have a somewhat irritable mood more generally, he did not appear to be depressed. His formal depression test scores remained within normal limits, even in the face of declining performance over time, and his motivation remained adequate for completing the tests presented in the examination. His wife's descriptions regarding continuing social interests and personal activities reflected behaviors that are contrary to depression. Also, the patient denied depression when asked directly during interview.

CAUSE/ETIOLOGY

While no cause/etiology was specified in the referral, the possible presence of depression or progressive dementia was mentioned; as was a history of possible medication-induced amnestic disorder. The classification of the patient's memory impairment in the current *case presentation* is dementia, probable Alzheimer's type. Although the specific cause of AD is not known presently, the diagnosis alone is used most often to explain a patient's symptoms of memory and other neurobehavioral abnormalities. This practice has practical utility because, in arriving at this conclusion, a number of competing explanations must be excluded, e.g., adverse affects of a potential toxicant (as in the current *case presentation*, a medication).

VERIFICATION OF CAUSE/ETIOLOGY

No specific cause/etiology was specified in the initial referral, and, therefore, there is no basis for formal verification. However, a history of possible medication-induced amnestic disorder was mentioned, with the implication that this medication history should be considered in explaining any finding of cognitive impairment. The patient's sleep medication, Ambien (zolpidem) was not explanatory to the patient's symptoms. While Ambien, a nonbenzodiazepine GABA$_A$ agonist with selective binding affinity for benzodiazepine receptor sites, can be accompanied by adverse psychomotor and amnestic effects, its half-life is very short (~2 hr) and any adverse effects have been shown to dissipate within approximately 8 hr of initial (10 mg) dosing (Swainston & Keating, 2005). There was some question regarding the patient's compliance with medication procedures, and conceivably this could have led to his being exposed to the drug without the physician's knowledge. However, the wife reported that, if anything, her husband had taken less of the medication than prescribed by his physician, and this suggested that Ambien was not an explanatory factor. Further, the history of sleep problems, for which the Ambien had been prescribed, was found on formal examination to be nonpathological and involved no apnea. That the previous problems with sleep were in remission suggested that neither sleep nor the treatment medication were contributory to the patient's cognitive status at the time of the present evaluation.

Conclusion

The behavioral condition of dementia can have devastating effects on the affected individual and, as much as any other illness, devastating effects on family and friends of that individual as well. Because of its dramatic effects, it is a condition that undoubtedly has been recognized since the beginning of human history. Understanding dementia is critical to neurobehavioral toxicology because its symptoms can mimic those of toxic disorder, yet they are nonspecific with regard to underlying disease or to its cause. Dementia presents the clinician and research investigator with multiple challenges. Its presence is obvious often only when relatively severe and, yet, even milder degrees of involvement can disrupt the person's normal routine and lead to lessened efficiency, emotional disturbance, and psychological pain. Many illnesses that cause dementia involve progressive neurodegeneration, but progression often is prolonged and mild impairments may go undetected for many years. Especially in the context of mild cognitive impairments or in the early stages of a progressively worsening dementia, the risk of misattributing symptoms to a specific cause is high. The predictive validity of clinical diagnoses is less than optimal even in some of the best researched and understood dementia-producing illnesses, e.g., AD.

Early and accurate classification of dementia depends on objective determination of the presence of specified impairments that define the condition and explain the patient's symptoms. This phase of the evaluation is accomplished relatively independently of causal considerations, at least beyond those that dictate the measurements needed ultimately to determine causality (e.g., indices of exposure to certain toxicants). Once the presence and nature of cognitive impairment is established, establishing the final, specific disorder will require the development of a differential diagnosis, often extensive in the case of dementia. The items on this list will dictate additional laboratory and other data as might be needed to validate the diagnosis. In large part, this aspect of diagnosis involves a process of exclusion. The final diagnosis and causal implications will need to meet objective criteria for establishing their accuracy. Because some dementias reflect underlying conditions for which a cause has not yet been scientifically determined (e.g., AD), the diagnosis itself is often treated as the (causal) explanation for the individual's symptoms and signs.

Headache

James W. Albers

Headache is a common complaint and one of the ten most common symptoms of patients presenting to clinicians in general. It was estimated that complaints of headache resulted in over 18 million office visits per year in the United States in the 1980s (Stang, Yanagihara, Swanson, & Beard, 1992). Chronic or recurrent headaches are classified into different groups based on clinical features such as frequency, pain quality (e.g., character, intensity, and location), and accompanying symptoms (e.g., photophobia, nausea, and vomiting) (Silberstein, 1992). The most frequent forms of headache are generally described as tension-type (muscle contraction) or migraine (vascular) headaches. Tension-type headache is near ubiquitous, with about 75% of the general population experiencing episodic or chronic tension-type headache in any given year (Rasmussen, Jensen, Schroll, & Olesen, 1992). Migraine also is a common disorder. On the basis of the population surveys of American households, over 11 million people experience migraine headaches that produce moderate-to-severe disability (Stewart, Lipton, Celentano, & Reed, 1992). Of these migraineurs, 3.4 million American females and 1.1 million American males experience at least one migraine headache each month. Similar results were found in other population-based studies, giving an overall age-adjusted incidence of migraine of 294 per 100,000 person-years for females and 137 per 100,000 person years for males (Stang et al., 1992). These clinic-based estimates undoubtedly underrepresented the true frequency of migraine because not all migraineurs seek medical attention. Regardless of the exact frequencies, tension headache and migraine are a source of substantial impairment impacting work, social functioning, and perception of general health status, particularly among young adults (Waldie & Poulton, 2002). There are many difficulties associated with occupational studies of nonspecific symptoms such as headache, for which no objective confirmatory tests exist (Taylor, Pocock, Hall, & Waters, 1970).

Clinical studies implicate numerous correlates of headache, including psychological factors like stress, personality type, and depression; foods; physical factors including disorders of the head and neck; and general systemic medical illnesses (Cook et al., 1989; Seltzer, 1982). Consider the numerous foods and beverages that have been implicated as causing headache syndromes. These include alcohol products, chocolate, coffee and tea, foods containing tyramine or aspartame, and numerous food coloring and flavoring agents (Seltzer, 1982). In a population-based cohort of elderly subjects, the prevalence of any headache type was strongly associated with concurrent pain other than headache, depression, bereavement, terminal sleep disturbance, and self-assessment of health (Cook et al.). It is not surprising that headache is commonly associated with exposure to toxic substances. Among the various headache classification schemes, the International Headache Society (IHS) includes a classification for headaches induced by substances or their withdrawal (Headache Classification Committee of the International Headache Society, 1988). In the setting of an inadvertent noxious exposure, headache may be a direct consequence of the exposure. Headache also may develop as an indirect consequence of the exposure, because of the stress and anxiety associated with real or perceived health concerns related to the toxic exposure. The following *case presentation* explores such an example.

Case presentation[2]

A 24-year-old graduate student presented with headaches that he attributed to a remote chemical exposure. He associated the onset of his headaches to new carpeting placed in his home several years earlier. At that time, he was aware of a strong smell of "new carpeting" when he first entered the home after the installation. The odor was unpleasant, and within hours he developed a diffuse, dull headache that was present the next morning when he awoke. The headache improved during the day at school but recurred shortly after returning home. The pattern continued, and he became alarmed because the severity and duration of the pain increased. A representative of the carpet company reassured him that there was no reason to be concerned about the installation, but he remained skeptical and consulted his family physician several weeks later.

By the time he saw his physician, the headache was described as constant, band-like, and nonpulsatile. It was bilateral and throughout his head with greatest intensity behind both eyes. He sometimes felt nauseated but never vomited. Eating did not seem to improve or worsen his headache. He had experienced headaches in the past, but no more than a few per month and none as severe as his current headaches. He drank one cup of coffee each day, during the week and on weekends, and he occasionally drank soft drinks that contained caffeine. There was no family history of headache. His examination was normal, and he was reassured that nothing serious was wrong.

His physician recommended several over-the-counter headache medications and prescribed a preparation that contained codeine. The medications initially improved his headaches, but the response was temporary. He refilled the prescription medication several times, because none of the over-the-counter medications had any persistent effect on the headaches that were present on awakening each morning. He developed a pattern of increasing the amount and frequency of the pain medications in order to get through the day. In addition, he complained of impaired concentration and difficulty sleeping, and he became increasingly anxious that something serious was wrong.

As his symptoms persisted and increased in severity, he became convinced that the new carpeting, which he could still smell, was the source of his escalating headaches. He sought the advice of a physician who specialized in chemical injuries. That physician concurred that chemicals in the carpeting could cause headache. Recommended evaluations included skin testing that showed hypersensitivity to numerous chemicals present in carpeting and glues. On the basis of the test results, he was told that he had developed a toxic headache syndrome. He was advised to remove the carpeting from his home, which he did. Improvement, if any, was limited, and his headaches remained controlled only by a codeine-containing medication. His family physician was reluctant to continue to prescribe codeine, and he began to seek additional opinions from numerous other physicians who provided him with a variety of headache medications, many of which were opiate-agonists.

When seen several years after the onset of persistent headaches, he could not remember being headache-free at any time in the past year. He was experiencing severe daily headaches that differed only in intensity. He had used many analgesic medications during the past year and had used some codeine-containing medication on a daily basis since codeine was first prescribed for him. He also was taking a selective serotonin reuptake inhibitor (SSRI) antidepressant. He acknowledged taking more of the pain medications than had been prescribed, but only when his headache was severe. Numerous neurodiagnostic tests had been performed in prior evaluations, including normal head MRI and cranial CT imaging studies, several normal electroencephalograms (EEGs), and unremarkable serological studies for "vasculitis."

On examination, he appeared depressed. He demonstrated poor eye contact and had difficulty concentrating. He also appeared angry, explaining that the carpeting had "ruined" his life. The general medical and neurological examinations, however, were normal, including auscultation for bruits (orbits, skull, and neck), ophthalmoscopy, and examination of the head and neck.

DIFFERENTIAL DIAGNOSIS

This patient's diagnosis at the time of his initial evaluation was "chemical-induced headaches," a diagnosis that remained essentially unchanged throughout the clinical course, including years after removal from exposure to the precipitating factor.

ALTERNATIVE CLINICAL DIAGNOSES

A single diagnosis does not explain this patient's headache syndrome. At onset, the original diagnosis of "chemical-induced" headaches is reasonable. However, as the headaches persisted after removal from additional exposure, a descriptive diagnosis of chronic daily headache syndrome is more appropriate. The nosology and pathophysiology of chronic daily headache is multifactorial, and uncertainty surrounds the definition (Bigal, Sheftell, Rapoport, Lipton, & Tepper, 2002; Welch & Goadsby, 2002). The category of chronic daily headache does not appear in the International Headache Society classification of 1988 (Headache Classification Committee of the International Headache Society, 1988), and this form of headache often evolves from episodic migraine (Sandrini, Cecchini, Tassorelli, & Nappi, 2001). Yet, this patient's headache description per se is consistent with diagnosis of muscle contraction headache, and the progression of headache occurred in association with chronic use of codeine-containing analgesic medications. In this setting, an additional consideration, and one similar to the original diagnosis of chemical-induced headaches, is medication overuse or "rebound" headache, a form of headache resulting from long-term overuse of analgesic and other headache medications. Rebound headache is, in fact, a form of chemical-induced headache, but the "chemical" in the *case presentation* is not the one originally felt to be contributing to the headache syndrome. Additional items that could have been considered in the differential diagnosis are discussed in the following paragraphs.

Discussion

The history is an important part of any neurological evaluation. Important elements of a headache history include a review of the patient's previous headache experience. This includes an attempt to determine if more than one type of headache is being experienced. The nature of individual headaches is described in terms of their spatial (e.g., primary location, spread, and radiation) and temporal patterns (onset, development, duration, and interval between headaches). Information of any warnings of impending headache is recorded. The characteristics of individual headaches are described (e.g., throbbing, boring, steady ache, periodic stabbing, lancinating, band-like pressure), as is the intensity (dull, moderate, severe, "worse headache of life"). The presence or absence of precipitating factors or "triggers" is explored, as are ameliorating factors, including medications. Associated symptoms surrounding the headache are important, including sensory (visual or somatic), motor (weakness), autonomic (nausea, vomiting, flushing, or tearing), and psychological (euphoria, depression, anxiety). A family history of migraine or "sick headaches" is relevant, because of the strong predilection of familial headache. Inquiry about previous carsickness or motion sickness as a child frequently accompanies migraine. Important elements of the headache examination, in addition to the neurological examination, include the general examination (blood pressure, cranial bruits, condition of teeth, jaw opening, sinus palpation, temporal arteries, and range of neck motion).

In terms of the *case presentation*, categorizing the patient's headache as a chronic tension-type headache is consistent with the criteria proposed by the Headache Classification Committee of the IHS (Headache Classification Committee of the International Headache Society, 1988). The reliability and validity of different forms of criteria, usually administered by questionnaire, have been addressed (Hagen, Zwart, Vatten, Stovner, & Bovim, 2000; Lipton, Stewart, & Merikangas, 1993). Because different types of headaches frequently coexist, it is reasonable to suspect that the different forms of headache simply represent a continuum having a common mechanism, differing only in severity. Recent epidemiological studies have identified different patterns, however, supporting the contention that tension-type and migraine headaches are distinct entities (Rasmussen et al., 1992).

There are very few headache types that produce neurological impairment during or independent of headache. The few headaches commonly associated with a positive neurological examination are summarized in Table 17.8. Most headaches are associated with a normal neurological examination (Table 17.9). Several kinds of neurodiagnostic tests are used to evaluate the different headache types, depending primarily on the type of neurological signs, if any,

Table 17.8 Headache syndromes associated with a positive neurological examination.

Syndrome	Features
Arterial insufficiency (ischemia)	Infarction, hypertension, focal signs, bruit
Glaucoma (acute)	Blurred vision, "halo" around lights, eye pain and redness
Mass lesions (neoplasm, subdural, malformation, hemorrhage, abscess)	Acute onset with hemorrhage, progressive, atypical headache, precipitate with change in posture, exercise, or valsalva
Meningitis/encephalitis	Progressive, severe, and diffuse pain, nuchal rigidity, confusion, personality change, focal signs
Migraine (during scotoma phase)	See Table 17.9
Pseudotumor cerebri	Visual obscurations, papilledema, enlarged blind spot
Subarachnoid hemorrhage	Abrupt onset, "worst headache of life," rigid neck
Temporal arteritis	Deep, boring headache in patient above 55 years of age, visual loss
Venous thrombosis (sagittal sinus)	Subacute, progressive somnolence with evidence of increased intracranial pressure

Table 17.9 Headache syndromes associated with a normal neurological examination.

Syndrome	Features
"Atypical" facial pain	Constant, boring pain usually present for years, unresponsive; abnormal psychological evaluation
Migraine (vascular)	Abrupt onset, associated with anorexia
Common	Nausea, vomiting, photophobia, unilateral, pulsatile
Classic	Prodrome (flashing lights, scintillating scotoma)
Complicated	Neurological impairment (hemiplegia, ophthalmoplegia)
Cluster	Unilateral boring pain just after falling asleep, tearing, nasal congestion, facial flushing
Muscle contraction (tension) headache	Slow onset, diffuse, "band-like" pressure
Rebound headache	Diffuse, severe, chronic analgesic "abuse"
Sleep apnea headache	Present on awakening, snoring, frequent arousals
Temporomandibular joint disease	Tender joint, pain with forceful jaw closure
Trigeminal neuralgia	Lancinating, "electric shock-like" pain

identified. Evaluations may include examination of the cerebrospinal fluid (CSF) (pressure, xanthochromia, bacteria, cell count, cytology, and protein), cranial CT or brain MRI, EEG, angiography, WESR, temporal artery biopsy, collagen vascular evaluation, tonometry (intraocular pressure), temporomandibular joint imaging, and dental examination.

NERVOUS SYSTEM LOCALIZATION

Several sources of head pain exist. Intracranial sources of pain include the venous sinuses, arteries, and the perivascular dura that is innervated by the trigeminal nerve. Extracranial sources include the skin, scalp (periosteum), muscles, arteries, cranial (V, VII, IX, X) and cervical (II, III) nerves, nasal and sinus mucosa, teeth, and ocular structures. Structures that are pain insensitive include the skull, most of the dura and pia, ependyma, choroid plexus, and the brain parenchyma. Stimulation of pain receptors includes mechanical (traction and distention of pain-sensitive structures) and chemical (blood and substances released by inflammation or ischemia, including histamine, serotonin, kinins, prostaglandins, and potassium) factors. The original models that associated tension-type headaches to muscle contraction and migraine headaches to vasoconstriction and subsequent reactive vasodilatation are dated and over-simplified explanations for the pathophysiology of headache. Newer hypotheses exist, including models of centrally generated or enhanced pain of hypothalamic neuronal origin (Silberstein, 1992). In these models, neurogenic inflammation mediated by the serotonergic and adrenergic pain modulating systems is proposed to account for some of the pain.

Neuronal degeneration, per se, does not produce headache. The concept that head pain reflects brain damage is a common misconception. Consider any of a number of central nervous system disorders such as AD, parkinsonism, multiple system atrophy, or cerebral infarction. All of these disorders are associated with neuronal degeneration. In some disorders, the degree of neuronal loss may be massive, and evidence of neuronal loss is apparent on imaging studies and documented on autopsy examinations. Yet, regardless of the magnitude of cerebral atrophy or tissue loss, headache does not accompany any of these disorders, with the exception of occasional headache pain during the acute phase of cerebral infarct in association with tissue swelling and mechanical displacement of surrounding tissues.

VERIFICATION OF THE CLINICAL DIAGNOSES

A scientific classification of headache remains inexact and relies on clinical descriptions in the absence of biological markers (Welch & Goadsby, 2002). On the basis of the normal examination and the description of headaches, the initial diagnosis of chemically-induced headache, and the subsequent diagnoses of chronic tension-type headache, chronic daily headache, and medication overuse or rebound headache all seem appropriate. The diagnosis of muscle contraction headache fulfills criteria proposed by the Headache Classification Committee of the IHS (Headache Classification Committee of the International Headache Society, 1988). This classification does not establish the cause of the headache type, but it requires that alternative explanations be explored. The diagnoses of chemically-induced headache and medication overuse or rebound headache imply that the cause of the headache syndrome is known.

CAUSE/ETIOLOGY

The unusual feature of this patient's headache was not so much that it was precipitated by exposure to a noxious odor. Rather, the persistence of headache that increased in severity long after removal from ongoing exposure remained unexplained and atypical of most headache types. The IHS criteria for headache induced by chronic substance exposure include the requirement that headache disappears within 1 month after withdrawal from the substance (Headache Classification Committee of the International Headache Society, 1988). The patient attributed the cause of his headaches to exposure to the new carpeting. He also came to believe that the substance damaged his brain, explaining both the persistence of headache and development of some symptoms attributed to altered cognition. This belief was supported by at least one of his treating physicians.

Very little is known about the cause of headache, and the pathophysiology of headache remains incompletely understood. What, then, is the relationship between "chemical" exposure and headache? Numerous substance and situations are capable of causing headache. The term "toxic headache" is frequently used to describe an headache that accompanies exposure to substances such as anticholinesterases, arsenic, benzene, carbon dioxide, carbon monoxide, carbon tetrachloride, ethyl alcohol, lead, pesticides, nitrates, and perhexiline, to name a few (Cory, 2003; Dalessio, 1987). However, toxic headache is more often used to describe the headache that accompanies several systemic illnesses, particularly those producing fever and including bacterial or viral septicemia. Toxic headaches also develop in response to withdrawal from an exposure to certain substances such as alcohol or caffeine (Dalessio, 1987).

The initial differential diagnosis for the patient in the *case presentation* appropriately included exposure to some noxious substance. Because headache developed in association with exposure to the new carpeting, it seems reasonable that some volatile chemical in the carpeting or the glues used to secure it were responsible for the initial headache syndrome. But certainly this transient exposure cannot explain the persistent headache still experienced by this patient, years after removal from exposure. Although numerous substances provoke the onset of a headache, no known substance produces a persistent or recurrent headache pattern independent of ongoing or recurrent exposure. What then should be considered in the differential diagnosis at the follow-up evaluations, after the headaches have persisted in spite of removal from additional exposure?

The differential diagnosis at the time of reevaluation was similar to the initial diagnosis, including the suspicion that the headaches were likely precipitated by a chemical exposure. The only difference reflected the chemical thought to cause the ongoing headaches. Included among the many substances capable of producing headache are numerous medications. Unfortunately, headache is one of the most common adverse symptoms reported for many common medications. For example, several of the SSRI antidepressants are used to treat chronic headache, but they also are known to precipitate headache in some patients. Codeine commonly provokes headache and, like many familiar substances including caffeine and alcohol, the headache often develops as part of a medication-withdrawal syndrome. The patient experiencing a codeine-withdrawal syndrome promptly responds to reintroduction of codeine, producing a pattern of pain—medication—temporary relief—recurrent pain—more medication. In this pattern, the source of the initial pain is usually irrelevant, as the pain is perpetuated by the medication, not the initial precipitant. Overuse of medications used to treat acute headache is thought to provoke headache, and the mean critical duration of use until onset of headache has been determined for several medications (Limmroth, Katsarava, Fritsche, Przywara, & Diener, 2002; Zwart, Dyb, Hagen, Svebak, & Holmen, 2003).

There are several models for the withdrawal-type headache syndrome. It has long been recognized that headache is a common postoperative problem. Only recently, however, was caffeine discovered to be a common source of this problem (Weber, Ereth, & Danielson, 1993). In a study of 233 patients admitted to the surgical service, postoperative headaches occurred in 22% of patients who routinely drank caffeinated beverages, but in only 7% of those who did not, and a significant dose–response relationship was demonstrated. Further, among those using caffeinated beverages regularly, those who drank caffeinated beverages on the day of surgery had a lower frequency of post-operative headaches than did those who abstained. The explanation is simple. Cessation of caffeine intake causes a withdrawal syndrome characterized by headache, malaise, and irritability. In a double-masked study of subjects who routinely consume caffeine, the caffeine-withdrawal syndrome resulted in a higher frequency of depression, anxiety, fatigue, and headache during the placebo period than at baseline or when administered caffeine (Silverman, Evans, Strain, & Griffiths, 1992). Despite these findings, others have found a lower frequency and severity of caffeine-withdrawal headache, particularly when participants were unaware of the caffeine-withdrawal focus of the study (Dews, Curtis, Hanford, & O'Brien, 1999).

The recognition of medication-induced headache, either as a direct effect or as part of a withdrawal syndrome, is important in understanding the headaches described in the *case presentation*. Medications are a common source of headache (Table 17.10). The most prominent contributor to this patient's headache syndrome is likely the codeine medication he had been taking for several years, although numerous medications produce a similar effect. Clinicians involved in the care of patients who have chronic headache confront serious medication overuse on a regular basis (Saper, 1987). In fact, it is estimated that as many as 50% of patients seeking help for headache indulge in excessive medication use to relieve their distress (Saper, 1989). The concept of medication rebound headaches was recognized in the 1980's (Saper & Jones, 1986; Rapoport, 1987). This syndrome involves daily or almost daily use of medications that inadvertently increase headache frequency and severity. Some headache specialists identify this problem as the single most important factor leading to chronic, treatment refractory headache (Rapoport, 1987; Saper, 1987). The special problems experienced by the patient in the *case presentation* are typical of patients who overuse medication. The overuse stems from the experience that the only symptomatic headache relief or improvement they experience follows administration of their medication. With increased medication usage, marital, employment, and social relationships deteriorate, and preexisting psychological problems intensify (Saper, 1990). Patients diagnosed with chemical-induced headache are occasionally "detoxified" to remove some purported causative neurotoxicants, few of which are ever identified as being present in unusual amount or available for removal. A perception that chemicals or substances we cannot measure or even identify are potentially more dangerous than medications is understandable, but such rationalization may impede removal from ongoing exposure to the "toxic" medication.

The patient in the *case presentation* is similar in many ways to a patient described by Schaumburg and Albers (2005) in the context of pseudoneurotoxic disease. The patient they described had a long history of migraine headaches, and she developed a headache shortly after a brief, trivial exposure

Table 17.10 Medications and substances which produce headache among their adverse effects.

Analgesics
 Nonsteroidal anti-inflammatory
 drugs (NSAIDs)
  Ibuprofen
  Indomethacin
  Ketoprofen
  Naproxen
  Phenylbutazone
Anesthetics
 Ether
 Ketamine
 Nitrous oxide
Antiasthmatics
 Aminophylline
 Budesonide
 Terbutaline
 Theophylline
 Zafirlukast
Antibiotics
 Aseptic meningitis
  Amoxicillin
  Cephalosporins
  Ciprofloxacin
  Isoniazid
  Penicillin
 Producing increased intracranial
 hypertension
  Ampicillin
  Minocycline
  Nalidixic acid
  Nitrofurantoin
  Tetracycline
  (intracranial hypertension)
 Nonspecific headache
  Amphotericin
  Chloroquine
  Griseofulvin
  Linezolid
Anticonvulsants
 Carbamazepine
 Gabapentin
 Valproate (withdrawal)
Antidepressants
 Selective serotonin reuptake
 inhibitors (SSRIs)
Antihistamines and histamine
Antihypertensive
 Atenolol
 Calcium channel blockers
  Nifedipine
  Mibefradil
  Nitrendipine
 Hydralazine
 Prazosin
Antiparkinsonian
 Bromocriptine
 Dopamine
 Pramipexole

Antiplatelet
 Dipyridamole
 Pentoxifylline
Caffeine (withdrawal)
Cardiovascular
 Amiodarone
 Ephedrine
 Isosorbide dinitrate
 Monoamine oxidase inhibitors
 Niacin
 Nitroglycerin
 Sympathomimetics
Foods and additives
 Aspartame
 Chocolate
 Citrus fruits
 Ice cream (cold induced)
 Monosodium glutamate (MSG)
 Sodium nitrate ("hot dog" headache)
Gastrointestinal
 Histamine (H2) receptor blockers
  Cimetidine
  Ranitidine
 Proton pump inhibitors
  Omeprazole
  Lansoprazole
Hormonal
 Anabolic steroids
 Danazol
 Oral contraceptives
 Antiestrogen agents (tamoxifen)
Illicit drugs
 Amphetamine (withdrawal)
 Cocaine
 Heroin cerebritis
Immunomodulators
 Azathioprine
 Corticosteroids
 Cyclosporin
 Intravenous immunoglobulin (IVIg)
Neuropsychiatric
 Benzodiazepine
 SSRIs
Oncologic
 Tacrolimus
 Muromonab (OKT3)
Radiological contrast
Vitamins
 Retinoids
 Vitamin A
Miscellaneous
 Allopurinol
 Intrathecal baclofen

"Medications and Substances as a Cause of Headache: A Systematic Review of the Literature," by T. Cory, 2003, *Clinical Neuropharmacology*, *26*, p. 122.

to a low-hazard organophosphate insecticide. The insecticide contained a hydrocarbon solvent vehicle that likely precipitated slight acute effects, including possibly a typical migraine headache. Following the brief exposure, she experienced intensification of her migraine headaches, eventually resulting in an erroneous diagnosis of "toxic brain syndrome." Like the patient in the *case presentation*, this patient's condition gradually evolved in the setting of chronic opiate analgesic use into a chronic daily headache syndrome, augmented by analgesic rebound. Unsubstantiated diagnoses of environmental-toxic related conditions promoted her psychological decline, during which time the consequences of chronic opiate administration, the only true toxic exposure, were not addressed.

How frequently does excessive use of over-the-counter or prescription analgesics lead to analgesic rebound headache? On the basis of a survey of 473 practitioners previously interested in the treatment of headache, more than 40% of respondents indicated that analgesic rebound headache was present in at least 20% of their patients (Rapoport et al., 1996). Most patients with rebound headache were women (almost 75%), and most were between 31 to 40 years of age. No one analgesic was consistently identified, and medications other than those containing caffeine were commonly implicated. In this study, depression was the most frequent psychological problem found to accompany analgesic rebound headache (Rapoport et al.).

Other factors may have caused or contributed to the present patient's headache syndrome, in addition to medication overuse. These factors include psychological features such as the progressive depression that developed in relation to his situation. A potential factor contributing to his depression included his strong belief that he has been permanently injured. In addition, a definite deterioration in his quality of life was produced by his continuous headache pain and increased medication use. Both resulted in progressive functional decline, with all of the attendant psychological features, many of which are capable of promoting or producing headache, independent of any medication effect. Somatic symptoms are clearly important features of depression, and the use of antidepressant medications in this patient was likely appropriate. Yet, there was no indication that headache was recognized as one of the possibly adverse medication effects.

It is established that patients with depression, particularly those seen by primary care physicians, frequently report somatic symptoms, including headache. How common are somatic symptoms among patients with depression? A large-scale study of 25,916 patients utilized data from the World Health Organization's study of psychological problems in general health care to explore the relation between somatic symptoms and depression (Simon, VonKorff, Piccinelli, Fullerton, & Ormel, 1999). Over 10% of the patients studied fulfilled criteria for major depression. Of these patients, 69% reported only somatic symptoms. About 50% of the depressed patients had multiple unexplained somatic symptoms, yet over 10% denied psychological symptoms of depression on direct questioning.

It might seem obvious that someone suffering severe intermittent or continuous headache would become depressed. In fact, the cross-sectional association between migraine and other forms of severe headache and major depression could reflect a psychological response to headache attacks. However, a similar relationship has been found for increased risk of developing headache among severely depressed patients (Breslau, Davis, Schultz, & Peterson, 1994). This observation suggests a shared mechanism for migraine and severe depression, not a simple causal explanation for the migraine-depression comorbidity.

Headache sufferers, particularly migraineurs but also patients with severe nonmigraine headaches, are frequently described as having psychopathologies other than depression. Such individuals are thought of as obsessional, rigid, angry personality types, and recent population-based studies have associated migraine and depression as well as migraine and panic disorder (Silberstein, Lipton, & Breslau, 1995). The association between migraine or severe headache and psychopathology has been investigated in several studies (Breslau & Andreski, 1995; Breslau, Chilcoat, & Andreski, 1996; Breslau, Schultz, Stewart, Lipton, & Welch, 2001; Merikangas, Merikangas, & Angst, 1993; Silberstein et al., 1995). While most of the studies have focused on the association between migraine and major depression, other relationships including an association between migraine and other severe headaches and panic disorder exist (Breslau, Merikangas, & Bowden, 1994; Merikangas et al., 1993). In a large survey of over 4700 subjects, the adjusted odds ratio of panic disorder was 3.7 (95% CI 2.2, 6.2) among subjects with migraine and 3.0 (95% CI 1.5, 5.8) among subjects with severe headache (Breslau et al., 2001). Panic disorder also was associated with an increased risk for first onset of migraine and for first onset of other severe headaches, although the influence was primarily from headaches to panic disorders. The presence of bi-directional associations makes selection bias an unlikely explanation for this finding, and suggests that shared environmental or genetic factors may explain the comorbidity of panic disorder and severe headaches (Breslau et al.). Other psychological factors, including neuroticism, appear to increase the risk for developing migraine (Breslau et al., 1996). This association persists even after controlling for potential confounders, including major depression and anxiety disorders at baseline, resulting in a relative risk for developing migraine of 2.9 (95% CI 1.1, 7.7). The relevance of these associations is poorly understood.

VERIFICATION OF CAUSE/ETIOLOGY

This patient's chronic headache syndrome likely had multiple contributing causes. Most prominent in the list of contributing factors was medication rebound headaches, resulted from long-term overuse of analgesic medications. Other considerations include a direct adverse medication effect from one of the medications, as well as psychological factors including depression. The rebound headache syndrome produced by numerous analgesic medications fulfills most criteria for causation. These criteria include animal models of withdrawal syndromes based on physiological changes, as it is unknown whether laboratory animals experience headache pain. Only by tapering and discontinuing the potentially offensive medications (detoxification), would it be possible to document criteria that are related to resolution of the headache. This recommendation to eliminate the potential offensive substance is frequently met with resistance from the patient, and psychological and physiological issues associated with dependency must be addressed. The daily headaches experienced by the patient in the *case presentation* eventually resolved after weaning from the offensive analgesic medications. He continued to experience intermittent headaches that were ultimately diagnosed as migraine and successfully treated with an anticonvulsant medication. Anticonvulsant drugs seem useful in clinical practice for the prophylaxis of migraine, an observation possibly explained by a variety of central nervous system actions that are probably relevant to the pathophysiology of migraine (Chronicle & Mulleners, 2004).

Summary

Headache is a common symptom that generally is nonspecific for a particular disorder. Yet, different patterns of headache can be identified, usually based on the clinical history. Numerous structures within and about the skull are known pain generators, but neuronal degeneration per se does not produce headache. The concept that pain is a symptom of "brain damage" is incorrect. Although many substances, including many foods and medications, are known to precipitate headache after acute exposure, no substance has ever been identified that is capable of producing persistent or recurrent headache independent of ongoing exposure. Patients with chronic daily headache frequently overuse medications in an attempt to control their pain. Rebound headache is a common clinical problem, not only from analgesic medications, but also from caffeine and alcohol. Not surprisingly, numerous psychological factors are important to headache that is common and sometimes predominant somatic symptom among patients experiencing depression, anxiety, panic attacks, and other forms of psychopathology.

Hepatic encephalopathy

James W. Albers

Numerous toxicants are hepatotoxic but not neurotoxic. Yet, in the presence of such toxins, neurologic dysfunction develops in the form of an encephalopathy from hepatic failure, not as a direct result of the hepatotoxin. The resultant hepatic encephalopathy is typical of most forms of encephalopathy, regardless of cause.

Case presentation[2]

A 20-year-old college student was brought to the emergency department by her roommates, who complained that she had been ill for almost 3 days after attending a campus party. Before attending the party, she had complained of not feeling well, and she borrowed acetaminophen from one of her roommates. She attended the party several hours later, where she ingested a substantial amount of alcohol. She returned home, took an unknown number of acetaminophen tablets, and went to bed. When she awoke, she complained of feeling nauseated and refused to eat. Over the next 24 hr, she remained in bed and began acting in a manner that was described by her roommate as "strange." Her past medical history was positive only for an isolated nocturnal seizure in her early teens. The seizure was not observed but only suspected. Nevertheless, she was prescribed phenytoin and had experienced no subsequent problems. She was using no other medications. The family history was negative for neurological disease.

On examination, vital signs were normal. The general medical examination revealed mild scleral icterus and a slightly enlarged, nontender liver that was palpable several centimeters below the costal margin. Neurological examination showed her to be alert and oriented. She was appropriately anxious about her situation, but she was easily distracted and complained only of feeling nauseous and fatigued. Her examination was otherwise normal.

Laboratory test results were remarkable for markedly elevated liver-function studies, including an elevated bilirubin level. A toxicology screen was positive for acetaminophen and phenytoin, the two medications she had taken. The alcohol level was not detectable. A cranial CT scan and an EEG were normal. The EEG was ordered in part because of the history of a remote seizure but also to identify evidence of a recent ictal event.

DIFFERENTIAL DIAGNOSIS

The medical diagnosis was acute hepatotoxicity, most likely due to the combination of phenytoin, ethyl alcohol, and acetaminophen. Additional considerations included infectious etiologies (hepatitis) or other hepatotoxins, all of which were excluded by laboratory testing, and congenital lever disorders, for which there was no supportive evidence.

Additional history

Over the next several days, the patient evidenced complete liver failure. Her only treatment options were general medical support and liver transplant, assuming a donor organ could be found. Her neurological condition progressively deteriorated. On the third day of hospitalization, the neurology consultant documented easy distractibility and disorientation to the day of the week and time of day. She appeared anxious and slightly agitated, refusing to answer what she termed, stupid questions. During the examination, she persistently picked at her clothing and rearranged the sheets and her clothing (akathisia). Reflexes were brisk, but not pathological. Over the next several days, she became increasingly drowsy and eventually lethargic. When awake, she had a prominent postural tremor of her outstretched hands and asterixis of her hands and feet. Her condition progressively deteriorated, and she appeared to sleep most of the time, being difficult to arouse. When awake, she was confused, combative, and disoriented. She had coarse saccadic eye movements and prominent nystagmus. Her language functions seemed normal, but she was grossly dysarthric. Muscle stretch reflexes became pathologically brisk with clonus, and she developed extensor Babinski and Chaddock signs. Occasionally, multifocal myoclonic jerks were observed, often in response to apparent volitional movement or startle. Several days later, she became unarousable. Her pupils were dilated but responded slowly to light. The ophthalmoscopy examination was otherwise normal, without papilledema. Painful stimulation produced decerebrate posturing, with forceful extension and inversion of her arms and legs. Cranial nerve brain stem function remained intact. Sequential EEG studies had shown deterioration with progressive slowing. Coincident with loss of consciousness, her EEG showed marked slowing in the delta range with prominent triphasic waves indicative of hepatic coma. Over the next several weeks, the EEG showed a progressive loss of amplitude, absent responsiveness to stimuli, and intermittent burst suppression.

FINAL DIAGNOSIS

The patient's physicians characterized her condition as representative of a severe, end-stage hepatic encephalopathy.

Discussion

The proposed diagnosis for this patient's neurological problem included both the neuroanatomical localization (encephalopathy) and the presumed cause (hepatic failure).

NERVOUS SYSTEM LOCALIZATION

All of the neurological symptoms and signs are referable to the supratentorial and posterior fossa levels of the nervous system, with the earliest and most prominent abnormalities involving the cerebrum.

VERIFICATION OF THE CLINICAL DIAGNOSES

On the basis of the history, clinical signs, and laboratory results, the diagnosis of hepatic failure was secure, as was the diagnosis of encephalopathy. Both diagnoses fulfill all criteria necessary to establish their validity. In the presence of hepatic failure, a diagnosis of hepatic encephalopathy is appropriate, although other conditions, such as a superimposed central nervous system infection, may coexist and contribute to the encephalopathy.

CAUSE/ETIOLOGY

This patient's medical problem (hepatic failure) was attributed to the combined use of phenytoin, ethyl alcohol, and acetaminophen. Each alone is a known hepatotoxin, and the three share common metabolic pathways in the liver (Artnak & Wilkinson, 1998; Makin, Wendon, & Williams, 1995; Walsh, Wigmore, Hopton, Richardson, & Lee, 2000). The combination of these and related substances is known to have a deleterious synergistic adverse effect on liver function, and toxic levels are easily established, resulting in complete and permanent liver failure (Schiodt, Lee, Bondesen, Ott, & Christensen, 2002; Wilson, Kasantikul, Harbison, & Martin, 1978). The epidemiology of hepatotoxicity is well established for a wide variety of substances, mostly medications. Elevated hepatic enzymes in response to starting a new medication is one of the most frequently observed indications of toxicity, and hepatic enzymes are routinely monitored for many medications. Animal models of hepatotoxicity are available for most of the known hepatotoxins.

In contrast, the cause of the neurological problem was only indirectly related to the combined ingestion of the medications and alcohol. Although acute ingestion of a sufficient quantity of alcohol, in and of itself, produces a transient intoxication that may progress to coma, in this case, all of the progressive neurological signs were interpreted to represent hepatic failure, not a direct neurotoxicant effect. Hepatic encephalopathy is a well-established syndrome, with a known progression of clinical impairments and EEG abnormalities in the presence of complete hepatic failure (Rothstein & Herlong, 1989). Among the different clinical tests, an abnormal EEG is strongly suggestive of overt hepatic encephalopathy (Saxena et al., 2002). In addition, correct prediction of future progression is one of the criteria important in confirming the clinical diagnosis of hepatic encephalopathy. The patient in the *case presentation* demonstrated almost all of the sequential signs associated with hepatic encephalopathy (Table 17.11). However, there are few, if any, characteristic features that distinguish hepatic encephalopathy from other forms of encephalopathy, absent evidence of liver failure.

The mechanism by which hepatic failure produces encephalopathy is unclear, although numerous hypotheses exist. Most neurologists agree that hepatic encephalopathy is a form of metabolic encephalopathy that has a multifactorial pathogenesis (Jones, 2002; Levine & Rothstein, 1996). The hyperammonemia associated with hepatic encephalopathy is thought to negatively impact central nervous system energy metabolism, but a causal relationship between the ammonia concentration and neurological effects has never been established (Bachmann, 2002). Moderate levels of hyperammonemia increase flux through the serotonin pathway due to increased transport of large neutral amino acids, including tryptophan, through the blood–brain barrier. The increasing levels of hyperammonemia increase cerebral blood flow and produce cerebral edema, in association with increased

Table 17.11 Symptoms and signs associated with increasing stages of hepatic encephalopathy.

Stage	Mental status/behavior	Clinical signs/EEG findings
1	Alert with mild confusion Anxious Irritable and agitated Depressed Impaired performance Short attention span Fatigue with altered sleep pattern	Postural tremor of outstretched hands Slowed coordination Restlessness (purposeless movements) EEG: normal to mild slowing (degree related to level of encephalopathy)
2	Drowsy Personality change Inappropriate behavior (disinhibited) Impaired cognition Disorientation to time Poor recall	Asterixis (flap of outstretched hands) Dysarthria (slurred speech) Akathisia (persistent purposeless movements) Primitive reflexes (snout, suck, grasp) Gross ataxia and paratonia EEG: progressive background slowing
3	Somnolent but arousable Bizarre behavior, paranoid Delirium Profound confusion Disorientation to time and place Incomprehensible speech	Progressive hyperreflexia Babinski and Chaddock signs Rapid respiration, incontinence Myoclonus Decreased seizure threshold EEG: delta waves (no alpha) and impaired reactivity
4	Progressively altered consciousness React to sound React to painful stimuli Coma	Decerebrate posturing (involuntary) Brisk oculocephalic reflexes Dilated pupils and nystagmus EEG: marked slowing with: Triphasic waves (hepatic coma) Unresponsive, burst suppression; flat

Modified from Office Practice of Neurology, by E. J. Levine and J. D. Rothstein; M. A. Samuels and S. Feske (Eds.), 1996, New York: Churchill Livingstone.

osmolytes in astrocytes and increased serotoninergic activity (Bachmann, 2002; Wendon, Harrison, Keays, & Williams, 1994). Ammonia levels are good predictors of impending cerebral herniation in patients with acute liver failure (Butterworth, 2002), and ammonia levels correlate significantly with the severity of hepatic encephalopathy (Ong et al., 2003). There is some evidence that hepatic encephalopathy may be caused by a decreased plasma ratio of branched-chain amino acids (BCAA) to aromatic amino acids, but the hypothesis is not supported by treatments that correct this abnormality (Als-Nielsen, Koretz, Kjaergard, & Gluud, 2003). There also is speculation that gamma-aminobutyric acid (GABA), the main inhibitory amino acid in the central nervous system, is involved in producing hepatic encephalopathy, perhaps via build-up and leakage of abnormal amino acids that mimic GABA in neurons (Albrecht & Zielinska, 2002). Functional brain imaging (e.g., PET) will undoubtedly be an important tool for investigating neuro-transmitter function in hepatic encephalopathy (Lockwood, 2002).

VERIFICATION OF THE CAUSE/ETIOLOGY

The association of encephalopathy and hepatic failure is well established, and application of the criteria for establishing causation to the diagnosis of hepatic encephalopathy is straightforward. Hepatic failure is a frequent cause of encephalopathy, fulfilling all of the Bradford Hill criteria for causation of hepatic encephalopathy.

Comment

In discussing encephalopathy, there are some things that can contribute to diagnostic confusion. For example, a diagnosis of *toxic encephalopathy* has been at times based on a classification scheme that some attribute to a 1985 meeting of the World Health Organization and Nordic Council of Ministers (World Health Organization and Nordic Council of Ministers, 1985) and occasionally refer to as the "WHO classification." In actuality, the classification (see Table 17.12) can be attributed to a series of meetings (World Health Organization and Nordic Council of Ministers, 1985; Baker et al., 1985; Baker & Seppalainen, 1987) and perhaps described in more detail in the report of the 1987 workshop (Baker & Seppalainen, 1987). When the "WHO classification" criteria are used to establish a clinical diagnosis, a use for which they are not well suited, individuals with nothing more than nonspecific symptoms may fulfill the criteria. In contrast, hepatic encephalopathy, one of the most common forms of encephalopathy diagnosed at any tertiary medical center, shows a spectrum of abnormalities that is far greater than considered in the "WHO classification." Contrast the symptoms, signs, and EEG results associated with different levels of hepatic encephalopathy (Table 17.11) to those listed in Table 17.12. Clearly, individuals fulfilling Type 1 or Type 2 encephalopathy would not even fulfill the entry criteria for Stage 1 hepatic encephalopathy. The criteria in Table 17.12, on the other hand, were better suited for epidemiological studies, not criteria to establish clinical diagnoses.

The prognosis for neurological recovery from such a profound level of cerebral dysfunction as demonstrated in the *case presentation* is remarkably

Table 17.12 Characteristics of encephalopathy as defined by the "WHO classification."

Type	Mental status/behavior	Clinical signs/EEG findings
1	Central nervous system "symptoms"	None
2	Mild toxic encephalopathy	
A	Predominant neurobehavioral deficit with mood or personality change	None
B	Intellectual impairment with abnormalities on neuropsychological testing	None
3	Severe chronic encephalopathy with features of dementia	None described

Modified from World Health Organization and Nordic Council of Ministers, 1985; Baker et al., 1985; Baker & Seppalainen, 1987.

good, assuming the hepatic failure can be resolved. It is known that the central nervous system is capable of showing remarkable potential for neurological recovery even after a severe level of metabolic encephalopathy. The common misconception that the brain is incapable of recovery is based on the limited ability at a cellular level for neurons to regenerate. However, substantial neurological dysfunction can result from profound metabolic problems that do not produce neuronal death. Surprisingly, the level of hepatic coma on admission prior to liver transplant is not a significant determinant of outcome (Schiodt et al., 1999). In the setting of hepatic encephalopathy, liver transplantation provides the means to successfully rescue such patients from near-certain death (Shakil, Mazariegos, & Kramer, 1999). Of course, liver transplantation is associated with neurological complications in over 25% of patients, with diffuse encephalopathy being the most common complication, occurring in 15% of patients (Lewis, 2003).

Contrast the information about the excellent prognosis for recovery from even severe hepatic encephalopathy to reports of persistent "toxic encephalopathy" characterized by irreversible intellectual impairment and persistent cognitive deficits resulting from exposure to some potential neurotoxicant producing minimal or arguable levels of impairment (Bruhn, Arlien-Soborg, Gyldensted, & Christensen, 1981; Feldman, Ratner, & Ptak, 1999). Review of such reports confirms that most are based on subjective symptoms as opposed to neurological signs, and normal imaging and EEG results, which are used to "exclude" other causes of encephalopathy. It is an interesting but a somewhat circular argument that the normal test results can be used to exclude other forms of encephalopathy, yet these same test results do not exclude the diagnosis of *toxic encephalopathy*. Similarly, subtle "abnormalities" on quantitative neuropsychological testing are used to confirm a diagnosis of toxic encephalopathy, yet they cannot be assumed to even represent deterioration from preexposure results, because preexposure test results usually are unavailable.

FOLLOW-UP CLINICAL INFORMATION

Within 6 weeks after admission, a donor liver became available and an orthotic liver transplant was performed successfully. For the first several days posttransplantation, there was little change in her neurological condition. However, as the level of coma began to recede, she became minimally responsive to painful stimuli and eventually showed purposeful withdrawal. Over several weeks, she progressively improved and eventually was transferred to the rehabilitation service. On the rehabilitation service, she showed continued improvement, and she was ultimately discharged to her parent's home after only 6 weeks of rehabilitation. She remained at home for the ensuing year, but she returned to college the following year, where she performed successfully academically and graduated 2 years later. On routine follow-up evaluations with the transplant service, she was described as completely recovered. A single neurological consultation confirmed that opinion, and there was complete resolution of all neurological signs of encephalopathy, including the EEG abnormalities, as expected (Ciancio et al., 2002). As an aside, the phenytoin was discontinued during her initial hospitalization and never restarted, despite the observation that status epilepticus may develop during hepatic encephalopathy (Eleftheriadis, Fourla, Eleftheriadis, & Karlovasitou, 2003). She remained seizure free.

Conclusion

Hepatic encephalopathy is one of the prototypical examples of cortical dysfunction characterized as encephalopathy. The progressive nature of hepatic failure permits evaluation of the neurological signs that develop sequentially in association with progressive levels of increasing encephalopathy. These signs become apparent when the mental status examination shows only relatively mild levels of abnormality. Untreated, the encephalopathy progresses to profound coma and ultimately to death. Accordingly, EEG abnormalities reflect the level of deterioration, and certain components of persistent EEG abnormality provide a quantitative index of the level of neurological dysfunction. Perhaps most important, patients with profound hepatic encephalopathy can experience complete recovery of neurological function if the underlying problem, hepatic failure, can be corrected. This degree of recovery demonstrates the impressive resilience of the nervous system to varying degrees of metabolic abnormality.

Hypothyroidism

Stanley Berent

The endocrine system, under the influence of the nervous system, works to maintain homeostasis, internally but also to maintain a balance between internal and external demands on the organism. Since these environments are changing continually, constant homeostatic adjustments are required. The ultimate viability of the organism depends on an effective messenger system to communicate between its constituent parts in order to coordinate internal and external inputs and needed actions. Hormones (from Greek, meaning to excite or stimulate to action) act as these messengers, integrating the information received with a biochemical program (Goldman & Bennett, 2000; McEwen, 1999), and select hormones mediate functions of the nervous system (Gill, 2000). Two classes of hormones bind to and communicate with two primary types of receptor sites. The two basic types of hormones are peptides and steroids, and they differ from each other in a number of ways, e.g., mode of synthesis, type of receptor site, and mechanisms of action. Hormones and their functional roles in the endocrine and nervous systems are complex and the interactions between the two systems compound the individual complexities. The illustration in Figure 17.1, reproduced from Siegel, Agranoff, Albers, Fisher, and Uhler (1999), provides a schematic representation of some of the known and possible interactions between the various constituents of the endocrine system.

The endocrine system, and thyroid-related processes more specifically, can become dysfunctional in multiple ways. In general, diseases or conditions that impair the production of hormones lead to states of deficiency, while diseases or conditions that cause overproduction of hormones result in excessive states. The excessive states frequently result from impaired feedback mechanisms, e.g., as occurs most commonly in neoplasia and autoimmunity (Gill, 2000). Increased production and release of thyroid hormone (*hyperthyroidism*), e.g., can result in *thyrotoxicosis*, a clinical syndrome that includes nervousness, emotional lability, and fine motor tremor in the hands and that results from exposure to excess thyroid hormone (Goldman & Bennett, 2000). *Grave's disease* represents a special instance of disorder resulting from hyperthyroidism. Patients

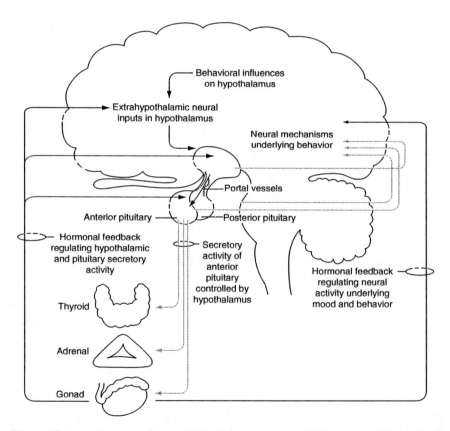

Figure 17.1 A schematic representation of known and possible reciprocal interactions among behavior, the brain, and hormonal systems. From *Basic neurochemistry: Molecular, cellular and medical aspects* (6th ed.) by G. J. Siegel, B. W. Agranoff, R. W. Albers, S. K. Fisher, & M. D. Uhler, 1999. Philadelphia: Lippincott-Raven. Reprinted with permission.

with hyperthyroidism can develop thyrotoxic crisis (*thyroid storm*), a life-threatening condition requiring appropriate medical treatment.

The most prevalent endocrine disorders, however, are those that result from states of deficiency (e.g., *hypothyroidism*) (Gill, 2000). Hypothyroidism results from decreased hormonal secretion from the thyroid gland. Hypothyroidism is termed *primary* when this condition results from the gland itself, *secondary* if caused by disease of the pituitary, and *tertiary* if the result of hypothalamic disease (Dillmann, 2000; Goldman & Bennett, 2000). When severe, hypothyroidism results in metabolic slowing and the manifestation of numerous symptoms and signs, including skin changes, myxedema, percussion myoedema, hair loss, weight gain, voice change, gait ataxia (due to midline cerebellar degeneration), myopathy, neuropathy (including compressive neuropathies), neurobehavioral abnormalities (including dementia or other impairments of cognition), and a variety of laboratory abnormalities, including elevated creatine kinase levels (American Thyroid Association, 2003; Davis, Stern, & Flashman, 2003; Dugbartey, 1998; Felz & Forren, 2004; Goldman & Bennett, 2000; Northam, 2004). Also, disruptions to normal thyroid function can have consequences for organ systems (e.g., cardiovascular) that, in turn, can adversely affect the central nervous system (Danzi & Klein, 2004).

Hypothyroidism that occurs early in life can have devastating developmental consequences when not identified and treated appropriately (Dugbartey, 1998; Frankton et al., 2000; Goldman & Bennett, 2000; Klein & Mitchell, 2002; Leger, Larroque, Norton, & Association Francaise pour le Depistage et la Prevetion des Handicaps de l'Enfant, 2001). When the disorder is present at birth, for instance, severe physical and intellectual abnormalities can occur (a condition termed *cretinism*) (Dillmann, 2000; Goldman & Bennett, 2000; Hirayama, Niho, Fujino, & Murakami, 2003; Lazarus, 2005). While cases of profound hypothyroidism are now rare in the United States, signs and symptoms of milder forms of hypothyroidism are fairly common, with estimates of prevalence that reportedly range from about 17% (Mayo Foundation for Medical Education and Research (MFMER), 2005) to 20% (Felz & Forren, 2004) depending on how cases are defined. The majority of these cases (90 to 95%) represent adult onset *primary hypothyroidism* (Goldman & Bennett, 2000). Also, Tunbridge et al. (1977) reported that many people may reflect some precursor of hypothyroidism without manifesting clinical findings sufficient to make a formal clinical diagnosis.

It has been estimated that about half of the approximately 27 million people in the United States who are believed to have thyroid disease are undiagnosed (Blackwell, 2004). There is wide agreement that, depending on severity of the hormone deficiency, the symptoms and signs of hypothyroidism vary between patients, the problems associated with hypothyroidism can develop slowly over a number of years, and that symptoms of hypothyroidism often are misattributed to simply getting older (American College of Obstetricians and Gynecologists, 2005; American Medical Association, 2003; Mayo Foundation for Medical Education and Research, 2005; Scatcherd, 2004); the last mentioned instance occurring perhaps especially in the elderly person with dementia (Lopponen et al., 2004). The attribution to aging is not surprising since symptoms associated with subclinical hypothyroidism can be nonspecific and, although hypothyroidism can occur at any age, including infancy and teenage years, the majority of cases involve the middle-aged and older, with women being seven times more likely than are men to develop thyroid dysfunction (Blackwell, 2004). Thyroid problems increase with age, and those over 40 years of age are more likely than younger people to have an underactive thyroid, even if not clinically diagnosable as hypothyroidism (Karlin, Weintraub, & Chopra, 2004). At the same time, symptoms in the early stages of hypothyroidism can be subtle, if not rare (Constant et al., 2006; Hepworth, Pang, & Rovet, 2006; Jha et al., 2006; Mayo Foundation for Medical Education and Research, 2005; Watt et al., 2006). Despite the paucity of overt symptoms, the presence of subclinical hypothyroidism has been associated with a number of neurobehavioral conditions (e.g., depression [Bhatara, Alshari, Warhol, McMillin, & Bhatara, 2004; Davis et al., 2003]) and medical disorders (e.g., Cardiovascular disease [Biondi & Klein, 2004; Imaizumi et al., 2004]). Also, spontaneous subclinical hypothyroidism can eventuate in overt hypothyroidism in the elderly over time (Diez & Iglesias, 2004).

Hypothyroidism that is left untreated, however, can cause many problems over time. Some of the more common symptoms and signs of hypothyroidism are listed in Table 17.13. Many of the symptoms listed in Table 17.13 are the same as or similar to the complaints made by persons suspected of having toxicant-induced injuries. This observation, together with the high prevalence of thyroid disorder in the general population, leaves it likely that patients who have thyroid dysfunction will be seen in the course of neurobehavioral toxicological examination, regardless of the stated reason for referral. The nonspecific nature of symptoms, the tendency for symptoms to be mild or absent in early stages of the disease, the aging-related nature of many of symptoms and signs, and the overlap of many these disease manifestations with psychiatric or psychological disorders likely explain why it is easy to overlook the early manifestations of thyroid disorder or to misattribute the findings to normal aging or other, nonthyroid-related illness. The following *case presentation* serves to underscore these points.

Case presentation[2]

A 47-year-old female was referred by her psychological counselor for neurobehavioral evaluation. The counselor had followed the patient off and on for the prior 6 years, having seen the patient initially for issues related to the breakup of her approximately 10 year marriage. At that time, the patient was diagnosed with anxiety and depression, which appeared to be entirely situational. She was initially in counseling for about a year, with no medications prescribed. Her depression and anxiety improved to the point that she no longer needed formal counseling. After her divorce, the patient completed a remaining year of college, graduated with a degree in business, and went to work for a national retailing chain.

Table 17.13 Symptoms and signs that are often attributed to hypothyroidism.

Abnormal menstrual periods

Abnormal physical and mental development (infants and children)

Anxiety

Ataxia

Brittle nails

Cardiac problems

Cognitive problems

Constipation

Constipation

Decreased libido

Decreased appetite

Delayed puberty

Delirium

Depression

Difficulty in school (children and adolescents)

Dry skin

Edema (myxedema)

Elevated blood cholesterol

Excitement
Fatigue

Forgetfulness

Gait ataxia

Goiter (with potential complications to breathing)

Hair loss (lateral 1/3 of eyebrows)

Hoarse voice

Late development of permanent teeth (developmental)

Mental retardation (*cretinism* in infants)

Muscle cramps

Muscle weakness

Myoedema

Painful, stiff, swollen joints

Paresthesias, upper or lower limbs

"Puffy" face

Sensitivity to cold

Short stature (developmental)

Slow relaxation phase of muscle stretch reflexes

Tender, stiff muscles

Weight gain

Taken from various sources, including the following: *Hypothyroidism,* Mayo Foundation for Medical Education and Research (MFMER), 2005; *Diagnostic and Statistical Manual of Mental Disorders,* by American Psychiatric Association, 2003, Washington DC: American Psychiatric Association; *Thyroid Disease,* American College of Obstetricians and Gynecologists, 2005; *Cecil Textbook of Medicine* (21st ed.), by L. Goldman and J.C. Bennett, 2000, Philadelphia: W.B. Saunders.

Following the completion of counseling, the patient stayed in touch with her counselor, contacting him periodically to provide reports of her progress. These reports had been consistently positive at first, but the patient most recently complained of a worsening of her mood and a general decline over the previous few years in her sense of personal well-being. Although there appeared to be no one event precipitating the change in her mood, the company she worked for had gone through a merger with some reorganization taking place during this same time period. She had been successful at her job and had appropriately risen through the ranks to her present position as a division head. She was not in danger of losing her job, but she had been asked to report to a new supervisor who was much more critical of her work than had been the previous manager. She was feeling stressed and found her work much less rewarding than in the past.

The referral asked for neurobehavioral evaluation in the face of gradual decline in behavioral efficiency with accompanying increase in depression.

INITIAL CLINICAL DIAGNOSIS

This patient's diagnosis at the time of referral was *major depression, recurrent*, with complaints of sadness, fatigue, and poor concentration.

CAUSE/ETIOLOGY

While no cause/etiology was specified in the referral, the initial clinical diagnosis and the history provided in the referral implied a change in mood that was reactive to life experiences (i.e., job-related stress and, perhaps, continuing adjustment difficulties).

RESULTS OF CLINICAL NEUROBEHAVIORAL EVALUATION

Clinical interview and history. The patient was cooperative and pleasant during interview. She related normally and efficiently in terms of interpersonal communications and appeared to be an accurate historian, reporting the major points conveyed in the referral. Some additional information in the current interview included her description of average performance throughout her school years, with no history of learning disability, or special education. She believed she had adjusted to her divorce well, stating that, in fact, she probably would not have completed college if the marriage had continued. She dated occasionally but said she had no interest in marrying again. She liked her job but recently had become concerned that she might be laid off as a result of the present reorganization. Her chief complaints included feeling mildly depressed and anxious (which she saw as including decline in her usual energy level, appetite, and libido), increased forgetfulness, and difficulty concentrating at work. In reviewing the complaints with her, she acknowledged that she viewed her present job situation as stressful. Her demeanor appeared to be consistent with mild depression, and she denied suicidal thinking or other serious symptoms of depression.

When asked about medications, she confided that she never liked taking medications and that she was at times negligent in remembering to take them. She reported a history of hypothyroidism that dated to her early adulthood, treated since that time with Synthroid (levothyroxine). When confronted directly, the patient admitted to not being as conscientious as she knew she should be about taking her medicine. Also, she confided that she had not seen her personal physician for several years. The patient was assisted in making an appointment with her primary care physician and given a return appointment to our clinic in 6 months.

Neuropsychological Examination. Table 17.14 contains selected results from the patient's two neuropsychological examinations, the current examination as well as the results obtained at a follow-up evaluation approximately 6 months later. In terms of the first of these examinations, the results indicated an average level of intellectual ability in verbal and nonverbal areas. These scores together with her measured average vocabulary and reading recognition levels were consistent with her reported educational and vocational history. Although the patient was well oriented to her surroundings and her

Table 17.14 Results of Serial Testing (6 months apart) in a patient with symptoms of hypothyroidism and depression.

Test administered	Domain measured	Test results time 1	Test results time 2
WAIS-III, VIQ	Verbal intellect	93	96
WAIS-III, PIQ	Performance intellect	90	97
WAIS-III, Vocabulary	Vocabulary level	10	9
WAIS-III, Similarities	Abstract conceptualization	8	9
WAIS-III, Block Design	Visual-motor problem solving	9	10
WAIS-III, Digit Symbol	Psychomotor problem solving	9	10
MMSE	General mental status	23/30	27/30
WMS-III, Auditory Immediate	Verbal, immediate learning	78	86
WMS-III, Auditory Delay	Verbal, delayed recall	69	82
WMS-III, Visual Reproductions I	Visual, immediate learning	10	10
WMS-III, Visual Reproductions II	Visual recall	8	9
WRAT-3, Reading	Reading recognition	105	102
MMPI-2 Clinical Scale 2 (D)	Clinical rating of depression	$T = 77$ Moderate depression	$T = 65$ Mild depression

Selected tests were chosen that were repeated across examinations and that reflected a range of neuropsychological domains sufficient to discern a meaningful clinical pattern.

general mental status judged to be normal by observation, her score on the MMSE (23 of 30) was at the border of normality. Her difficulties on the MMSE were limited to missing two of three items on the delayed recall and all items on serial sevens subtraction. She was able to spell a word backwards without error. Also, the patient earned mildly impaired scores on verbal and visual learning and memory on the WMS-III. Other than these instances of difficulty in attention and concentration on the MMSE and learning and memory on the WMS-III, the patient scored normally in other areas of cognitive function. Also, she appeared to be normal in terms of language and psychomotor abilities.

From an emotional viewpoint, the patient admitted to a history of depression that she dated to early adulthood and described herself as moderately depressed at present. Although her depression waxed and waned in terms of severity, she said that she recently seemed always to be at least mildly depressed. Her primary physician had at times prescribed antidepressants, especially around the time of her divorce; but she had not been compliant with them because of her aversion to medication in general. She completed a valid MMPI-2, with a depression scale score that placed her within the moderately severe level of affectual disturbance (scale 2, T = 77). Other scale scores within the clinical range included scale 7 (T = 66), most likely reflecting very mild anxiety, and scale 0 (T = 68), suggesting mild tendencies to social withdrawal. There was no indication from interview or testing for the presence of thought disturbance or other psychoses.

ADDITIONAL INFORMATION

The patient was seen by her primary physician shortly after her first neuro-behavioral evaluation, who reported a normal physical examination, including neurological examination. However, hypothyroidism was diagnosed based on laboratory (elevated TSH = 7.0 and below normal T_4 = 3.8) and clinical findings that included forgetfulness and difficulties with concentration. The patient was given a new prescription for levothyroxine and counseled regarding the importance of complying with the medication regimen.

The patient again was seen for neurobehavioral evaluation about 6 months following her initial visit. She reported feeling better in general, physically and emotionally on this occasion than she did on the first visit. While some of her difficulties at work continued, these did not seem to bother her as much as before. Her neuropsychological examination was repeated. The results (Table 17.14) reflected generally improved scores in most areas tested. The most substantial changes in scores occurred on the MMSE, where she was now able to complete two of the three delayed recall items and three of the five items on serial subtractions. On the WMS-III, her scores were higher in comparison to her first testing and essentially normal on verbal and visual delayed recall. Her depression score on the MMPI-2 was now at the border of normality, an improvement in test result consistent with her self-report in interview. The neurobehavioral evaluation results were communicated to the patient's counselor, with the recommendation that special attention be given to medication compliance issues.

The initial diagnosis was revised to include cognitive impairment (likely reversible) due to a primary medical condition, hypothyroidism. The diagnosis of *major depression, recurrent* was changed to *mood disorder due to a general medical condition*, i.e., *hypothyroidism* (American Psychiatric Association, 1994).

Comment

A clinical neurobehavioral diagnosis of dementia was excluded from the differential diagnosis in favor of a more general designation of *cognitive impairment*. In fact, impaired cognition was documented on the basis of test findings, e.g., below normal verbal memory. However, the criteria for diagnosing dementia also include multiple cognitive impairments in addition to memory, a decline from prior levels of functioning, and impaired social or occupational functioning (American Psychiatric Association, 1994). In addition to memory impairment, a decline in functioning could be established most likely on the basis of interview and history. The patient was able, however, to continue her work and other daily social and personal activities without significant impairment, leading to the exclusion of dementia. The finding of improved functioning following reinstatement of her treatment for hypothyroidism warranted the added designation of "reversible."

Both the cognitive impairment and mood disorder were seen as due to the patient's hypothyroidism. The diagnostic history of *major depressive disorder* was noted, as was the presence of work-related stress, as both could have contributed to some extent to the patient's symptoms.

Discussion

Establishing a diagnosis of hypothyroidism in adults is relatively straight forward once the proper examination and laboratory tests are conducted. The endocrine system is responsible for maintaining appropriate and coordinated responses between the environment and the nervous system, i.e., maintaining homeostasis. Communication between cells is critical to maintaining homeostatic regulation, and hormones serve as the messengers in this process. Just as there are several types of hormones, each with specific functional capacities, so too there are a number of glands and feedback systems associated with these glands. The thyroid is one such gland, and it accomplishes its functions via feedback loops that include the hypothalamus, pituitary, and thyroid (Barchas & Altemus, 1999; Goldman & Bennett, 2000; McEwen, 1999) (see Figure 17.1). Each component in this system has a role to perform, the hypothalamus produces *thyroid-releasing hormone* (TRH), which energizes *thyroid-stimulating hormone* (TSH) that, in turn, signals the production of thyroid hormone. This last hormone feeds back on both pituitary and hypothalamus to complete the process. The main secretion of the thyroid is *thyroxine* (T_4), which is produced by the thyroid gland exclusively. *Triiodothyronine* (T_3) is derived partly from thyroid secretion but mostly by conversion of T_4. Normal thyroid function depends on normal TSH levels and adequate intake of iodine (Goldman & Bennett, 2000).

The results of physical and laboratory examinations are important to the neurobehavioral toxicological evaluation, and should include evaluation of endocrine function whenever clinical suspicion of hypothyroidism is present. Evaluation for possible thyroid disease involves physical examination of the thyroid, laboratory tests of thyroid function, and may also include other specific tests such as ultrasonography and radioactive iodine uptake scan.

As mentioned in the introduction, hypothyroidism reflects a state of deficiency in the trace mineral, iodine. Iodine is found naturally in many seafoods and seaweed, and iodized salt represents an important nutritional source of this mineral. Iodine is essential in the production of thyroid hormones. Although severe deficiency in the United States is rare currently, thyroid disorders were fairly common before the 1920s, most likely because of lack of iodine in the diet. Even today as many as 200 million people worldwide may suffer from iodine deficiency (Mayo Foundation for Medical Education and Research, 2005). The problem appeared to be eliminated in the United States by adding iodine to table salt. Nevertheless, milder symptoms and signs of hypothyroidism continue to be fairly common. A population study of 25,000 patients in the United States, for instance, reported the prevalence of hypothyroidism as 21% of the females and 16% of the males studied (Canaris, Manowitz, Mayor, & Ridgway, 2000). Exposure to some medications and other substances (e.g., lithium) also can adversely affect thyroid function, as can a number of medical illnesses and treatments (e.g., autoimmune disease, radiation treatment, thyroid surgery) (Mayo Foundation for Medical Education and Research, 2005).

In addition, many people may reflect some precursor of hypothyroidism even though they do not manifest clinical findings sufficient to diagnose the disorder. Tunbridge et al. (1977) reported finding elevated levels of thyroid-stimulating hormone (TSH) in 7.5% of the females and 2.8% of the males in their study of 2,779 patients in England. Over a 20 year follow-up with these same patients, the investigators found an 8-fold increase in the odds ratio for developing hypothyroidism on the basis of initial elevation of TSH alone, but a greater than 30-fold increase if TSH were elevated along with elevated antithyroid antibodies. The odds ratios for men were even greater than for women using the same predictor variables (Felz & Forren, 2004; Tunbridge et al.).

NERVOUS SYSTEM LOCALIZATION

This *case presentation* reflects the involvement of the interaction between endocrine and nervous systems, and more specifically involvement of the thyroid and its interaction with the nervous system. The neurobehavioral symptoms and test findings in the current *case presentation* reflected involvement of the supratentorial level of the central nervous system (e.g., depression, memory, and concentration).

VERIFICATION OF THE INITIAL CLINICAL DIAGNOSIS

The sole diagnosis of *major depression, recurrent* was not adequate to explain the most important findings in the *case presentation*. The lack of specification of an underlying medical condition lacked coherence and did not fit the overall pattern of the patient's illness, e.g., it left the recurrence of depression following successful treatment of that condition unexplained. Difficulties with concentration were mentioned by the referring clinician, with specification of any possible neuropsychological impairment deferred to specialty examination. Other objective criteria used to verify a clinical diagnosis were not met and, overall, the diagnosis failed to predict the subsequent illness course.

VERIFICATION OF THE REVISED CLINICAL DIAGNOSIS

The revised diagnoses are adequate to explain the most important, if not all, of the findings in the clinical presentation. While cognitive impairment can occur in depression (Zakzanis et al., 1999), the separate diagnoses reflecting her various symptoms were justified, and necessary to account for the neuropsychological findings as well as being coherent and to best fit the illness pattern and subsequent course. Together, the revised clinical diagnosis provided the simplest explanation for the clinical findings.

VERIFICATION OF CAUSE/ETIOLOGY

No specific cause was advanced to explain the initial clinical diagnosis. While the diagnosis of major depression can be considered to be idiopathic, requiring no causal specification, the revised diagnoses do carry such a demand.

VERIFICATION OF REVISED CAUSE/ETIOLOGY

The patient met *DSM-IV* criteria for both *mood disorder due to a general medical condition*, i.e., hypothyroidism, and cognitive impairment (American Psychiatric Association, 1994). However, the finding of hypothyroidism, with verification of improved cognitive and emotional functioning following the successful treatment of this medical condition, necessitated specifying that these conditions were most likely due to the underlying medical condition. The patient reflected a history of major depression, but she did not appear to reflect continuing low mood as to justify a *dysthymic* disorder. Although she acknowledged that she had been under some work-related stress, the clinical evidence did not appear to alone justify this as sufficient to explain the magnitude of her depression or difficulties with cognition. Depression is known to sometimes occur early in hypothyroidism and can increase in severity over time (Demet et al., 2003; Karlin et al., 2004; Mayo Foundation for Medical Education and Research, 2005). Also, some of the symptoms that purportedly occur in hypothyroidism (see Table 17.13) are similar to those associated with depression, even when depression is not formally specified in a given case (e.g., decreased libido, change in weight, fatigue). The presence of psychological stress is common in hypothyroidism and may even play an interactive role in some of the cognitive impairments seen in this medical condition. For instance, Gerges, Alzoubi, Park, Diamond, and Alkadhi (2004) used a rat model to show that while learning and memory were adversely affected by either chronic stress or hypothyroidism, the combination of both stress and hypothyroidism produced more severe and longer-lasting memory impairment than did either condition alone.

The proposed causal role for hypothyroidism in the current *case presentation* meets objective criteria for verification. As reviewed earlier, the risks and clinical manifestations of changes in thyroid function are well established and include the symptoms reported by this patient. The timing of her complaints is appropriate, and the relationship between signs, symptoms, and the proposed physiological cause is biologically plausible. This plausibility is strengthened further by the sensibility of the severity of thyroid deficiency and neurobehavioral impairments and the improved neurobehavioral functioning following improved thyroid functioning. The neurobehavioral manifestations in the *case presentation* included only those that are known to occur in hypothyroidism, including the relatively specific as opposed to general nature of her cognitive impairments (Burmeister et al., 2001). The diagnoses and causal determinations in this case were developed within a differential diagnosis model that considered a variety of potential causes for the patient's problems.

Comment

Depression affects motivation and energy level and can be a factor that interferes with treatment compliance (Sevinc & Savli, 2004). While not made as a formal diagnosis, the patient's medication compliance issues, in themselves contributory to her clinical problems, were communicated to others concerned with the patient's clinical treatment. Also, it is possible that the patient's history of depression, job-related stress, or other factors yet unknown contributed in some part to the findings in this case presentation. Emotional or other psychological disorders can interact with thyroid dysfunction, resulting in more severe psychopathology than might otherwise be the case and with each component of the patient's condition requiring independently targeted treatment (Bhatara et al., 2004). Bhatara et al. (2004), for instance, reported a 10 year follow-up study of a patient who developed hypothyroidism and psychosis at age 13 years. He was treated initially with a combination of antipsychotic medications and levothyroxine. At age 21, however, he discontinued his psychotropic medications while continuing to take levothyroxine. His psychotic symptoms returned within 2 months of his terminating his medications, requiring hospitalization. The patient's levothyroxine was discontinued, and he was placed on antipsychotic medication alone. However, his psychosis continued and it was only after being placed on a combination of levothyroxine and psychotropic medications that his symptoms subsided. The patient's symptoms in the current *case presentation* were never as severe as those described by Bhatara and colleagues. It would not be unexpected, however, if at some point the patient required counseling or similar clinical treatment for her emotional symptoms. While her thyroid dysfunction may have been corrected, this would not remove the stresses she might experience at work or in other aspects of her life. With the successful treatment of her thyroid dysfunction, however, she should be better able than in the past to cope effectively with such stresses.

Conclusion

Whether over- or under-active, thyroid disorders can lead to emotional problems and cognitive difficulties. Hyperthyroidism can be associated with anxiety, irritability, or an overly excited state, while depression and fatigue can be a result of hypothyroidism. Manifestations of emotional symptoms alone that result from thyroid dysfunction are considered rare and not specific to thyroid dysfunction when these symptoms occur in an individual patient; however, hypothyroidism has been reported to worsen depression even when it is not the direct cause of the emotional disturbance (Demet et al., 2003). When present, depressive symptoms can be expected to improve with effective treatment of the underlying thyroid disorder (Mayo Foundation for Medical Education and Research, 2005). Nevertheless, the possibility of thyroid dysfunction, as well as other underlying medical conditions, should be considered always in forming the differential diagnosis related to mood and other neurobehavioral disorders.

Hypoxic encephalopathy

James W. Albers

Numerous substances are considered neurotoxicants because they are associated with hypoxia, either by competing with oxygen for hemoglobin binding (e.g., carbon monoxide) or by producing sedation and a resultant respiratory arrest (e.g., central nervous system depressants). It remains unclear for many of the neurotoxic substances that produce hypoxia whether or not they are neurotoxicants in and of themselves, in the absence of hypoxia. In general, however, for most substances producing loss of conscious and depressed cardiopulmonary function, the consequences of excessive exposure can be explained by the resultant hypoxia/ischemia, as opposed to an independent direct neurotoxic effect. Principles important to this concept are discussed in reference to the following case presentation.

Case presentation[2]

A coworker found a 62-year-old custodian unconscious in a remote area of the company's storage facility. The custodian was on the floor in an area that he had been cleaning. There was no evidence of obvious trauma and no unusual odors suggestive of exposure to some noxious substance. It was unknown how long he had been unconscious, and it was unclear exactly what he had been doing immediately prior to becoming unconscious. His cleaning cart was nearby, and his mop was on the floor beside him. The floor was still damp, and his cleaning bucket contained only a soapy material. Because he was found in an area of the building that contained many chemicals, the possibility of an inadvertent overexposure to some yet unidentified substance was considered. The coworker sounded an alarm calling for help, opened a nearby door to the outside of the building, and began to administer cardiopulmonary resuscitation because the custodian did not appear to be breathing.

The rescue squad arrived within 10 min. Cardiopulmonary resuscitation was continued after it was established that he was pulseless. Upon their arrival, a few jerking extremity movements that were thought to resemble a seizure were noted. The rescue squad verified that there were no obvious signs of trauma. The custodian was placed on a spine board for transportation, an intravenous line was started and glucose was given, blood was obtained for subsequent analyses, oxygen was provided by mask, and a cardiac monitor and a pulse oximeter were placed on the patient. A blood pressure was unobtainable. The cardiac monitor showed a severe bradycardia (pulse rate of about 30) and complete atrial-ventricular blockade. The SaO_2 level was 52%. Intubation was attempted, but the attempt was unsuccessful. The patient was transported to the emergency department of a local hospital.

In the emergency department, asystole developed. Intubated was completed successfully and he underwent successfully cardioversion. After resuscitation, his vital signs were stable with a respiratory rate of 18 per min, a blood pressure of 150/90 mmHg, and a pulse rate of 130 bpm. His postresuscitation cardiogram was unremarkable. On examination, he was deeply comatose and showed no response to deep pain. On admission to the emergency department, the pupils were not dilated, but they did not respond to light. Shortly after intubation, however, he had normal pupillary, corneal, oculovestibular (Doll's eye movements), and gag reflexes. Muscle stretch reflexes were brisk (3 to 4+), with unsustained knee and ankle clonus. Bilateral Babinski and Chaddock responses (abnormal) were elicited.

Initial laboratory results included arterial blood gases obtained after arrival at the emergency department just prior to intubation. Those studies showed evidence of a respiratory acidosis, with a low pH (7.21), an elevated $PaCO_2$ (50 mmHg), and a normal PaO_2 (recorded while receiving oxygen by mask). A carboxyhemoglobin level was slightly elevated (2%), but all other laboratory studies were unremarkable, including normal glucose, urea nitrogen, liver enzyme, and electrolyte levels. A toxicology panel of blood and urine was obtained and later reported as normal. The initial cardiac evaluation, which included an urgent cardiac catheterization, was unremarkable. Serial cardiac enzymes and electrocardiograms showed no evidence of cardiac ischemia or infarction. A cranial CT scan, performed emergently to exclude the presence of cerebral hemorrhage, was interpreted as normal. An EEG, performed several hours following admission to the hospital, was of low amplitude with moderate diffuse slowing in the theta range. The EEG responded poorly to any stimuli (auditory, visual, or tactile). On the basis of the history and test results, the patient was assumed to have experienced a cardiac dysrhythmia resulting in cerebral hypoxic ischemia. It was impossible to establish the magnitude or duration of hypoxia.

The family was contacted and the past medical history was said to be negative, as were the social and occupational histories. He was taking no medicines on a regular basis. He smoked cigarettes (40 pack year history), and he used alcohol occasionally. The initial diagnosis of cerebral hypoxic ischemia was attributed to a cardiac dysrhythmia, although other causes had not been eliminated. The plant physician was concerned that the findings could represent a toxic encephalopathy or a toxic exposure producing hypoxia. An industrial hygiene evaluation identified evidence of a small spill near the site of the incident, which was later identified as the cleaning solution containing soap. Air monitoring analyses identified no unusual substances. No other evidence of any toxic substance was identified in the vicinity, and none of the laboratory studies of blood or urine raised concern for a toxic exposure (other than the slightly elevated carboxyhemoglobin level).

DIFFERENTIAL DIAGNOSIS

This patient's diagnosis was acute hypoxic encephalopathy due to cardiopulmonary arrest. Primary diagnostic considerations included a myocardial infarction or a cardiac dysrhythmia. Additional differential diagnosis items listed in the record, all of which were related to his unconsciousness, included a possible seizure disorder with a prolonged postictal episode and acute intoxication due to some unidentified substance (e.g., carbon monoxide). Initial concerns about possible head trauma, cerebral or subarachnoid hemorrhage, or acute metabolic abnormality (hypoglycemia or electrolyte abnormality) were excluded by the initial examination and by the cranial CT and laboratory evaluations performed emergently.

Additional information

Examination after 6 hr of admission showed little change in the neurological examination. Brain stem reflexes remained intact. There were no volitional or purposeful movements, and painful stimuli resulted in limited movement but no decerebrate posturing or forced extension of the arms and legs. Reflexes remained diffusely hyperactive with unsustained clonus and plantar responses remained extensor. Over the next 8 hr, he began to improve, showing purposeful movements and withdrawal from painful stimuli. He opened his eyes to auditory stimuli, and he followed moving objects with conjugate eye movements. His chest x-ray was normal, without evidence of aspiration, and he was extubated shortly thereafter.

The morning after admission, this patient showed dramatic improvement in his neurological status. He had regained consciousness and was responding appropriately to simple questions. However, he remained somewhat confused and had no memory of events of the previous day, including the events many hours before he was found unconscious. A brain MRI performed 72 hr after admission showed subtle, diffuse white matter abnormalities compatible with ischemia/hypoxia, and numerous small, discrete areas of possible infarction. There was no cerebral atrophy, but there was blurring of the white and gray matter junction, suggestive of mild edema due to diffuse hypoxia. He continued to show clinical improvement, and within an additional 24 hr, his family felt he had returned to his baseline level of function. The bedside neurological examination of mental status was said to be normal, and plans were made to complete his cardiac evaluations.

Shortly after transfer from the intensive care unit to a monitored bed in the step-down unit, he experienced a second acute event during which he suddenly lost consciousness and his cardiac monitor showed prolonged asystole. He again underwent emergent cardioversion. His subsequent electrocardiogram showed bradycardia with a complete atrial-ventricular block requiring insertion of a temporary cardiac pacemaker. He regained consciousness, but remained confused most of the day. By the following morning, however, he again returned to his baseline level of function. His subsequent cardiac evaluation resulted in a diagnosis of atrial-ventricular block associated with sinus node dysfunction. He fulfilled criteria for implantation of a permanent cardiac pacemaker, and the procedure was completed uneventfully.

After discharge, this patient did well from a cardiac standpoint. Within the next month, he showed gradual but progressive improvement and returned to all previous activities excluding work. His family felt he had returned to baseline, other than being slightly forgetful, and he complained of a similar problem, particularly related to short-term memory. A repeat neurological examination found an MMSE score of 25. His general fund of knowledge seemed appropriate for his education (he had completed the 11th grade in high school). He had difficulty with tasks involving short-term memory, consistently remembering one of three items at 5 min. Language function was intact without evidence of aphasia. He demonstrated relatively good problem-solving skills, without evidence of concrete thinking, and he generally was able to follow three step commands that crossed the midline. Motor examination showed equivocal limb ataxia but was otherwise unremarkable. His reflexes remained slightly brisk, but there were no pathological reflexes. A follow-up EEG showed equivocal slowing for age, most prominent over the temporal lobe leads. A cranial CT scan performed approximately 6 months after discharge showed very mild ventriculomegaly and mild, diffuse cerebral atrophy.

REVISED CLINICAL DIAGNOSIS

The final neurological diagnosis was "mild cerebral hypoxic encephalopathy due to cardiac arrest." The cardiac events were attributed to sinus node dysfunction.

Discussion

Establishing the diagnosis of acute cerebral hypoxic ischemia usually is not difficult. The presence of hypoxia is based on the setting, the respiratory and other clinical signs, and laboratory confirmation of hypoxia.

NERVOUS SYSTEM LOCALIZATION

This patient's neurological signs indicate a bilateral supratentorial abnormality. Loss of consciousness results from bilateral supratentorial dysfunction or brain stem (posterior fossa) dysfunction involving the midbrain and rostral pons. In this *patient presentation*, the only neurological signs potentially referable to the posterior fossa involved the brief period during which the pupillary light reflexes were absent, possibly due to oculomotor dysfunction or to abnormality of the pupillary light reflex arc within the midbrain. Although the efferent limb of the pupillary reflex is subserved by the oculomotor cranial nerve, the response may be absent by other mechanisms. In the setting of diffuse hypoxia, it is relatively common to experience temporary loss of pupillary reflexes, as in this *case presentation*. All other tests of the posterior fossa function, such as those involving the cranial nerves subserving the oculovestibular, corneal, and gag reflexes, were intact. The brief extremity twitching movements thought to represent a seizure likely originated from the cortex. During hypoxia, cortical neurons depolarize and jerking limb movements are observed as the cellular membrane potential crosses the threshold for discharge. Similarly, as oxygen levels are restored and depolarized cells re-establish a normal resting membrane potential, diffuse or multifocal discharges sometimes result in limb twitching.

VERIFICATION OF THE CLINICAL DIAGNOSIS

The diagnosis of acute encephalopathy satisfies all of the criteria for that diagnosis. This diagnosis explains the neurological findings, best fits the pattern of clinical signs, provides the simplest (most parsimonious) explanation, fits the observed pathophysiology as based on electrodiagnostic and imaging studies, and correctly anticipated the clinical course for partial recovery.

CAUSE/ETIOLOGY

Localizing the region of neurological dysfunction does not identify the cause of the problem. In this case, the general physical examination readily identified at least part of the explanation for the neurological dysfunction, namely generalized cerebral hypoxia or ischemia. That explanation does not,

Table 17.15 Potential causes of syncope associated with hypoxia (individual causes are not mutually exclusive).

Cardiac origin
   Conduction defects
   Ischemic cardiac disease
   Sinus node disease
   Ventricular arrhythmia

Other causes of vascular origin
   Vertebral-basilar artery thrombosis
   Pulmonary embolism

Noncardiovascular origin
   Acute airway obstruction
   Decreased environmental oxygen
   Insufficient mechanical respiratory function
      Myopathy
      Impaired neuromuscular transmission
      Major motor seizure

Impaired oxygen diffusion
   Intoxication
   Systemic hypotension
      Anaphylaxis
      Hemorrhage
      Infection (arterial-venous shunt)
   Vasovagal syncope

"Syncope: General Characteristics and Its Relation to Age," by A. Dougnac, A. Kychenthal, S. Loyola, R. Rubio, R. Gonzalez, D. Arriagada, et al., 1989, *Revista Medica de Chile, 117,* p. 1236. "Evaluation of Acute Mental Status Change in the Nonhead Injured Trauma Patient," by M. L. Cheatham, E. F. Block, and L. D. Nelson, 1998, *American Surgeon, 64,* p. 900.

however, identify the original causes for the hypoxia or ischemia, for which there are many causes. A few examples are listed in Table 17.15. The final diagnosis related to the cause of the hypoxia may be established by physical examination, or ancillary testing may be required, including EKG, echocardiography, Holter monitoring, or more prolonged cardiac monitoring. For the purpose of this review, the ultimate cause, although important in terms of treatment and prognostic considerations, does not influence the adverse neurological effects of decreased oxygen to cerebral neurons.

Neurons in the central nervous system do not receive sufficient oxygen under several conditions. Ischemia refers to reduced blood supply, either to a localized region (e.g., the cerebrum) or generalized. Anoxia refers to the absence of oxygen in the lungs, whereas hypoxia refers to reduced oxygen tension in the lungs. Hypoxia results in hypoxemia, an abnormally low arterial oxygen tension (pressure in mmHg; PaO_2) in the arterial blood. The terms hypoxia and hypoxemia frequently are interchanged, as the physiological results associated with each are identical. The PaO_2 level reflects the amount of dissolved oxygen in blood. Anemia indicates insufficient hemoglobin, the oxygen carrier in the blood. Substantial anemia can interfere with the oxygen carrying capacity in the blood, but anemia alone rarely produces hypoxemia. Other conditions can interfere with oxygen utilization irrespective of blood circulation or the oxygen level in the lungs. For example, carbon monoxide has an affinity to bind with hemoglobin (carboxyhemoglobin) that exceeds oxygen by more than 240-fold (Graham, 2000). When carboxyhemoglobin levels exceed about 20%, symptoms of exertional dyspnea and headache develop. A carboxyhemoglobin level of 30% is associated with severe headache and impaired cognition. Levels of 60% to 70% result in loss of consciousness, and levels exceeding 70% are rapidly fatal (Graham, 2000). Substances that poison the respiratory enzymes in nerve cells, such as cyanide, also produce hypoxic or anoxic cell death, irrespective of sufficient oxygen and blood flow.

A normal PaO_2 level ranges from 80 to 100 mmHg. When the PaO_2 falls below a level of approximately 60 mmHg, a level considered to be moderate hypoxia, arterial oxygenation is inadequate, a condition associated with hypoxic respiratory failure (Weitzenblum, Chaouat, & Kessler, 2002). In the cortex, neuronal ischemia due to inadequate oxygen may result in irreversible infarction (producing neuronal degeneration), depending on the magnitude and duration of ischemia. In the *case presentation*, the combined findings of an absent palpable pulse, unobtainable blood pressure, and a markedly reduced SaO_2 level established the presence of systemic hypoxia/ischemia. The relationship between the SaO_2 level and PaO_2 level is shown in the oxygen saturation curve (Figure 17.2). A SaO_2 level greater than 95% is considered acceptable. The sustained PaO_2 level associate with irreversible

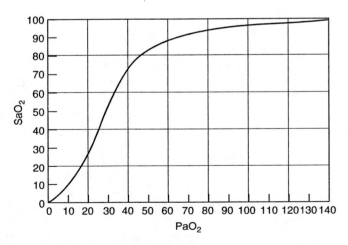

Figure 17.2 Normal oxyhemoglobin dissociation curve, showing the relationship between systemic arterial oxygen saturation (SaO_2) and oxygen tension (PaO_2).

neuronal death is difficult to identify precisely because it depends on many additional factors, of which the most important is maintained blood flow. Experimental nonhuman primate models of the effects of progressive hypoxemia with preserved cerebral circulation indicated that there is no effect on brain metabolism, function, or histopathology until the PaO_2 falls below 35 mmHg (Brierley, Prior, Calverley, Jackson, & Brown, 1980). Even levels of 25 mmHg were tolerated without affecting the EEG or producing permanent structural damage. Only when the PaO_2 levels were reduced to 21–24 mmHg for at least 8 min did irreversible damage occur.

The underlying neuronal pathophysiology resulting from hypoxia is complicated, involving two fundamental processes, ischemia and infarction. Ischemia is a reversible alteration in neuronal function. Infarction is the result of a reversible neuronal degeneration. The approximate response to various levels of hypoxia is summarized in Table 17.16 for a healthy adult. In association with hypoxia of sufficient magnitude, changes occur involving the production of high-energy phosphate bonds. Hypoxia also interferes with glucose metabolism, such that glucose metabolism terminates at the end of glycolysis. Under conditions of hypoxia, ATP production is compromised and glycolysis is accelerated, rapidly depleting glucose stores. In a setting of rapidly depleting substrates and inefficient ATP generation, ATP levels fall. The result of ATP and glucose depletion in association with hypoxia deprives the neuron of its

Table 17.16 The response to increasing levels of sustained hypoxia in healthy adults.

Approximate oxygenation levels		Symptoms and signs
PaO_2 (mmHg)	*SaO_2 (%)*	
90–100	95–100	Normal range; no known adverse effect
60–89	90–94	Impaired night vision, tunnel vision or scotoma
45–59	80–89	Shortness of breath with exertion Drowsiness Light-headedness, dizziness, and palpitations Headache Dim vision ("gray-out") Impaired judgment Incoordination
40–45	70–79	Increased symptoms of impaired vision, hearing, and sensation Inability to concentrate Further impaired judgment Impaired memory and cognition Weakness on attempted exertion
30–40	60–69	Syncope Seizure Progressive coma Cardiopulmonary arrest Death

two major sources of high-energy phosphate bonds, resulting in altered neuronal function. Interference with the cellular sodium–potassium pump produces decreased neuronal potassium, a decline in the membrane resting potential, and the loss of neuronal function (ability to generate an action potential). The result of persistent hypoxia and reduced glucose levels is an acute increase in intracellular water (intracellular edema). If the duration of hypoxia is relatively brief, all of these processes are reversible. If the duration of hypoxia is sufficiently long, neuronal degeneration results. All changes depend on the magnitude of hypoxia. Under conditions of anoxia (complete oxygen deprivation), depletion of ATP and glucose occurs within 1–2 min, and neuronal degeneration occurs. Under less severe conditions (partial hypoxia as opposed to complete anoxia), ATP depletion occurs more slowly and the period of reversible ischemia is extended. In the setting of partial hypoxia, however, increased levels of lactate develop, as lactate is the product of glycolysis. The resultant local acidosis associated with increased levels of lactate also contributes to neuronal degeneration.

The material above describes primarily the influence of hypoxia on neuronal necrosis, a process that begins with cellular edema, damage to the mitochondria, and ultimate breakdown of the cell nucleus with disintegration and necrosis of the cell. Another type of neuronal death is apoptosis, a programmed cell death that is encountered during brain development and which is controlled by the activity and balance of several genes. There is some evidence that the magnitude and duration of hypoxia determine whether neurons undergo rapid necrosis or apoptosis, a slow form of programmed cell death (Graham, 2000). On a larger scale, the summation of the cellular effects of hypoxia results in accumulation of carbon dioxide and increased levels of lactic acid, both of which result in local vasodilatation in an attempt to increase local blood flow. In association with anabolic neuronal changes, the blood–brain barrier fails and the resultant cerebral edema reduces cerebral blood flow and further compromises function of surviving neurons.

VERIFICATION OF CAUSE/ETIOLOGY

Hypoxia and ischemia, as potential bases of encephalopathy, fulfill all of the criteria for causation, including strength of association, reproducibility, dose–response, animal models showing the same pathophysiology, and biological coherence.

Adverse effects of cerebral hypoxia

Issues related to hypoxemia resulting from hypoxia or ischemia are important to understanding the adverse effects of many neurotoxicants. The neurological effects of hypoxia/ischemia sometimes appear confusing, particularly in terms of the variety of outcomes following seemingly similar levels of hypoxia. Much of this confusion likely reflects the interaction between the magnitude and duration of hypoxia. The concept of duration is particularly important in this context, but even duration depends on additional factors, such as preserved blood flow during hypoxia and the concentration of circulating oxygen-binding red blood cells. For example, in the presence of cerebral anoxia due to complete vascular occlusion, the tissue oxygen pressure rapidly falls and within about 5 min irreversible neuronal damage occurs. In contrast, during respiratory arrest or removal of oxygen from the environment, the time to irreversible neuronal damage is substantially longer, because tissues continue to extract small amounts of oxygen from the circulation. Similarly, the outcome following similar durations of complete cardiac standstill differs from situations involving inadequate but persistent degrees of cardiac output. These and other issues are reviewed briefly in the following paragraphs.

Predicting outcome after hypoxic ischemia is difficult, and the implications of an incorrect prognosis are important in clinical practice. In the context of clinical neurobehavioral toxicology, cerebral hypoxia must be considered in terms of magnitude and duration, but also in terms of the interaction between the two measures vis-à-vis the long-term temporal profile. The temporal profile is important to this discussion because of the potential for physiological response, whereby individuals accommodate to gradually increasing levels of hypoxia and are able to tolerate substantially larger degrees of slowly developing hypoxia compared to more rapidly developing levels of hypoxia. For purposes of discussion, three different temporal profiles of hypoxia will be considered and the consequences of each reviewed in terms of prognosis: acute (cardiac arrest and related conditions), subacute (high altitude sickness), and chronic (chronic pulmonary disease). Also, sleep disturbance (e.g., obstructive sleep apnea) has increasingly become an area of interest as a model for the study of hypoxia, both as a secondary consequence of another primary disorder (e.g., COPD) and in its own right (see discussion below on COPD and chapter 18). The primary consideration for each of these different situations is the ultimate degree of hypoxia. On an individual level, numerous other factors influence cerebral blood flow and neuronal hypoxia. In addition to systemic blood pressure and cardiopulmonary function, these factors included blood viscosity and factors that influence the degree of cerebral vasodilatation, such as carbon dioxide levels, pH, lactic acid, and intracranial pressure. In addition, there are individual differences in susceptibility to hypoxic-induced injury that include both genetic and acclimatization factors (Virués-Ortega, Buela-Casal, Garrido, & Alcazar, 2004).

Acute hypoxia is associated with cardiac or cardiopulmonary arrest. The prognosis among patients who survive a cardiac arrest can generally be established in terms of successful return of brainstem function, purposeful extremity movements, and the duration of coma. As a generalization, patients who show return of brain stem function, purposeful limb movements, and improved level of consciousness within 24 hr of onset generally have a good prognosis for complete neurological recovery. Patients who do not show improvement in these three levels of function within 24–72 hr have a very poor prognosis for complete neurological recovery, although exceptions exist. Such information is important in terms of recovery anticipated after less severe degrees of hypoxia, such as those associated with momentary loss of consciousness.

Levy, Caronna, Singer, Lapinski, Frydman, & Plum (1985) prospectively evaluated neurological function among 210 patients who sustained cerebral hypoxia-ischemia due to cardiac arrest. At initial examination, 52 patients (25%) who had had nonresponsive pupils never regained independent function. Among patients who had responsive pupils, spontaneous eye movements, and any response to painful stimuli (extensor, flexor, or withdrawal) at initial examination, 11 of 27 (41%) regained independent function. However, 24 hr after cardiac arrest, only 1 of 93 patients who had absent motor responses, decorticate posturing, or decerebrate posturing and disconjugate eye movements regained independent function. Among 30 patients who opened their eyes and followed simple commands or withdrew from painful stimuli at 24 hr after onset, 19 (63%) recovered independent function.

In contrast, there are few studies that describe cognitive outcome after out-of-hospital cardiac arrest of the type experienced by the patient in the *case presentation*. Roine, Kajaste, and Kaste (1993a) studied neuropsychological sequelae of cardiac arrest following restoration of spontaneous circulation. They identified 155 patients who were successfully resuscitated from among 677 resuscitation attempts during the study period. Of the 155 patients, survivors underwent neurological and neuropsychological examinations 3 months and 12 months after arrest ($n = 68$ and 54, respectively). The mean MMSE score of all 143 surviving patients 24 hr after arrest was 4 (95% CI, 3 to 6). Improvement was rapid: at 1 week the average MMSE score ($n = 120$) was 13 (95% CI, 11 to 16), and by 3 months the mean score ($n = 73$) was 25 (95% CI, 23 to 27). At 12 months, the mean MMSE score was 26 (95% CI, 25 to 28). The mean level of performance on standardized memory and intelligence measures 3 and 12 months after arrest was within normal limits, except for the Wechsler Memory Scale (WMS) delayed recall, which was subnormal. The Wechsler memory quotient was normal, but the standard deviations of most test results exceeded those in normal populations, consistent with the presence of outlying values. The difference in the level of performance between the two examinations at 3 and 12 months was not significant. Nevertheless, 3 months after arrest, 60% of the patients had moderate-to-severe cognitive deficits, and at 12 months, 48% of survivors still had moderate-to-severe deficits. In addition, 45% of these patients were depressed, 24% severely so. The investigators concluded that moderate-to-severe neuropsychological sequelae are identified in approximately one-half of out-of-hospital cardiac arrest survivors at 12 months, suggesting the impairments may be permanent. The most resistant function tested was speech, being affected only in the presence of clinically severe dementia. Reading, writing, and visual perception also showed little evidence of abnormality, whereas memory, visuoconstructive functions, programming of activity, voluntary hand movements, and arithmetic abilities seemed more likely to be affected. On the basis of the WAIS testing, performance intelligence was somewhat more affected than the verbal intelligence.

An important question involves identification of objective measures of neurological dysfunction that develop under similar conditions. Using the same cardiac arrest model described in the previous paragraph, Roine, Raininko, Erkinjuntti, Ylikoski, and Kaste (1993b) assessed brain MRI among 52 of the cardiac arrest survivors described above. Cardiac arrest was associated with discrete deep cerebral infarctions but not with diffuse abnormalities in the cerebral white matter (leukoaraiosis), as evidenced by confluent high signal T2 weighted abnormalities that are typically associated with ischemia. Diffuse white matter abnormalities were associated with increasing age, however. After adjusting for age, delayed advanced life support was inversely correlated with the magnitude of atrophy ($r = -.62, p < .0001$). Conversely, an absence of age-related atrophy predicted poor outcome after cardiac arrest, perhaps implicating the presence of brain edema. None of the MRI findings predicted the level of functional outcome at 12 months. These observations related to acute cardiac arrest are relevant to neurotoxicants that exert their effects by producing hypoxia. All of the patients described in the paragraphs above had loss of consciousness, many for prolonged periods. Yet, despite profound neurological impairment at onset, many later showed normal or near normal performance on neuropsychological testing. In addition, follow-up neuroimaging demonstrated evidence of neuronal loss in the form of cerebral atrophy.

Another situation potentially associated with cerebral hypoxia-induced cognitive dysfunction occurs in association with coronary artery bypass graft (CABG) surgery. Neurological outcome after CABG surgery is one area that has been relatively well investigated, and which is relevant to the consideration of subtle cognitive impairments associated with potential cerebral hypoxic/ischemia. During this procedure, patients are vulnerable to micro emboli and episodic or temporary cerebral hypoxia and ischemia. In general, the magnitude of hypoxia or ischemia during CABG surgery should be mild relative to unattended cardiac arrest models, making these results of interest as a less severe model of cerebral hypoxia compared to the cardiac arrest model. There are numerous reports of impaired cognition following CABG surgery. However, some evaluations of patients who reported reduced cognitive function after CABG surgery did not demonstrate impaired cognition on neuropsychological testing (Newman et al., 1989). Instead, those patients who report deterioration in cognition tended to have significantly higher levels of depression (Beck Depression Inventory) and higher levels of state anxiety than did remaining patients who did not report deterioration in cognition. Such findings confirm that subjective reports of impaired cognition do not always reflect demonstrable cognitive impairment, but may be attributed to other factors, including altered mood state.

An evaluation, similar to that reported in the preceding paragraph, administered neuropsychological tests to 245 patients before and 6 months after CABG surgery or cardiac valve surgery (Savageau, Stanton, Jenkins, & Frater, 1982a). The results of initial post-operative assessments were reported separately for a slightly different cohort (Savageau, Stanton, Jenkins, & Klein, 1982b). Although the immediate postoperative evaluations found that 28% of the patients showed deterioration in one or more test scores compared to the preoperative evaluation, over 80% of these patients returned to normal by 6 months (Savageau, et al., 1982a). Somewhat unexpectedly, the majority of patients who showed a significant decline in performance at 6 months acquired their decrements after the postoperative examination. The remaining 5% of patients showed a postoperative deterioration that persisted through 6 months. Postoperative factors such as higher levels of fatigue, depression, and worries related to the operation and the recovery process were associated with decrements of function at 6 months, suggesting that emotional factors may have contributed to their residual neuropsychological deficits. Some of these results were replicated by Sellman, Holm, Ivert, and Semb (1993) who evaluated 54 patients before and 1 and 6 months after CABG surgery. At 1 month 9 patients (17%) and at 6 months 4 patients (7%) showed neuropsychological deficits defined as a reduction of one standard deviation in two or more tests. They concluded that a risk of neuropsychological dysfunction after extracorporeal circulation exists, although improvement occurs within the subsequent 6 months. In a study of similar design, Hammeke and Hastings (1988) evaluated the incidence and course of neuropsychological sequelae among 46 patients studied before and shortly after CABG surgery, comparing their performance with noncardiac surgery patients and a nonsurgical referent group. A subset of all patients was reexamined 6 months later. They identified postsurgical neuropsychological deficits, which included impaired attention, psychomotor speed, and fine motor dexterity. They also found considerable interpatient performance variability, and the deficits they identified often were subtle. The deficits generally resolved within 6 months. They concluded that nonspecific factors associated surgery may contribute to the immediate postoperative deficit in patients who have cardiac operations. Whether deficits associated with extracorporeal circulation reflect a model of hypoxia/ischemia intermediate between cardiac arrest and other more benign conditions is unknown. The important information is that the deficits associated with these conditions, whether attributable to cerebral hypoxia or to psychological factors, tend to improve or resolve over time.

A model of relatively subacute hypoxia is related to the decreased oxygen levels associated with increasing altitude, as in high altitude climbing without supplementary oxygen. On exposure to high altitude, cerebral blood flow increases, PaO_2 and SaO_2 levels decrease, and pulmonary artery pressure increases (Berre, Vachiery, Moraine, & Naeije, 1999; Levine, Zuckerman, & deFilippi, 1997). Rapid ascent to high altitude can result in hypoxia, altitude sickness, and cerebral edema. It is therefore common practice to increase altitude gradually over a period of days to weeks, to permit physiological acclimation such as increased blood viscosity due to increasing numbers of red blood cells. Performance impairments associated with high altitude normalize after return to lower altitudes (Levine et al., 1997). Nevertheless, definite cerebral hypoxia frequently results from high altitude climbs. At extreme high altitude, SaO_2 decreases substantially, to levels below 60% (Tannheimer, Thomas, & Gerngross, 2002). An additional important and usually unrecognized variation in the hypoxic stimulus is desaturation during sleep at high altitude (Reeves & Weil, 2001). Regardless of the degree of acclimation, the magnitude of cerebral hypoxia is a primary component of high altitude sickness and high altitude cerebral edema. MRI suggests that the cerebral edema associated with high altitude has a prominent vasogenic mechanism, characterized by leakage of protein and water through the blood–brain barrier (Hackett, 1999). The mechanisms producing increased blood–brain barrier permeability are poorly understood, but they may reflect increased capillary pressure, ischemia, and adrenergic and cholinergic activation (Hackett, 1999). In the presence of vasogenic edema, intracellular cytotoxic edema likely follows, resulting neuropsychological sequelae characteristic of a subcortical dementia and imaging evidence of ischemic lesions in the globus pallidus bilaterally (Usui et al., 2004). More typically, only transient neurological signs are observed during brief exposures to high altitude. The mechanisms are thought to reflect hypocapnic cerebral vasoconstriction which occurs in response to severe hypoxic hyperventilation (Cauchy et al., 2002). Nevertheless, individual susceptibility (such as individuals with known migraine), rate of ascent, and preexposure acclimation are major independent determinants of acute altitude sickness (Schneider, Bernasch, Weymann, Holle, & Bartsch, 2002).

The best recognized long-term adverse functional effect of high altitude climbing in the absence of overt high altitude sickness is the occurrence of impaired memory performance in some climbers, based on neuropsychological testing before and 75 days after the ascent after return to sea level (Cavaletti, Garavaglia, Arrigoni, & Tredici, 1990). Others have demonstrated that climbers who demonstrate a more vigorous ventilatory response to hypoxia have more residual neurobehavioral impairment after returning to lower elevations than do climbers with lesser levels of ventilatory response (Hornbein, Townes, Schoene, Sutton, & Houston, 1989). This observation is thought to reflect poorer cerebral oxygenation despite greater ventilation, possibly due to a relative decrease in cerebral blood flow caused by hypocapnia, a factor that more than offsets the increase SaO_2 levels (Hornbein et al., 1989). These complex relationships between completing degrees of hypercapnia and SaO2 levels vis-à-vis tissue oxygenation highlight the difficulties involved in explaining and predicting the results of prolonged hypoxia.

Patients with chronic obstructive pulmonary disease (COPD) provide yet another model of the effects of chronic or intermittent hypoxia, hypercapnia, and respiratory acidosis on neurological function. Patients with COPD show systemic signs that include decreases body weight, loss of skeletal muscle mass (cachexia), osteoporosis, hypercapnia-induced peripheral edema, sleep disturbances, and neurobehavioral abnormalities such as cognitive impairment (attributed to hypoxemia) and depression (Grassi, Carminati, Cossi, Marengoni, & Tantucci, 2003). The influence of disturbed sleep among COPD patients is of interest, particularly in the context of the cognitive complaints associated with nocturnal hypoxia and obstructive sleep apnea (see *patient with neuropsychological complaints attributed to diet drugs,* in chapter 18). Nocturnal oxygen desaturation during sleep is frequently observed among patients with COPD. However, hypoventilation, not sleep apnea, is thought to be the most relevant factor producing oxygen desaturation, and a $PaCO_2$ exceeding 50 mmHg is highly indicative for a nocturnal oxygen desaturation (De Angelis et al., 2001). Patients with severe hypoxic COPD have clear cerebral dysfunction, with loss of consciousness being associated, on average, with a pH of 7.17 and a mean pCO_2 of about 100 mmHg (Duenas-Pareja et al., 2002). There is some evidence to suggest that chronic hypoxia of less magnitude may cause peripheral neuropathy among patients with COPD, a hypothesis confirmed in cross-sectional evaluations of patients with COPD (Kayacan, Beder, Deda, Karnak, 2001). Furthermore, measures of central nervous system physiology suggest similar performance decrements (Kayacanet al., 2001). Specifically, COPD patients who had resting PaO_2 levels less than 55 mmHg (a level associated with tissue hypoxia) showed nerve conduction evidence of neuropathy and delayed brain stem evoked responses indicative of chronic hypercapnia and respiratory acidosis. Oxygen therapy is recommended for treatment of patients with resting arterial hypoxemia as demonstrated by a resting PaO_2 lower than 55–60 mmHg (Man, McAlister, Anthonisen, & Sin, 2003). It has been shown that nonhypoxemic COPD does not increase the risk of subclinical cognitive dysfunction (Weitzenblum et al., 2002). However, it is suspected that there is cognitive impairment identified among hypoxemic COPD patients, and this impairment is thought to resemble the impairment associated with AD. Brain perfusion single photon emission computed tomography (SPECT) identified anterior cerebral hypoperfusion among hypoxemic COPD patients (Antonelli Inc et al., 2003). The imaging abnormalities were associated with impairments on select neuropsychological tests, and the combined results are thought to herald frontal-type cognitive decline with the worsening of the hypoxemia.

Consequences of hypoxia on neuropsychological testing

The neurobehavioral effects of hypoxia have been studied in both animals and humans. Aside from usually minor individual differences in susceptibility to impairment, the fact that different mechanisms of hypoxic injury are accompanied by different effects on the nervous system has frustrated attempts to determine a specific neuropsychological profile that results from hypoxia (Virues-Ortega et al., 2004). Technical and research methodological problems have complicated such efforts as well. These problems relate to a lack of standardization of tests used in studies in this area and with lack of standard definitions in terms of variables (independent as well as dependent variables) studied. These problems have been discussed at various times in these volumes (see, e.g., volume I). Virués-Ortega et al. summarized some of these factors specifically with regard to hypoxia. Given the variability of clinical response to varying degrees of hypoxia discussed earlier in this section, there is no reason to expect a uniform profile specific to hypoxia even if all problems with standardization and methodology were removed. At the same time, there are some predictable neurological outcomes, documented in animal and human models, that have been associated with hypoxia, and these, in turn, predict expectations with regard to neuropsychological findings.

The hippocampus and limbic system (Huber, Kasischke, Ludolph, & Riepe, 1999; Krnjevic, 1999; Zola-Morgan & Squire, 1986; Zola-Morgan, Squire, & Amaral, 1986) as well as some portions of the cerebellum (Pae, Chien, & Harper, 2005; Serrano et al., 2003) and possibly frontal lobes (Peskine, Picq, & Pradat-Diehl, 2004; Petiet, Townes, Brooks, & Kramer, 1988) are especially vulnerable to hypoxic damage, again depending on a host of factors regulating the extent and nature of damage. Given these observations, it is not surprising that changes in the behaviors that are known to be associated with these brain structures have most often been listed as resulting from hypoxia. At the risk of oversimplifying, and again depending on the extent of neurological damage, these behaviors include learning new information, short-term memory (but, not retrieval of long-term information), dysphasia and other language impairment (e.g., verbal fluency), abstract reasoning, comprehension, and affect (including the development of emotional disorder). Changes in psychomotor speed have also been listed, but with the caveat that impairments in this area of functioning could be secondary to changes in attention or related to emotional responses (e.g., motivation) (Virues-Ortega et al., 2004). These various functions reflect areas of behavior (behavioral domains) that are measured regularly in neuropsychological examination, i.e., intellectual functions, language, cognition, psychomotor function, and affect (see volume 1, also Berent & Trask, 2000).

Neuropsychological examination can be an important tool in the evaluation of hypoxic injury. It can be used to document the presence and nature of behavioral impairments, to aid in the differential diagnosis, e.g., determination of preexisting conditions, as well as to monitor disease progression. When the results of neuropsychological testing are viewed in the context of clinical evaluation and objective causal criteria, they also can aid in causal determination. To maximize the potential of such tests requires the use of validated and reliable measures within the context of professionally acceptable standardization. There is no one battery (i.e., collection) of specific tests that has been agreed upon as "the battery to use in evaluating hypoxia." However, the considerations just mentioned (e.g., use of standardized measures with technically documented validity and reliability and measurement of specified behavioral domains) do narrow the choices considerably. A list of suggested instruments meeting technical criteria for use is presented in Table 17.17.

Conclusion

The effects of hypoxia on cerebral function are complicated, and they depend on many factors in addition to the absolute level of hypoxemia. Each of these models presented in this section, including cardiopulmonary arrest, high altitude sickness, and COPD makes important contributions to our understanding of outcome following cerebral hypoxia. In the context of clinical neurobehavioral toxicology, important considerations relevant to toxic encephalopathy include the magnitude and duration of hypoxia and preservation of cerebral

Table 17.17 Some specific psychometric instruments for use in the evaluation of hypoxic injury.

Behavioral domain	Specific function measured	Suggested test instrument
Intellectual	Current ability, verbal and nonverbal	Wechsler Intelligence Scales (WAIS, WISC, or WASI)
	Historical baseline	Wechsler subtests sensitive to historical functioning, e.g., Vocabulary, Information
		Wide Range Achievement Test, Reading Subtest (WRAT)
Language	Aphasic disturbance	Boston Naming Test
	Verbal fluency	CFL, or similar procedure
	Reading level	WRAT-Reading
	Writing	Sentence Completion
Cognition	Mental Status	Mini-Mental Status Examination
	Memory, initial (new learning) and delayed (short-term memory), verbal and nonverbal (visual)	Wechsler Memory Scale
	Long-term memory	Information subtest of the Wechsler Scales
	Attention	Wechsler subtests: Arithmetic, Digit-Span
		Reaction time procedures
		Continuous performance test procedures
	Abstract conceptualization	Similarities subtest from Wechsler Scales
	Complex problem solving	Halstead Category Test Wisconsin Card Sorting
Psychomotor	Fine motor dexterity	Grooved Pegs
	Visual-motor	Trails B
	Motor speed	Halstead Tapping, Trails A
	Strength	Dynamometer grip strength
	Visual construction	WAIS Block design
	Steadiness	Handwriting, line drawings, motor steadiness battery
Affect	Emotional disturbance, Coping style	Minnesota Multiphasic Personality Inventory
	Motivation/effort	Rey-15, TOMM, or similar

circulation. Notably, many cerebral neurotoxicants exert their influence of cerebral neurons by producing hypoxia, not neurotoxicity. In this context, many issues related to central nervous system neurotoxicity can be considered in terms of whether or not exposure was sufficient to produce loss of consciousness. In terms of our understanding of the intensity of hypoxia required to produce permanent measurable declines in neurobehavioral performance, the prognosis for complete recovery is established in terms of the duration of unconsciousness. In terms of neurotoxicants that produce their adverse effects by producing hypoxia, it is nonsensical to expect larger impairments for less severe "exposures," particularly those that produce only limited duration of unconsciousness or no period of unconsciousness. Similarly, the various forms of hypoxic encephalopathy sufficient to produce measurable behavioral decrements all result in identifiable histopathology and all produce measurable changes in objective tests of cerebral function, including measures of physiology (EEG and evoked responses) and structure (imaging studies).

Parkinson's disease and parkinsonism

James W. Albers

Parkinson's disease is a degenerative disease of unknown cause, but a disease for which a complex interplay between genetic and environmental factors are thought to be important considerations (Huang, Fuente-Fernandez, & Stoessl, 2003; Warner & Schapira, 2003). The relationship between striatal (caudate nucleus–putamen) dopaminergic deficiency and the severity of the motor abnormalities in Parkinson's disease is established (Broussolle et al., 1999). The molecular basis of Parkinson's disease involves degeneration of dopamine-containing neurons in the substantia nigra, deposition of Lewy bodies in the midbrain, a near complete loss of the neurotransmitter dopamine in the basal ganglia (caudate/putamen), and emergence of motor impairments (Guilarte, 2001; Le Couteur, Muller, Yang, Mellick, & McLean, 2002). This selective depletion of dopamine reflects the degree of degeneration observed in the substantia nigra. The discovery of 1-methyl-4-phenyl-1,2,3,6-tetrahydropyridine (MPTP) as a dopamine neuron neurotoxicant stimulated interest in environmental causes of this disorder (Langston, Ballard, Tetrud, & Irwin, 1983). By definition, Parkinson's disease requires neuropathologic confirmation. Therefore, the term "parkinsonism" is the term used to describe forms of hyperkinetic and hypokinetic movement disorders involving the basal ganglia that clinically resemble Parkinson's disease. Idiopathic Parkinson's disease is described as primary parkinsonism, whereas patients whose parkinsonian signs reflect another underlying condition are said to have symptomatic or secondary parkinsonism (Yahr, 1989).

Case presentation[2]

A 57-year-old professor was referred for reevaluation of his antiparkinsonism medications. He was well until about 7 years earlier when, at age 50, he developed a resting tremor of his right hand. This tremor was present variably. It was exacerbated by fatigue or stress and disappeared completely during sleep. The tremor was described by his physician as a low frequency, rhythmic tremor present only at rest. The initial evaluation included a normal head

MRI. Over several years, there was progression of his tremor and extension to the opposite arm and to the right leg. In addition, he noted difficulty with fine hand movements and problems with his balance. The family history was negative for neurologic disorders. The social history also was unremarkable. He was a humanities professor. None of his hobbies involved exposure to potential neurotoxicants. He had never smoked, and he used alcohol sparingly. The past medical history was unremarkable and he had never taken any medications on a regular basis.

When seen 3 years after onset of his tremor, examination showed normal cognition, masked facies with decreased blink rate, saccadic eye movements, resting tremor of three extremities, cogwheel rigidity and increased resistant to passive limb movement, a shuffling gait with decreased arm movement and flexed posture, a decreased alternate motion rate of the fingers, hands, and feet, and a positive glabellar reflex (inability to suppress the blink reflex to percussion of the forehead). The remainder of the neurological examination was unremarkable.

DIFFERENTIAL DIAGNOSIS

On the basis of the history and clinical findings, a diagnosis of idiopathic Parkinson's disease was established. Other disorders that could have been considered included multiple system atrophy (MSA), progressive supranuclear palsy (PSP), olivopontocerebellar atrophy (OPCA), and medication-induced parkinsonism. The absence of any prior medication use excluded a drug-induced disorder, and neurologic features in addition to parkinsonism suggestive of each of the other diagnoses were absent. For example, there was no evidence of cerebellar ataxia (MSA, PSP, OPCA), dysautonomia (MSA), and no paresis of extraocular muscles (PSP). A repeat head MRI showed no evidence of hydrocephalus or any structural basal ganglia abnormalities.

Discussion

Parkinson's disease is a degenerative disease of unknown cause. However, much is known about the clinical features of the disease, including the localization, underlying neuropathology, and epidemiology. Parkinson's disease is a common neurological condition, with an estimated prevalence of about 341/100,000 (Schoenberg et al., 1988). The prevalence of parkinsonism, by definition, is even higher, because individuals with movement disorders characteristic of parkinsonism may not yet fulfill the definition of Parkinson's disease, or they may have identifiable problems that exclude the diagnosis of idiopathic Parkinson's disease.

NERVOUS SYSTEM LOCALIZATION

All of this patient's neurological signs can be located to the supratentorial level of the nervous system within the basal ganglia, the same localization for the motor signs associated with Parkinson's disease. Specific abnormalities can be attributed to striatal (caudate nucleus–putamen) dopaminergic deficiency, produced by selective depletion of dopamine due to degeneration of substantia nigra neurons (Broussolle et al., 1999).

VERIFICATION OF THE CLINICAL DIAGNOSIS

Cardinal manifestations of Parkinson's disease include rest tremor, rigidity, bradykinesia–hypokinesia, flexed posture, loss of postural reflexes, and freezing phenomenon. Of these signs, at least two, one of which must include rest tremor or bradykinesia, must be present to establish a clinical diagnosis of Parkinson's disease (Fahn, 1995). All of the signs demonstrated by this patient fulfilled explicit questions required to verify the clinical diagnosis of Parkinson's disease.

ADDITIONAL CLINICAL INFORMATION

Because the diagnosis seemed secure and his functional impairment was sufficient to interfere with activities of daily living, he was started on the dopamine agonists carbidopa/levodopa (Sinemet) and selegiline (Eldepryl). Following initiation of the dopamine agonist medications, there was a dramatic reduction in the clinical signs of parkinsonism. Over time, however, he required increasing amounts of medications to achieve the same level of improvement. In addition, he began to experience episodic "freezing," during which he was momentarily unable to initiate movement. For example, when attempting to walk, he would initially remain immobile, followed by rapid short festinating steps. Freezing occurred primarily in the morning and improved somewhat with increased medication, but he simultaneously developed substantial periods of dyskinesias characterized by restlessness and involuntary writhing movements of the head, trunk, and extremities. These dyskinetic movements were not particularly bothersome to him, but he was conscious of their cosmetic appearance. They were considered preferable to the parkinsonian signs that developed just prior to his scheduled medication time, when he felt virtually immobile and experienced a severe resting tremor.

CAUSE/ETIOLOGY

The diagnosis of "idiopathic" parkinsonism is based primarily on the absence of any known exposures or conditions associated with Parkinson's disease. By definition, the "cause" of an idiopathic disorder cannot be verified.

Comment

Consider for a moment how the diagnosis of idiopathic parkinsonism would be influenced if the history reported in the *case presentation* had included any of the following information: existence of several relatives who also showed signs of parkinsonism; a history of severe head injury preceding onset of his symptoms; onset of symptoms after a transient, high-level exposure to carbon monoxide producing unconsciousness; recreational exposure to (1-methyl-4-phenyl-1,2,3,6-tetrahydropyridine (MPTP); occupational exposure to carbon disulfide, occupational exposure to the rotenone, a pesticide; or an occupational history that included labor in a manganese mine? Each of these situations or substances has been identified as a possible risk factor for Parkinson's disease or parkinsonism. Although some of these potential risk factors have been inconsistently reported in the literature, accumulating evidence supports an adverse association. For example, case-control study among 93 twins discordant for Parkinson's disease showed an increased risk of developing Parkinson's disease decades after mild-to-moderate closed head injury (odds ratio [OR] 3.8, 95% confidence interval [CI] = 1.3, 11.0) (Goldman et al., 2006). In terms of chemical risk factors, it is generally accepted that sufficient exposure to substances such as manganese, carbon disulfide, or carbon monoxide may lead to parkinsonism following substantial latent period after exposure, a feature atypical of most neurotoxic disorders (Belongia et al., 1990; Hageman et al., 1999; Tanner, 1992).

Review of all situations potentially associated with Parkinson's disease or parkinsonism is beyond the scope of this section, although a few of the best-studied associations will be described. The material that follows attempts to distinguish between parkinsonism and Parkinson's disease, although referenced materials sometimes refer to both the syndrome and the disease. The causal determinations are based primarily, but not exclusively, on available case-control studies in which cases were diagnosed with Parkinson's disease or parkinsonism. Case-control studies were select because, along with cohort studies, they are the only forms of epidemiological studies potentially capable of establishing causation. Like all epidemiological evaluations, methodological problems such as incorrect definition, selection bias, and failure to identify confounding associations limit even these hypothesis-testing studies. Substances associated with parkinsonism are discussed in terms of common sources of exposure, clinical course, and proposed mechanisms of toxicity. Agents discussed include manganese, carbon disulfide, and MPTP. In addition, the experimental evidence that associates the pesticide rotenone with selective nigrostriatal dopaminergic degeneration is reviewed.

MANGANESE

The central nervous system is an important target of manganese neurotoxicity, particularly the basal ganglia (Crossgrove & Zheng, 2004; Normandin & Hazell, 2002; Olanow, 2004). Manganese intoxication is generally considered an occupational disease, and chronic manganese intoxication was recognized in the early 19th century (Albin, 2000; Couper, 1837). Although well recognized, the risk of developing manganese poisoning appears to be very low considering the numbers of workers exposed (Trimble & Krishnamoorthy, 2000). Excessive manganese exposure, frequently in response to inhalation of manganese dioxide containing dust particles, is associated with accumulation of manganese in brain tissue and a syndrome with many clinical features suggestive of parkinsonism (Albin, 2000; Crossgrove & Zheng, 2004; Huang, Weng, Lu, Chu & Yen, 2003). Consistent with this, the adverse consequences of manganese intoxication are thought to mainly affect the basal ganglia (McAlpine & Araki, 1958). Chronic manganese intoxication usually occurs after 1 or 2 years of exposure, but patients with manganese-induced parkinsonism may develop neurological progression many years after cessation of exposure (Calne, Chu, Huang, Lu, & Olanow, 1994). Excessive exposure also has been attributed to medicinal administration of manganese, or compounds that readily release manganese (Crossgrove & Zheng, 2004).

Early symptoms of manganese intoxication are nonspecific and include asthenia, anorexia, insomnia, and headache (Trimble & Krishnamoorthy, 2000). The neurological syndrome is characterized by extrapyramidal signs that include mask facies, bradykinesia, impaired balance, and rigidity, but with little evidence of resting tremor, one of the cardinal manifestations of Parkinson's disease (Albin, 2000). There are other purported features of manganese intoxication not typically attributed to Parkinson's disease, including dementia, cerebellar dysfunction, dystonia, and neuropsychiatric features (Albin, 2000; Bahiga, Kotb, & El Dessoukey, 1978; Ballard, Tetrud, & Langston, 1985). The neuropsychiatric component of manganese intoxication is said to include mental excitement, aggressive behavior, and incoherent speech, sometimes associated with hallucinations and delusions (manganese mania or psychosis) (Trimble & Krishnamoorthy, 2000). Many of the clinical features resemble parkinsonism, yet the complete clinical syndrome is distinct from that disorder (Albin, 2000; Paulsen, 1977). Consistent with the concept that manganese does not produce a syndrome identical to idiopathic Parkinson's disease, Koller, Lyons, and Truly (2004) found levodopa therapy ineffective for the management of manganese-induced parkinsonism. Given the high prevalence of Parkinson's disease in the general population, it is of particular relevance that patients with parkinsonism due to manganese intoxication be distinguished from patients with idiopathic Parkinson's disease who have incidental manganese exposure. Manganese-induced parkinsonism differs from idiopathic Parkinson's disease in terms of its predilection to accumulate in and damage the pallidum and striatum rather than the substantia nigra (Olanow, 2004). As such, the clinical signs, response to levodopa, imaging studies, and neuropathology typically distinguish these two conditions (Olanow, 2004).

Although manganese intoxication is a recognized cause of a parkinsonian-like disorder, this metal has not been identified as a major cause in epidemiological investigations of Parkinson's disease (Schoenberg, 1987). The association between parkinsonism and manganese was initially supported by case reports of workers occupationally exposed to manganese (Couper, 1837; Huang et al., 1989; Whitlock, Amuso, & Bittenbender, 1966). The six patients reported by Huang et al. had chronic manganese exposure confirmed by elevated tissue and environmental air levels. Signs of a bradykinetic-rigid syndrome plus hallucinations and aberrant behavior appeared after at least 6 months exposure. The extrapyramidal signs included hypokinesia, rigidity, dystonia, and tremor. Unlike subsequent reports (e.g., Koller et al., 2004), the parkinsonian features described by Huang et al. (1989) responded to dopaminergic treatment. These individuals also had sialorrhea, increased sweating, impotence, and insomnia. Symptoms and signs progressed with increasing exposure. Improvement was described in some workers after removal from exposure, but recovery was described as rare once the syndrome became advanced (Huang et al.). Later reports by the same investigators described progression after exposure had ceased, as mentioned above (Huang et al., 1993).

The epidemiology of Parkinson's disease and metal exposure is complicated. Parkinson's disease mortality rates have been calculated in geographic regions with respect to potential occupational exposures to metals (e.g., iron, zinc, copper, mercury, magnesium, and manganese) (Rybicki, Johnson, Uman, & Gorell, 1993). Regions with heavy paper, chemical, iron, or copper related-industrial categories had significantly ($p < .05$) higher death rates attributed to parkinsonism than counties without these industries. Significant correlations between industry density and parkinsonism death rates existed for the chemical, paper, and iron industries. Potential confounders included population density, farming density, and exposure to well water. Nevertheless, the ecological findings suggested a geographic association between Parkinson's disease mortality and the industrial use of heavy metals (Rybicki et al., 1993).

Surveys among workers exposed to manganese dust showed a similar prevalence of most subjective complaints among exposed and referent groups except for some nonspecific symptoms (fatigue, tinnitus, trembling of fingers, increased irritability) that were more frequent in exposure subjects (Roels et al., 1987). Psychomotor tests were reported to be more sensitive than the standardized neurological examination for the preclinical detection of adverse effects of manganese exposure, but no dose–response relationships between performance and biological measure of exposure were identified. Cross-sectional evaluation workers in a manganese ore milling plant compared with a referent group identified an increased frequency of neurological symptoms (Chia, Foo, Gan, Jeyaratnam, & Tian, 1993a) and poorer performance for measures of motor speed, visual scanning, visuomotor coordination, visuomotor and response speed, and visuomotor coordination, and postural sway among exposed workers compared to referent subjects (Chia et al., 1993b). However, neither clinical examination nor nerve conduction studies showed any group differences. Like Roels et al., these investigators concluded that the neurobehavioral test battery might be a more sensitive method than a clinical examination in detecting early changes in motor function among manganese-exposed workers (Chia et al., 1993a). In contrast, Myers et al. (2003) evaluated 489 manganese mineworkers in a cross-sectional investigation of nervous system effects of medium to low-level occupational manganese exposures. Multivariate analyses found no significant associations among symptoms or test results with any manganese exposure measures, after adjustment for confounders. They concluded that manganese miners exposed on average at levels near the American Conference of Governmental Industrial Hygienists Threshold Limit Value (ACGIH TLV) are unlikely to show subclinical neurotoxicity (Myers et al.).

A population-based case-control study evaluated the potential role of occupational exposure to iron, copper, manganese, mercury, zinc, and lead as risk factors for idiopathic Parkinson's disease (Gorell et al., 1997). Subjects completed a risk-factor questionnaire detailing actual work conditions of all jobs held for more than 6 months from age 18 onward. Exposures were based on an occupational rating by a masked industrial hygienist. Controls were frequency-matched for age (within 5 years), race, and sex. After adjusting for sex, race, age, and smoking status, individuals with more than 20 years of exposure showed a significantly increased association of Parkinson's disease for manganese exposure [OR 10.61, 95% CI 1.06, 105.83]. Lower, yet still significant, ORs were identified for exposure to other metals, either alone or in combination. These findings were interpreted to strongly suggest that chronic exposure to several different metals, acting alone or together over time, was associated with Parkinson's disease (Gorell et al.). Other attempts to evaluate the possible role of manganese in the risk of developing Parkinson's disease have been less convincing. A hospital-based, case-control study that used occupational histories to identify potential occupational exposures found no significant association between exposure to hazardous materials, especially manganese, and Parkinson's disease (Park et al., 2004). In an extension of the previous study, Park et al. (2005) interviewed 367 consecutive outpatients with Parkinson's disease and 309 control subjects. The interview included a range of industrial categories, as used in the study described previously, to identify potential exposures. In this extended study, ever having worked in agriculture, hunting, and forestry industries was positively associated with Parkinson's disease (OR 1.88), as was work in agriculture production crops (OR 1.96). In contrast, having worked with hazardous substances did not identify a significantly increased risk of developing Parkinson's disease. Unexpectedly, more subjects in the control group than the Parkinson's disease patient group had worked in the occupations with potential exposure to manganese ($p < .001$). Comparison of serum and 24-hr manganese urine excretion levels among patients with Parkinson's disease and matched controls showed no significant group differences, suggesting that serum levels and urinary excretion of manganese as measured when neurological signs of the disease are evident are apparently unrelated to the risk of developing Parkinson's disease (Jimenez-Jimenez et al., 1995). Similar negative results were found for CSF concentrations of copper, iron, and manganese among patients with Parkinson's disease and referents. The findings did not support the hypothesis that CSF levels of these metals are potential markers of Parkinson's disease (Gazzaniga et al., 1992). Although low-level exposure to manganese has been implicated in various neurologic and neurobehavioral changes, including decreased learning ability in school-aged children and increased propensity for violence in adults, a literature review conducted by Finley found very weak cause–effect relationships that did not justify concern about environmental exposure to manganese for most of the North American population (Finley et al., 2004).

The pathology attributed to manganese intoxication differs from that of parkinsonism, despite the numerous similarities. The mechanism for the neurodegenerative damage specific to select brain regions is not clearly understood (Crossgrove & Zheng, 2004). There is experimental evidence that astrocytes are a primary target of early dysfunction and damage, and that chronic manganese exposure leads to selective dopaminergic dysfunction, neuronal loss, and gliosis in basal ganglia structures together with characteristic astrocytic changes (Normandin & Hazell, 2002). The pathology attributed to chronic manganese intoxication includes neuronal degeneration in the pallidum, the striatum, and the substantia nigra (Yamada et al., 1986), a distribution similar to that seen in carbon monoxide intoxication (Albin, 2000). The neuropathology also has been replicated in nonhuman primate models of manganese intoxication (Olanow et al., 1996; Pentschew, Ebner, & Kovatch, 1962), and chronic manganese intoxication has been proposed as a model for Parkinson's disease analogous to MPTP (Huang et al., 1993). Nevertheless, none of the models produces the loss of dopaminergic neurons characteristic of Parkinson's disease (Albin, 2000).

CARBON DISULFIDE

The association between carbon disulfide and neurological impairment relies strongly on information derived from occupational workers who had chronic exposures of many years duration (Albin, 2000). Early reports included description of rayon workers who were noted to have an increased frequency of parkinsonism. Carbon disulfide was implicated as a possible cause of their syndrome because it had widespread use in the production of rayon fibers (Quarelli, 2001; Seppalainen & Haltia, 1980, 2001) (as referenced by Albin, 2000). Although parkinsonism is the most frequent neurological syndrome attributed to carbon disulfide intoxication, carbon disulfide exposed workers also show behavioral problems, ataxia, hearing loss, tremulousness, and sensory loss with nerve conduction abnormalities (Peters, Levine, Matthews, & Chapman, 1988; Seppalainen & Haltia, 1980; Spencer, Schaumburg, & Ludolph, 2000). Although some of the reports are based on evaluation of self-selected workers (Peters et al., 1988), the incidence of atypical parkinsonism among workers exposure to carbon disulfide is thought to be increased compared to the general population (Seppalainen & Haltia, 1980). Animals exposed to carbon disulfide demonstrate symmetric lesions of the pallidum and the substantia nigra pars reticulum (Alpers & Lewy, 1940; Richter, 1945). These studies were performed more than a half-century ago using conventional neuropathological techniques of that time, but the central nervous system pathological abnormalities appear robust.

1-METHYL-4-PHENYL-1,2,3,6-TETRAHYDROPYRIDINE (MPTP)

The discovery of MPTP as a dopamine neuron neurotoxicant surfaced in the 1980s after a chemist attempting to produce a meperidine analog, 1-methyl-4-phenyl-4-proprionoxypiperidine (MPPP), inadvertently produced a mixture of MPPP and MPTP (Langston et al., 1983). This mixture was sold illicitly as a heroin substitute, and approximately 400 intravenous drug abusers purchased and used the designer drug (Langston & Ballard, 1984; Langston, Ballard,

Tetrud, & Irwin, 1984a; Ruttenber, Garbe, Kalter, et al., 1986). Following use of the MPPP and MPTP mixture, several of these individuals developed an acute onset form of parkinsonism.

After recognition of this syndrome, other individuals who had also used the illicit drug were found to have a milder form of parkinsonism, and some users who did not develop clinical abnormalities were found to have an abnormal number of striatal dopamine terminals on PET evaluation (Calne, Langston, Martin, et al., 1985). Follow-up PET studies demonstrated evidence of progressive loss of the dopamine neurons, consistent with the concept that normal neuronal attrition would predict that these individuals would develop clinically evident parkinsonism in the future. MPTP-induced parkinsonism reproduced all of the major features of Parkinson's disease, as well as many minor features including seborrhea and mild neuropsychological deficits (Williams, 1986), and these patients responded to dopamine agonists. Subsequent laboratory studies identified the mechanism of MPTP neurotoxicity as inhibition of complex I of the electron transport chain in dopamine neurons (Przedborski & Jackson-Lewis, 1998). Toxicity depends on conversion of MPTP to the neurotoxicant 1-methyl-4-phenylpyridinium ion (MPP+) by monoamine oxidase B. The first detailed human neuropathological studies of MPTP-induced parkinsonism revealed moderate-to-severe deletion of pigmented nerve cells in the substantia nigra but no Lewy bodies (Langston et al., 1999), the cytoplasmic proteinaceous aggregates associated with idiopathic Parkinson's disease (Sherer, Betarbet, & Greenamyre, 2001). The neuropathology was interpreted as supporting the hypothesis that a time-limited injury to the nigrostriatal system can produce a self-perpetuating process of neurodegeneration. MPTP has been used to develop animal models of Parkinson's disease (Burns et al., 1983; Langston, Forno, Rebert, & Irwin, 1984b), which have proven an excellent means to study the pathophysiology of idiopathic parkinsonism (Albin, 2000).

ROTENONE

For many years, an association between Parkinson's disease and farming as an occupation, rural living, or use of well water (Rajput et al., 1987) has been suspected (Table 17.18 for additional references). One of the common connections between these factors is potential exposure to pesticides or herbicides. The structural similarities between Paraquat, an agricultural pesticide, and MPTP, a chemical capable of inducing neuronal damage in the zona compacta of the substantia nigra, seemed to support the connection (Calne, Eisen & McGeer, 1986; Tanner, 1989). Systemic administration of rotenone, a lipophilic pesticide that inhibits mitochondrial complex I, has recently been shown in rats to cause a highly selective nigrostriatal dopaminergic degeneration that produces hypokinesia and rigidity (Betarbet et al., 2000; Betarbet, Sherer, Di Monte, & Greenamyre, 2002b). Recent evidence suggests rotenone produces specific features of Parkinson's disease in rodents via oxidative damage of catecholaminergic neurons (Betarbet, Sherer, & Greenamyre, 2002a). The nigral neurons of rotenone-treated rats accumulate fibrillar cytoplasmic inclusions that contain ubiquitin and alpha-synuclein, thereby reproducing the anatomical, neurochemical, behavioral, and neuropathological features of Parkinson's disease (Betarbet et al., 2000).

VERIFICATION OF CAUSE/ETIOLOGY

Three of the substances described above, manganese, carbon disulfide, and MPTP, satisfactorily fulfill criteria supporting a causal relation with a parkinson-ism-like disorder. Of these substances, MPTP-intoxication most closely resembles idiopathic parkinsonism, clinically and pathologically, yet all of these neurotoxic disorders share many of the motor abnormalities of Parkinson's disease. Rotenone-induced parkinsonism has been demonstrated in experimental animals, but has not been established as producing parkinsonism in humans. Despite the numerous associations between some occupations and parkinsonism or Parkinson's disease, only a few occupational risk factors so far have been identified to date. At present, occupations related to the health care industry, teaching, and farming have been associated inconsistently with increased risk of parkinsonism, whereas among patients with diagnosed Parkinson's disease, working as a welder has been proposed to be associated with younger age of onset relative to other clinical patients (Goldman et al., 2005). In a retrospective case-control survey, medical records of 2,249 consecutive patients with Parkinson's disease or parkinsonism from three specialty clinics were reviewed to identify each patient's primary lifetime occupation, and the results were compared to Department of Labor regional statistics. The results of this large study suggested that occupation as a physician or dentist, farmer, or teacher was significantly more common than expected among patients with Parkinson's disease, as were lawyers, scientists, and religion-related jobs. Those employed as computer programmers had a younger age at diagnosis. Welders were not over-represented. Despite the association identified, the investigators warned that the results could reflect biases inherent in specialty clinic surveys related to over-representation of younger, employed, and insured patients, an observation relevant to many of the studies referenced in this chapter (Goldman et al.).

The cause of Parkinson's disease is largely unknown, but pharmacological, environmental, and genetic factors are all important. Neuroleptic drug exposure probably represents the best-established iatrogenic association with parkinsonism and extrapyramidal effects (Avorn et al., 1995). The extrapyramidal effects of neuroleptic medications are, at least in part, pharmacological, and they frequently are reversible. For some agents, the risk of developing extrapyramidal side effects correlates with occupancy of the dopamine receptor by the drug (Yamada et al., 2002). However, epidemiological studies implicate numerous other substances and conditions with a form of progressive parkinsonism that resembles Parkinson's disease. A summary of several recent case-control studies is shown in Table 17.18, identifying some of the positive, negative, and neutral associations.

Epidemiological studies clearly suggest that environmental and genetic factors are important in the pathogenesis of Parkinson's disease (Anderson

Table 17.18 Case-control studies investigating potential associations between Parkinson's disease or parkinsonism and various exposures or conditions.

Exposure or condition	Studies showing positive causal association	OR (odds ratio)[a]	No. of events cases/controls	Studies showing no or negative (protective) causal association	OR (odds ratio)[a]	No. events cases/controls
Anesthetic (inhalation) exposure						
Animal fat intake	Zorzon et al., 2002	2.2; 1.3–3.8	136/272	Chen, Zhang, Herman, Willett, & Ascherio, 2003	M 1.4; 0.9–2.2 F 0.7; 0.4–0.9	191/NA 168/NA
Carbon monoxide exposure/poisoning	Seidler et al., 1996	1.9; 1.2–3.0	83/55	Hertzman, Wiens, Bowering, Snow, & Calne, 1990; Kuopio, Marttila, Helenius, & Rinne, 1999; Seidler et al., 1996	1.3; 0.8–2.4 1.2; 0.8–1.8	123/246 84/81
Chemical exposure	Smargiassi et al., 1998; Tsui et al., 1999; Tanner et al., 1989; Werneck & Alvarenga, 1999	2.1; 1.2–3.9 3.8; 1.7–8.4 2.4; 1.3–4.3 5.9; 1.5–27.3	86/86 425/5661 22/21 92/100	Liou et al., 1997; Stern et al., 1991; Tsui et al., 1999; Smargiassi et al., 1998	2.0; 0.2–24.7 NS NS 2.6; 1.0–6.6	120/240 69/149 425/5661 16/7
Exhaust fumes	Seidler et al., 1996	2.4; 1.5–3.6 1.6; 1.1–2.4	134/94 135/119			
Family history Parkinson's disease	Zorzon et al., 2002	41.7; 12.2–143	136/272			
Family history essential tremor	Zorzon et al., 2002	10.8; 2.6–43.7	136/272			

(continued)

Table 17.18 (continued) Case-control studies investigating potential associations between Parkinson's disease or parkinsonism and various exposures or conditions.

	Positive causal association	OR (odds ratio)[a]	No. of events cases/controls	No or negative (protective) causal association	OR (odds ratio)[a]	No. events cases/controls
Fungicide exposure				Gorell, Johnson, Rybicki, Peterson, & Richardson, 1998; Semchuk, Love, & Lee, 1992	1.5; 0.4–5.3 1.6; 0.81–3.3	144/464 130/260
Gases and vapors	Seidler et al., 1996	1.7; 1.2–2.4 1.6; 1.1–2.2	175/140 177/145			
Gasoline, fuels, oils				Chaturvedi, Ostbye, Stoessl, Merskey, & Hachinski, 1995	1.2; 0.6–2.1	87/2070
Glues and paints	Seidler et al., 1996	1.6; 1.1–2.4	140/124	Seidler et al., 1996; Chaturvedi et al., 1995	1.5; 1.0–2.3 0.7 NS	140/124 87/2070
Herbicide exposure occupational	Gorell et al., 1998; Ho, Woo, & Lee, 1989; Kuopio et al., 1999; Liou et al., 1997; Semchuk et al., 1992; Semchuk, Love, & Lee, 1993; Seidler et al., 1996	3.4; 1.1–10.3 3.6; 1.0–12.9 1.7; 0.9–3.2 2.9; 2.3–3.7 3.1; 1.3–7.0 2.9; 1.2–7.3 2.4; 1.0–6.0	144/464 34/105 123/246 120/240 130/260 130/260 380/379	Nuti, 2004; Stern et al., 1991; Werneck et al., 1999	NS 0.9; 0.6–1.5 2.5; 0.5–13.1	69/149 92/110

Exposure	Reference	Mean; range	Cases/controls	Reference	Mean; range	Cases/controls
Metal exposure (including welders)				Goldman et al., 2005;	NS	2,249/DOL[b]
				Liou et al., 1997;	1.6; 0.0–1416	120/240
				Semchuk et al., 1993;	NS	130/260
				Hertzman et al., 1990;	NS	105/230
				Park et al., 2004;	NS	367/309
				Park et al., 2005	NS	87/2070
Paints, stains, varnishes				Chaturvedi et al., 1995	1.4; 0.7–2.5	
Pesticide exposure or occupation in farming	Butterfield, Valanis, Spencer, Lindeman, & Nutt, 1993;	5.8	53/68	Chan et al., 1998;	0.8; 0.3–2.22	215/213
	Liou et al., 1997;	2.9; 2.3–3.7	120/240	Kirkey et al., 2001;	1.7; 0.8–3.6	144/464
	De Palma, Mozzoni, Mutti, Calzetti, & Negrotti, 1998;	2.9; 1.4–6.1	100/200	Kuopio et al., 1999;	1.0; 0.6–1.0	123/246
	Gorell et al., 1998;	2.8; 1.0–7.6	144/464	Rocca et al., 1996;	0.6; 0.3–1.3	62/124
	Hertzman et al., 1990;	3.7; 1.3–10.4	57/122	Tsui et al., 1999;	0.7; 0.3–1.4	414/6659
	Ho et al., 1989;	5.2; 1.6–17.7	34/105	Seidler et al., 1996;	1.5; 0.9–2.5	380/379
	Park et al., 2005;	1.96	367/309	Stern et al., 1991;	0.7; 0.3–1.4	69/149
	Seidler et al., 1996;	4.6; 1.0–12.9	380/379	Smargiassi et al., 1998;	1.2; 0.6–2.4	25/20
	Semchuk et al., 1992;	2.3; 1.3–4.0	130/260	Chaturvedi et al., 1995;	1.8; 0.9–3.4	87/2070
	Zorzon et al., 2002;	7.7; 1.4–44.1	136/272	Firestone et al., 2005	1.0; 0.7–1.4	156/241
	Goldman et al., 2005	3.0; 2.1–4.2	2,249/DOL[b]			
Petroleum products	Werneck et al., 1999	6.6	92/100			
Printing, inks/dyes	Tanner et al., 1989	2.6; 1.2–5.4	15/8	Chaturvedi et al., 1995	1.4; 0.7–2.8	87/2070

(continued)

Table 17.18 (continued) Case-control studies investigating potential associations between Parkinson's disease or parkinsonism and various exposures or conditions.

	Positive causal association	OR (odds ratio)[a]	No. of events cases/ controls	No or negative (protective) causal association	OR (odds ratio)[a]	No. events cases/ controls
Service occupation				Kirkey et al., 2001	0.7; 0.5–1.0	144/464
Solvent exposure	Seidler et al., 1996; self-report, not confirmed by job assessment; Smargiassi et al., 1998	1.6; 1.1–2.4 1.8; 1.2–2.7 2.8; 1.2–6.3	100/79 99/73 23/10	De Palma et al., 1998; Chaturvedi et al., 1995	1.2; 0.7–2.0 1.3; 0.7–2.4	100/200 87/2070
Solvent exposure and CYP2D6 polymorphism genotype	De Palma et al., 1998; Elbaz et al., 2004	14.5; 1.2–185 ~2	100/200			
Teaching, and health services occupations	Tsui et al., 1999;	2.5; 1.7–3.7	425/5661			
Physicians/dentists	Goldman et al., 2005	2.1; 1.8–2.4	2,249/DOL[b]			
Excluding physicians/dentists	Goldman et al., 2005	9.6; 6.9–13	2,249/DOL[b]	Goldman et al., 2005	0.5; 0.3–0.6	2,249/DOL[b]
Well water use	Zorzon et al., 2002; Firestone et al., 2005	2.0; 1.1–3.6 1.81; 1.0–3.2	136/272 250/388			

[a] Mean, 95% confidence interval; [b] DOL = Department of Labor regional statistics.

et al., 1999; Bandmann, Vaughan, Holmans, Marsden, & Wood, 1997; Chan et al., 1998; Kirkey et al., 2001; Sherer, Betarbet, & Greenamyre, 2002; Zorzon, Capus, Pellegrino, Cazzato, & Zivadinov, 2002). Priyadarshi, Khuder, Schaub, and Priyadarshi (2001) performed a meta-analysis of peer-reviewed studies to examine the association between Parkinson's disease and exposure to environmental factors such as rural or farm living, well water use, and pesticide exposure. The majority of studies identified increased risk of Parkinson's disease for rural living (OR 1.56; 95% CI 1.18–2.07) and a borderline-increased risk for well water use (OR 1.26; 95% CI 0.97–1.64). The combined risk for farming, exposure to farm animals, or living on a farm was 1.42 (95% CI 1.05–1.91). The OR for pesticides exposure was 1.85 (95% CI 1.31–2.60). These analyses could not establish dose–response relationships because of the imprecise nature of the data. Despite the growing body of information linking pesticide exposure and Parkinson's disease, the strength of the associations identified suggests that pesticides do not play a substantial etiologic role (Firestone et al., 2005). Others have found that early exposure to well water may trigger the appearance of young-onset Parkinson's disease (Tsai et al., 2002). Overall, the influence of some as of yet unidentified environmental factor(s) associated with farming or rural living seems likely (Priyadarshi et al., 2001) but not supported by all studies (Baldi et al., 2003; Firestone et al., 2005).

In contrast, most epidemiological studies of Parkinson's disease have identified protective factors, such as a significantly reduced risk for Parkinson's disease among cigarette smokers and perhaps coffee drinkers (Betarbet et al., 2000). A reduced risk of Parkinson's disease was found for ever having smoke cigarettes (OR 0.5, 95% CI 0.4, 0.8), or among current smokers (OR 0.3, 95% CI 0.1, 0.7) compared to former smokers (OR 0.6, 95% CI 0.4, 0.9), and there was an inverse gradient with pack-years smoked (trend $p < 0.001$) (Checkoway et al., 2002). The explanation for these protective observations is unclear.

Genetic factors also are important in the pathogenesis of Parkinson's disease. Familial studies have identified mutations in genes, including alpha-synuclein, that are thought to be important in development of the disease (Sherer et al., 2001). Alpha-synuclein is a component of the Lewy body, and mutations or oxidative modification of alpha-synuclein causes it to aggregate, perhaps in association with mitochondrial dysfunction (Sherer et al.). The underlying molecular basis for Parkinson's disease may involve mitochondrial dysfunction (e.g., due to genetic defects, environmental toxicants, or a combination of the two), which induces a configurational change in alpha-synuclein, causing aggregation and resulting in selective neurodegeneration of dopaminergic neurons through mechanisms involving oxidative stress and excitotoxicity (Sherer et al.; Uversky, Li, & Fink, 2001). A common final pathway that is influenced by aging, environmental factors, and genetic mechanisms exists, which involves direct neurotoxicity and alpha-synuclein aggregation (Le Couteur et al., 2002). It is possible that abnormal protein handling increases susceptibility to oxidative stress; whereas numerous other factors, including impaired mitochondrial function, lead to impaired protein degradation and selective nigral cell death (Huang et al., 2003).

Review of Table 17.18 shows the importance of genetic factors, and the presence of a positive family history for Parkinson's disease is a principal risk factor for developing the disease. For example, Zorzon et al. found an increased OR of 41.7 (CI 12.2, 143) for developing Parkinson's disease among individuals with a positive family history of Parkinson's disease (Zorzon et al., 2002). The diagnosis of Parkinson's disease requires expert assessment of clinical signs and careful exclusion of alternative diagnoses (Tsui, Calne, Wang, Schulzer, & Marion, 1999). It is therefore possible that disorders other than Parkinson's disease or parkinsonism explain some of the associations shown in the tables. It is also possible that referral bias contributes to some of the identified associations. Despite these problems, it is likely that occupational exposures account for at least some of the suspected associations. A predominant cause of Parkinson's disease has not as of yet been established, and the causes of parkinsonism are undoubtedly multifactorial. A reasonable hypothesis proposes an interaction between genetics and the environment renders some individuals susceptible to developing the disease. Although unproven, the numerous occupational associations suggest that some neurotoxic exposure, alone or in combination with other factors, may contribute to development of parkinsonism. Even this observation remains speculative, however, as an alternative explanation unrelated to a specific neurotoxicant involves a putative infectious agent (Tsui et al., 1999). The occupational associations could therefore simply represent working in conditions conductive to the spread of respiratory infections (Tsui et al). Results of the numerous epidemiological studies remain inconclusive. Presumably, a hypothesis will emerge that is capable of explaining most of the available data involving genetic, geographic, occupational, and other environmental factors.

Summary

The cause of idiopathic Parkinson's disease remains unknown, yet several causes of parkinsonism are suspected including head trauma (Maher et al., 2002) and some infectious causes such as the influenza epidemic during the early last century (Schoenberg, 1987). The recognition that exposure to MPTP, a designer drug meperidine analogue, could produce degeneration of nigrostriatal dopaminergic neurons, renewed interest in environmental factors important in the development of Parkinson's disease. It is known that several other exogenous toxins are capable of damaging basal ganglia neurons. For reasons that are currently unclear, the globus pallidus and putamen neurons are particularly susceptible to mitochondrial toxins. Animal models are important in understanding the pathogenesis of human diseases. Parkinson's disease was the first neurological disease modeled by agents that selectively disrupt or destroy catecholaminergic systems and subsequently treated by neurotransmitter replacement therapy (Betarbet et al., 2002a). Identification of the role of oxidative phosphorylation in degeneration of these neurons may explain the host of agents and conditions that appear capable of producing parkinsonism in the susceptible individual. The generally accepted hypothesis is that Parkinson's disease reflects the pathological endpoint resulting from an interaction of environmental and genetic risk factors, and that the risk attributable to any given factor is likely to be small (Firestone et al., 2005).

Summary

The various presentations in this chapter were chosen to highlight the importance of a complete differential diagnosis in neurobehavioral toxicology. Demographics, medical and psychiatric illnesses, and even normal variations in physiology and behavior can present with clinical findings that mimic those expected to occur as a result of toxicant-induced disorders. Failure to recognize the part played by one or more of these factors in a given case can lead to faulty diagnostic conclusions and erroneous causal attributions. AD, for instance, and other progressive dementias involve brain regions and neural pathways in common with the pathophysiology associated with many toxicant-induced disorders. Especially during the early phases of these progressive dementias, when clinical symptoms are mild and objective signs of disease may be absent, it is relatively easy to mistakenly attribute the patient's complaints to some other cause (e.g., toxicant exposure or other illness or injury). Even seemingly normal conditions can influence examination results. The demographic of aging, for instance, is closely related to onset of dementia, to the extent that normal changes in brain function almost always serve as alternatives in the differential diagnosis of dementia. Likewise, aging and other normal variations in function need to be considered before concluding a toxic etiology in a given case.

Exposure to toxicants can induce symptoms that are seen in a host of normal and abnormal psychological conditions, ranging from mild-to-severe alterations in emotional and cognitive functions as well as changes in perception, judgment, and consciousness. Likewise, similar symptoms and signs are manifest in a host of medical disorders that involve disruption of normal physiological functions (e.g., endocrine dysregulation, hepatic encephalopathy, or cerebral hypoxia from cardiopulmonary arrest, high altitude sickness, or COPD). Any or all of the clinical presentations associated with the various psychological and medical conditions listed here can mimic those expected in toxicant-induced disorders. In fact, the mechanisms that underlie the observed symptoms and signs of abnormality may be the same regardless of cause (e.g., hypoxia resulting from cardiopulmonary arrest or from toxicant exposure).

The various sections and *case presentations* discussed in this chapter emphasized the recurrent theme in these volumes, i.e., the important distinction between diagnosis and causal attribution and the need to recognize and consider objectively all potential alternatives in formulating clinical conclusions. The diagnosis of dementia in a given case, e.g., may be entirely accurate, independent of any causal specification. An important additional question is whether the patient's dementia is due to neuronal loss as a result of progressive neurodegenerative disease, toxicant-induced hypoxic injury, or some other psychiatric or medical condition?

Notes

1   This *case presentation* is based on a description by Donald W. Black in a 2002 letter to the editor (Black, 2002).
2   Details of the history have been modified to preserve the anonymity of the patient and her family.
3   This case presentation is based on a description by Ali Ahmed et al. in a 2006 letter to the editor, published in the *Journal of the American Geriatrics Society* (Ahmed et al., 2006).
4   This case presentation is based on a description by V. J. Vorhees, in a 2003 article published in *The Journal of the American Board of Family Practice*.
5   This case presentation is based on a description by J. Hepple, in a 2004 article published in the *International Journal of Geriatric Psychiatry* (Hepple, 2004).
6   Details of this case were obtained from published reports by Grabski (1961) and by Knox and Nelson (1966).

References

Ahmed, A., Yaffe, M. J., Thornton, P. L., & Kinney, F. C. (2006). Depression in older adults: The case of an 82-year-old woman with dizziness. *Journal of the American Geriatrics Society, 54*, 187–188.

Albers, J. W. & Berent, S. (2000a). *Clinical neurobehavioral toxicology*. Philadelphia: W. B. Saunders.

Albers, J. W. & Berent, S. (2000b). Controversies in neurotoxicology: Current status. *Neurologic Clinics, 18*, 741–764.

Albers, J. W., Wald, J. J., Garabrant, D. H., Trask, C. L., & Berent, S. (2000). Neurologic evaluation of workers previously diagnosed with solvent-induced toxic encephalopathy. *Journal of Occupational and Environmental Medicine, 42*, 410–423.

Albin, R. L. (2000). Basal ganglia neurotoxins. *Neurology Clinics, 18*, 665–680.

Albrecht, J. & Zielinska, M. (2002). The role of inhibitory amino acidergic neurotransmission in hepatic encephalopathy: A critical overview. *Metabolic Brain Disease, 17*, 283–294.

Allen, D. N., Goldstein, G., & Warnick, E. (2003). A consideration of neuropsychologically normal schizophrenia. *Journal of the International Neuropsychological Society, 9*, 56–63.

Alpers, B. J. & Lewy, F. H. (1940). Changes in the nervous system following carbon disulfide poisoning in animals and man. *Archives of Neurology and Psychiatry, 44*, 725–731.

Als-Nielsen, B., Koretz, R. L., Kjaergard, L. L., & Gluud, C. (2003). Branched-chain amino acids for hepatic encephalopathy. *Cochrane Database of Systematic Reviews*, CD001939.

Alzheimer, A. (1907). Über eine eigenartige erkrankung der himrinde. *Allgemeine Zeitschrift fur Psychiatrie, 64*, 146–148.

Amella, E. J. (2004). Presentation of illness in older adults. *American Journal of Nursing, 104*, 40–51.

American Academy of Neurology. (2001). AAN guideline summary for point of care: Detection, diagnosis and management of dementia. Retrieved from http://www.aan.com/public/practiceguidelines/md_summary.htm

American College of Obstetricians and Gynecologists. (2005). Thyroid disease. Retrieved from http://www.medem.com/search/default.cfm

American Medical Association. (2003). Hypothyroidism. Retrieved from http://www.medem.com/search/default.cfm

American Psychiatric Association. (1968). *Diagnostic and statistical manual of mental disorders (DSM-II)* (2nd ed.). Washington, DC: Author.

American Psychiatric Association. (1987). *Diagnostic and statistical manual of mental disorders (DSM-III)* (3rd ed.). Washington, DC: Author.

American Psychiatric Association. (1994). *Diagnostic and statistical manual of mental disorders* (4th ed.). Washington, DC: Author.

American Psychiatric Association. (2000). *Diagnostic and statistical manual of mental disorders: DSM-IV-TR.* (4th ed.) Washington, DC: Author.

American Thyroid Association. (2003). *ATA hypothyroidism booklet.* Falls Church, VA: Author.

Anderson, C., Checkoway, H., Franklin, G. M., Beresford, S., Smith-Weller, T., & Swanson, P. D. (1999). Dietary factors in Parkinson's disease: The role of food groups and specific foods. *Movement Disorders, 14*, 21–27.

Anderson, M. D. (1976). *Logan's Run.* Jenny Agutter, Richard Jordan, Michael York, and Peter Ustinov. USA, Metro-Goldwyn-Mayer.

Andreasen, N., Minthon, L., Vanmechelen, E., Vanderstichele, H., Davidsson, P., Winblad, B. et al. (1999). Cerebrospinal fluid tau and Abeta42 as predictors of development of Alzheimer's disease in patients with mild cognitive impairment. *Neuroscience Letters, 273*, 5–8.

Antonelli Inc, Marra, C., Giordano, A., Calcagni, M. L., Cappa, A., Basso, S. et al. (2003). Cognitive impairment in chronic obstructive pulmonary disease—a neuropsychological and SPECT study. *Journal of Neurology, 250*, 325–332.

Arnold, G. L., Kramer, B. M., Kirby, R. S., Plumeau, P. B., Blakely, E. M., Sanger Cregan, L. S. et al. (1998). Factors affecting cognitive, motor, behavioral and executive functioning in children with phenylketonuria. *Acta Paediatrica, 87*(5), 565–70.

Artnak, K. E. & Wilkinson, S. S. (1998). Fulminant hepatic failure in acute acetaminophen overdose. *DCCN—Dimensions of Critical Care Nursing, 17*, 135–144.

Attard, O., Dietemann, J. L., Diemunsch, P., Pottecher, T., Meyer, A., & Calon, B. L. (2006). Wernicke encephalopathy: A complication of parenteral nutrition diagnosed by magnetic resonance imaging. *Anesthesiology, 105*, 847–848.

Avorn, J., Bohn, R. L., Mogun, H., Gurwitz, J. H., Monane, M., Everitt, D. et al. (1995). Neuroleptic drug exposure and treatment of parkinsonism in the elderly: A case-control study. *American Journal of Medicine, 99*, 48–54.

Bachmann, C. (2002). Mechanisms of hyperammonemia. *Clinical Chemistry and Laboratory Medicine, 40*, 653–662.

Baelum, J. (1999). Acute symptoms during non-inhalation exposure to combinations of toluene, trichloroethylene, and *n*-hexane. *International Archives of Occupational and Environmental Health, 72*, 408–410.

Bahiga, L. M., Kotb, N. A., & El Dessoukey, E. A. (1978). Neurological syndromes produced by some toxic metals encountered industrially or environmentally. *Zeitschrift fur Ernahrungswissenschaft, 17*, 84–88.

Baker, E. L., Bus, J. S., Cranmer, J. M., Curtis, M. F., Golberg, L., Grasso, P., Keller, W. L., Morgan, R. W., Scala, R. A., & Seppalainen, A. M. (1985). International workshop on neurobehavioral effects of solvents. Consensus workshop summary. *Neurotoxicology, 6*, 99–102.

Baker, E. L. & Seppalainen, A. M. (1987). Human aspects of solvent neurobehavioral effects. Report of the workshop session on clinical and epidemiological topics. Session three of the proceedings of the workshop on neurobehavioral effects of solvents. *Neurotoxicology, 7*, 43–56.

Baldi, I., Lebailly, P., Mohammed-Brahim, B., Letenneur, L., Dartigues, J. F., & Brochard, P. (2003). Neurodegenerative diseases and exposure to pesticides in the elderly. *American Journal of Epidemiology, 157*, 409–414.

Bale, T. L., Contarino, A., Smith, G. W., Chan, R., Gold, L. H., Sawchenko, P. E. et al. (2000). Mice deficient for corticotropin-releasing hormone receptor-2 display anxiety-like behaviour and are hypersensitive to stress. *Nature Genetics, 24*, 410–414.

Ballard, C. G., Ayre, G., O'Brien, J., Sahgal, A., McKeith, I. G., Ince, P. G. et al. (1999). Simple standardised neuropsychological assessments aid in the differential diagnosis of dementia with Lewy bodies from Alzheimer's disease and vascular dementia. *Dementia and Geriatric Cognitive Disorders, 10*, 104–108.

Ballard, P. A., Tetrud, J. W., & Langston, J. W. (1985). Permanent human parkinsonism due to 1-methyl-4-phenyl-1,2,3,6-tetrahydropyridine (MPTP): Seven cases. *Neurology, 35*, 949–956.

Baloh, R. W. (2000). Hearing and equilibrium. In L. Goldman & J. C. Bennett (Eds.), *Cecil textbook of medicine* (21st ed., pp. 2250–2257). Philadelphia: W.B. Saunders.

Bandmann, O., Vaughan, J., Holmans, P., Marsden, C. D., & Wood, N. W. (1997). Association of slow acetylator genotype for N-acetyltransferase 2 with familial Parkinson's disease. *Lancet, 350*, 1136–1139.

Barbee, J. G. (1998). Mixed symptoms and syndromes of anxiety and depression: Diagnostic, prognostic, and etiologic issues. *Annals of Clinical Psychiatry, 10*, 15–29.

Barchas, J. D. & Altemus, M. (1999). Biochemical hypotheses of mood and anxiety disorders. In G. J. Siegel, B. W. Agranoff, S. K. Fisher, R. W. Albers, & M. D. Uhler (Eds.), *Basic neurochemistry: Molecular, cellular and medical aspects* (6th ed., pp. 1074–1093). Philadelphia: Lippincott-Raven.

Belongia, E. A. & et al. (1990). An investigation of the cause of the eosinophilia-myalgia syndrome associated with tryptophan use. *New England Journal of Medicine, 323*, 357–365.

Bennet, A. & Stirling, J. (1998). Vulnerability factors in the anxiety disorders. *British Journal of Medical Psychology, 71*, 311–321.

Bennett, D. A. (2000). Diabetes and change in cognitive function. *Archives of Internal Medicine, 160*, 141–143.

Berent, S. & Trask, C. L. (2000). Human neuropsychological testing and evaluation. In E. Massaro (Ed.), *Neurotoxicology handbook, Vol. 2* (pp. 551–576). Totowa, NJ: Humana press.

Berent, S. (1986). Psychopathology and other behavioral considerations for the clinical neuropsychologist. In S. Filskov & T. J. Boll (Eds.), *Handbook of clinical neuropsychology, Vol. 2* (pp. 279–304). New York: John Wiley and Sons.

Berent, S., Giordani, B., Foster, N., Minoshima, S., Lajiness-O'Neill, R., Koeppe, R. et al. (1999). Neuropsychological function and cerebral glucose utilization in isolated memory impairment and Alzheimer's disease. *Journal of Psychiatric Research, 33*, 7–16.

Bernstein, A. M., Willcox, B. J., Tamaki, H., Kunishima, N., Suzuki, M., Willcox, D. C. et al. (2004). First autopsy study of an Okinawan centenarian: Absence of many age-related diseases. *Journals of Gerontology Series A-Biological Sciences and Medical Sciences, 59*, 1195–1199.

Berre, J., Vachiery, J. L., Moraine, J. J., & Naeije, R. (1999). Cerebral blood flow velocity responses to hypoxia in subjects who are susceptible to high-altitude pulmonary oedema. *European Journal of Applied Physiology and Occupational Physiology, 80*, 260–263.

Betarbet, R., Sherer, T. B., & Greenamyre, J. T. (2002a). Animal models of Parkinson's disease. *Bioessays, 24*, 308–318.

Betarbet, R., Sherer, T. B., Di Monte, D. A., & Greenamyre, J. T. (2002b). Mechanistic approaches to Parkinson's disease pathogenesis. *Brain Pathology, 12*, 499–510.

Betarbet, R., Sherer, T. B., MacKenzie, G., Garcia-Osuna, M., Panov, A. V., & Greenamyre, J. T. (2000). Chronic systemic pesticide exposure reproduces features of Parkinson's disease. *Nature Neuroscience, 3*, 1301–1306.

Bhatara, V., Alshari, M. G., Warhol, P., McMillin, J. M., & Bhatara, A. (2004). Coexistent hypothyroidism, psychosis, and severe obsessions in an adolescent: A 10-year follow-up. *Journal of Child and Adolescent Psychopharmacology, 14*, 315–323.

Bigal, M. E., Sheftell, F. D., Rapoport, A. M., Lipton, R. B., & Tepper, S. J. (2002). Chronic daily headache in a tertiary care population: Correlation between the International Headache Society diagnostic criteria and proposed revisions of criteria for chronic daily headache. *Cephalalgia, 22*, 432–438.

Biondi, B. & Klein, I. (2004). Hypothyroidism as a risk factor for cardiovascular disease. *Endocrine, 24*, 1–13.

Birren, J. E. & Botwinck, J. (1955). Speed response as a function of perceptual difficulty and age. *Journal of Gerontology, 10*, 433–436.

Birren, J. E. & Fisher, L. M. (1995). Aging and speed of behavior: possible consequences for psychological functioning. *Annual Review of Psychology, 46*, 329–353.

Black, D. W. (2002). Paroxetine for multiple chemical sensitivity syndrome. *American Journal of Psychiatry, 159*, 1436–1437.

Blackwell, J. (2004). Evaluation and treatment of hyperthyroidism and hypothyroidism. *Journal of the American Academy of Nurse Practitioners, 16*, 422–425.

Blasko, I., Lederer, W., Oberbauer, H., Walch, T., Kemmler, G., Hinterhuber, H. et al. (2006). Measurement of thirteen biological markers in CSF of patients with Alzheimer's disease and other dementias. *Dementia and Geriatric Cognitive Disorders, 21*, 9–15.

Bleeker, M. L. (1994). *Occupational neurology and clinical neurotoxicology.* Baltimore: Williams & Wilkins.

Boyd, R. C. & Amsterdam, J. D. (2004). Mood disorders in women from adolescence to late life: An overview. *Clinical Obstetrics and Gynecology, 47*, 515–526.

Boyes, W. K., Evans, M. V., Eklund, C., Janssen, P., & Simmons, J. E. (2005). Duration adjustment of acute exposure guideline level values for trichloroethylene using a physiologically-based pharmacokinetic model. *Risk Analysis, 25*, 677–686.

Bozoki, A., Giordani, B., Heidebrink, J. L., Berent, S., & Foster, N. L. (2001). Mild cognitive impairments predict dementia in nondemented elderly patients with memory loss. *Archives of Neurology, 58*, 411–416.

Braak, H. & Braak, E. (1991). Neuropathological stageing of Alzheimer-related changes. *Acta Neuropathologica, 82*, 239–259.

Breslau, N. & Andreski, P. (1995). Migraine, personality, and psychiatric comorbidity. *Headache, 35*, 382–386.

Breslau, N., Chilcoat, H. D., & Andreski, P. (1996). Further evidence on the link between migraine and neuroticism. *Neurology, 47*, 663–667.

Breslau, N., Davis, G. C., Schultz, L. R., & Peterson, E. L. (1994a). Joint 1994 Wolff Award Presentation. Migraine and major depression: A longitudinal study. *Headache, 34*, 387–393.

Breslau, N., Merikangas, K., & Bowden, C. L. (1994b). Comorbidity of migraine and major affective disorders. *Neurology, 44*, S17–S22.

Breslau, N., Schultz, L. R., Stewart, W. F., Lipton, R., & Welch, K. M. (2001). Headache types and panic disorder: Directionality and specificity. *Neurology, 56*, 350–354.

Brierley, J. B., Prior, P. F., Calverley, J., Jackson, S. J., & Brown, A. W. (1980). The pathogenesis of ischaemic neuronal damage along the cerebral arterial boundary zones in Papio anubis. *Brain, 103*, 929–965.

Brockington, I. (2006). Wernicke–Korsakoff syndrome. *Archives of Women's Mental Health, 9*, 58–59.

Broussolle, E., Dentresangle, C., Landais, P., Garcia-Larrea, L., Pollak, P., Croisile, B. et al. (1999). The relation of putamen and caudate nucleus 18F-Dopa uptake to motor and cognitive performances in Parkinson's disease. *Journal of the Neurological Sciences, 166*, 141–151.

Brown, E. S., Rush, A. J., & McEwen, B. S. (1999). Hippocampal remodeling and damage by corticosteroids: Implications for mood disorders. *Neuropsychopharmacology, 21*, 474–484.

Brown, G. C., Brown, M. M., & Sharma, S. (2004). Health care economic analyses. *Retina, 24*, 139–146.

Brown, J. S. (2002). *Environmental and chemical toxins and psychiatric illness.* Washington, DC: American Psychiatric Publishing.

Brown, P., Cathala, F., Castaigne, P., & Gajdusek, D. C. (1986). Creutzfeldt-Jakob disease: Clinical analysis of a consecutive series of 230 neuropathologically verified cases. *Annals of Neurology, 20*, 597–602.

Bruhn, P., Arlien-Soborg, P., Gyldensted, C., & Christensen, E. L. (1981). Prognosis in chronic toxic encephalopathy. A two-year follow-up study in 26 house painter with occupational encephalopathy. *Acta Neurologica Scandinavica, 64*, 259–272.

Burmeister, L. A., Ganguli, M., Dodge, H. H., Toczek, T., DeKosky, S. T., & Nebes, R. D. (2001). Hypothyroidism and cognition: Preliminary evidence for a specific defect in memory. *Thyroid, 11*, 1177–1185.

Burns, R. S., Chiueh, C. C., Markey, S. P., Ebert, M. H., Jacobowitz, D. M., & Kopin, I. J. (1983). A primate model of parkinsonism: Selective destruction of dopaminergic neurons in the pars compacta of the substantia nigra by N-methyl-4-phenyl-1,2,3,6-tetrahydropyridine. *Proceedings of the National Academy of Sciences of the United States of America, 80*, 4546–4550.

Bush, S. S. & Martin, T. A. (2005). *Geriatric neuropsychology: Practice essentials.* London and New York: Taylor & Francis.

Butterfield, P. G., Valanis, B. G., Spencer, P. S., Lindeman, C. A., & Nutt, J. G. (1993). Environmental antecedents of young-onset Parkinson's disease. *Neurology, 43*, 1150–1158.

Butterworth, R. F. (2002). Pathophysiology of hepatic encephalopathy: A new look at ammonia. *Metabolic Brain Disease, 17*, 221–227.

Calne, D. B., Chu, N. S., Huang, C. C., Lu, C. S., & Olanow, W. (1994). Manganism and idiopathic Parkinson; similarities and differences. *Neurology, 44*, 1583.

Calne, D. B., Eisen, A., & McGeer, E. (1986). Alzheimer's disease, Parkinson's disease, and motoneuron disease: Abiotrophic interaction between aging and environment? *Lancet*, 2, 1067–1070.

Calne, D. B., Langston, J. W., Martin, W. R. W., et al. (1985). Positron emission tomography after MTPT: Observations relating to the cause of Parkinson's disease. *Nature*, *317*, 246–251.

Canaris, G. J., Manowitz, N. R., Mayor, G., & Ridgway, E. C. (2000). The Colorado thyroid disease prevalence study. *Archives of Internal Medicine*, *160*, 526–534.

Carrigan, M. H. & Randall, C. L. (2003). Self-medication in social phobia: A review of the alcohol literature. *Addictive Behaviors*, *28*, 269–284.

Cauchy, E., Larmignat, P., Boussuges, A., Le Roux, G., Charniot, J. C., Dumas, J. L. et al. (2002). Transient neurological disorders during a simulated ascent of Mount Everest. *Aviation Space and Environmental Medicine*, *73*, 1224–1229.

Cavaletti, G., Garavaglia, P., Arrigoni, G., & Tredici, G. (1990). Persistent memory impairment after high altitude climbing. *International Journal of Sports Medicine*, *11*, 176–178.

Chan, D. K., Woo, J., Ho, S. C., Pang, C. P., Law, L. K., Ng, P. W. et al. (1998). Genetic and environmental risk factors for Parkinson's disease in a Chinese population. *Journal of Neurology, Neurosurgery and Psychiatry*, *65*, 781–784.

Chaouloff, F. (2000). Serotonin, stress and corticoids. *Journal of Psychopharmacology*, *14*, 139–151.

Chaturvedi, S., Ostbye, T., Stoessl, A. J., Merskey, H., & Hachinski, V. (1995). Environmental exposures in elderly Canadians with Parkinson's disease. *Canadian Journal of Neurological Sciences*, *22*, 232–234.

Cheatham, M. L., Block, E. F., & Nelson, L. D. (1998). Evaluation of acute mental status change in the nonhead injured trauma patient. *American Surgeon*, *64*, 900–905.

Checkoway, H., Powers, K., Smith-Weller, T., Franklin, G. M., Longstreth, W. T., Jr., & Swanson, P. D. (2002). Parkinson's disease risks associated with cigarette smoking, alcohol consumption, and caffeine intake. *American Journal of Epidemiology*, *155*, 732–738.

Chen, H., Zhang, S. M., Hernan, M. A., Willett, W. C., & Ascherio, A. (2003). Dietary intakes of fat and risk of Parkinson's disease. *American Journal of Epidemiology*, *157*, 1007–1014.

Chia, S. E., Foo, S. C., Gan, S. L., Jeyaratnam, J., & Tian, C. S. (1993a). Neurobehavioral functions among workers exposed to manganese ore. *Scandinavian Journal of Work, Environment and Health*, *19*, 264–270.

Chia, S. E., Goh, J., Lee, G., Foo, S. C., Gan, S. L., Bose, K. et al. (1993b). Use of a computerized postural sway measurement system for assessing workers exposed to manganese. *Clinical and Experimental Pharmacology and Physiology*, *20*, 549–553.

Chronicle, E. & Mulleners, W. (2004). Anticonvulsant drugs for migraine prophylaxis. *Cochrane Database of Systematic Reviews*. (3):CD003226.

Ciancio, A., Marchet, A., Saracco, G., Carucci, P., Lavezzo, B., Leotta, D. et al. (2002). Spectral electroencephalogram analysis in hepatic encephalopathy and liver transplantation. *Liver Transplantation*, *8*, 630–635.

Clark, D. M. (1999). Anxiety disorders: Why they persist and how to treat them. *Behaviour Research and Therapy*, *37*(Suppl. 1), S5–27.

Cohen, S. I., Silverman, A. J., & Shmavonian, B. M. (1961). Influence of psychodynamic factors on central nervous system functioning in young and aged subjects. *Psychosomatic Medicine*, *23*, 123–137.

Comeau, N., Stewart, S. H., & Loba, P. (2001). The relations of trait anxiety, anxiety sensitivity, and sensation seeking to adolescents' motivations for alcohol, cigarette, and marijuana use. *Addictive Behaviors, 26*, 803–825.

Constant, E. L., Adam, S., Seron, X., Bruyer, R., Seghers, A., & Daumerie, C. (2006). Hypothyroidism and major depression: A common executive dysfunction? *Journal of Clinical and Experimental Neuropsychology: Official Journal of the International Neuropsychological Society, 28*, 790–807.

Cook, N. R., Evans, D. A., Funkenstein, H. H., Scherr, P. A., Ostfeld, A. M., Taylor, J. O. et al. (1989). Correlates of headache in a population-based cohort study of elderly. *Archives of Neurology, 46*, 1338–1344.

Cory, T. (2003). Medications and substances as a cause of headache: A systematic review of the literature. *Clinical Neuropharmacology, 26*, 122–136.

Couper, J. (1837). On the effects of black oxide of magnesium when inhaled into the lungs. *Annals of Medical Pharmacology, 1*, 41.

Crimmins, E. M. & Finch, C. E. (2006). Infection, inflammation, height, and longevity. *Proceedings of the National Academy of Sciences of the United States of America, 103*, 498–503.

Crossgrove, J. & Zheng, W. (2004). Manganese toxicity upon overexposure. *NMR in Biomedicine, 17*, 544–553.

Dalessio, D. J. (1987). *Wolff's headache and other head pain* (5th ed.). New York: Oxford University Press.

Danzi, S. & Klein, I. (2004). Thyroid hormone and the cardiovascular system. *Minerva Endocrinologica, 29*, 139–150.

Davidson, L. L. & Heinrichs, R. W. (2003). Quantification of frontal and temporal lobe brain-imaging findings in schizophrenia: A meta-analysis. *Psychiatry Research, 122*, 69–87.

Davis, J. D., Stern, R. A., & Flashman, L. A. (2003). Cognitive and neuropsychiatric aspects of subclinical hypothyroidism: Significance in the elderly. *Current Psychiatry Reports, 5*, 384–390.

De Angelis, G., Sposato, B., Mazzei, L., Giocondi, F., Sbrocca, A., Propati, A. et al. (2001). Predictive indexes of nocturnal desaturation in COPD patients not treated with long term oxygen therapy. *European Review for Medical and Pharmacological Sciences, 5*, 173–179.

de Leon, M. J., Convit, A., DeSanti, S., Bobinski, M., George, A. E., Wisniewski, H. M. et al. (1997a). Contribution of structural neuroimaging to the early diagnosis of Alzheimer's disease. *International Psychogeriatrics, 9*(Suppl. 90), 183–190.

de Leon, M. J., George, A. E., Golomb, J., Tarshish, C., Convit, A., Kluger, A. et al. (1997b). Frequency of hippocampal formation atrophy in normal aging and Alzheimer's disease. *Neurobiology of Aging, 18*, 1–11.

De Masi, F. (2004). The psychodynamic of panic attacks: A useful integration of psychoanalysis and neuroscience. *International Journal of Psycho-Analysis, 85*, 311–336.

De Palma, G., Mozzoni, P., Mutti, A., Calzetti, S., & Negrotti, A. (1998). Case-control study of interactions between genetic and environmental factors in Parkinson's disease. *Lancet, 352*, 1986–1987.

Defilippis, N. A. & McCampbell, E. (1997). *Booklet category test, 2nd edition, professional manual.* (2nd ed.). Odessa, Florida: Psychological Assessment Resources.

Demet, M. M., Ozmen, B., Deveci, A., Boyvada, S., Adiguzel, H., & Aydemir, O. (2003). Depression and anxiety in hypothyroidism. *West Indian Medical Journal, 52*, 223–227.

Dews, P. B., Curtis, G. L., Hanford, K. J., & O'Brien, C. P. (1999). The frequency of caffeine withdrawal in a population-based survey and in a controlled, blinded pilot experiment. *Journal of Clinical Pharmacology, 39,* 1221–1232.

Dietemann, J. L., Botelho, C., Nogueira, T., Vargas, M. I., Audibert, C., Abu, E. M. et al. (2004). Imaging in acute toxic encephalopathy. *Journal of Neuroradiology, Journal de Neuroradiologie, 31,* 313–326.

Diez, J. J. & Iglesias, P. (2004). Spontaneous subclinical hypothyroidism in patients older than 55 years: An analysis of natural course and risk factors for the development of overt thyroid failure. *Journal of Clinical Endocrinology and Metabolism, 89,* 4890–4897.

Dillmann, W. H. (2000). The thyroid. In L. Goldman & J. C. Bennett (Eds.), *Cecil textbook of medicine* (21st ed., pp. 1231–1250). Philadelphia: W.B. Saunders.

Dougnac, A., Kychenthal, A., Loyola, S., Rubio, R., Gonzalez, R., Arriagada, D. et al. (1989). Syncope: General characteristics and its relation to age. *Revista Medica de Chile, 117,* 1236–1242.

Drane, D. L., Yuspeh, R. L., Huthwaite, J. S., & Klinger, L. K. (2002). Demographic characteristics and normative observations for derived trail making test indices. *Neuropsychiatry, Neuropsychology, and Behavioral Neurology, 15,* 39–43.

Duenas-Pareja, Y., Lopez-Martin, S., Garcia-Garcia, J., Melchor, R., Rodriguez-Nieto, M. J., Gonzalez-Mangado, N. et al. (2002). Non-invasive ventilation in patients with severe hypercapnic encephalopathy in a conventional hospital ward. *Archivos de Bronconeumologia, 38,* 372–375.

Dugbartey, A. T. (1998). Neurocognitive aspects of hypothyroidism. *Archives of Internal Medicine, 158,* 1413–1418.

Duverne, S. & Lemaire, P. (2005). Arithmetic split effects reflect strategy selection: An adult age comparative study in addition comparison and verification tasks. *Canadian Journal of Experimental Psychology, 59,* 262–278.

Elbaz, A., Levecque, C., Clavel, J., Vidal, J. S., Richard, F., Amouyel, P. Alperovitch, A., Chartier-Harlin, M. C., Tzourio, C. (2004). CYP2D6 polymorphism, pesticide exposure, and Parkinson's disease. *Annals of Neurology, 55,* 430–434.

Eleftheriadis, N., Fourla, E., Eleftheriadis, D., & Karlovasitou, A. (2003). Status epilepticus as a manifestation of hepatic encephalopathy. *Acta Neurologica Scandinavica, 107,* 142–144.

Fahn, S. (1995). Parkinsonism. In L. P. Rowland (Ed.), *Merrit's textbook of neurology* (9th ed.). Baltimore: Williams and Wilkins.

Feldman, R. G. (1998). *Occupational and environmental neurotoxicology.* Philadelphia: Lippencott-Raven.

Feldman, R. G., Ratner, M. H., & Ptak, T. (1999). Chronic toxic encephalopathy in a painter exposed to mixed solvents. *Environmental Health Perspectives, 107,* 417–422.

Felz, M. W. & Forren, A. C. (2004). Profound hypothyroidism—a clinical review with eight recent cases: Is it right before our eyes? *Southern Medical Journal, 97,* 490–498.

Fenichel, O. (1945). *The psychoanalytic theory of neurosis.* New York: W.W. Norton and Company, Inc.

Fera, F., Weickert, T. W., Goldberg, T. E., Tessitore, A., Hariri, A., Das, S. et al. (2005). Neural mechanisms underlying probabilistic category learning in normal aging. *Journal of Neuroscience, 25,* 11340–11348.

Festinger, L. (1957). *A theory of cognitive dissonance.* Stanford: Stanford University Press.

Festinger, L. (1962). Cognitive dissonance. *Scientific American, 207*, 93–98.

Filley, C. M. (1998). The behavioral neurology of cerebral white matter. *Neurology, 50*, 1535–1540.

Filley, C. M. (2001). *The behavioral neurology of white matter*. New York: Oxford University Press.

Filley, C. M. & Kleinschmidt-DeMasters, B. K. (2001). Toxic leukoencephalopathy. *New England Journal of Medicine, 345*, 425–432.

Filley, C. M., Halliday, W., & Kleinschmidt-DeMasters, B. K. (2004). The effects of toluene on the central nervous system. *Journal of Neuropathology and Experimental Neurology, 63*, 1–12.

Filley, C. M., Heaton, R. K., & Rosenberg, N. L. (1990). White matter dementia in chronic toluene abuse. *Neurology, 40*, 532–534.

Finley, J. W. (2004). Does environmental exposure to manganese pose a health risk to healthy adults? *Nutrition Reviews, 62*, 148–153.

Firestone, J. A., Smith-Weller, T., Franklin, G., Swanson, P., Longstreth, W. T., Jr., & Checkoway, H. (2005). Pesticides and risk of Parkinson disease: A population-based case-control study. *Archives of Neurology, 62*, 91–95.

Fleischer, R. D., Greenberg, S. R. W., & Harrison, H. W. (1973). *Soylent Green*. Charlton Heston, Edward G. Robinson, Leigh Taylor-Young, Chuck Connors, and Joseph Cotten. USA, Metro-Goldwyn-Mayer.

Folks, D. G. (1995). Munchausen's syndrome and other factitious disorders. In M. I. Weintraub (Ed.), *Malingering and conversion disorders* (13th ed., pp. 267–281). Philadelphia: W. B. Saunders Company.

Folstein, M. F., Folstein, S. E., & McHugh, P. R. (1975). "Mini-mental state." A practical method for grading the cognitive state of patients for the clinician. *Journal of Psychiatric Research, 12*, 189–198.

Forsell, Y. (2000). Predictors for depression, anxiety and psychotic symptoms in a very elderly population: Data from a 3-year follow-up study. *Social Psychiatry and Psychiatric Epidemiology, 35*, 259–263.

Francis, J. & Kapoor, W. N. (1990). Delirium in hospitalized elderly. *Journal of General Internal Medicine, 5*, 65–79.

Francis, J., Martin, D., & Kapoor, W. N. (1990). A prospective study of delirium in hospitalized elderly. *The Journal of the American Medical Association 263*, 1097–1101.

Franco, K., Tamburino, M., Campbell, N., Zrull, J., Evans, C., Bronson, D. et al. (1995). The added costs of depression to medical care. *Pharmacoeconomics, 7*, 284–291.

Frankton, S., Karmali, R., Mirkine, N., Bergmann, P., Fuss, M., & Williams, G. R. (2000). Pituitary-thyroid feedback hypersensitivity as a novel cause of hypothyroidism in children. *Lancet, 356*, 1238–1240.

Freud, S. (1966). *The complete introductory lectures on psychoanalysis*. New York: W. W. Norton.

Freud, S. (1997). *Dora: An analysis of a case of hysteria*. New York: Simon & Schuster.

Frick, P. J., Lilienfeld, S. O., Ellis, M., Loney, B., & Silverthorn, P. (1999). The association between anxiety and psychopathy dimensions in children. *Journal of Abnormal Child Psychology, 27*, 383–392.

Fullerton, C. S., Ursano, R. J., Reeves, J., Shigemura, J., Grieger, T., Fullerton, C. S. et al. (2006). Perceived safety in disaster workers following 9/11. *Journal of Nervous and Mental Disease, 194*, 61–63.

Gazzaniga, G. C., Ferraro, B., Camerlingo, M., Casto, L., Viscardi, M., & Mamoli, A. (1992). A case control study of CSF copper, iron and manganese in Parkinson disease. *Italian Journal of Neurological Sciences, 13,* 239–243.

Geller, A. M. & Zenick, H. (2005). Aging and the environment: A research framework. *Environmental Health Perspectives, 113,* 1257–1262.

Gerges, N. Z., Alzoubi, K. H., Park, C. R., Diamond, D. M., & Alkadhi, K. A. (2004). Adverse effect of the combination of hypothyroidism and chronic psychosocial stress on hippocampus-dependent memory in rats. *Behavioural Brain Research, 155,* 77–84.

Gershenfeld, H. K. & Paul, S. M. (1998). Towards a genetics of anxious temperament: From mice to men. *Acta Psychiatrica Scandinavica, Supplementum, 393,* 56–65.

Gill, G. N. (2000). Principles of endocrinology. In L. Goldman & J. C. Bennett (Eds.), *Cecil textbook of medicine* (21st ed., pp. 1179–1189). Philadelphia: W.B. Saunders.

Gold, G., Giannakopoulos, P., Montes-Paixao, J. C., Herrmann, F. R., Mulligan, R., Michel, J. P. et al. (1997). Sensitivity and specificity of newly proposed clinical criteria for possible vascular dementia. *Neurology, 49,* 690–694.

Goldman, L. & Bennett, J. C. (2000). *Cecil textbook of medicine* (21st ed.). Philadelphia: W. B. Saunders.

Goldman, S. M., Tanner, C. M., Oakes, D., Bhudhikanok, G. S., Gupta, A., & Langston, J. W. (2006). Head injury and Parkinson's Disease risk in twins. *Annals of Neurology, 60,* 65–72.

Goldman, S. M., Tanner, C. M., Olanow, C. W., Watts, R. L., Field, R. D., & Langston, J. W. (2005). Occupation and parkinsonism in three movement disorders clinics. *Neurology, 65,* 1430–1435.

Gorell, J. M., Johnson, C. C., Rybicki, B. A., Peterson, E. L., & Richardson, R. J. (1998). The risk of Parkinson's disease with exposure to pesticides, farming, well water, and rural living. *Neurology, 50,* 1346–1350.

Gorell, J. M., Johnson, C. C., Rybicki, B. A., Peterson, E. L., Kortsha, G. X., Brown, G. G. et al. (1997). Occupational exposures to metals as risk factors for Parkinson's disease. *Neurology, 48,* 650–658.

Goswami, S., Mattoo, S. K., Basu, D., & Singh, G. (2004). Substance-abusing schizophrenics: Do they self-medicate? *American Journal on Addictions, 13,* 139–150.

Goswami, S., Singh, G., Mattoo, S. K., & Basu, D. (2003). Courses of substance use and schizophrenia in the dual-diagnosis patients: Is there a relationship? *Indian Journal of Medical Sciences, 57,* 338–346.

Gould, R., Miller, B. L., Goldberg, M. A., & Benson, D. F. (1986). The validity of hysterical signs and symptoms. *Journal of Nervous and Mental Disease, 174,* 593–597.

Grabski, D. A. (1961). Toluene sniffing producing cerebellar degeneration. *American Journal of Psychiatry, 118,* 461–462.

Graham, D. I. (2000). Response to brain to hypoxia. In A. Crockard, R. Hayward, & J. T. Hoff (Eds.), *Neurosurgery. The scientific basis of clinical practice. Vol. 1* (3rd ed., pp. 429–447). London: Blackwell Science.

Grassi, V., Carminati, L., Cossi, S., Marengoni, A., & Tantucci, C. (2003). Chronic obstructive lung disease. Systemic manifestations. *Recenti Progressi in Medicina, 94,* 217–226.

Greenberg, P. E., Kessler, R. C., Birnbaum, H. G., Leong, S. A., Lowe, S. W., Berglund, P. A. et al. (2003). The economic burden of depression in the United States: How did it change between 1990 and 2000? *Journal of Clinical Psychiatry, 64,* 1465–1475.

Gui, Q. P., Zhao, W. Q., & Wang, L. N. (2006). Wernicke's encephalopathy in nonalcoholic patients: Clinical and pathologic features of three cases and literature reviewed. *Neuropathology, 26,* 231–235.

Guilarte, T. R. (2001). Is methamphetamine abuse a risk factor in parkinsonism? *Neurotoxicology, 22,* 725–731.

Hachinski, V. C., Iliff, L. D., Zilhka, E., Du Boulay, G. H., McAllister, V. L., Marshall, J. et al. (1975). Cerebral blood flow in dementia. *Archives of Neurology, 32,* 632–637.

Hackett, P. H. (1999). High altitude cerebral edema and acute mountain sickness. A pathophysiology update. *Advances in Experimental Medicine and Biology, 474,* 23–45.

Hageman, G., van der Hoek, J., van Hout, M., van der Laan, G., Steur, E. J., et al. (1999). Parkinsonism, pyramidal signs, polyneuropathy, and cognitive decline after long-term occupational solvent exposure. *Journal of Neurology, 246,* 198–206.

Hagen, K., Zwart, J. A., Vatten, L., Stovner, L. J., & Bovim, G. (2000). Head-HUNT: Validity and reliability of a headache questionnaire in a large population-based study in Norway. *Cephalalgia, 20,* 244–251.

Haines, J. D. (2005). A case of pseudoseizures. *Southern Medical Journal, 98,* 122–123.

Hammeke, T. A. & Hastings, J. E. (1988). Neuropsychologic alterations after cardiac operation. *Journal of Thoracic and Cardiovascular Surgery, 96,* 326–331.

Hanninen, T., Hallikainen, M., Koivisto, K., Helkala, E. L., Reinkainen, K. J., Mykkanen, L. et al. (1994). A follow-up study of subjects with age-associated memory impairment. Neurology *44*(Suppl. 2), A143.

Hardy, J. (2006). A hundred years of Alzheimer's disease research. *Neuron, 52,* 3–13.

Harris, K. M. & Edlund, M. J. (2005). Self-medication of mental health problems: New evidence from a national survey. *Health Services Research, 40,* 117–134.

Headache Classification Committee of the International Headache Society. (1988). Classification and diagnostic criteria for headache disorders, cranial neuralgia, and facial pain. *Cephalalgia, 8*(Suppl. 7), 1–96.

Heinrichs, R. W. & Zakzanis, K. K. (1998). Neurocognitive deficit in schizophrenia: A quantitative review of the evidence. *Neuropsychology, 12,* 426–445.

Henningsen, P., Jakobsen, T., Schiltenwolf, M., & Weiss, M. G. (2005). Somatization revisited: Diagnosis and perceived causes of common mental disorders. *Journal of Nervous and Mental Disease, 193,* 85–92.

Hepple, J. (2004). Conversion pseudodementia in older people: A descriptive case series. *International Journal of Geriatric Psychiatry, 19,* 961–967.

Hepworth, S. L., Pang, E. W., & Rovet, J. F. (2006). Word and face recognition in children with congenital hypothyroidism: An event-related potential study. *Journal of Clinical and Experimental Neuropsychology: Official Journal of the International Neuropsychological Society, 28,* 509–527.

Hertzman, C., Wiens, M., Bowering, D., Snow, B., & Calne, D. (1990). Parkinson's disease: A case-control study of occupational and environmental risk factors. *American Journal of Industrial Medicine, 17,* 349–355.

Heyman, A., Fillenbaum, G. G., Gearing, M., Mirra, S. S., Welsh-Bohmer, K. A., Peterson, B. et al. (1999). Comparison of Lewy body variant of Alzheimer's disease with pure Alzheimer's disease: Consortium to Establish a Registry for Alzheimer's Disease, Part XIX. *Neurology, 52,* 1839–1844.

Hirayama, T., Niho, K., Fujino, O., & Murakami, M. (2003). The longitudinal course of two cases with cretinism diagnosed after adolescence. *Journal of Nippon Medical School Nihon Ika Daigaku Zasshi, 70,* 175–178.

Ho, S. C., Woo, J., & Lee, C. M. (1989). Epidemiologic study of Parkinson's disease in Hong Kong. *Neurology, 39,* 1314–1318.

Hornbein, T. F., Townes, B. D., Schoene, R. B., Sutton, J. R., & Houston, C. S. (1989). The cost to the central nervous system of climbing to extremely high altitude. *New England Journal of Medicine, 321,* 1714–1719.

Huang, C. C., Weng, Y. H., Lu, C. S., Chu, N. S., & Yen, T. C. (2003). Dopamine transporter binding in chronic manganese intoxication. *Journal of Neurology, 250,* 1335–1339.

Huang, C., Chu, N., Lu, C., Wang, J., Tsai, J., Tzeng, J. et al. (1989). Chronic manganese intoxication. *Archives of Neurology, 46,* 1104–1106.

Huang, C. -C., Lu, C. -S., Chu, N. -S., Hochberg, F., Lilienfeld, D., Olanow, W. et al. (1993). Progression after chronic manganese exposure. *Neurology, 43,* 1479–1483.

Huang, Z., Fuente-Fernandez, R., & Stoessl, A. J. (2003). Etiology of Parkinson's disease. *Canadian Journal of Neurological Sciences, 30*(Suppl. 1), S10–S18.

Huber, R., Kasischke, K., Ludolph, A. C., & Riepe, M. W. (1999). Increase of cellular hypoxic tolerance by erythromycin and other antibiotics. *Neuroreport, 10,* 1543–1546.

Imaizumi, M., Akahoshi, M., Ichimaru, S., Nakashima, E., Hida, A., Soda, M. et al. (2004). Risk for ischemic heart disease and all-cause mortality in subclinical hypothyroidism. *Journal of Clinical Endocrinology and Metabolism, 89,* 3365–3370.

Interian, A., Guarnaccia, P. J., Vega, W. A., Gara, M. A., Like, R. C., Escobar, J. I. et al. (2005). The relationship between ataque de nervios and unexplained neurological symptoms: A preliminary analysis. *Journal of Nervous and Mental Disease, 193,* 32–39.

Janet, P. (1920). *The major symptoms of hysteria: Fifteen lectures given in the medical school of Harvard University.* New York: The Macmillan Company.

Janssens, J. P. & Krause, K. H. (2004). Pneumonia in the very old. *The Lancet Infectious Diseases, 4,* 112–124.

Jessen, F., Feyen, L., Freymann, K., Tepest, R., Maier, W., Heun, R. et al. (2006). Volume reduction of the entorhinal cortex in subjective memory impairment. *Neurobiology of Aging, 27,* 1751–1756.

Jha, A., Sharma, S. K., Tandon, N., Lakshmy, R., Kadhiravan, T., Handa, K. K. et al. (2006). Thyroxine replacement therapy reverses sleep-disordered breathing in patients with primary hypothyroidism. *Sleep Medicine, 7,* 55–61.

Jimenez-Jimenez, F. J., Molina, J. A., Aguilar, M. V., Arrieta, F. J., Jorge-Santamaria, A., Abrera-Valdivia, F. et al. (1995). Serum and urinary manganese levels in patients with Parkinson's disease. *Acta Neurologica Scandinavica, 91,* 317–320.

Jones, E. A. (2002). Ammonia, the GABA neurotransmitter system, and hepatic encephalopathy. *Metabolic Brain Disease, 17,* 275–281.

Jorm, A. F., Christensen, H., Korten, A. E., Henderson, A. S., Jacomb, P. A., & Mackinnon, A. (1997). Do cognitive complaints either predict future cognitive decline or reflect past cognitive decline? A longitudinal study of an elderly community sample. *Psychological Medicine, 27,* 91–98.

Karlin, N. J., Weintraub, N., & Chopra, I. J. (2004). Current controversies in endocrinology: Screening of asymptomatic elderly for subclinical hypothyroidism. *Journal of the American Medical Directors Association, 5,* 333–336.

Katzman, R., Aronson, M., Fuld, P., Kawas, C., Brown, T., Morgenstern, H. et al. (1989). Development of dementing illnesses in an 80-year-old volunteer cohort. *Annals of Neurology, 25,* 317–324.

Kayacan, O., Beder, S., Deda, G., & Karnak, D. (2001). Neurophysiological changes in COPD patients with chronic respiratory insufficiency. *Acta Neurologica Belgica, 101,* 160–165.

Kessler, R. C. (2004). The epidemiology of dual diagnosis. *Biological Psychiatry, 56,* 730–737.

Kessler, R. C., Barber, C., Birnbaum, H. G., Frank, R. G., Greenberg, P. E., Rose, R. M. et al. (1999). Depression in the workplace: Effects on short-term disability. *Health Affairs, 18,* 163–171.

Kessler, R. C., Berglund, P. A., Bruce, M. L., Koch, J. R., Laska, E. M., Leaf, P. J. et al. (2001). The prevalence and correlates of untreated serious mental illness. *Health Services Research, 36,* 987–1007.

Kirkey, K. L., Johnson, C. C., Rybicki, B. A., Peterson, E. L., Kortsha, G. X., & Gorell, J. M. (2001). Occupational categories at risk for Parkinson's disease. *American Journal of Industrial Medicine, 39,* 564–571.

Klaassen, C. D. & Watkins, J. B. (2003). *Casarett and doul's essentials of toxicology.* New York: McGraw-Hill Medical Publishers.

Klein, R. Z. & Mitchell, M. L. (2002). Maternal hypothyroidism and cognitive development of the offspring. *Current Opinion in Pediatrics, 14,* 443–446.

Knapp, D. J., Saiers, J. A., & Pohorecky, L. A. (1993). Observations of novel behaviors as indices of ethanol withdrawal-induced anxiety. *Alcohol and Alcoholism, 2,* 489–493.

Knight, J. R. (2004). A 35-year-old physician with opioid dependence. *The Journal of the American Medical Association, 292,* 1351–1357.

Knopman, D. S., DeKosky, S. T., Cummings, J. L., Chui, H., Corey-Bloom, J., Relkin, N. et al. (2001). Practice parameter: Diagnosis of dementia (an evidence-based review). Report of the Quality Standards Subcommittee of the American Academy of Neurology. *Neurology, 56,* 1143–1153.

Knox, J. W. & Nelson, J. R. (1966). Permanent encephalopathy from toluene inhalation. *New England Journal of Medicine, 275,* 1494–1496.

Koller, W. C., Lyons, K. E., & Truly, W. (2004). Effect of levodopa treatment for parkinsonism in welders: A double-blind study. *Neurology, 62,* 730–733.

Kraepelin, E. (1909). *Psychiatry.* Leipzig, Germany: Barth.

Kraepelin, E. (1910). Das senile und prasenile irresein. *Psychiatrie, ein lehrbuch fur studierende und arzte, 1910,* 593–632.

Krnjevic, K. (1999). Early effects of hypoxia on brain cell function. *Croatian Medical Journal, 40,* 375–380.

Kuhl, D. E., Metter, E. J., & Riege, W. H. (1985). Patterns of cerebral glucose utilization in depression, multiple infarct dementia, and Alzheimer's disease. *Research Publications—Association for Research in Nervous and Mental Disease, 63,* 211–226.

Kuopio, A. M., Marttila, R. J., Helenius, H., & Rinne, U. K. (1999). Environmental risk factors in Parkinson's disease. *Movement Disorders, 14,* 928–939.

Langston, J. W. & Ballard, P. (1984). Parkinsonism induced by methly-4-phenly-1,2,3,6-tetrahyrdopyridine (MPTP): Implications for treatment and the pathogenesis of Parkinson's disease. *Canadian Journal of Neurological Sciences, 11,* 160–165.

Langston, J. W., Ballard, P. A., Tetrud, J. W., & Irwin, I. (1984). Chronic parkinsonism in humans due to a product of meperidine-analog synthesis. *Science, 11,* 160–165.

Langston, J. W., Ballard, P., Tetrud, J. W., & Irwin, I. (1983). Chronic Parkinsonism in humans due to a product of meperidine-analog synthesis. *Science, 219,* 979–980.

Langston, J. W., Forno, L. S., Rebert, C. S., & Irwin, I. (1984). Selective nigral toxicity after systemic administration of 1-methyl-4-phenyl-1,2,5,6-tetrahydropyrine (MPTP) in the squirrel monkey. *Brain Research, 292*, 390–394.

Langston, J. W., Forno, L. S., Tetrud, J., Reeves, A. G., Kaplan, J. A., & Karluk, D. (1999). Evidence of active nerve cell degeneration in the substantia nigra of humans years after 1-methyl-4-phenyl-1,2,3,6-tetrahydropyridine exposure. *Annals of Neurology, 46*, 598–605.

Lazarus, J. H. (2005). Thyroid disease in pregnancy and childhood. *Minerva Endocrinologica, 30*, 71–87.

Lazarus, R. S. (1991). *Emotion and adaptation.* New York: Oxford University Press.

Le Couteur, D. G., Muller, M., Yang, M. C., Mellick, G. D., & McLean, A. J. (2002). Age-environment and gene-environment interactions in the pathogenesis of Parkinson's disease. *Reviews on Environmental Health, 17*, 51–64.

Leger, J., Larroque, B., Norton, J., & Association Francaise pour le Depistage et la Prevetion des Handicaps de l'Enfant. (2001). Influence of severity of congenital hypothyroidism and adequacy of treatment on school achievement in young adolescents: A population-based cohort study. *Acta Paediatrica, 90*, 1249–1256.

Levenson, M. R., Kiehl, K. A., & Fitzpatrick, C. M. (1995). Assessing psychopathic attributes in a noninstitutionalized population. *Journal of Personality and Social Psychology, 68*, 151–158.

Levine, B. D., Zuckerman, J. H., & deFilippi, C. R. (1997). Effect of high-altitude exposure in the elderly: The Tenth Mountain Division study. *Circulation, 96*, 1224–1232.

Levine, E. J. & Rothstein, J. D. (1996). Hepatic encephalopathy. In M. A. Samuels & S. Feske (Eds.), *Office practice of neurology.* New York: Churchill Livingstone.

Levy, D. E., Caronna, J. J., Singer, B. H., Lapinski, R. H., Frydman, H., & Plum, F. (1985). Predicting outcome from hypoxic-ischemic coma. *Journal of the American Medical Association, 253*, 1420–1426.

Lewis, M. B. H. (2003). Neurologic complications of liver transplantation in adults. *Neurology, 61*, 1174–1178.

Limmroth, V., Katsarava, Z., Fritsche, G., Przywara, S., & Diener, H. C. (2002). Features of medication overuse headache following overuse of different acute headache drugs. *Neurology, 59*, 1011–1014.

Liou, H. H., Tsai, M. C., Chen, C. J., Jeng, J. S., Chang, Y. C., Chen, S. Y. et al. (1997). Environmental risk factors and Parkinson's disease: A case-control study in Taiwan. *Neurology, 48*, 1583–1588.

Lipton, R. B., Stewart, W. F., & Merikangas, K. R. (1993). Reliability in headache diagnosis. *Cephalalgia, 13*(Suppl. 12), 29–33.

Lockwood, A. H. (2002). Positron emission tomography in the study of hepatic encephalopathy. *Metabolic Brain Disease, 17*, 431–435.

Lopponen, M. K., Isoaho, R. E., Raiha, I. J., Vahlberg, T. J., Loikas, S. M., Takala, T. I. et al. (2004). Undiagnosed diseases in patients with dementia—a potential target group for intervention. *Dementia and Geriatric Cognitive Disorders, 18*, 321–329.

Maaranen, P., Tanskanen, A., Haatainen, K., Honkalampi, K., Koivumaa-Honkanen, H., Hintikka, J. et al. (2005). The relationship between psychological and somatoform dissociation in the general population. *Journal of Nervous and Mental Disease, 193*, 690–692.

Maher, N. E., Golbe, L. I., Lazzarini, A. M., Mark, M. H., Currie, L. J., Wooten, G. F. et al. (2002). Epidemiologic study of 203 sibling pairs with Parkinson's disease: The GenePD study. *Neurology, 58*, 79–84.

Maher, S. (2004). Sleep in the older adult. *Nursing Older People, 16,* 30–34.

Maier, W. & Falkai, P. (1999). The epidemiology of comorbidity between depression, anxiety disorders and somatic diseases. [Review] [28 refs]. *International Clinical Psychopharmacology, 14*(Suppl. 2), S1–S6.

Makin, A. J., Wendon, J., & Williams, R. (1995). A 7-year experience of severe acetaminophen-induced hepatotoxicity (1987–1993). *Gastroenterology, 109,* 1907–1916.

Man, S. F., McAlister, F. A., Anthonisen, N. R., & Sin, D. D. (2003). Contemporary management of chronic obstructive pulmonary disease: Clinical applications. *Journal of the American Medical Association, 290,* 2313–2316.

Marjama, J., Troster, A. I., & Koller, W. C. (1995). Psychogenic movement disorders. In M. I. Weintraub (Ed.), *Malingering and conversion reactions* (13th ed., pp. 283–297). Philadelphia: W.B. Saunders Company.

Masur, D. M., Sliwinski, M., Lipton, R. B., Blau, A. D., & Crystal, H. A. (1994). Neuropsychological prediction of dementia and the absence of dementia in healthy elderly persons. *Neurology, 44,* 1427–1432.

Matarazzo, J. D. (1972). *Wechsler's measurment and appraisal of adult intelligence.* Baltimore: Williams and Wilkins.

Mattay, V. S., Fera, F., Tessitore, A., Hariri, A. R., Berman, K. F., Das, S. et al. (2006). Neurophysiological correlates of age-related changes in working memory capacity. *Neuroscience Letters, 392,* 32–37.

Mayeux, R., Saunders, A. M., Shea, S., Mirra, S., Evans, D., Roses, A. D. et al. (1998). Utility of the apolipoprotein E genotype in the diagnosis of Alzheimer's disease. Alzheimer's Disease Centers Consortium on Apolipoprotein E and Alzheimer's Disease. *New England Journal of Medicine, 338,* 506–511.

Mayo Foundation for Medical Education and Research (MFMER). (2005). Hypothyroidism. Retrieved from http://www.mayoclinic.com/health/hypothyroidism/DS00353

McAllister-Williams, R. H., Ferrier, I. N., & Young, A. H. (1998). Mood and neuropsychological function in depression: The role of corticosteroids and serotonin. *Psychological Medicine, 28,* 573–584.

McAlpine, D. & Araki, S. (1958). Minamata disease. An unusual neurological disorder caused by contaminated fish. *Lancet, 2,* 629–631.

McClellan, J., Prezbindowski, A., Breiger, D., & McCurry, C. (2004). Neuropsychological functioning in early onset psychotic disorders. *Schizophrenia Research, 68,* 21–26.

McEwen, B. S. (1999). Endocrine effects on the brain and their relationship to behavior. In G. J. Siegel, B. W. Agranoff, S. K. Fisher, R. W. Albers, & M. D. Uhler (Eds.), *Basic neurochemistry: Molecular, cellular and medical aspects* (6th ed., pp. 1007–1026). Philadelphia: Lippincott-Raven.

McEwen, B. S. (2004). Protection and damage from acute and chronic stress: Allostasis and allostatic overload and relevance to the pathophysiology of psychiatric disorders. *Annals of the New York Academy of Sciences, 1032,* 1–7.

McKeith, I. G., Galasko, D., Kosaka, K., Perry, E. K., Dickson, D. W., Hansen, L. A. et al. (1996). Consensus guidelines for the clinical and pathologic diagnosis of dementia with Lewy bodies (DLB): Report of the consortium on DLB international workshop. *Neurology, 47,* 1113–1124.

McKeith, I., Mintzer, J., Aarsland, D., Burn, D., Chiu, H., Cohen-Mansfield, J. et al. (2004). Dementia with Lewy bodies. *Lancet, Neurology, 3,* 19–28.

McKhann, G., Drachman, D., Folstein, M., Katzman, R., Price, D., & Stadlan, E. M. (1984). Clinical diagnosis of Alzheimer's disease: Report of the NINCDS-ADRDA Work Group under the auspices of Department of Health and Human Services Task Force on Alzheimer's Disease. *Neurology, 34,* 939–944.

Merikangas, K. R., Merikangas, J. R., & Angst, J. (1993). Headache syndromes and psychiatric disorders: Association and familial transmission. *Journal of Psychiatric Research, 27,* 197–210.

Metter, E. J., Schrager, M., Ferrucci, L., & Talbot, L. A. (2005). Evaluation of movement speed and reaction time as predictors of all-cause mortality in men. *Journals of Gerontology Series A-Biological Sciences and Medical Sciences, 60,* 840–846.

Miller, B. L., Darby, A., Benson, D. F., Cummings, J. L., & Miller, M. H. (1997a). Aggressive, socially disruptive and antisocial behaviour associated with fronto-temporal dementia. *British Journal of Psychiatry, 170,* 150–154.

Miller, B. L., Ikonte, C., Ponton, M., Levy, M., Boone, K., Darby, A. et al. (1997b). A study of the Lund-Manchester research criteria for frontotemporal dementia: Clinical and single-photon emission CT correlations. *Neurology, 48,* 937–942.

Mineka, S. & Zinbarg, R. (2006). A contemporary learning theory perspective on the etiology of anxiety disorders: It's not what you thought it was. *American Psychologist, 61,* 10–26.

Mitrushina, M., Boone, K. B., Razani, J., & D'Elia, L. F. (2005). *Handbook of normative data for neuropsychological assessment, 2nd edition.* (2nd ed.). New York: Oxford University Press.

Moroney, J. T., Bagiella, E., Desmond, D. W., Hachinski, V. C., Molsa, P. K., Gustafson, L. et al. (1997). Meta-analysis of the Hachinski Ischemic Score in pathologically verified dementias. *Neurology, 49,* 1096–1105.

Morris, J. C. (1994). Conflicts of interest: Research and clinical care. *Alzheimer Disease and Associated Disorders, 8*(Suppl. 4), 49–57.

Morris, J. C. (2005a). Dementia update 2005. *Alzheimer Disease and Associated Disorders, 19,* 100–117.

Morris, J. C. (2005b). Early-stage and preclinical Alzheimer disease. *Alzheimer Disease and Associated Disorders, 19,* 163–165.

Munroe, R. L. (1955). *Schools of psychoanalytic thought: An exposition, critique, and attempt at integration.* New York: Holt, Rinehart and Winston.

Myers, J. E., teWaterNaude, J., Fourie, M., Zogoe, H. B., Naik, I., Theodorou, P. et al. (2003). Nervous system effects of occupational manganese exposure on South African manganese mineworkers. *Neurotoxicology, 24,* 649–656.

Nardi, A. E., Lopes, F. L., Valenca, A. M., Nascimento, I., Mezzasalma, M. A., Zin, W. A. et al. (2004a). Psychopathological description of hyperventilation-induced panic attacks: A comparison with spontaneous panic attacks. *Psychopathology, 37,* 29–35.

Nardi, A. E., Valenca, A. M., Lopes, F. L., Nascimento, I., Mezzasalma, M. A., & Zin, W. A. (2004b). Clinical features of panic patients sensitive to hyperventilation or breath-holding methods for inducing panic attacks. *Brazilian Journal of Medical and Biological Research, 37,* 251–257.

National Institute on aging (NIH-NIA). (2006). Alzheimer's disease fact sheet. Retrieved from http://www.nia.nih.gov/Alzheimers/Publications/adfact.htm

Newman, S., Klinger, L., Venn, G., Smith, P., Harrison, M., & Treasure, T. (1989). Subjective reports of cognition in relation to assessed cognitive performance following coronary artery bypass surgery. *Journal of Psychomatic Research, 33,* 227–233.

Nixon, R. D., Resick, P. A., & Griffin, M. G. (2004). Panic following trauma: The etiology of acute posttraumatic arousal. *Journal of Anxiety Disorders, 18,* 193–210.

Nordlund, A., Rolstad, S., Hellstrom, P., Sjogren, M., Hansen, S., Wallin, A. et al. (2005). The Goteborg MCI study: Mild cognitive impairment is a heterogeneous condition. *Journal of Neurology, Neurosurgery and Psychiatry, 76,* 1485–1490.

Normandin, L. & Hazell, A. S. (2002). Manganese neurotoxicity: An update of pathophysiologic mechanisms. *Metabolic Brain Disease, 17,* 375–387.

Northam, E. A. (2004). Neuropsychological and psychosocial correlates of endocrine and metabolic disorders—a review. *Journal of Pediatric Endocrinology, 17,* 5–15.

Nuti, A., Ceravolo, R., Dell'Agnello, G., Gambaccini, G., Bellini, G., Kiferle, L. et al. (2004). Environmental factors and Parkinson's disease: A case-control study in the Tuscany region of Italy. *Parkinsonism and Related Disorders, 10,* 481–485.

O'Donohue, W. & Cucciare, M. A. (2005). The role of psychological factors in medical presentations. *Journal of clinical psychology in medical settings, 12*(1), 13–24.

Olanow, C. W. (2004). Manganese-induced parkinsonism and Parkinson's disease. *Annals of the New York Academy of Sciences, 1012,* 209–223.

Olanow, C. W., Good, P. F., Shinotoh, H., Hewitt, K. A., Vingerhoets, F. et al. (1996). Manganese intoxication in the rhesus monkey: A clinical, imaging, pathologic, and biochemical study. *Neurology, 46,* 492–498.

Ong, J. P., Aggarwal, A., Krieger, D., Easley, K. A., Karafa, M. T., Van Lente, F. et al. (2003). Correlation between ammonia levels and the severity of hepatic encephalopathy. *American Journal of Medicine, 114,* 188–193.

Pae, E. K., Chien, P., & Harper, R. M. (2005). Intermittent hypoxia damages cerebellar cortex and deep nuclei. *Neuroscience Letters, 375,* 123–128.

Pao, M., Lohman, C., Gracey, D., & Greenberg, L. (2004). Visual, tactile, and phobic hallucinations: Recognition and management in the emergency department. *Pediatric Emergency Care, 20,* 30–34.

Park, J., Yoo, C. I., Sim, C. S., Kim, H. K., Kim, J. W., Jeon, B. S., Kim, K. R., Bang, O. Y., Lee, W. Y., Yi, Y., Jung, K. Y., Chung, S. E., & Kim, Y. (2005). Occupations and Parkinson's disease: A multi-center case-control study in South Korea. *Neurotoxicology, 26,* 99–105.

Park, J., Yoo, C. I., Sim, C. S., Kim, J. W., Yi, Y., Jung, K. Y. Chung, S. E., & Kim, Y. (2004). Occupations and Parkinson's disease: A case-control study in South Korea. *Industrial Health, 42,* 352–358.

Pasquier, F. (1999). Early diagnosis of dementia: Neuropsychology. *Journal of Neurology, 246,* 6–15.

Paulsen, G. W. (1977). Environmental effects on the central nervous system. *Environmental Health Perspectives, 20,* 75–96.

Pentschew, A., Ebner, F. F., & Kovatch, R. M. (1962). Experimental manganese encephalopathy in monkeys: A preliminary report. *Journal of Neuropathology and Experimental Neurology, 22,* 488–493.

Peskine, A., Picq, C., & Pradat-Diehl, P. (2004). Cerebral anoxia and disability. *Brain Injury, 18,* 1243–1254.

Peters, H. A., Levine, R. L., Matthews, C. G., & Chapman, L. J. (1988). Extrapyramidal and other neurologic manifestations associated with carbon disulfide fumigant exposure. *Archives of Neurology, 45,* 537–540.

Petersen, R. C., Doody, R., Kurz, A., Mohs, R. C., Morris, J. C., Rabins, P. V. et al. (2001). Current concepts in mild cognitive impairment. *Archives of Neurology, 58,* 1985–1992.

Petersen, R. C., Smith, G. E., Ivnik, R. J., Kokmen, E., & Tangalos, E. G. (1994). Memory function in very early Alzheimer's disease. *Neurology, 44,* 867–872.

Petiet, C. A., Townes, B. D., Brooks, R. J., & Kramer, J. H. (1988). Neurobehavioral and psychosocial functioning of women exposed to high altitude in mountaineering. *Perceptual and Motor Skills, 67,* 443–452.

Poser, S., Mollenhauer, B., Kraubeta, A., Zerr, I., Steinhoff, B. J., Schroeter, A. et al. (1999). How to improve the clinical diagnosis of Creutzfeldt-Jakob disease. *Brain, 122,* 2345–2351.

Priyadarshi, A., Khuder, S. A., Schaub, E. A., & Priyadarshi, S. S. (2001). Environmental risk factors and Parkinson's disease: A metaanalysis. *Environmental Research, 86,* 122–127.

Przedborski, S. & Jackson-Lewis, V. (1998). Mechanisms of MPTP toxicity. *Movement Disorder, 13*(Suppl. 1), 35–42.

Quarelli, G. (2001). Les syndrome strio-pallidal dans l'intoxication chronique par sulfure de carbon (syndrome de Quarelli). *Presse Medicale, 1,* 533.

Rajput, A. H., Uitti, R. J., Stern, W., Laverty, W., O'Donnell, K., O'Donnell, D. et al. (1987). Geography, drinking water chemistry, pesticides and herbicides and the etiology of Parkinson's disease. *Canadian Journal of Neurological Sciences, 14,* 414–418.

Rapoport, A. (1987). Analgesic rebound. *American Journal of Psychiatry, 144,* 813–814.

Rapoport, A., Stang, P., Gutterman, D. L., Cady, R., Markley, H., Weeks, R. et al. (1996). Analgesic rebound headache in clinical practice: Data from a physician survey. *Headache, 36,* 14–19.

Rasmussen, B. K., Jensen, R., Schroll, M., & Olesen, J. (1992). Interrelations between migraine and tension-type headache in the general population. *Archives of Neurology, 49,* 914–918.

Reed, L. J., Lasserson, D., Marsden, P., Stanhope, N., Stevens, T., Bello, F. et al. (2003). FDG-PET findings in the Wernicke–Korsakoff syndrome. *Cortex, 39,* 1027–1045.

Reeves, J. T. & Weil, J. V. (2001). Chronic mountain sickness. A view from the crow's nest. *Advances in Experimental Medicine and Biology, 502,* 419–437.

Reuler, J. B., Girard, D. E., & Cooney, T. G. (1985). Current concepts. Wernicke's encephalopathy. *New England Journal of Medicine, 312,* 1035–1039.

Richter, R. (1945). Degeneration of the basal ganglia in monkeys from chronic carbon disulfide poisoning. *Journal of Neuropathology and Experimental Neurology, 4,* 324–329.

Rocca, W. A., Anderson, D. W., Meneghini, F., Grigoletto, F., Morgante, L., Reggio, A. et al. (1996). Occupation, education, and Parkinson's disease: A case-control study in an Italian population. *Movement Disorders, 11,* 201–206.

Roels, H., Lauwerys, R., Buchet, J. P., Genet, P., Sarhan, M. J., Hanotiau, I. et al. (1987). Epidemiological survey among workers exposed to manganese: Effects on lung, central nervous system, and some biological studies. *American Journal of Industrial Medicine, 11,* 307–327.

Roine, R. O., Kajaste, S., & Kaste, M. (1993a). Neuropsychological sequelae of cardiac arrest. *Journal of the American Medical Association, 269,* 237–242.

Roine, R. O., Raininko, R., Erkinjuntti, T., Ylikoski, A., & Kaste, M. (1993b). Magnetic resonance imaging findings associated with cardiac arrest. *Stroke, 24,* 1005–1014.

Roman, G. C., Tatemichi, T. K., Erkinjuntti, T., Cummings, J. L., Masdeu, J. C., Garcia, J. H. et al. (1993). Vascular dementia: Diagnostic criteria for research studies. Report of the NINDS-AIREN International Workshop. *Neurology, 43,* 250–260.

Roth, W. T. (2005). Physiological markers for anxiety: Panic disorder and phobias. *International Journal of Psychophysiology, 58,* 190–198.

Rothstein, J. D. & Herlong, H. F. (1989). Neurologic manifestations of hepatic disease. In J. E. Riggs (Ed.), *Neurologic manifestations of systemic disease* (pp. 563–579). Philadelphia: W. B. Saunders & Co.

Rowland, R. W. (1989). *Merritt's textbook of neurology.* (8th ed.). Philadelphia: Lea & Febiger.

Ruff, R. M. & Parker, S. B. (1993). Gender- and age-specific changes in motor speed and eye-hand coordination in adults: Normative values for the finger tapping and grooved pegboard tests. *Perceptual and Motor Skills, 76,* 1219–1230.

Ruttenber, A. J., Garbe, P. L., Kalter, H. D. et al. (1986). Meperidine analogue exposure in California narcotics abusers: Initial epidemiologic findings. In S. P. Markey, N. Castagnoli, A. G. Trevor, et al. (Eds.), *MPTP: A neurotoxin producing a parkinsonian syndorme* (pp. 339). New York: Academic Press.

Rybicki, B. A., Johnson, C. C., Uman, J., & Gorell, J. M. (1993). Parkinson's disease mortality and the industrial use of heavy metals in Michigan. *Movement Disorders, 8,* 87–92.

Sackellares, J. C. & Berent, S. (1996). *Psychological disturbances in epilepsy.* Boston: Butterworth-Heinemann.

Sacuiu, S., Sjogren, M., Johansson, B., Gustafson, D., & Skoog, I. (2005). Prodromal cognitive signs of dementia in 85-year-olds using four sources of information. *Neurology, 65,* 1894–1900.

Sandrini, G., Cecchini, A. P., Tassorelli, C., & Nappi, G. (2001). Diagnostic issues in chronic daily headache. *Current Pain and Headache Reports, 5,* 551–556.

Saper, J. R. & Jones, J. M. (1986). Ergotamine tartrate dependency: Features and possible mechanisms. *Clinical Neuropharmacology, 9,* 244–256.

Saper, J. R. (1987). Drug treatment of headache: Changing concepts and treatment strategies. *Seminars in Neurology, 7,* 178–191.

Saper, J. R. (1989). Chronic headache syndromes. *Neurology Clinics, 7,* 387–412.

Saper, J. R. (1990). Daily chronic headache. *Neurology Clinics, 8,* 891–901.

Savageau, J. A., Stanton, B. A., Jenkins, C. D., & Frater, R. W. (1982). Neuropsychological dysfunction following elective cardiac operation. II. A six-month reassessment. *Journal of Thoracic and Cardiovascular Surgery, 84,* 595–600.

Savageau, J. A., Stanton, B. A., Jenkins, C. D., & Klein, M. D. (1982). Neuropsychological dysfunction following elective cardiac operation. I. Early assessment. *Journal of Thoracic and Cardiovascular Surgery, 84,* 585–594.

Saxena, N., Bhatia, M., Joshi, Y. K., Garg, P. K., Dwivedi, S. N., & Tandon, R. K. (2002). Electrophysiological and neuropsychological tests for the diagnosis of subclinical hepatic encephalopathy and prediction of overt encephalopathy. *Liver, 22,* 190–197.

Scatcherd, J. A. (2004). Critique of the hyperthyroidism and hypothyroidism CPG. *Journal of the American Academy of Nurse Practitioners, 16,* 426–427.

Schaumburg, H. H. & Albers, J. W. (2005). Pseudoneurotoxic disease. *Neurology, 66,* 22–26.

Schiodt, F. V., Atillasoy, E., Shakil, A. O., Schiff, E. R., Caldwell, C., Kowdley, K. V. et al. (1999). Etiology and outcome for 295 patients with acute liver failure in the United States. *Liver Transplantation and Surgery*, 5, 29–34.

Schiodt, F. V., Lee, W. M., Bondesen, S., Ott, P., & Christensen, E. (2002). Influence of acute and chronic alcohol intake on the clinical course and outcome in acetaminophen overdose. *Alimentary Pharmacology and Therapeutics*, 16, 707–715.

Schneider, M., Bernasch, D., Weymann, J., Holle, R., & Bartsch, P. (2002). Acute mountain sickness: Influence of susceptibility, preexposure, and ascent rate. *Medicine and Science in Sports and Exercise*, 34, 1886–1891.

Schoenberg, B. S. (1987). Environmental risk factors for Parkinson's disease: The epidemiological evidence. *Canadian Journal of Neurological Sciences*, 14, 407–413.

Schoenberg, B. S., Osuntokun, B. O., Adeuja, A. O. G., Bademosi, O., Nottidge, V., Anderson, D. W. et al. (1988). Comparison of the prevalence of Parkinson's disease in black populations in ther rural United States and in rural Nigeria: Door-to-door community studies. *Neurology*, 38, 645–646.

Schurhoff, F., Golmard, J. L., Szoke, A., Bellivier, F., Berthier, A., Meary, A. et al. (2004). Admixture analysis of age at onset in schizophrenia. *Schizophrenia Research*, 71, 35–41.

Seidler, A., Hellenbrand, W., Robra, B. P., Vieregge, P., Nischan, Joerg, J. et al. (1996). Possible environmental, occupational, and other etiologic factors for Parkinson's disease: A case-control study in Germany. *Neurology*, 46, 1275–1284.

Sellman, M., Holm, L., Ivert, T., & Semb, B. K. (1993). A randomized study of neuropsychological function in patients undergoing coronary bypass surgery. *Thoracic and Cardiovascular Surgeon*, 41, 349–354.

Seltzer, S. (1982). Foods, and food and drug combinations, responsible for head and neck pain. *Cephalalgia*, 2, 111–124.

Semchuk, K. M., Love, E. J., & Lee, R. G. (1992). Parkinson's disease and exposure to agricultural work and pesticide chemicals. *Neurology*, 42, 1328–1335.

Semchuk, K. M., Love, E. J., & Lee, R. G. (1993). Parkinson's disease: A test of the multifactorial etiologic hypothesis. *Neurology*, 43, 1173–1180.

Seppalainen, A. M. & Haltia, M. (1980). Carbon disulfide. In P. S. Spencer & H. H. Schaumburg (Eds.), *Experimental and clinical neurotoxicology* (pp. 356–373). Baltimore: Williams & Wilkins.

Serrano, J., Encinas, J. M., Salas, E., Fernandez, A. P., Castro-Blanco, S., Fernandez-Vizarra, P. et al. (2003). Hypobaric hypoxia modifies constitutive nitric oxide synthase activity and protein nitration in the rat cerebellum. *Brain Research*, 976, 109–119.

Sevinc, A. & Savli, H. (2004). Hypothyroidism masquerading as depression: The role of noncompliance. *Journal of the National Medical Association*, 96, 379–382.

Shakil, A. O., Mazariegos, G. V., & Kramer, D. J. (1999). Fulminant hepatic failure. *Surgical Clinics of North America*, 79, 77–108.

Sherer, T. B., Betarbet, R., & Greenamyre, J. T. (2001). Pathogenesis of Parkinson's disease. *Current Opinion in Investigational Drugs*, 2, 657–662.

Sherer, T. B., Betarbet, R., & Greenamyre, J. T. (2002). Environment, mitochondria, and Parkinson's disease. *Neuroscientist*, 8, 192–197.

Siegel, G. J., Agranoff, B. W., Albers, R. W., Fisher, S. K., & Uhler, M. D. (1999). *Basic neurochemistry: Molecular, cellular and medical aspects* (6th ed.). Philadelphia: Lippincott-Raven.

Silberstein, S. D. (1992). Advances in understanding the pathophysiology of headache. *Neurology*, 42(Suppl. 2), 6–10.

Silberstein, S. D., Lipton, R. B., & Breslau, N. (1995). Migraine: Association with personality characteristics and psychopathology. *Cephalalgia, 15,* 358–369.

Silverman, K., Evans, S. M., Strain, E. C., & Griffiths, R. R. (1992). Withdrawal syndrome after the double-blind cessation of caffeine consumption. *New England Journal of Medicine, 327,* 1109–1114.

Simon, G. E., VonKorff, M., Piccinelli, M., Fullerton, C., & Ormel, J. (1999). An international study of the relation between somatic symptoms and depression. *New England Journal of Medicine, 341,* 1329–1335.

Simon, R. P. (2000). Syncope. In L. Goldman & J. C. Bennett (Eds.), *Cecil textbook of medicine* (21st ed., pp. 2028–2030). Philadelphia: W.B. Saunders.

Smargiassi, A., Mutti, A., De Rosa, A., De Palma, G., Negrotti, A., & Calzetti, S. (1998). A case-control study of occupational and environmental risk factors for Parkinson's disease in the Emilia-Romagna region of Italy. *Neurotoxicology, 19,* 709–712.

Sonino, N., Fava, G. A., Raffi, A. R., Boscaro, M., & Fallo, F. (1998). Clinical correlates of major depression in Cushing's disease. *Psychopathology, 31,* 302–306.

Spencer, P. S., Schaumburg, H. H., & Ludolph, A. C. (2000). *Experimental and clinical neurotoxicology* (2nd ed.). New York: Oxford University Press.

Spurgeon, A. (2002). Models of unexplained symptoms associated with occupational and environmental exposures. *Environmental Health Perspectives, 110* (Suppl. 4), 601–605.

Spurgeon, A., Gompertz, D., & Harrington, J. M. (1996). Modifiers of non-specific symptoms in occupational and environmental syndromes. *Occupational and Environmental Medicine, 53,* 361–366.

Spurgeon, A., Gompertz, D., & Harrington, J. M. (1997). Non-specific symptoms in response to hazard exposure in the workplace. *Journal of Psychosomatic Research, 43,* 43–49.

Stang, P. E., Yanagihara, T., Swanson, J. W., & Beard, C. M. (1992). Incidence of migraine headache: A population-based study in Olmsted County, Minnesota. *Neurology, 42,* 1657–1662.

Steinberg, B. A., Bieliauskas, L. A., Smith, G. E., & Ivnik, R. J. (2005a). Mayo's Older Americans Normative Studies: Age- and IQ-Adjusted Norms for the Trail-Making Test, the Stroop Test, and MAE Controlled Oral Word Association Test. *Clinical Neuropsychologist, 19,* 329–377.

Steinberg, B. A., Bieliauskas, L. A., Smith, G. E., Ivnik, R. J. (2005b). Mayo's Older Americans Normative Studies: Age- and IQ-Adjusted Norms for the Wechsler Memory Scale—Revised. *Clinical Neuropsychologist, 19,* 378–463.

Steinberg, B. A., Bieliauskas, L. A., Smith, G. E., Ivnik, R. J., & Malec, J. F. (2005c). Mayo's Older Americans Normative Studies: Age- and IQ-Adjusted Norms for the Auditory Verbal Learning Test and the Visual Spatial Learning Test. *Clinical Neuropsychologist, 19,* 464–523.

Stephens, R. (2006). Age-related decline in digit–symbol performance: Eye-movement and video analysis. *Archives of Clinical Neuropsychology, 21,* 101–107.

Stern, M., Dulaney, E., Gruber, S. B., Golbe, L., Bergen, M., Hurtig, H. et al. (1991). The epidemiology of Parkinson's disease. A case-control study of young-onset and old-onset patients. *Archives of Neurology, 48,* 903–907.

Stewart, W. F., Lipton, R. B., Celentano, D. D., & Reed, M. L. (1992). Prevalence of migraine headache in the United States. Relation to age, income, race, and other sociodemographic factors. *Journal of the American Medical Association, 267,* 64–69.

Stone, J., Carson, A., & Sharpe, M. (2005). Functional symptoms in neurology: Management. *Journal of Neurology, Neurosurgery and Psychiatry, 76*(Suppl. 1), i13–i21.

Stowell, C. P. & Barnhill, J. W. (2005). Acute mania in the setting of severe hypothyroidism. *Psychosomatics, 46,* 259–261.

Sullivan, C. (2002). The boogie man is coming. Retrieved from http://www.common-dreams.org/views02/1118–06.htm

Sunderland, T., Wolozin, B., Galasko, D., Levy, J., Dukoff, R., Bahro, M. et al. (1999). Longitudinal stability of CSF tau levels in Alzheimer patients. *Biological Psychiatry, 46,* 750–755.

Swainston, H. T. & Keating, G. M. (2005). Zolpidem: A review of its use in the management of insomnia. *CNS Drugs, 19,* 65–89.

Swan, G. E., DeCarli, C., Miller, B. L., Reed, T., Wolf, P. A., & Carmelli, D. (2000). Biobehavioral characteristics of nondemented older adults with subclinical brain atrophy. *Neurology, 54,* 2108–2114.

Tanner, C. M. (1989). The role of environmental toxins in the etiology of Parkinson's disease. *Trends in Neurosciences, 12,* 49–54.

Tanner, C. M. (1992). Occupational and environmental causes of parkinsonism. *Occupational Medicine, 7,* 503–513.

Tanner, C. M., Chen, B., Wang, W., Peng, M., Liu, Z., Liang, X. et al. (1989). Environmental factors and Parkinson's disease: A case-control study in China. *Neurology, 39,* 660–664.

Tannheimer, M., Thomas, A., & Gerngross, H. (2002). Oxygen saturation course and altitude symptomatology during an expedition to broad peak (8047 m). *International Journal of Sports Medicine, 23,* 329–335.

Taylor, P. J., Pocock, S. J., Hall, S. A., & Waters, W. E. (1970). Headaches and migraine in colour retouchers. *British Journal of Internal Medicine, 27,* 364–367.

Tesar, G. (2002). Depression and other mood disorders. Retrieved from http://www.clevelandclinicmeded.com/diseasemanagement/psychiatry/depression/depression.htm

The University of Michigan. (2006). America's war against terrorism. Retrieved from http://www.lib.umich.edu/govdocs/usterror.html

Thomson, A. D. & Marshall, E. J. (2006). The natural history and pathophysiology of Wernicke's Encephalopathy and Korsakoff's Psychosis. *Alcohol and Alcoholism, 41,* 151–158.

Tisserand, D. J., McIntosh, A. R., van der Veen, F. M., Backes, W. H., & Jolles, J. (2005). Age-related reorganization of encoding networks directly influences subsequent recognition memory. *Cognitive Brain Research, 25,* 8–18.

Tombaugh, T. N., Kozak, J., & Rees, L. (1999). Normative data stratified by age and education for two measures of verbal fluency: FAS and animal naming. *Archives of Clinical Neuropsychology, 14,* 167–177.

Trimble, M. R. & Krishnamoorthy, E. S. (2000). The role of toxins in disorders of mood and affect. *Neurology Clinics, 18,* 649–664.

Trimble, M. R. (1988). *Biological psychiatry.* Chichester, England, UK: John Wiley & Sons.

Tsai, C. H., Lo, S. K., See, L. C., Chen, H. Z., Chen, R. S., Weng, Y. H. et al. (2002). Environmental risk factors of young onset Parkinson's disease: A case-control study. *Clinical Neurology and Neurosurgery, 104,* 328–333.

Tsui, J. K., Calne, D. B., Wang, Y., Schulzer, M., & Marion, S. A. (1999). Occupational risk factors in Parkinson's disease. *Canadian Journal of Public Health, 90,* 334–337.

Tull, M. T., Gratz, K. L., Salters, K., Roemer, L. (2004). The role of experiential avoidance in posttraumatic stress symptoms and symptoms of depression, anxiety, and somatization. *Journal of Nervous and Mental Disease, 192,* 754–761.

Tunbridge, W. M., Evered, D. C., Hall, R., Appleton, D., Brewis, M., Clark, F. et al. (1977). The spectrum of thyroid disease in a community: The Whickham survey. *Clinical Endocrinology, 7,* 481–493.

Turner, R. S. (2006). Alzheimer's disease. *Seminars in Neurology, 26,* 499–506.

Usui, C., Inoue, Y., Kimura, M., Kirino, E., Nagaoka, S., Abe, M. et al. (2004). Irreversible subcortical dementia following high altitude illness. *High Altitude Medicine and Biology, 5,* 77–81.

Uversky, V. N., Li, J., & Fink, A. L. (2001). Pesticides directly accelerate the rate of alpha-synuclein fibril formation: A possible factor in Parkinson's disease. *FEBS Letters, 500,* 105–108.

van Boxtel, M. P., Buntinx, F., Houx, P. J., Metsemakers, J. F., Knottnerus, A., Jolles, J. et al. (1998). The relation between morbidity and cognitive performance in a normal aging population. *Journals of Gerontology Series A-Biological Sciences and Medical Sciences, 53,* M147–M154.

Vander, B. T., Minoshima, S., Giordani, B., Foster, N. L., Frey, K. A., Berent, S. et al. (1997). Cerebral metabolic differences in Parkinson's and Alzheimer's diseases matched for dementia severity. *Journal of Nuclear Medicine, 38,* 797–802.

Virues-Ortega, J., Buela-Casal, G., Garrido, E., & Alcazar, B. (2004). Neuropsychological functioning associated with high-altitude exposure. *Neuropsychology Review, 14,* 197–224.

Volkan, V. (1970). Typical findings in pathological grief. *Psychiatric Quarterly, 44,* 231–250.

Vorhees, V. J. (2003). "I can't move." *Journal of the American Board of Family Practice, 16,* 560–561.

Voyer, P., McCubbin, M., Cohen, D., Lauzon, S., Collin, J., & Boivin, C. (2004). Unconventional indicators of drug dependence among elderly long-term users of benzodiazepines. *Issues in Mental Health Nursing, 25,* 603–628.

Waldie, K. E. & Poulton, R. (2002). The burden of illness associated with headache disorders among young adults in a representative cohort study. *Headache, 42,* 612–619.

Waller, E., Scheidt, C. E., & Hartmann, A. (2004). Attachment representation and illness behavior in somatoform disorders. *Journal of Nervous and Mental Disease, 192,* 200–209.

Walsh, T. S., Wigmore, S. J., Hopton, P., Richardson, R., & Lee, A. (2000). Energy expenditure in acetaminophen-induced fulminant hepatic failure. *Critical Care Medicine, 28,* 649–654.

Warner, T. T. & Schapira, A. H. (2003). Genetic and environmental factors in the cause of Parkinson's disease. *Annals of Neurology, 53*(Suppl. 3), S16–S23.

Watt, T., Groenvold, M., Rasmussen, A. K., Bonnema, S. J., Hegedus, L., Bjorner, J. B. et al. (2006). Quality of life in patients with benign thyroid disorders. A review. *European Journal of Endocrinology, 154,* 501–510.

Weber, J. G., Ereth, M. H., & Danielson, D. R. (1993). Perioperative ingestion of caffeine and postoperative headache. *Mayo Clinic Proceedings, 68,* 842–845.

Wechsler, D. (1997). *WAIS-III: Wechsler adult intelligence scale. Administration and scoring manual.* (3rd ed.). San Antonio: The Psychological Corporation (Harcourt Brace & Company).

Weiss, S. M., Lightowler, S., Stanhope, K. J., Kennett, G. A., & Dourish, C. T. (2000). Measurement of anxiety in transgenic mice. *Reviews in the Neurosciences, 11,* 59–74.

Weitzenblum, E., Chaouat, A., & Kessler, R. (2002). Long-term oxygen therapy for chronic respiratory failure. Rationale, indications, modalities. *Revue de Pneumologie Clinique, 58,* 195–212.

Welch, K. M. & Goadsby, P. J. (2002). Chronic daily headache: Nosology and pathophysiology. *Current Opinion in Neurology, 15,* 287–295.

Wendon, J. A., Harrison, P. M., Keays, R., & Williams, R. (1994). Cerebral blood flow and metabolism in fulminant liver failure. *Hepatology, 19,* 1407–1413.

Werneck, A. L. & Alvarenga, H. (1999). Genetics, drugs and environmental factors in Parkinson's disease. A case-control study. *Arquivos de Neuro-Psiquiatria, 57,* 347–355.

Whalley, L. J., Dick, F.D., & McNeill, G. (2006). A life-course approach to the aetiology of late-onset dementias. *Lancet Neurology, 5,* 87–96.

Whitlock, C. M., Jr., Amuso, S. J., & Bittenbender, J. B. (1966). Chronic neurological disease in two manganese steel workers. *American Industrial Hygiene Association Journal, 27,* 454–459.

Williams, A. (1986). MPTP toxicity: Clinical features. *Journal of Neural Transmission, 20*(Suppl), 5–9.

Wilson, J. T., Kasantikul, V., Harbison, R., & Martin, D. (1978). Death in an adolescent following an overdose of acetaminophen and phenobarbital. *American Journal of Diseases of Children, 132,* 466–473.

Wilson, R. K., Kuncl, R. W., & Corse, A. M. (1958). Wernicke's encephalopathy: Beyond alcoholism. *Nature Clinical Practice Neurology, 2,* 54–58.

World Health Organization and Nordic Council Ministers (1985). *Chronic effects of organic solvents on central nervous system and diagnostic criteria: report on WHO/Nordic Council of Ministers Working Group (Environmental Health 5), Copenhagen, 10–14 June, 1985.* Copenhagen: World Health Organization and Nordic Council of Ministers.

World Health Organization. (2001). *International classification of functioning, disability and health (ICF).* Geneva: World Health Organization.

Xu, Y., Jack, C. R., Jr., O'Brien, P. C., Kokmen, E., Smith, G. E., Ivnik, R. J. et al. (2000). Usefulness of MRI measures of entorhinal cortex versus hippocampus in AD. *Neurology, 54,* 1760–1767.

Yahr, M. D. (1989). Parkinsonism. In L. P. Rowland (Ed.), *Merrits's textbook of neurology* (8th ed., pp. 658–671). Philadelphia: Lea & Febiger.

Yamada, M., Ohno, S., Okayasu, I., Okeda, R., Hatakeyama, S., Watanabe, H. et al. (1986). Chronic manganese poisoning: A neuropathological study with determination of manganese distribution in the brain. *Acta Neuropathologica, 70,* 273–278.

Yamada, Y., Ohno, Y., Nakashima, Y., Fukuda, M., Takayanagi, R., Sato, H. et al. (2002). Prediction and assessment of extrapyramidal side effects induced by risperidone based on dopamine D(2) receptor occupancy. *Synapse, 46,* 32–37.

Yeung, A., Chang, D., Gresham, R. L., Jr., Nierenberg, A. A., Fava, M., Yeung, A. et al. (2004). Illness beliefs of depressed Chinese American patients in primary care. *Journal of Nervous and Mental Disease, 192,* 324–327.

Young, E. A., Haskett, R. F., Grunhaus, L., Pande, A., Weinberg, V. M., Watson, S. J. et al. (1994). Increased evening activation of the hypothalamic-pituitary-adrenal axis in depressed patients. *Archives of General Psychiatry, 51,* 701–707.

Zakzanis, K. K. & Heinrichs, R. W. (1999). Schizophrenia and the frontal brain: A quantitative review. *Journal of the International Neuropsychological Society*, *5*, 556–566.

Zakzanis, K. K., Leach, L., & Kaplan, E. (1999). *Neuropsychological differential diagnosis*. Lisse: Swets & Zeitlinger.

Zola-Morgan, S. & Squire, L. R. (1986). Memory impairment in monkeys following lesions limited to the hippocampus. *Behavioral Neuroscience*, *100*, 155–160.

Zola-Morgan, S., Squire, L. R., & Amaral, D. G. (1986). Human amnesia and the medial temporal region: Enduring memory impairment following a bilateral lesion limited to field CA1 of the hippocampus. *Journal of Neuroscience*, *6*, 2950–2967.

Zorzon, M., Capus, L., Pellegrino, A., Cazzato, G., & Zivadinov, R. (2002). Familial and environmental risk factors in Parkinson's disease: A case-control study in north-east Italy. *Acta Neurologica Scandinavica*, *105*, 77–82.

Zwart, J. A., Dyb, G., Hagen, K., Svebak, S., & Holmen, J. (2003). Analgesic use: A predictor of chronic pain and medication overuse headache. The Head-HUNT study. *Neurology*, *61*, 160–164.

18 Consequences of an incomplete differential diagnosis

The symptoms of toxicant exposure often are nonspecific. As a result, the symptoms observed in a given *case presentation* might implicate a number of potentially explanatory medical and nonmedical conditions. The nature of symptoms, even when they are found ultimately to be in response directly to chemical exposure, also can be influenced by other nontoxicant factors (e.g., historical medical disease, psychiatric disorders, or variations in normal behavior). Developing a complete differential diagnosis is an essential step toward solving the problems associated with the reality of nonspecificity. The clinical approaches presented in volume I should occur within a model that includes consideration of the patient's history, results of physical examination, and findings from other medical and neurobehavioral tests and examinations. Finally, considerable emphasis has been placed in these volumes on the requirement to separate clinical diagnosis from causal determination. The cases that follow reflect situations where failure to attend to one or more aspects of these four themes resulted in initial clinical diagnoses or proposed causes that were either incorrect or incomplete. In each case, the specific problems are identified, discussed, and verified within an evidence-based approach to diagnostic and causal determination.

Selected presentations

Child with behavioral and learning problems attributed to ethylmercury

Christine L. Trask and Sherri Provencal

On July 19, 2005 the directors of the centers for disease control and prevention (CDC) and the National Institute of Child Health Development and the acting deputy commissioner for international and special programs at the Food and Drug Administration (FDA) held a joint news conference to discuss the heated debate surrounding Thimerosal in vaccines and autism (Harris, 2005). They reiterated publicly that there is no proven link between vaccines and autism. Nevertheless, during the press conference several parents sat in vigil outside, one holding a sign claiming that a vaccine caused her child's autism.

In the past two decades, substantial attention has become focused on the increasing incidence of children diagnosed with autism or an autistic-spectrum disorder, as well as the potential link between these disorders and environmental exposures. Following the Food and Drug Administration (FDA) Modernization Act of 1997, the FDA reviewed and evaluated the risk of all food and drugs containing mercury. In June 1999, it was reported that children vaccinated with agents containing a preservative, Thimerosal, could be exposed to a level of organic mercury that exceeded the existing guidelines for exposure to methylmercury (Ball, Ball, & Pratt, 2001). Although the prevalence of autistic-spectrum disorders began to rise slightly in the later half of the 1980s, the increase in diagnosis was steeper in the beginning of the 1990s. It has been unclear if the increase in reported cases of autistic-spectrum disorders reflects an actual increase in incidence, an increase in diagnosis related to improved coverage of psychological services and better detection, changes in diagnostic criteria, or changes in insurance reimbursement which may indirectly affect diagnosis (Parker, Schwartz, Todd, & Pickering, 2004). Nevertheless, the general public and several researchers have assumed that the sharp increase in diagnosis corresponds, at least in part, to some true increase in incidence.

As greater attention has become focused on autism, greater interest has been generated on uncovering the potential cause for this disorder. One theory has been that the increase in autism is related to the vaccination schedules, given the temporal relationship between the increase in diagnosis of autism and the change in vaccination schedules. In particular, Thimerosal was identified as a potential causal agent. Thimerosal is a preservative used in vaccines since the 1930s (Institute of Medicine, 2001). Added in minute amounts to vaccines, it helped prevent bacteria from contaminating multidose vials of vaccines (Meadows, 2001). Thimerosal is almost 50% ethylmercury by weight (Institute of Medicine, 2001). In 1990 and 1991, *Haemophilus influenzae* b (Hib) and hepatitis B (hep B) were first universally recommended, significantly increasing the exposure to vaccines with Thimerosal. The only other childhood vaccine that included Thimerosal was diphtheria-tetanus-pertussis (DTP). Two-year-old children in 1999 who received the series of recommended vaccines (e.g., four doses of DTP, four doses of Hib, three doses of hep B) were estimated to have been exposed to a 237.5 μg cumulative dose of ethylmercury (Stehr-Green, Tull, Stellfeld, Mortenson, & Simpson, 2003), with an estimated exposure of 187.5 mg within the first 6 months of life (Institute of Medicine, 2001). Since 2001, however, thimerosal was largely removed from most immunizations for young children, with the exception of some influenza vaccines (Food and Drug Administration [FDA], 2005) (Table 18.1). The reduction of vaccines containing thimerosal has economic implications, especially for developing countries, in that alternative vaccines are typically single-dose vials that are more expensive and that require the use of refrigeration (Parker et al., 2004).

Case presentation[1]

A neuropsychological evaluation was sought for a 6-year-old boy by his parents. In particular, the mother reported that she felt her child had been

Table 18.1 Current Thimerosal content of routinely used pediatric vaccines (Food and Drug Administration [FDA], 2005).

Thimerosal vaccine	Trade name/ manufacturer	Thimerosal concentration	History of Thimerosal
DTaP	Infanrix (GSK)	Free	Never contained
	Deptacel (AP)	Free	Never contained
	Tripedia (AP)	Trace (<0.3 µg Hg/ 0.5 ml dose)	
DTaP-HepB-IPV	Pediatrix (GSK)	Trace (<0.0125 µg Hg/ 0.5 ml dose)	Never more than trace
Pneumococcal conjugate	Prevanar (WL)	Free	Never contained
Inactivated poliovirus	IPOL (AP)	Free	Never contained
Varicella (chicken pox)	Varivax (M)	Free	Never contained
Mumps, measles, and rubella	MMR-II (M)	Free	Never contained
Hepatitis B	Recombivax HB (M)	Free	
	Engerix B (GSK)	Trace (<0.5 µg Hd/ 0.5 ml dose)	
Haemophilus influenzae Type B conjugate (Hib)	ActHIB (AP)/ OmniHIB (GSK)	Free	Never contained
	PedvaxHIB (M)	Free	
	Hib TITER (WL)	Free	Never contained
Hib/Hepatitis B Combination	Comvax (M)	Free	Never contained
Influenza	Fluzone (AP)	0.01% Ages 6 months– 3 years: 12.5 µg/0.25 ml	
	Fluzone (AP) no Thimerosal	Free	
	Fluvirin (Chiron/Evans)	0.01% (25 µg/ 0.5 ml dose)	
	Fluvirin (Chiron/Evans) no preservative	Free	
Influenza, live	FluMist (MedImmune)	Free	Never contained
Meningococcal	Menactra (AP)	Free	Never contained

poisoned by a series of childhood vaccines. Up through age 3, development was reported to be normal. He was speaking in two to three word sentences, would scribble with a crayon, could feed himself independently, and could pull on and take off a pair of sweatpants. He regularly engaged in parallel play and appeared interested in the activities of other children. He received all recommended childhood immunizations and shortly after his 4-year-old well-visit during which he was given a series of vaccines (DtaP, MMR), he began to demonstrate a decline in his expressive language, as well as decreased awareness of sounds, hypersensitivity to light, increased tantrums, withdrawal from social contact, and sleep difficulties. When the boy was seen at age 4 years, 6 months, his oral language was markedly impaired, but he was demonstrating early written language skills. He could point to individual printed letters and could write his first name. He also successfully completed toilet training. Family medical history was generally benign, but limited because the child had been adopted. The child's parents were seeking a second opinion at this time because of a more recent loss of skills, in the absence of any known toxic exposure or progressive medical condition. At age 6 years, his language consisted of only single words, used inconsistently and often in inappropriate contexts. He had lost his early written language skills, could no longer identify individual letters or numbers, and had demonstrated declines in graphomotor skills. He also demonstrated a regression in toileting skills, and he was currently wearing pull-ups and depended on others for most self-care activities.

INITIAL CLINICAL DIAGNOSIS

The family physician had also noticed significant declines in the child's development, but had failed to identify any clear medical causes. As a result, he noted in his diagnostic conclusion that mercury poisoning seemed likely, given the clear loss of previously acquired skills, and the temporal association between the onset of the decline and the administration of childhood vaccinations. In particular, he commented to the mother that, although the literature on group studies have not supported a relationship between mercury in vaccines and autistic-like symptoms, that did not rule out the possibility of a causal effect for a particular child.

ADDITIONAL INFORMATION

At the onset of the decline, the child had undergone multiple medical studies. A neurologic consultation noted that the child's head circumference was large for age, at the 95th percentile, and he currently demonstrated a mildly asymmetric gait. Past medical history was unremarkable. Routine blood chemistry, urine metabolic screen, and blood lead levels were normal. Chromosomal studies, including fragile X, were negative. A formal hearing evaluation was reported to be normal and a brain magnetic resonance imaging (MRI) scan was normal. There also were some nonspecific abnormalities. In particular, an electroencephalography (EEG) showed the presence of left temporal delta slowing, suggestive of nonspecific left temporal neuronal dysfunction. A sleep-deprived EEG showed some sharp spikes in the left frontal region during sleep, but no clear epileptiform activity. A video EEG sleep study also did not record any epileptiform activity, but noted diffuse background slowing, particularly in the left temporal area.

Neuropsychological testing. During the neuropsychological evaluation, the child appeared to tolerate only 5–10 min of externally imposed activities. He tended to treat other people as furniture, readily climbing on the examiner's lap or leaning against the examiner's leg, but maintained minimal to no eye contact. He also tended to "sniff" new people upon introduction to them. In the testing room, he frequently attempted to turn off the light, and would spin, twirl, and hum in the darkness. His verbalizations had an expressive intonation pattern to them, following the length and phrasing of sentences, but it was difficult to discern individual words. Occasional head banging and toe walking were observed. Given the level of behavioral disruption, formal testing was difficult to accomplish but most results reflected functioning in a mild to moderately impaired range (Table 18.2).

ALTERNATIVE CLINICAL DIAGNOSIS

The child in this *case presentation* reflected mild-to-moderate neurobehavioral dysfunction and clear developmental abnormalities. On the basis of

Table 18.2 Neuropsychological test results.

Measure	Result
Peabody Picture Vocabulary Test–Revised	Age-equivalence = 2 years, 2 months
Stanford Binet Intelligence Scales—4th Edition (mean = 50, SD = 8)	
Vocabulary	Standard score = 38, 7th percentile Articulation difficulties (e.g., "fladder" for "flower")
Pattern Analysis	Standard Score = 33, 1st percentile
Bayley Scales of Infant Development—2nd Edition	Only able to complete nonverbal items Estimated age equivalency = 2 years, 10 months
Beery Butkenica Developmental Test of Visual-Motor Integration	Drew an approximation of a vertical line and a circle
Vineland Adaptive Behavior Scales (mean = 100, SD = 15)	
Communication	Standard score = 53, age-equivalence = 2 years
Social skills	Standard score = 59, age-equivalence = 1 year, 11 months
Daily living skills	Standard score = 73, age-equivalence = 3 years, 11 months
Motor skills	Standard score = 73, age-equivalence = 3 years, 11 months

the patient's evaluation, history, and examination results, the differential diagnosis included adverse reaction to Thimerosal in a vaccine, adverse reaction to another aspect associated with vaccination, a pediatric seizure disorder such as Landau–Kleffner syndrome (LKS), and a pervasive developmental disorder, such as autism or Childhood Disintegrative Disorder (CDD). Given the length of progressive declines and the lack of medical findings, an acute infectious or metabolic disorder appeared unlikely.

Discussion

The childhood immunization program has been considered to be one of the most important health interventions of the 20th century (Bonanni, 1999; CDC, 1999). Nevertheless, distrust of the immunization program has increased public, as well as professional concerns about a possible link between autism and immunizations (Bernard, Enayati, Roger, Binstock, & Redwood, 2002). For example, Koger, Schettler, and Weiss (2005) have asserted that between 3% and 25% of developmental defects, such as autism, are caused by neurotoxic environmental exposures. Autistic symptoms are known to be associated with several medical conditions, including LKS, tuberous sclerosis, and other metabolic diseases. Nevertheless, approximately 70–90% of instances of autism have an unknown etiology and pathogenesis (Bailey, Phillips, & Rutter, 1996; Gillberg & Coleman, 1992).

MERCURY AND THIMEROSAL

There are two major forms of mercury: inorganic and organic. Inorganic mercury is associated with neurodevelopmental difficulties and renal toxicity in young children (Winship, 1986; Pichichero et al., 2002). For organic mercury, methylmercury is one of the forms of mercury that has been most studied (see chapter 15, for further discussion). Ethylmercury is another form of organic mercury that is believed to have properties similar to methylmercury. In contrast to methylmercury, however, ethylmercury has a shorter half-life and ethylmercury is more rapidly excreted through the gut and stool (Folb et al., 2004). In addition, in animal studies, ethylmercury has been reported to be less toxic than methylmercury (Magos et al., 1985).

Guidelines have been created by various international and national agencies to limit the cumulative exposures to methylmercury. These guidelines reflect a wide range, with the most stringent being set by the Environmental Protection Agency (EPA) in the United States (Andrews et al., 2004) at 0.1 to 0.47 µg/kg body weight/day (World Health Organization; WHO). When the level of Thimerosal in vaccines was reviewed, it was noted that this level would have been exceeded by some children by the age of 6 months. Despite the absence of research supporting that this level of exposure to ethylmercury was likely to result in harm, the American Academy of Pediatrics and the Public Health Service in 1999 recommended the removal of Thimerosal from vaccines, as a precautionary measure.

Human and animal studies of methylmercury have found impairments in vision, learning disabilities, attention, and motor skills. At high levels of exposure, mercury may be associated with smaller brain size, cellular distortions of the brain, and mental retardation (Koger, Schettler, & Weiss, 2005). Symptoms of autism and methylmercury toxicity have been reported to be similar (Bernard, Enayati, Redwood, Roger, & Binstock, 2001). Two of the most prominent studies of the effect of methylmercury on children were conducted in communities that consume large quantities of seafood (e.g., Seychelle Islands by Myers et al., 2003; and Faroe Islands by Grandjean et al., 1997) and have yielded inconsistent results.

There have been some cases of acute toxicity from Thimerosal-containing agents in the literature (FDA, 2005). In general, the range of exposure has been from 3 to several 100 mg/kg, including one suicide attempt with Thimerosal (Pfab, Muckter, Roider, & Zilker, 1996). At high levels, symptoms were obtundation, coma, and death. Other symptoms included local necrosis, acute hemolysis, disseminated intravascular coagulation, and acute renal tubular necrosis (FDA, 2005).

A limited number of animal studies with Thimerosal have been conducted. The earliest study was reported by Powell and Jamieson (1931), who noted the maximum tolerated doses in several animal species, such as rabbits and rats. Blair, Clark, Clarke, and Wood (1975) reported that there were no histopathological changes in the brain or kidney of squirrel monkeys associated with administration of Thimerosal intranasally for 190 days.

In 2002, a strategic advisory group of experts reported that the review of evidence of toxicity from Thimerosal-containing vaccines was not supported and that these vaccines should continue to be used (Folb et al., 2004). The Global Advisory Committee (2005) on vaccine safety established by WHO reported that several of the features associated with autism, such as increased brain weight, total brain volume, cortical gray matter volume and neuronal cell density of Purkinje cells in the cerebellum, and the absence of gliosis were not biologically consistent with an external toxic agent, such as mercury exposure. They also noted that there was no clear animal model of autism, although some animal models of deficits in social play exist, and that these models typically reflect a genetic basis for the deficit. On the basis of the studies of twins, if one monozygotic twin develops autism, the risk for the other twin to develop an autistic-spectrum disorder has been estimated to be 92%, whereas the risk falls to 10% for dizygotic twins (Bailey et al., 1995; Wong, 2001). This difference in concordance rates supports the theory that autism has a strong genetic component (Libbey, Sweeten, McMahon, & Fujinami, 2005). It has been suggested that as many as 20 different genes may be involved (Cook, 2001; Risch et al., 1999).

The relationship between vaccinations and autistic-spectrum disorders has been investigated through several computerized database systems. The vaccine adverse event reporting system (VAERS) was created in 1990 and is overseen by the FDA and the CDC. Reports about adverse effects can be submitted by a wide range of people including individuals, health care providers, and manufacturers (Woo et al., 2004). Woo et al. searched the VAERS for reports of autistic symptoms following vaccination from 1990 until 2001. From the cases identified, a total of 124 reporters participated. In this study, the average age of symptom onset was 19.2 months. Reported diagnoses included autism or autistic-spectrum disorder (75.0%), mental retardation (4.0%), and/or developmental delay, not otherwise specified. The majority of reports (65.3%) were filed in response to an MMR vaccine. Many of the reporters (86.3%) believed that Thimerosal or mercury played a very strong or moderate role in the person's current problems. The temporal association between receipt of the vaccine and symptom development was the main foundation for the belief that vaccines cause autism. Approximately half (46%) of the children for whom a VAERS report was filed had not received any other immunizations since the symptoms began. In particular, MMR and diphtheria-tetanus-acellular pertussis were the vaccines most likely to be withheld.

Geier and Geier (2004) also used data from the VAERS to compare children receiving Thimerosal-containing DtaP vaccines to a group receiving Thimerosal-free DtaP vaccines (1997–2000) on the number and type of adverse events reported. A borderline significant odds ratio (OR) for autism was reported (OR $= 1.8$, 95% CI $= 1.0$–3.3, $p < .05$), with significantly increased odds ratio for speech disorders, mental retardation, personality disorders, and thinking abnormalities.

In the United Kingdom, the general practitioner research database (GPRD) is a computerized database that includes records of vaccination and diagnoses of autism or other pervasive developmental disorders (Smeeth et al., 2004). The GPRD was created in 1987 and includes records from contributing general practices that are broadly representative of practices in England and Wales with regard to geographical location, practice size, and age and sex of registered patient. The only vaccine with Thimerosal used routinely in the infant immunization program in the United Kingdom since the 1980s is diphtheria-tetanus-whole-cell pertussis (DTP) or diphtheria tetanus (DT) vaccine or vaccines containing DTP or DT. These vaccines contain 50 μg of Thimerosal, which equates to 25 μg of mercury per dose (Andrews et al., 2004). Given the immunization schedule in the United Kingdom, many children would have had a cumulative exposure of 150 μg of Thimerosal by 4 months of age (Andrews et al.). Andrews et al. examined data of children born during 1988–1997 who had at least 2 years of continuous follow-up after birth, with a total of 103,043 children who met inclusionary criteria. The majority of children (>96%) had received all three doses of DTP/DT. The authors noted that there appeared to be an unexpected protective effect of DTP/DT vaccination on general developmental disorders, unspecified development delay, and attention deficit hyperactivity disorder (ADHD). The only area of potential increased risk associated with Thimerosal exposure was for tics in a smaller subgroup.

In Denmark, Makela, Nuorti, and Peltola (2002) examined data on nearly 3 million people. A total of 440 cases of autism and 787 cases of autistic-spectrum disorders were identified. Within the sample, 4.4% did not receive any whole-cell pertussis vaccine (which is associated with greater adverse effects than acellular pertussis vaccines; Zimmerman, 1998), 95.6% received at least one dose, 89.0% received at least two doses, and 62.7% received all three doses. There was no evidence of a dose–response relationship between the number of doses received and the incidence of autism or autistic-spectrum disorders.

In 2001, the Institute of Medicine completed a review of the available scientific literature on the association between Thimerosal in vaccines and autism. At that time, they concluded that there was insufficient evidence to support a causal relationship between Thimerosal and autism. In 2004, the Institute of Medicine reviewed five new epidemiological studies in Sweden, Denmark, the United States, and the United Kingdom and nine controlled observational studies, three ecological studies, and two studies based on a passive reporting system in Finland. None of these studies found a relationship between Thimerosal in vaccines and autism. As a result, the Institute of Medicine revised their previous conclusion to report that Thimerosal-containing vaccines are not associated with autism.

VIRAL INFECTIONS

In addition to hypotheses about the relationship between Thimerosal and autistic-spectrum disorders, an alternative hypothesis that has received considerable attention from the media is that autistic-spectrum disorders are linked to the MMR vaccine. A relationship between autism and viral infections had been previously studied (e.g., Deykin and MacMahon, 1979; Jorgensen, Goldschmidt, & Vestergaard, 1982). Chess (1971) found that children who had congenital rubella had a higher rate of autism, and Stubbs (1976) reported that children with autism appeared to have an altered immune response to rubella vaccination, suggesting a congenital infection with the rubella virus. Similarly, Singh, Lin, Newell, and Nelson (2002) and Singh, Lin, and Yang (1998) reported that children with autism had higher levels of anti-measle-mumps-rubella antibodies. This theory of a specific link between the MMR vaccine and autism first received attention in 1998 following the publication of Wakefield et al. (1998) of an association between autism, MMR vaccines, and gastrointestinal problems in 12 children with pervasive developmental disorders. Unlike the DTP vaccine, live viral vaccines such as measles vaccine, do not use preservatives such as Thimerosal, because they would interfere with the active ingredients in the vaccine (Folb et al., 2004). Wakefield et al. reported an autistic enterocolitis, which was described as a developmental regression and gastrointestinal symptoms that developed following administration of the MMR vaccine. Almost all children were reported to show some general developmental regression (e.g., loss of acquired skills after uneventful health visits for the first year of life) and gastrointestinal symptoms, including constipation, diarrhea, abdominal pain, and bloating. Behavioral symptoms developed within 2 weeks of receiving the

MMR vaccine in 8 of the original 12 children studied (Wakefield et al., 1988). They went on to report that there was evidence of the measles' virus genome in the peripheral white blood cells and bowel biopsy specimens of some of the patients (Kawashima et al., 2000; Uhlmann et al., 2002).

In 1988, the MMR vaccine was introduced in Great Britain for all children aged 12–15 months. In a study reviewing records from June 1, 1987 until December 31, 2001, Smeeth et al. (2004) identified cases of autism (76.6%) and other pervasive developmental or autistic-spectrum disorders (23.4%). A total of 1,294 cases and 4,469 controls were included in this study. They found no significant differences between cases and controls in any of the measures of vaccination status, including median age at first MMR vaccination, MMR vaccination between third birthday, MMR vaccination before age 18 months, receipt of MMR vaccination at any age (cases, 78.1%; controls, 82.1%).

Fombonne and Chakrabarti (2001) compared 96 children born in Great Britain between 1992 and 1995 who had been diagnosed with a pervasive developmental disorder with two clinical samples: one from Maudsley Hospital born between 1987 and 1996 with a confirmed diagnosis of a pervasive developmental disorder and believed to have received an MMR vaccine and the other from Maudsley family study born between 1954 and 1979 with a diagnosis of autism who were not given MMR vaccines. Almost all of the cases ($n = 95$) received an MMR vaccine (median age $= 13.5$ months). There was no evidence of an increased incidence of CDD in children receiving an MMR vaccine. For children who had been exposed to MMR vaccines and those that had not, the age of onset of autistic symptoms, as reported by parents, was similar (19.3 and 19.2 months versus 19.5 months). Gastrointestinal symptoms were reported in 18.8% of the sample and were not associated with an increased risk for developmental regression.

A retrospective cohort study from Denmark failed to find a relationship between use of the MMR vaccine and autism or autistic-spectrum disorders (Madsen, Hviid, & Vestergaard, 2002). They reviewed data on more than 500,000 children, including nearly 100,000 children who had not received an MMR vaccine. On the basis of relative risk, there was not an association between the MMR vaccine and autism or autistic-spectrum disorders.

Because the concerns about the relationship between vaccines and autism have been raised, declines in vaccination coverage have been reported in Australia, Great Britain, Germany, and Japan (Bardenheier et al., 2004). In particular, the number of children in Great Britain receiving MMR vaccinations has declined from 92% in 1995–1996 to 82% in 2002–2003 and as low as 65% in some areas (Owens, 2002). In a telephone survey that compared beliefs of parents whose children were up to date with recommended vaccines (control) and those that were not (case), they found that parents whose children were not up to date had more specific concerns regarding side effects from vaccines, including the belief that autism was associated with vaccination (Bardenheier et al.). Current immunization schedules recommend 20 vaccines within the first 2 years of life (Table 18.3), which reflects an increase of 25% over the past 5 years (Bardenheier et al.). Information

Table 18.3 Schedule of recommended immunizations in the United States.

Vaccine	Number of doses	Age ranges Birth–6 months	6–24 months	4–6 years
Hepatitis B	4 (if birth dose given)	First dose soon after birth, second dose at least 4 weeks later; combination vaccines cannot be given before age 6 weeks	Third dose at least 16 weeks after the first dose. Last dose—not before 24 weeks of age	
DTaP	4	First dose at 2 months, second dose at 4 months, third dose at 6 months		Fourth dose
MMR	2		First dose at 12–18 months	Second dose
Haemophilus influenzae Type B (Hib)	2–3	First dose at 2 months, second dose at 4 months, third dose (if required) at 6 months		
Inactivated poliovirus	3	First dose at 2 months, second dose at 4 months		Third dose
Varicella	1		Any time after age 12 months	
Pneumococcal	3–4	First dose at 2 months, second dose at 4 months, third dose at 6 months	Fourth dose, if necessary, ages 12 months–5 years	

from another telephone survey noted that approximately 25% of parents believe that the immune system becomes weak from too many vaccines and 23% also reported believing that children get too many shots (Gellin, Maibach, & Marcuse, 2000).

AUTISTIC REGRESSION

In addition to possible associations between immunizations and developmental neurobehavioral declines, the literature has also noted spontaneous regression to occur in a subset of children with an autistic disorder. The data demonstrate that regression in children with a diagnosis of autism occurs in only a minority of the cases. Reported prevalence rates of regression in autism vary between 20% and 49%, with most studies reporting about one-third (Goldberg, et al., 2003; Hoshino et al., 1987; Kobayashi & Murata, 1998; Kurita, 1985; Tuchman & Rapin, 1997). Differences in prevalence rates are due to varying research methods, including the operational definition of regression, the heterogeneity and size of the sample, and the setting from which the sample was drawn (Davidovitch, Glick, Holtzmon, Tirosh, & Safir, 2000; Taylor, Miller, & Lingam, 2002).

Across autistic-spectrum disorders, there are several identified patterns of onset: children who have autistic symptoms present since early infancy, children who develop early achievement milestones then plateau in their development, and children who have a clear developmental loss of previously acquired neurodevelopmental skills (Rogers & DiLalla, 1990). For autistic children with the third pattern of onset, regression typically occurs between the first and third year of life, with most parents reporting loss of skills between 18 and 24 months of age (Davidovitch et al., 2000; Goldberg et al., 2003; Kobayashi & Murata, 1998; Tuchman & Rapin, 1997). The loss of skills usually is gradual, although language loss can sometimes have a more sudden onset in children with autism or other diagnosed pervasive developmental disorders (Goldberg et al.; Rapin & Katzman, 1998).

Perhaps the most challenging factor contributing to the nature and course of autistic regression lies in the reliance on parental history of the child's development. When parents are asked about the course of the regression in their autistic children, approximately 20% report normal development for 12–18 months before the development of more typical autistic features (Volkmar, Steir, & Cohen, 1985). There is some evidence, however, that many children with a history of autistic regression actually demonstrated subtle communicative and social deficits prior to the reported loss of skills or demonstrated a plateau in their development versus a loss of acquired skills. Siperstein and Volkmar (2004) found that parents of children with autism are more likely to report a loss of skills compared to parents of children with other developmental disorders, but the percentage of clear or even probable loss of skills using a standardized method based on a review of records was only 11.8% of the autistic children. Research based on experimenter ratings of early videotapes supports the finding that some children may have atypical development in certain areas that precedes the regression (Osterling, Dawson, & Munson, 2002). More obvious developmental milestones, such as crawling and speaking first words, are readily noticed and more accurately reported; however, parents are less likely to accurately report the quality of their child's type of play, the use of joint attention, response to name, amount of time spent referencing faces, and the use of early communicative gestures (Rogers, 2004).

The role of subclinical epileptiform activity in autism is a topic of current debate, especially as it relates to autistic regression. There is increasing evidence that subclinical epilepsy in the absence of clinical seizures, as seen in partial epilepsies or EEG-diagnosed syndromes, such as electrical status epilepticus during slow wave sleep (ESES), can cause specific cognitive, language, and behavioral dysfunction (Fejerman, Caraballo, &, Tenembaum, 2000; Gordon, 2000; Yung, Park, Cohen, & Garrison, 2000). In autistic-spectrum disorders, the prevalence of subclinical epileptiform activity using EEG or magnetoencephalography ranges from 8% to 85% (Kawasaki, Yokota, Shinomiya et al., 1997; Lewine et al., 1999; Tuchman & Rapin, 1997). Some hypothesize a direct relationship between epileptiform discharges and autistic regression (Nash, Gross, & Devinsky, 1998; Nash & Petrucha, 1990).

Developmental outcome for children with a history of regression may be poorer than other children with autism. According to one study, which inter-viewed parents about their children's regression, many of the children regained some of the lost skills 2–4 years later, with improvements attributed largely to therapeutic and instructional interventions (Goldberg et al., 2003). Studies suggest children who regressed reportedly have had lower levels of intellectual abilities, more severe speech problems, more severe behavioral problems, and lower adaptive skills at schools or institutions than children with autism with no loss of expressive language or other regression (Hoshino et al., 1987; Rogers & DiLalla, 1990). Kobayashi and Murata (1998) con-firmed the lower level of language development in children with a history of regression, but did not find lower levels of adaptive skills upon entering elementary school.

LANDAU–KLEFFNER SYNDROME

Declines in cognitive skills have also been associated with specific seizure disorders. Landau–Kleffner syndrome (LKS) is a condition of an acute, acquired auditory agnosia and developmental aphasia following normal devel-opment (Beaumanoir, 1985; Deonna, 1991; Gordon, 1997). A defining feature of LKS is that the EEG during stage III sleep shows a nearly continuous spike-wave epileptiform pattern, a physiological criterion that is necessary for a diagnosis of LKS. A related syndrome, electrical status epilepticus in slow wave sleep (ESES), is considered a variant of LKS, with both considered a type of epileptic encephalopathy in which cognitive and behavioral regression occurs in the context of abnormal EEG activity (Tassinar, Rubboli, Volpi et al., 2000). The epidemiology of LKS is unknown, but is considered an extremely rare neurological disorder of childhood. In a population-based study in Tel Aviv, 1 out of 440 children presenting with epilepsy over 20 years were diagnosed with LKS (Kramer et al., 1998).

Children with LKS develop normally, but at some time after age 3 years, there is a rapid loss of receptive and expressive language skills typically associated with either seizures or epileptiform abnormalities on EEG. Most commonly, loss of receptive language skills, termed verbal auditory agnosia, is the initial feature and often leads parents to question deafness. Expressive aphasia usually follows the loss of receptive skills. Although the most striking feature of LKS regression is the loss of acquired receptive and expressive language abilities, children commonly demonstrate behavioral abnormalities similar to those seen in autistic children (Roulet Perez, Davidoff, Despland, & Deonna, 1993).

The role of abnormal brain activity in LKS is not clear. In addition to required abnormal EEG patterns during sleep, approximately 70% of children with LKS have clinical seizures (Hirsch et al., 1990). Because functional neuroimaging techniques implicate the intrasylvian cortex as the foci of epileptiform discharges in classic LKS (Chez, Major, & Smith, 1992; Lewine et al., 1999), it is possible that epileptiform activity has a specific, negative effect on language processing, interfering with the neural circuitry of the brain and directly causing LKS. Given the lack of a distinct correlation between the status of the epileptiform activity and cognitive and behavioral functioning, other investigators consider the epileptiform activity an epiphenomenon reflecting underlying brain pathology rather than a direct cause of the language, cognitive, and behavioral disorder (Eslava-Cobos & Mejia, 1997; Holmes, McKeever, & Saunders, 1981; Rapin, 1995).

Improvement in language, cognition, and behavior associated with LKS has been reported following treatment with corticosteroids (Lerman, Lerman-Sagie, & Kivity, 1991; Sinclair & Snyder, 2005; Stefanos, Grover, & Geller, 1995). Recovery of language function, some to age-appropriate level, has also been reported in children who underwent multiple subpial transection (MST) surgeries (Grote, van Slyke, & Hoeppner, 1999; Irwin, et al., 2001; Sawhney, Robertson, Polkey et al., 1995). MST is a surgical technique developed to treat refractory seizures in eloquent areas of cortex by protecting neural function, while disrupting epileptic discharges, by severing horizontal intracortical fibers at 5 mm intervals, but preserving vertical fibers and penetrating blood vessels from the pia (Liu, 2000; Morrell & Hanbery, 1969). Although prognosis for seizure control for LKS is quite good, cognitive declines and permanent neuropsychological deficits are common (Smith & Hoeppner, 2003). Not all children with LKS respond to seizure-control interventions and, in general, the developmental outcome for children with LKS can be quite poor, especially if not treated early and effectively by available treatments (Robinson, Baird, Robinson, & Simonoff, 2001; Van Hout, 1997).

CHILDHOOD DISINTEGRATIVE DISORDER

Within the autistic-spectrum or pervasive developmental disorders, there is a specific disorder that has been associated with the loss of developmental skills. Childhood disintegrative disorder (CDD) is characterized by a regression in acquired cognitive functions and behavior following a period of typical development for at least 2 years. Behaviorally, the child displays symptoms characteristic of autism, but CDD is diagnostically distinct from autism in its requirement of a period of normal development followed by a loss of skills (American Psychiatric Association, 1994). Compared to other pervasive developmental disorders, the nosology and causes of CDD are poorly understood.

In contrast to other pervasive developmental disorders, CDD is extremely rare and estimated to occur in 0.1 to 1.7 per 100,000 cases (Burd, Fisher, & Kerbeshian, 1987; Fombonne, 2002, 2003). Reports of CDD prevalence from clinic settings report 1.64 to 8% in children with varied childhood psychoses, autism, and other developmental disorders (Kurita, Kita, & Miyake, 1992; Rogers & DiLalla, 1990; Volkmar & Cohen, 1989; Volkmar et al., 1994). In a clinic-based study, the reported rate of CDD was 0.22% of all cases attending a child psychiatric clinic over a 5-year period (Malhotra & Singh, 1993).

In contrast to regression in autism, language and behavioral regression in CDD is delayed and occurs after at least 2 years of normal development and up to 10 years of age (Malhotra & Gupta, 1999). According to Volkmar (1992), the onset of regression is typically insidious and develops over weeks to months. Loss of language skills is the most striking feature. Other associated features include development of social abnormalities, stereotypical behaviors, hyperactivity, self-injurious/aggressive behaviors, and affective disturbances (Volkmar, Klin, Marans, & Cohen, 1997). In contrast to autistic regression, in which delays are present early in development and/or skills plateau, early delays in CDD are absent or relatively mild and followed by a more distinct onset of regression and continued developmental difficulties (Rogers & DiLalla, 1990; Volkmar, 1992; Volkmar, Steir, & Cohen, 1985).

The severity of psychopathology is more severe and the outcome is worse for children with CDD compared to those with autism (Malhotra & Gupta, 2002; Mouridsen, Rich, and Isager, 1998; Rogers & DiLalla, 1990; Volkmar & Cohen, 1989; Volkmar & Rutter, 1995). Intellectual abilities are significantly compromised in children with CDD, as most function in the severe to profound mentally retarded range (Malhotra & Singh, 1993; Volkmar & Cohen, 1989; Volkmar & Rutter, 1995). In one recent study, however, no differences were found in intellectual ability between children with CDD and autism (Kurita, Osada, & Miyake, 2004).

NERVOUS SYSTEM LOCALIZATION

The symptoms, signs, and test findings in the *case presentation* implicate the supratentorial level of the central nervous system.

VERIFICATION OF THE INITIAL CLINICAL DIAGNOSIS

On the basis of the child's history and evaluation, the original diagnosis of "poisoning" or exposure to mercury in vaccines could not be verified.

Although the present evaluation clearly supported the finding of significant cognitive decline, there was no clear evidence identifying exposure to Thimerosal in vaccines as the cause of the decline. Importantly, there is a lack of biological plausibility, and the scientific literature fails to provide convincing evidence that the level and type of mercury present in Thimerosal could produce the type of symptom pattern found in the *case presentation*.

VERIFICATION OF THE ALTERNATIVE CLINICAL DIAGNOSIS

The final diagnosis for the case presented was CDD based on *DSM-IV* criteria (American Psychiatric Association, 1994).

CAUSE/ETIOLOGY

The family physician had assumed that because a medical condition was not clearly identified, mercury poisoning from Thimerosal in vaccines was the causal agent.

VERIFICATION OF CAUSE/ETIOLOGY

Mercury can be measured in urine, hair, and blood samples. Given the age of the child, the length of time since vaccination, and the reported half-life of ethylmercury, even if elevated levels of ethylmercury were present at the time of symptom onset, they would not be expected to persist at this time. Although the child reportedly exhibited declines following a vaccination after his third birthday, he had received multiple vaccinations in the preceding years with no adverse reactions noted. In addition, the child continued to acquire other development skills during this period, only to show a later decline in those skills, as well. Nevertheless, some of the features of this case, such as macrocephaly, are not consistent with a toxic etiology, such as mercury exposure.

COMMENT

This child demonstrated apparently normal development up until age 3 years. After that point, he began to demonstrate a regression in multiple skills areas, including receptive and expressive language, social skills, bladder control, play, and motor skills. The timing of the declines in functioning is consistent with that reported in CDD. The presence of nonspecific EEG abnormalities is also a common feature. Although there are abnormalities present on EEG, they do not reflect the specific patterns seen in a specific seizure disorder, such as LKS. Although CDD is at times attributed to some underlying medical condition, the discovery of such a condition may be delayed for some years after the diagnosis is behaviorally apparent (American Psychiatric Association, 1994). For all practical purposes, therefore, the cause of the disorder is unknown.

Conclusion

Childhood is an especially vulnerable time. There is little more disturbing than witnessing a young child losing, as opposed to acquiring, developmental skills. Arriving at an accurate and timely diagnosis in such a case is critical, and it is understandable that parents, researchers, and clinicians want to discover a "smoking gun" that would explain such a devastating condition. It is essential that clinicians attempt to maintain objectivity and develop an appropriate differential diagnosis prior to attempting to establish a causal attribution, as it is often difficult, if not impossible, to make a conclusive statement regarding causality or etiology. Unfortunately, the link between autism and vaccines appears at the current time to be based largely on emotional responses, rather than on an objective evaluation of the data. Media attention and continued research on the link between autism and vaccines have served to undermine the public's confidence in this life-saving health initiative. As a result, fewer and fewer children are receiving vaccines, and we are beginning to see the health consequences of this behavior (Allred, Shaw, Santibanez, Rickert, & Santoli, 2005; Bardenheier et al., 2004; Owens, 2002).

Depression in a chronic medical condition

Stanley Berent

Depression has come to be expected in medical illness. Major depression develops in up to 25% of patients with diabetes, carcinoma, stroke, and other medical conditions, and even higher in specified illnesses (e.g., up to 40% in certain neurological conditions like Parkinson's disease and Alzheimer's disease and up to 60% in Cushing's disease) (American Psychiatric Association, 1994). The debilities associated with many illnesses can seriously interfere with the affected person's normal lifestyle, raising stress levels and preventing the pursuit of previously pleasurable work and recreational activities. Although it is likely that all depression that accompanies illness has an experiential component (Berent et al., 1996), the disease mechanisms involved in specific illnesses can include the central nervous system and produce an endogenous depression. In such instances, the differential diagnosis becomes complicated since symptoms and signs such as headache, memory loss, and sleep difficulties may overlap between depression and medical illness. To make matters even more complicated, it has been shown that the presence of even mild depression affects the primary illness in comparison to what might otherwise be expected (Miller, Stetler, Carney, Freedland, & Banks, 2002; O'Donohue & Cucciare, 2005; Rowan, Davidson, Campbell, Dobrez, & MacLean, 2002; Watkins et al., 2003). The following *case presentation* reflects the difficulties inherent in establishing an accurate and complete diagnosis in such situations.

Case presentation[1]

A 45-year-old female patient was seen on two occasions for neuropsychological evaluation, before and 1 year following adrenalectomy for a benign adenoma. The patient's symptoms had begun about 1 year before her initial evaluation, with significant weight gain, increased facial hair, facial flushing, and irregular menstruation. The patient had been referred to neuropsychology because her treating physician noted that she was not consistent in following treatment procedures, appeared to be depressed, and was having difficulty with her performance at work. Her past medical history was positive for diet-treated diabetes mellitus. On her initial medical examination, she was hypertensive with rounded (moon) facies, truncal obesity, and abdominal striae. The remainder of her examination was normal, including neurological examination. Her urinary free cortisol and adrenocorticotropic hormone (ACTH) levels were elevated. A CT scan revealed an adrenal mass, and she underwent adrenalectomy, at which time a benign adrenal adenoma was identified.

At the time of her first neuropsychological examination and prior to her adrenalectomy, the patient was found to be functioning essentially within the normal range (Table 18.4) for scores earned on selected measures. She was of normal intellect and with no significant discrepancy between verbal and performance IQ indices. Language functions were normal and she displayed normal mental status. She was normal cognitively, including learning and memory. Some psychomotor tasks were performed relatively poorly in comparison to her general ability, but her scores remained at or near normal. Depression inventories revealed mild levels of depression.

Table 18.4 Selected scores from neuropsychological examinations for patient with Cushing's syndrome and adrenalectomy.

Test name	Examination I: scores	Examination II: scores
WAIS-R FSIQ	96	97
WAIS-R VIQ	97	95
WAIS-R PIQ	94	99
Vocabulary	10	9
Comprehension	9	9
Similarities	11	10
Digit Span	9	10
Digit Symbol	9	12
WMS MQ	103	103
WMS IV % recall	76	90
WMS VI % recall	85	87
WMS VII % recall	87	98
Grooved Pegs, total time	180 s	115 s
Self-Rating scale	Moderately depressed	Not depressed
SCL-90-R, Depression	$T = 57$	$T = 37$
MMSE	26 of 30	28 of 30

INITIAL CLINICAL DIAGNOSIS

This patient was diagnosed initially with Cushing's syndrome and depression. Neurobehavioral disorders at that time included mood disorder as well as adjustment and treatment compliance issues.

ADDITIONAL INFORMATION

Following adrenalectomy, all systemic signs of Cushing's syndrome slowly resolved. Her weight returned to her baseline levels, her facial hair disappeared, and her menses became regular. Urine cortisol and ACTH levels normalized. The second neuropsychological evaluation was concerned primarily with the patient's possible continuation of depression and changes that might have occurred in her cognitive status between the two examinations. Scores from selected tests that were administered to her are contained in Table 18.4. In comparison to her initial scores, the results from her second examination revealed improvements in a number of areas. Notable, the results on depression inventories were markedly improved and within the normal range. The most dramatic change occurred in areas of psychomotor performance, where her scores on the second examination were unambiguously normal. Although her formal scores on measures of learning and memory had been essentially normal initially, she showed improved scores on her second testing. Arguing against a practice effect as explanatory to these changes are the length of time between examinations (1 year) and those scores that remained unchanged despite repeat testing.

FINAL CLINICAL DIAGNOSIS

At the time of her second evaluation, the patient's neuropsychological diagnoses included history of Cushing's disease with depression (i.e., mood disorder due to a general medical condition), which had resolved.

Discussion

The diagnosis of Cushing's syndrome is accurate and accounts for the patient's clinical symptoms, signs, laboratory findings, and clinical course following resection of the adrenal adenoma. The patient received a secondary diagnosis of depression, with cognitive and emotional involvement. The contributions made to the patient's clinical picture by these secondary findings, as well as the implications they have from a differential diagnostic viewpoint, are discussed in the following paragraphs.

NEUROBEHAVIORAL LOCALIZATION

The distribution of this patient's problem and localization is relatively straightforward. Although many of the patient's cognitive and emotional symptoms could be viewed as experiential or motivational, depression and cognitive impairments are referable to supratentorial regions of the brain. The diagnosis of Cushing's syndrome potentially implicates the central nervous system, as well, because the central nervous system is a direct target of resultant endocrine dysfunction in this disorder.

VERIFICATION OF THE CLINICAL DIAGNOSIS

The diagnosis of Cushing's syndrome satisfies objective criteria for verification, including issues related to adequacy, primacy, coherence, parsimony, robustness, and prediction. Of interest here, is whether or not the cognitive and emotional findings are related directly to this diagnosis, or whether other factors that are unrelated to the biology of Cushing's might be explanatory. As will be discussed more fully below, there is a large body of consistent research evidence, including epidemiological and animal modeling, that links excess cortisol to the kinds of symptoms experienced by the patient, including the secondary neurobehavioral diagnosis given to the patient, i.e., depression (Sonino, Fava, Raffi, Boscaro, & Fallo, 1998). In addition, surgical removal from endogenous exposure and subsequent lowering of cortisol levels were accompanied by improved function in affect and cognition (Table 18.4).

The diagnosis of mood disorder due to a general medical condition, in this case Cushing's disease, requires that the condition be known to produce such symptoms and judgment on the part of the clinician that the disturbance is not better explained by another behavioral condition, e.g., the stress that accompanies having a serious medical illness (American Psychiatric Association, 1994). The differential diagnosis, therefore, is extensive and importantly includes delirium, dementia, substance-induced mood disorder, major depressive disorder, bipolar disorder, and adjustment disorder with depressed mood.

The diagnosis of mood disorder due to Cushing's syndrome in the present case is verifiable because it best explains the patient's symptoms and signs. The disturbance is not better explained by another mental disorder. Except for a clear and mild situational depression from which the patient recovered some years before the current evaluation, there is no personal or family history of mood disturbance. Although the patient appears to have evidenced some compromise in terms of cognitive function, she was clearly not demented. Cushing's disease is known to produce mood disturbance. Both Cushing's disease and depression are known to share common neurochemical substrates. The patient's mood disturbance began following the onset of her medical condition and improved concomitantly with the successful treatment of her medical condition.

CAUSE/ETIOLOGY

The term "Cushing's syndrome" has been applied traditionally to a clinical picture that results from excess of cortisol, regardless of cause. The term "Cushing's disease" has been used to refer specifically to hyperfunction of the adrenal cortex as a result of excess pituitary ACTH (Berkow, 1982; Hudson, Hudson, Griffing, Melby, & Pope, 1987). Both disorders can be accompanied by cognitive dysfunction (Starkman, Gebarski, Berent, & Schteingart, 1992), and glucocorticoid medications can lead to disturbances of both mood and cognition (Wolkowitz, Reus, Canick, Levin, & Lupien, 1997). A number of steroid hormones, including cortisol and other hormones involved in Cushing's disease, have been shown to be important in the regulation of memory and other cognitive functions (Carlson & Sherwin, 1998). Also, psychiatric disturbances are common among patients with endocrine disturbance (Barchas & Altemus, 1999), and depression is known to occur regularly in Cushing's disease (Sapolsky, 2000; Sonino et al., 1998). This should not be surprising because the limbic system is involved in the regulation of glucocorticoids and these hormones, in turn, play an important role in the regulation of emotion (Greden et al., 1983). The hypothalamic-pituitary-adrenal (HPA) axis, in fact, is a focus of research on mood (Barchas & Altemus, 1999). Consistent with the idea of a regulatory role for these hormonal systems in depression is the apparent coincidence of reversibility in depression and in levels of potentially contributory hormones. Young et al. (1994), for instance, demonstrated that some depressed patients secrete excessive cortisol when depressed, but not following amelioration of their depression.

Despite scores on formal tests that remained essentially within the normal range, the patient in the *case presentation* was considered to be reflecting mild cognitive impairment. This judgment was based on the clinical analyses of her neuropsychological test results and the changes in those results across time. Also, she was found at the time of her first examination to have a mood disturbance. The improvement in her mood between the first and second neuropsychological examinations mirrored her improved scores on cognitive and psychomotor tests, and this too was considered to be important in deciding on the presence of mild cognitive impairment. There is considerable published evidence that cognitive disturbance often accompanies depression (Zakzanis, Leach, & Kaplan, 1999). As mentioned earlier, both cognitive and emotional symptoms occur in Cushing's disease, as well. As in depression, the cognitive impairments can improve following successful treatment of the medical condition (Starkman et al., 1992, 1999). On the basis of these various observations, Cushing's disease has been proposed as a model to employ in the study of depression (Starkman et al., 1992).

The coincidence of cognitive impairment and depression presents a challenge for the biological study of depression. This is because depression affects motivation and can compromise concentration and performance on cognitive tasks that depend on attention for successful completion (Berent, 1986). Although much is known about the interactions between experience and physiology (McEwen, 2000), this problem of coincidence has continued to confound the scientific study of depression. It serves also as a basis for the "chicken or egg" type dilemma for the clinician who tries to discern cause from effect. That is, which came first? Or more specifically in this instance, did depression interfere with the patient's cognitive performance, or were both depression and cognitive abilities adversely affected by a third variable, i.e., biological changes associated with a medical condition?

VERIFICATION OF CAUSE/ETIOLOGY

The presence of affectual disorder in the *case presentation* introduces the dilemma we just discussed. That is, did the depression arise independently of the primary medical disorder or was the depression caused by the medical disorder? Also, and regardless of the answer to the first question, which of the patient's complaints derived primarily from the depression and which from her Cushing's? Here, the most likely answer to this question is that the patient's depression (as well as the cognitive changes) derived from her medical condition, or more precisely from the neurobiology of her medical condition. This conclusion meets objective criteria (e.g., Hill, 1965) for establishing causality. For instance, the timing of the patient's depressive symptoms coincided with the onset of her symptoms and signs of Cushing's disease. Mood disturbance is known to accompany Cushing's disease in a majority of cases (as is cognitive impairments independent of affectual disturbance [Starkman et al., 1992]). The cause and effect relationship is biologically plausible, and improvement in her medical condition was accompanied by improved neurobehavioral functioning, in addition to improvement in her mood. Animal models have been developed that reflect the proposed biological relationships in Cushing's and depression. Multiple studies have yielded consistent results with regard to the relationship between cortisol and depression. The cause and effect relationship is relatively specific, and other possible explanations for the clinical findings were investigated and excluded.

Conclusion

This *case presentation* illustrates how a medical condition that involves an endogenous toxin, cortisol in this instance, can lead to a complicated clinical presentation that involves multiple systems and could even mimic other toxicant-induced disorders, including the effects of exogenous toxicants. Most important, this example illustrates how affectual and cognitive disturbance can manifest as a consequence of a medical condition. In addition, the case demonstrates the complexity of determining the independence of these neuropsychological impairments vis-à-vis the primary medical condition.

Neurobehavioral complaints attributed to mold exposure

Christopher J. Graver and Linas A. Bieliauskas

Molds are multicellular, microscopic fungi that form cobweb-like masses of branching threads. These threads project into the air bearing the part of the plant from which spores develop. On a cellular level, they have a nucleus bounded by an organized membrane (Davis, 1999), which helps to differentiate them from bacteria. In addition, fungi can be distinguished from most other plants and algae by their lack of chlorophyll. Molds reproduce through the growth of conidium (asexual spores) on the ends of tubular filamentous structures called hypha (Medoff & Kobayashi, 1991). From the hypha, spores can be spread by the wind or attached to various structures for transportation (e.g., feathers, fur, or clothing).

Molds may be of brilliant colors or black and white, depending on the type. They can be found year-round in virtually any environment both indoors and outdoors. Although they tend to grow best in warm, damp, and humid conditions, mold spores can survive in harsh environmental conditions, such as cool and dry environments. Depending on growth conditions and temperature, molds can exist in a filamentous state or as yeast (Medoff & Kobayashi, 1991). The exact number of fungi species is unknown, but experts estimate that there are over 100,000 distinct fungi species (Terr, 2001). The more common molds that are found in homes and offices include *Cladosporium*, *Penicillium*, and *Aspergillus*, and less often, *Stachybotrys chartarum* (see Figure 18.1).

Potential health consequences of mold exposure have been gaining both lay and professional interest in recent years. Exposure to most molds commonly occurs through inhalation, but exposure also can occur through direct dermal

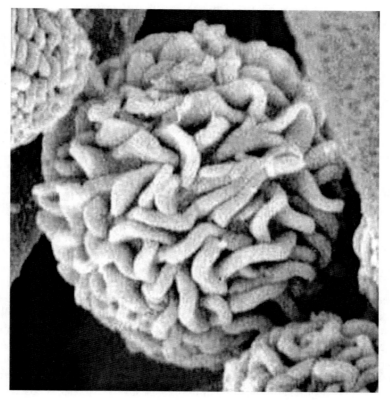

Figure 18.1 A conidium of *Stachybotrys chartarum*. Scanning electron micrograph. Photo by Berlin Nelson; courtesy of the American Phytopathological Society.

contact or ingestion of food products. For example, Drobotko (1945) fed horses pure cultures of the saprophytic mold, *Stachybotrys*, mixed with regular feed. Abnormally high amounts of pure mold culture (10–30 dishes in a 24-hr period) mixed with feed were toxic to the horses and proved fatal within 5–32 days depending on the amount of mold culture in the feed. Mold levels that more closely approximated natural mold exposure (five dishes or less in a 24-hr period) resulted in irritation of the mouth, throat, nose, and lips, as well as leukopenia in one horse; these findings fully resolved within 3 months. Regardless of the amount of mold culture ingested, the illness induced by mold exposure was not found to be contagious or infectious, even with artificial attempts to infect healthy horses. This was one of the first reported studies on the toxic effects of *Stachybotrys*.

In subsequent years, some research has suggested that molds also have the potential to cause health problems in humans. Molds produce allergens (substances that can cause allergic reactions), irritants, and in some cases, potentially toxic substances (mycotoxins). Inhaling or touching mold or mold spores may cause allergic reactions that are not uncommon in sensitive individuals. These allergic responses include hay fever-type symptoms, such as sneezing, runny nose, red eyes, and skin rash. Molds also can cause asthma attacks in people with asthma who are allergic to mold. In addition, mold exposure can irritate the eyes, skin, nose, throat, and lungs of both mold-allergic and nonallergic people. Symptoms other than the allergic and irritant types are not commonly reported as a result of inhaling mold, which is the most frequent mode of exposure in humans.

There are an increasing number of reports of people exposed to mold in their homes or offices and who are described as subsequently developing a "toxic mold syndrome" (Edmondson, Nordness, Zacharisen, Kurup, & Fink, 2005). The complaints associated with a toxic mold syndrome frequently include nonspecific symptoms such as headache, cough, diarrhea, dizziness, nausea, weakness, fatigue, difficulty concentrating, memory loss, and mood changes. Nevertheless, these complaints may result from a variety of causes other than exposure to mold, such as an illness contracted outside the home or office, acute sensitivity (e.g., allergies), job-related stress or dissatisfaction, and other psychosocial factors. Toxic mold syndrome is thought by some to be related etiologically directly to the neurotoxic properties of mold, with neurotoxic involvement related more specifically to mycotoxin exposure (Osuchowski, Edwards, & Sharma, 2005). Many of these same mycotoxins, of course, have medicinal properties that are familiar worldwide, including penicillin, cyclosporine, and the cholesterol-lowering statins, all of which are of fungal origin (Manzoni & Rollini, 2002). Thus, the precise relationship between mold exposure and "toxic" neurological or neuropsychological effects remains incompletely resolved. There are presently no known patterns of neuropsychological or psychological symptoms that constitute a specific toxic mold syndrome, and the clinical diagnosis of this disorder is based often only on self-reported symptoms (Lees-Haley, 2002).

The lack of a clear scientific understanding of mold induced neurotoxicity and the tendency to base a clinical diagnosis solely on self-reported symptoms have contributed to controversy about the validity of the diagnosis. Given the growing public awareness of potential mold exposure, it is not unusual for such cases to be seen by clinicians within the context of litigation. Two such cases are described in the following paragraphs.

Case presentation[1]

This 50-year-old, single white female was referred for neuropsychological evaluation by her attorney. The referral asked for an independent evaluation of her cognitive complaints and the possible association to reported in-home mold exposure that occurred in 1999. The patient reported completing a GED in her 20s and 2 years of coursework at a community college where she earned mostly B to C grades. After she left school without a degree, she worked as a secretary, a waitress, and most recently as a factory worker. The patient reported developing carpal tunnel syndrome and has not worked for the past 7 years due to carpal tunnel problems. Her presenting complaints were somewhat vague and included tired eyes, headaches, an inability to read, difficulty following a plot, and poor memory for complex information. The patient indicated that she was not initially aware of any health risks associated with mold and did not experience symptoms immediately following exposure. The previously mentioned symptoms developed over a 2–3 month period following the onset of a molding condition in her house.

There were indications in the patient's history of long-term psychiatric problems with a turbulent childhood and multiple inpatient hospitalizations. Past psychiatric diagnoses included paranoid schizophrenia, bipolar disorder, and passive–aggressive personality disorder. A neuropsychological evaluation performed 2 years earlier reported the presence of depression and anxiety, as well as a distorted performance on cognitive tests such that they were judged unreliable with regard to her cognitive functioning. Neurological examinations from several neurologists at the same time were essentially normal and one neurologist remarked that the patient seemed to have a functional overlay to her symptoms.

INITIAL CLINICAL DIAGNOSIS

The patient reported receiving multiple clinical diagnoses to explain her symptoms, including migraines, possible multiple sclerosis, and asthmatic bronchitis. She herself, however, was convinced that her symptoms were due to an undiagnosed disorder that was due to mold exposure.

VERIFICATION OF THE INITIAL CLINICAL DIAGNOSIS

Other than a report from one neurologist diagnosing the patient with benign essential tremor, no other positive neurological findings were available from case records. She had stated to her neurologist that she had brain demyelination, decreased memory, burning feet, and fluctuating vision in one eye. The neurologist concluded that this was an unusual presentation and likely represented a functional overlay. The patient's constellation of symptoms did not meet the criteria for a specific neurological disorder aside from possible benign essential tremor or migraine headache (Richardson et al., 2000). There were no clinical findings which would explain the symptoms, no known diagnosis for the constellation of symptoms, and there is thus no good fit for any specific neurological disorder. Alternatively, the neurologist's impression of a functional overlay appeared to be more probable than the patient's self-diagnosis.

ADDITIONAL INFORMATION

Review of the previous evaluations showed normal EEG, serum lyme (*Borrelia burgdorferi*) titers, fungal titers, thyroid function studies, blood counts, protein electrophoresis, brain stem auditory evoked potential, audiogram, and EKG. One clinician who examined the patient in the past reported that her brain MRI showed evidence of multiple lesions, and it was suggested that these findings represented a multifocal demyelinating process. Review of the MRI report, however, revealed only increased signal intensity and focal encephalomalacia in the left parietal area but no other evidence of increased signal intensity or an inflammatory disease. The MRI findings were thought to be related to a motor vehicle accident that occurred earlier. Further testing, including cerebrospinal fluid (CSF) evaluation, was negative for multiple sclerosis or infection.

Results of neuropsychological evaluation. Selected results from the patient's neuropsychological examination are presented in Table 18.5. On examination, the patient was agitated, defensive, and prone to interrupting the examiner, but she was superficially co-operative after the first couple hours of testing. The results showed poor orientation, variable attention/concentration, poor learning and memory, and psychomotor slowing. On the other hand, her intellectual abilities did not show a decline from estimated premorbid levels and she preformed within normal limits on two higher order conceptual reasoning tasks. The patient's apparent cognitive dysfunction was qualified by notable dissimulation on several tasks formally assessing motivation and effort. Personality testing was consistent with the presence of a potential thought disorder and numerous somatic complaints. She also was thought to have characteristics of borderline personality disorder. A conversion reaction and hypochondriacal concerns were suspected.

NERVOUS SYSTEM LOCALIZATION

The symptoms, signs, and test findings in the *case presentation* implicate the supratentorial level of the central nervous system.

Table 18.5 Selected neuropsychological examination scores for the *case presentation*

Procedure	Domain measured	Test results
MMSE	General mental status	20/30
WRAT-3, Reading	Single-word reading ability	86
WRAT-3, Spelling	Spelling achievement	78
WRAT-3, Arithmetic	Mathematical achievement	89
WAIS-III FSIQ	Overall intellect	91
WAIS-III VIQ	Verbal intellect	89
WAIS-III PIQ	Performance intellect	97
WAIS-III Working Memory Index	Working memory	90
WAIS-III Processing Speed Index	Cognitive processing speed	81
WMS-III Immediate Memory	Immediate memory abilities	78
WMS-III General Memory	Delayed memory abilities	62
WMS-III Auditory Recognition Memory	Delayed recognition memory	60
California Verbal Learning Test	List learning and memory	$T = 17$
Benton Visual Naming Test	Confrontation naming	7th percentile
Controlled Oral Word Association Test	Verbal fluency	48th percentile
Trail Making Test A	Visuomotor speed	27th percentile
Trail Making Test B	Mental flexibility	38th percentile
Booklet Category Test	Complex problem solving	51st percentile
Validity Indicator Profile	Effort and engagement in testing	Invalid
MMPI-2	Personality/psychopathology	$L = 66$ $F = 61$ $K = 54$ $Hs = 97$ $D = 97$ $Hy = 89$ $Sc = 67$ All other MMPI-2 Scales within normal

ALTERNATIVE CLINICAL DIAGNOSIS

On the basis of the patient's evaluation, history, and examination results, there was no evidence that she sustained brain dysfunction, on the basis of mold exposure or any other basis. There was ample evidence, however, of incomplete effort during testing, a preoccupation with somatic symptoms, and unusual notions of neurological disturbance (such as the belief that she was suffering a demyelinating disease) in the context of significant lifelong psychiatric difficulties.

VERIFICATION OF THE ALTERNATIVE CLINICAL DIAGNOSIS

The final diagnoses were determined to be borderline personality disorder, conversion reaction, and incomplete effort. A long history of severe psychiatric disturbance was verified, including inpatient psychiatric hospitalizations as a child. A review of medical and psychiatric records starting in childhood showed evidence of frequent and vague somatic complaints, including headache, shortness of breath, tightness in her chest, itching, sore throat, aches, and pains. Given that her vague somatic complaints had been ongoing for quite some time, it was unlikely that they were linked to mold exposure in her 40s. In addition, her complaints began 2–3 months after the reported exposure to mold, only after she was informed that mold exposure can have detrimental health effects. Thus, it is likely that her new assumptions about the effects of mold exposure led her to believe that her cluster of symptoms was causally related to her mold exposure, which is not an uncommon phenomenon according to the psychological literature (Lees-Haley, 2002; Rosenthal & Jacobson, 1968).

Further evidence of the impact of susceptibility to suggestion comes from a study by Edmondson et al. (2005) who acknowledged the significant role of psychological distress, secondary gain, and the legal and media promotion of the mold toxicity symptoms "thereby influencing patient responses during the medical interview." In their study, they found that children did not exhibit or complain of central nervous system symptoms following mold exposure, whereas adults from the same families did complain of central nervous system symptoms. The authors concluded that this is the case because children are less likely to be influenced by these other factors than adults.

Although the patient performed in the impaired range on some neuropsychological tests, she also failed tests formally measuring effort. This is important to note in light of the study of Green, Rohling, Lees-Haley, and Allen (2001), which found that a patient's effort during neuropsychological testing has a larger impact on test scores than the degree of injury, even when including severe traumatic brain injury. Therefore, her poor effort would likely explain most, if not all, of her impairments on neuropsychological testing. Although other etiologies may be contributing to her complaints (e.g., migraine, asthmatic bronchitis, or others), a final argument against toxic mold syndrome in this patient is the fact that central nervous system fungal infection usually develops only in individuals who are immunocompromised, presenting as a subacute meningitis (Davis, 1999). This patient had no indication of a compromised immune system or any neurological signs of a central nervous system infection.

Case presentation[1]

This 30-year-old, married male was referred for neuropsychological evaluation by his attorney. He was referred for an independent medical examination regarding cognitive difficulties following mold exposure two years earlier as a result of faulty cable installation in his home. The patient reported earning a high school diploma and later completed approximately one year of college coursework. His overall grades were generally in the "C" range, but reported specific life-long difficulties with reading comprehension and math. He had many years of experience in law enforcement and was still working in that field at the time of the evaluation. The patient's presenting complaints included "mental fogginess," difficulty multi-tasking, decreased attention span, feeling "at a loss for words," and difficulty remembering conversations.

INITIAL CLINICAL DIAGNOSIS

The patient had been diagnosed by a neuropsychologist with an amnestic disorder based on an evaluation two years earlier. The patient felt his symptoms were likely due to mold exposure, and he was involved with litigation to that effect.

ADDITIONAL INFORMATION

Other than being involved in marriage counseling previously, the patient denied any psychiatric illnesses or treatment. As already mentioned, however, an earlier neuropsychological evaluation concluded that the patient suffered from an amnestic disorder based on his normal cognitive functioning with isolated difficulty on a visuospatial memory task. A neurological examination at the same time was normal, as was an EEG that was completed in the same month. The patient was taking an antihypertensive medication at the time of testing. The past medical history included a prior diagnosis of obstructive sleep apnea, for which he was not receiving treatment.

NEUROPSYCHOLOGICAL CONSULTATION

Results of neuropsychological evaluation. Selected results from the patient's current neuropsychological examination are presented in Table 18.6. He was a casually dressed and well-groomed individual who was polite and cooperative throughout the testing process. He worked quickly through tasks, but did not appear to be impulsive or rushed. The patient's mood appeared to be euthymic and his affect was broad and appropriate. His speech was clear and articulate, and the rate, volume, and prosody of his speech were unremarkable. During this evaluation, he performed within normal limits and expectation on all tests administered, including tests of visuospatial memory. Attention/concentration, processing speed, and language skills were all within normal limits. He scored somewhat lower on spelling achievement, which likely reflected a long-standing spelling disability as mentioned in the previous neuropsychological report. His general intellectual abilities were measured in the average range and personality testing revealed no significant psychopathology.

ALTERNATIVE CLINICAL DIAGNOSIS

Based on the patient's evaluation, history, and examination results, there was no evidence that he sustained brain dysfunction. The main discrepancy was

Table 18.6 Selected neuropsychological examination scores for *case presentation*

Procedure	Domain measured	Test results
MMSE	General mental status	28/30
WRAT-3, Reading	Single-word reading ability	95
WRAT-3, Spelling	Spelling achievement	88
WRAT-3, Arithmetic	Mathematical achievement	96
WAIS-III FSIQ	Overall intellect	98
WAIS-III VIQ	Verbal intellect	98
WAIS-III PIQ	Performance intellect	97
WAIS-III Working Memory Index	Working memory	94
WAIS-III Processing Speed Index	Cognitive processing speed	93
WMS-III Immediate Memory	Immediate memory abilities	100
WMS-III General Memory	Delayed memory abilities	105
WMS-III Auditory Recognition Memory	Delayed recognition memory	100
California Verbal Learning Test	List learning and memory	$T = 49$
Benton Visual NamingTest	Confrontation naming	87th percentile
Controlled Oral Word Association Test	Verbal fluency	81st percentile
Trail Making Test A	Visuomotor speed	76th percentile
Trail Making Test B	Mental flexibility	64th percentile
Booklet Category Test	Complex problem solving	51st percentile
Validity Indicator Profile	Effort and engagement in testing	Valid
MMPI-2	Personality/psychopathology	All MMPI-2 scales within normal

between his normal results on tests of memory function and his perception of impaired memory.

VERIFICATION OF THE INITIAL CLINICAL DIAGNOSES

The initial neuropsychology evaluation resulted in a diagnosis of "amnestic disorder" due to impaired visuospatial memory. A review of the data from that neuropsychological evaluation revealed that although the patient's immediate visuospatial memory was slightly lower than was expected based on his general intellectual abilities, his delayed visuospatial memory was solidly in the average range with 100% retention of this material. Further inspection revealed that the immediate visual memory score was slightly low due to poor single-trial learning; however, his learning over repeated trials was above average. Therefore, it was judged that there was no indication on previous objective testing of memory impairment. In addition, the previous neuropsychological report indicated that because the patient's Personality Assessment Inventory was within normal limits, emotional factors could not explain the patient's complaints of poor memory. The report, however, neglected to include data from the Beck Depression Inventory (raw score = 18) and Beck Anxiety Inventory (raw score = 30), which together indicated mild to moderate symptoms of depression and anxiety. Consistent with these measures, the patient reported during a clinical interview that he was experiencing considerable stress around the time of the evaluation, providing another possible explanation for his perceived memory difficulties (normal memory variation associated with periods of increased stress or anxiety).

CAUSE/ETIOLOGY

Assuming for a moment that this patient was experiencing variation in his memory, is it reasonable that it could be attributed to an exposure to mold? As mentioned above, previous neurological and neuropsychological examinations, as well as an EEG, were within normal limits. The current neuropsychological assessment also did not find evidence of any impairment and concluded that his neuropsychological performance was consistent with estimated premorbid cognitive abilities.

While it is possible that this individual was exposed to mold, he did not show any signs of mold exposure and no symptoms were evident on objective examinations. The patient was originally complaining of mental fogginess, difficulty multi-tasking, decreased attention span, feeling "at a loss for words," and difficulty remembering conversations, but he did not report symptoms of rhinitis, cough, or other respiratory symptoms, which have been found to be the most common symptoms in the scientific literature associated with mold exposure (Edmondson et al., 2005). Suspected etiologies for his complaints included in the differential diagnosis were obstructive sleep apnea, antihypertensive medications, and his previously documented anxiety and depression symptoms, the latter of which are also associated with cognitive inefficiency and problems with attention and short-term memory (Caine, 1981; Eysenck, 1991; Paterniti, Dufouil, Bisserbe, & Alpérovitch, 1999).

Beta blockers have been implicated in difficulties with working memory (Muller, Mottweiler, & Bublak, 2005) and verbal short term memory (Dimsdale, Newton, & Joist, 1989; Rosen & Kostis, 1984; Solomon, Hotchkiss, Saravay et al., 1983). Attentional capacity and vigilance deficits and impairments in attention-biased scores on neuropsychological tests have also been reported in numerous studies concerning sleep apnea syndromes (Durmer & Dinges, 2005; Engleman, Kingshott, Martin, & Douglas, 2000; Verstraeten & Cluydts, 2004). Nevertheless, there were no objective findings of cognitive problems on neuropsychological testing for this patient, making it moot to establish a "cause" for his normal memory function.

Discussion

What is toxic mold syndrome? Technically, mold itself is not toxic. When the term "toxic mold" is used, it usually refers to the secondary metabolites of fungi called mycotoxins, which can be harmful under some circumstances. The allegation of mold toxicity, and more specifically mold neurotoxicity, has been gaining in popularity in personal injury litigation. For example, Lees-Haley (2004) conducted a survey of toxic mold topics on the Internet, which found approximately 120,000 "hits" to the phrase toxic mold on a popular search engine. At the time of this writing several years later, that same search phrase on the same search engine returned over 800,000 hits, 1,600 photos, and 681 Internet discussion groups devoted to toxic mold. In addition, many of the top matches for toxic mold are Web sites claiming to be information resources on the topic, but are often sponsored by attorney groups or law firms and have copious links to legal services. Other media coverage of mold toxicity also has been conspicuous, including an article in *Time* magazine (Hamilton, 2001) that referred to mold as "some sort of biblical plague," but goes on to admit that the biggest winners are the "industries feeding off mold mania" (e.g., the legal profession, inspection and cleanup companies, and, ironically, the media). Despite all this publicity and readily available information on mold, there are few scientific studies that show a consistent pattern of symptoms or deficits that would indicate neurotoxic effects of mold exposure in the home or office.

Proponents of the causal relationships between mold exposure and physical and cognitive symptoms often state the belief that there are no other factors that can explain the symptoms, no other reasons why someone would make subjective complaints and sue for large sums of money, and no scientific studies that have "disproved" the relationship (Lees-Haley, 2002). Some individuals argued that they had seen enough patients whose problems with memory, learning, and concentration occurred only after exposure to *Stachybotrys* that they were convinced there is a relationship (see the *Time* magazine article by Hamilton, 2001).

Embedded in these arguments are several types of persuasions, such as the use of social proof, which involves the use of a few "credible" people who repeatedly go public with their claims. The complaints of popular figures, such as Ed McMahon (O'Neill, 2002; Guccione, 2003) and Erin Brockovich (Hendrix, 2001), have helped perpetuate this argument, as have the overwhelming number of personal stories about toxic mold exposure in the popular media. The use of dramatic case histories or sensationalized lawsuits can perpetuate a belief, such as that of Melinda Ballard of Dripping Springs, Texas, who sued Farmer's Insurance for $100 million due to her family's exposure to mold in their home (*Ballard v. Fire Insurance Exchange*, 2002). The story of her case now appears on over 3,000 Web sites, some with such theatrical titles as "Haunted by Mold." Although media stories regarding the case lead the reader to believe that she was awarded millions for her family's toxic exposure to mold, allegations of bodily injury and mental anguish were dismissed by the court due to lack of supporting studies (*Alison et al. v. Fire Insurance Exchange, et al.*, 2002).

Although the courts may have cited a lack of supporting studies for a toxic mold syndrome in 2001, there are a few studies in the current scientific literature that support a relationship between mold exposure and neurobehavioral problems. Several articles report an association between mycotoxins and cognitive complaints, such as attention, learning and memory, executive function, and psychomotor speed (Baldo, Ahmad, & Ruff, 2002; Crago et al., 2003; Gordon et al., 2004; Rea et al., 2003).

For example, Gordon et al. (2004) found that subjects exposed to mold in their home or work showed evidence of cognitive dysfunction in the areas of processing speed, attention, working memory, executive functions, learning, and short- and long-term memory. Subjects in this study exposed to mold were found to perform similarly on neuropsychological tasks as those with mild-to-moderate traumatic brain injury. Similar to these findings, Crago et al. (2003) reported that the neuropsychological impairments found in mold-exposed subjects were similar to subjects who suffered a mild traumatic brain injury. Furthermore, they found a dose–response relationship between measures of mold exposure and abnormal neuropsychological performance, suggesting that mold is responsible for significant and measurable cognitive deficits in exposed individuals.

In an earlier study by Baldo et al. (2002), it was reported that individuals exposed to mold were impaired in their visuospatial learning and memory, verbal memory, and psychomotor speed. Rea et al. (2003) expanded the previously reported neuropsychological findings to include neurological abnormalities, autonomic nervous system dysfunction, and abnormal SPECT scans of the brain. They concluded that the relationship between these abnormal findings was indicative of direct toxic damage. As a result of mold exposure, the subjects in their study were reported to have a mycotoxin-induced chronic fatigue which caused them to miss school or work, prevented them from performing manual tasks, and made it difficult to move from their homes, even though evacuation was necessary for their survival.

Although these studies may seem to lend support to the relationship between mycotoxin exposure and neurobehavioral deficits, there are several methodological limitations to these studies that require more careful review before definitive conclusions can be drawn. Lees-Haley, Greiffenstein, Larrabee, and Manning (2004) point out several methodological problems with neurotoxicity research in general, many of which apply to the above-mentioned studies. For example, a literature review by Rea et al. (2003) consists of a single statement that "Toxic exposure to molds and mycotoxins in public buildings, office buildings, and homes is becoming commonplace." This one sentence does not adequately address the state of the literature, provide a rationale for conducting the study, or help to frame the relevant issues. This same problem occurs in other literature reviews, which include information about studies that support the relationships between mold exposure and neurobehavioral deficits, but often neglect alternate theories and research findings, such as the findings by Hodgson et al. (1998) who found evidence of better memory performance in those exposed to mold as compared to normal control subjects.

It can be difficult to carry out scientifically sound studies on mold exposure due to the relatively low degree of control over many variables. For example, the above-mentioned studies included participants who were exposed to different types of molds or mycotoxins, had different levels of mold exposure, and whose duration of exposure varied widely (months to years). Furthermore, no clear independent variables were defined. Terr (2001) reported that every human on earth has been exposed to mold and estimates that there are 100,000 fungi with varying properties, thus making it critical to rigidly define the independent variables (in this case, particular mycotoxins).

In addition to the difficulty selecting patients based on similar mold exposures, selection bias is a major issue with which to contend, especially in research involving potential litigants. Given that subjects ethically cannot be randomly assigned to a mold-exposure group or a placebo control group, studies on mold exposure will inherently have some degree of selection bias, but attempts should still be made to minimize confounding factors. Unfortunately, studies such as those by Gordon et al. (2004) and Baldo et al. (2002) included nonrandomly selected participants of which 94% and 100%, respectively, were involved in litigation.

The choice of litigants is problematic for several reasons. Studies have found strong evidence that patients involved in civil litigation perform differently than nonlitigants with the same claimed etiology (Binder & Willis, 1991; Feinstein, Ouchterlony, Somerville, & Jardine, 2001; Gervais et al., 2001; Larrabee, 2003; Suhr, Tranel, Wefel, & Barrash, 1997). Additionally, board certified neuropsychologists performing forensic evaluations have reported that approximately 29% of individuals with any type of toxic exposure claim are malingering (Mittenberg, Patton, Canyock, & Condit, 2002) and that number increased to approximately 46% when evaluating individuals claiming to have toxic encephalopathy (van Hout, Schmand, Wekking, Hageman, & Deelman, 2003).

Other problems include the appropriate matching of educational attainment between groups. It is well known that education is a significant contributor to differences in neuropsychological performance (Heaton, Grant, & Matthews, 1991; Le Carret, Lafont, & Letenneur, 2003; Lezak, 1988; Mortimer, 1988) and that normal patients with lower education can perform worse than "impaired" individuals with higher education (Adams, Boake, & Crain, 1982; Stern, Andrews, & Pittman, 1992; Zarit, Miller, & Kahn, 1978). Yet, one study included a mold-exposure group that had 32.3% of participants with less than or equal to a high school education, while only 17% of the control group had a similar level of education (Gordon et al., 2004). Therefore, it is possible that the findings by Gordon et al. were impacted by educational differences between the groups.

In summary, it can be quite difficult to design and carry out research on the relationships between mold exposure and neurobehavioral consequences given the multitude of factors that are problematic to control. Therefore, the conclusions drawn from these studies substantiate some type of association between mold exposure and neurobehavioral impairment, but a definitive causal relationship has not, at this time, been demonstrated. With such an expansive field of investigation and relatively few studies in the literature, the complete effect of mold exposure on humans remains unclear at this time. There are many additional factors worthy of investigation that may explain the neurobehavioral symptoms observed in patients exposed to mold, including civil litigation, secondary gain, suboptimal effort, preexisting health problems, and psychiatric symptoms, which could explain changes in both neuropsychological and physiological functionings (Binder & Campbell, 2004; Brambilla et al., 1992; Condren, O'Neill, Ryan, Barrett, & Thakore, 2002; Furlan, DeMartinis, Schweizer, Rickels, & Lucki, 2001).

CURRENT OCCUPATIONAL MEDICINE VIEWS REGARDING MOLD TOXICITY

According to recent guidelines of the American College of Occupational and Environmental Medicine (Hardin, Kelman, & Saxon, 2003), mold is ubiquitous, unavoidable (unless extreme measures are taken), and part of normal life. Although there is no evidence that neuropsychological dysfunction occurs as a result of mold exposure, there is evidence that ingestion of foods containing mycotoxins can cause illness. This does not, however, mean that exposure to mold through inhalation can produce the same illness. Mold inhalation and mold ingestion generally have very different effects on health. For example, Drobotko (1945) found that horses that ingested moldy hay developed signs of illness within 36 hr, whereas there was no evidence of mold-related illness in horses that did not ingest the moldy hay, despite being housed in the same stables for a month. Certainly, allergic reactions to fungi occur in approximately 5% of the population as a result of mold inhalation, but these reactions usually present as asthma or rhinitis (Binder & Campbell, 2004). Edmondson et al. (2005) support this view and have found evidence that a majority of health problems associated with mycotoxin exposure are allergic, not toxic, in nature.

Physical symptoms that may be caused by indoor fungi include respiratory complaints that involve the nose and lungs, eye symptoms, and mucous membrane irritation (Cox-Ganser et al., 2005). These adverse effects can occur by a variety of mechanisms, including IgE-mediated hypersensitivity, fungal infection, irritant reaction to spores or fungal metabolites, and possibly toxic reaction to mycotoxins (Portnoy, Kwak, Dowling, VanOsdol, & Barnes, 2005). These physical reactions, however, are not common in response to mold exposure; otherwise, the abundance of mold in our environment would result in widespread mycotoxicoses on a daily basis. Fortunately for humans, the musty odor associated with mold is not caused by mycotoxins (Binder & Campbell, 2004). Mycotoxins are minimally volatile, do not off gas into the environment, and cannot pass through solid substances, which reduces the chance of airborne illnesses. Nonetheless, actively growing fungal colonies are sometimes visually objectionable and can release volatile substances that have an unpleasant smell, leading to psychological responses such as fatigue and nausea. The only major concern with respect to airborne fungal pathogens is with immunocompromised individuals, such as those taking immunosuppressant medications, those with AIDS, and those with severe diabetes. In such cases, a fungal meningitis is possible, and often presents acutely (Davis, 1999).

It is difficult to pinpoint a specific etiology for the somewhat vague symptoms reported in patients reporting mold neurotoxicity. Such vague symptoms, as Crago et al. (2003) mention, are also seen in those complaining of traumatic brain injury. Similar symptoms also have be reported in connection with other illnesses covered in this volume, including amalgam illness, suggesting significant symptom overlap and the lack of a well-defined constellation of symptoms. Rare cases of leukoencephalopathy have been reported following exposure to mycotoxins, but if this occurs, concomitant exposure to other toxins also needs to be considered. For example, other leukotoxic agents that are commonly found in our environment include cranial irradiation, current and past medications, alcohol, illicit drugs, over-the-counter (OTC) preparations (including herbal supplements), and other environmental or occupational toxins (Filley & Kleinschmidt-DeMasters, 2001).

One of the major problems in specifying mycotoxins as the causal agent in patients' complaints is the lack of a neurobiological criterion. Studies conducted to date reporting a relationship between mold exposure and neuropsychological impairments have relied heavily on self-reported mold exposure. A significant recall bias exists regarding information on toxic exposure (Hilsabeck, Gouvier, & Bolter, 1998; Korgeski and Leon, 1983), highlighting the need for objective measurements of mycotoxin levels. Although some studies claim to have measured mold content in the participants' environment, this is problematic because "toxigenic mold," as Crago et al. (2003) describe it, does not mean that mycotoxins are definitively present, only that there is a potential risk for mycotoxin exposure (Costa & Scussel, 2002).

A better method for evaluating the relationship between mycotoxin exposure and adverse health effects would be a direct measurement of mycotoxin levels in patients. Accurate measurements of mold, however, can be problematic. Rea et al. (2003) state that "mold counts are crude and have large variations in reported mold quantity." The authors go on to state that the "technology to evaluate quantitative mycotoxin exposure and virulence is unavailable." Furthermore, Edmondson et al. (2005) suggest that skin prick/puncture tests and intracutaneous tests are not reliable in isolation to diagnose even a clinical allergy to molds and report that "there are no standardized, reliable urine, serum, or environmental mycotoxin detection assays." This may be one of the most significant hurdles to overcome in this line of research. Without objective method to determine mycotoxin levels in humans, any conclusions about the causal relationship of mycotoxin exposure to neuropsychological and physiological abnormalities are purely speculative. Although there is evidence of allergic reactions to mold in the form of irritated noses, lungs, eyes, skin, and mucous membranes, the current scientific evidence does not support a causal relationship between adverse neurobehavioral effects in healthy individuals and mycotoxin inhalation in home, school, or office environments (Burge, 2001; Kuhn & Ghannoum, 2003; Robbins, Swenson, Neally, Gots, & Kelman, 2000).

Conclusion

Disorders with no readily available medical explanation, such as toxic mold syndrome, are often characterized by subjective complaints and symptoms, rather than objective findings (Labarge & McCaffrey, 2000). According to Binder and Campbell (2004), medically unexplained disorders may have etiologies that consist of biological-genetic substrates, the accumulation of stressful experiences, and/or the way in which experiences are psychologically organized. Disorders like toxic mold syndrome have characteristics of what Ford (1997) described as "fashionable illnesses." These are illnesses characterized by vague, subjective symptoms, quasi-scientific explanations, and symptoms consistent with anxiety and depression, in the absence of objective laboratory findings. Patients complaining of these disorders often reject psychosomatic explanations for their symptoms and rather embrace biomedical explanations (Butler, Chalder, & Wessely, 2001; Nimnuan, Hotopf, & Wessely, 2001).

Many of these medically unexplained disorders have overlapping symptoms and do not present with a coherent or distinct pattern of deficits, especially from a neuropsychological perspective (Deary, 1999). Also important to note is that fact that many of the complaints of mold-exposure patients occur commonly in healthy individuals. For example, Paniak et al. (2002) found that 33% of healthy individuals complained of fatigue, 58% reported experiencing headaches, 58% complained of forgetfulness, and 35% reported poor concentration.

Patients complaining of medically unexplained syndromes also often have subjective complaints out of proportion to objective findings (Barsky & Borus, 1999). Such patients may view themselves as severely disabled and often enter litigation or apply for disability payments (Wolfe et al., 1997). Furthermore, patients with pseudoneurological symptoms, in the absence of objective neurological evidence, can still have abnormalities on neuropsychological testing (Mace & Trimble, 1996), but these are usually associated with nonneurological etiologies such as poor effort or other psychological factors (Brown, Levin, Ramsay, Katz, & Duchowny, 1991). Inhalation of mold spores can cause hay fever-type symptoms, such as sneezing, runny nose, red eyes, and dermatitis, as well as asthma attacks in individuals who are allergic to mold. In addition, mold exposure can irritate the eyes, skin, nose, throat, and lungs of both mold-allergic and nonallergic people. On the other hand, more serious health consequences usually occur only in immunocompromised individuals exposed to mold, and this most often presents as subacute meningitis (Davis, 1999).

Although all cases are unique and need to be approached within the context of each individual's history and differential diagnosis, currently the scientific literature is not supportive of a relationship between mold exposure and severe health problems or neuropsychological abnormalities, except in extraordinary circumstances such as direct ingestion of large amounts of mold, as was found with horses (Drobotko, 1945), or the exposure of immunocompromised individuals to mycotoxins. With each case, health professionals should rely on past mental health and medical records, as well as objective findings, rather than the patient's self report alone to make a diagnosis (Coyne, Thomspon, & Racioppo, 2001). In individuals with suspected mold exposures, careful consideration must be given to potential etiologies other than mold exposure, including psychological factors that can lead to functional somatic syndromes. Other factors to consider include potential secondary gain, attorney coaching, media influence, other medical history, and past psychiatric history. As in all clinical cases, the patient's complaints should be dealt with objectively and thoroughly to arrive at an accurate diagnosis and explanation for the patient's symptoms as well as appropriate and effective treatment.

Patient with neurobehavioral symptoms attributed to dental amalgams

Stanley Berent

An increasing number of patients who attribute their complaints to dental amalgams are being seen in clinical practices (Gottwald et al., 2001). The complaints made by these patients vary but usually include some or all of a number of nonspecific symptoms. These commonly include depression, anxiety, weakness, fatigue, muscle and joint pain, headache, dizziness, difficulties with sleep, problems with concentration and other cognitive functions, gastrointestinal distress, and impaired sensation (World Health Organization & International Programme on Chemical Safety, 1991; World Health Organization, 1997). Diagnosed largely on the basis of the patient's own attribution of their symptoms to amalgam, this phenomenon has been referred to by a variety of names, including "amalgam disease" (Gottwald et al.), "amalgam syndrome" (Leonhardt, 2001) or "amalgam attributed illness" (World Health Organization, 1997). The chemical agent underlying this condition is presumed by its adherents to be elemental mercury (Hg), a metal capable of producing toxic effects (Agency for Toxic Substances and Disease Registry, 1999; American Conference of Governmental Industrial Hygienists, 2001; World Health Organization, 1997; World Health Organization et al., 1991).

Case presentation[1]

This 64-year-old, divorced white female was referred for neuropsychological evaluation by her primary care physician. The referral asked for evaluation of cognitive and emotional functioning to help confirm a diagnosis of amalgam disease. The patient was born and raised in Czechoslovakia and came to this country as a young adult. She had learned to speak English while growing up in her native country and spoke fluently and with only a very slight accent. She had worked for the U.S. government in Europe, where she met her husband. When he was transferred back to the United States, she came with him. They had no children and were divorced soon after that move. Her complaints in interview were vague and many, consisting of recurrent headaches, occasional but persistent dizziness, allergies, stiffness in various body locations at different times, pains in joints and muscles, unable to lift anything heavy, general fatigue, severe dental problems (gums and teeth), frequent cramps, motion sickness, depression, and "nervous trouble." She listed a host of substances to which she believed she was allergic, but past tests for specific allergens had all been negative.

Records that the patient brought to the evaluation reflected evaluation on these and other symptoms, with negative findings on all objective tests and evaluations. The only exception was the referring physician's conclusion that her symptoms were the result of amalgam disease, and the patient remarked to me in interview that her physician was the only person who had been able to accurately diagnose the nature of her difficulty.

INITIAL DIAGNOSIS

The referring clinician diagnosed amalgam disease and attributed all of the patient's symptoms to this condition, adding that mercury had "off gassed" over time from her amalgams and as a result had damaged the patient's brain. No other considerations were included in the differential diagnosis.

ADDITIONAL INFORMATION

Review of the previous evaluations included report of a normal EEG and a normal brain MRI study, showing no evidence of atrophy or other abnormality. Urine mercury was reported as 7.2 μg Hg/L and interpreted by the referring physician as representing an "elevated level of mercury." Prior medical records reflected past diagnoses of anxiety and depression and treatments for those conditions with psychotropic medications. The referring physician's notes commented that the patient's mood disturbance was resistant to "traditional psychiatric" treatment attempts because the mood disturbance was a manifestation of amalgam disease. He indicated that several of her amalgams had been removed by a dentist who specialized in "removal of toxic filings," with immediate and partial relief of her symptoms, but that the symptoms returned as her mercury levels again increased as a result of the remaining amalgams. The patient had been scheduled to return at a future date for completion of her amalgam removal.

Comment

Urine mercury concentration is considered to be the most accurate measure for estimating chronic exposure to mercury vapor, and levels of mercury in blood reflect peak exposures (Agency for Toxic Substances and Disease Registry [ATSDR], 1999). Analysis of mercury in hair reflects methylmercury exposure (Agency for Toxic substances and Disease Registry [ATSDR], 1999), whereas less than 10% of the mercury measured in urine is methylmercury

(Klaassen, 1996). The relationship between urine mercury levels and dental amalgam will be discussed later in this section. For now, it should be pointed out that these levels, while eventually lowered as a result of amalgam removal, actually rise immediately following removal. In fact, the level of urine mercury may almost double in the month following removal, gradually falling to the preremoval baseline during the second month and continuing to lower over the course of the next months to a year (Clarkson, Friberg, Hursh, & Nylander, 1988a; Clarkson, Friberg, Nordberg, & Sager, 1988b). Reports of immediate symptom relief with amalgam removal, therefore, are certainly not related to lessened mercury levels. It is more likely that a patient's subjective perception of improvement is the reflection of a placebo effect.

RESULTS OF NEUROPSYCHOLOGICAL EVALUATION

Selected results from the patient's neuropsychological examination are presented in Table 18.7. These results reflect essentially normal functioning in terms of cognitive ability. The significant difference between WAIS-R PIQ and VIQ most likely resulted from a lack of optimal motivation to perform. This conclusion is strengthened by the patient's tendency to perform relatively

Table 18.7 Selected neuropsychological examination scores for a patient complaining of amalgam-related illness.

Test administered	Domain measured	Test results
MMSE	General mental status	29 of 30
WAIS-R, VIQ	Verbal intellect	103
WAIS-R, PIQ	Performance intellect	86
WAIS-R, Vocabulary	Vocabulary level	10
WAIS-R, Similarities	Abstract conceptualization	11
WAIS-R, Block Design	Visual-motor problem solving	9
WAIS-R, Digit Symbol	Psychomotor problem solving	7
WAIS-R, Picture completion	Attention/concentration and visual problem solving	8
WMS, MQ	General memory and orientation	120
WMS, Passages	Verbal recall, percent retained	92%
WMS, Visual Reproductions	Visual recall, percent retained	82%
WRAT-3, Reading	Reading recognition	107
Depression Self-Ratings	Clinical ratings of depression	Mild depression
MMPI-2	Personality/psychopathology	$L = 68$ $F = 48$ $K = 60$ $Hs = 55$ $D = 68$ $Hy = 72$ All other scales within normal

less well on tasks that demanded motor involvement as opposed to her performance on verbal, analytic tasks that were less physically effortful. The elevated scores on tests of emotional functioning suggested that mild emotional disturbance may have influenced her performance, leading to the pattern of strengths and weaknesses just noted. This conclusion is strengthened by the absence of positive findings from neurological examination or brain imaging studies that might suggest any neurological abnormality. Given that her elevations on emotional testing remained in the mild range, the persistence of her belief that she has an illness related to amalgam also needs to be considered as contributory to her symptoms.

ALTERNATIVE CLINICAL DIAGNOSIS

On the basis of the patient's evaluation, history, and examination results, an alternative (working) clinical diagnosis was made: somatoform disorder.

Discussion

AMALGAM-RELATED DISEASE

What is amalgam disease? There is relatively little mention of amalgam disease in the published professional literature. In fact, as of 2004, a search for this term using Medline produced only five publications that mentioned the disorder by this specific term or by some similar diagnostic phrase. Aside from the papers by Gottwald et al. (2001), Leonhardt (2001), and the 1991 WHO report (World Health Organization et al., 1991) two additional papers included a publication in the Norwegian by Kringlen (1999) and one by Mutter and Daschner (2003) commenting on the Gottwald paper. There are, however, a number of studies that have addressed the relationship between dental amalgam and illness without designating a specific disease. Other studies have addressed potential adverse effects of elemental mercury exposure on neurobehavioral functions using formal neuropsychological measures. Still others have concerned themselves with the potential relationship between mercury exposure and progressive neurological diseases such as Alzheimer's disease and Parkinson's disease. Some of the more important of these studies will be reviewed briefly.

Mercury from dental amalgam does not convert to methylmercury (Clarkson et al., 1988a; Clarkson, 1997, 2002), the latter resulting from methylation of mercury by bacteria in the environment and entering the food chain via fish and fish-eating mammals (National Research Council, 2000; U.S. Environmental Protection Agency Office of Air Quality Standards, 1997). The numerous research papers that address the toxic effects of methylmercury, therefore, are not reviewed, except as these might have relevance for the issue of mercury from dental amalgams. Also excluded are the papers that deal specifically with ethylmercury, a form of mercury with many properties similar to methylmercury (Clarkson, 2002). A potential source of ethylmercury exposure is Thimerosal, which has been used as a preservative in diphtheria, tetanus, influenza, and other vaccines (Institute of Medicine, 2001).

The composition of dental amalgam typically contains about 50% elemental mercury (U.S. Department of Health and Human Services, 1993; U.S. Department of Health and Human Services, 1997). Dental amalgams are a combination of mercury with other metals, e.g., copper, tin, and silver. According to Clarkson (Clarkson et al., 1988b), the impetus for identifying mercury as the primary source of toxicity from dental amalgams may have been fueled by a 1939 German study wherein Stock (Stock, 1939) reported that amalgam fillings could release mercury vapor. Although mercury is a liquid at room temperature (elemental or metallic mercury), mercury vapor is endemic and results primarily from natural degassing of the earth's crust (Klaassen & Watkins, 2003). Mercury vapor (Hg^0) is much more toxic than is elemental mercury (Klaassen & Watkins, 2003). It has long been known that in sufficient amounts, exposure to mercury vapor can produce a severe acute reaction that, if not fatal, can produce adverse neurological effects that include tremor and hyper-excitability (Feldman, 1999). This result has been termed by some as *asthenic-vegetative syndrome* (Klaassen & Watkins, 2003) or by others as *micromercuralism* (Feldman, 1999) and described as a condition with very specific diagnostic criteria said to include neurasthenic symptoms and the presence of three or more clinical findings of tremor, thyroid enlargement, increased uptake of radioiodine in thyroid, labile pulse rate, tachycardia, dermographism, gingivitis, hematological changes, and increased excretion of mercury in urine (Klaassen & Watkins, 2003). Feldman (1999) wrote that early complaints of micromercuralism may be subtle and include fatigue, general weakness, loss of appetite, diarrhea, insomnia, changes in mood, and tremor that resembles that seen in patients with hyperthyroidism. Since all of the symptoms listed by Feldman are nonspecific in terms of underlying disease, he emphasized the need for a well-documented exposure history in arriving at a diagnosis of micromercuralism (Feldman, 1999). It should be noted, further, that the nonspecific nature of these symptoms leaves micromercuralism controversial as an actual disorder. Nevertheless, growing concern has been expressed by some that exposure to mercury vapor from dental amalgams may produce a condition perhaps similar to what has been described as micromercuralism.

The rationale for thinking that mercury toxicity can occur from dental amalgams is based on the fact that mercury vapor exposure does result from dental amalgam. It is known that the number of dental amalgam surfaces is significantly correlated with concentrations of mercury in urine. Kingman (Kingman, Albertini, & Brown, 1998b), e.g., studied the relationship between amalgam exposure and urine mercury levels. The authors of that study estimated that each ten amalgam surface increases were associated with an increase of 1 μg/L mercury in urine concentration. This was a large study ($n = 1,127$) but limited to mostly male military personnel, between the ages of 40 and 70 years. A person with seven to eight amalgam filings (the average number in the general population) will absorb an estimated 2–17 μg Hg/day in addition to the amount of mercury exposure from other sources, which can be two or three times that amount (Clarkson et al., 1988b). Chronic gum chewing or other stimulation of dental amalgams can lead to increased Hg^0 exposure in the oral cavity (Sallsten, Thoren, Barregard, Schutz, & Skarping, 1996). An exact "normal range" for urine mercury (HgU) is difficult to specify for several reasons. Values differ across cultures and age groups as well as over time and as a result of interaction with individual difference factors. The mean levels for the nonoccupationally exposed general population reported by WHO in their 1991 publication (World Health Organization et al., 1991) were 4–5 µg Hg/L. More recent surveys, however, have reported values that are lower, e.g., a study of 1,748 American women with a mean urine value of 0.72 µg Hg/L, with 95% less than or equal to 5.0 µg Hg/L (U.S. Department of Health and Human Services, 2003) and another study of 1,073 American males with a mean urine value of 1.97 µg Hg/L (Kingman, Albertini, & Brown, 1998a). In this last study, the number of amalgams significantly correlated with HgU, lending support to the idea that mercury from dental amalgams does, in fact, increase the body burden of this metal. Further, the amalgam-related illness proposition appears to be similar to a number of other conditions that remain to be documented conclusively. We have discussed such proposed syndromes (e.g., multiple chemical sensitivity, chronic fatigue syndrome, painters' encephalopathy, and others) at various places in the present book and elsewhere (Albers & Berent, 2000). We have at times labeled these conditions as controversial because of their incomplete scientific documentation in the face of strongly expressed views by adherents of the concept and those in opposition, and we have described certain characteristics that appear to be common to all of these phenomena. For instance, the proposed phenomena usually include both the symptoms of the disorder and the presumed cause in the diagnosis. As is the case with amalgam-related illness, allergic reactions and local side effects aside, scientific review groups often have attended to the issues surrounding the proposed illness phenomenon and determined that no definitive scientific evidence exists that documents it as a diagnosable disease or to document the proposed causal relationship between the identified symptoms and the specified causal agent (U.S. Department of Health and Human Services, 1997; Brownawell, 2005). At the same time, such reviews usually have resulted in a statement regarding the need for additional research on the topic (U.S. Department of Health and Human Services, 1997). A very important characteristic, and one that reflects a coherent rationale in terms of hypothesis generation, can be described as an extension of some already known problem to include the newer proposed condition. This last rationale often appears to rest on a presumption of continuity. That is, if exposure on one level is known to produce an adverse effect on the organism, then exposure to a lesser amount of the same chemical should produce a similar effect albeit to a lesser extent. While such a linear relationship will apply to some substances, many substances will reflect toxicokinetics that do not lend to this proposition. An alternative to the continuity approach that also would be consistent with the idea that relatively small amounts of mercury exposure from dental amalgam might produce symptoms of illness is an additive model, e.g., that the added exposure to mercury vapors from dental amalgam increases the body burden of mercury to a toxic level.

STUDIES OF AMALGAM-RELATED ILLNESS

What is the scientific evidence for amalgam-related disease? There are few published studies that have approached the topic of amalgam-related illnesses. The majority of studies that have addressed this issue have been cross-sectional in design with the exception of one (Langworth, Bjorkman, Elinder, Jarup, & Savlin, 2002), which can be best described as a case report since no control group was employed. In the Langworth study, 428 subjects were referred for evaluation by their treating physicians. The urine mercury levels among this group (2 μg Hg/L) were said to be within the normal range in comparison to historical controls. The author administered a symptom check list (SCL-90-R) and on the basis of results from this instrument concluded that there was a "clear tendency" to somatization, with 40% of the sample scoring above the cutoff on the SCL-90-R for anxiety, depression, and obsessions. Bratel, Haraldson, and Ottosson (1997) and Bratel et al. (1997) compared 50 "noncontact allergic to mercury" individuals who complained of problems associated with their amalgam restorations to 50 control subjects matched for age, sex, and socioeconomic status. A subjective self-rating scale (Comprehensive Psychopathological Rating Scale [CPRS]) was employed, the results of which revealed that the amalgam group scored higher than the controls on "asthenia," anxiety, and depression. Also, the authors reported that a psychiatric diagnosis was clinically established in 70% of the amalgam group. Interestingly, 36% of the controls also had a psychiatric diagnosis.

Using the Karolinska Scales of Personality (KSP), Bagedahl-Strindlund et al. (1997) compared 67 subjects with complaints that were self-attributed to their amalgams to 64 age, sex, and socioeconomically matched persons and reported a higher prevalence of psychiatric disturbance in the amalgam complaint group (89%) versus the controls (6%). Also, subjects in the amalgam complaint group were said to exhibit increased psychasthenia, somatic anxiety, muscle tension, and "low socialization." A study by Bailer et al., 2001 compared 40 subjects who claimed that their dental amalgams had adversely affected their health to 43 controls. Subjects were excluded if physical examination revealed underlying disease that accounted for the self-reported complaints. Also excluded was any subject with a positive patch test for allergic reaction to mercury. There was no statistically significant difference between groups in terms of urine mercury levels (subjects: 1.7 μg Hg/L; controls: 1.4 μg Hg/L). Results from administration of the SCL-90-R showed subjects to be significantly higher than controls on the somatization and obsessive-compulsive subscales. Also, a screening test for somatization symptoms was administered and subjects were again found to be higher than controls for the presence of medically unexplained physical symptoms. Finally, in the study by Gottwald et al. mentioned earlier (Gottwald et al., 2001), the investigators reported no significant difference between subjects with amalgam-related complaints and age, sex, and dental disease matched controls in terms of urine mercury, with both groups showing HgU within the normal range. However, results from the SCL-90-R revealed significantly higher scores for the subjects in comparison to controls on somatization, depression, and anxiety.

Surveys were conducted in two additional studies, in an attempt to describe directly individuals who report symptoms that they associate with their dental amalgams. Similar to the five studies reviewed earlier, Malt et al. (1997) reported higher survey responses among 99 self-referred subjects than among a comparison group in areas of depression, somatization disorder, and chronic fatigue syndrome. Melchart, Wuhr, Weidenhammer, and Kremers (1998) in a survey of 6,744 dental patients found no significant correlation between severity or type of self-reported symptoms and number of amalgam fillings.

The studies reviewed appear to provide little support for amalgam-related illness in other than psychological terms. All of these studies suffer from methodological problems, not the least of which is the reliance on self-selected subjects who have already decided that their various complaints are due to dental amalgams. Further, there is lack of masking of subjects and probably investigators, which adds another element of potential bias. The reliance on self-report devices for determining the subjects' symptoms is troubling as well since in a population that has already voiced their complaints, such self-report instruments do little more that document and possibly quantify what is already known by verbal report. This is especially the case in the absence of corroborating signs of illness. Finally, exposures were low in these studies, with a lack of difference between groups in terms of measured mercury levels. On the positive side, the studies were fairly consistent in reporting symptoms that were similar across studies. Of most importance perhaps is the common report of somatization or somatic concerns in five studies, anxiety in four, depression in four, and an obsessional coping style in two studies.

Although the research designs that were employed do not allow for causal determination, the results of these studies provide a description of some behavioral characteristics of a relatively large number of persons who believe that their health has been adversely affected by dental amalgam ($n = 628$ across all studies that employed psychological self-report instruments and $n > 7,000$ when the survey studies are combined with self-report indices). A fictitious "model individual" can be described in terms of personality on the basis of the composite findings across studies as one who employs an obsessional, somatization coping style that is only partially successful in dealing with the person's anxious depression. Of course, others might argue that this mood disturbance is but a manifestation of mercury exposure and that the heightened somatic concerns and obsessional personal styles are by-products of the affectual symptoms. If that is so, the studies reviewed do not lend support to such a conclusion and can do no more than provide the descriptions noted. Also, the lack of significant correlation between symptom type or severity and number of amalgams is inconsistent with an amalgam-induced illness hypothesis. On the basis of those studies reviewed to this point, one can conclude that traditional psychiatric or psychological diagnoses (primarily somatoform and affectual disturbance) account fully for the complaints made by the individual research subjects. We will need to look elsewhere for evidence in support of a hypothesis of amalgam-specific disease.

AMALGAM AND NEUROPSYCHOLOGICAL FUNCTIONS

Since the symptoms of amalgam-related illness are said to include difficulties with concentration and other cognitive abilities, presumably because of the adverse effects of mercury on the central nervous system, studies that address neuropsychological functioning in relation to dental amalgam are relevant. Factor-Litvak et al. (2003) reported the results of a correlational study of cognitive function and dental amalgam in 550 nonoccupationally exposed persons between the ages of 30 and 49 years. The mean urine mercury level in this group was 1.7 µg Hg/L, with a range of 0.09–17.8 µg Hg/L. The number of amalgam surfaces calculated in this study was determined (mean: 6.1, range: 0–46) and compared to urine mercury measurements. A significant linear correlation between the number of surfaces and HgU was reported. However, no significant correlation was found to exist between formal neuropsychological test results and HgU or number of amalgam surfaces. The neuropsychological functions measured in the Factor-Litvak study included verbal and nonverbal memory, attention, motor, and some aspects of problem solving. Strengths in the Factor-Litvak study included the documentation of exposure variables and documentation of the relationship between amalgam surfaces and HgU, but the study has a number of weaknesses as well. Despite the relatively large number of subjects, for instance, mean scores on neuropsychological measures were reported to be within the normal range. This could potentially reflect a sampling bias toward less seriously affected individuals. Similarly, about 95% of the subjects were found to have HgU levels that were <5 µg Hg/L, essentially within the normal range.

Two other studies also failed to establish a relationship between amalgam and neuropsychological dysfunction. Nitschke, Muller, Smith, & Hopfenmuller (2000c) divided 300 subjects, ages 70–103 years, into three groups on the bases of age and dental status, i.e., number of amalgams. Twelve percent of the total sample was found on the basis of clinical criteria to be "demented," but there was no significant correlation between dementia and dental state. Interestingly, the group with the most amalgams was found to be the highest functioning in terms of reasoning, general knowledge, and intelligence. Unfortunately, this study may be confounded by age, intellectual level and other factors. In a relatively large study ($n = 587$) that was part of what has been referred to as "the Swedish Adoption/Twin Study of Aging" (Bjorkman, Pedersen, & Lichtenstein, 1996), mental and general well-being and some specific cognitive functions were evaluated in relation to dental status. No significant relationships were found between general well-being and cognitive function. Also, a co-twin control design was added as a component of this overall study with twin pairs discordant for exposure to amalgam. Again, no evidence for negative effects of amalgam was detected, and the authors of the study concluded that their findings did not indicate any negative effects from dental amalgam on physical, mental health, or memory functions in a general population over 50 years of age.

THE USE OF DENTAL AMALGAMS IN CHILDREN

It was mentioned earlier that few prospective, longitudinal research designs have been employed to study the behavioral effects of mercury from dental amalgam. An exception is the study by DeRouen et al. (2006) which was designed to examine the safety in children of dental amalgam restorations in comparison to the use of a resin composite. Five hundred and seven Portuguese children aged 8–10 years were randomly assigned to either an amalgam or a resin group for restorative dental treatment and evaluated annually for 7 years. Annual evaluations included formal assessments of neurobehavioral functions (e.g., attention, memory, and motor) and nerve conduction studies. Over the course of the study, both groups underwent similar restorative treatments (e.g., similar tooth surfaces were repaired), but with more repairs required in the composite than in the amalgam group. Baseline creatinine-adjusted urinary mercury levels were approximately the same between the two groups (1.8 μg/g for the amalgam group, and 1.9 μg/g for the composite group). Over the course of the study, however, the urine levels of mercury in the amalgam group were significantly higher (1.0 to 1.5 μg/g) than in the composite group ($p < .001$). After 7 years, no statistically significant differences were found between the two groups in neurobehavioral measures of attention, memory, or visuomotor function; or in nerve conduction velocities (DeRouen et al., 2006).

In the United States, Bellinger et al. (2006) also followed 534 children whose dental caries were randomly treated with amalgam or resin composite materials. The primary outcome measure in the Bellinger study (also referred to as "The New England Children's Amalgam Trial") was a 5-year change in full-scale IQ, with secondary outcome measures of memory and visuomotor function and renal function (i.e., creatinine-adjusted albumin in urine). No statistically significant differences in neurobehavioral or renal effects between the two groups after 5 years were noted. Also, and while the authors of this study said they could not rule out completely the possibility for "very small" effects on IQ over time, the two groups did not differ in IQ change scores at 5 years. Bellinger et al. concluded that their study suggested that health concerns about amalgam based restorations need not be the basis for treatment decisions related to the use of restorative materials.

Overall, the studies reviewed fail to provide any support for a relationship between dental amalgam and neuropsychological dysfunction. However, all of these studies reflect one or more methodological problems. For instance, all employed a limited number of formal neuropsychological measures and at times used tests that can be described as esoteric and of uncertain validity (Nitschke, Muller, Smith, & Hopfenmuller, 2000). In addition, the reliance on the number of amalgam surfaces as an analog to actual mercury levels in some studies leaves the actual exposure in those studies difficult to determine precisely.

Despite their shortcomings, the results of these studies of neuropsychological functioning suggest that any possible adverse affects of amalgam on neurobehavioral functioning are likely to be subtle and most likely limited in terms of type of ability affected.

Alzheimer's disease and dental amalgams. As mentioned earlier, some have suggested a possible association between mercury from dental amalgams and neurodegenerative disease. If such an association were found to exist, it would have import not only for our understanding of disorders such as Alzheimer's disease (AD), but also it would speak to the possible relationship between amalgam and neuropsychological dysfunction and, therefore, amalgam-related illness, as well (Nitschke et al., 2000). 12% of the subjects were diagnosed clinically with AD, but no relationship was found between AD and dental amalgams. In a study by Fung et al. (1996), nine nursing home residents who had been diagnosed with AD using NINCDS/ADRDA criteria (National Institutes of Health, 1993) were compared to nine residents from the same home but with no dementia or other central nervous system-related diseases. There was no significant difference between these two groups in terms of either current number of dental amalgam surfaces or in currently measured HgU. Although not statistically significant, the AD group did have a higher average number of amalgams than did the controls (6.2 versus 3.0), and the mean HgU level was higher in the AD group than in the controls (2.96 versus 1.86 μg Hg/L). It is unfortunate that no attempt was apparently made in this study to determine historical exposure to Hg by way of lifetime number of amalgams or other sources for Hg exposure. However, Gun et al. (1997) did evaluate and compare the occupational exposure histories of 170 AD patients to 170 age and sex-matched controls. Subjects had all been diagnosed with AD using NINCDS/ADRDA criteria. Gun employed occupational hygienists and masked them to the neurological status of individual subjects. Using an exposure matrix, the hygienists assessed each subject's exposure to mercury. Although no association was found to exist in this study between occupational exposure to mercury and the diagnosis of AD, a major study weakness is in the relatively small proportion of subjects with evidence of historical occupational exposure to mercury. The results of the studies reviewed failed to provide evidence for an association between dental amalgams and subsequent neurodegenerative, dementing illness. The question of such an association cannot be established nor ruled out completely on the basis of these studies, however, since each of the studies mentioned suffers from one or more methodological weaknesses.

Comment

Taken together, the studies reviewed in this section do not support a concept of amalgam disease as a specific diagnostic entity. Nor do the results of these studies provide evidence for a causal connection between dental amalgams, or mercury at levels associated with amalgams, and the neurobehavioral and other symptoms complained about by individuals who feel they have this condition. The studies are consistent with a coherent psychological picture that appears to characterize a large number of individuals who complain they have been injured by their dental amalgams. Thus, psychological conditions such as anxiety, depression, and somatoform disorder should be a regular component of the differential diagnosis in cases where dental amalgam is thought to play a role in the patient's symptoms.

NERVOUS SYSTEM LOCALIZATION

The proposed initial diagnosis for this patient's neurobehavioral problem included both the neuroanatomical localization (damage to the patient's brain) and the presumed cause (exposure to mercury as a chemical by-product of dental amalgam).

The patient described in the *case presentation* was thought to show evidence of impaired cognition, but no other signs were described by her physician. Cognitive dysfunction of organic origin is localized to the supratentorial level of the central nervous system, although this localization does not necessarily infer an organic explanation for the disorder.

VERIFICATION OF THE ORIGINAL CLINICAL DIAGNOSES

On the basis of the patient's history and evaluation, the original diagnosis of amalgam disease could not be verified. The original diagnosis implied both a cause (i.e., mercury from the patient's amalgams) and an effect (i.e., the symptoms of disease). The present evaluation did not corroborate the presence of cognitive impairment as complained about by the patient and concluded by her clinician (the diagnosis was neither adequate nor parsimonious) (Richardson et al., 2000). Further, historical records failed to substantiate the presence of neurological abnormality as would be predicted by the initial diagnosis (the diagnosis was not coherent). Finally, the review of the literature on the topics relevant to the initial diagnosis failed to produce convincing evidence of formal acceptance by the professional community of the diagnosed disorder (the diagnosis did not fit the pattern of the patient's signs and symptoms, nor was it robust or predictive).

CAUSE/ETIOLOGY

As mentioned, the initial diagnosis contained causal attribution, i.e., mercury from the patient's dental amalgams.

VERIFICATION OF CAUSE/ETIOLOGY

Setting aside for the moment the lack of scientific support for illness resulting from exposure to dental amalgam, the proposed cause in this case still can not be verified. Applying objective causal criteria (Hill, 1965), the timing of the exposure in this case does not fit a toxicant-induced disorder. For instance, her symptoms improved at a time when exposure would have been greater (i.e., immediately upon removal of her dental fillings), even though the patient believed the exposure to be lessened. As already mentioned, the literature reviewed earlier does not support the presence of "high risk" associated with amalgam restorations. Perhaps most important, other diagnostic explanations for the patient's complaints had not been adequately investigated and eliminated.

VERIFICATION OF THE ALTERNATIVE CLINICAL DIAGNOSIS

The final diagnosis for the *case presentation* was determined to be *undifferentiated somatoform disorder* based on *DSM-IV* criteria (American Psychiatric Association, 1994). In addition to alternative somatoform disorders (i.e., *somatization disorder, conversion disorder, and hypochondriasis*), the differential diagnosis included depression, obsessive-compulsive disorder, and amalgam disease. The last was included because of its having been diagnosed previously, and the alternative psychiatric disorders were included because the research reviewed above consistently identified these attributes in persons complaining of amalgam-related illnesses. This same body of research influenced the diagnostic decision but was not the determining factor in excluding amalgam disease from the final diagnostic conclusion. In this case, a more important consideration was the lack of physical finding that might support a toxicant-induced disorder. This included the history of normal neurological examination, normal results from brain scan examinations, and a urine mercury level that was judged on the basis of published normative data to be within the normal range. In addition, the report of remission of symptoms immediately following partial removal of her dental amalgams did not appear to be biologically plausible although it was sensible from the point of view of placebo effect or suggestibility.

In terms of the psychiatric conditions aside from somatoform disorders, one could argue that this patient was obsessed with the idea that her amalgams were the source of all of her ills and that her intent to have them extracted represented compulsive-like behavior to alleviate the anxiety associated with their presence. However, the criteria associated with a diagnosis of obsessive-compulsive disorder contain a number of behaviors that simply do not fit her unique situation. For one, the recurrent and persistent thoughts in obsessive-compulsive disorder, thoughts which she certainly exhibited, are to be seen as not simply excessive worries about real-life problems. To her, and to a relatively large number of others, the idea that dental amalgams are harmful is very real. Even though scientific studies have not yet been able to substantiate these phenomena as fact, it also has not ruled out the possibility completely. For the patient to adhere to the idea is, in the face of the scientific evidence, a matter of personal belief. To conclude that the idea is implausible would be a matter of subjective personal belief as well. Therefore, from a scientific perspective one must accept that it is possible, even if at the moment it is highly unlikely. More importantly, the diagnostic criteria for obsessive-compulsive disorder state that the actions of the person with this disorder are not connected in a realistic way with what they are designed to prevent or neutralize or they are clearly excessive. Given the last discussion about her beliefs, her motivation to have her amalgams removed is logically tied to an outcome of eliminating the adverse reactions she fears. Finally with regard to *obsessive-compulsive disorder*, the criteria indicate that the person should have at some point in the course of the disorder recognized that her actions are excessive or unreasonable. We have no evidence that the patient has ever reflected such insight.

With regard to depression, the patient can certainly be described as depressed. In fact, her history is positive for such diagnosis and treatment. However, she was not overtly depressed at the time of the present evaluation. On the basis of this observation, she would fail to meet DMS criteria for major depression, which states that the individual should reflect five of the following: Depressed mood for at least a 2-week period, diminished interest or pleasure in almost all activities, significant weight loss, sleep disturbance, psychomotor retardation or agitation, fatigue or loss of energy, feelings of worthlessness, diminished ability to concentrate, and recurrent thoughts of death or suicidal related thoughts or actions. Of these nine factors, she met only three—fatigue, loss of energy, and concentration difficulties. Although it is possible that her mood had been depressed for some 2-week period in the past, e.g., at the time she was diagnosed with depression, there was no objective historical confirmation of this, and the patient did not admit to such.

Within the family of somatoform disorders, somatization disorder does not fit the *case presentation* because of its very strict criteria and emphasis on multiple system involvement. Although the patient did complain of pain in muscles and joints and headache, these two areas are not sufficient to meet the four areas required by the formal diagnostic criteria. Nor did the patient complain of gastrointestinal symptoms to the extent required by the criteria. Conversion disorder must be ruled out on the same logical basis as was obsessive-compulsive disorder. That is, conversion disorder requires that the symptom or deficit not be explainable on the basis of culturally sanctioned behavior or experience. That conclusion can not be made in this instance given the fact that her treating clinician sanctioned the disorder, if for no other reason. Aside from this last observation, there are a relatively large number of people who firmly believe that the symptoms as complained about in this case do reflect the toxic effects of dental amalgam. Likewise, a formal diagnosis of hypochondriasis does not best fit the *case presentation*. Although this last diagnosis is conceivable, there is too little known about the patient's past medical, psychological, and social history to decide if she is routinely prone to fears of having a serious medical disease despite appropriate medical evaluation or treatment. We do know that following partial removal of her amalgams, she reported feeling better. This in itself might argue against a diagnosis of hypochondriasis. Finally, this clinical picture is better explained by another somatoform disorder, *undifferentiated somatoform disorder*.

Undifferentiated somatoform disorder is described in *DSM-IV* (American Psychiatric Association, 1994) as a *residual disorder*. The diagnosis is similar to but less stringent in terms of diagnostic criteria than somatization disorder. It is reserved for those patients with a persistent somatoform clinical presentation who do not meet the entire criteria for somatization or other somatoform disorder. Important to the current *case presentation*, there may be one or more unexplained medical complaints that have led to formal consultation, often as in this instance with a primary care physician. To render a diagnosis of undifferentiated somatoform disorder all of the criteria required for somatization disorder do not have to be met and there is no duration requirement. Otherwise the two disorders are similar. In this case, the criteria met for undifferentiated somatoform disorder included physical complaints comprised of fatigue and loss of appetite symptom that could not be fully explained by a known general medical condition. In addition, she met a second criterion: if a medical condition is believed to be related, the complaints and psychosocial impairments must be in excess of laboratory findings the symptoms cause distress in important areas of functioning, the disturbance is not better accounted for by another somatoform disorder, and as far as is discernable, the symptoms were not intentionally produced (American Psychiatric Association, 1994).

REVISED CAUSE/ETIOLOGY

The cause of the symptoms in this *case presentation* is seen as reflecting issues based on the belief that she has a disorder that is due to a specific chemical contained in her dental amalgams, i.e., elemental mercury. Other related psychological dynamics may play a contributory role as well, e.g., anxiety based on (as yet unknown to us) aspects of her personal history that have been "converted" symbolically to fears regarding her dental amalgams.

VERIFICATION OF REVISED CAUSE/ETIOLOGY

Although criteria such as those presented by Hill (1965) have been used extensively by us and others as a basis for verifying a causal relationship between a chemical and its toxic affect on the individual, the application of such criteria to psychological disorders has been less prevalent. Nevertheless, and aside from the observation that a diagnosis of amalgam disease fails to meet the criteria proposed by Hill, the psychological diagnosis concluded in this case, undifferentiated somatoform disorder, does appear to meet the majority of these criteria. That is, this diagnosis fits the timing aspects in that the patient attributes her complaints to the placement of her amalgams, the studies reviewed above yielded results in many instances of behavioral characteristics in persons with similar complaints that are consistent with the final diagnosis, the absence of physical test findings as observed in the current *case presentation* is listed as a criterion for undifferentiated somatoform disorder and leaves the diagnosis biologically plausible, a dose–response relationship that was counter to what would be expected in mercury poisoning is compatible with a psychological mechanism, and the studies reviewed above were consistent in the reported clinical findings in this *case presentation*. In addition, the criterion of disease specificity is difficult for psychological disorders as our knowledge of the pathophysiology in these conditions is evolving. On the other hand and at the time of presentation, this case was seen as best fitting the stated diagnosis and psychological cause. This diagnosis was accomplished within the context of a differential diagnosis that included the initial diagnosis of amalgam disease, which satisfies objective criteria that speak to the consideration of other possible explanations. To our knowledge, there is no animal model that has been discovered that addresses specifically the disorders under consideration. Although some *in vitro* or animal models might speak indirectly to the diagnoses, these were not discussed in this section because the research variables employed in those studies were too far removed from the specific topic of amalgam disease.

Conclusion

Although in this case a specific diagnostic conclusion that represented an alternative to the initial diagnosis made at the time of referral, not every case presenting with previously diagnosed amalgam disease will have the same explanations for the patient's symptoms. While somatization was seen as a characteristic exhibited by many of the subjects in the studies reviewed earlier, not all subjects in those studies reflected this factor and studies were not uniform in their conclusions even when somatization was present. Every case, as has been said repeatedly in these volumes, will need to be approached on its own merits and within the context of the differential diagnosis.

This *case presentation* calls our attention to another phenomenon. This is the occurrence of diseases and disorders that have not necessarily gone through all the steps called for by the scientifically and evidence-based disciplines that are concerned with clinical health care. We discussed such entities to some extent in our earlier works (Albers, Wald, Garabrant, Trask, & Berent, 2000), and we have described many of the clinical and scientific issues relevant to this topic in volume I of the present work (see especially, chapters 2, 4, and 8). In chapter 8 of volume I, we discussed issues of causality from several perspectives. One of these perspectives is related to how science deals with the issue of causality. With that as a background, one could think of less than completely verified diseases not so much as "controversial" but more as "opportunistic." They are opportunistic because the proponents at times seize the opportunity to address science at its weakest points. What are these weak points? The answer to this question can be complex. One weak point that has special relevance for the current *case presentation* is that science is poorest at proving the negative. As a result, the door is left open for less scientifically inclined individuals to advance their beliefs without the benefit of scientific proof. If the concept is not dispelled, then it is still possible. Since the scientist is unable to disprove the existence and recognizes that until such is done, the concept will remain "possible," others who believe in the phenomenon may call for methods alternative to science, e.g., consensus within some specified peer group, describing the alternative as, in fact, more powerful than is scientifically justified. Or, an emotional argument might be made in support of the concept, like, "We do not have time to wait for science to do its slow and tedious work, as patients are suffering." Besides, the argument might continue "on the basis of my substantial clinical experience, I can think of nothing else it could be." Looked at in this way, the controversy is not so much around the proposed diagnosis since every scientist is eager to discover something new, and every scientist we are familiar with would rather arrive at a positive than a negative finding in a research project. What is the basis of controversy then, if not the proposed disorder itself? We would argue that the controversy revolves around maintaining the integrity of the scientific method as the most accurate way to make the presently unknown, known.

Patient with history of head injury

Stanley Berent

Why discuss head injury (HI) in a book on neurobehavioral toxicology? There are two primary answers to this question. The first reason relates to the fact that HIs are relatively common and, therefore, have a good chance of appearing in a given patient's medical history. The number of traumatic brain injuries (TBI), a term often used synonymously with HI, is close to 1.5 million people a year in the United States, with about 50,000 deaths related to these injuries (U.S. Department of Health and Human Services [DHHS], 2005). Also, each year 80,000–90,000 people begin onset of long-term or lifelong TBI-related disability (Thurman, Alverson, Dunn, Guerrero, & Sniezek, 1999; U.S. Department of Health and Human Services [DHHS], 2005). For children, the figures related to TBI are approximately a half million emergency department visits, 37,000 hospitalizations, and 2,685 deaths (Langlois, Rutland-Brown, & Thomas, 2004). In the occupational setting, the incidence of work-related HI is similar to that for work-related poisonings (National Institute for Occupational Safety and Health [NIOSH], 2004).

The second reason for including a discussion of HI relates to the nature of the symptoms associated with TBI, especially mild TBI. The nonspecific nature of TBI-related symptoms is in many respects similar to that reported in some cases of toxicant exposure (Table 18.8). Also, the findings from neuropsychological examination and other test results may be similar to those associated with some toxicant exposures (Filley & Kleinschmidt-DeMasters, 2001; Zakzanis, Leach, & Kaplan, 1999).

Because of the relatively high incidence of TBI in the general population, it would not be unexpected that patients suspected of having suffered toxicant-induced disorder also might reflect a history of TBI. When present, this historical factor, along with the known commonality of symptoms and similarities of some test findings in toxicant exposure and TBI, suggests that both should be included in the differential diagnosis in many if not all cases where one or the other is the suspected cause of the patient's symptoms.

Table 18.8 Symptoms associated with concussion or mild traumatic brain injury (TBI) in adults.*

Headache

Neck pain

Memory complaints

Concentration difficulties

Decision making problems

Slowed thinking

Easily confused

Getting lost

Lack of energy and easily fatigued feeling

Changes in mood

Sleep difficulties

Dizziness

Loss of balance

Nausea

Increased sensitivity to lights or sounds

Easy distractibility

Blurred vision

Changes in sense of smell or taste

Ringing in ears (tinnitus)

* Symptoms in children mirror those in adults; however, the children may be less able to verbalize these complaints or they may show themselves indirectly through such behaviors as irritability, changes in eating patterns, becoming overly tired, changes in sleep patterns, changes in school performance, loss of interest in toys or play, loss of balance, regression to earlier behaviors (e.g., regressing to pretoilet training after the skill had been obtained). Adapted from "Traumatic Brain Injury (TBI): Topic Home" U.S. Department of Health and Human Services (DHHS)," 2005, C. f. D. C. a. P. C., http://www.cdc.gov/node.do/id/0900f3ec8000dbdc

Case presentation[1]

A 42-year-old male was referred by his primary care physician for neuro-psychological evaluation. The patient was said to be complaining of symptoms that he (the patient) attributed to toxicant exposure at work. Primary complaints included difficulties with memory (e.g., going to get something and forgetting what he intended to retrieve), concentration (especially on the job but also when listening to conversational speech), and comprehension (especially understanding what others are saying). Also, he complained of not being able to perform as well as previously in his job as a "maintenance engineer" at a large manufacturing plant where he had worked for the last 22 years.

His medical and neurological examinations were said to be normal. The only possible exception to these normal findings was a relatively low score on formal mental status testing using the Mini-Mental State Examination (MMSE) (Folstein, Folstein, & McHugh, 1975). He scored 23 of 30 on the MMSE, losing points for serial subtractions (4 errors on 5 trials), 2 errors (of 3 items) on delayed recall, and 1 error in properly carrying out a three-step command. This score placed him at the border between normal and deficient mental status on the basis of the MMSE. At the same time, he was described as well oriented during his medical and neurological examinations.

The history he provided included no substantial past injuries or illnesses. The patient reported having been involved in a motor vehicle accident (MVA) about 2 years previously but stated that he was not seriously injured in that accident. He was raised in a rural area where his father was a maintenance worker at a nearby factory. His mother was a homemaker. He said he did "OK" in school, "got by" but was "not a scholar." He married his high school sweetheart shortly after graduation, and they have been together since. They have two grown children in good health.

The patient placed his concerns regarding toxicant exposure to an event that occurred at work about 6 years before the present appointment. He reported that he had become dizzy while cleaning out a "grease pit" at work and "passed out" before he could leave the pit. One of his coworkers saw him fall and rescued him from the pit. He was unconscious for about 10–15 min and awoke to see the emergency vehicle arrive at the scene. He recalled that an oxygen mask was placed over his face, and he was taken to the hospital emergency department (ED), where he was evaluated and released after about 6–8 hr. He said he continued to feel lightheaded and found it difficult to think. He believes he had some memory difficulties for awhile, but this improved within a year. Since that time, however, he has experienced an increase in the symptoms listed earlier. When directly questioned, he said that there had been some improvement in his symptoms over the last year, but that they still cause him problems.

There was no formal record of the exact chemical involved in the exposure incident, but the patient said he had been told by coworkers that it was a solvent they used regularly at work, one containing trichloroethylene (TCE).

INITIAL CLINICAL DIAGNOSIS

The patient's physician had diagnosed the patient with cognitive impairments possibly resulting from exposure to solvents, resolving.

ADDITIONAL INFORMATION

With the patient's permission, past hospital and other medical records were retrieved. These included records from the time of his exposure approximately 6 years previously, as well as records related to his MVA about 2 years before the present evaluation. The EMS report from the time of his exposure indicated that he was found in a semiconscious state and being assisted by his coworkers. He was said to have lost consciousness while cleaning out a pit and subsequently taken outside and laid on the ground. The period of unconsciousness was estimated to be 5–15 min (fairly consistent with the patient's report in interview described earlier). Vital signs were normal, aside from a slight increase in pulse rate. He was administered O_2 by mask and transferred to the hospital. In the ED, he was described as slightly groggy and mildly confused. His mental status was rated as mildly abnormal because of inability to specify the exact date or where he was located at the time. He was oriented to person and historical events. Also, he was described as anxious and slightly agitated, but no formal psychiatric diagnosis was assigned. He was kept under observation for a few hours, during which time his mental status returned to normal. At his insistence, the patient was discharged, and advised to see his own doctor within a week or so. The discharge diagnosis was acute intoxication with transient loss of consciousness as result of work-related solvent exposure.

The patient returned to work after about 3 weeks, but in the face of continued complaints over a period of about 6 months concerning primarily memory and concentration difficulties, the patient's physician referred him for EEG and MRI evaluations, both of which were normal. Within the next few months, his physician described the patient's symptoms as "much improved."

About 2 years before the present examination, the patient was involved in a MVA, in which he was the sole occupant of an automobile that was struck from behind by a pickup truck. An attempt to retrieve police and EMS reports related to this accident were unsuccessful. His ED records were obtained, however. These records indicated that the patient arrived at the ED with multiple, minor abrasions and altered state of consciousness, with a Glasgow Coma Score (GCS) = 13 (specifying that the patient was confused, disoriented, and inappropriate speech [profanity]). Also, he was said to have been unconscious at the scene of the accident and had to be extracted from the vehicle. Vital signs showed increased blood pressure (140/90 mmHg), increased respiratory rate, and increased pulse rate. All vital signs returned to normal during the course of symptomatic treatment (e.g., hydration). Also, his behavior returned to normal over the course of about 4 hr (with GCS = 15). He was referred for a cranial CT, which was interpreted as showing a small subdural hematoma in the left frontal–temporal region. An EEG showed abnormal slowing, left > right. The patient was hospitalized for 8 days, during which time his condition continued to improve. Repeat CT and EEG evaluations were normal, as was an MRI performed 1 week after the MVA. Following discharge, he remained off work for 6 weeks. A note from his physician about 1 year post-MVA said the patient still complained of difficulties with concentration and memory, but that these symptoms had lessened considerably since his MVA. There was no mention of the earlier toxicant exposure.

COMMENT ON NEUROPSYCHOLOGICAL TEST RESULTS

Selected results from the patient's neuropsychological examination are contained in Table 18.9. These results reflected a person who is of generally average intellectual ability. His normal, average level scores on vocabulary

Table 18.9 Neuropsychological testing results in a patient with complaints of solvent exposure and history of head injury.

Test administered	Domain measured	Test results
WAIS-III, VIQ	Verbal intellect	92
WAIS-III, PIQ	Performance intellect	108
WAIS-III, Vocabulary	Vocabulary level	9
WAIS-III, Similarities	Abstract conceptualization	6
WAIS-III, Block Design	Visual-motor problem solving	11
WAIS-III, Digit Symbol	Psychomotor problem solving	5
MMSE	General mental status	24/30
WMS-III, Aud. Immd.	Verbal memory, immediate	72
WMS-III, Aud. Delay	Verbal memory, delayed	80
WMS-III, Visual Immd.	Visual memory, immediate	93
WMS-III, Visual Delay	Visual memory, delayed	100
WRAT-3, Reading	Reading recognition	102
MMPI-2	Clinical ratings of psychopathology	All scales within normal, except D = 68
TOMM	Test of effort	50, 50

Selected tests were chosen that reflected a range of neuropsychological domains sufficient to discern a meaningful clinical pattern.

and the WRAT-III suggest that, if anything, he understated his past school performance, or that he was able to acquire these skills despite not having done that well in formal schooling. The MMSE showed a mental status picture that remained relatively unchanged from that reported in the referral information, with continuing problems with serial seven subtraction and delayed item recall. At the same time, his mental status was judged by observation in interview to be normal, and his score on the formal MMSE, though borderline-low, remained in the normal range (24 of 30). The striking finding in these results was the significant difference in his verbal and nonverbal scores. His verbal IQ was significantly lower than his performance IQ. There was also a significant difference between verbal and nonverbal memory scores, with verbal (immediate and delayed memory scores) in the below normal range and visual scores within normal limits. In addition, the patient produced impaired scores on some tasks that demanded problem solving and abstract conceptualization. Although his depression score on the MMPI-2 was slightly within the range indicating very mild clinical depression, there was no indication of more severe psychopathology. A test of effort was performed normally. There was no indication, therefore, that lack of effort influenced his test results.

These test results are consistent with underlying supratentorial dysfunction, lateralized to the dominant hemisphere. Frontal and temporal regions are also implicated.

The patient was described diagnostically as suffering from cognitive impairment. When using the *DSM* (American Psychiatric Association, 1994), the formal diagnosis would be *dementia* (with qualification that the dementia is "due to other general medical conditions" once the specific medical condition has been confirmed as causal to the dementia.

Discussion

Seventy-five percent of all annual occurrences of TBI are represented by concussions that are generally rated as "mild" and most often occur in the context of a closed-head injury (CHI) (U.S. Department of Health and Human Services [DHHS], 2005). Unfortunately, the terms used in reference to HI are not well standardized. The term closed-head injury, for instance, is used variously in the literature but generally appears to refer to injuries to the brain that do not involve penetration of the skull.[2] Concussion, too, lacks precise definition. Here, we will define concussion in relation to TBI as a transient loss of consciousness that results from a physical trauma and is most often associated with minimal or even no long-term residua (Goldman & Bennett, 2000). The severity of TBI is usually based on the GCS (Teasdale & Jennett, 1974), where "mild" is defined as a GCS $\geq$ 13, "moderate" = GCS 9–12, and "severe" $\leq$ GCS 8[3] (see Table 18.10). Others have employed the term "brief" in place of "transient" but this term is subject to interpretation as

Table 18.10 Items rated in the Glasgow Coma Scale.

Item to be rated	Criteria	Assigned score
Eyes	Open spontaneously (independent of awareness)	4
	Open in response to speech (not necessarily command)	3
	Open in response to pain (not to eyes)	2
	Never open	1
Best verbal response	Fully oriented (person, time, place)	5
	Confused (disoriented)	4
	Inappropriate (profanity, overly loud, etc.)	3
	Incomprehensible (groaning, moans)	2
	No verbal responses	1
Best motor response	Follows commands	6
	Localizes pain with motor gesture (deliberate)	5
	Withdraws from stimulation	4
	Abnormal flexion	3
	Abnormal extension	2
	None (flaccid)	1

Scale items based on original work by Teasdale and Jennett (1974). The overall GCS is a summation of item scores, with 3 being the lowest and 15 the highest possible scores.

well. Rowland (1989) defined concussion as a "brief loss of consciousness after head injury, with no immediate or delayed evidence of structural brain damage." Rowland attempted to address the lack of precision reflected by the term, "brief," by defining the period of unconsciousness as limited to 6 hr, beyond which damage to brain tissue, again according to Rowland, can be presumed to have occurred. When loss of consciousness exceeds 6 hr, the presumed tissue damage is said to involve diffuse axonal injury (DAI). DAI may reflect in focal or diffuse microscopic lesions (Rowland, 1989). This last observation may be important in explaining why symptoms, and even impaired scores on quantitative neurobehavioral tests, may be present when the results of structural brain imaging and other clinical tests might remain within normal limits.

Estimates are that 15% of people who suffer even a mild brain injury continue to experience problems from that injury a year later (Guerrero, Thurman, & Sniezek, 2000), and that about 2% of the population in the United States lives with TBI-related disabilities (Thurman et al., 1999). The last figure most likely reflects an underestimate, however, as the data are based only on hospitalized cases and do not include those persons seen in emergency departments but not admitted, those seen in outpatient offices, or those who did not receive treatment for their injuries (U.S. Department of Health and Human Services [DHHS], 2005). Also, changes in hospital practices that have led to reductions in hospitalization for many patients who in the past would likely have been admitted probably contribute to the underestimation (Thurman & Guerrero, 1999).

Everyone is at risk for TBI, with males twice as likely as females to suffer such injury (U.S. Department of Health and Human Services [DHHS], 2005). In terms of age, the groups at highest risk are those aged 15–24 years and those over 75 years (Thurman et al., 1999). As might be expected, occupational injuries involving TBI are not uncommon. Analyses of data using the NIOSH Work-RISQS reveal that for 1999 (the latest date for which data were available), there were approximately 13,000 work-related concussions treated in U.S. hospital emergency departments (workers aged 20–64 years). The rate estimate (incidents/100 FTE) for concussion for this same group of workers was reported as 0.011. For comparison, the rate estimate reported for work-related poisonings in the same age range was 0.018. The injury/illness rate for work-related injuries of any type requiring emergency department visits was 2.9.

Zakzanis et al. (1999) reported that executive dysfunction (e.g., planning and complex problem solving), memory acquisition, and delayed recall were found to be the most sensitive measures of mild TBI based upon their quantitative review of the scientific literature. Others (e.g., Binder, Rohling, & Larrabee, 1997) also have implicated attention/concentration as likely to be impaired in patients with mild TBI. Compare these neuropsychological test findings with those suggested by Filley and Kleinschmidt-DeMasters (2001), who in addressing toxic leukoencephalopathy described findings of abnormality in sustained attention, information processing speed, memory retrieval, and visual-spatial skills with sparing of language functions. We have discussed the lack of disease specificity inherent not only in neuropsychological test scores but in some other medical tests as well (see, e.g., the section on *Solvents* in chapter 15). Although it is important to quantitatively document behavioral abnormalities, diagnostic possibilities and their potential causes must be included in a differential diagnosis and analyzed within the context of objective criteria that consider both test and extra-test findings in reaching clinical conclusions. In other words, a final, disease-specific clinical conclusion results usually from the entirety of the clinical evaluation rather than from one component of the evaluation.

Similarities between symptoms of some toxicant exposures and TBI are not surprising because consequences of the resultant cerebral injury can be common in both. The pathology of TBI, even when mild, can be multiple, and some years ago, Levin, Benton, and Grossman (1982) divided the various types of injuries into primary and secondary occurrences. Primary injuries following TBI, according to Levin et al., include microscopic (widespread neuronal damage resulting from the physical forces of shearing and stretching of nerve fibers) and macroscopic lesions such as contusions and lacerations to brain tissue that result directly from impact. Secondary mechanisms of injury include hemorrhage, edema, hyperemia, ischemia, increased intracranial pressure, herniation, hypoxia, and embolism. Especially as the severity of TBI increases (GCS $\leq$ 8), cerebral hypoxia and hypoperfusion can be present and are related to clinical outcome (Dunham, Ransom, Flowers, Siegal, & Kohli, 2004) (see section on *Hypoxia*, chapter 17). In a study using positron emission tomography (PET) to study patients with severe-to-moderate TBI (GCS = 4–10), Wu et al. (2004) reported a significant reduction in subcortical white matter oxygen to glucose utilization ratio following TBI in comparison to normal control values. Although mean cortical gray matter and whole brain values remain unchanged following TBI, white matter O_2 metabolism was reduced diffusely throughout the cerebral hemispheres (Wu et al.). White matter lesions have been shown to be an important component in toxic induced injury as well (Filley & Kleinschmidt-DeMasters, 2001; Filley, Heaton, & Rosenberg, 1990). Also, more general disturbances involving neurotransmission can result from TBI (Arciniegas et al., 1999), and this factor could provide a basis for commonality between the two sources of injury, TBI and toxicant exposure. Common underlying mechanisms of injury could be expected to result in common symptoms and even clinical signs. In such cases, the history may become critical in making an accurate causal attribution.

NERVOUS SYSTEM LOCALIZATION

Although the patient in the *case presentation* had a neurological examination that was normal, except for mild alterations in mental status, findings from neuropsychological and other tests (e.g., past CT, EEG) reflected abnormalities. These findings implicated the supratentorial level of the central nervous system, with further localization to the hemisphere dominant for language (probably the left cerebral hemisphere in this right-handed person), frontal and temporal regions specifically.

VERIFICATION OF THE ORIGINAL CLINICAL DIAGNOSIS

The initial diagnosis in this case—cognitive impairment—can be confirmed on the basis of neuropsychological testing. This diagnosis explains all or the most important of the patient's symptoms. The aspects of the original diagnostic statement regarding the etiology of the patient's impairments will be addressed separately.

VERIFICATION OF THE ALTERNATIVE CLINICAL DIAGNOSIS

As already mentioned, the presence of cognitive impairment was confirmed by the neuropsychological examination results. A more formal and specific diagnosis based on *DSM* nomenclature would be "dementia." If only memory were impaired, the correct *DSM* diagnosis would be amnestic disorder. The presence of disturbances in cognitive function beyond memory alone (e.g., problem solving, abstraction), together with a conclusion that the cognitive deficits reflected a decline in comparison to previous levels of functioning, justifies the dementia designation.

The MMPI depression scale score suggests the additional diagnosis of dysthymia. However, the patient did not overtly complain of symptoms of depression. Nor did he meet other *DSM* criteria for dysthymia (e.g., depressed mood most of the time over a prolonged time period) (American Psychiatric Association, 1994). His score on the depression scale of the MMPI-2, although slightly within the clinical range ($T = 68$ [normal cutoff: $T = 65$]) is not sufficient in itself to justify a formal diagnosis, especially since there was no indication that depression served to impair his effort or performance. Put another way, the cognitive component was sufficient to explain all of the clinical findings. As in any case where depression is possible, this aspect of the clinical findings was carefully explored with the patient before excluding it as an alternative diagnosis. One final technical note, if depression was indicated and found subsequently to be due to a medical condition, the proper diagnosis would be "mood disorder due to a general medical condition," with specification of the medical condition.

CAUSE/ETIOLOGY

The initial diagnosis was confounded with a causal statement that the patient's symptoms were the result of acute toxicant exposure some 6 years before.

VERIFICATION OF CAUSE/ETIOLOGY

The cause for the patient's impairments cannot be verified using objective criteria. The reasons for this conclusion in entirety are probably best discussed within the context of the differential diagnostic considerations that derived from the present evaluation and are discussed in addressing the alternative cause/etiology.

REVISED CAUSE/ETIOLOGY

Head injury resulting from an MVA 2 years before is seen as explanatory to the patient's present condition.

VERIFICATION OF THE REVISED CAUSE/ETIOLOGY

The attribution of the clinical findings in the *case presentation* to TBI can be verified on the basis of three primary criteria. These include the pattern of neurobehavioral strengths and weaknesses, the coherence of the relationship between examination results and independently documented regions of physical abnormalities, and the timing of injury in relation to subsequent symptoms and test findings.

The pattern of neurobehavioral strengths and weaknesses revealed in the psychometric examination is consistent with underlying neurological dysfunction that is focal and lateralized to the language dominant cerebral hemisphere. This pattern while biologically plausible with damage induced by TBI is not consistent with toxicant-induced disorder, where bilateral effects are expected (Albers & Berent, 2000; Schaumburg & Spencer, 1987). Also, the observed neurobehavioral pattern is consistent with findings reported from imaging studies that were conducted following the patient's MVA. The neuroanatomical areas implicated by CT and EEG were those that mediate the behavioral domains that were found on neuropsychological examination to be deficient (e.g., verbal intellect, learning, memory, abstraction, and problem solving). Importantly, cognitive domains not mediated by these neuroanatomical regions appeared to remain intact (e.g., nonverbal intellectual skills, visual learning and memory). Effort was excluded as explanatory on the basis of formal testing.

In terms of timing, both the toxicant exposure and the TBI occurred before the current examination. Records, however, documented a course of improvement following the exposure incident, with worsening of symptoms following the subsequent MVA and TBI. Most telling, however, was the availability of normal brain imaging results following the patient's exposure, with findings consistent with head injury, i.e., subdural hematoma, after his TBI. Also, the clinical course following his accident and resultant TBI is coherent, with subjectively reported improved function over time.

What if the medical history records in this case had not been available? The patient had understated the impact of his past MVA. Since he appeared to understate his educational successes as well, his misrepresentation of these events could have reflected a personality style. We may never know the exact reasons for his approach in reporting his history. He may have been motivated in some way to emphasize the past toxicant exposure, or perhaps his cognitive impairments interfered with his ability to give an accurate history. Nevertheless, and even if none of these events had been known, the focal and lateralizing nature of the neuropsychological results and other clinical findings in this case would have implicated an acute injury that was not the reported toxicant exposure.

What if the neuropsychological results had shown a more general as opposed to focal pattern of impairments? Traumatic brain injury can manifest in bilateral, multifocal, or generalized neurological dysfunction, depending on the nature and severity of the injury (Levin et al., 1982; Rowland, 1989). In the present case, the history of medical test results and reported clinical course of his symptoms would have allowed for the TBI diagnosis, while excluding toxicant exposure as explanatory.

Does TBI explain all of his impairments, or might there be some contribution from his past exposure to toxicants? Though possible, the normal examination results that were reported following the patient's exposure incident argue against a causal relationship to any impairment noted later. The history does document acute effects immediately following the exposure, but the subsequent clinical course appeared to reflect a return to normal functioning before his subsequent MVA and TBI. When the results of his current neuropsychological examination are considered, the patient appears to be functioning normally, and at levels consistent with his estimated baseline level of ability, in areas other than those designated as impaired as a result of his current examination. This pattern argues against a generalized decline in performance as would be predicted if toxicant exposure were contributory.

Conclusion

This *case presentation* underscores the importance of history in differentiating between toxicant exposure and other potential causes for a patient's symptoms and signs. The pattern of neurobehavioral strengths and weaknesses was meaningful in reaching clinical conclusions in this specific case. Even without the history of TBI, the behavioral measurements would have allowed for an accurate description of the patient's difficulties, contributing importantly to prognostic statements and treatment planning. Nevertheless, the discovery of a past MVA that resulted in TBI was critical in arriving at the most likely cause for the patient's diagnosis.

Patient with neuropsychological complaints attributed to diet drugs

Stanley Berent

Obesity is a major problem for a great many people. Obesity is defined as a body mass index (BMI) greater than 29 (Gallagher et al., 2000), where BMI is calculated as the weight in kilograms divided by height in meter square (kg/m^2). A desirable BMI from a health viewpoint is usually considered to be between 20 and 25, but about 5 million or more Americans have a BMI equal to or greater than 35 kg/m^2, with more than a million over 40 kg/m^2 (Heiat, A., National Institutes of Health [NIH]: the NIH Consensus Conference on Health Implications of Obesity in, United States Department of Agriculture (and the National Heart, Lung, and Blood Institute., 2003).

Aside from aesthetic, economic, social, and personal identity concerns, obesity has other major health implications. Some of these implications include increased risk for hypertension and other cardiovascular disease, diabetes mellitus, dyslipidemia, gallbladder disease, sleep disturbances, and increased morbidity and mortality in general. A variety of treatment interventions, alone and in combination, have been advanced in attempts to deal with the problem of obesity. Aside from surgical and psychosocial treatments, various medications, commonly referred to as "diet drugs," have been advanced as well. Fenfluramine is one such medication.

Case presentation[1]

A 41-year-old female presented for a "second opinion" with complaints of memory loss, headache, difficulty sleeping, depression, anxiety, severe emotional distress, and fears associated with what she perceived as an increased risk for "fatal illness" associated with her use of diet drugs in the past. She reported that the last clinician she saw told her that her past use of diet drugs was the most likely cause of her symptoms. The patient's complaints were made against a background of numerous physical problems that included hypertension and tachycardia. She believed she had suffered "brain damage" as a result of her use of diet drugs, and she reported that she intended to sue the makers of these drugs.

She had a problem with her weight all of her life. As a teenager, she tried to lose weight by dieting, purging, and through the use of illegally obtained "speed." She had seen a therapist for counseling in the past, beginning as a teenager, and continuing until she was prescribed diet drugs by her physician. She also was diagnosed at that time with depression and prescribed an antidepressant medication. The patient began taking fenfluramine and phentermine ("fen-phen") and dexfenfluramine (Redux) about 10 years before the current evaluation and continued to take these medications for about 2 years. She discontinued these medications, however, after she read an article in a lay publication about adverse effects, including possible valvular heart disease, associated with their use. Following termination of fen-phen and Redux, she regained the weight she had lost while being treated, and she became increasingly concerned that the medications had injured her. However, she did not complain of problems associated with her use of these medications until some years after she terminated use of the diet drugs. Despite there being no recorded history of such complaints, she reported that her present symptoms of memory loss, headache, and difficulty sleeping began about 1 year after discontinuing her diet drugs. She reported that the symptoms had grown progressively worse. Memory loss was described as difficulty concentrating and recalling everyday events. The headaches were described as bilateral and nonpulsatile. There were no associated features, and, in particular, she denied nauseousness. These headaches occurred almost daily. They typically were present upon awakening but improved later in the day. She reported always being a light sleeper. She denied problems falling asleep, but she felt restless and awoke numerous times during the night. She never felt rested and fell asleep easily during the day, if given the opportunity. She denied episodes of sleep paralysis or cataplexy.

The family history was positive for depression (mother), alcoholism (father), and obesity (parents and daughter). She described herself as having been raised in "an alcoholic family." She reported that she had been employed for about 18 years as a bookkeeper for a major manufacturer. Her last physician had recommended a thorough cardiopulmonary evaluation, the results of which were unremarkable.

INITIAL CLINICAL DIAGNOSIS

The physician last seen by the patient had established a diagnosis of depression and memory problems due to a fenfluramine-induced "serotonin neurotoxic syndrome." No additional diagnoses were considered, and possible preexisting conditions were considered only in the sense that they had left her vulnerable to the adverse effects of fenfluramine.

INITIAL CAUSE/ETIOLOGY

The patient's symptoms of depression and memory impairment were attributed to her use of diet pills, which was said to have resulted in fenfluramine-induced serotonin neurotoxic syndrome.

Discussion

The initial clinical diagnosis for this patient's problems proposed by her physician included both a biochemical explanation (*serotonin neurotoxic syndrome*) and the presumed cause of her problem (exposure to the diet drug, fenfluramine).

Fenfluramine has been used for some time to study eating behaviors in animals and the relationship between feeding and the serotonergic system. Fenfluramine elicits the release of 5-hydroxytryptamine (5-HT, serotonin) and inhibits its reuptake. It is believed that a number of metabolites of 5-HT have differential effects on various neuronal sites and, hence, on various aspects of eating. For example, postsynaptic receptors regulate the size of meals eaten while another site regulates rate of eating (Frazer & Hensler, 1999). The relationship between serotonin and behavior goes well beyond eating and includes psychiatric disorders such as schizophrenia and depression. Chemicals with the capacity to affect the serotonergic system have been used to treat psychiatric problems. For instance, fenfluramine has been used in treating autistic children with ADHD (Aman, Kern, McGhee, & Arnold, 1993). As with all medications, side effects can occur with the use of diet drugs. A study of 3000 obese patients taking Redux for 6 months to a year (Laudignon & Rebuffe-Scrive, 1997) revealed minor, subjective, and mostly transient (tending to disappear within a couple of weeks of starting the drug) central nervous system side effects similar to those seen with serotonin reuptake inhibitors (often referred to as selective serotonin reuptake inhibitors [SSRIs]). Side effects included asthenia, diarrhea, dry mouth, and somnolence. Adverse side effects occurred in less than 20% of patients.

At very high dose levels, these drugs have been reported to deplete brain serotonin in a dose-dependent manner in animal models, leading at times to irreversible alterations in brain chemistry (Christensen et al., 1999). A comparable effect in humans at therapeutic levels has not been documented. Nevertheless, some have argued that an adverse effect comparable to that seen in animals also occurs in humans under some conditions (Schenck & Mahowald, 1996). Christensen et al. used fluorine magnetic resonance spectroscopy to measure dexfenfluramine (DF) and its active metabolite, dex-norfenfluramine (dNF) in humans. These investigators found very low, nontoxic concentrations of DF and dNF in human brain by this method. The animals were found to have levels that were 35–70 times greater than the humans. Despite the objective evidence that these compounds did not have effects in humans similar to those in animals, a continuing controversy over the presence of serotonergic-like symptoms developed.

Controversy over these drugs intensified when they were taken off the market in 1997 because of concerns over the potential for development of cardiopulmonary related adverse reactions that included primarily valvular heart disease, a condition not experienced by the patient. While not directly ascribing the effects of these drugs to central nervous system serotonergic mechanisms, Curzon and Gibson (1999) listed primary pulmonary hypertension and valvular heart disease as potential medication-induced disorders. Others have also reported on these cardiopulmonary side effects (Kolanowski, 1999; Scheen & Lefebvre, 1999; Vivero, Anderson, & Clark, 1998).

Fenfluramine does influence serotonin levels in the central nervous system; however, the notion that the use of fenfluramine at therapeutic levels can lead to a serotonin neurotoxic syndrome is hypothetical at best. There is no conclusive evidence at this time that fenfluramine or its related compounds are neurotoxic at therapeutic levels in humans. The controversy over the neurotoxicity of this substance appears to have begun with an article by Ricaurte, Yuan, Hatzidimitriou, Cord, and McCann (2002). Ricaurte et al. (2002) speculated that these drugs in humans might cause disturbances in mood, sleep, impulse control, sexual disturbance, and neuroendocrine function. In contrast, other controlled studies have shown that the central nervous system side effects that occur with these medications are mostly minor, subjective, and transient (Laudignon & Rebuffe-Scrive, 1997). Noble (1997) used a brief battery of psychological measures and found no differences on any measures between a group treated with Redux and controls. MMSE scores remained normal throughout the study, and there were no differences in reports of psychiatric disturbances. In a review article, McCann, Seiden, Rubin, and Ricaurte (1997) looked at animal and human study results published between 1966 and 1997. They reported that fenfluramine caused long-lasting reductions in serotonin markers in all animal species studied, but they found no human studies reporting comparable findings. In a later publication (McCann, Eligulashvili, & Ricaurte, 1998), however, these same authors reported 31 case studies purportedly evidencing adverse, severe and at times persistent "neuropsychiatric syndromes." Most of these cases reflected memory-related problems and depression. McCann et al. related these adverse events to alterations in serotonin brain chemistry. Although McCann et al. admitted that some of these cases had positive personal histories for similar disturbances, there appears to have been little effort to factor in these potential confounders. Fenfluramine was at one time the largest used of the diet drugs (Curzon & Gibson, 1999). Despite this widespread use, the literature on this drug contains relatively few reports of central nervous system-related adverse effects. The representativeness of the McCann et al. sample and general applicability of findings based on that sample, therefore, might be limited.

VERIFICATION OF THE INITIAL CLINICAL DIAGNOSIS

The clinical diagnosis of serotonin neurotoxic syndrome given to this patient by her treating physician cannot be verified using objective criteria, such as presented by Richardson et al. (2000). The diagnosis is not adequate in that it does not explain the clinical findings. The diagnosis also does not fit the illness pattern, in that many of her symptoms predated her use of diet medications and appeared to be little changed in type or severity since. This conclusion is based on historical records that are in contrast to the patient's report of progressive worsening of her symptoms. The diagnosis lacks parsimony because other aspects of the patient's history might better and more simply explain the reported symptoms. Further, the diagnosis of serotonin neurotoxic syndrome is not coherent in that the presumed pathophysiology has not been scientifically established. A MEDLINE search of the medical literature published between 1966 and 2003, for instance, failed to yield a publication with the named condition in the title.

VERIFICATION OF INITIAL CAUSE/ETIOLOGY

The cause/etiology proposed initially in this *case presentation* cannot be verified using objective criteria. If one assumes that serotonin neurotoxic syndrome is a diagnosable condition, what is the likelihood that it could be caused by use of the diet drugs prescribed for this patient? This patient's neurologic and psychological problems were attributed to abnormalities in the serotonergic system of the brain, yet the primary reason for this diagnosis appeared to be the historical use of a diet drug, fenfluramine, whose mechanism of action involves the manipulation of serotonin. Serotonin reuptake inhibitors (SRIs) have been fairly extensively employed as antidepressants and include such medicines as fluoxetine (Prozac), sertraline (Zoloft), paroxetine (Paxil), and flovoxatine (Luvox). While these drugs have been associated with a "fatal serotonin syndrome," this condition has been reported to occur with the concomitant overdose of SRIs and MAO inhibitors (Goldman & Bennett, 2000). Serotonin reuptake inhibitors antidepressant overdoses in the context of monotherapy are believed to generally cause only sedation (Goldman & Bennett, 2000).

Comment

Other than the history of medicinal treatment for obesity, no substantial review by her physician of past medical, psychosocial, or other history is evident. There appears to have been little attention paid to more than the most primary of the patient's complaints, with no attempt to elicit further symptoms or signs or to engage more than minimally in differential diagnosis. The patient's self-ascribed causal link between her complaints and her use of diet drugs seems to have been uncritically accepted by her last physician. There was a notable lack of consideration, even identification, of other factors that might explain this patient's symptoms.

Given the patient's belief that she had been "brain damaged," it is especially notable that until the present evaluation no referrals were made for EEG or MRI or other imaging studies. When administered, the EEG and MRI examinations were reported to be normal.

There were several transient symptoms reported in the history related to the *case presentation* that can be attributed to use of diet drugs. That is, there were symptoms experienced by this patient shortly after she began taking these diet medications. These initial medication side effects were well documented and included dry mouth, diarrhea, and altered time perception. All of these side effects were mild. All are known physiological side effects associated with use of these drugs. These side effects cleared quickly with adjustment to her medication dose, and the record indicated that she remained symptom free following such adjustment until her presentation some years later.

ALTERNATIVE CLINICAL DIAGNOSIS

If serotonin neurotoxic syndrome is not the correct diagnosis, what explains the patient's symptoms? Because of the long-standing complaint of sleep difficulty, the patient's husband was asked about her sleep habits. He indicated that she tends to fall asleep in minutes and begins snoring loudly. He said that she had always snored loudly, but that her snoring had become progressively louder as she gained weight. He also indicated that she would demonstrate long periods when she seemed not to breath, followed by a loud gasp, awakening herself from sleep. He said such episodes had occurred dozens of times per night for as long as he could remember and to the extent that he was awake to witness them.

On the basis of this additional information, a sleep study was recommended. Polysomnography showed frequent hypopneas with respiratory disturbances lasting up to 1 min and substantial oxygen desaturation diagnostic of severe obstructive sleep apnea (OSA).

What is OSA? OSA is a sleep disorder in which complete (apnea) or partial (hypopnea) obstruction of the upper airway occurs. This obstruction produces loud snoring, often with choking or gasping sounds, desaturation of hemoglobin with hypoxia, frequent arousals and sleep disruption, and excessive daytime sleepiness (Ahmed, Chung-Park, & Tomashefski, 1997; Davey, 2003). The adverse consequences of OSA were not recognized until recently, when it became clear that OSA had serious neuropsychological, neurological, and cardiovascular consequences. Common neurological associations, in addition to excessive daytime sleepiness, include headaches that are typically present on awakening, poor memory and concentration, and increased risk for stroke (Ahmed et al., 1997; Bliwise, 1996; Decary, Rouleau, & Montplaisir, 2000; Kelly, Claypoole, & Coppel, 1990; Lattimore, Celermajer, & Wilcox, 2003; Sateia, 2003; Wolk & Somers, 2003; Yaggi & Mohsenin, 2003). Additional neurobehavioral associations include depressed mood and nocturnal panic attacks (Aikens, Caruana-Montaldo, Vanable, Tadimeti, & Mendelson, 1999; Baran & Richert, 2003), as well as daytime performance inefficiencies (Cheshire, Engleman, Deary, Shapiro, & Douglas, 1992). Cardiovascular consequences include hypertension, angina, and increased risk for myocardial infarction (Ahmed, Chung-Park, & Tomashefski, 1997; Roux & Hilbert, 2003; Wolk & Somers, 2003). The association with hypertension is especially important, and many patients diagnosed with OSA were previously assumed to have essential (idiopathic) hypertension. The frequency of headache, particularly headaches that are present on awakening, has been reported to be increased among patients with sleep apnea (Larner, 2003; Neau, et al., 2002). This patient complained of a number of discrete symptoms and each can be explained on the basis of the patient's history and examination findings (Table 18.11).

Table 18.11 Symptoms with their initial and alternative explanations in a case of suspected diet drug toxicity.

Symptom	Initial explanation	Alternative explanation
Daytime sleepiness, impaired sleep	Diet drug	Preexisting obstructive sleep apnea (OSA)
Memory problems and difficulty concentrating	Diet drug	OSA and depression
Headache	Diet drug	OSA
Depression	Diet drug	Preexisting family and personal difficulties, OSA
Hypertension	Idiopathic	OSA
Anxiety	Diet drug	Component of depression and worries about health
Fear	Diet drug	Belief by the patient that diet drugs injured her
Brain damage	Diet drug	No evidence for brain damage
Stress	Diet drug	Family and interpersonal difficulties as well as misinformation from professionals
Dry mouth, past	Diet drug	Diet drug
Transient forgetfulness, past	Diet drug	Diet drug
Time misperception, past	Diet drug	Possible diet drug

The patient was prescribed treatment with continuous positive airway pressure (CPAP), with reported improvement of her sleep-related symptoms, including a reduction in nocturnal awakening, daytime sleepiness, and restlessness. Her husband reported that she no longer snored. A repeat sleep study documented improvement in apneic episodes and sleep disruption, and she no longer demonstrated significant oxygen desaturation. She also experienced improvement in her memory and ability to concentrate, and her headaches resolved. The positive results of her treatment with CPAP is consistent with the idea that OSA is likely and substantially explanatory to her clinical picture (McMahon, Foresman, & Chisholm, 2003).

VERIFICATION OF ALTERNATIVE CLINICAL DIAGNOSES

This patient had numerous clinical symptoms, including memory loss, headache, difficulty sleeping, and depression, all of which suggested a diagnosis of OSA. She also experienced anxiety and concern that her difficulties were related to prior use of diet medications, producing symptoms of a situational depression. From a neuropsychological and neurologic viewpoint, the patient evidences problems that reflect multiple, long-standing conditions that are unrelated to her use of fenfluramine and other diet drugs. Chief among these are the problems of OSA and depression. Whether or not a component of her depression is attributable to OSA is uncertain, as depression is a common component of OSA, independent of other considerations. Nevertheless, these two diagnoses explain the majority of her symptoms and fulfill the explicit questions needed to verify the diagnoses—adequacy, predominance, coherence, parsimony, robustness, and prediction.

Comment

Although the patient ascribed her symptoms to the diet drugs she took over a 2-year period before the current evaluation, her primary and present complaints were self-reported and brought to her physician's attention some years after termination of those drugs. In her presentation to the physician, she also implied a worsening of symptoms, occurring gradually over the immediately proceeding 2-year period. The temporal course of illness is an important factor to consider in solving any diagnostic problem. Here, it is a critical factor, as it does not fit the hypothesized fenfluramine etiology. That is, there is no indication in the literature of progressive worsening of fenfluramine-induced dysfunction, even in those instances of positive reports.

The delayed onset of symptoms is also inconsistent with drug-induced dysfunction. Aside from these considerations of onset and course, the patient's symptoms can be explained on the basis of preexisting difficulties or consequences of those difficulties. For instance, the patient's reported symptoms and test findings included the majority, if not all, of the problems associated with OSA reviewed above. In addition, her chronic obesity can in itself be expected to contribute to the patient's symptoms (Chin & Ohi, 1999).

The patient denied past psychological difficulties, but records indicated depression some years before she began treatment with diet drugs, e.g., a formal diagnosis of depression with obsessive-compulsive tendencies more than 2 years before beginning diet medications. Also, records indicated a history of past family problems and probable substance abuse that dated at least to adolescence. The patient, herself reported an alcoholic family picture. She was a chronic smoker for many years and complained of fatigue at least 2 years before starting fenfluramine.

With regard to her complaints about stress, there are indications of family-related stresses predating her medical treatment for obesity. In addition, in interviews with previous clinicians, she had indicated stress associated with such nonmedicine related factors as family strife and household moves, factors apparently not considered by the physician who diagnosed serotonin neurotoxic syndrome.

Conclusion

This *case presentation* serves as a reminder that unproved hypotheses about cause and effect relationships between toxicants and the nervous system cannot be assumed to exist in a given clinical case. As mentioned in volume I, even when something has been shown to be possible, or even probable, it may not be explanatory.

As a final note, the authors have seen repeatedly the remarkable effects that comments made by professionals can have on patients. In this case, such information contributed to the patient's belief that the reason for all of her symptoms rested with her past use of diet drugs and may have delayed accurate diagnosis and proper treatment.

Patient with presumed arsenic-induced neurotoxicity

James W. Albers

Laboratory evidence of an elevated level of some specific toxin can be among the most important information used to establish causation. The following *case presentation* illustrates how the inadvertent request for a laboratory study produced results that led to a flawed diagnosis and possibly resulted in failure to establish the correct diagnosis.

Case presentation[1]

A 25-year-old male who had always been athletic and active in organized sports presented with clumsiness, numbness in his distal extremities, mild aching back pain, difficulty walking, and urinary urgency. The symptoms appeared 2 months earlier, progressed over several days, and then remained static. He denied other symptoms at present. He was not using any medications and reported a normal diet. His history was remarkable only for a several year history of migratory joint pain, which he attributed to over-exercise. The family history was unremarkable.

The general examination was normal. Neurological examination showed an asymmetric spastic paraparesis with moderate weakness of hip flexion (3+/3−). There was increased resistance to passive movement of the lower extremities with "clasp-knife" give-away weakness. The gait was unsteady and moderately spastic, producing prominent foot circumduction. Strength was normal in his arms, but he showed dysmetria on finger-to-nose testing and had a slow alternate motion rate. Vibration and pinprick sensations were reduced to the mid-cervical level, with decreased joint position sensation in the toes and ankles. Reflexes were brisk except for the masseter and ankle reflexes, which were normal. Positive Hoffmann, Babinski, and Chaddock reflexes were present bilaterally. Abdominal reflexes were absent.

DIFFERENTIAL DIAGNOSIS

The patient's physician diagnosed a myelopathy, possibly progressive, and localized the neurological findings to the level of the mid-cervical spinal cord. On the basis of the focal localization and the progressive course, a mass lesion producing a compressive myelopathy (e.g., cervical spondylosis) or inflammatory myelopathy (e.g., transverse myelitis) was suspected. However, the physician recognized that some of the findings (e.g., the dysmetria) were not likely localized to the cervical spinal cord, suggesting a multifocal localization such as associated with a central nervous system disorder.

ADDITIONAL INFORMATION

MRI studies of the spine (cervical and thoracic) were remarkable for non-specific signal changes in the mid-cervical and upper thoracic spine. Conventional tests of urine and blood were unrevealing, other than providing evidence of a mild anemia with moderate thrombocytopenia, findings not further evaluated. Studies for collagen vascular diseases and vasculitis (W-ESR, ANA, rheumatoid factor, anti-DNA) gave normal results. Additional tests for vitamin E, vitamin B_{12}, and thyroid function gave normal results. Cerebrospinal fluid (CSF) examination showed an elevated total protein (153 mg%) and a border-line-low glucose level. MRI of the brain showed multiple small white matter hyperintensities of unknown significance.

There was no progression of his deficit until 3 months later when he developed severe vertigo and constant movement of his vision (oscillopsia). Repeat examination showed course nystagmus to lateral gaze, increased dysmetria, and generalized hyperreflexia with bilateral ankle clonus. Although a diagnosis of multiple sclerosis was clinically suspected, there were no other findings on the eye examination or on ophthalmoscopy suggestive of that disorder (i.e., visual field defects, red desaturation, disc pallor, or venous sheathing). The patient did not experience paresthesias with neck flexion (Lhermitte's sign), and he was unaware of any effect of body temperature on his symptoms (Uhthoff's phenomenon). A clinical trial of corticosteroids produced no clear improvement.

Reevaluation 4 months later followed a nocturnal major motor seizure observed by his wife. He had no personal or family history of seizure, and there was no evidence that this was a symptomatic or provoked seizure. His wife and children reported that he had deteriorated for several weeks before experiencing the seizure. Specifically, he had been confined to bed with nausea, progressive leg weakness, and difficulty voiding, and he had exhibited mild confusion at times.

On examination, he was lethargic and incontinent. He had a left gaze preference and coarse nystagmus. There was asymmetric upper extremity weakness, worse on the right, with incoordination of both arms and a slow alternate motion rate of the hands and fingers. Dystonic posturing of the hands was present. The legs were flaccid. Sensation was absent in the distal lower extremities and impaired in the upper extremities, with a mid-cervical sensory level. There was loss of rectal tone and no volitional contraction of the rectal sphincter. The sphincter was described as flaccid, and the anal reflex was absent. Muscle stretch reflexes were brisk in the arms, but reflexes that had been brisk at the knees and ankles at the time of his initial examination were now absent.

Laboratory testing showed a low hematocrit with pancytopenia, mild thrombocytopenia, and evidence of increased hemolysis. The blood urea nitrogen (BUN) and creatinine levels were moderately elevated. The CSF showed an elevated total protein and a moderately reduced glucose relative to the serum glucose level (hypoglycorrhachia). Evaluation of the urine for abnormal excretion of porphyrins gave normal results. An EEG showed asymmetric persistent slowing in the theta range consistent with diffuse encephalopathy. The numerous laboratory studies included an elevated serum arsenic level that had been ordered inadvertently. A lumbosacral MRI was requested but never performed because of the rapid deterioration.

The evidence of flaccid, areflexic weakness, and sensory loss involving the legs in the presence of abnormal arsenic levels leads to a diagnosis of possible arsenical neuropathy. Additional history was obtained of the intermittent appearance of white lines under the nails over a several year period. Inspection of the nails revealed faint, short lines in several fingernails resembling those shown in Figure 18.2. The nail abnormalities were interpreted as Mees' lines, supporting a diagnosis of arsenic intoxication. Repeat laboratory testing confirmed elevated arsenic levels. During the hospitalization, renal function deteriorated and dialysis was initiated. The patient's wife found a half-empty container of an arsenic-containing pesticide in the basement workshop, and she recalled that her husband had complained of finding ants in the basement.

The possible diagnosis of arsenic intoxication was not considered definitive by his physicians. However, they were unable to confirm an alternative explanation or recommend specific treatment. The patient and his wife became increasingly convinced that the diagnosis of arsenic intoxication was without alternative. The patient's wife sought out physicians who shared their belief in the diagnosis of arsenic intoxication. They ultimately consulted another physician who was familiar with arsenic poisoning and treatment with

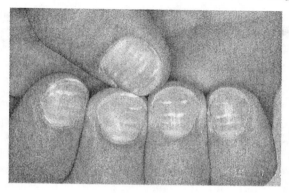

Figure 18.2 Fingernails showing evidence of leuconychia due to local trauma to the nail bed. The white lines on the nails associated with leuconychia differ from Mees' lines in that the former are nonuniform, involve individual nails at different levels, and do not transverse the entire nail.

chelation therapy. This physician acknowledged that the diagnosis was unclear, as was the likelihood that chelation therapy would be beneficial. However, she felt that chelation was safe and the risk-to-benefit ratio was favorable. Chelation therapy was recommended and initiated by the family despite mildly impaired renal function which remained unchanged during chelation. Subsequent serum arsenic levels were reduced from the previously elevated values and chelation was discontinued.

The patient agreed to a nephrology consultation in response to subsequently deteriorating renal function. That consultation resulted in a diagnosis of "acute tubular necrosis and glomerulonephritis, possible secondary to vasculitis." Serum laboratory screening tests for vasculitis returned normal results. A recommended renal biopsy demonstrated acute tubular necrosis with evidence of a thrombotic microangiopathy. This information became available as the patient showed deterioration with multiorgan failure, including renal failure requiring dialysis. Consultation with a physician specializing in the treatment of vasculitis resulted in administration of intravenous corticosteroids and interval therapeutic plasma exchange without dramatic improvement but with apparent stabilization of his multiorgan deterioration. Additional immune-modulating treatments included use of intermittent immunoglobulin therapy and chronic immunosuppressive medications, including cyclophosphamide. His severe neurological impairment did not improve and he was transferred to a chronic care facility.

During his treatment, a hair arsenic level was noted to be slightly elevated, whereas arsenic levels in fingernail clippings were undetectable.

Discussion

For this patient, the neurological localization to the peripheral nervous system that resulted in a diagnosis of "neuropathy" appeared inconsistent with available information, and the differential diagnosis for the combined abnormalities was incomplete, in part because of the patient's decision to defer further evaluations and because of his ultimate deterioration. These factors rendered the subsequent causation conclusions related to the diagnosis of neuropathy inaccurate and inappropriate.

NERVOUS SYSTEM LOCALIZATION

The patient's symptoms or signs do not support localization to the peripheral nervous system. The most important neurological finding was that of a sensory level (see chapter 6, volume I). The only localization that explains this finding is a lesion in the cervical spinal cord. The persistent lethargy reflects bilateral supratentorial dysfunction (cerebrum), as does the presence of dystonia and development of a major motor seizure. The dysmetria and course nystagmus likely reflect localization to the posterior fossa. The left gaze preference is evidence of asymmetry, either at the supratentorial or posterior fossa levels. Brisk reflexes in the arms reflect central nervous system, upper motor neuron involvement. Because the reflex arc includes the final common pathway of the motor system, a neuropathy of any magnitude, such as one sufficient to produce flaccid, areflexic leg paralysis, would undoubtedly result in hypoactive or absent arm reflexes. In this setting, the lower extremity signs, when combined with absent rectal sphincter tone and urinary incontinence, reflect involvement of the caudal spinal cord. The combination of flaccid paralysis, severe sensory loss, areflexia, and loss of sphincter control reflects severe lumbosacral spinal cord dysfunction, likely from myelomalacia, not peripheral neuropathy. Taken together with the other nervous system signs, these findings reflect multifocal central nervous system involvement over the rostral-to-caudal length of the neuraxis.

VERIFICATION OF THE CLINICAL DIAGNOSIS

There was not agreement among the numerous treating and consulting physicians on a final diagnosis. However, the clinical diagnosis of neuropathy cannot be verified. The diagnosis of neuropathy was based on signs of sensory loss, weakness, and absent reflexes in the lower extremities. Although superficially reasonable, the diagnosis ignored important evidence that localized these finding to the central, not the peripheral, nervous system. In contrast, the neuroanatomical diagnosis of multifocal central nervous system dysfunction incorporates all of the neurological findings and satisfies all questions required to verify the localization. The most parsimonious localization is to the central nervous system with asymmetric involvement of multiple levels (supratentorial, posterior fossa, and spinal cord). This "diagnosis" represents a functional description of the site of abnormality, as opposed to a diagnosis of a specific disease or disorder.

CAUSE/ETIOLOGY

The neurological disorder was attributed to arsenic poisoning, and justified by the presence of "peripheral neuropathy," Mees' lines, elevated blood arsenic levels, and lack of an alternative explanation. The diagnosis was "confirmed" by demonstrating slightly elevated hair arsenic levels. However, the impression of arsenic poisoning fulfills few of the explicit questions necessary to verify the diagnosis. It is true that arsenic is a systemic poison capable of producing multiorgan failure, with primary hematological, peripheral nervous system, and hepatic involvement. Of those features, only the hematological findings were present and even those findings were not specific for arsenic toxicity. In addition, a common hematological manifestation of arsenic poisoning, basophilic stippling of red blood cells, was absent. The nervous system is a common target for arsenic, but this patient had primary central nervous system involvement, not a peripheral neuropathy that reflects the most common neurological target of acute arsenic poisoning. As discussed, the terminal findings attributed to peripheral neuropathy reflected involvement of the central nervous system and were consistent with myelomalacia of the caudal spinal cord. The asymmetric central nervous system manifestations were atypical for most neurotoxicants, but characteristic of a multifocal vascular or autoimmune disorder. The features of the fingernail findings were not those described by Mees, but typical of leuconychia, the result of local trauma to the nail bed (Figure 18.2). Finally, the elevated serum arsenic level, the information interpreted as most supportive of arsenic poisoning, simply reflected the patient's renal failure. The serum arsenic level, like virtually all substances measured in the serum, was elevated because of the inability of the kidneys to clear the blood of any toxic substance. All other measures indicative of an increased body burden of arsenic, such as direct tissue measures, were not substantially elevated.

VERIFICATION OF CAUSE/ETIOLOGY

Application of criteria for establishing causation to the diagnosis of arsenic poisoning for this patient is straightforward. Arsenic toxicity is a well-established disorder, but there is no generally accepted information that would associate arsenic with the syndrome described here.

ALTERNATIVE CLINICAL DIAGNOSIS

Thrombotic microangiopathy, such as associated with systemic lupus erythematosus (SLE) or an SLE-like disorder, producing multifocal central nervous system ischemic infarctions, including spinal cord myelomalacia, and progressive renal failure best explains this patient's clinical and laboratory findings.

VERIFICATION OF THE ALTERNATIVE CLINICAL DIAGNOSIS

Although the asymmetric, multifocal central nervous system manifestations described in the *case presentation* were atypical for most neurotoxicants, they were typical of those associated with most forms of vasculitis involving the nervous system. There are numerous neurological manifestations of the different forms of vasculitis and collagen vascular disease (Nadeau, 1985). Systemic disorders characterized by a thrombotic microangiopathy produce multifocal ischemia in all involved organs, including the central nervous system. The resultant neurological findings are indistinguishable from those associated with other forms of central nervous system vasculitis (Moore & Cupps, 1983). As such, a diagnosis of an SLE-like disorder with thrombotic microangiopathy fulfills all of the explicit questions necessary to verify the diagnosis. Specifically, a systemic thrombotic microangiopathy is characterized by hemolytic anemia, thrombocytopenia, central nervous system ischemia and infarction, and renal dysfunction, all features of the patient's illness (Hughson, McCarty, Sholer, & Brumback, 1993; Jain, Chartash, Susin, & Furie, 1994). The CSF abnormalities, including the unexplained hypoglycorrhachia and elevated protein, are characteristic of a lupus-associated myelomalacia, usually from distal spinal cord ischemia (Levine, Langer, Albers, & Welch, 1988). The resultant neurological impairment associated with myelomalacia is characterized by a flaccid areflexic paralysis, dense sensory loss, and impaired sphincter function.

An electrodiagnostic evaluation was not performed as part of this patient's evaluation, but it undoubtedly would have excluded the diagnosis of neuropathy. Nerve conduction studies and needle EMG studies of patients with myelomalacia show low amplitude motor responses, normal sensory responses (in spite of dense clinical sensory loss), and denervation involving distal and proximal muscles, including the paraspinal muscles. Such a pattern of abnormality is consistent with an anatomical diagnosis of "polyradiculopathy without neuropathy" (McGonagle, Levine, Donofrio, & Albers, 1990). Although most forms of polyradiculopathy without neuropathy are associated with extradural lesions or with intradural—extra-axial lesions, intra-axial lesions produce electrodiagnostic findings that are indistinguishable from those associated with the other two anatomical localizations. Forms of intra-axial lesions producing polyradiculopathy without neuropathy are listed in Table 18.12, accounting for about 15% of the patients with electrodiagnostic evidence of polyradiculopathy reported by McGonagle et al. (1990). The absence of pain as a prominent complaint was the most important feature that distinguished these patients from those with extra-axial disease.

Information used to exclude the presence of a systemic vasculitis in the *case presentation* relied entirely on the normal serology measures. Unfortunately, such measures are frequently normal in vasculitis and other SLE-like disorders. Tests that would have been helpful in clarifying the diagnosis, such as a leptomeningeal biopsy or angiography, were never requested. However, even tissue biopsy of brain or leptomeninges frequently is nondiagnostic among patients ultimately found to have an isolated central nervous system angiitis (Schmidley, 2000a). Whether or not cerebral angiography would have identified abnormalities is unclear, because some forms of vasculitis, such as central nervous system angiitis, involve vessels that are below the size of those visualized on cerebral angiography (Schmidley, 2000a). Vasculitis and thrombotic microangiopathy are both established causes of lacunar infarctions (Arboix & Marti-Vilalta, 2004).

Table 18.12 Conditions and disorders associated with polyradiculopathy without neuropathy produced by intra-axial lesions.

Acute or chronic spinal cord ischemia
    Atherosclerotic vascular disease
    Central nervous system vasculitis
    Spinal cord arteriovenous malformation or fistula

Chronic effects of spinal cord trauma

Degenerative central nervous system disorders (e.g., spinocerebellar degeneration)

Intraspinal neoplasm

Malignant atrophic papulosis (Dego's syndrome)

Motor neuron disease

Multiple sclerosis (associative with spinal cord gliosis)

Postpolio muscular atrophy

Post-traumatic anterior horn cell degeneration

Post-traumatic conus medullaris syndrome

Post vaccination in encephalomyeloradiculopathy

Syringomyelia

Transverse myelitis

Modified from "Spectrum of Patients with EMG Features of Polyradiculopathy without Neuropathy," by T. K. McGonagle, S. R. Levine, P. D. Donofrio, and J. W. Albers, 1990, *Muscle and Nerve, 13*, p. 63.

    The cause of thrombotic microangiopathy is unknown. Microangiopathy has been associated with some forms of vasculitis and as a manifestation of several autoimmune disorders including SLE. However, other associations or causes have been identified, including a paraneoplastic syndrome attributed to cancer (Kwaan & Gordon, 2001), pregnancy (Pisoni, Ruggenenti & Remuzzi, 2001), solid organ and bone marrow recipients (Ramasubbu et al., 2003), and a variety of infections, including HIV infection (Ahmed, Siddiqui, Siddiqui, Zaidi & Cervia, 2002). Among infectious agents, thrombotic microangiopathy also has been reported in association with parvovirus B19 isolated by PCR from renal biopsy specimens of some immunosuppressed patients (Murer et al., 2000). The temporal association between the onset of thrombotic microangiopathy, isolation of the viral genome in renal specimens, seroconversion, and endothelial tropism of the virus suggests that this parvovirus could be the etiologic agent of thrombotic microangiopathy in these cases. The onset after infection also could depend on other illness-related cofactors, which make the patient more susceptible to microthrombi formation in the renal microvasculature (Murer et al.). Finally, and important in the context of the possible relationship to toxicants, the pathogenesis of microangiopathy has been associated with numerous medications (Pisoni et al., 2001; Teixeira et al., 2002). Among the different medications are included mitomycin, cyclosporine, tacrolimus, interferon, antiaggregating agents, and quinine (Pisoni et al.). The mechanism by which different drugs induce thrombotic microangiopathy is unclear, but the associations make it difficult to definitively exclude without careful examination the possibility that other toxicants, including arsenic, could also be linked to thrombotic microangiopathy.

Patients with lupus nephritis occasionally develop renal biopsy evidence of vasculitis and thrombotic microangiopathy (Descombes, Droz, Drouet, Grunfeld, & Lesavre, 1997). There also are patients with SLE who develop a thrombotic microangiopathy in association with diffuse vasculitis producing cerebritis and multiorgan involvement. The clinical course in these patients is usually progressive deterioration to death (Santiago, Batuman, & Meleg-Smith, 1996). In a small series of patients with SLE or SLE-like disease who had evidence of a thrombotic microangiopathy, prominent features of the acute illness included fever, hemolytic anemia, thrombocytopenia, nervous system involvement, and renal dysfunction. For most of these patients, the prognosis was poor, despite aggressive immunosuppressive treatment. The authors concluded that the spectrum of vascular diseases in SLE extends beyond vasculitis to include noninflammatory vascular processes that can cause equally devastating complications (Jain, 1996).

Among patients with SLE and antiphospholipid antibodies, a distinctive type of chronic cerebral vasculopathy has been identified in the small leptomeningeal arteries (Hughson et al., 1993). These patients had evidence of cerebrovascular disease. Autopsy study that included multiple blocks of brain tissue using serial histological sections and histochemical and immunohistochemical methods disclosed fibrin thrombi and widespread obstruction by a proliferation of intimal fibrous tissue or myointimal cells. The fibrous and cellular segments of obstructed arteries frequently contained fibrin thrombi and displayed varying stages of recanalization. Obstructed arteries were identified without evidence of active or healed inflammatory vasculitis. The authors concluded that cerebrovascular changes of the antiphospholipid syndrome are derived from a chronic thrombotic microangiopathy, supporting the hypothesis that antiphospholipid antibodies can cause recurring episodes of intravascular thrombosis (Hughson et al.). Nevertheless, thrombotic microangiopathy is not specific for any single disease, and other disorders, including polyarteritis nodosa (PAN), have been associated with thrombotic microangiopathy producing central nervous system lacunar infarctions in the absence of an underlying vasculitis (Reichart, Bogousslavsky, & Janzer, 2000).

Numerous forms of vasculitis are known to involve the nervous system (Table 18.13). Neurological manifestations vary greatly, depending on the primary site of involvement. Among patients with isolated central nervous system angiitis, major motor seizures, dementia, altered consciousness, encephalitis-like presentations, neurobehavioral and psychiatric features, asymmetric weakness or sensory loss, visual abnormalities, nystagmus, cranial nerve abnormalities, lumbosacral radiculopathy, myelopathy, parkinsonism, and transient ischemic-like episodes are reported (Schmidley, 2000b).

Table 18.13 Forms of vasculitis involving the central and peripheral nervous systems.

Peripheral nervous system
  Polyarteritis nodosa (PAN)
  Hypersensitivity angiitis
Central nervous system
  Granulomatous angiitis
  Isolated central nervous system angitis
  Takayasu's arteritis
  Temporal arteritis
Both
  Lymphoid granulomatosis
  Systemic lupus erythematosus
  Wegener's granulomatosis

Modified from "Collagen Vascular Disease: Vasculitis, Systemic Lupus Erythematosus, and Rhuemoid Arthritis," by S. E. Nadeau, 1985, *5*, p. 324. *Central Nervous System Angiitis* (pp. 1–22), by J. W. Schmidley, 2000b, Boston: Butterworth Heinemann.

Similar combinations of neurological problems are associated with other forms of collagen vascular disease, including SLE (Nadeau, 1985). Neurodiagnostic findings in vasculitis may include nonspecific imaging abnormalities, abnormal EEG and EMG evaluations, CSF evidence of elevated protein without pleocytosis (albuminocellular dissociation), or nondiagnostic results (Nadeau, 1985; Schmidley, 2000b).

VERIFICATION OF THE CAUSE/ETIOLOGY

Applying causation criteria to the diagnosis of thrombotic microangiopathy is inappropriate, because this descriptive clinicopathological syndrome does not claim to establish the cause of the patient's problem. However, the diagnosis of thrombotic microangiopathy fulfills all criteria required to establish the clinical diagnosis (Richardson, Wilson, Williams, Moyer, & Naylor, 2000). In addition, application of the Hill criteria essentially excludes arsenic as a cause of thrombotic microangiopathy, despite the association of thrombotic microangiopathy with numerous medications.

Conclusion

The consideration that arsenic was related to this patient's problem was the result of misinterpretation of an elevated serum arsenic level. However flawed the neuroanatomical diagnoses, failure to recognize that the elevated arsenic level reflected renal failure, not excessive arsenic exposure, contributed to the incorrect diagnostic reasoning. For this patient who had multiple systemic abnormalities, evidence suggesting a possible abnormal exposure to a known systemic poison provided an attractive explanation for all of the numerous medical abnormalities. As the suspicion of excessive exposure to a neurotoxicant escalated, all subsequent findings were attributed on occasion to arsenic toxicity, despite their implausibility. Even the primary finding of impaired renal function, of essential importance in establishing alternative diagnoses, was attributed to arsenic, an unlikely occurrence. The correct diagnosis of thrombotic microangiopathy was identified by renal biopsy, a finding unlikely to be explained by arsenic toxicity.

Solvent-exposed mechanic with dementia

James W. Albers and Stanley Berent

Dementia is a common neurological disorder. The essential feature of dementia, according to the *DSM-IV*, is the development of multiple cognitive impairments (American Psychiatric Association, 1994). Memory impairment must be included with a significant deficit in at least one additional area of cognition (e.g., aphasia, agnosia, or executive functioning). The significance of the impairment can be determined by the magnitude of disability it causes. That is, the deficit (i.e., cognitive impairment) should be of sufficient severity to cause occupational or social dysfunction (i.e., disability). Most important, the deficits must represent a decline from a previously higher level of functioning. This is in contrast to some forms of static encephalopathy, such as those associated with a birth injury, e.g., The differential diagnosis for adult-onset dementia includes degenerative, hereditary, infectious, inflammatory, metabolic, neoplastic, vascular, and toxic etiologies. The following case highlights the consequences of failing to formulate a complete differential diagnosis for this common syndrome. Because the patient who is presented below had occupational exposure to several potential neurotoxicants, particularly solvents, these exposures were mistakenly assumed to explain his neurological problems. As emphasized a number of times in the present work, reaching a seemingly obvious diagnostic conclusion on the basis of initial impression and before completing the clinical diagnostic process in its entirety can inadvertently lead to biased results.

Case presentation[1]

A 31-year-old mechanic was referred by his family physician to a specialist in toxicant-induced disorders for evaluation of the patient's complaints. The patient and his wife provided the history. He had been well until about 18 months previously, when he experienced an insidious onset of what was described as difficulty concentrating and confusion. His family physician attributed these complaints to occupational exposure to chemicals.

His work as a mechanic for the previous 5 years included exposure to a variety of solvents that he could identify only as "degreasers" and "paint thinner-like" chemicals. He typically used the solvents to degrease equipment and small parts. He described working in an area where there were open 55-gallon drums of solvents. He would obtain a "bucket" of solvent, which he would take to his work area and apply with a rag or by emerging small parts in the bucket. He never wore a respirator. Almost daily he developed a headache and became dizzy and nauseated if he used solvents for more than 15 or 20 min. These symptoms were relieved by fresh air. He denied loss of consciousness during these episodes. However, on one occasion, he remembered being lightheaded, and next remembered being outside of the building. He was uncertain how he got outside or how long he had been there. He tried to return to work that day, but he had a severe headache and was unable to stand without assistance. The headache resolved about 20 min later, and he went home. Because of the problems described above, he had taken leave of absence from work. He tried to return to work several times, but he was unable to perform his usual activities because of difficulty concentrating. He subsequently was reprimanded at work for making inappropriate comments to coworkers and exhibiting bizarre behavior, which his employer felt posed a safety concern.

The social history was negative for excessive use of alcohol, either in the past or at present. He was using no prescription medications, and only occasional over-the-counter medications for headache. The social and family histories were described as unremarkable. His father was deceased, but his mother was in good health. He was an only child and had no children of his own, although his wife had one child from a previous marriage. His only known occupational history was as described above. The employer's industrial hygiene records showed that there were no reports of unusual exposures or other employees with similar complaints, nor did the company have any history of safety violations. His only other complaint was that of "difficulty gaining weight." A thorough medical examination found him to be in good health.

DIFFERENTIAL DIAGNOSIS

The specialist agreed with the referring physician's diagnosis, and he also attributed the cognitive difficulties to solvent-induced toxic encephalopathy (described as psycho-organic painters' encephalopathy). No other considerations were included in the differential diagnosis.

Discussion

The proposed diagnosis for this patient's neurological problem included both the neuroanatomical localization (encephalopathy) and the presumed cause (solvent exposure).

NERVOUS SYSTEM LOCALIZATION

The patient described in the *case presentation* was thought to show evidence of impaired cognition, but no other signs were described by his physician. Cognitive dysfunction of organic origin is localized to the supratentorial level of the central nervous system, although this localization does not necessarily infer an organic explanation for the disorder. The headaches reported by this patient were nonspecific, but they appeared by history to be precipitated by exposure to solvents at work. Nevertheless, this symptom almost never has importance in localizing a neurological problem. As discussed elsewhere in the present work, "headache" does not imply evidence of brain damage.

VERIFICATION OF THE CLINICAL DIAGNOSIS

On the basis of the history provided, the transient symptoms associated with acute solvent exposure could be considered consistent with a mild solvent intoxication. However, there was little information to support a diagnosis of chronic or persistent encephalopathy.

The term "encephalopathy" is typically used to describe altered behavior characterized by confusion and impaired cognition. Patients with acute but mild encephalopathy of any cause may experience headache and lightheadedness, but show little in the way of objective neurological dysfunction. At this mild level of involvement, symptoms rapidly resolve without sequelae following correction of the underlying problem causing the encephalopathy, whether it is related to hypoxia, metabolic dysfunction, or exposure to a neurotoxicant. More severe forms of acute encephalopathy are associated with nonspecific behavioral abnormalities that include irritability, confusion, and anxiety, in association with personality change, inappropriate behavior, impaired cognition, and disorientation. Neurological signs include postural tremor, slowed coordination, and restlessness, typically in association with asterixis, dysarthria, akathisia, gross ataxia, and the appearance of additional abnormal signs such as primitive snout, suck, and grasp reflexes. With increasing levels of encephalopathy, delirium appears, reflexes become hyperactive, and pathologic Babinski and Chaddock reflexes become evident, sometimes in association with myoclonus. At this level of encephalopathy, symptomatic major motor seizures may develop. These neurological signs and manifestations reflect widespread central nervous system dysfunction.

In contrast, signs of dementia reflect impaired cognition. Dementia is distinguished from delirium, which, according to *DSM-IV* criteria (American Psychiatric Association 1994, p. 123), is defined by disturbance in consciousness (e.g., reduced ability to focus, sustain, or shift attention) and change in cognition that evolves over a brief period of time (i.e., hours to days) and usually fluctuates in severity during the course of the day. These changes are not explainable by preexisting disorders or as a consequence of a neurodegenerative disorder like Alzheimer's disease, although delirium and dementia may coexist.

If disability is limited solely to learning new material or retention of previously learned information, amnestic disorder should be considered (*DSM-IV*, 1994, pp. 156 ff); (American Psychiatric Association, 1994). Isolated Memory Impairment (IMI) (Berent et al., 1999) is another condition to consider in the differential diagnosis. In IMI, there is a documented impairment in ability to learn new information in the face of normal general mental status and essentially normal cognitive functioning otherwise. Unlike amnestic disorders, individuals with IMI may continue to function in their social or occupational roles, although the continued success in these roles may be more apparent than real. There is some evidence that IMI may represent an early stage in the development of progressive dementia (Berent et al.).

On the basis of the available information, the diagnosis of encephalopathy seems inappropriate for this patient. In contrast, a diagnosis of possible dementia is more fitting, based on the history of progressive intellectual decline.

CAUSE/ETIOLOGY

What are the possible causes for this patient's chronic cognitive symptoms? Disregarding for a moment the likelihood that this patient had a progressive dementia, not encephalopathy, what are some of the numerous causes of encephalopathy? Transient hypoxia and liver failure are among the two most common causes of encephalopathy observed by neurologists in any major medical center. It is conceivable that the single episode associated with confusion could have involved loss of consciousness. A period of prolonged unconsciousness could have been caused by or resulted in respiratory insufficiency. Respiratory insufficiency of sufficient magnitude and duration could produce hypoxia. Nevertheless, his neurological problems developed before this episode. The possibility of loss of consciousness was equivocal, and the episode was unobserved and did not result in a medical evaluation. The diagnosis of hypoxic encephalopathy was never considered. Further, if he had a hypoxic encephalopathy, the subsequent temporal course would have been one of the progressive improvements until a plateau was reached, not deterioration as described by the patient.

Among the most common neurotoxic syndromes involving the central nervous system are those producing an acute or chronic encephalopathy (Albers & Berent, 1999). Numerous substances, including solvents, are capable of producing central nervous system abnormalities described as encephalopathy. This patient's neurological problem was attributed to a solvent-induced toxic encephalopathy, yet the only features used to establish this diagnosis appeared to be the opportunity for solvent exposure together with his self-reported cognitive decline. The nonspecific psycho-organic syndrome referred to as painter's encephalopathy is attributed by some to chronic low-level or repeated high-level exposures to solvents. This syndrome is controversial and poorly described (Albers & Berent, 2000). The controversy relates to whether or not solvent exposure, in the absence of hypoxia, produces permanent nervous system damage characterized by a toxic encephalopathy. The spectrum of involvement is narrow, and solvent-induced toxic encephalopathy typically produces no objective neurological signs of the type associated with other, established forms of encephalopathy. At this mild or equivocal level of abnormality, conventional neuropsychological testing is important, yet these abnormalities are nonspecific as well (Report of the Therapeutics and Technology Subcommittee of the American Academy of Neurology, 1996). While the neuropsychological examination is capable of documenting the presence of cognitive impairment, the results in isolation will be nonspecific with regard to etiology (see chapter 5, volume 1 of the present work).

The controversy about "solvent-induced toxic encephalopathy" probably reflects the definition used to establish the diagnosis. The most commonly referenced definition, which is attributed by some to the World Health Organization (WHO), has potential application as an epidemiological instrument for classification purposes. It does not have diagnostic utility in individual cases, however. The most important reason that it cannot be used to establish a diagnosis of toxic encephalopathy in an individual patient is because it rests heavily on nonspecific symptoms and disregards competing diagnoses. For example, neurological evaluations of solvent-exposed workers who fulfilled the 1985 definition of toxic encephalopathy revealed no evidence of specific neurological abnormalities, and no worker demonstrated evidence of dementia (Albers et al., 2000). An unusual feature of the syndrome of solvent-induced toxic encephalopathy is its inability to predict a prognosis in individual cases. In one study, 51% of 87 patients with this diagnosis felt subjectively improved 3–9 years after diagnosis, 21% felt worse, and 27% reported no change (Antti-Poika, 1982b). Essentially all forms of acute cerebral dysfunction, including the toxic, hypoxic, or metabolic encephalopathies, improve if the responsible condition is alleviated. This failure to show improvement following removal from ongoing exposure is a feature of solvent-induced toxic encephalopathy that calls the existence of the syndrome into question. In this context, the syndrome of toxic encephalopathy fails to distinguish itself from other existing forms of minor or equivocal neurological dysfunction, including those associated with individual differences attributable to hereditary and educational causes. Further, it is conceptually bothersome from a diagnostic viewpoint that reports of confirmed solvent-induced toxic encephalopathy progressing to a point of death or severe impairment requiring hospitalization are nonexistent, and equally concerning that no neuropathological difference have been identified among subjects diagnosed during life with chronic toxic encephalopathy, compared to referent subjects (Klinken & Arlien-Soborg, 1993; Ridgway, Nixon, & Leach, 2003).

With respect to this patient's headaches, encephalopathy of any cause is not generally associated with head pain. It is true that numerous substances capable of producing an acute toxic encephalopathy also produce headache. However, consider for a moment that headache is not associated with disorders like Alzheimer's disease, parkinsonism, hypoxic encephalopathy, or multiple-infarct dementia, all of which are characterized by loss of neuronal tissue. The chronic headaches described by this patient are characteristic of muscle contraction headaches, the most common headache syndrome, and are not indicative of a neurological injury.

VERIFICATION OF CAUSE/ETIOLOGY

On the basis of the available information, the diagnosis of solvent-induced toxic encephalopathy (psycho-organic "painter's" encephalopathy) does not fulfill criteria required for verification, and this patient is left without an adequate or alternative explanation for his neurological problem.

ADDITIONAL INFORMATION

Because of his persisting complaints and the suspected association between solvent exposure and development of cognitive problems, he was referred for a neurological evaluation approximately 1 year after the initial evaluation described previously. The patient's wife was adamant that his cognitive function had progressively declined to the point that he needed help with some activities of daily living, such as putting away his clothes. He now required almost continued monitoring within his home because he "couldn't be trusted." She reported that his headaches had improved and that his dizziness had resolved once he stopped working. His wife attributed this improvement to his avoiding solvent exposure at work. He had, however, developed severe behavior problems that were described as bad "temper tantrums" and episodes of violent behavior. These tantrums seemed provoked by minor frustrations.

On examination, the patient was a thin, apathetic, bored-appearing male. His general medical examination was unremarkable, as previously reported. The neurological examination showed moderately abnormal mental status and motor examinations. Specifically, he responded slowly and deliberately to questioning. He was oriented to person and place but not time. His memory was grossly intact. He repeated five digits forward and three in reverse, and he recalled two of three items at 5 min. He could name the current president, but he could name only four past presidents. A test of similarities was normal given his high school education, but his judgment was difficult to evaluate because of vague, tangential responses. Proverb testing was abnormal, producing very concrete responses. He followed simple commands, including two-step commands that crossed the midline. The remainder of the neurological examination showed saccadic eye movements with impaired pursuit but no nystagmus. He had normal strength, but the alternate motion rate was generally slow. He had a mild dysmetria with minimal past pointing on finger-to-nose and impaired heel-to-shin testing. The gait was wide-based and ataxic, and he was unable to tandem walk. He also displayed mild truncal ataxia. He required support to walk on his heels or his toes because of unsteadiness. During the examination, he showed occasional, small-amplitude "flickering," choreiform movements of his fingers bilaterally. These movements were accentuated greatly by asking him to sustain a posture, as in the examination of sustension tremor. There was no startle myoclonus.

A neuropsychological evaluation was requested as part of the evaluation. The psychometric part of the neuropsychological evaluation resulted in test scores that indicated some cognitive and some emotional impairment. Although relatively mild in terms of level of severity (Halstead Impairment Index: 0.5), areas of difficulty were more likely to be nonverbal than verbal (e.g., WAIS-R Digit Symbol: 5, Vocabulary: 8). His general mental status (MMSE: 26/30) and general intellectual ability (WAIS-R FSIQ: 96 [PIQ: 98, VIQ: 96]; WMS: 94) were normal and about average. The patient completed high school; and his current reading, spelling, and arithmetic as measured with the WRAT were low normal (7th to 8th grade level). He was slow on speeded psychomotor tasks, reflected mild difficulty in constructing angles and lines on qualitatively analyzed visual-constructive tasks (e.g., drawing geometric figures), but his grip strength and finger tapping speed were normal and consistent with his right hand dominance. The MMPI reflected mild depression (scale 2; $t = 82$), with clinically relevant scores on Scale 0 ($t = 84$) and Scale 8 ($t = 74$).

The neuropsychological examination report summary depicted the patient as low normal in terms of general mental status and intellect. Mild cognitive impairment was noted, predominantly in psychomotor and other nonverbal domains and including initial learning and delayed recall of nonverbal materials. While there was no evidence for major disturbance of thought or affect, the patient was described as mildly depressed with tendencies toward disturbed and intrusive thinking and social isolation.

The results of the initial diagnostic testing included cranial CT and brain MRI examinations showing diffuse, mild to moderately severe cortical atrophy. A prior EEG examination showed mild slowing of the background rhythm, but no epileptiform activity or other focal or projected dysrhythmia. There were no abnormal electrical discharges associated with the choreiform movements.

As part of the neurological evaluation, all of the patient's medical records were requested. When received, the records included medical information about the patient's father. Those records revealed that the father, who was no longer living, also had developed in early mid-life progressive memory and behavior problems associated with abnormal movements. The father's evaluation had resulted in a diagnosis of possible Huntington disease, a diagnosis apparently not shared with the family at that time. Additional information about the father was unavailable. Despite the new information about the family history, the patient declined further diagnostic testing.

ALTERNATIVE CLINICAL DIAGNOSIS

This patient had impaired mental status that, by history, was consistent with an acquired dementia characterized by slow progression. The dementia was associated with behavioral problems, and a movement disorder (chorea and ataxia). A differential diagnosis applicable to progressive, acquired dementia is shown in Table 18.14. The table is not inclusive but lists many of the degenerative, hereditary, infectious, inflammatory, metabolic, neoplastic, structural, and vascular causes of progressive dementia.

On the basis of the available information, including many routine laboratory investigations of blood and urine and imaging studies that are not described,

Table 18.14 Differential diagnosis of progressive dementia.

Degenerative
  Alzheimer's disease
  Basoganglionic degeneration
  Frontotemporal dementia
  Multiple system atrophy "Parkinsonism-plus"
  Pick's disease

Hereditary
  Familial Alzheimer's disease
  Huntington disease
  Some forms of epilepsy

Infectious
  Creutzfeldt–Jacob disease (CJD)
  Fungal
  Human immunodeficiency virus (HIV)
  Lyme
  Sarcoid
  Syphilis
  Viral encephalitis; e.g., herpes simplex virus (HSV)
  Whipple disease

Inflammatory (autoimmune)
  Acute disseminated encephalomyelitis
  Cerebral amyloid angiopathy with vasculitis
  Isolated central nervous system angiitis
  Lupus anticoagulant disorders
  Multiple sclerosis
  Neuro-Bechet's disease
  Subacute sclerosing panencephalitis (SSPE)
  Sjogren's disease
  Systemic lupus erythematosus
  Varicella-zoster (VZ) vasculitis

Metabolic
  Hypothyroidism
  Vitamin B_{12} deficiency
  Wilson's disease

Neoplasm
  Cerebral gliomatosis
  Intravascular lymphomatosis
  Lymphomatoid granulomatosis
  Paraneoplastic vasculitis
  Primary central nervous system lymphoma (PCNSL)
  Progressive multifocal leukoencephalopathy
  Other paraneoplastic syndrome

Seizure
  Myoclonic epilepsy
  Nonconvulsive status epilepticus

Toxic[a]

Vascular
  Diffuse cortical ischemia (hypoxia or anoxia)
  Disseminated intravascular coagulation (DIC)
  Hypertensive encephalopathy
  Endocarditis
  Multi-infarct dementia
  Normal pressure hydrocephalus
  Subdural hematoma
  Thrombotic thrombocytopenia (TTP)

[a] Numerous substances, when present in sufficient dose and over sufficient time, may lead to dementia (primary or secondary to hypoxia, e.g.).

the differential diagnosis thought to be most appropriate for this patient focused on two areas: Huntington disease versus small vessel vasculitis (e.g., isolated central nervous system angiitis). Given the information about the family history, the most likely explanation for the patient's cognitive and movement disorders was Huntington disease.

VERIFICATION OF THE ALTERNATIVE CLINICAL DIAGNOSIS

The primary diagnosis of Huntington disease successfully fulfills most of the explicit questions required to verify the diagnosis, including those related to adequacy, primacy, coherence, parsimony (except for headache which was unrelated to this diagnosis), and robustness. Long-term follow-up information was unavailable for this patient, but, nevertheless, would represent important information. Failure to demonstrate the expected continued progression would have been inconsistent with the diagnosis of Huntington disease, demonstrating the importance of all of the questions, not just a selected few, used to verify the diagnosis.

CAUSE/ETIOLOGY

Huntington disease is a progressive neurodegenerative disorder with autosomal dominant transmission of an unstable expanded trinucleotide (CAG) repeat that occurs in the IT15 gene (Williams, Hegde, Herrera, Stapleton, & Love, 1999).

VERIFICATION OF CAUSE/ETIOLOGY

Had genetic testing been performed at the time of this patient's evaluation, it could have been used to verify or refute the presence of this genetic disorder, as molecular confirmation of the clinical diagnosis in Huntington disease can address this question.

Comment

Huntington disease is a dominantly inherited disorder. Symptoms usually begin around age 40, but onset can occur at anytime in individuals at risk, and progression occurs over a 10- to 30-year period (Martin, 1984; Sandberg & Coyle, 1984). Early neurological signs in Huntington disease include chorea, decreased fine motor coordination, and slowed saccadic eye movements (Folstein & Folstein, 1983; Hayden, 1981; Shoulson, 1981, 1982, 1984; Young et al., 1986, 1987). Memory function may decline precipitously around the time of clinical onset, although functional deficits do not evolve uniformly among patients with known Huntington disease (Snowden, Craufurd, Thompson, & Neary, 2002). With progression, dysarthria, rigidity, bradykinesia, and dystonia appear (Folstein & Folstein, 1983; Hayden, 1981; Shoulson, 1981, 1982, 1984; Young et al., 1986, 1987). Occasional patients who are ultimately diagnosed with Huntington disease present with chorea and prominent spasticity and cerebellar ataxia suggestive of a spinocerebellar degeneration (Kageyama, Yamamoto, Ueno, & Ichikawa, 2003). This observation would be consistent with the gait and truncal ataxia described in the *case presentation*. Both general and specific neurobehavioral impairments can occur at any time and are usually mild in the beginning and progressively worsen (Berent et al., 1988). Behavioral changes such as increased irritability often occur early in the course of Huntington disease and are accompanied by other cognitive impairments, e.g., memory disturbance (Brandt & Butters, 1986). Although a nonspecific observation, weight loss appears to be a common feature in the early stage of Huntington disease (Djousse et al., 2002). Several electrophysiological tests (e.g., sympathetic skin responses, blink reflexes, somatosensory evoked potentials) have purported use in the evaluation of Huntington disease, but these tests have not had widespread application (Lefaucheur et al., 2002).

Since the discovery of the genetic abnormality, a mouse model has been developed that is transgenic for exon 1 of the HD gene containing an expanded CAG sequence and that exhibits neuronal changes pathognomonic for the disease (Turmaine et al., 2000). In humans, progressive neuronal loss follows the onset of Huntington disease, with corresponding and increased cognitive impairment and capacity to perform activities of daily living. In terms of pathology, Huntington disease is characterized by marked neuronal loss in the caudate nucleus and putamen (Bruyn, 1968; Lange, 1981). Although there appears to be little or no cortical pathology early in the course of Huntington disease (Young et al., 1987), severe loss of cerebral cortical tissue has been said to occur in later stages of the disease (Martin & Beal, 1992). The globus pallidus and thalamus are mildly affected, as is the cerebellum (Bruyn, 1968; Dom, Malfroid, & Baro, 1976; Lange, 1981). Some investigators have suggested that frontal-subcortical connections become disrupted in Huntington disease and result in behavioral symptoms mediated by these mechanisms (Cummings, 1993).

Behavioral impairment in Huntington disease is progressive and includes a wide range of cognitive, psychomotor, and emotional domains (Berent et al., 1988). The general, behavioral decline in Huntington disease has been evaluated using standardized rating scales of the functional capacities of afflicted individuals (Folstein & Folstein, 1983; Hayden, 1981; Shoulson, 1981, 1982, 1984; Young et al., 1986, 1987). Although less is known about specific cognitive impairments that contribute to this general decline, impairments that have been documented in Huntington disease appear to proceed in a systematic fashion that mirrors the subserving neuroanatomical deterioration (Berent et al.; Butters, Sax, Montgomery, & Tarlow, 1978; Caine, Ebert, & Weingartner, 1977; Hayden, 1981).

Partially successful attempts have been made to profile the behavioral manifestations in Huntington disease. A profile that differentiates patients with Huntington disease from other degenerative supratentorial neurological diseases is difficult to specify (Zakzanis, Leach, & Kaplan, 1999). There are a number of reasons for the difficulty. One important reason involves the large individual variation in the rate of progression in Huntington disease. Neuro-pathology also interacts with individual differences in premorbid ability, perhaps adversely impairing some people more than others even when the neuropathology changes are similar. Variations in onset could also interact with individual differences in development. Nevertheless, there is consider-able predictable regularity in Huntington disease, at least in the early stages of its course, and this results in some generalities about expected behavioral symptoms. Impairment of delayed recall for recently learned verbal and visual material, for instance, appears to occur early in the course of the disease (Zakzanis et al., 1999).

Until fairly recently, there was little opportunity to study in vivo the relationships between observed behavior and underlying physiological pro-cesses. The availability of brain imaging techniques, especially positron emission tomography (PET), has enabled us to make direct comparison between behavior, metabolism, and the structural integrity of the nervous system. For instance, studies with PET have revealed a marked reduction in caudate metabolism in patients with early Huntington disease who, at the same time, show little or no atrophy as measured structurally by computerized x-ray tomography (CT) (Kuhl et al., 1982; Young et al., 1986, 1987). These various studies have shown that changes in metabolism can be detected with PET before structural changes in brain are evident using other imaging tech-niques. These studies, for instance, revealed that Huntington disease patients are significantly lower that normal in fluoro-deoxyglucose (FDG) metabolism in the caudate and putamen nuclei but not significantly so in thalamus (Young et al., 1986, 1987). Further, many, but not all, of the behavioral changes that occur in Huntington disease reflect significant correlation to these specific areas of brain hypometabolism (Berent et al., 1988).

The mapping of areas of brain hypometabolism to corresponding behavioral domains is a complex process that remains incomplete. In addition, not all behavior will fit conveniently with our notions of functional localization. Aside from complex interactive relationships between brain regions (e.g., cortical to subcortical structures), some complex behaviors (e.g., coping and adaptation) depend on adequate functioning in other, sometimes multiple, behavioral variables (Berent, 1986; Berent et al., 1988). There is an intimate relationship, e.g., between verbal learning and coping and adaptation (Berent, 1986). Since impairment of verbal learning ability can be a symptom in Huntington disease, correlating significantly with other and seemingly non-verbal symptoms like rapid alternating movements as well as with regions of FDG hypometabolism in Huntington disease, difficulties in this area might contribute importantly to disruption in other complex behaviors such as coping and adaptation (Berent et al.). Depression and other behavioral disturbances are known to manifest in Huntington disease as well, and these can adversely affect the patient's motivation or otherwise detract from general behavioral efficiency in the individual.

Testing for Huntington disease by DNA-linkage was developed in the late 1980s and became available by direct mutation analyses in the mid-1990s

(Williams et al., 1999). Genetic testing for Huntington disease was not yet clinically available at the time of this patient's evaluation. If testing had been available, and if the diagnosis of Huntington disease was excluded by test results, additional testing would have included examination of the CSF and repeat neuropsychometric testing to address the question of progression. Evidence of CSF pleocytosis would raise concern for chronic inflammation, as seen in some chronic infections. Evidence of an increased CSF protein would indicate a defective blood–brain barrier. Although elevated CSF protein is a nonspecific finding, it usually is associated with inflammation of the meninges and would, therefore, be supportive of the initial concern regarding an isolated central nervous system angiitis. Central nervous system angiitis occasionally can be confirmed with cerebral angiography, but confirmation usually requires a meningeal biopsy (Koo & Massey, 1988; Schmidley, 2000). Central nervous system angiitis is an alternative diagnosis that would have provided both headache and dementia with a common explanation. Nevertheless, taken together, a diagnosis of solvent-induced headaches independent from the cognitive and behavioral problems is a much more likely explanation for this nonspecific symptom that is so prevalent in the general population.

Conclusion

It cannot be assumed that information that is not available for review would have been unhelpful. In this patient with an adult-onset, progressive dementia, the family history was reported to be negative for neurological or behavioral problems. Neurological examination showed evidence of subtle choreiform movements, coexisting with an abnormal mental status examination. Only when medical records were recovered that described the patient's father was it discovered that the father had experienced problems similar to those of his son. The father's evaluation showing dementia and a movement disorder was suspected to represent familial Huntington disease, information apparently never shared with the family. The presence of headache is not suggestive of brain damage, and, in fact, most disorders associated with neuronal loss are painless.

Solvent-exposed machinist with behavioral and neurological complaints

James W. Albers

In the late-1970s, trichloroethylene (TCE), trichloroethane (TCA), perchloroethylene (PERC) and similar solvents became associated by some with a controversial syndrome identified in the following material as solvent-induced toxic encephalopathy (Albers & Berent, 2000a; Arlien-Soborg, Bruhn, Gyldensted, & Melgaard, 1979; Baker & Fine, 1986; Bauer & Rabins, 1977).

The controversy involving TCE-associated toxic encephalopathy, like several similar controversial syndromes, has been highly publicized in the past several decades. The controversy involves the most fundamental question about the existence of the neurobehavioral disorder as a specific and clinically diagnosable entity. The merit of the very existence of the purported syndrome has been argued in the courtroom, where the legal system was required to resolve difficult causation questions and scientists who have polarized opinions regarding the presence or absence of the solvent-induced encephalopathy fuel arguments. Regardless of one's belief about the existence of this syndrome, most would agree that no scientific consensus has been reached that would establish this syndrome as a diagnosable disorder with characteristic symptoms, signs, course, treatment, and clear etiology (Frumkin, Ducatman, & Kirkland, 1997). The following *case presentation* highlights several features of this syndrome.

Case Presentation[1]

An internist referred a 48-year-old medically disabled machinist for a second opinion regarding the allegation that the machinist's relatively long-standing clinical complaints reflected occupational exposure to trichloroethylene (TCE). Chief complaints included poor short-term memory, balance problems and dizziness, mood swings with difficulty controlling his temper, headaches, and intermittent numbness and tingling of his feet and hands. All of these problems developed insidiously several years before. The treating physician had developed doubts about the toxic origin of his patient's complaints when the removal from opportunity for further exposure failed to result in any improvement.

Examples of the memory problems included telling his children to do something and having his wife tell him that he made the same request several minutes before, forgetting items at the grocery store unless he used a shopping list, walking into a room and being unable to remember what he was retrieving, momentary lapses while driving when he would forget where he was going, difficulty recalling names, and difficulty following conversations in a large group. His balance problems consisted of momentary unsteadiness of gait. Dizziness was described as lightheadedness (not spinning) occurring several times per day and lasting seconds. Sudden head movements sometimes made him dizzy. Dizziness frequently developed just after standing from a seated or lying position, but it also occurred for no reason or in association with stress.

The mood swings were unpredictable. They were attributed to an explosive temper, usually over trivial things. He was unaware that this was a problem until it brought it to his attention by his wife. He also described feeling depressed for many years. He reported difficulty sleeping, awakening two to three times per night. He had trouble falling asleep, awakening early in the morning and being unable to go back to sleep. He had been treated with several antidepressant medications with little improvement.

He experienced daily headaches that he described as a tight band around his head. They developed over a 45-min period every morning and resolved in about an hour. He was not nauseated during a headache. There was no family history of vascular headaches and he was not carsick as a child. He did not use caffeine. His headaches developed when he was exposed to TCE at work, but they persisted despite removal from exposure to solvents. He had never taken any medications for his headaches. Intermittent numbness of his hands more than his feet was difficult for him to describe. The numbness sometimes developed while working, but more commonly, he would awaken from sleep with numb hands.

Occupational exposure to TCE began about 15 years previously. He worked as a machinist for a company that made small kitchen appliances and reported being exposed to TCE daily, usually when he was cleaning small machine parts in his shop with the solvent. While cleaning parts with TCE, he would develop a headache and feel drunk. As soon as he left work, the headache and other symptoms would resolve.

He was referred by a coworker to a physician knowledgeable about issues related to occupational exposure to solvents. After undergoing an evaluation, he was notified by letter that he had evidence of a solvent-induced toxic encephalopathy and a toxic neuropathy. He also had a brain MRI, an EEG, and an EMG, the results of which were unknown to him. He used the letter to obtain a medical disability but sought no additional evaluations. After leaving work, there was no change in his condition, other than a feeling of increasing boredom and decreased libido.

The past medical history was remarkable only for a brief hospitalized for depression 5 years before his first occupational exposure to solvents. Additional details were unavailable. He rarely used alcohol. He used no drugs other than his antidepressant medications.

The general physical and neurological examinations were normal. This included examination of mental status. The MMSE score was 27 (normal). Despite prominent memory complaints, his memory, as judged during the extensive account of his history, was normal. There was no abnormality of language. He performed simple calculations correctly, although he did so in a slow, deliberate manner. He correctly and quickly identified similarities between objects. He interpreted simple proverbs appropriately, without evidence of concrete thinking. Tests of recent memory were performed with great difficulty. This performance was inconsistent with his interactions during informal conversation. Digit span was performed in a deliberate, stressed manner and his responses were not suggestive of an organic defect. For example, he was able to remember only four digits forward, always missing the fifth digit when five digits were given. Nevertheless, when asked to repeat digits backwards, after several seconds he would always correctly begin with the fifth digit. When performing "serial 7s," his responses were consistently off by one digit. He performed multiple three-step commands crossing the midline without error.

Another finding relevant to his complaints included a normal casual gait. During formal testing, he regularly included a side step to the right. When observed walking in the hallway, independent of the formal evaluation, his gait was normal. His standing posture similarly was normal at all times except during formal testing. During testing, he leaned far to either side, but never fell. In spite of this posture, he could stand with his feet together and with his eyes open or closed without breaking stance (normal Romberg). The test he performed was actually far more difficult than that usually performed without leaning. He could walk on his heels and toes and was able to hop on either foot. He had normal strength without evidence of atrophy. Sensory testing also was normal. He identified small objects in his hands with his eyes closed, manipulating them in his hands without difficulty. Reflexes were normal (2+) in the upper and lower extremities, including the ankle reflexes. There were no pathological reflexes. Brief volitional hyperventilation (10–15 s) reproduced the lightheadedness, and it also produced numbness and tingling of his hands and lips.

DIFFERENTIAL DIAGNOSIS

This patient had an essentially normal neurologic examination with no abnormalities suggestive of an encephalopathy or peripheral neuropathy. The mental status abnormalities on formal testing were not consistent with an organic disorder. The rapid and dramatic response to a brief period of volitional hyperventilation reproduced several of his primary symptoms. The complaints of intermittent dizziness and lightheadedness were consistent with hyperventilation syndrome, a disorder sometimes associated with anxiety. The balance and short-term memory difficulties were thought to reflect a manifestation of anxiety. The headaches were characteristic of muscle contraction headaches, complaints common in individuals who are anxious or depressed. There was a long history of intermittent depression antedating any occupational exposure to solvents, and the mood swings and difficulty with temper have a psychological basis. The findings specifically are not those of an encephalopathy. Other complaints such as decreased libido and a terminal sleep disturbance also were characteristic of depression and anxiety. The decreased libido was thought to reflect an adverse medication effect.

Symptoms that were temporally associated with TCE exposure, including headaches, dizziness, and drunken feeling, and that rapidly resolved when exposure ceased, likely represented acute intoxication if the exposure description is accurate. However, there was no evidence that any of the complaints that persisted years after the last exposure were related to the previous occupational exposures to solvents.

ADDITIONAL INFORMATION

Routine evaluations of serum and urine were unremarkable. An electrodiagnostic examination demonstrated normal nerve conduction studies and a normal needle EMG examination with no evidence of neuropathy. The study also included normal blink responses, demonstrating intact trigeminal and facial nerve function. Review of the previous evaluations included report of a normal EEG and of two normal brain MRI studies, showed no evidence of atrophy or other abnormality.

NEUROPSYCHOLOGICAL EVALUATION

The patient reflected normal mental status, with good orientation to his surroundings. Intellect was normal (based on a WAIS-R FSIQ: 92, VIQ: 96,

PIQ: 88). With a reported high school education, a normal and approximately average vocabulary level (WAIS-R Vocabulary: 9) and fund of general information (WAIS-R Information: 9), and normal reading recognition level (WRAT-3 Reading: 100), the observed intellectual level was seen as consistent with his reported education. Some variability was reflected in the results of cognitive testing, but his memory was judged to be normal, based upon normal levels of delayed recall for verbal and visual materials from the Wechsler memory Scale (WMS MQ: 120, Verbal percent recall: 80%, Visual percent recall: 84%). A valid MMPI-2 reflected moderately severe emotional disturbance with clinical emphases on depression (Scale 2: $T = 76$), anxiety (Scale 7 [Pt]: $T = 84$ and MMPI-2 ANX Content Scale: $T = 76$), and strong tendencies to somatization (Scale 1 [Hs]: $T = 72$, Scale 3 [Hy]: $T = 80$). There was no indication of major affective or thought disorder from formal testing or interview. A normal score on Scale 4 ($T = 52$) argued against a characterological basis for the patient's complaints, and personal, interpersonal (MMPI Scale 0: $T = 78$), and family concerns revealed in interview indicated a situational basis for these emotional difficulties. For instance, the patient reported that he and his wife had been experiencing marital difficulties for approximately the last 5 years and that they were contemplating divorce. He also reflected strong concerns about his physical health that centered on his exposure to toxicants in the workplace and the fact that a "doctor" had told him he could expect to suffer continuing difficulties because of that exposure.

ALTERNATIVE CLINICAL DIAGNOSIS

Dysthymic disorder (depression) and generalized anxiety disorder.

Discussion

The patient in the *case presentation* reported symptoms typical of workers diagnosed with "painters' encephalopathy," a purported form of solvent-induced toxic encephalopathy. Initial reports of painters' encephalopathy appeared in the 1970s; however, the association between neurologic dysfunction and occupational exposure to organic solvents has remained unproven (Baker & Fine, 1986; Bleecker, Bolla, Agnew, & Schwartz, 1991; Chang et al., 1993; Herskowitz, Ishii, & Schaumburg, 1971; Maizlish, Fine, Albers, Whitehead, & Langolf, 1987; Paulson & Waylonis, 1976; Spencer & Schaumburg, 1985; Spencer, Schaumburg, Raleigh, & Terhaar, 1975). The acceptance of painters' encephalopathy as a formal clinical diagnosis can be characterized as controversial, and this controversy centers around the question of whether occupational exposure to trichloroethylene (TCE), trichloroethane (TCA), perchloroethylene (PERC), mineral spirits, or similar solvents alone or in combination at low doses over long periods of time are capable of causing permanent neurologic damage (Albers & Berent, 2000a; Albers et al., 2000; Albers, Wald, Werner, Franzblau, & Berent, 1999).

The initial reports of what came to be called painters' encephalopathy described workers, mainly painters, who were awarded disability for neurological consequences attributed to chronic, low-dose occupational exposure to organic solvents (Arlien-Soborg et al., 1979; Juntunen, Hupli, Hernberg, & Luisto, 1980; Seppalainen, 1981; Seppalainen, Husman, & Martinson, 1978). Before the appearance of these case reports, there had been little concern about low-dose occupational exposure to solvents. Nevertheless, it was recognized that many solvents had neurotoxic potential when present in sufficient amount, and it was well established that a high solvent exposure could produce unconsciousness and depressed respiration with a resultant hypoxia or anoxia. Prolonged hypoxia or anoxia can produce neurologic injuries, including death. The ability to produce reversible unconsciousness at high exposure levels was so predictable that several solvents used as industrial degreasers, including TCE, were also used as anesthetics (Leech, 1936; Rosenberg, 1995; Waters, Gerstner, & Huff, 1977).

As an anesthetic, TCE was associated with a syndrome of multiple cranial mononeuropathies that was initially attributed to the anesthetic use of TCE. This syndrome eventually was linked to a decomposition product, dichloroacetylene, as described in chapter 10 of volume II of this book (Buxton & Hayward, 1967; Feldman, Mayer, & Taub, 1970; Humphrey & McClelland, 1944). Trichloroethylene was replaced as an anesthetic agent, not so much because of its neurotoxicity, but because better anesthetic agents became available (Albers & Berent, 2000a). There was little general concern that chronic low-level or even transient high-level exposures to TCE or similar solvents were dangerous, as long as there was not resultant hypoxia and loss of consciousness (Spencer & Schaumburg, 1985). Those who postulate an association between occupational solvent exposure and neurological symptoms often site reports of altered affect, memory loss, impaired cognition, and dementia among workers with occupational exposure to solvents (Baker, Smith, & Landrigan, 1985). Such workers are described as typically having years of solvent exposure at levels sufficient to produce frequent symptoms of acute intoxication (Frumkin et al., 1997).

NERVOUS SYSTEM LOCALIZATION

The patient presented has several symptoms and a few signs that localize to the supratentorial level. However, there were no neurological signs that would confirm any anatomical abnormality or neurological diagnosis.

VERIFICATION OF THE ORIGINAL CLINICAL DIAGNOSIS

Few of the explicit questions used to verify the diagnosis of encephalopathy or toxic encephalopathy can be answered affirmatively. The diagnosis was originally based on nonspecific symptoms, in the absence of any neurological or psychometric signs specific for a diagnosis of encephalopathy. Using the syndrome of hepatic encephalopathy as an example (chapter 17), none of characteristic features of encephalopathy was manifest in the present case.

VERIFICATION OF THE ALTERNATIVE CLINICAL DIAGNOSIS

The two *DSM-IV* based diagnoses, dysthymic disorder and anxiety disorder, are adequate in explaining all of the patient's symptoms and serve to "best fit" the illness pattern in a simple and coherent manner. The diagnoses are robust in that no findings are inconsistent with the diagnoses. They anticipate all aspects of the clinical course in this *case presentation*. While the patient does not fully meet formal criteria for somatoform disorder, his tendencies to somatize are important to note because of their implications for treatment intervention. For instance, his concerns about his health are understandable in light of what he has reportedly been told about his condition by professionals in the past. As a result of this "education," his conclusions appear to be reasonable. That is, his conclusions are not pathological, i.e., irrational. At the same time, his belief that his health-related complaints are due to his past exposure to toxicants is overly learned and somewhat intractable at this point. To argue against his "reasonable conclusions" might well perturb the development of rapport between the treating person and the patient. Further and more generally, the patient tends to prefer physical explanations over psychological reasons for his complaints. This tendency may leave the patient somewhat resistant to what he perceives as nonmedical explanations for his symptoms even though such explanations will need to be considered in any future treatment intervention he receives.

CAUSE/ETIOLOGY

A reasonable question, in addition to the question involving the diagnosis of the patient presented, is whether the syndrome of toxic encephalopathy, as applied to chronic, low-level occupational exposure to solvents, exists as a diagnosable entity. In more than 25 years since the first reports of painters' encephalopathy, the syndrome has failed to gain general acceptance. As more data have become available, rather than becoming better established, painters' encephalopathy has become increasingly controversial (Frumkin et al., 1997; Ridgway, Nixon, & Leach, 2003; Rosenberg, 1995; Schaumburg & Albers, 2005). To date, subsequent studies of workers with chronic, low-level solvent exposures have produced disparate results, with the bulk of scientific evidence failing to support a consistent association between solvent exposure and encephalopathy. Critical literature reviews concluded that the evidence that chronic occupational exposure to solvents produced a syndrome resembling presenile dementia was weak (Errebo-Knudsen & Olsen, 1986). At best, only a "tendency" to dose–response relationships could be identified (Gregersen, Angels, Nielsen, Nrgaard, & Uldal, 1987; Juntunen, Antti-Poika, Tola, & Partanen, 1982). More recent reviews have come to similar conclusions (Ridgway et al., 2003).

The debate about the existence of painters' encephalopathy often involves expert opinions, equally as often in the context of litigation, providing polarized views that represent self-declared positions. At times, lists of publications are presented in support of one point of view or another. However, interpretation of the evidence depends on more than just a tabulation of the number of studies supporting one point of view. Interpretation should reflect an understanding of the methodologies used to evaluate the association between occupational solvent exposure and encephalopathy (McLaughlin & Blot, 1997). This review of the basic methodologies should de-emphasize the importance of those studies incapable of establishing causation or those with insufficient power to find an association if it existed (Albers et al., 1999, 2000; Schoenberg, 1982; Taubes, 1995).

Most would agree that it is unusual for a purported disorder to remain in question more than 25 years after being proposed. There may be reasons for this, ranging from nonexistence of the syndrome to reduced opportunities for exposure. How robust is the evidence to support the existence of the syndrome? Most of the supportive evidence is in the form of case reports or cross-sectional studies, and frequently of a descriptive study of a small number of workers without a referent comparison group (Linz, Morton, Wiens, Coull, & Maricle, 1986). In addition, incongruous reports including "chronic brain syndrome" with cerebral atrophy (Arlien-Soborg et al., 1979), autonomic nervous system dysfunction (Matikainen & Juntunen, 1985), vestibular dysfunction (Arlien-Soborg, Zilstorff, Grandjean, & Milling Pedersen, 1981), and large fiber peripheral neuropathy (Husman & Karli, 1980) are difficult to reconcile with an identifiable syndrome. Similarly, reports of failure to improve after removal from exposure, with most workers remaining unchanged and approximately equal numbers of workers deteriorating as improving, are atypical of most all other nervous system injuries (Antti-Poika, 1982a; Bruhn, Arlien-Soborg, Gyldensted, & Christensen, 1981). Furthermore, the limited spectrum of severity attributed to painters' encephalopathy, a syndrome characterized primarily by symptoms or neuropsychological test abnormalities without neurological signs of impairment, is atypical of most neurotoxic disorders or conditions. Case reports provide an important starting point for recognition of a new syndrome. However, they cannot provide evidence of causal associations because they are based on individuals who are selected on the bases of both disease and exposure. Even when the selection criteria are clearly defined, it cannot be determined how such selected individuals relate to the underlying population from which they were selected.

Properly conducted cross-sectional studies provide more reliable evidence of associations between exposures and disease. But, these study designs, too, are limited by an inherent inability to reconcile the timing between exposure and impairment onset. This is a critical issue. Although numerous studies purport to identify subtle neurotoxicity of chronic solvent exposure, an equally impressive literature exists demonstrating that people who perform solvent-exposed jobs may differ in terms of their preexposure cognitive abilities compared to workers in other trades to which they are often compared (Gade, Mortensen, & Bruhn, 1988). The result is that the associations between subtle cognitive deficits and solvent exposure may reflect deficits that existed before the exposure occurred. An important finding that increases the likelihood that an association identified in a cross-sectional study is valid is the presence of a strong dose–response relationship. Nevertheless, a positive cross-sectional study is incapable of demonstrating the cause of an identified association. A negative cross-sectional study, when conducted properly, e.g., one that is masked and one that quantitatively measures exposure, is capable of reducing concern that an important association exists (Maizlish et al., 1985, 1987). While it remains plausible that some neurodegenerative processes may be influenced by occupational exposure to solvents, and that the cross-sectional reports of residual neuropsychological difficulties deserve further scientific consideration (Daniell et al., 1999), the proof of causality will require that more rigorous studies be performed than have been reported to date.

Cohort and case-control studies provide more reliable evidence of causality than do the other research designs just described (Garabrant, 2000) (also, see chapter 3 in volume I of this book). Cohort studies based on historic exposure information that is recorded before subjects are diagnosed with encephalopathy can help to establish that exposure preceded disease. To date, only 3 of the 14 available cohort studies found an association between occupational exposure to solvent and any diagnoses relevant to encephalopathy (Lundberg, Gustavsson, Hogberg, & Nise, 1992; Mikkelsen, 1980; Nilson, Sallsten, Hagberg, Backman, & Barregard, 2002). Of the three that reported positive findings, one found an elevated risk of being awarded a disability pension for presenile dementia among painters compared to bricklayers after excluding subjects with secondary diagnoses of alcohol abuse, cerebral concussion, or other etiologic factors (Mikkelsen, 1980). This retrospective study relied on review of union membership files, as the diagnosis of presenile dementia was based on registers of disability pension (pension diagnoses codes). The authors acknowledged that the diagnosis of presenile dementia is sometimes misinterpreted and misdiagnosed. No excess risk was found for any other neuropsychiatric disease or condition (Mikkelsen, 1980). The second study that reported positive findings was confounded by alcohol consumption (Lundberg et al., 1992). In this study, the incidence of neuropsychiatric disorders was higher in painters than in carpenters, but alcoholism showed the highest relative risk. Excessive alcohol consumption or injury due to alcohol, or both, was common among painters, and an interaction between occupational solvent exposure and alcohol intake was proposed to explain the increase frequency of alcoholism among painters.

The third cohort study that attributed abnormalities with occupational solvent exposure involved a follow-up evaluation of 41 solvent-exposed floor layers and 40 unexposed carpenter referents (Nilson et al., 2002). The reevaluation occurred 18 years after the baseline assessment, using the same ten neuropsychological tests from the test battery for investigating functional disorders. The floor layers did not deteriorate significantly more over time than did the carpenters. However, among subjects over 60 years of age, only floor layers showed decline in visual memory, and the most highly exposed floor layers deteriorated significantly more than their referents in visual memory and perceptual speed. The hypothesis that floor layers would deteriorate more in cognitive performance than their unexposed referents over a period of 18 years was partly supported by the results of this study. The results are consistent with the view that the negative effects of exposure to solvents may interact with the normal aging process, primarily at heavy exposure. The findings as reported, however, were based on only a small number of older subjects and a small subset of tests (1 of 12 tests). An alternative explanation is that confounding due to their work activities explained the differences. Carpenters work in a three-dimensional space, whereas floor layers work in a two-dimensional space. The single test showing a significant three-way interaction with group and age was "Block Design," a test that required spatial skills, possibly of the type developed by carpenters. Further, the only significant three-way interaction (exposure × time × age) involved reasoning, where, contrary to the hypothesis, the older referents deteriorated more over time than any other subgroup.

In contrast to the three cohort studies attributing adverse consequences to occupational solvent exposure, 12 remaining cohort studies failed to identify a statistically significant relationship between solvent exposure and neurological abnormality or a risk ratio exceeding 2.0. Several of these studies have been described in greater detail previously (Albers & Berent, 2000a) and will only be summarized here. One of the negative cohort studies evaluated only acute short-term solvent exposure and did not address chronic effects (Muttray et al., 2005). Guberan et al. found that disability risk was higher among painters than among electricians for neuropsychiatric causes, but the risk ratio was less than 2.0 and not a single case of presenile dementia was diagnosed among the 1,916 painters (Guberan, Usel, Raymond, Tissot, & Sweetnam, 1989). Similarly, Riise, Kyvik, and Moen (1995) performed a retrospective cohort study of painters. They found a slightly increased risk for disability pensioning due to neuroses among the painters compared to construction workers and food processors, but the risk ratio again was less than 2.0. As found previously by Guberan et al., painters were at increased risk for alcoholism (Riise et al., 1995). van Vliet, Swaen, Slangen, and de Boorder (1987) found no significant differences in terms of neuropsychiatric disability pensions between painters and construction workers, no support for a dose–effect relationship, and no indication of a "typical" organic solvent syndrome. In a prospective cohort study, Williamson and Winder (1993) found no significant neurobehavioral changes apprentice painters after 2 years of occupational solvent exposure.

Kiesswetter et al. evaluated neurobehavioral performance and a hypothesized age-exposure interaction among a group of printers who had homogenous exposure to a single organic solvent, toluene (Kiesswetter, Sietmann, Zupanic, & Seeber, 2000). Workers were examined two times over an interval of 1 year. Multivariate analyses revealed a significant performance decrease with age, and an interaction between age and exposure was found. Although this study could be considered a fourth "positive" study, the results were contrary to the hypothesis. Specifically, the group with higher exposures (printers) and older age revealed better performance and fewer symptoms than the group with lower exposure. They found no evidence of adverse delayed effects of former toluene exposure in a possible vulnerable phase in age over 50 years.

Lash, Becker, So, and Shore (1991) evaluated a group of 1,758 retired airline mechanics to examine the hypothesis that long-term exposure to methyl chloride produced long-term central nervous system effects. A group of eligible retirees having long-term solvent exposure and another group with a low probability of solvent exposure were given a comprehensive battery of physiological and psychological tests. No significant group differences were detected on outcome measures, aside from subtle differences in attention and memory. Thus, no firm evidence was found to support the hypothesis of lasting central nervous system effects among retired mechanics with long-term methylene chloride exposure.

Seeber et al. (2004) performed a follow-up evaluation over 5 years of 192 printers exposed to toluene below 50 ppm. Stepwise regressions models did not exhibit remarkable exposure effects on the performance variables, and repeated-measures analyses also did not exhibit significant impacts of prior or current exposure on functions. They found no evidence for psychological performance effects due to long-term toluene exposure below 50 ppm. Sethre, Laubli, Hangartner, Berode, and Krueger (2000) studied short-term solvent exposure in a longitudinal study. With the neurobehavioral tests used, no solvent effect in relation to the dose could be identified.

Orbaek and Lindgren (1988) reevaluated 62 patients with chronic toxic encephalopathy diagnosed in 1976–1981. During the interval after solvent exposure ceased (median 48 months), 13 had been found to have other diseases that might contribute to brain dysfunction. The remaining group of 32 men (median age 55 years) was reexamined applying the same methods used initially. The subjects reported some improvement in their neurasthenic problems (less fatigue, headache, and dizziness). The psychometric retesting showed significant deterioration in verbal memory, improvement in visual memory, and unchanged results on the other tests. In conclusion, these patients diagnosed with toxic encephalopathy improved subjectively when exposure stopped. Psychometrically they performed very close to the initial testing, excluding a progressive brain disease or subacute pharmacological solvent intoxication. Ihrig, Dietz, Bader, and Triebig (2005) examined on two occasions over a 2-year period 127 workers occupationally exposed to solvents; no significant associations were identified between neuropsychological test results and solvent exposure. Finally, Schaper et al. (2004) found no change in color vision, a test use as an index of possible neurotoxicity, on repeat examinations of workers occupational exposed to toluene. Overall, the combined evidence from existing cohort studies does not support the hypothesis that occupational exposure to organic solvent alone is a risk factor for central or peripheral neurotoxicity.

Among the numerous case-control studies investigating the relationship between solvent exposure and a particular condition or disorder, 17 studies involve Alzheimer's disease (5), dementia or dementia-like syndrome (4), or a neuropsychiatric diagnosis (9) (the total reflects one study included both dementia and neuropsychiatric diagnoses). One of the five case-control studies investigating the association between occupational solvent exposure and Alzheimer's disease identified an elevated risk. In the only positive study involving Alzheimer's disease, Kukull et al. (1995) found an elevated adjusted odds ratio (OR) of 2.3 (95% CI 1.1–4.7) between Alzheimer's disease and solvent exposure. One of the authors from that study subsequently reported (2001) evidence that the apolipoprotein 4 allele (APOE 4) may modify the associations between father's occupation, early-life environmental factors, and development of AD in late life (Moceri et al., 2001). None of the remaining four studies addressing Alzheimer's disease (Graves, Rosner, Echeverria, Mortimer, & Larson, 1998; Gun et al., 1997; Harmanci et al., 2003; Shalat, Seltzer, & Baker, 1988) identified an increased risk or an OR exceeding 2.0. Two of four studies investigating the association between occupational solvent exposure and dementia identified an increased risk. The first of the two, however, was confounded by alcohol use. Cherry, Labreche, and McDonald (1992) reported a slightly elevated relative risk (risk ratio = 2.3) for organic brain damage in association with combined alcohol intake and occupational solvent exposure. Olsen and Sabroe (1980) also reported a slightly higher risk of being awarded disability for dementia attributed to occupational solvent exposure, although the relative risk of receiving a diagnosis of dementia was not greater than that of other neuropsychiatric diagnosis in this study and potential sources of bias were acknowledged. The remaining two studies (O'Flynn, Monkman, & Waldron, 1987; Palmer, Inskip, Martyn, & Coggon, 1998) found no support for the hypothesis that occupational exposure to solvents is a cause of dementia.

Three of nine case-control studies investigating the association between occupational solvent exposure and any neuropsychiatric diagnosis or condition exposure reported an elevated risk that they attributed to solvent exposure. Included was a study by Riise and Moen (1990) that reported a significant relationship between disability pension due to neuropsychiatric diagnoses and occupational solvent exposure among solvent-exposed tanker workers. Chen, Dick, and Seaton (1999), in a nested case-control study, found an increased risk for developing neuropsychological symptoms, but this study was not disease or diagnosis based, limiting the importance of the observation. The study performed by Olsen and Sabroe (1980), and described above in terms of the association between solvent expose and dementia, also found an increased risk for being awarded a disability pension for a neuropsychiatric disorder attributed to solvent exposure. Among the remaining case-control studies, van Vliet et al. (1989) identified some trends indicating positive exposure–outcome relationships between high occupational exposure to organic solvents and the likelihood for receiving disability benefits due to neuropsychiatric disorders, although they acknowledged that bias may have influenced their results. In a subsequent study by many of the same authors (van Vliet et al., 1990), a possible association between "neuroses" and occupational solvent exposure was identified but attributed to classification bias. They found no elevated risk for neuropsychiatric disorders, and they concluded that although they could not exclude the possibility, their data did not confirm that Dutch painters were at increased risk of being prematurely disabled due to neuropsychiatric disorders. Among remaining case-control studies, risk ratios less than 2.0 or absence of significant exposed versus nonexposed group differences have been reported for the association between occupational exposure to solvents and nonspecific neuropsychiatric disorders (Axelson, Hane, & Hogstedt, 1976; Labreche, Cherry, & McDonald, 1992; Nelson, Robins, White, & Garrison, 1994) or neuropsychiatric disability (Brackbill, Maizlish, & Fischbach, 1990). Overall, however, most of the case-control studies found either no association or a weak association (sometimes confounded by alcoholism) between solvent exposure and the named disorder.

In summary, and as reported in previous reviews (Albers & Berent, 2000a; Lees-Haley & Williams, 1997; Ridgway et al., 2003; Spurgeon, 2002), available epidemiological results do not clearly identify a relationship between chronic, low-level occupational exposure to organic solvents and encephalopathy. In the intervening years, the bulk of scientific evidence failed to support a causal relationship between chronic, low-level occupational exposure to mixtures of organic solvents and encephalopathy, dementia, or any specific neuropsychiatric condition. *Chronic painters' encephalopathy* and other similar proposed syndromes seem to represent unnecessary concepts which are based upon inadequate scientific data.

Few neurological disorders produce damage to nervous system tissue or neurodegeneration for which pathological confirmation does not exist. In contrast, there are few reports of autopsy or pathological investigation of workers with purported neurological injury attributed to occupational solvent exposure. One exception to this lack of information is the autopsy study conducted by Klinken and Arlein-Soborg (1993) and summarized by Ridgway et al. (2003). This neuropathology study was based on review of autopsies of 103 subjects suspected of having chronic toxic encephalopathy and included approximately 50% of cases who had received compensation for solvent-related health problems. The results of the autopsy findings were compared to two referent groups. One referent group included 643 subjects whose deaths had been of forensic interest but unrelated to organic solvent exposure. The second referent group consisted of 733 hospitalized controls, whose deaths also were unrelated to solvent exposure. The pathology evaluations for all included standardized gross and histopathological examinations of selected brain sections. No differences were identified between the solvent and referent materials in terms of body weight/age-corrected brain weights or the frequency of pathological brain changes. The investigators concluded that individuals diagnosed with chronic toxic encephalopathy had no obvious morphological changes in the nervous system.

A major limitation of most studies is a lack of exposure information. Because of the difficulties inherent in quantifying the magnitude of remote solvent exposures, most studies rely on the worker's memory to establish exposure. Alternatively, exposure levels are inferred based on job titles, without measurements to confirm either the identity of the solvents or the actual exposure circumstances. Nevertheless, case-control studies have not provided convincing support for the conclusion that solvent exposure causes neurological and psychiatric disorders.

If painters' encephalopathy is not an established disorder, then how do we explain the large number of workers who have been diagnosed with this syndrome? If they do not have painters' encephalopathy, what do they have and how are their symptoms explained? The answer to the first question is that much of the controversy reflects social and legal, not medical, debate. One study reported the results of standard neurological evaluations performed on railroad workers who had long-term occupational solvent exposures (average 22 years) (Albers et al., 2000), addressing the second question.

It had been postulated by others that these workers had a solvent-induced toxic encephalopathy, and all were involved in litigation against their employer, alleging that occupational solvent exposures produced the encephalopathy and, in some cases, neuropathy. The workers all recounted episodes of transient intoxication that was associated with solvent exposure at work. The most common chief complaints among the 52 workers included impaired memory (38), altered mood (21), imbalance (18), and headache (17). These persistent symptoms developed on average 16 years after the first exposure opportunity. Thirteen workers had mild mental status abnormalities. None, however, fulfilled conventional clinical criteria for encephalopathy or dementia. Furthermore, none had abnormal blink reflex (51) or abnormal EEG (39) studies. Forty-seven of the workers had conventional brain MRI studies. Only one MRI was interpreted to show evidence of any cortical atrophy, and the neuroradiologist in this instance reported the atrophy as mild. Eight of the MRI studies showed scattered ischemic lesions among workers with known diabetes mellitus (2), elevated blood pressure (4), or peripheral vascular disease (two conditions frequently associated with the nonspecific imaging abnormalities). This is in contrast to the expected MRI abnormalities indicative of the "toxic leukoencephalopathy" associated with numerous neurotoxicants (Filley & Kleinschmidt-DeMasters, 2001). These findings are in agreement with recent work that reviewed the scientific evidence for an association between occupational exposure to organic solvents and long-term nervous system damage detectable by imaging, neurophysiology, or histopathology (Ridgway et al., 2003). In this review, Ridgway concluded that existing brain imaging data (MRI and CT) provided strong evidence of an absence of neurological damage among selected individuals with occupational solvent exposure. Further, no dose–response abnormalities could be inferred from existing studies and those positive studies had reporting and/or designs weaknesses, including limited consideration of potential confounding.

Among workers who had long-term occupational solvent exposures averaging 22 years, stepwise multiple linear and logistic regression models identified no statistically significant ($p < .05$) dose–response relationships between exposure duration and symptoms or signs suggestive of encephalopathy (Albers et al., 2000). The number of symptoms ($p < .001$) and the number of signs ($p = .05$) were associated with current use of central nervous system-active medications. Further, lower Mini-Mental Status Examination (MMSE) scores were associated with a history of alcohol abuse ($p = .01$) and a lower educational level ($p = .03$). The number of symptoms involving memory, mood, balance, or headache differed significantly between workers in different geographical sites ($F(3,48) = 2.94$, $p = .04$). This finding was not explained by job title or exposure duration. Perhaps the most illustrative finding resulting from this cross-sectional study was a highly significant ($p = .0001$) inverse relationship between the worker's initial solvent exposure year ($r^2 = 0.60$) or total years of solvent exposure through 1987 ($r^2 = 0.56$) and the interval to major neurologic symptom onset (Figure 18.3) (Albers et al.). In other words, a worker first occupationally exposed to solvents in 1955 required about 30 years to develop his first neurologic symptom, whereas a worker first exposed in 1980 required only 5 years to develop persistent symptoms. The latent period from onset of exposure to onset of

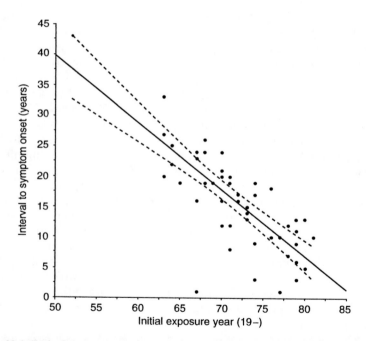

Figure 18.3 Interval from initial exposure to neurologic symptom onset (years) versus the initial year of occupational exposure to solvents (brackets around regression line indicate 95% confidence bands for true mean of Y). From "Neurologic evaluation of workers previously diagnosed with solvent-induced toxic encephalopathy," by J. W. Albers, J. J. Wald, D. H. Garabrant, C. L. Trask, and S. Berent, 2000, *Journal of Occupational and Environmental Medicine*, *42*, 410. With permission.

persistent symptoms was inconsistent with development of a toxic-induced disorder and atypical of any neurotoxic or pharmacological effect. This observation provided strong evidence that factors other than solvent exposure accounted for the neurologic complaints reported by these workers. Importantly, no objective neurologic evidence was found to support a diagnosis of toxic encephalopathy, toxic neuropathy, or any other coherent medical syndrome among these individuals. The limited number of signs suggestive of neurologic dysfunction argues against substantial neurotoxic injury of any type in this group of workers. For the most part, abnormalities were either nonspecific, isolated findings, or variations of normality common in the general population. Conventional application of the differential diagnosis technique indicated that most complaints expressed by these workers were readily explained by neuropsychological factors or conditions completely unrelated to occupational solvent exposure.

Many of these workers described symptoms suggestive of situational anxiety and depression (Albers et al., 2000). Patients frequently present for evaluation with symptoms for which medical explanations cannot be found (Nimnuan, Hotopf, & Wessely, 2000). These symptoms are often attributable to common psychological disorders such as anxiety or depression (Goldberg, 1990; Marks, Goldberg, & Hillier, 1979). Not infrequently, symptoms first appeared among the workers we described after they "learned" from others that they had evidence of "toxic encephalopathy" attributable to solvents. Speaking speculatively, perhaps the communication to the worker that he or she might have a serious neurological illness might explain the unusual latency from exposure to first symptoms discussed earlier and shown in Figure 18.3. This information and the method by which it was obtained could explain the negative emotional reactions expressed by these workers as well. Many workers had limited understanding about their problem, reporting only that they had been diagnosed with brain damage. Several expressed anxiety or concern about their future, believing (some, because they had been told my others) that they had a progressive condition with a poor prognosis akin to Alzheimer's disease. Many workers reported never returning after the initial evaluation to the physician who established the diagnosis of toxic encephalopathy. Frequently, there was no evidence that any reassurance or emotional support had been provided about whether or not the worker was likely to become mentally or physically incapacitated. These workers frequently described increased stress and anxiety caused by common life events such as misplacing their keys or forgetting a neighbor's name. They interpreted these events as symptoms and as further evidence of their toxicant-induced injury. One of the most common causes of apparent dementia is "pseudo-dementia," a treatable form of cognitive impairment that has a psychological, not a neurological, basis (Newman et al., 1989; Sahakian, 1991; Strub & Black, 1992). Patients with depressed mood may display disinterest and poor concentration, both of which result in memory difficulties. This was a likely explanation for many of the cognitive complaints expressed by these workers.

How was the previous diagnosis of toxic encephalopathy established by others for these workers (Albers et al., 2000)? For the most part, a neurologist, the medical specialist who typically evaluates patients suspected of having encephalopathy, had not established the initial diagnosis. In fact, despite the implications of the diagnosis, only 13 of the 52 workers had been referred to a neurologist for any reason. Four of the 13 workers had the diagnosis of encephalopathy confirmed by the neurologist. However, the neurological diagnoses were as follows for these four patients: probable Alzheimer's disease versus small vessel ischemia (1), multiple chemical sensitivity syndrome (1), anxiety and depression associated with solvent exposure (1), and possible presenile dementia (1). All four of these workers had normal EEG studies. Two of the four had MRI evidence of scattered ischemic lesion. Both had explanations other than occupational solvent exposure for the findings. One had diabetes mellitus and one had elevated blood pressure; both reported a history of alcohol abuse. For most workers, an explanation other than solvent exposure explained their complaints. Often the alternative explanation had been identified by the worker's personal physician, only to be replaced by a physician involved in the litigation process with a diagnosis of toxic encephalopathy. Workers with memory complaints frequently provided examples of their difficulties that were characteristic of normal memory variation, not impaired cognition or dementia. Examples such as forgetting names of familiar people, forgetting where they had placed their tools, needing lists when shopping, and being unable to remember specifics of their trip after driving to and from work were provided as evidence of encephalopathy. Interpretation of such complaints was complicated by use of medications known to interfere with cognitive function. Many workers were prescribed medications known to influence coordination and balance, potentially contributing to their complaints, as well. Workers frequently denied knowledge of such potential medication side effects. Memory complaints frequently occurred in association with depressed mood or history of increased anxiety, making it difficult to separate the role of psychological factors in their complaints.

After publication of the results of standard neurologic evaluations performed on railroad workers who had long-term occupational solvent exposures (Albers et al., 2000), Morton (2002) expressed concern that neuropsychological evaluations were not performed and that the symptoms of depression and/or anxiety were secondary and reactive to loss of cognitive abilities. Actually, the results of detailed neuropsychological examinations were available for these workers. However, other important factors exist in addition to results of neuropsychological testing. These factors include information of baseline function such as past school performance, motivation, and known medical and psychological conditions, any of which may influence results and explain positive findings. This additional information is important because neuropsychological test results, while sensitive indicators of impairment, are not specific for toxic-induced dysfunction. Morton also hypothesized that workers with chronic encephalopathy who are removed from further solvent exposure experience some improvement, if only because they develop better coping skills (Morton, 2002). As described earlier, however, there was no evidence that improved function followed removal from exposure. Importantly, and as already mentioned, evaluations performed after removal from exposure demonstrated a striking inverse relationship between initial exposure year and the time interval to onset of major neurologic symptoms (Figure 18.3). This observation strongly suggests that factors other than solvent exposure accounted for the workers' symptoms. Such factors almost certainly included dissemination of incorrect information and generation of unnecessary anxiety and depression due to improperly communicated or even incorrect diagnoses and incorrect prognoses for many of these workers.

Several of Morton's comments (Morton, 2002) are at the heart of the debate involving solvent encephalopathy as an identifiable entity. At least some of the controversy about solvent-induced encephalopathy involves the methods sometimes used to diagnose solvent-induced encephalopathy (see Table 17.12 and related comments on page 1098ff). Most of the workers reported above were said to fulfill the definition of toxic encephalopathy developed at a series of meetings (World Health Organization and Nordic Council of Ministers, 1985; Baker, Bus, & Cranmer, et al., 1985; Baker & Seppalainen, 1987). This classification was described in greater detail in the 1987 workshop reported by Baker & Seppalainen (1987) and has been referred to by some as the "WHO classification." This classification scheme has potential use in epidemiological studies, but it does not have clinical diagnostic application in individual cases. The primary limitation of the definition is its apparent disregard for competing diagnoses or explanations. Although the term toxic encephalopathy implies both a neurological condition (encephalopathy) and its etiology (toxic-induced), the "WHO classification" can only categorize or grade the severity of the condition. It cannot establish a cause. Behavior can be influenced by a variety of factors, only some of which are neurological. An individual with a depression reactive to life experiences but no solvent exposure could easily have memory complaints and even demonstrate some intellectual impairment on clinical testing or interview, yet have no neurologically based dysfunction. With change in life situation, the depression and intellectual decline might improve with subsequent improvement in intellectual function. Such an individual would initially meet criteria for "Type 2A encephalopathy" using the "WHO classification" of sustained change in mood or personality change. However, it would be erroneous and improper to conclude that the cause of the problem could be attributed to organic solvent exposure.

The emphasis on symptoms, in contrast to objective measures of neurological function, has contributed to the use of questionnaires (often non- or poorly standardized) to evaluate heath effects associated with long-term solvent exposures. While such instruments have utility in epidemiological studies, they have limited application in clinical medicine. For example, questionnaire results were compared among patients with suspected solvent-induced toxic encephalopathy, subjects from a random sample from the general population, and a sample of occupationally active spray painters. Questions concerning memory and concentration symptoms alone were found to show better sensitivity for identifying toxic encephalopathy than other subsets of questions. However, the diagnosis of toxic encephalopathy was said to require information in addition to exposure data and questionnaire responses. The investigators concluded that questionnaire screening instruments did not replace current clinical diagnostic procedures (Carter et al., 2002).

Regarding the issue of painters' encephalopathy more specifically, Rosenberg reviewed the literature used to establish the association between symptoms and underlying exposure (Rosenberg, 1995). He summarized his review as follows: "In conclusion, current literature does not support previously published studies relating chronic occupational solvent exposure to any permanent central nervous system or peripheral nervous system injury. In particular, there is no compelling evidence to suggest that chronic low-level exposure to solvent mixtures causes adverse neurobehavioral effects" (Rosenberg, 1995).

Several reports appeared in the past decade associating exposure to low-levels of TCE in residential water supplies with neurobehavioral impairments (Feldman, Chirico-Post, & Proctor, 1988; Feldman et al., 1994; Landrigan, Kominsky, & Ruhe, 1987; White, Feldman, Eviator, Jabre, & Niles, 1997). Many of the reports involved studies of litigants in a series of widely publicized and controversial toxic tort cases. Given the inability of epidemiological studies to establish a causal relationship between chronic, low-level occupational exposure to TCE or similar organic solvents and neurologic dysfunction, it is unlikely and even illogical to expect that residential exposure at levels lower by several orders of magnitude than occupational exposure levels would produce a neurotoxic syndrome. In a recent review of the literature associated with resident TCE exposure, Lees-Haley et al. concluded "the existing literature is complicated by serious and often fatal methodological errors, confusion and speculation, contradictory findings, nonspecific findings and findings which are misapplied or improperly generalized. It is important to examine the literature with a critical eye for its methodology rather than relying on the author's conclusions alone" (Lees-Haley, 1992).

To date, there is no credible animal model that has demonstrated neurotoxic injury resulting from chronic, low-level exposure at levels consistent with those experienced in occupational settings. A recent review of key animal toxicity studies involving representative solvents found no consistent solvent-associated effect detectable by histopathology examination of the nervous system or by electrophysiological evaluations (Ridgway et al., 2003).

VERIFICATION OF CAUSE/ETIOLOGY

Application of the criteria for causation to the syndrome of toxic encephalopathy caused by occupational exposure to solvent cannot verify a toxic etiology for the clinical *case presentation* and, also, results in serious doubts about the very existence of the syndrome as a diagnosable entity. Concerning the alternative clinical diagnoses of dysthymic disorder and anxiety disorder, it is well established that both may be attributable to exogenous stimuli (e.g., life events). The verification of the ability of life events to cause depression and anxiety was addressed elsewhere in the present volumes.

Conclusion

The bulk of scientific evidence at the present time fails to support a causal relationship between chronic, low-level occupational exposure to solvents and toxic encephalopathy, toxic neuropathy, or any other identifiable neurological disorder. Chronic painters' encephalopathy and other similar proposed syndromes, therefore, appear to represent unnecessary concepts, which are based on inadequate scientific data. For the individual presented, traditional psychiatric diagnoses adequately explained all aspects of the patient's clinical presentation. These conclusions are not meant to suggest that individual exposures to solvents cannot result in harm (see section on *solvents* in chapter 15). Rather, the viewpoint suggested is that each patient needs to be considered in terms of the unique neurobehavioral toxicological history that person brings to the evaluation.

Summary

Things are not always what they appear, an adage with considerable relevance when attempting to conclude toxicant-induced disorder. The nine *case presentations* described in this chapter reflect important factors to consider in arriving at accurate and verifiable clinical (and research) conclusions. Many of these factors are extra-clinical, in that they reflect personal and societal beliefs and pressures that superficially might not seem directly related to the clinical diagnostic process, yet, still contribute to inaccurate clinical conclusions.

The discussion in this chapter pertaining to a child with learning and other behavioral problems by Trask and Provencal, for instance, implicated factors far removed from the suspected toxicant (ethylmercury) that influenced initial conclusions in the *case presentation*. The discussion on *causality* in volume I emphasized that people seek explanations for the events they experience, at times seemingly less concerned about accuracy than with having an answer. Anxiety is motivating. It is likely that obtaining an answer to the question of what caused a symptom reduces anxiety that accompanies the unknown, reinforcing the causal conclusion irrespective of its correctness. Concerns related to the well-being of our children may be among the most anxiety-provoking situations one might encounter. As emphasized by Trask and Provencal, people wanted an explanation for the apparent increase in childhood autism and its seeming correlation with the increased use of Thimerosal in vaccines. Although a causal relationship between the mercury contained in Thimerosal and autism might have been a reasonable hypothesis, its ready acceptance by many individuals was premature. In fact, the data suggesting that there was an increase in the incidence of autism may itself have been inaccurate. Nevertheless, the acceptance of this idea was widespread and may have influenced the physician's initial conclusions in the *case presentation*.

Toxicants, naturally occurring and man-made, are ubiquitous, and it is reasonable to consider the part these agents might play in producing illness, either as explanatory to well established but still incompletely understood diseases (e.g., Alzheimer's disease) or representing unique illnesses that provide alternatives to traditional diagnostic entities (e.g., amalgam-related illness, toxic mold-induced illness, or illnesses resulting from chronic, low-dose exposure to solvents). Unproven hypotheses, of course, are not a basis for diagnosis or causal determination, but there is another important consideration is this instance. That is, it is never appropriate to make a causal conclusion that is based solely on exclusion, e.g., as reflected in the statement sometimes heard "I can't think of anything else it could be."

It is important to recognize that toxicant-induced illness can reflect endogenous as well as environmental exposures. Like anxiety, depression is frequently present in patients who may have been injured by exposure to a toxicant. Depression is frequent in medical disorders, regardless of cause, and the symptoms and signs of mood disorder can mimic those seen in toxicant-induced disorder. Also, alterations in mood have the capacity to influence the clinical presentation, leaving the depressed patient more difficult to diagnose accurately than might be the case if mood disorder was not present. Depression can at times be the direct result of a primary medical disorder, waxing and waning in severity as a consequence of changes in the patient's primary medical disorder. Such changes in the patient's medical condition can serve as a basis for the pseudo- or reversible dementias seen in depression and some medical disorders (e.g., Cushing's syndrome). Depending on the circumstances in a give case, however, these changes can be easily mistaken for improved function following removal from exposure to a toxic substance.

The sections in this chapter have all emphasized the need to develop a complete differential diagnosis in evaluating the patient with suspected toxicant-induced disorder. The various *case presentations* and discussions reflected the ways in which errors can occur in a given case. Also, these sections described objective clinical evaluations that resulted in accurate diagnostic conclusions through a systematic clinical approach that was based on knowledge of the various clinical and extra-clinical factors that can influence a given case, identification of these factors through interview and history, recognition of their presence in developing the differential diagnosis, and performing independent evaluations of diagnosis and etiology.

Notes

1   Details of the history have been modified to preserve the anonymity of the patient and the patient's family.

2   One of the most famous cases describing a penetrating head injury involved a railroad foreman Phineas Gage, who in 1848 while setting an explosive charge suffered injury when a premature explosion caused the 43-in.tapping iron, which he was using, to penetrate the left side of his skull. The tapping iron entered under the left cheek bone and exited through the top of his skull. He suffered damage to

most of the left frontal lobe of his brain. Although he was said to be described by his coworkers as "no longer Gage," he recovered from the trauma and died in 1860 (Haas, 2001).

3   Note that a GCS score alone conveys little information other than allowing for severity rating and monitoring the patient's level of consciousness (Goldman & Bennett, 2000). The scale contains three component parts (i.e., best eye response, best verbal response, and best motor response), and convention is to break the GCS into its component parts, e.g., GCS 9 (E2V3M4) (Trauma.Org, 2005). The GCS may be combined with other clinical findings to classify the patient's condition more precisely, e.g., differentiating between "minor head injury" and "moderate head injury" on the basis of GCS (13–15) with return to normal level of consciousness and mentation within 24 hr for the former and GCS (9–12) with a depressed level of consciousness for several hours or days, with or without coma, in the latter instance (Goldman & Bennett, 2000).

References

Adams, R. L., Boake, C., & Crain, C. (1982). Bias in a neuropsychological test classification related to education, age, and ethnicity. *Journal of Consulting and Clinical Psychology, 50*, 143–145.

Agency for Toxic substances and Disease Registry (ATSDR). (1999). Toxicological profile for mercury. Retrieved from www.atsdr.cdc.gov/toxprofiles/tp46.html

Ahmed, Q., Chung-Park, M., & Tomashefski, J. F., Jr. (1997). Cardiopulmonary pathology in patients with sleep apnea/obesity hypoventilation syndrome. *Human Pathology, 28*, 264–269.

Ahmed, S., Siddiqui, R. K., Siddiqui, A. K., Zaidi, S. A., & Cervia, J. (2002). HIV associated thrombotic microangiopathy. *Postgraduate Medical Journal, 78*, 520–525.

Aikens, J. E., Caruana-Montaldo, B., Vanable, P. A., Tadimeti, L., & Mendelson, W. B. (1999). MMPI correlates of sleep and respiratory disturbance in obstructive sleep apnea. *Sleep, 22*, 362–369.

Albers, J. W., & Berent, S. (1999). Neurotoxicology. In R. W. Evans (Ed.), *Diagnostic testing in neurology* (pp. 257–271). Philadelphia: WB Saunders Co.

Albers, J. W., & Berent, S. (2000). *Clinical neurobehavioral toxicology*. Philadelphia: W. B. Saunders.

Albers, J. W., & Berent, S. (2000a). Controversies in neurotoxicology: Current status. *Neurology Clinics, 18*, 741–763.

Albers, J. W., Wald, J. J., Garabrant, D. H., Trask, C. L., & Berent, S. (2000). Neurologic evaluation of workers previously diagnosed with solvent-induced toxic encephalopathy. *Journal of Occupational and Environmental Medicine, 42*, 410–423.

Albers, J. W., Wald, J. J., Werner, R. A., Franzblau, A., & Berent, S. (1999). Absence of polyneuropathy among workers previously diagnosed with solvent-induced toxic encephalopathy. *Journal of Occupational and Environmental Medicine, 41*, 500–509.

Alison et al. v. Fire Insurance Exchange, et al. (2002). No. 03-01-00717-CV (Texas App., 3d Dist., Austin, Dec. 19, 2002).

Allred, N. J., Shaw, K. M., Santibanez, T. A., Rickert, D. L., & Santoli, J. M. (2005). Parental vaccine safety concerns: Results from the National Immunization Survey, 2001–2002. *American Journal of Preventive Medicine, 28*, 221–224.

Aman, M. G., Kern, R. A., McGhee, D. E., & Arnold, L. E. (1993). Fenfluramine and methylphenidate in children with mental retardation and attention deficit hyperactivity disorder: Laboratory effects. *Journal of Autism and Developmental Disorders, 23,* 491–506.

American Conference of Governmental Industrial Hygienists. (2001). *Documentation of the threshold limit values and biological exposure indices.* (7th ed.) Cincinnati, Ohio: Author.

American Psychiatric Association. (1994). *Diagnostic and statistical manual of mental disorders* (4th ed.). Washington, DC: Author.

Andrews, N., Miller, E., Grant, A., Stowe, J., Osborne, V., & Taylor, B. (2004). Thimerosal exposure in infants and developmental disorders: A retrospective cohort study in the United Kingdom does not support a causal association. *Pediatrics, 114,* 584–591.

Antti-Poika, M. (1982a). Overall prognosis after chronic organic solvent intoxication. *International Archives of Occupational and Environmental Health, 51,* 127–138.

Antti-Poika, M. (1982b). Prognosis of symptoms in patients with diagnosed chronic organic solvent intoxication. *International Archives of Occupational and Environmental Health, 51,* 81–89.

Arboix, A., & Marti-Vilalta, J. L. (2004). New concepts in lacunar stroke etiology: The constellation of small-vessel arterial disease. *Cerebrovascular Diseases, 17,* 58–62.

Arciniegas, D., Adler, L., Topkoff, J., Cawthra, E., Filley, C. M., & Reite, M. (1999). Attention and memory dysfunction after traumatic brain injury: Cholinergic mechanisms, sensory gating, and a hypothesis for further investigation. *Brain Injury, 13,* 1–13.

Arlien-Soborg, P., Bruhn, P., Gyldensted, C., & Melgaard, B. (1979). Chronic painters' syndrome. Chronic toxic encephalopathy in house painters. *Acta Neurologica Scandinavica, 60,* 149–156.

Arlien-Soborg, P., Zilstorff, K., Grandjean, B., & Milling Pedersen, L. (1981). Vestibular dysfunction in occupational chronic solvent intoxication. *Clinical Otolaryngology and Allied Sciences, 6,* 285–290.

Axelson, O., Hane, M., & Hogstedt, C. (1976). A case-referent study on neuropsychiatric disorders among workers exposed to solvents. *Scandinavian Journal of Work, Environment and Health, 2,* 14–20.

Bagedahl-Strindlund, M., Ilie, M., Furhoff, A. K., Tomson, Y., Larsson, K. S., Sandborgh-Englund, G. et al. (1997). A multidisciplinary clinical study of patients suffering from illness associated with mercury release from dental restorations: Psychiatric aspects. *Acta Psychiatrica Scandinavica, 96,* 475–482.

Bailer, J., Rist, F., Rudolf, A., Staehle, H. J., Eickholz, P., Triebig, G. et al. (2001). Adverse health effects related to mercury exposure from dental amalgam fillings: Toxicological or psychological causes? *Psychological Medicine, 31,* 255–263.

Bailey, A., LaCouteur, A., Gottesman, I., Bolton, P., Simonoff, E., Yuzda, E., & Rutter, M. (1995). Autism as a strongly genetic disorder: Evidence from a British twin study. *Psychological Medicine, 25,* 63–77.

Bailey, A., Phillips, W., & Rutter, M. (1996). Autism: Towards an integration of clinical, genetic, neuro-psychological and neurobiological perspectives. *Journal of Child Psychology and Psychiatry, 37,* 89–126.

Baker, E. L., Bus, J. S., Cranmer, J. M., Curtis, M. F., Golberg, L., Grasso, P., Keller, W. L., Morgan, R. W., Scala, R. A., & Seppalainen, A. M. (1985). International workshop on neurobehavioral effects of solvents. Consensus workshop summary. *Neurotoxicology, 6*, 99–102.

Baker, E. L., & Fine, L. J. (1986). Solvent neurotoxicity: The current evidence. *Journal of Occupational Medicine, 28*, 126–129.

Baker, E. L., & Seppalainen, A. M. (1987). Human aspects of solvent neurobehavioral effects. Report of the workshop session on clinical and epidemiological topics. *Neurotoxicology, 7*, 43–56.

Baker, E. L., Jr., Smith, T. J., & Landrigan, P. J. (1985). The neurotoxicity of industrial solvents: A review of the literature. *American Journal of Industrial Medicine, 8*, 207–217.

Baldo, J. V., Ahmad, L., & Ruff, R. (2002). Neuropsychological performance of patients following mold exposure. *Applied Neuropsychology, 9*, 193–202.

Ball, L. K., Ball, R., & Pratt, R. D. (2001). An assessment of Thimerosal use in childhood vaccines. *Pediatrics, 107*, 1147–1154.

Ballard v. Fire Insurance Exchange. (2002). Case No. 99-05252 (Texas Dist., 345th Dist. Travis County, filed May 5, 1999).

Baran, A. S., & Richert, A. C. (2003). Obstructive sleep apnea and depression. *CNS Spectrums, 8*, 120–134.

Barchas, J. D., & Altemus, M. (1999). Biochemical hypotheses of mood and anxiety disorders. In G. J. Siegel, B. W. Agranoff, S. K. Fisher, R. W. Albers, & M. D. Uhler (Eds.), *Basic neurochemistry: Molecular, cellular and medical aspects* (6th ed., pp. 1074–1093). Philadelphia: Lippincott-Raven.

Bardenheier, B., Yusuf, H., Schwartz, B., Gust, D., Barker, L., & Rodewald, L. (2004). Are parental vaccine safety concerns associated with receipt of measles-mumps-rubella, diphtheria and tetanus toxoids with acellular pertussis or Hepatitis B vaccines by children. *Archives of Pediatric and Adolescent Medicine, 158*, 569–575.

Barsky, A. J., & Borus, J. F. (1999). Functional somatic syndromes. *Annals of Internal Medicine, 130*, 910–921.

Bauer, M., & Rabins, S. F. (1977). Trichlorethylene toxicity. Review. *International Journal of Dermatology, 16*, 113–116.

Beaumanoir, A. (1985). The Landau–Kleffner syndrome. In J. Roger, C. Dravet, M. Bureau, F. E. Dreifull, & P. Wolf (Eds.), *Epileptic syndromes in infancy, childhood, and adolescence* (pp. 181–191). Paris: John Libbery Eurotext Ltd.

Bellinger, D. C., Trachteuberg, F., Barregard, L., Taveres, M., Ceonichiari, E., Daniel, D., et al. (2006). Neuropsychological and renal effects of dental amalgam in children: a randomized clinical trial. *Journal of the American Medical Association, 295*, 1775–1783.

Berent, S. (1986). Psychopathology and other behavioral considerations for the clinical neuropsychologist. In S. Filskov & T. J. Boll (Eds.), *Handbook of clinical neuropsychology* (Vol. 2). New York: John Wiley and Sons.

Berent, S., Giordani, B., Foster, N., Minoshima, S., Lajiness-O'Neill, R., Koeppe, R. et al. (1999). Neuropsychological function and cerebral glucose utilization in isolated memory impairment and Alzheimer's disease. *Journal of Psychiatric Research, 33*, 7–16.

Berent, S., Giordani, B., Gilman, S., Junck, L., Kluin, K. J., & Koeppe, R. A. (1996). Psychological factors and PET measured glucose metabolism in olivopontocerebellar atrophy. *Assessment, 3*, 335–351.

Berent, S., Giordani, B., Lehtinen, S., Markel, D., Penney, J. B., Buchtel, H. A. et al. (1988). Positron emission tomographic scan investigations of Huntington's disease:

Cerebral metabolic correlates of cognitive function. *Annals of Neurology, 23,* 541–546.

Berkow, R. (1982). *The Merck manual.* (14th ed.). Rahway, NJ: Merck & Co., Inc.

Bernard, S., Enayati, A., Redwood, L., Roger, H., & Binstock, T. (2001). Autism: A novel form of mercury poisoning. *Medical Hypotheses, 56,* 462–471.

Bernard, S., Enayati, A., Roger, H., Binstock, T., & Redwood, L. (2002). The role of mercury in the pathogenesis of autism. *Molecular Psychiatry, 7,* S42–S43.

Binder, L. M., & Campbell, K. A. (2004). Medically unexplained symptoms and neuropsychological assessment. *Journal of Clinical and Experimental Neuropsychology, 26,* 369–392.

Binder, L. M., Rohling, M. L., & Larrabee, J. (1997). A review of mild head trauma. Part I: Meta-analytic review of neuropsychological studies. *Journal of Clinical and Experimental Neuropsychology, 19,* 421–431.

Binder, L. M., & Willis, S. C. (1991). Assessment of motivation after financially compensable minor head trauma. *Psychological Assessment, 3,* 175–181.

Bjorkman, L., Pedersen, N. L., & Lichtenstein, P. (1996). Physical and mental health related to dental amalgam fillings in Swedish twins. *Community Dentistry and Oral Epidemiology., 24,* 260–267.

Blair, A. M. J. N., Clark, B., Clarke, A. J., & Wood, P. (1975). Tissue concentrations of mercury after chronic dosing of squirrel monkeys with Thimerosal. *Toxiciology, 3,* 171–176.

Bleecker, M. L., Bolla, K. I., Agnew, J., & Schwartz, B. S. (1991). Dose-related subclinical neurobehavioral effects of chronic exposure to low levels of organic solvents. *American Journal of Industrial Medicine, 19,* 715–728.

Bliwise, D. L. (1996). Is sleep apnea a cause of reversible dementia in old age? *Journal of the American Geriatrics Society, 44,* 1407–1409.

Bonanni, P. (1999). Demographic impact of vaccination: A review. *Vaccine, 17*(Suppl. 3), S120–S125.

Brackbill, R. M., Maizlish, N., & Fischbach, T. (1990). Risk of neuropsychiatric disability among painters in the United States. *Scandinavian Journal of Work, Environment and Health, 16,* 182–188.

Brambilla, F., Bellodi, L., Perna, G., Battaglia, M., Sciuto, G., Diaferia, G., Petraglia, F., Panerai, A., & Sacerdote, P. (1992). Psychoimmunoendocrine aspects of panic disorder. *Neuropsychobiology, 26,* 12–22.

Brandt, J., & Butters, N. (1986). The neuropsychology of Huntington's disease. *Trends in Neuroscience, 9,* 118–120.

Bratel, J., Haraldson, T., Meding, B., Yontchev, E., Ohman, S. C., & Ottosson, J. O. (1997). Potential side effects of dental amalgam restorations. (I). An oral and medical investigation. *European Journal of Oral Sciences, 105,* 234–243.

Bratel, J., Haraldson, T., & Ottosson, J. O. (1997). Potential side effects of dental amalgam restorations. (II). No relation between mercury levels in the body and mental disorders. *European Journal of Oral Sciences, 105,* 244–250.

Brown, M. C., Levin, B. E., Ramsay, R. E., Katz, D. A., & Duchowny, M. S. (1991). Characteristics of patients with nonepileptic seizures. *Journal of Epilepsy, 4,* 225–229.

Brownawell, A. M., Berent, S., Brent, R. L., Bruckner, J. V., Doull, J., Gershwin, E. M., Hood, R. D., Matanoski, G. M., Rubin, R., Weiss, B., & Karol, M. H. (2005). The potential adverse health effects of dental amalgam. *Toxicological Reviews, 24,* 1–10.

Bruhn, P., Arlien-Soborg, P., Gyldensted, C., & Christensen, E. L. (1981). Prognosis in chronic toxic encephalopathy. A two-year follow-up study in 26 house painter with occupational encephalopathy. *Acta Neurologica Scandinavica, 64*, 259–272.

Bruyn, G. W. (1968). Huntington's chorea: Historical, clinical and laboratory synopsis. In P. Vinkin & G. W. Bruyn (Eds.), *Handbook of clinical neurology* (pp. 298–378). New York: Elsevier.

Burd, L., Fisher, W., & Kerbeshian, J. (1987). A prevalence study of pervasive developmental disorders in North Dakota. *Journal of the American Academy of Child and Adolescent Psychiatry, 26*, 700–703.

Burge, H. A. (2001). Fungi: Toxic killers or unavoidable nuisances? *Annals of Allergy, Asthma, and Immunology, 87*, 52–56.

Butler, J. A., Chalder, T., & Wessely, S. (2001). Causal attributions for somatic sensations in patients with chronic fatigue syndrome and their partners. *Psychological Medicine, 31*, 97–105.

Butters, N., Sax, D., Montgomery, K., & Tarlow, S. (1978). Comparison of the neuropsychological deficits associated with early and advanced Huntington's disease. *Archives of Neurology, 35*, 585–589.

Buxton, P. H., & Hayward, M. (1967). Polyneuritis cranialis associated with industrial trichloroethylene poisoning. *Journal of Neurology, Neurosurgery and Psychiatry, 30*, 511–518.

Caine, E. D. (1981). Pseudodementia: Current concepts and future directions. *Archives of General Psychiatry, 38*, 728–733.

Caine, E. D., Ebert, M. H., & Weingartner, H. (1977). An outline for the analysis of dementia. The memory disorder of Huntington's disease. *Neurology, 27*, 1087–1092.

Carlson, L. E., & Sherwin, B. B. (1998). Steroid hormones, memory and mood in a healthy elderly population. *Psychoneuroendocrinology, 23*, 583–603.

Carter, N., Iregren, A., Soderman, E., Olson, B. A., Karlson, B., Lindelof, B., et al. (2002). EUROQUEST—a questionnaire for solvent related symptoms: Factor structure, item analysis and predictive validity. *Neurotoxicology, 23*, 711–717.

Centers for Disease Control and Prevention (CDC). (1999). Ten great public health achievements—United States, 1990–1999. *MMWR Morbity and Mortality Weekly, 48*, 243–248.

Chang, C. M., Yu, C. W., Fong, K. Y., Leung, S. Y., Tsin, T. W., Yu, Y. L., et al. (1993). *n*-Hexane neuropathy in offset printers. *Journal of Neurology, Neurosurgery and Psychiatry, 56*, 538–542.

Chen, R., Dick, F., & Seaton, A. (1999). Health effects of solvent exposure among dockyard painters: Mortality and neuropsychological symptoms. *Occupational and Environmental Medicine, 56*, 383–387.

Cherry, N. M., Labreche, F. P., & McDonald, J. C. (1992). Organic brain damage and occupational solvent exposure. *British Journal of Industrial Medicine, 49*, 776–781.

Cheshire, K., Engleman, H., Deary, I., Shapiro, C., & Douglas, N. J. (1992). Factors impairing daytime performance in patients with sleep apnea/hypopnea syndrome. *Archives of Internal Medicine, 152*, 538–541.

Chess, S. (1971). Autism in children with congenital rubella. *Journal of Autism and Child Schizophrenia, 1*, 33–47.

Chez, M., Major, S., & Smith, M. (1992). SPECT evaluation of cerebral perfusion in LKS. *Epilepsia, 33*, 52.

Chin, K., & Ohi, M. (1999). Obesity and obstructive sleep apnea syndrome. *Internal Medicine, 38*, 200–202.

Christensen, J. D., Yurgelun-Todd, D. A., Babb, S. M., Gruber, S. A., Cohen, B. M., & Renshaw, P. F. (1999). Measurement of human brain dexfenfluramine concentration by 19F magnetic resonance spectroscopy. *Brain Research, 834*, 1–5.

Clarkson, T. W. (1997). The toxicology of mercury. *Critical Reviews in Clinical Laboratory Sciences, 34*, 369–403.

Clarkson, T. W. (2002). The three modern faces of mercury. *Environmental Health Perspectives, 110*(Suppl. 1), 11–23.

Clarkson, T. W., Friberg, L. T., Hursh, J. B., & Nylander, M. (1988a). The prediction of intake of mercury vapor from amalgams. In T. W. Clarkson, L. T. Friberg, G. F. Nordberg, & P. R. Sager (Eds.), *Biological monitoring of toxic metals* (pp. 247–264). New York: Plenum Press.

Clarkson, T. W., Friberg, L., Nordberg, G. F., & Sager, P. R. (1988b). Mercury. In *Biological monitoring of toxic metals* (pp. 199–246). New York: Plenum Press.

Condren, R. M., O'Neill, A., Ryan, M. C., Barrett, P., & Thakore, J. H. (2002). HPA axis response to a psychological stressor in generalized social phobia. *Psychoneuroendocrinology, 27*, 693–703.

Cook, E. H. Jr. (2001). Genetics of autism. *Child and Adolescent Psychiatry Clinics of North America, 10*, 333–350.

Costa, L. L. F., & Scussel, V. M. (2002). Toxigenic fungi in beans (phaseolus vulgaris L.) classes black and color cultivated in the state of Santa Catarina, Brazil. *Brazilian Journal of Microbiology, 33*, 138–144.

Cox-Ganser, J. M., White, S. K., Jones, R., Hilsbos, K., Storey, E., Enright, P. L., Rao, C. Y., & Kreiss, K. (2005). Respiratory morbidity in office workers in a water-damaged building. *Environmental Health Perspectives, 113*, 485–490.

Coyne, J. C., Thompson, R., & Racioppo, M. W. (2001). Validity and efficiency of screening for history of depression by self-report. *Psychological Assessment, 13*, 163–170.

Crago, B. R., Gray, M. R., Nelson, L. A., Davis, M., Arnold, L., & Thrasher, J. D. (2003). Psychological, neuropsychological, and electrocortical effects of mixed mold exposure. *Archives of Environmental Health, 58*, 452–463.

Cummings, J. L. (1993). Frontal-subcortical circuits and human behavior. *Archives of Neurology, 50*, 873–880.

Curzon, G., & Gibson, E. L. (1999). The serotonergic appetite suppressant fenfluramine. Reappraisal and rejection. *Advances in Experimental Medicine and Biology, 467*, 95–100.

Daniell, W. E., Claypoole, K. H., Checkoway, H., Smith-Weller, T., Dager, S. R., Townes, B. D., et al. (1999). Neuropsychological function in retired workers with previous long-term occupational exposure to solvents. *Occupational and Environmental Medicine, 56*, 93–105.

Davey, M. J. (2003). Understanding obstructive sleep apnoea. *Nursing Times, 99*, 26–27.

Davidovitch, M., Glick, L., Holtzmon, D., Tirosh, E., & Safir, M. P. (2000). Developmental regression in autism: Maternal perception. *Journal of Autism and Developmental Disorders, 30*, 113–119.

Davis, L. E. (1999). Fungal infections of the central nervous system. *Neurologic Clinics, 17*, 761–781.

Deary, I. J. (1999). A taxonomy of medically unexplained symptoms. *Journal of Psychosomatic Research, 47*, 51–59.

Decary, A., Rouleau, I., & Montplaisir, J. (2000). Cognitive deficits associated with sleep apnea syndrome: A proposed neuropsychological test battery. *Sleep, 23*, 369–381.

Deonna, T. W. (1991). Acquired epileptiform aphasia in children (Landau–Kleffner syndrome). *Journal of Clinical Neurophysiology, 8*, 288–298.

Department of Health. *Statistical bulletin.NHS Immunisation Statistics, England. 2002–2003.* Retrieved October 21, 2005, from http://www.publications.doh.gov. uk/public/sb0316 htm

DeRouen, T. A., Martin, M. D., Leroux, B. G., Townes, B. D., Woods, J. S., Leitao, J., et al. (2006). Neurobehavioral effects of dental amalgam in children: A randomized clinical trial. *Journal of the American Medical Association, 295*, 1784–1792.

Descombes, E., Droz, D., Drouet, L., Grunfeld, J. P., & Lesavre, P. (1997). Renal vascular lesions in lupus nephritis. *Medicine, 76*, 355–368.

Deykin, E. Y., & MacMahon, B. (1979). Viral exposure and autism. *American Journal of Epidemiology, 109*, 628–638.

Dimsdale, J. E., Newton, R. P., & Joist, T. (1989). Neuropsychological side effects of beta-blockers. *Archives of Internal Medicine, 149*, 514–525.

Djousse, L., Knowlton, B., Cupples, L. A., Marder, K., Shoulson, I., & Myers, R. H. (2002). Weight loss in early stage of Huntington's disease. *Neurology, 59*, 1325–1330.

Dom, R., Malfroid, M., & Baro, F. (1976). Neuropathology of Huntington's chorea. Studies of the ventrobasal complex of the thalamus. *Neurology, 26*, 64–68.

Drobotko, V. G. (1945). Stachybotryotoxicosis: A new disease of horses and humans. *American Review of Soviet Medicine, 2*, 238–242.

Dunham, C. M., Ransom, K. J., Flowers, L. L., Siegal, J. D., & Kohli, C. M. (2004). Cerebral hypoxia in severely brain-injured patients is associated with admission Glasgow Coma Scale score, computed tomographic severity, cerebral perfusion pressure, and survival. *Journal of Trauma-Injury Infection and Critical Care, 56*, 482–489.

Durmer, J. S., & Dinges, D. F. (2005). Neurocognitive consequences of sleep deprivation. *Seminars in Neurology, 25*, 117–129.

Edmondson, D. A., Nordness, M. E., Zacharisen, M. C., Kurup, V. P., & Fink, J. N. (2005). Allergy and "toxic mold syndrome." *Annals of Allergy, Asthma, and Immunology, 94*, 234–239.

Engleman, H. M., Kingshott, R. N., Martin, S. E., & Douglas, N. J. (2000). Cognitive function in the sleep apnea/hypopnea syndrome (SAHS). *Sleep, 23*(Suppl. 4), S102–S108.

Errebo-Knudsen, E. O., & Olsen, F. (1986). Organic solvents and presenile dementia (the painters' syndrome). A review of the Danish literature. *Science of the Total Environment, 48*, 45–67.

Eslava-Cobos, J., & Mejia, L. (1997). Landau–Kleffner syndrome: Much more than aphasia and epilepsy. *Brain and Language, 57*, 215–224.

Eysenck, M. W. (1991). Cognitive factors in clinical anxiety: Potential relevance to therapy. In M. Briley and S. E. File (Eds.), *New concepts in anxiety* (pp. 419–433). London: Macmillan.

Factor-Litvak, P., Hasselgren, G., Jacobs, D., Begg, M., Kline, J., Geier, J. et al. (2003). Mercury derived from dental amalgams and neuropsychologic function. *Environmental Health Perspectives, 111*, 719–723.

Feinstein, A., Ouchterlony, D., Somerville, J., & Jardine, A. (2001). The effects of litigation on symptoms expression: A prospective study following mild traumatic brain injury. *Medicine, Science and the Law, 41*, 116–121.

Fejerman, N., Caraballo, R., & Tenembaum, S. N. (2000). Atypical evolutions of benign localization-related epilepsies in children: Are they predictable. *Epilepsia, 41*, 380–390.

Feldman, R. G. (1999). *Occupational and environmental neurotoxicology*. Philadelphia: Lippencott-Raven.

Feldman, R. G., Chirico-Post, J., & Proctor, S. P. (1988). Blink reflex latency after exposure to trichloroethylene in well water. *Archives of Environmental Health, 43*, 143–148.

Feldman, R. G., Mayer, R. M., & Taub, A. (1970). Evidence for peripheral neurotoxic effect of trichloroethylene. *Neurology, 20*, 599–606.

Feldman, R. G., White, R. F., Eriator, I. I., Jabre, J. F., Feldman, E. S., & Niles, C. A. (1994). Neurotoxic effects of trichloroethylene in drinking water: Approach to diagnosis. In R. L. Isaacson & R. F. Jensen (Eds.), *The vulnerable brain and environmental risks* (pp. 3–23). New York: Plenum Press.

Filley, C. M., & Kleinschmidt-DeMasters, B. K. (2001). Toxic leukoencephalopathy. *The New England Journal of Medicine, 345*, 425–432.

Filley, C. M., Heaton, R. K., & Rosenberg, N. L. (1990). White matter dementia in chronic toluene abuse. *Neurology, 40*, 532–534.

Folb, P. I., Bernatowska, E., Chen, R., Clemens, J., Dodoo, A. N., Ellenberg, S. S., et al. (2004). A global perspective on vaccine safety and public health: The global advisory committee on vaccine safety. *American Journal of Public Health, 94*, 1926–1931.

Folstein, M. F., Folstein, S. E., & McHugh, P. R. (1975). "Mini-mental state." A practical method for grading the cognitive state of patients for the clinician. *Journal of Psychiatric Research, 12*, 189–198.

Folstein, S. E., & Folstein, M. F. (1983). Psychiatric features of Huntington's disease: Recent approaches and findings. *Psychiatric Developments, 1*, 193–205.

Fombonne, E. (2002). Prevalence of childhood disintegrative disorder. *Autism, 6*, 149–157.

Fombonne, E. (2003). Epidemiological surveys of autism and other pervasive developmental disorders: An update. *Journal of Autism and Developmental Disorders, 33*, 365–382.

Fombonne, E., & Chakrabarti, S. (2001). No evidence for a new variant of measles-mumps-rubella-induced autism. *Pediatrics, 108*, 58–65.

Food and Drug Administration. (FDA). (2005). *Thimerosal in vaccines*. Retreived July 18, 2005, from http://www.fda.gov/cber/vaccine/thimerosal.htm.

Ford, C. V. (1997). Somatization and fashionable diagnoses: Illness as a way of life. *Scandinavian Journal of Work and Environmental Health, 23*(Suppl. 3), 7–16.

Frazer, A., & Hensler, J. G. (1999). Serotonin. In G. J. Siegel, B. W. Agranoff, R. W. Albers, S. K. Fisher, & M. D. Uhler (Eds.), *Basic neurochemistry: Molecular, cellular and medical aspects* (6th ed., pp. 263–292). Philadelphia: Lippincott-Raven.

Frumkin, H., Ducatman, A., & Kirkland, K. (1997). Solvent exposure in the railroad industry (letter). *Journal of Occupational and Environmental Medicine, 39*, 926–930.

Fung, Y. K., Meade, A. G., Rack, E. P., Blotcky, A. J., Claassen, J. P., Beatty, M. W., et al. (1996). Mercury determination in nursing home patients with Alzheimer's disease. *Genetic Dentistry, 44*, 74–78.

Furhoff, A. K., Tomson, Y., Ilie, M., Bagedahl-Strindlund, M., Larsson, K. S., Sandborgh-Englund, G., et al. (1998). A multidisciplinary clinical study of patients suffering from illness associated with release of mercury from dental restorations. Medical and odontological aspects. *Scandinavian Journal of Primary Health Care, 16*, 247–252.

Furlan, P. M., DeMartinis, N., Schweizer, E., Rickels, K., & Lucki, I. (2001). Abnormal salivary cortisol in response to acute psychological but not physical stress. *Biological Psychiatry, 50*, 254–259.

Gade, A., Mortensen, L., & Bruhn, P. (1988). "Chronic painter's syndrome." A reanalysis of psychological test data in a group of diagnosed cases, based on comparisons with matched controls. *Acta Neurologica Scandinavica, 77*, 293–306.

Gallagher, D., Heymsfield, S. B., Heo, M., Jebb, S. A., Murgatroyd, P. R., & Sakamoto, Y. (2000). Healthy percentage body fat ranges: An approach for developing guidelines based on body mass index. *American Journal of Clinical Nutrition, 72*, 694–701.

Garabrant, D. H. (2000). Epidemiologic principles in the evaluation of suspected neurotoxic disorders. In J. W. Albers & S. Berent (Eds.), *Clincial neurobehavioral neurotoxicology* (pp. 631–648). Philadelphia: W.B. Saunders Co.

Geier, D. A., & Geier, M. R. (2004). Neurodevelopmental disorders following thimerosal-containing childhood immunizations: A follow-up analysis. *International Journal of Toxicology, 23*, 369–376.

Gellin, B. G., Maibach, E. W., & Marcuse, E. K. (2000). Do parents understand immunizations? A national telephone survey. *Pediatrics, 106*, 1097–1102.

Gervais, R. O., Russell, A. S., Green, P., Allen, L. M., Ferrari, R., & Pieschl, S. D. (2001). Effort testing in patients with fibromyalgia and disability incentives. *Journal of Rheumatology, 28*, 1892–1899.

Gillberg, C., & Coleman, M. (1992). *The biology of the autistic syndromes* (2nd ed.). Cambridge, UK: MacKeith Press.

Gillberg, C., & Coleman, M. (2000). *The biology of the autistic syndromes* (3rd ed.). Cambridge, UK: MacKeith Press.

Global Advisory Committee on Vaccine Safety, 2–3 December 2004. (2005). *Weekly Epidemiological Record, 80*, 3–7.

Goldberg, D. (1990). Reasons for misdiagnosis. In N. Sartorius, D. Goldberg, G. de Girolamo, J. Costa de Silva, Y. Lecrubier, & U. Wittchen (Eds.), *Psychological disorders in general medical settings* (pp. 139–145). Toronto: Hogrefe & Huber.

Goldberg, W. A., Osann, K., Filipek, P. A., Laulhere, T., Jarvis, K., Modahl, C., Flodman, P., & Spence, M. A. (2003). Language and other regression: Assessment and timing. *Journal of Autism and Developmental Disorders, 33*, 607–615.

Goldman, L., & Bennett, J. C. (2000). *Cecil textbook of medicine* (21st ed.). Philadelphia: W.B. Saunders.

Gordon, N. (1997). The Landau–Kleffner syndrome: Increased understanding. *Brain Development, 19*, 311–316.

Gordon, N. (2000). Cognitive functions and epileptic activity. *Seizure, 9*, 184–188.

Gordon, W. A., Cantor, J. B., Johanning, E., Charatz, H. J., Ashman, T. A., Breeze, J. L., Haddad, L., & Abramowitz, S. (2004). Cognitive impairments associated with toxigenic fungal exposure: A replication and extension of previous findings. *Applied Neuropsychology, 11*, 65–74.

Gottwald, B., Traenckner, I., Kupfer, J., Ganss, C., Eis, D., Schill, W. B. et al. (2001). "Amalgam disease"—poisoning, allergy, or psychic disorder? [comment]. *International Journal of Hygiene and Environmental Health, 204*, 223–229.

Grandjean, P., Weihe, P., White, R. F., Klintsova, A., Bates, K. E., & Weiler, I. J. (1997). Cognitive deficit in 7-year-old children with prenatal exposure to methylmercury. *Neurotoxicology and Teratology, 19*, 417–428.

Graves, A. B., Rosner, D., Echeverria, D., Mortimer, J. A., & Larson, E. B. (1998). Occupational exposures to solvents and aluminium and estimated risk of Alzheimer's disease. *Occupational and Environmental Medicine, 55*, 627–633.

Greden, J. F., Gardner, R., King, D., Grunhaus, L., Carroll, B. J., & Kronfol, Z. (1983). Dexamethasone suppression tests in antidepressant treatment of melancholia. The process of normalization and test-retest reproducibility. *Archives of General Psychiatry, 40*, 493–500.

Green, P., Rohling, M. L., Lees-Haley, P. R., & Allen, L. M. (2001). Effort has a greater effect on test scores than severe brain injury in compensation claimants. *Brain Injury, 15*, 1045–1060.

Gregersen, P., Angels, B., Nielsen, T. E., Nrgaard, B., & Uldal, C. (1987). Neurotoxic effects of organic solvents in exposed workers: An occupational, neuropsychological, and neurological investigation. *American Journal of Industrial Medicine, 5*, 201–225.

Grote, C., van Slyke, P., & Hoeppner, J. (1999). Language outcome following multiple subpial transaction for Landau–Kleffner syndrome. *Brain, 122*, 464–470.

Guberan, E., Usel, M., Raymond, L., Tissot, R., & Sweetnam, P. M. (1989). Disability, mortality, and incidence of cancer among Geneva painters and electricians: A historical prospective study. *British Journal of Industrial Medicine, 46*, 16–23.

Guccione, Jean (2003, May 9). Ed McMahon settles suit over mold for $7.2 Million. Los Angeles Times.

Guerrero, J. L., Thurman, D. J., & Sniezek, J. E. (2000). Emergency department visits associated with traumatic brain injury: United States, 1995–1996. *Brain Injury, 14*, 181–186.

Gun, R. T., Korten, A. E., Jorm, A. F., Henderson, A. S., Broe, G. A., Creasey, H., et al. (1997). Occupational risk factors for Alzheimer's disease: A case-control study. *Alzheimer's Disease and Associated Disorders, 11*, 21–27.

Haas, L. F. (2001). Phineas Gage and the science of brain localisation. *Journal of Neurology, Neurosurgery and Psychiatry, 71*, 761.

Hamilton, A. (2001). Beware: Toxic mold. *Time Magazine, 157*, 54–55.

Hardin, B. D., Kelman, B. J., & Saxon, A. (2003). Adverse human health effects associated with mold in the indoor environment. *Journal of Occupational and Environmental Medicine, 45*, 470–478.

Harmanci, H., Emre, M., Gurvit, H., Bilgic, B., Hanagasi, H., Gurol, E., et al. (2003). Risk factors for Alzheimer's disease: A population-based case-control study in Istanbul. *Alzheimer's Disease and Associated Disorders, 17*, 139–145.

Harris, G. (2005, July 19). No vaccine-autism link, parents are told. *The New York Times*. Retrieved July 22, 2005, from http://query.nytimes.com/gst/health/article-page.html?res=9D01EED8173CF933A15754C0A9639C8B63.

Hayden, M. (1981). *Huntington's chorea*. Berlin: Springer Verlag.

Heaton, R. K., Grant, I., & Matthews, C. G. (1991). *Comprehensive norms for an expanded Halstead-Reitan battery*. Odessa, FL: Psychological Assessment Resources, Inc.

Heiat, A., National Institutes of Health (NIH: The NIH Consensus Conference on Health Implications of Obesity in, United States Department of Agriculture (the, & National Heart, L. A. B. I. (2003). Impact of age on definition of standards for ideal weight. *Preventive Cardiology, 6,* 104–107.

Hendrix, A. (2001, March 8). Erin Brockovich crusades against mold. *San Francisco Chronicle,* p. A3.

Herskowitz, A., Ishii, N., & Schaumburg, H. H. (1971). *n*-Hexane neuropathy: A syndrome occurring as a result of industrial exposure. *New England Journal of Medicine, 285,* 82–85.

Hill, A. B. (1965). The environment and disease: Association or causation. *Proceedings of the Royal Society of medicine, 58,* 295–300.

Hilsabeck, R. C., Gouvier, W. D., & Bolter, J. F. (1998). Reconstructive memory bias in recall of neuropsychological symptomatology. *Journal of Clinical and Experimental Neuropsychology, 20,* 328–338.

Hirsch, E., Marescaux, C., Maquet, P., Metz-Lutz, M. N., Kiesmann, M., Salmon, E., et al. (1990). Landau–Kleffner syndrome: A clinical and EEG study of five cases. *Epilepsia, 31,* 756–767.

Hodgson, M. J., Morey, P., Leung, W., Morrow, L., Miller, D., Jarvis, B., Robbins, H., Halsey, J. F., & Storey, E. (1998). Building-associated pulmonary disease from exposure to stachybotrys chartarum and aspergillus vericolor. *Journal of Occupational and Environmental Medicine, 40,* 241–249.

Holmes, H., McKeever, M., & Saunders, Z. (1981). Epileptiform activity in aphasia of childhood: An epiphenomenon. *Epilepsia, 22,* 631–639.

Hoshino, Y., Kaneko, M., Yashima, Y., Kumashiro, H., Volkmar, F. R., & Cohen, D. J. (1987). Clinical features of autistic children with setback course in their infancy. *Japanese Journal of Psychiatry and Neurology, 41,* 237–246.

Hudson, J. I., Hudson, M. S., Griffing, G. T., Melby, J. C., & Pope, H. G., Jr. (1987). Phenomenology and family history of affective disorder in Cushing's disease. *American Journal of Psychiatry, 144,* 951–953.

Hughson, M. D., McCarty, G. A., Sholer, C. M., & Brumback, R. A. (1993). Thrombotic cerebral arteriopathy in patients with the antiphospholipid syndrome. *Modern Pathology, 6,* 644–653.

Humphrey, J. H., & McClelland, M. (1944). Cranial-nerve palsies with herpes following general anaesthesia. *British Medical Journal, 4,* 315–318.

Husman, K., & Karli, P. (1980). Clinical neurological findings among car painters exposed to a mixture of organic solvents. *Scandinavian Journal of Work, Environment and Health, 6,* 33–39.

Ihrig, A., Dietz, M. C., Bader, M., & Triebig, G. (2005). Longitudinal study to explore chronic neuropsychologic effects on solvent exposed workers. *Industrial Health, 43,* 588–596.

Iida, M. (1982). Neurophysiological studies in *n*-hexane polyneuropathy in the sandal factory. *Electroencephalography and Clinical Neurophysiology, 36*(Suppl.), 671–681.

Institute of Medicine. (2001). *Immunization safety review. Thimersol-containing vaccines and neurodevelopmental disorders.* Washington, DC: The National Academy Press.

Institute of Medicine. (2004). *Immunization safety review: Vaccines and autism.* Washington, DC: The National Academies Press.

Irwin, K., Birch, V., Lees, J., Polkey, C., Alarcon, G., Binnie, C., Smedley, M., Baird, G., & Robinson, R. O. (2001). Multiple subpial transection in Landau–Kleffner syndrome. *Developmental Medicine and Child Neurology, 43,* 248–252.

Jain, K. K. (1996). Drug-induced peripheral neuropathies. In *Drug-Induced Neurological disorders* (pp. 209–234). Seattle: Hogrefe & Huber Publishers.

Jain, R., Chartash, E., Susin, M., & Furie, R. (1994). Systemic lupus erythematosus complicated by thrombotic microangiopathy. *Seminars in Arthritis and Rheumatism, 24*, 173–182.

Jorgensen, O. S., Goldschmidt, V. V., & Vestergaard, B. F. (1982). Herpes simplex virus (HSV) antibodies in child psychiatric patients and normal children. *Acta Psychiatrica Scandinavica, 66*, 42–49.

Juntunen, J., Antti-Poika, M., Tola, S., & Partanen, T. (1982). Clinical prognosis of patients with diagnosed chronic solvent intoxication. *Acta Neurologica Scandinavica, 65*, 488–503.

Juntunen, J., Hupli, V., Hernberg, S., & Luisto, M. (1980). Neurological picture of organic solvent poisoning in industry. *International Archives of Occupational and Environmental Health, 46*, 219–231.

Kageyama, Y., Yamamoto, S., Ueno, M., & Ichikawa, K. (2003). A case of adult-onset Huntington disease presenting with spasticity and cerebellar ataxia, mimicking spinocerebellar degeneration [Japanese]. *Rinsho Shinkeigaku—Clinical Neurology, 43*, 16–19.

Kawasaki, Y., Yokota, K., Shinomiya, M., Shimizu, Y., & Niwa, S. (1997). Brief report: Electroencephalographic paroxysmal activities in the frontal area emerged in middle childhood and during adolescents in a follow-up study of autism. *Journal of Autism and Developmental Disorders, 27*, 605–630.

Kawashima, H., Mori, T., Kashiwagi, Y., Takekuma, K., Hoshika, A. & Wakefield, A., (2000). Detection and sequencing of measles virus from peripheral mononuclear cells from patients with inflammatory bowl disease and autism. *Digestive Diseases and Sciences, 45*, 723–729.

Kelly, D. A., Claypoole, K. H., & Coppel, D. B. (1990). Sleep apnea syndrome: Symptomatology, associated features, and neurocognitive correlates. *Neuropsychology Review, 1*, 323–342.

Kiesswetter, E., Sietmann, B., Zupanic, M., & Seeber, A. (2000). Neurobehavioral study on the interactive effects of age and solvent exposure. *Neurotoxicology, 21*, 685–695.

Kingman, A., Albertini, T., & Brown, L. J. (1998). Mercury concentrations in urine and whole blood associated with amalgam exposure in a US military population. *Journal of Dental Research, 77*, 461–471.

Klaassen, C. D. (1996). Heavy metals and heavy metal antagonists. In J. G.Hardman, L. E. Limbird, P. B. Molinoff, R. W. Ruddon, & A. G. Gilman (Eds.), *Goodman & Gilman's: The pharmacological basis of therapuetics* (9th ed., pp. 1649–1672). New York: McGraw-Hill.

Klaassen, C. D., & Watkins, J. B. (2003). *Casarett and Doull's essentials of toxicology.* New York: McGraw-Hill Medical Publishers.

Klinken, L., & Arlien-Soborg, P. (1993). Brain autopsy in organic solvent syndrome. *Acta Neurologica Scandinavica, 87*, 371–375.

Kobayashi, R., & Murata, T. (1998). Setback phenomenon in autism and long-term prognosis. *Acta Psychiatrica Scandinavica, 98*, 296–303.

Koger, S. M., Schettler, T., & Weiss, B. (2005). Environmental toxicants and developmental disabilities: A challenge for psychologists. *American Psychologist, 60*, 243–255.

Kolanowski, J. (1999). Obesity and hypertension: From pathophysiology to treatment. *International Journal of Obesity and Related Metabolic Disorders, 23*(Suppl. 1), 42–46.

Koo, E. H., & Massey, E. W. (1988). Granulomatous angiitis of the central nervous system: Protean manifestations and response to treatment. *Journal of Neurology, Neurosurgery and Psychiatry, 51*, 1126–1133.

Korgeski, G. P., & Leon, G. R. (1983). Correlates of self-reported and objectively determined exposure to Agent Orange. *American Journal of Psychiatry, 140*, 1443–1449.

Kramer, U., Nevo, Y., Neufeld, M. Y., Fatal, A., Leitner, Y., & Harel, S. (1998). Epidemiology of epilepsy in childhood: A cohort of 440 consecutive patients. *Pediatric Neurology, 18*, 46–50.

Kringlen, E. (1999). Psychiatric aspects of the "amalgam disease." *Tidsskrift for Den Norske Laegeforening, 119*, 3461–3464.

Kuhl, D. E., Phelps, M. E., Markham, C. H., Metter, E. J., Riege, W. H., & Winter, J. (1982). Cerebral metabolism and atrophy in Huntington's disease determined by 18FDG and computed tomographic scan. *Annals of Neurology, 12*, 425–434.

Kuhn, D. M., & Ghannoum, M. A. (2003). Indoor mold, toxigenic fungi, and *Stachybotrys chartarum*: Infectious disease perspective. *Clinical Microbiology Review, 16*, 144–172.

Kukull, W. A., Larson, E. B., Bowen, J. D., McCormick, W. C., Teri, L., Pfanschmidt, M. L. et al. (1995). Solvent exposure as a risk factor for Alzheimer's disease: A case-control study [published erratum appears in Am J Epidemiol Aug 15;142 (4):450 (1995)]. *American Journal of Epidemiology, 141*, 1059–1071.

Kurita, H. (1985). Infantile autism with speech loss before the age of thirty months. *Journal of the American Academy of Child and Adolescent Psychiatry, 24*, 191–196.

Kurita, H., Kita, M., & Miyake, Y. (1992). A comparative study of development and symptoms among disintegrative psychosis and infantile autism with and without speech loss. *Journal of Autism and Developmental Disorders, 22*, 175–188.

Kurita, H., Osada, H., & Miyake, Y. (2004). External validity of childhood disintegrative disorder in comparison with autistic disorder. *Journal of Autism and Developmental Disorders, 34*, 355–362.

Kwaan, H. C., & Gordon, L. I. (2001). Thrombotic microangiopathy in the cancer patient. *Acta Haematologica, 106*, 52–56.

Labarge, A. S., & McCaffrey, R. J. (2000). Multiple chemical sensitivity: A review of the theoretical and research literature. *Neuropsychology Review, 10*, 183–211.

Labreche, F. P., Cherry, N. M., & McDonald, J. C. (1992). Psychiatric disorders and occupational exposure to solvents. *British Journal of Industrial Medicine, 49*, 820–825.

Landrigan, P. J., Kominsky, J. R., & Ruhe, R. L. (1987). Common-source community and industrial exposure to trichloroethylene. *Archives of Environmental Health, 42*, 327–332.

Lange, H. W. (1981). Quantitative changes of telencephalon, diencephalon and mesencephalon in Huntington's chorea, postencephalitic and idiopathic parkinsonism. *Verth Anat Ges, 75*, 923–925.

Langlois, J. A., Rutland-Brown, W., & Thomas, K. E. (2004). *Traumatic brain injury in the United States: Emergency department visits, hospitalizations, and deaths.* Atlanta, Georgia, USA: U.S. Government, CDC, National Center for Injury Prevention and Control.

Langworth, S., Bjorkman, L., Elinder, C. G., Jarup, L., & Savlin, P. (2002). Multidisciplinary examination of patients with illness attributed to dental fillings. *Journal of Oral Rehabilitation, 29*, 705–713.

Larner, A. J. (2003). Obstructive sleep apnoea syndrome presenting in a neurology outpatient clinic. *International Journal of Clinical Practice, 57,* 150–152.

Larrabee, G. J. (2003). Exaggerated pain report in litigants with malingered neurocognitive dysfunction. *The Clinical Neuropsychologist, 17,* 395–401.

Lash, A. A., Becker, C. E., So, Y., & Shore, M. (1991). Neurotoxic effects of methylene chloride: Are they long lasting in humans? *British Journal of Industrial Medicine, 48,* 418–426.

Lattimore, J. D., Celermajer, D. S., & Wilcox, I. (2003). Obstructive sleep apnea and cardiovascular disease. *Journal of the American College of Cardiology, 41,* 1429–1437.

Laudignon, N., & Rebuffe-Scrive, M. (1997). Overview of the safety data. In S. Nicoadis (Ed.), *Obesity management and redux* (pp. 105–111). San Diego: Academic Press, Ltd.

Le Carret, N., Lafont, S., & Letenneur, L. (2003). The effect of education on cognitive performances and its implication for the constitution of the cognitive reserve. *Developmental Neuropsychology, 23,* 317–337.

Leech, P. N. (1936). The use of trichloroethylene for general anesthesia. *Journal of the American Medical Association, 107,* 1302.

Lees-Haley, P. R. (1992). Neuropsychological complaint base rates of personal injury claimants. *Forensic Reports, 5,* 385–391.

Lees-Haley, P. R. (2002). Mold neurotoxicity: Validity, reliability, and baloney. Presented at the conference, "Mold Medicine and Mold Science: Its Practical Applications for Patient Care, Remediation, and Claims," hosted by the International Center for Toxicology and Medicine and the Georgetown University Department of Pharmacology. May 13–14, 2002.

Lees-Haley, P. R. (2004). Commentary on neuropsychological performance of patients following mold exposure. *The Scientific Review of Mental Health Practice, 3,* 60–66.

Lees-Haley, P. R., Greiffenstein, M. F., Larrabee, G. J., & Manning, E. L. (2004). Methodological problems in the neuropsychological assessment of effects of exposure to welding fumes and manganese. *The Clinical Neuropsychologist, 18,* 449–464.

Lees-Haley, P. R., & Williams, C. W. (1997). Neurotoxicity of chronic low-dose exposure to organic solvents: A skeptical review. *Journal of Clinical Psychology, 53,* 699–712.

Lefaucheur, J. P., Bachoud-Levi, A. C., Bourdet, C., Grandmougin, T., Hantraye, P., Cesaro, P. et al. (2002). Clinical relevance of electrophysiological tests in the assessment of patients with Huntington's disease. *Movement Disorders, 17,* 1294–1301.

Leonhardt, T. (2001). The "dental amalgam syndrome"—an environmental somatization Syndrome? A comparison between chronic carbon monoxide intoxication and illness related to dental amalgam. *Dansk Medicinhistorisk Arbog,* 177–186.

Lerman, P., Lerman-Sagie, T., & Kivity, S. (1991). Effect of early corticosteroid therapy for Landau–Kleffner syndrome. *Developmental Medicine and Child Neurology, 33,* 257–260.

Levin, H. S., Benton, A. L., & Grossman, R. G. (1982). *Neurobehavioral consequences of closed head injury.* New York: Oxford University Press.

Levine, S. R., Langer, S. L., Albers, J. W., & Welch, K. M. (1988). Sneddon's syndrome: An antiphospholipid antibody syndrome?. *Neurology, 38,* 798–800.

Lewine, J. D., Andrews, R., Chez, M., Patil, A. A., Devinsky, O., Smith, M., et al. (1999). Magnetoencephalographic patterns of epileptiform activity in children with regressive autism spectrum disorders. *Pediatrics, 104,* 405–418.

Lezak, M. D. (1988). IQ: R.I.P. *Journal of Clinical and Experimental Neuropsychology*, *10*, 351–361.

Libbey, J. E., Sweeten, T. L., McMahon, W. M., & Fujinami, R. S. (2005). Autistic disorder and viral infections. *Journal of NeuroVirology*, *11*, 1–10.

Linz, D. H., Morton, W. E., Wiens, A. N., Coull, B. M., & Maricle, R. A. (1986). Organic solvent-induced encephalopathy in industrial painters. *Journal of Occupational Medicine*, *28*, 119–125.

Liu, Z. (2000). The surgical treatment of intractable epilepsy. *Stereotactic and Functional Neurosurgery*, *75*, 81–89.

Lundberg, I., Gustavsson, A., Hogberg, M., & Nise, G. (1992). Diagnoses of alcohol abuse and other neuropsychiatric disorders among house painters compared with house carpenters. *British Journal of Industrial Medicine*, *49*, 409–415.

Mace, C. J., & Trimble, M. R. (1996). Ten-year prognosis of conversion disorder. *British Journal of Psychiatry*, *169*, 282–288.

Madsen, K. M., Hviid, A., Vestergaard, M., et al. (2002). A population-based study of measles, mumps, and rubella vaccination and autism. *New England Journal of Medicine*, *347*, 1477–1482.

Magos, L., Brown, A. W., Sparrow, S., Bailey, E., Snowden, R. T., & Skipp, W. R. (1985). The comparative toxicology of ethyl- and methylmercury. *Archives of Toxicology*, *57*, 260–267.

Maizlish, N. A., Fine, L. J., Albers, J. W., Whitehead, L., & Langolf, G. D. (1987). A neurological evaluation of workers exposed to mixtures of organic solvents. *British Journal of Internal Medicine*, *44*, 14–25.

Maizlish, N. A., Langolf, G. D., Whitehead, L. W., Fine, L. J., Albers, J. W., Goldberg, J., et al. (1985). Behavioural evaluation of workers exposed to mixtures of organic solvents. *British Journal of Internal Medicine*, *42*, 579–590.

Makela, A., Nuorti, J. P., & Peltola, H. (2002). Neurologic disorders after measles-mumps-rubella vaccination. *Pediatrics*, *110*, 957–963.

Malhotra, S., & Gupta, N. (1999). Childhood disintegrative disorder. *Journal of Autism and Developmental Disorders*, *29*, 491–498.

Malhotra, S., & Singh, S. (1993). Disintegrative psychosis of childhood: An appraisal and case study. *Acta Paedopsychiatricia*, *56*, 37–40.

Malhotra, S., & Singh, S. (2002). Childhood disintegrative disorder: A re-examination of the current concept. *European Child and Adolescent Psychiatry*, *11*, 108–114.

Malt, U. F., Nerdrum, P., Oppedal, B., Gundersen, R., Holte, M., & Lone, J. (1997). Physical and mental problems attributed to dental amalgam fillings: A descriptive study of 99 self-referred patients compared with 272 controls. *Psychosomatic-Medicine*, *59*, 32–41.

Manzoni, M., & Rollini, M. (2002). Biosynthesis and biotechnological production of statins by filamentous fungi and application of these cholesterol-lowering drugs. *Applied Microbiology and Biotechnology*, *58*, 555–564.

Marks, J. N., Goldberg, D. P., & Hillier, V. F. (1979). Determinants of the ability of general practitioners to detect psychiatric illness. *Psychological Medicine*, *9*, 337–353.

Martin, J. B. (1984). Huntington's disease: New approaches to an old problem. The Robert Wartenberg lecture. *Neurology*, *34*, 1059–1072.

Martin, J. B., & Beal, M. F. (1992). Huntington's disease and neurotoxins. In J. W. Langston & A. Young (Eds.), *Neurotoxins and neurodegenerative disease* (pp. 169–175). New York: The New York Academy of Sciences.

Matikainen, E., & Juntunen, J. (1985). Autonomic nervous system dysfunction in workers exposed to organic solvents. *Journal of Neurology, Neurosurgery and Psychiatry, 48*, 1021–1024.

McCann, U. D., Eligulashvili, V., & Ricaurte, G. A. (1998). Adverse neuropsychiatric events associated with dexfenfluramine and fenfluramine. *Progress in Neuro-Psychopharmacology and Biological Psychiatry, 22*, 1087–1102.

McCann, U. D., Seiden, L. S., Rubin, L. J., & Ricaurte, G. A. (1997). Brain serotonin neurotoxicity and primary pulmonary hypertension from fenfluramine and dexfenfluramine. A systematic review of the evidence. *Journal of the American Medical Association, 278*, 666–672.

McEwen, B. S. (2000). The neurobiology of stress: From serendipity to clinical relevance. *Brain Research, 886*, 172–189.

McGonagle, T. K., Levine, S. R., Donofrio, P. D., & Albers, J. W. (1990). Spectrum of patients with EMG features of polyradiculopathy without neuropathy. *Muscle and Nerve, 13*, 63–69.

McLaughlin, J. K., & Blot, W. J. (1997). A critical review of epidemiology studies of trichloroethylene and perchloroethylene and risk of renal-cell cancer. *International Archives of Occupational and Environmental Health, 70*, 222–231.

McMahon, J. P., Foresman, B. H., & Chisholm, R. C. (2003). The influence of CPAP on the neurobehavioral performance of patients with obstructive sleep apnea hypopnea syndrome: A systematic review. *Wisconsin Medical Journal, 102*, 36–43.

Meadows, M. (2001). Understanding vaccine safety: Immunization remains our best defense against deadly disease. *FDA Consumer Magazine, 35*, 18–23.

Medoff, G., & Kobayashi, G. S. (1991). Systemic fungal infections: An overview. *Hospital Practice, 26*, 41–52.

Melchart, D., Wuhr, E., Weidenhammer, W., & Kremers, L. (1998). A multicenter survey of amalgam fillings and subjective complaints in non-selected patients in the dental practice. *European Journal of Oral Sciences, 106*, 770–777.

Mikkelsen, S. (1980). A cohort study of disability pension and death among painters with special regard to disabling presenile dementia as an occupational disease. *Scandanavian Journal of Social Medicine Suppl. 16*, 34–43.

Miller, G. E., Stetler, C. A., Carney, R. M., Freedland, K. E., & Banks, W. A. (2002). Clinical depression and inflammatory risk markers for coronary heart disease. *American Journal of Cardiology, 90*, 1279–1283.

Mittenberg, W., Patton, C., Canyock, E. M., & Condit, D. C. (2002). Base rates of malingering and symptoms exaggeration. *Journal of Clinical and Experimental Neuropsychology, 24*, 1094–1102.

Moceri, V. M., Kukull, W. A., Emanual, I., van Belle, G., Starr, J. R., Schellenberg, G. D. et al. (2001). Using census data and birth certificates to reconstruct the early-life socioeconomic environment and the relation to the development of Alzheimer's disease. *Epidemiology, 12*, 383–389.

Moore, P. M., & Cupps, T. R. (1983). Neurological complications of vasculitis. *Annals of Neurology, 14*, 155–167.

Morrell, F., & Hanbery, J. W. (1969). A new surgical technique for the treatment of focal cortical epilepsy. *EEG Clinical Neurophysiology, 26*, 120.

Mortimer, J. A. (1988). Do psychosocial factors contribute to Alzheimer's disease? In J. H. Henderson and A. S. Henderson (Eds.), *Etiology of dementia of Alzheimer's type* (pp. 39–52). New York: Wiley.

Morton, W. E. (2002). Solvent-induced toxic encephalopathy. *Journal of Occupational and Environmental Medicine, 44,* 393–394.

Mouridsen, S. E., Rich, B., & Isager, T. (1998). Validity of childhood disintegrative psychosis. General findings of a long-term follow-up study. *British Journal of Psychiatry, 172,* 263–267.

Muller, U., Mottweiler, E., & Bublak, P. (2005). Noradrenergic blockade and numeric working memory in humans. *Journal of Psychopharmacology, 19,* 21–28.

Murer, L., Zacchello, G., Bianchi, D., Dall'Amico, R., Montini, G., Andreetta, B. et al. (2000). Thrombotic microangiopathy associated with parvovirus B 19 infection after renal transplantation. *Journal of the American Society of Nephrology, 11,* 1132–1137.

Mutter, J., & Daschner, F. D. (2003). Commentary regarding the article by Gottwald et al.: "Amalgam disease"—poisoning, allergy, or psychic disorder? Int J Hyg Environ Health 204, 223–229 (2001). *International Journal of Hygiene and Environmental Health, 206,* 69–70.

Muttray, A., Martus, P., Schachtrup, S., Muller, E., Mayer-Popken, O., & Konietzko, J. (2005). Acute effects of an organic solvent mixture on the human central nervous system. *European Journal of Medical Research, 10,* 381–388.

Myers, G. J., Davidson, P. W., Cox, C., Shamlaye, C. F., Palumbo, D., Cernichiari, E., et al. (2003). Prenatal methylmercury exposure from ocean fish consumption in the Seychelles Child Development Study. *Lancet, 361,* 1686–1692.

Nadeau, S. E. (1985). Collagen vascular disease: Vasculitis, systemic lupus erythematosus, and rhuemoid arthritis. *Seminars in Neurology, 5,* 324–343.

Nash, R., Gross, A., & Devinsky, O. (1998). Autism and autistic epileptiform regression with occipital spikes. *Developmental Medicine and Child Neurology, 40,* 453–458.

Nash, R., & Petrucha, D. (1990). Epileptic aphasia: A pervasive developmental disorder variant. *Journal of Child Neurology, 5,* 327–328.

National Institute for Occupational Safety and Health (NIOSH). (2004). Work-related injury statistics query system (Work-RISQS). Retrieved from http://www2.cdc.gov/risqs/default.asp

National Institutes of Health. (1993). *Advisory panel on Alzheimer's disease. Fourth report of the advisory panel on Alzheimer's disease, 1992* (Rep. No. NIH pub. No. 93–3520). Washington, DC: Superintendent of documents, U.S. Government Printing Office.

National Research Council. (2000). *Toxicological effects of methylmercury.* Washington, DC: National Academy Press.

Neau, J. P., Paquereau, J., Bailbe, M., Meurice, J. C., Ingrand, P., & Gil, R. (2002). Relationship between sleep apnoea syndrome, snoring and headaches. *Cephalalgia, 22,* 333–339.

Nelson, N. A., Robins, T. G., White, R. F., & Garrison, R. P. (1994). A case-control study of chronic neuropsychiatric disease and organic solvent exposure in automobile assembly plant workers. *Occupational and Environmental Medicine, 51,* 302–307.

Newman, S., Klinger, L., Venn, G., Smith, P., Harrison, M., & Treasure, T. (1989). Subjective reports of cognition in relation to assessed cognitive performance following coronary artery bypass surgery. *Journal of Psychomatic Research, 33,* 227–233.

Nilson, L. N., Sallsten, G., Hagberg, S., Backman, L., & Barregard, L. (2002). Influence of solvent exposure and aging on cognitive functioning: An 18 year follow up of formerly exposed floor layers and their controls. *Occupational and Environmental Medicine, 59,* 49–57.

Nimnuan, C., Hotopf, M., & Wessely, S. (2000). Medically unexplained symptoms: How often and why are they missed? *Quarterly Journal of Medicine, 93,* 21–28.

Nimnuan, C., Hotopf, M., & Wessely, S. (2001). Medically unexplained symptoms: An epidemiological study in seven specialties. *Journal of Psychosomatic Research, 51,* 361–367.

Nitschke, I., Muller, F., Smith, J., & Hopfenmuller, W. (2000). Amalgam fillings and cognitive abilities in a representative sample of the elderly population. *Gerodontology., 17,* 39–44.

Noble, R. E. (1997). An 18-month study of the effects of dexfenfluramine on cognitive function in obese american patients. In S. Nicoadis (Ed.), *Obesity management and redux* (pp. 93–97). San Diego, CA: Academic Press, Ltd.

O'Donohue, W., & Cucciare, M. A. (2005). The role of psychological factors in medical presentations. *Journal of Clinical Psychology in Medical Settings, 12*(1), 13–24.

O'Flynn, R. R., Monkman, S. M., & Waldron, H. A. (1987). Organic solvents and presenile dementia: A case referent study using death certificates. *British Journal of Industrial Medicine, 44,* 259–262.

Olsen, J., & Sabroe, S. (1980). A case-reference study of neuropsychiatric disorders among workers exposed to solvents in the Danish wood and furniture industry. *Scandanavian Journal of Social Medicine, 16,* 44–49.

Olsson, I., Steffenburg, S., & Gillberg, C. (1998). Epilepsy in autism and autistic-like conditions: A population-based study. *Archives of Neurology, 45,* 666–668.

O'Neill, A. (2002, April 10). Ed McMahon Sues Over Mold in House; Courts: Entertainer seeks $20 million from insurer, alleging he was sickened by substance after botched repair. *The Los Angeles Times,* pp. C1.

Orbaek, P., & Lindgren, M. (1988). Prospective clinical and psychometric investigation of patients with chronic toxic encephalopathy induced by solvents. *Scandinavian Journal of Work, Environment and Health, 14,* 37–44.

Osterling, J. A., Dawson, D., & Munson, J. A. (2002). Early recognition of 1-year-old infants with autism spectrum disorder versus mental retardation. *Development and Psychopathology, 14,* 239–251.

Osuchowski, M. F., Edwards, G. L., & Sharma, R. P. (2005). Fumonisin B1-induced neurodegeneration in mice after intracerebroventricular infusion is concurrent with disruption of sphingolipid metabolism and activation of proinflammatory signaling. *Neurotoxicology, 26,* 211–221.

Owens, S. R. (2002). Injection of confidence: The recent controversy in the UK has led to falling MMR vaccination rates. *EMBO Reports, 3,* 406–409.

Palmer, K., Inskip, H., Martyn, C., & Coggon, D. (1998). Dementia and occupational exposure to organic solvents. *Occupational and Environmental Medicine, 55,* 712–715.

Paniak, C., Reynolds, S., Phillips, K., Toller-Lobe, G., Melnyk, A., & Nagy, J. (2002). Patient complaints within 1 month of mild traumatic brain injury: A controlled study. *Archives of Clinical Neuropsychology, 17,* 319–334.

Parker, S. K., Schwartz, B., Todd, J., & Pickering, L. K. (2004). Thimerosal-containing vaccines and autistic-spectrum disorder: A critical review of published original data. *Pediatrics, 114,* 793–804.

Paterniti, S., Dufouil, C., Bisserbe, J. C., & Alpérovitch, A. (1999). Anxiety, depression, psychotropic drug use and cognitive impairment. *Psychological Medicine, 29,* 421–428.

Paulson, G. W., & Waylonis, G. W. (1976). Polyneuropathy due to *n*-hexane. *Archives of Internal Medicine, 136,* 880–882.

Pfab, R., Muckter, H., Roider, G., & Zilker, T. (1996). Clinical course of severe poisoning with thiomersal. *Clinical Toxicology, 34,* 453–460.

Pichichero, M. E., Cernichiari, E., Lopreiato, J., & Treanor, J. (2002). Mercury concentrations and metabolism in infants receiving vaccines containing thiomerisal: A descriptive study. *Lancet, 360,* 1737–1741.

Pisoni, R., Ruggenenti, P., & Remuzzi, G. (2001). Drug-induced thrombotic micro-angiopathy: Incidence, prevention and management. *Drug Safety, 24,* 491–501.

Portnoy, J. M., Kwak, K., Dowling, P., VanOsdol, T., & Barnes, C. (2005). Health Effects of Indoor Fungi. *Annals of Allergy, Asthma, Immunology, 94,* 313–319.

Powell, H. M., & Jamieson, W. A. (1931). Merthiolate as a germicide. *American Journal of Hygiene, 13,* 296–310.

Ramasubbu, K., Mullick, T., Koo, A., Hussein, M., Henderson, J. M., Mullen, K. D., & Avery, R. K. (2003). Thrombotic microangiopathy and cytomegalovirus in liver transplant recipients: A case-based review. *Transplant Infectious Disease, 5,* 98–103.

Rapin, I. (1995). Autistic regression and disintegrative disorder: How important the role of epilepsy?. *Seminars in Pediatric Neurology, 2,* 278–285.

Rapin, I., & Katzman, R. (1998). Neurobiology of autism. *Annals of Neurology, 43,* 7–14.

Rea, W. J., Didriksen, N., Simon, T. R., Pan, Y., Fenyves, E. J., & Griffiths, B. (2003). Effects of toxic exposure to molds and mycotoxins in building-related illnesses. *Archives of Environmental Health, 58,* 399–405.

Reichart, M. D., Bogousslavsky, J., & Janzer, R. C. (2000). Early lacunar strokes complicating polyarteritis nodosa: Thrombotic microangiopathy. *Neurology, 54,* 883–889.

Report of the Therapeutics and Technology Subcommittee of the American Academy of Neurology. (1996). Assessment: Neuropsychological testing in adults. Considerations for neurologists. *Neurology, 47,* 592–599.

Ricaurte, G. A., Yuan, J., Hatzidimitriou, G., Cord, B. J., & McCann, U. D. (2002). Severe dopaminergic neurotoxicity in primates after a common recreational dose regimen of MDMA ("ecstasy"). *Science, 297,* 2260–2263.

Richardson, W. S., Wilson, M. C., Williams, J. W. J., Moyer, V. A., & Naylor, C. D. (2000). Users' guides to the medical literature: XXIV. How to use an article on the clinical manifestations of disease. *Journal of the American Medical Association, 284,* 869–875.

Ridgway, P., Nixon, T. E., & Leach, J. P. (2003). Occupational exposure to organic solvents and long-term nervous system damage detectable by brain imaging, neurophysiology or histopathology. *Food and Chemical Toxicology, 41,* 153–187.

Riise, T., & Moen, B. E. (1990). A nested case-control study of disability pension among seamen, with special reference to neuropsychiatric disorders and exposure to solvents. *Neuroepidemiology, 9,* 88–94.

Riise, T., Kyvik, K. R., & Moen, B. (1995). A cohort study of disability pensioning among Norwegian painters, construction workers, and workers in food processing. *Epidemiology, 6,* 132–136.

Risch, N., Spiker, D., Lotspeich, L., Nouri, N., Hinds, D., Hallmayer, J., et al. (1999). A genomic screen of autism: Evidence for a multilocus etiology. *American Journal of Human Genetics, 65,* 493–507.

Robbins, C. A., Swenson, L. J., Neally, M. L., Gots, R. E., & Kelman, B. J. (2000). Health effects of mycotoxins in indoor air: A critical review. *Applied Occupational and Environmental Hygiene, 15,* 773–784.

Robinson, R. O., Baird, G., Robinson, G., & Simonoff, E. (2001). Landau–Kleffner syndrome: Course and correlates with outcome. *Developmental Medicine and Child Neurology, 43,* 243–247.

Rogers, S. (2004). Developmental regression in autism spectrum disorders. *Mental Retardation and Developmental Disabilities Research Reviews, 10,* 139–143.

Rogers, S. J., & DiLalla, D. L. (1990). Age of symptom onset in young children with pervasive developmental disorders. *Journal of the American Academy of Child and Adolescent Psychiatry, 29,* 863–872.

Rosen, R. C., & Kostis, J. B. (1985). Biobehavioral sequelae associated with adrenergic-inhibiting antihypertensive agents: A critical review. *Health Psychology, 4,* 579–604.

Rosenberg, N. L. (1995). Neurotoxicity of organic solvents. In N. L. Rosenberg (Ed.), *Occupational and environmental neurology* (pp. 71–113). Boston: Butterworth-Heinemann.

Rosenthal, R., & Jacobson, L. (1968). *Pygmalion in the Classroom: Teacher expectation and Pupils' intellectual development.* New York: Holt, Rinehart & Winston, Inc.

Roulet Perez, E., Davidoff, V., Despland, P. A., & Deonna, T. (1993). Mental and behavioural deterioration of children with epilepsy and CSWS: Acquired epileptic frontal syndrome. *Developmental Medicine and Child Neurology, 35,* 661–674.

Roux, F. J., & Hilbert, J. (2003). Continuous positive airway pressure: New generations. *Clinics in Chest Medicine, 24,* 315–342.

Rowan, P. J., Davidson, K., Campbell, J. A., Dobrez, D. G., & MacLean, D. R. (2002). Depressive symptoms predict medical care utilization in a population-based sample. *Psychological Medicine, 32,* 903–908.

Rowland, R. W. (1989). *Merritt's textbook of neurology* (8th ed.). Philadelphia: Lea & Febiger.

Sahakian, B. J. (1991). Depressive pseudodementia in the elderly. *International Journal of Geriatric Psychiatry, 6,* 453–458.

Sallsten, G., Thoren, J., Barregard, L., Schutz, A., & Skarping, G. (1996). Long-term use of nicotine chewing gum and mercury exposure from dental amalgam fillings. *Journal of Dental Research, 75,* 594–598.

Sandberg, P. R., & Coyle, J. T. (1984). Scientific approaches to Huntington's disease. *CRC Critical Reviews in Clinical Neurobiology, 1,* 1–44.

Santiago, K., Batuman, V., & Meleg-Smith, S. (1996). A 31-year-old woman with lupus erythematosus and fatal multisystem complications. *Journal of the Louisiana State Medical Society, 148,* 379–384.

Sapolsky, R. M. (2000). Glucocorticoids and hippocampal atrophy in neuropsychiatric disorders. *Archives of General Psychiatry, 57,* 925–935.

Sateia, M. J. (2003). Neuropsychological impairment and quality of life in obstructive sleep apnea. *Clinics in Chest Medicine, 24,* 249–259.

Sawhney, I. M., Robertson, I. J., Polkey, C. E., et al. (1995). Multiple subpial transactions: A review of 21 cases. *Journal of Neurology, Neurosurgery, and Psychiatry, 58,* 344–349.

Scelsi, R., Poggi, P., Fera, L., & Gonella, G. (1981). Industrial neuropathy due to n-hexane: Clinical and morphological findings in three cases. *Clinical Toxicology, 18,* 1387–1393.

Schaper, M., Demes, P., Kiesswetter, E., Zupanic, M., & Seeber, A. (2004). Colour vision and occupational toluene exposure: Results of repeated examinations. *Toxicology Letters, 151,* 193–202.

Schaumburg, H. H., & Albers, J. W. (2005). Pseudoneurotoxic disease. *Neurology*, *65*, 22–26.

Schaumburg, H. H., & Spencer, P. S. (1987). Recognizing neurotoxic disease. *Neurology*, *37*, 276–278.

Scheen, A. J., & Lefebvre, P. J. (1999). Pharmacological treatment of obesity: Present status. *International Journal of Obesity and Related Metabolic Disorders*, *23*(Suppl. 1), 47–53.

Schenck, C. H., & Mahowald, M. W. (1996). Potential hazard of serotonin syndrome associated with dexfenfluramine hydrochloride (Redux). *Journal of the American Medical Association*, *276*, 1220–1221.

Schmidley, J. W. (2000). Isolated central nervous system angiitis: Clinical aspects. In *Central nervous system angiitis* (pp. 1–28). Boston: Butterworth Heinemann.

Schmidley, J. W. (2000a). Diagnosis and therapy: Isolated CNS angiitis. In *central nervous system angiitis* (pp. 43–59). Boston: Butterworth Heinemann.

Schmidley, J. W. (2000b). Isolated CNS angiitis: Clinical aspects. In *central nervous system angiitis* (pp. 1–22). Boston: Butterworth Heinemann.

Schoenberg, V. S. (1982). Descriptive neuroepidemiology: Applications to occupational neurology. *Acta Neurologica Scandinavica*, *66*(Suppl. 92), 1–9.

Seeber, A., Schaper, M., Zupanic, M., Blaszkewicz, M., Demes, P., Kiesswetter, E. et al. (2004). Toluene exposure below 50 ppm and cognitive function: A follow-up study with four repeated measurements in rotogravure printing plants. *International Archives of Occupational and Environmental Health*, *77*, 1–9.

Seppalainen, A. M. (1981). Neurophysiological findings among workers exposed to organic solvents. *Scandinavian Journal of Work, Environment and Health*, *7* (Suppl.), 29–33.

Seppalainen, A. M., Husman, K., & Martinson, C. (1978). Neurophysiological effects of long-term exposure to a mixture of organic solvents. *Scandinavian Journal of Work, Environment and Health*, *4*, 304–314.

Sethre, T., Laubli, T., Hangartner, M., Berode, M., & Krueger, H. (2000). Isopropanol and methylformate exposure in a foundry: Exposure data and neurobehavioural measurements. *International Archives of Occupational and Environmental Health*, *73*, 528–536.

Shalat, S. L., Seltzer, B., & Baker, E. L., Jr. (1988). Occupational risk factors and Alzheimer's disease: A case-control study. *Journal of Occupational Medicine*, *30*, 934–936.

Shoulson, I. (1981). Huntington disease: Functional capacities in patients treated with neuroleptic and antidepressant drugs. *Neurology*, *31*, 1333–1335.

Shoulson, I. (1982). Care of patients and families with Huntington's disease. In C. D. Marsden (Ed.), *Movement disorders* (pp. 277–290). London: Butterworth.

Shoulson, I. (1984). Huntington's disease. A decade of progress. *Neurologic Clinics*, *2*, 515–526.

Sinclair, D. B., & Snyder, T. J. (2005). Corticosteroids for the treatment of Landau–Kleffner syndrome and continuous spike-wave discharge during sleep. *Pediatric Neurology*, *32*, 300–306.

Singh, V. K., Lin, S. X., Newell, E., & Nelson, C. (2002). Abnormal measles-mumps-rubella antibodies and central nervous system autoimmunity in children with autism. *Journal of Biomedical Science*, *9*, 359–364.

Singh, V. K., Lin, S. X., & Yang, V. C. (1998). Serological association of measles virus and human herpesvirus 6 with brain autoantibodies in autism. *Clinical Immunology and Immunopathology*, *89*, 105–108.

Siperstein, R., & Volkmar, F. (2004). Brief report: Parental reporting of regression in children with pervasive developmental disorders. *Journal of Autism and Developmental Disorders, 34,* 731–734.

Smeeth, L., Cook, C., Fombonne, E., Heavey, L., Rodriguqes, L. C., Smith, P. G., & Hall, A. J. (2004). MMR vaccination and pervasive developmental disorders: A case control study. *The Lancet, 364,* 963–969.

Smith, M. C., & Hoeppner, T. J. (2003). Epileptic encephalopathy of late childhood: Landau–Kleffner syndrome and the syndrome of continuous spikes and waves during slow-wave sleep. *Journal of Clinical Neurophysiology, 20,* 462–472.

Snowden, J. S., Craufurd, D., Thompson, J., & Neary, D. (2002). Psychomotor, executive, and memory function in preclinical Huntington's disease. *Journal of Clinical and Experimental Neuropsychology, 24,* 133–145.

Solomon, S., Hotchkiss, E., Saravay, S. M., Bayer, C., Ramsey, P., & Blum, R. S. (1983). Impairment of memory function by antihypertensive medication. *Archives of General Psychiatry, 40,* 1109–1112.

Sonino, N., Fava, G. A., Raffi, A. R., Boscaro, M., & Fallo, F. (1998). Clinical correlates of major depression in Cushing's disease. *Psychopathology, 31,* 302–306.

Spencer, P. S., & Schaumburg, H. H. (1985). Organic solvent neurotoxicity: Facts and research needs. *Scandinavian Journal of Work, Environment and Health, 11* (Suppl. 1), 53–60.

Spencer, P. S., Schaumburg, H. H., Raleigh, R. L., & Terhaar, C. J. (1975). Nervous system degeneration produced by the industrial solvent methyl *n*-butyl ketone. *Archives of Neurology, 32,* 219–222.

Spurgeon, A. (2002). *A Review of the literature relating to the chronic neurobehavioural effects of occupational exposure to organic solvents.* Birmingham, UK: Institute of Occupational Health, University of Birmingham.

Starkman, M. N., Gebarski, S. S., Berent, S., & Schteingart, D. E. (1992). Hippocampal formation volume, memory dysfunction, and cortisol levels in patients with Cushing's syndrome. *Biological Psychiatry, 32,* 756–765.

Starkman, M. N., Giordani, B., Gebarski, S. S., Berent, S., Schork, M. A. et al. (1999). Decrease in cortisol reverses human hippocampal atrophy following treatment of Cushing's disease. *Biological Psychiatry, 46,* 1595–1602.

Stefanos, G. A., Grover, W., & Geller, F. (1995). Case study: Corticosteroid treatment of language regression in pervasive developmental disorders. *Journal of American Academy of Child and Adolescent Psychiatry, 34,* 1107–1111.

Stehr-Green, P., Tull, P., Stellfeld, M., Mortenson, P. B., & Simpson, D. (2003). Autism and thimerosal-containing vaccines. *American Journal of Preventive Medicine, 25,* 101–106.

Stern, Y., Andrews, H., & Pittman, J. (1992). Diagnosis of dementia in a heterogeneous population: Development of a neuropsychological paradigm-based diagnosis of dementia and quantified correction for the effects of education. *Archives of Neurology, 49,* 453–460.

Stock, A. (1939). Die chronische quecksilber—un amalgam-vergiftung. *Zahnarztl, 10,* 403–407.

Strub, R. L., & Black, F. W. (1992). *Neurobehavioral disorders: A clinical approach.* Philadelphia: F. A. Davis.

Stubbs, E. G. (1976). Autistic children exhibit undetectable hemagglutination-inhibition antibody titers despite previous rubella vaccination. *Journal of Autism and Child Schizophrenia, 6,* 269–274.

Suhr, J., Tranel, D., Wefel, J., & Barrash, J. (1997). Memory performance after head injury: Contributions of malingering, litigation, status, psychological factors, and medication use. *Journal of Clinical and Experimental Neuropsychology, 19*, 500–514.

Tassinar, C. A., Rubboli, G., Volpi, L., et al. (2000). Encephalopathy with electrical status epilepticus during slow wave sleep or ESES syndrome including the acquired aphasia. *Clinical Neurophysiology, 111*, 94–102.

Taubes, G. (1995). Epidemiology faces its limits. *Science, 269*, 164–169.

Taylor, B., Miller, E., Lingam, R., et al. (2002). Measles, mumps, and rubella vaccination and bowel problems or developmental regression in children with autism: Population study. *British Medical Journal, 324*, 393–396.

Teasdale, G., & Jennett, B. (1974). Assessment of coma and impaired consciousness. A practical scale. *Lancet, 304*, 81–84.

Teixeira, L., Debourdeau, P., Zammit, C., Estival, J. L., Pavic, M., & Colle, B. (2002). Gemcitabine-induced thrombotic microangiopathy. *Presse Medicale, 31*, 740–742.

Terr, A. I. (2001). Stachybotrys: Relevance to human disease. *Annals of Allergy, Asthma, and Immunology, 87*, 57–63.

Thurman, D., & Guerrero, J. (1999). Trends in hospitalization associated with traumatic brain injury. *The Journal of the American Medical Association, 282*, 954–957.

Thurman, D. J., Alverson, C., Dunn, K. A., Guerrero, J., & Sniezek, J. E. (1999). Traumatic brain injury in the United States: A public health perspective. *Journal of Head Trauma Rehabilitation, 14*, 602–615.

Trauma.Org (2005). Trauma.org: Traumabank information repository. Retrieved from http://www.trauma.org/index.html

Tuchman, R. F., & Rapin, I. (1997). Regression in pervasive developmental disorders: Seizures and epileptiform electroencephalogram correlates. *Pediatrics, 99*, 560–566.

Turmaine, M., Raza, A., Mahal, A., Mangiarini, L., Bates, G. P., & Davies, S. W. (2000). Nonapoptotic neurodegeneration in a transgenic mouse model of Huntington's disease. *Proceedings of the National Academy of Sciences of the United States of America, 97*, 8093–8097.

Uhlmann, V., Martin, C. M., Sheils, O., Pilkington, L., Silva I., Killalea, A., Murch, S. B., Walker-Smith, J., Thomson, M., Wakefield, A. J., & O'Leary, J. J. (2002). Potential viral pathogenic mechanism for new variant inflammatory bowel disease. *Molecular Pathology, 55*, 84–90.

U.S. Department of Health and Human Services. (1993). Dental amalgam: A scientific review and recommended public health service strategy for research, education and regulation. U.S. Department of Health and Human Services. Retrieved from http://www.health.gov/environment/amalgam1/ct.htm

U.S. Department of Health and Human Services. (1997). Dental amalgam and alternative restorative materials. U.S. Department of Health and Human Services. Retrieved from http://www.health.gov/environment/amalgam2/contents.html

U.S. Department of Health and Human Services. (2003). Second national report on human exposure to environmental chemicals. [NCEH Pub. No. 01-0716]. Centers for Disease Control and Prevention. Retrieved from http://www.cdc.gov/exposurereport/pdf/SecondNER.pdf

U.S. Department of Health and Human Services (DHHS), C. f. D. C. a. P. C. (2005). Traumatic brain injury (TBI): Topic home. Retrieved from http://www.cdc.gov/node.do/id/0900f3ec8000dbdc.

U.S. Environmental Protection Agency Office of Air Quality Standards. (1997). Mercury Report to Congress. U.S. Eninvironmental Protection Agency. Retrieved from http://www.epa.gov/oar/mercover.html

Van Hout, A. (1997). Acquired aphasia in children. *Seminars in Pediatric Neurology*, 4, 102–108.

van Hout, M. S., Schmand, B., Wekking, E. M., Hageman, G., & Deelman, B. G. (2003). Suboptimal performance on neuropsychological tests in patients with suspected chronic toxic encephalopathy. *Neurotoxicology*, 24, 547–551.

van Vliet, C., Swaen, G. M. H., Slangen, J. J. M., & de Boorder, T. (1987). The organic solvent syndrome. A comparison of cases with neuropsychiatric disorders among painters and construction workers. *International Archives of Occupational and Environmental Health*, 59, 493–501.

van Vliet, C., Swaen, G. M., Volovics, A., Slangen, J. J., Meijers, J. M., de Boorder, T. et al. (1989). Exposure-outcome relationships between organic solvent exposure and neuropsychiatric disorders: Results from a Dutch case-control study. *American Journal of Industrial Medicine*, 16, 707–718.

van Vliet, C., Swaen, G. M., Volovics, A., Tweehuysen, M., Meijers, J. M., de Boorder, T. et al. (1990). Neuropsychiatric disorders among solvent-exposed workers. First results from a Dutch case-control study. *International Archives of Occupational and Environmental Health*, 62, 127–132.

Verstraeten, E., & Cluydts, R. (2004). Executive control of attention in sleep aponea patients: Theoretical concepts and methodological considerations. *Sleep Medicine Reviews*, 8, 257–267.

Vivero, L. E., Anderson, P. O., & Clark, R. F. (1998). A close look at fenfluramine and dexfenfluramine. *Journal of Emergency Medicine*, 16, 197–205.

Volkmar, F. R. (1992). Childhood disintegrative disorder: Issues for DSM-IV. *Journal of Autism and Developmental Disorders*, 22, 625–642.

Volkmar, F. R., & Cohen, D. J. (1989). Disintegrative disorder of "late onset" autism. *Journal of Child Psychology and Psychiatry and Allied Disciplines*, 30, 717–724.

Volkmar, F. R., & Rutter, M. (1995). Childhood disintegrative disorder; results of the DSM-IV autism field trials. *Journal of American Academy of Child and Adolescent Psychiatry*, 34, 1092–1095.

Volkmar, F. R., Klin, A., Marans, W., & Cohen, D. J. (1997). Childhood disintegrative disorder. In D. J. Cohen & F. R. Volkmar (Eds.), *Handbook of autism and pervasive developmental disorders* (2nd ed., pp 47–59). New York: Wiley.

Volkmar, F. R., Klin, A., Siegel, B., Szatmari, P., Lord, C., Campbell, M., et al. (1994). Field trial for autistic disorder in DSM-IV. *American Journal of Psychiatry*, 142, 1450–1452.

Volkmar, F. R., Steir, D. M., & Cohen, D. J. (1985). Age of recognition of pervasive developmental disorder. *American Journal of Psychiatry*, 142, 1450–1452.

Wakefield, A. J., Murch, S. H., Anthony, A., Linnell, J., Casson, D. M., Malik, M., et al. (1998). Ileal-lymphoid-nodular hyperplasia, non-specific colitis, and pervasive developmental disorder in children. *Lancet*, 351, 637–641.

Waters, E. M., Gerstner, H. B., & Huff, J. E. (1977). Trichloroethylene. I. An overview. *Journal of Toxicology & Environmental Health*, 2, 671–701.

Watkins, L. L., Schneiderman, N., Blumenthal, J. A., Sheps, D. S., Catellier, D., Taylor, C. B. et al. (2003). Cognitive and somatic symptoms of depression are associated with medical comorbidity in patients after acute myocardial infarction. *American Heart Journal*, 146, 48–54.

White, R. F., Feldman, R. G., Eviator, I. I., Jabre, J. F., & Niles, C. A. (1997). Hazardous waste and neurobehavioral effects: A developmental perspective. *Environmental Research, 73,* 113–124.

Williams, L. C., Hegde, M. R., Herrera, G., Stapleton, P. M., & Love, D. R. (1999). Comparative semi-automated analysis of (CAG) repeats in the Huntington disease gene: Use of internal standards. *Molecular and Cellular Probes, 13,* 283–289.

Williamson, A. M., & Winder, C. (1993). A prospective cohort study of the chronic effects of solvent exposure. *Environmental Research, 62,* 256–271.

Winship, K. A. (1986). Organic mercury compounds and their toxicity. *Adverse Drug Reactions and Acute Poisoning Reviews, 5,* 141–180.

Wolfe, F., Anderson, J., Harkness, D., Bennet, R. M., Caro, X. J., Goldenberg, D. L., Russell, I. J., & Yunus, M. B. (1997). Work and disability status of persons with fibromyalgia. *Journal of Rheumatology, 24,* 1171–1178.

Wolk, R., & Somers, V. K. (2003). Cardiovascular consequences of obstructive sleep apnea. *Clinics in Chest Medicine, 24,* 195–205.

Wolkowitz, O. M., Reus, V. I., Canick, J., Levin, B., & Lupien, S. (1997). Glucocorticoid medication, memory and steroid psychosis in medical illness. *Annals of the New York Academy of Sciences, 823,* 81–96.

Wong, K. (2001). The search for autism's roots. *Nature, 411,* 882–884.

Woo, E. J., Ball, R., Bostrom, A., Shadomy, S., Ball, L. K., Evans, G., et al. (2004). Vaccine risk perception among reporters of autism after vaccination: Vaccine adverse event reporting system 1990–2001. *American Journal of Public Health, 94,* 990–995.

World Health Organization & International Programme on Chemical Safety. (1991). *Inorganic mercury: Environmental health criteria* (Rep. No. 118). Geneva: World Health Organization.

World Health Organization and Nordic Council of Ministers (1985). *Chronic effects of organic solvents on the central nervous system and diagnostic criteria: report on joint WHO/Nordic Council of Ministers Working Group (Environmental Health 5), Copenhagen, 10–14 June, 1985.* Copenhagen: World Health Organization and Nordic Council of Ministers.

World Health Organization. (1997). WHO consensus statement on dental amalgam. FDI World Dental Federation. *FDI. World, 6,* 9.

Wu, H. M., Huang, S. C., Hattori, N., Glenn, T. C., Vespa, P. M., Hovda, D. A., et al. (2004). Subcortical white matter metabolic changes remote from focal hemorrhagic lesions suggest diffuse injury after human traumatic brain injury. *Neurosurgery, 55,* 1306–1315.

Yaggi, H., & Mohsenin, V. (2003). Sleep-disordered breathing and stroke. *Clinics in Chest Medicine, 24,* 223–237.

Young, A. B., Penney, J. B., Starosta-Rubinstein, S., Markel, D. S., Berent, S., Giordani, B. et al. (1986). PET scan investigations of Huntington's disease: Cerebral metabolic correlates of neurological features and functional decline. *Annals of Neurology, 20,* 296–303.

Young, A. B., Penney, J. B., Starosta-Rubinstein, S., Markel, D., Berent, S., Rothley, J., et al. (1987). Normal caudate glucose metabolism in persons at risk for Huntington's disease. *Archives of Neurology, 44,* 254–257.

Young, E. A., Haskett, R. F., Grunhaus, L., Pande, A., Weinberg, V. M., Watson, S. J., et al. (1994). Increased evening activation of the hypothalamic-pituitary-adrenal axis in depressed patients. *Archives of General Psychiatry, 51,* 701–707.

Yung, A. W., Park, Y. D., Cohen, M. J., & Garrison, T. N. (2000). Cognitive and behavioral problems in children with centrotemporal spikes. *Pediatric Neurology, 23,* 191–195.

Zakzanis, K. K., Leach, L., & Kaplan, E. (1999). *Neuropsychological differential diagnosis.* Lisse, the Netherlands: Swets & Zeitlinger.

Zarit, S. H., Miller, N. E., & Kahn, R. L. (1978). Brain function, intellectual impairment and education in the aged. *Journal of the American Geriatrics Society, 26,* 58–67.

Zimmerman, R. K. (1998). AAFP, AAP and ACIP Release 1998: Recommended childhood immunization schedule. *American Family Physician, 57,* 153–154, 157.

19 Issues and controversies involving the central nervous system evaluation

The complexity of the neurobehavioral examination

There are few simple or straightforward problems involving the clinical evaluation of disorders of the central nervous system and behavior. There are multiple reasons for this, including the complexity of the behaviors being measured and a tendency for the patient to change over time (as in the case of normal aging) or in response to numerous other factors (such as changes in behavior that result from the introduction of or modifications made in the patient's medications). Many of the complaints made by patients reflect changes in function that, in addition to competing physiological influences, can be explained by non-neurological mechanisms, even normal behaviors, and at times including measurement idiosyncrasies themselves. A major problem to the clinician or researcher seeking to understand the functional aspects of the central nervous system has to do with the nature of behavior and its relationship to the brain. The central nervous system is the executive of the behavior used in the neurobehavioral evaluation to evaluate its integrity. It is the seat of normal behavior, and abnormalities can be viewed as departures from that normality. Functional indices (e.g., the various behaviors required for everyday survival of the organism and that are employed in the examination of the nervous system) are extremely sensitive to the biology from which they derive. But, these indices also are quite variable normally, within a given organism as well as in terms of individual differences. How to identify abnormality within this context of variability, then, becomes a major challenge in evaluating the central nervous system.

Patient with toxic exposure and multiple explanations for his complaints

In this chapter, we focus on some of the more regularly occurring issues in clinical neurobehavioral toxicology that confound accurate diagnosis and causal determination. Fortunately, not all cases that are seen in clinical practice are as complicated as the one presented below. Nevertheless, the various issues inherent in this *case presentation* are those that are seen regularly in clinical practice.

Case presentation[1]

A 58-year-old Hispanic male was referred for a neuropsychological evaluation about 5 years after being hospitalized for exposure to carbon monoxide (CO) at his place of employment. The referral asked for documentation of the nature and severity of cognitive and intellectual impairments that were suspected to be the result of CO exposure. Very little information about the patient was provided, but he was said to have been married and divorced several times, with an unknown number of grown children. The only available information about the episode of CO exposure was that he had been found by a co-worker, "asleep" in a utility area he had been cleaning. The co-worker summoned EMS when he was unable to arouse the patient. He was transported to the hospital where he was found to be conscious at the time of admission, about 1 hr after he had been found. On admission, he was described as evidencing symptoms that included dizziness, incoordination, difficulty seeing, headache, feeling tired, and anxious. It was unknown whether or not he had been unconscious prior to admission, but there was no conclusive evidence that he had been. Laboratory tests revealed a carboxyhemoglobin (COHb) level of 16% on admission, but no other relevant abnormalities. His symptoms dissipated within 24 hr, and he was discharged about 3 days after hospital admission.

The neurological examination

A neurological examination performed shortly after discharge from the hospital was reported as normal with a few minor exceptions. The MMSE score was 26 of 30, with points lost on serial sevens subtraction (missed two of five), delayed recall of objects (missed one of three), and language (repetition, left out an article that was contained in the stimulus phrase). He was described as having a normal mental status by observation, oriented to person, place, and time. Motor activities were performed slowly and deliberately, but there was no evidence of weakness, incoordination, or abnormal tone in response to passive manipulation. Bilateral palmomental reflexes were present, but no other pathological reflexes were demonstrated.

COMMENT ON THE FINDINGS FROM THE NEUROLOGICAL EXAMINATION

Signs of central nervous system dysfunction that are demonstrated on the clinical neurological examination vary in their importance. Some signs, such as hemianopsia, e.g., are strongly indicative of central nervous system pathology. Similarly, some pathological reflexes, such as a Babinski reflex, are strongly indicative of a central nervous system abnormality, although even the presence of a Babinski sign can vary over time, possibly as a result of physiological variation or the result of examiner technique. Still other signs, including some that are considered to be highly objective and representing a clinical "abnormality," have little clinical importance in isolation. Finally, some neurological findings (such as strength) may be influenced by subject motivation, although poor effort on neurological testing is readily identified by experienced clinicians.

In the *case presentation* described above, the only neurological abnormalities aside from the few errors in the formal mental status examination involved the motor system and identification of bilateral palmomental reflexes. Also, the motor system evaluation revealed that all activities, including test of alternate motion rate, were performed very slowly and deliberately. This observation is not the type of finding that would be considered an abnormal "sign" in the absence of other motor system abnormalities. There was no evidence of weakness, incoordination, tremor, abnormal tone, impaired station or gait, abnormal muscle stretch reflexes, or any reflex abnormalities suggestive of corticospinal tract involvement. The rate at which a motor activity is performed is highly influenced by motivation. Although there are many neurological diseases that adversely affect the rate at which motor activities are performed (e.g., disorders of the basal ganglia), speed is not selectively impaired in these disorders. The rate at which motor activities are performed influences other components of the neurological examination as well as many aspects of a formal psychometric examination. For example, routine, automatic motor activities, such as reaching for a pencil, scratching the skin, adjusting one's clothing, or recovering from an inadvertent stumble all involve motor activity. The built-in redundancy in the neurological evaluation, which includes both subjective and objective measures, allows the neurologist to identify consistency in the overall results. This consistency is an important component in identifying a true neurological abnormality. In the case of isolated slow motor responses, motivation is the most important factor explaining this behavior. This can take the form of deliberate poor performance or, more commonly, simply reflect disinterest or manifestation of impaired mood (e.g., depressed affect).

The only other neurological abnormality identified in this case was the presence of bilateral palmomental reflexes. The palmomental reflex is an example of an objective neurologic sign. It is also a sign that is not influenced to any extent by the subject's volition, and it is unlikely that any subject is even aware of the presence of such a reflex, let alone its relative clinical importance. A positive palmomental reflex involves visible involuntary contraction of the mentalis muscles in response to ipsilateral stimulation of the palm. It is a complex reflex that represents a continuum from barely observable to pronounced. The palmomental reflex is one of the several primitive reflexes that exist frequently in asymptomatic, otherwise neurologically intact adults. For example, a palmomental reflex is present in over one-third of subjects in the third to ninth decade of age (Jacobs & Gossman, 1980), and, among all of the primitive reflexes, the palmomental reflex is the most frequently elicited at any age (Jacobs & Gossman, 1980). When recorded using an EMG needle electrode from the mentalis muscle, most subjects, including those with no visible contraction of the mentalis muscle, show a positive response (Brown, Smith, & Knepper, 1998). This reflex rapidly extinguishes in some subjects, being present initially but disappearing in response to repeated stimulations. Features of the palmomental reflex explain the substantial variability in recording the presence or absence of this primitive reflex. Importantly, the presence of an isolated palmomental reflex has no clinical importance and is not indicative of an underlying neuropathology. It cannot be used in isolation to identify evidence of central nervous system pathology.

Differential diagnosis

The referring diagnosis was "cognitive difficulties as a result of CO poisoning." No other diagnoses were listed by the referring clinician.

The neuropsychological evaluation

The current evaluation eight months post-hospitalization included review of past history, clinical interview, and psychometric examination. Some information from the *clinical interview* included the following: The patient stated his primary complaints as including headache, difficulty falling asleep and maintaining sleep, depression, anxiety, and difficulties with his memory. He stated that he had never experienced any of these problems before he was exposed to CO, and that his symptoms had progressively worsened since his exposure. Early in the interview, the patient sat slumped in his chair, with his arms hanging beside him, and he spoke only when questioned directly. As the interview proceeded, however, his manner and posture changed. He became more animated when talking, using his arms and hands to emphasize his verbal statements. Eventually, he began to smile and make humorous remarks. English, he said, was his second language and he had learned to speak English as an adult and after arriving in this country. Later in the interview, however, he mentioned that his favorite subject in school (in his home country) had been English.[2] By observation, the patient was conversant in English, reflecting facile speech and good comprehension, even in the face of the examiner's purposeful use of increasingly sophisticated words and phrases. He reflected a good awareness of culture-specific knowledge, both historical and more recent knowledge. The patient reported that he had never been injured prior to his exposure to CO, specifically denying a history of motor vehicle or other accident or illness. Also, he denied any history of psychiatric treatment or emotional illness or difficulty. Other than the exposure, he stated, his life had been happy and stress free. Since the exposure he had become anxious most of the time. He added that he worries about anything related to CO, such as heaters and stoves, and avoids these as much as possible, to the extent that he had the heating in his home changed from gas to electric. He will not use a gas range and had not returned to work for fear of another exposure. He said that he loved his job, did it well, and that he desired to be able to return to work. He denied history of alcohol, tobacco, or other drug use.

Briefly, *historical records* contained information that was at times discrepant with what the patient presented in interview (Table 19.1). For instance, the patient reported that he had no history of accident or injury before his

Table 19.1 Primary complaints made by the patient before his exposure to carbon monoxide (CO).

Primary complaint	Record of complaint before exposure
Headache	Yes, multiple complaints in records, with previous diagnosis of migraine
Sleep problems	Yes, no formal studies reported but numerous complaints over a 10-year period before exposure and multiple prescriptions for sleep medications
Depression	Yes, past formal diagnosis of depression and several diagnostic statements regarding work and personal stresses and periodic, brief counseling around these issues
Anxiety	No formal diagnosis of anxiety but numerous complaints noted of general "fearful" feelings
Memory	No mention in record regarding memory or other cognitive related diagnoses but work records reflected numerous instances of "forgetfulness" on the job

exposure at work; however, records indicated multiple motor vehicle accidents that occurred some years before and in which he suffered a possible head injury in one and a back injury in another. These injuries were severe enough to result in a disability award. Also, the patient denied any psychiatric history, but again records reflected a past diagnosis of depression, occurring before his CO exposure, for which he was hospitalized and treated with antidepressants and counseling. He claimed in the interview that his life was stress free except for issues related to his exposure. Records indicated, however, that he complained of stress on several occasions and had been seen in counseling around issues related to two divorces. A child, now an adult, from an extramarital relationship had been incarcerated for a violent criminal act and later released from prison. The patient had sought counseling related to his adult son out of fear that his son wanted to harm him. Finally, a record reflected that one of his ex-wives had threatened to harm him and that he had sought a restraining order against her. He indicated in the interview that he performed well at work and that his bosses had consistently praised his work and wanted him to get well and come back. Work records, however, reflected multiple work-related reprimands that included warnings of termination on several occasions.

With regard to the patient's primary complaints, historical records painted a picture that differed from that presented during the interview (Table 19.2). The patient stated in the interview that all of his complaints were new following his exposure to CO. Records, however, indicated a history prior to the time of exposure that included multiple complaints of headache, with a diagnosis of "migraine." There was no indication of formal sleep studies, but records reflected numerous complaints of sleep problems and multiple prescriptions for sleep medications. In addition to his past treatment for

Table 19.2 Conflicting findings for *case presentation.*

Variable	Finding	Conflicting finding
English as a second language	Low Vocabulary Score on WAIS-III (SS = 6) and Information (SS = 5)	Adequate, near fluent language usage as well as adequate knowledge of current and historical culture-specific knowledge in interview
When English was learned	Self-reported in interview that learned English informally when came to USA as an adult 20 years before	Self-reported in interview that his favorite subject when in school was English
History of prior illness or injury	Denied history of prior injuries in interview	Historical records reflected three prior motor vehicle accidents, at lease one of which resulting in neck and possible head injury; and a severe back injury that resulted in disability designation
History of prior psychiatric or emotional problems	Denied in interview	Historical records reflected past diagnosis of depression, with one hospitalization, pharmacological treatment and counseling
Life stresses	Denied existence of stressors, except for primary complaint of anxiety specific to concerns of recurrent exposure to CO	Historical records reflected stress and need for counseling on several occasions, including two divorces, difficulties with ex-wife, incarceration of one child, concerns surrounding child's later release from prison, work-related reprimands that included warnings of termination

depression, other records reflected numerous episodes of what were termed "personal stresses" and counseling around those issues. Also, there was mention in one record that he had complained of having fearful feelings. No mention was found of cognitive complaints or memory disturbance more specifically, but his work records dated before the CO exposure described him as being "forgetful" on the job.

The results of the *neuropsychological (psychometric) examination* are reported in Table 19.3. The results reflected an individual who was functioning below average, in the borderline range between normal and deficient, in terms of general intellectual ability (with a WAIS-III FSIQ: 75, PIQ: 78, VIQ: 77, and PPVT: 79). Vocabulary level, fund of general information, and WAIS-III Arithmetic were all below the cutoff for normal ability. At the same time, his scores were in the normal range on tasks that demanded

Table 19.3 Results from the neuropsychological examination.

Test variable	Behavior measured	Test score
PPVT-III	Nonverbal intelligence	79
WAIS-III FSIQ	General intellect	75
WAIS-III VIQ	Verbal intelligence	77
WAIS-III PIQ	Nonverbal intelligence	78
Vocabulary	Vocabulary level	6
Similarities	Abstract conceptualization	9
Arithmetic	Calculation ability	6
Digit Span	Concentration and working memory	7
Information	Fund of general (culturally shared) information	5
Block Design	Timed psychomotor problem solving	8
Matrix Reasoning	Abstract visual-conceptual problem solving	8
Trails A	Timed psychomotor sequential problem solving	40 s
Trails B	Timed psychomotor alphanumeric problem solving	90 s
WRAT-III Reading	English reading recognition	9th grade
WMS-III General Memory	General memory	75
WMS-III Auditory Immediate	Verbal learning	86
WMS-III Auditory Delay	Delayed recall, verbal	92
WMS-III Visual Immediate	Visual learning	82
WMS-III Visual Delay	Delayed recall, visual	92
Grooved Pegboard	Timed fine motor	Dominant hand (R): 100 s Nondominant: 75 s
Hooper VOT	Visual organization and problem solving	$T = 50$
SCL-90-R	Self-report scale: psychiatric complaint	All scales $> T = 60$, with highest scores (>80) on depression, anxiety, isolation
Beck Depression Inventory	Self-report scale: depression	37
Rey-15	Effort	7 of 15

good abstract conceptualization and reasoning (Similarities), nonverbal reasoning (Matrix Reasoning), and nonverbal problem solving (Block Design). He scored at the border of normal on a task that required sustained concentration and working memory (Digit Span). His reading recognition level (9th grade) was relatively low for someone who reportedly completed high school, and as already mentioned his vocabulary was limited. Despite this, he appeared in interview to be reasonably conversant in English, and his reading level was sufficient to allow for administration of paper and pencil rating scales. Psychomotor tasks were performed slowly but most remained around the cutoff for normal in comparison to normal, native speakers of English who were high school graduates. Memory scores were at or near normal level, and he performed better on delayed recall tasks than he did on initial learning tasks, with no discrepancies noted between verbal and visual learning and memory tasks. In the emotional area, he consistently scored in the range of pathology, with his highest scores reflecting depression, anxiety, and isolation. A test of effort (Rey-15) resulted in a score that placed him in the range of less than adequate motivation to perform.

COMMENT ON THE NEUROPSYCHOLOGICAL EXAMINATION RESULTS

Although these scores appear to be low in general, they most likely reflect an underestimate of this person's actual ability. His relatively low scores on language tests in general and more specifically on vocabulary and reading level suggest a less than optimal educational background. Also, these scores are consistent with someone for whom their first, and most proficient, language is other than English. They also are consistent with a person whose cultural background differs from the normative group with which they are being compared, especially considering the very low score on fund of general information. Another important factor in interpreting the present results comes from his low score on the test of effort, suggesting that he may not have been putting forth his best effort in taking these tests, all of which are volitional in nature. The implications of this score can be seen as consistent with his slow performance on motor tasks and even in his lower initial learning scores in comparison to his relatively higher scores on the recall portions of the test. The suggestion that he may not have been giving full effort in the examination does not imply malingering, as other explanations might more likely result from emotional factors (his test findings of depressed mood), from personality factors such as lack of self-confidence in being examined in a second language, or even in test-taking anxiety itself.

What can be said about these examination results in terms of normality? There are two ways to approach this question. First, when one weighs in factors identified as likely affecting this patient's performance (e.g., English as a second language of uncertain facility, probable educational limitations, a cultural and possibly socioeconomic background that differs from the normative comparison groups, the presence of depressed mood and anxiety, and indication of less than optimal effort) against a background of scores that even at their lowest on the examination rests near normal; the examiner can conservatively conclude that the patient is most likely normal in terms of cognitive and intellectual abilities. A problem with this first approach is that it mixes explanations with findings, in a sense disregarding the objective test findings in favor of subjective (although seemingly reasonable) conclusions. An alternative approach, and one that the authors prefer, is to accept the measurements for what they are. They provide a picture of how this person has performed in comparison to some norm. From this perspective, the patient can reasonably be seen as functioning outside of normal limits. Next steps would include the determination of patterns of strengths (normal scores) and weaknesses (low or abnormal scores) and to compare these patterns against a knowledge base that includes the clinician's experience and judgment as to what kinds of conditions can be consistent with such patterns. In other words, to use the neuropsychological examination results, together with information from interview, history, other examinations and ancillary tests to construct and test a differential diagnosis of possible explanations for his performance. A later step in this process would be to explain the test findings, as opposed to explaining them away. The question becomes, why were this person's examination results abnormal? It is in answering this question that issues of education, language, and other demographic factors are considered.

Neuroanatomical localization

The patient's complaints and neuropsychological test findings all implicate the supratentorial level of the nervous system.

Additional information

CT and MRI scans done several months after his purported exposure were both read as "normal for age."

Factors influencing the evaluation

Individual differences

The interview and review of historical records left it apparent that the explanations for this patient's problems were not as simple as was implied by the information contained in the referral. A preliminary differential diagnosis developed following review of pertinent case-related information and during the course of evaluation is listed in Table 19.4. A number of unresolved issues need to be addressed before a final diagnostic statement can be made. These issues occur regularly in the clinical practice of neurobehavioral toxicology—as competing or additional diagnoses or as confounding variables that obscure an accurate diagnosis. Many of these considerations relate to underlying neuropathology (congenital or acquired) or to behavioral phenomena (pathological or normal variation). Neuropathology includes conditions that compete to explain the findings for a specific patient, such as underlying medical conditions and physiological phenomena; encompassing iatrogenic disorders and treatment effects that may be explanatory as well. Relevant behavioral phenomena include the individual's style of coping that characterizes his or

Table 19.4 Differential diagnosis for *case presentation.*

Developmental
  Neonatal or early childhood neurological injury
  Intellectual deficiency
  Learning disability
  Educational limitation
  Language/cultural differences

Degenerative
  Progressive dementia

Infectious
  HIV/AIDS
  Syphilis

Vascular
  Diffuse cortical ischemia (hypoxia or anoxia)
  Multi-infarct dementia

Psychopathology
  Depression
  Anxiety
  Character disorder

Extra-disease considerations
  Malingering or factitious disorder
  Motivation/effort

---

her reaction to specified aspects of the environment (e.g., anxiety reactions that might accompany an act of bioterrorism or defensive reactions that result from being involved in litigation, as well as his or her usual approach to the environment, i.e., a reflection of personality, usual coping style, or character). Also, potentially confounding variables include technical considerations of the tests and methods we employ to measure behavior. Some of the most important of all of these considerations are discussed in the following pages and within the context of analyzing the present *case presentation.*

Other considerations that influence or even explain the patient's complaints and examination findings

Every patient reflects a personal history that is unique to that individual, e.g., the culture in which the patient was born or raised, his or her primary language, the extent and nature of his or her educational history and how well he or she profited from their unique education, vocational, and socio-economic backgrounds. These and similar demographic factors can impact the individual's clinical presentation and interact with the technical aspects of behavioral measures during the neurobehavioral examination. Such factors contribute to individual differences and need to be understood in a given case in order to arrive at an accurate diagnosis.

Language and culture

As described in volume I and elsewhere in this book, the neuropsychological evaluation includes a history[3] and interview in addition to psychometric evaluation. In the *case presentation*, English was said to be the patient's second language (Spanish being his primary language). Therefore, consideration was given to the level of the patient's mastery of the English language. This issue can be addressed in three primary ways. First, the patient's facility with English is subjectively rated through direct observation in interview and, second, formal tests of English reading efficiency can be administered. Third, the patient can periodically be asked to explain his or her understanding of the test directions.

How relevant are language considerations in terms of the neuropsychological evaluation? Rosal, Carbone, and Goins (2003) studied a sample of low-literate Spanish speaking individuals and reported several problems that interfered with accurate behavioral measurement in the group. Although their results might reflect low literacy as much as language itself, the problems they listed are likely to generalize, at least in the sense of the need for their consideration, to all persons with some limitation in language proficiency. The problems they reported can be paraphrased as including difficulties with understanding general instructions, some test items generating varying interpretations, unfamiliar wording or terms that could lead to confusion, difficulty in comprehending abstract concepts, and incorrect word definitions. The findings reported by Rosal et al. (2003) can be interpreted to mean that an interview that includes special attention to the patient's proficiency and level of understanding in English should supplement formal testing in cases where English is the person's second language. The problems listed by Rosal et al. provide additional, helpful guides as to what to observe in such an interview.

In the current case, historical records contained mixed reports regarding the patient's facility with the English language. For example, one report described the patient as unable to speak English and needing an interpreter in order to undergo that particular evaluation, whereas another physician on a different occasion described the patient as fluent in English. Interestingly, both reports were based on evaluations performed within a year of one another and reflected examinations completed within 3 years of the present encounter. By observation during the present evaluation, the patient appeared to be fluent in both receptive and expressive uses of English. Also, he reflected an adequate understanding of the test directions when asked to explain these. On the formal test of reading in English, he was found to have a ninth grade reading level, a level sufficient, at least from the viewpoint of ability to read, for administration in English of the tests chosen for the examination. At the same time, formal literature reflects mixed opinions regarding the propriety of administering standard neuropsychological tests in English to persons with English as a second language (ESL) or to those who reside in or who were raised in a culture different from the examiner or place of test development (Gil & Bob, 1999). Also, there is the important consideration of the normative data associated with interpretation of the test results. Numerous studies have addressed the difficulties associated with not only the translation of tests into another language (Beck & Gable, 2003; Bowden & Fox-Rushby, 2003; Fortuny & Mullaney, 1997; Gil & Bob, 1999; Hendrickson, 2003) but also with the development of normative data that are appropriate for use even within the person's home culture (D'Elia, Satz, & Schretlen, 1989; Fiedler, Feldman, Jacobson, Rahill, & Wetherell, 1996; La Rue, Romero, Ortiz, Liang, & Lindeman, 1999; Stewart & Napoles-Springer, 2003). Even when a test is used that has been translated into the patient's primary language and administered by a native speaker, difficulties can remain. Levav, Mirsky, French, and Bartko (1998) studied neuropsychological assessment data obtained using four languages on subjects from five countries and at varying levels of age and education. With regard to country of origin, the investigators reported minimal effect on reaction time when measured within the context of measuring sustained attention. However, and despite the lack of difference in reaction time, tests that assessed ability to focus attention, problem-solving, shift strategies, and inhibit automatic response tendencies differed significantly as a product of country of origin (Levav et al., 1998). Interestingly, the latter effects mostly disappeared by the age of 54 years (Levav et al.).

Words have both denotations as well as connotations, and the meanings attributed to words can vary between cultures, even when a literal translation is made (Mkoka, Vaughan, Wylie, Yelland, & Jelsma, 2003). While participating on the World Health Organization's functional classification (ICF) project (World Health Organization, 2001), for instance, one of the present authors personally observed that the phrase "executive dysfunction," a term that is familiar and used fairly regularly by neuropsychologists in the West to refer to a type of cognitive difficulty, was consistently interpreted by the Japanese professionals as referring to business-related difficulties, with no cognitive implications. In informal attempts to translate this term into Japanese, the back-translation invariably referred to "managerial business incompetence."

The development of appropriate normative data is a challenging endeavor even within a given culture and, once developed, these normal values can change over time (La Rue et al., 1999; Marshall, Mungas, Weldon, Reed, & Haan, 1997). Uttl and Van Alstine (2003), for instance, have found through meta-analysis that WAIS Vocabulary test scores have been rising at rates that predict changes in IQ of 1.52 points/decade for younger adults and 4.79 points/decade for older adults. The explanation for this rise is a matter of speculation, and there is no reason to assume that the finding would generalize to all cultures.

Although there are studies that can be read to support the use of standard neuropsychological tests across cultures (Penley, Wiebe, & Nwosu, 2003) or the use of interview techniques to ensure that tests are used that are appropriate to the patient's understanding of instructions (Rosal et al., 2003), cultural and language differences remain a factor that the clinician must recognize and account for in interpreting the examination findings. These considerations extend to tasks that might appear on the surface to be culturally fair or to have relatively little language demand. At least one study, in fact, reported the somewhat counter intuitive finding that scores between English and Spanish speakers from a similar culture and matched for age and education were comparable on many of the language-based tasks, but scores were significantly lower for the Spanish speakers on most of the nonverbal measures in this study (Jacobs et al., 1997). Lee, Cheung, Chan, and Chan (2000) compared the performance of Chinese–English bilingual speakers to that of a group of monolingual English speakers on two versions of the trail making test. One version of the test (using color instead of alphanumeric characters) was said to be more "culturally fair" than the standard alphanumeric version. In fact, the authors found no significant difference in performance between the two groups using either version of the test; however, the within group performance between the two tests was highly correlated for the monolingual group while essentially absent in the bilingual group. The authors concluded that mastery of the English language, because of its emphasis on temporal sequencing, may provide some advantage in completing a task like trail making.

At the least, the clinician should take the conservative approach when interpreting test results based on a second language or a different culture. It seems appropriate to assume that an obtained score on a given test is likely to represent some underestimate of the patient's actual ability in the functional area measured. The test results themselves are likely to provide some support for the hypothesis just mentioned, as when the patient's productions reflect higher scores on tasks with relatively less language demand (e.g., Block Design) than on those tasks that are more dependent on language (e.g., Vocabulary) or culturally based knowledge (e.g., Information). Nevertheless, given the discussion above, one cannot assume that there exists a discrete difference in terms of the effects of language on verbal versus seemingly nonverbal tasks. Also, and while the effects of language may be primary (e.g., reduced vocabulary or verbal fluency when tested in a second language), many of these "primary" skills serve as intermediaries in the performance of other tasks, e.g., learning and memory. Ardila (2003), for instance, reviewed the topic of language representation and working memory in bilingual individuals being tested in their primary language versus their secondary language. Ardila concluded that processing information is more complex in a second language. As a result, working memory may be less efficient in a second language than in the person's primary language. In addition to the comparison of efficiency in primary versus secondary language, the findings from Ardila's review (2003) can be said to underscore the importance of language as an intermediary in performing cognitive tasks that on the surface might appear to be somewhat removed from language itself.

Literacy

Setting aside the native versus second language considerations, literacy itself can impact on test performance. In a study of the effects of illiteracy on test scores, Reis, Guerreiro, and Petersson (2003) compared literate and illiterate individuals on a number of neuropsychological measures. The investigators chose a relatively homogenous group of subjects, all from a small fishing village with common language and socioeconomic backgrounds. They found that some tests were more affected by literacy status than were others. The main findings were that naming and identification of objects, verbal fluency, verbal memory, and orientation appeared not to be affected in their sample by either literacy or educational level; whereas verbal working memory (digit span), verbal abstraction, long-term semantic memory, and calculation (multiplication) were significantly and adversely related to level of literacy. It may be that the illiterate person has failed to learn the skills needed to effectively complete some tests that might be employed to measure cognitive abilities. Folia and Kosmidis (2003), for instance, examined the hypothesis that it is the nature of the test that determines success or failure for the illiterate. They found that an illiterate group was able to perform comparably to the literate group when learning a list of objects but did significantly more poorly on word-list learning. They concluded that poor memory performance by illiterates can be attributed to a combination of the nature of the task (whether the task is more or less ecologically valid for this group) and the use of cognitive strategies by illiterate persons that differs from that employed by the literate individuals. Folia and Kosmidis (2003) further suggested that formal education might enhance ability through the acquisition of efficient learning and retrieval strategies. It appears to be well established that literacy, or the lack thereof, is a factor to consider in evaluating central nervous system function. It is tied closely to the issue of education, but reported education level, or even grades earned in school, is no guarantee of literacy. Each will need to be considered independently, not only in terms of tests and test scores but also in terms of comprehension as well.

Education

The patient in the *case presentation* was educated in a rural and economically poor region of South America before coming to the United States. Attempts to get records from his past schooling proved to be impossible. He reported completing the tenth grade in public school and, subsequently, completing one more year of trade school. Although the exact trade he studied remained unknown, the patient's description of his major, "industrial hygiene," together with his description of what he studied in class (e.g., procedures for cleaning carpets and draperies, removing and preventing stains, working as part of a team) and his work history that included employment solely as a school custodian left the impression that the subject matter of his trade-related training was consistent with his subsequent employment. Historical records revealed a discrepancy between the educational attainment he reported to his physician and that reported during the present evaluation. For instance, he reportedly told his physician that he had completed high school and one year of additional trade school, earning grades of "mostly 'Bs' and some 'Cs'." Also, he indicated to his physician that he had learned to speak English as an adult after coming to this country. Contrary to that report, he indicated during the present interview that he had done "OK" in school, that he did not have a high school diploma but would like to obtain a GED, and that his favorite school subject as a child had been English.

Aside from issues related to literacy discussed earlier, other skills that are learned in school can influence the interpretations of test results. Karzmark (2000), for instance, administered the MMSE version (Folstein, Folstein, & McHugh, 1975) of the serial sevens subtraction test and showed through multiple regression analysis that calculation skill was equal in importance to concentration in predicting performance on this task. At the same time, general cognitive dysfunction, psychopathology, and even education level were not predictive of success on the serial sevens subtraction test in the Karzmark (2000) study. The results of the Karzmark study serve to underscore the importance of measuring not only attention and concentration as cognitive abilities but also to include achievement tests that address arithmetic proficiency as well as reading and spelling.

Socioeconomic status

Socioeconomic status (SES) is closely related to education and often correlated with immigration and language status. Although much has been written about minority populations, a gap remains between what has been learned and the implementation of this knowledge to standard practice, research as well as clinical practice (Gil & Bob, 1999). Also, little has been written directly about the effects of SES on the formal behavioral examinations and on neuropsychological test productions more specifically. There is reason from a common sense viewpoint to believe that SES is related to test performance. However, the concept is confounded by the variables that are most often used to define SES, e.g., occupational status and educational attainment. As discussed earlier, some attention has been given to the relationship between education and neuropsychological test performance. However, much less has been done in the area of employment. Recognizing this as a somewhat neglected area, Kalechstein, Newton, and van Gorp (2003) reported the results of their meta-analysis involving the relationship between cognitive function and employment. This investigation found that employment status was significantly associated with a number of cognitive domains. The strongest of these associations included intellectual, executive, and memory functioning. In addition to minority and language corollaries to SES, the concept also has nutritional and other health implications that in themselves can impact on neurobehavioral status.

Motivation

What is "motivation?" We discussed the topic of motivation a number of times in these volumes. In chapter 4 of volume I, e.g., we called attention to the role of motivation as a variant of normal behavior that has the capacity to confound and obscure an otherwise sensible clinical diagnosis. We emphasized those aspects of motivation that involve a person's cooperation and effort, especially in the completion of volitional task performance as occurs in the psychometric examination. *Motivation* was an early topic of interest to formal, scientific psychology. The concept of *motive* in human behavior was of interest to philosophers even before the development of modern psychology, appearing in the writings of Spinoza as early as 1677 (Murphy, 1949). This early and sustained interest in motivation arose not from the viewpoint of pathology but from the recognition that the concept speaks to an important aspect of normal behavior necessary for survival of the organism. Motivation is actually a concept that extends well beyond effort alone. In fact, an accurate understanding of individual behavior cannot be achieved without consideration of motivation. While aspects of motivation can, and do, become altered in various pathological states, the clinician is challenged to differentiate between the type of pathology involved in a given case and what amounts to normal individual differences in motivation.

Many people, especially outside of the field of psychology and at times within the discipline itself, have a misunderstanding of the concept of motivation. To many, the term implies volitional intent. From this viewpoint, the person is seen as either energetically intent on performing well (i.e., highly motivated) or lacking sufficient reason or enthusiasm to fully engage in a task or activity (i.e., poorly motivated). This interpretation of motivation reflects the common or lay meaning of the term (Merriam-Webster, 1993). Historically for psychology, however, the concept of motivation has been approached through the study of *drives* (sometimes referred to as *needs*) and *incentives* (Lindzey, Hall, & Thompson, 1975; Woodworth & Schlosberg, 1938, 1964). Drives can be learned (e.g., parental approval) or they can be primary (e.g., hunger). Incentives are environmental conditions that stimulate action. Viewed in this way, motivation appears multifaceted and not exclusively dependent on the person's conscious awareness, or even intent. Anything that affects either factor in such a model of motivation, drive or incentive, might serve to alter motivational behavior. Such alterations may be positive or negative from the perspective of some specified outcome. A drug that alters hunger (such as those that elicit or inhibit the release of 5-hydroxytryptamine [5-HT, serotonin] for example) also will affect hunger-driven behaviors (Frazer & Hensler, 1999). From the perspective of incentive, a variety of environmental stimuli can serve to alter goal directed behaviors. Examples include the presence or absence of food, or the smell of food, in the examination room, the time of day, or even the ring of a telephone. The professional should always be aware of the possible occurrence of such altered behaviors during the examination as their occurrence may be obvious, but they can occur subtly or imperceptibly as well. In one instance known to the authors, e.g., a clinician interpreted some low scores on the behavioral examination as reflecting signs of poor sustained concentration and attributed these results to underlying neurological dysfunction. The behavioral notes made by the technician who assisted in the examination, however, mentioned that a faulty fire alarm had sounded periodically during the examination. Since the problem with the alarm was well known to the clinician and his assistants, the patient was told to ignore the alarm so the examination could be completed in the allotted time frame. Although we may never know the proper interpretation of the results of that compromised examination, the patient's incentive for self-protection would likely be stronger than the need to concentrate on the neurobehavioral test items. Likewise, distractibility as a result of the patient's concerns regarding safety would appear to be a more parsimonious explanation for the low test scores than brain damage. At the least, one would wish to repeat the examination under appropriate circumstances. This, in fact, was done, and on this occasion, the patient's scores on alternate tests of attention and concentration were within normal limits.

Other conditions can lead to interaction between drives and incentives and lead to changes in the person's motivational state as well. While the *Diagnostic and Statistical Manual of Mental Disorders, Fourth Edition (DSM-IV)* (American Psychiatric Association, 1994) does not speak directly to the concept of motivation, a number of disorders that are listed in this manual describe symptoms that are directly related to alterations in some aspect of motivation. The diagnostic criteria for dysthymic disorder, for instance, include poor appetite, insomnia, low energy, fatigue, and poor concentration (American Psychiatric Association, 1994). Any or all of these manifestations of dysthymia have the capacity to affect an individual's performance in formal psychometric examination. When present, these various conditions can explain in part or in whole an individual's primary complaints or test findings in a given clinical evaluation. Their effect, less than optimal effort on the examination, can be determined through careful observation of the patient's performance, with special attention to variations in performance during the examination, e.g., poorer performance later in the day in comparison to earlier. The test results themselves can reveal motivational intrusions, as when inconsistent performance is noted on redundant measures within a given examination or between repeated examinations. Nonclinically sensible changes are especially important to note. One patient, for instance, was found to perform normally on a nonverbal memory task, with impaired scores on the verbal portion of the test. In an earlier examination, however, the opposite result had been obtained, adequate verbal memory with poor nonverbal test scores. There had been no change in the patient's complaints or other clinical findings, and the changes in performance were judged to be neither clinically nor biologically sensible. There also are direct measures of effort that can be employed, e.g., the Rey-15 Item Test (Rey, 1964).

Attention

Like motivation, *attention* is a complex process that varies normally within and between individuals. It is reflective of neurobiological processes, with the reticular formation of the brain playing a critical role through communication to the cerebrum. A relatively early experiment by Moruzzi and Magoun (1949) demonstrated the importance of this neuroanatomical structure in maintaining arousal by stimulating the ascending reticular formation to produce an EEG response pattern of low-voltage, high-frequency cortical activity, a pattern characteristic of the awake organism. Without such arousal, the organism is asleep or stuporous. The ability to attend, therefore, is a basic function that is necessary to the organism's survival. While basic to all living organisms that depend on active (motivated) interaction with their environment to avoid danger and find nutrients, the process of attention is perhaps most highly evolved in humans. At all phylogenetic levels, however, the process of attention is modified by experience. Such responsiveness to the "outside" world occurs even at the basic levels of attention, the *orienting response* (Schlag & Schlag-Rey, 1982). An instructor in a graduate level physiology course once asked the class to design a living organism, including in the design every basic function the organism would need in order to survive. Interestingly, many of the students neglected this crucial ability to orient to the environment, while others left out the ability to track a target once it had elicited an orienting response. It has long been known, in fact, that even at this relatively basic level, the organism modifies the nature of its orienting response in the face of experience, with multiple steps in orienting response being demonstrable experimentally (Schlag & Schlag-Rey, 1982). As discussed in volume I, the hormonal system plays a critical role in this bridge between experience and physiology (Lupien & McEwen, 1997; McEwen, de Kloet, & Rostene, 1986).

Despite the complexity of basic concepts like attention, most clinical evaluations include only a relatively cursory treatment of this important behavior. Even during formal psychometric examinations, it would be somewhat extraordinary to find documentation of the patient's orienting response. Of course, attention is involved in almost all responses that the patient makes, such that the observation of any general inability should lead to a more detailed analysis of cognitive processes that underlie that observation. Here, however, we wish to emphasize the importance of normal variations in a function such as attention because too often this demand to separate normality from pathology is treated casually. As discussed elsewhere (see, e.g., chapter 4 of volume I) attention normally varies from time to time and for many reasons. Again, closely tied to motivation, these variations might result from inadvertent distractions, thoughts the person has judged to be of higher priority than the task(s) presented by the clinician, or even as a normal characteristic of the attention process itself, including the effects of historical and present experiences on attention. With regard to the last point, Schlag and Schlag-Rey (1982) demonstrated that if a stimulus was terminated immediately after elicitation of an orienting response in the cat, and before the animal was given opportunity to "consider" the stimulus for a longer time, the cat developed different behaviors from those manifested when it did have the opportunity to observe. Briefly, in such a paradigm, the cat developed the strategy of ignoring the initial stimulus presentation, manifesting what is thought of as a characteristic cat-like behavior of ignoring its prey, presumably to catch it by surprise. Regardless of the interpretation, a factual outcome of this experiment was that the initial orienting response time increased, from response times of about 200–400 ms to delays of up to 10 s. To the extent that these animal findings generalize to human beings, one might ask what effect an individual personal history of failure to obtain positive outcomes via attention to desired rewards would have on sustained attention during an interview or examination. Even more important is the profound role played by such *normal* variations on the patient's ability to learn, remember, or engage in other cognitive tasks during the clinical examination.

Our knowledge and understanding of the nervous system has increased substantially over the last few decades. In large part due to the advent of increasingly sophisticated imaging tools and other new technology, the field of neuroscience has increasingly become more defined as a specific discipline and has expanded its areas of interest to include intact animal and human organisms. Neurobehavioral toxicology of the future will need to incorporate these neuroscience-derived data into its research and clinical applications. Especially the area of behavioral measurement (neuropsychology), collaborating between the applied and more basic science aspects of neurobehavioral toxicology, will develop. As mentioned in the last few paragraphs, neuropsychology does not routinely attend as well as it might to what are really the basic foundations of more global functional behaviors, e.g., orienting, attending, concentration. When such basic behavioral mechanisms are quantified presently, it is usually in the context of their involvement indirectly with some higher order behavior, e.g., learning or memory. Although it is true that neuropsychology would benefit from measuring these behaviors directly, our scientific understanding of these basic functions has grown to such an extent that it will become increasingly important to attend to their measurement. In doing so, neuropsychology might obtain a number of unanticipated benefits. Consider, e.g., the study by Sailer, Flanagan, and Johansson (2005). In this work, the relationship between gaze behavior and changes in eye–hand coordination was evaluated in the context of learning a novel and complex visuomotor task. Such a task can be studied in terms of its component parts, e.g., apparatus-related factors such as grip, hand movements, pressure exerted, in aspects of gaze such as focus point, tracking, and so forth; and, with incorporation of imaging the functional and structural aspects of the central nervous system. To make such an approach a reality would require task standardization and the establishment of psychometric technical requirements. A part of the technical demand for such testing as proposed here would be to establish scientifically that the behaviors measured were in fact relevant to the pathology of interest, and that the measurement was sensitive and relatively specific. This type of approach is not as radical as it might appear, since it is really a repetition of how the first behavioral tests were developed over 100 years ago. The only real interval change is that our technology and knowledge base have become more sophisticated (e.g., from pencils to digital recording devises; from a capacity to establish predictive validity over time to *in vivo* construct validity).

Earlier it was suggested that the approach to behavioral measurement being described here might have some unanticipated benefits. What are these benefits? At present, an important weakness in the neurobehavioral examination relates to the fact that most aspects of the tasks presented require volition on the patient's, or subject's, part in completing the task. Although procedures exist that allow for some detection of individuals who are expending less than ideal effort in task performance, there currently is no method that is ideal in such detection. Complex computerized tasks that reflect the integration of several functional systems and measure separately the various components at work in task completion would create a situation of transparency in terms of the individual's effort. Such tasks would include too many aspects involved in their completion for the individual to fake effectively. How much pressure does the normal person exert when operating a control mechanism? How long does a person's gaze dwell on a target before moving to the next? Although the examiner may have the answers to these and other questions, the examinee will not. And even if he or she did have these information, these automatic behaviors would be outside of their volitional control.

Personality and coping style

We earlier referred to these individualized and relatively enduring human characteristics as "para-neurotoxic" considerations in arriving at a clinical diagnosis, in addition to their role as potential confounders in research. These characteristics not only compete with other possible conclusions in terms of diagnosis or causal explanation but also are identified often as influencing the nature of clinical symptoms. We spoke in volume I of the importance of *context* in which a given injury occurs, citing as example the terrorist Sarin gas attacks in Japan in 1994 and 1995 (Morita et al., 1995; Matsui, Ohbu, & Yamashina, 1996). While over 6,000 people were said to have been injured in these attacks, there were 18 fatalities; and physical symptoms among most of the survivors were relatively mild and transient, including visual changes and ocular pain, vomiting, dyspnea, headaches, and some mild cognitive problems (Matsui et al., 1996). Most patients were released from the hospital within a few hours and all physical signs and symptoms were said to have disappeared within a few weeks. What were labeled as "traumatic stress reactions" were an exception to this general picture of improvement. While even these emotional reactions were said to have resolved within a couple of months, some persisted longer. It is likely that individual differences in personality and coping style played an important role in predicting the nature of the emotional reaction and its course over time.

Human-made disasters, which include acts of terrorism, are known to produce emotional effects that last longer than those from natural disasters (e.g., the occurrence of a flood or storm), in some cases becoming chronic (Baum, 1991). Stress and emotional reactions to stress are common to all disasters (VandenBos & Bryant, 1991), but acts of terror are believed to produce some degree of emotional disturbance in the majority of those involved (Frederick, 1991), with reactions that adversely impact on all aspects of the affected person's life. In addition, such reactions are thought to be persistent, to the extent that recovery may never be complete in some individuals (Frederick, 1991). In the Sarin attacks in Japan, the most frequent emotional reactions were anxiety, with a specific diagnosis of post-traumatic stress disorder (PTSD) being most common. While factors associated with a given traumatic event influence the development of an emotional disorder such as PTSD, individual differences in personality, social, cultural factors, as well as history of preexisting mental disorders are believed to play important roles as well (American Psychiatric Association, 1994). Individual coping style might influence the expression of an anxiety disorder, but it may also influence communication between patient and doctor. A shy, introverted personality style, for instance, might inhibit the patient from sharing information with the clinician. A repressive coping style (a tendency to *flight* on the fight-flight continuum) might leave the patient less able than might otherwise be the case to share the information, or such a style might even affect the patient's self-insight and awareness of having experienced a traumatic event. When the coping style is sensitizing in nature (a *fight* or controlling style), such a patient may present the clinician only with those elements of the perceived condition as he or she believes is necessary. It is not uncommon, in fact, for individuals with such a coping style to become irritated with the clinician who persists in asking questions that appear to the patient to be unrelated to the clinical condition as the patient views it.

Practical or cultural factors can also affect communication, e.g., an individual who does not wish to divulge the occurrence of an event for fear of reprisal against him or against relatives or friends who are still at risk. In terms of toxicants specifically, a worker might not wish to admit to everything he or she knows about unsafe practices at their company for fear of losing their job, or perhaps their personality style is one that leads to some sense of loyalty that they interpret to mean that one should not talk about such issues outside or work. Malingering, or course, can be viewed as a special instance of practicality, even though it can properly be viewed as an expression of character as well. Malingering is relatively common, estimated to occur anywhere from about 7–30% in persons where potential benefits may be contingent on the outcome of an evaluation (Binder, 1993; Trueblood & Schmidt, 1993). Despite this frequency, malingering represents what is likely the most difficult behavior for a clinician to document. There are exceptions to this as when the malingered symptom is so specific as to be objectively disproved through tests or direct observation. A patient, e.g., complained in interview that he had no appetite and could eat no more than a bite or two of food before feeling bloated and nauseated, which he attributed to pesticide fumes in his home. When the physician passed the cafeteria at lunchtime, however, this same patient was observed to be starting on a second cheeseburger and talking to his friends about getting a third.

When the patient is a child, or intellectually limited adult, communication is even more challenging in that complaints often are made indirectly, through play or dreams, or they are presented by another, e.g., a parent. At times, complaints are made by way of what can be termed "acting out." Common in children, who may feel guilty or disloyal to someone, and in the intellectually impaired, "acting out" can often be recognized by a, usually dramatic, change in the individual's enduring behavior pattern (i.e., personality). A child, for instance, might begin breaking their toys or refusing to obey parental demands. An institutionalized adult might start refusing to queue for meals or clean up their living area. Knowledge of normal personality and coping styles, together with a sensitive approach to the patient, will be required of the clinician who wishes to understand the true diagnostic implications of these indirect expressions of complaint.

Also, anxiety symptoms often coexist with depression (Nisenson, Pepper, Schwenk, & Coyne, 1998). These emotional conditions are common in clinical practice, whether or not a toxicant is involved. An understanding of psychopathology is important for the neurobehavioral toxicologist because symptoms of anxiety and depression often are nonspecific and can overlap with those of toxicant exposure, e.g., headache, dyspnea, vertigo, nausea, lack of energy, changes in mental status, and memory problems. As mentioned in volume I, some have argued that in the face of exposure, the manifestation of emotional disturbance is the direct result of that exposure (Bolla & Roca, 1994). As we have said before, it is theoretically possible that this could occur, especially since many medicines (themselves with toxic potential) are known to produce depression or anxiety, as well as dizziness, memory disturbances, confusion, and the like. However, and as in the case of therapeutic drug-induced adverse reactions, such symptoms are likely to occur in isolation only rarely and are expected to remit once the drug, or other toxic substance, has been removed from the body. Consideration of the medications the patient may be taking, in fact, is an important item to include in a differential diagnosis. This includes not only the specific medication being taken but also the personality and coping styles of the patient since adverse drug reactions often can be the result of compliance problems on the part of the patient.

Approaching the differential diagnosis from a neurobehavioral perspective

The primary complaints made by the patient in the *case presentation* are all behavioral (see Table 19.1). So, too, are the various conditions listed in the differential diagnosis in Table 19.4. While the differential diagnosis in practice most often contains pathological conditions that potentially explain a patient's complaints, with normality an alternative explanation. Normality is often determined by exclusion, but here we included it in the diagnostic list to emphasize the importance of considering normal variation in the diagnostic process. All of the factors with the capacity to affect the findings of the neurobehavioral evaluation that we listed earlier have the capacity to do so to a pathological extent but also to exert a relative influence while remaining within normal limits. Even when normal, the patient may interpret the effect as pathological. It is one task of the clinician to apply an objective approach to the evaluation and to bring to the patient an accurate explanation for his or her concerns. To accomplish this end, the neurobehavioral evaluation will involve medical, neurological, and neuropsychological examinations, all of which include a clinical interview and history.

The role of neuropsychological testing in the examination

The neuropsychological examination is a major part of the neuropsychological evaluation (see chapter 5, volume I). It represents the best way we have to apply principles of physical measurement to behavioral variables. The test results from such examination can be viewed as similar to clinical signs that reflect a different view of the reported symptoms than that provided subjectively by the patient. The examination is not totally objective, however. If for no other reason, some subjectivity remains as a result of the need to measure behaviors that include those that are volitional, requiring the patient's cooperation to apply his or her best effort to complete the tasks. Neuropsychologists have devised a number of approaches to overcome this potential weakness to neuropsychological testing, e.g., providing redundant tests that measure the same or similar behaviors in different ways and the administration of tests that are designed to measure effort directly. A good knowledge of the tests' psychometric properties (e.g., issues of sensitivity, specificity, validity, reliability, and standard error of measurement) is needed for accurate interpretation of the results. Very important, the results of testing (within a given examination and between serial examinations) should reflect patterns of strengths and weaknesses that are biologically and clinically sensible. Consider, e.g., a case where the examination results on one occasion reflected a pattern of verbal learning and memory that was significantly weaker than visual learning whereas on repeat testing, the pattern was found to be reversed (i.e., visual weaker than verbal), with no change in the nature of the patient's complaints. While such a change in pattern might be consistent with some medical condition, this is a very unusual occurrence and should lead the clinician to consider closely the role of motivation in producing the results.

Issues of sensitivity and specificity

As we discussed in more detail in volume I, neuropsychological tests are quite sensitive for the most part. For instance, intertest variability between two administrations of the Wechsler Intelligence Scales has been reported to be well within the range of acceptance for most routine medical tests (Berent & Trask, 2000). The error of measurement for the Wechsler scales of $+/-5$ points means that these instruments can detect relatively slight variations not only in scores across time but also in comparison to normative populations. While such sensitivity is important to a clinical test, depending on how the scores are interpreted, sensitivity also can be a liability. Normal individual variations in behavior are relatively high, such that great care must be taken when concluding that a given score represents pathology of the nervous system. This is especially true when scores remain within the normal range. What is the normal range? A conservative approach would suggest that a score that is 1.5–2 SD below the mean can be said to be clinically relevant, that is, outside of normal. This is consistent with most other tests used in medicine. When talking about changes from "baseline" measurements, a change of similar magnitude should be employed.

It is important to bear in mind that while neuropsychological tests are highly sensitive, they are not specific to any one underlying physical or psychological mechanism. Nor are these tests specific to pathology, except in those few instances where test criteria are used to define a specific diagnosis, e.g., intellectual deficiency, isolated memory impairment, and some types of learning disabilities. Even then, they are never specific to cause. As emphasized in this chapter, and many times throughout these volumes, a multitude of factors might contribute to an observed score on psychometric examination. Even highly trained professionals can sometimes lose sight of the simple fact of lack of specificity in neuropsychological examination. In the heat of a deposition, for instance, an expert referring to the neuropsychological results was heard to say, "These (results) are measures of the brain, not just behavior." In fact, the truth is just the opposite of what the expert claimed. Neuropsychological tests measure *behavior*, and only behavior. The value of neuropsychological testing rests on the accuracy of these behavioral measurements. Behavior can be influenced by extraneurological factors such as attitudes and beliefs (Spurgeon, Gompertz, & Harrington, 1997). But when combined with knowledge of brain–behavior relationships and within the context of an appropriate differential diagnosis, behavior represents the best indicator of the functional integrity of the central nervous system.

Aside from being critical in the diagnoses of a host of central nervous system disorders, the results of neuropsychological examination are employed to provide clinical meaning to other tests that might be more specific to the brain but lack that behavioral specificity, e.g., EEG, PET, and MRI. Also, neurobehavioral measurement provides the ability to create objective baselines with which to monitor changes in clinically important areas such as disease progression, monitoring of medications, and treatment effectiveness. Changes in behavior over time are often critical to directly arrive at an accurate diagnosis in specific disorders such as progressive dementia, pseudo-dementia, multi-infarct dementia, and, of course, toxicant-induced illnesses.

Measurement of behavior in isolation

Patterns of strengths and weaknesses are important to sensible interpretation of neuropsychological test results. Not only are factors such as redundancy of measurement important (e.g., a test score in isolation could represent a momentary distraction, a lapse in effort, or a transient pathological condition such as absence seizure) but also patterns can reveal the nature of the weakness, e.g., generalized versus focal impairments. Patterns help to determine when effort might be explanatory, e.g., worse on easier than on hard items, good and bad performance on different tasks that carry similar cognitive demands, or that reflect similar central nervous system functional relationships. They allow for testing of hypotheses associated with specific disorders, e.g., the expectation of bilateral involvement of the central nervous system in most toxicant-induced disorders as opposed to lateralized presentations. A pattern can be suggestive of lifelong low functioning as a result of educational limitations (a low vocabulary in the face of adequate learning ability) or learning disability (low reading, spelling, or writing, within the code of more adequate nonverbal skills; or a low intellect with historical indications of poor school performance). Or a specific pattern of neuropsychological strengths and weaknesses may suggest acquired deficits in a person who functioned higher at an earlier time (e.g., a high vocabulary and fund of general information with currently poor working memory). It is the pattern of behavioral strengths and weaknesses revealed by the neuropsychological examination that is critical, and as a general rule, one isolated score is almost always of very little value.

The importance of ancillary test results

Ancillary test results almost always compliment the neuropsychological findings and may often be necessary in order to arrive at an accurate clinical conclusion. Most of the tests with relevance to neurobehavioral toxicology were reviewed in chapter 7 of volume I. These included tests with relevance specifically to the peripheral nervous system as well as others more specific to the central nervous system. Aside from various laboratory tests (e.g., the value of results from measurement of COHb in a case of suspected CO poisoning) and results of objective test scores contained in a patient's past school records (e.g., IQ test results showing a consistent result over a period of years in school), a number of techniques have been developed over the last 20 or 30 years that allow for structural and functional nuclear and radiographic scanning of the brain. When correlated with the findings from objective behavioral testing, the results from such tests can be invaluable, and efforts to obtain the results of such tests should always be made.

The value of combining findings from these diverse views of the central nervous system goes both ways. In their work on toxic leukoencephalopathy, e.g., Filley and Kleinschmidt-DeMasters (2001) described MRI and CT images of the brain that revealed lesions in multiple anatomical regions (see section on *toluene* in chapter 16). Importantly, however, toxic leukoencephalopathy also is accompanied by neurobehavioral impairments in attention, memory, and other cognitive and emotional behaviors in the face of preserved language functions (Filley & Kleinschmidt-DeMasters, 2001). MRI and CT results such as described by Filley and Kleinschmidt-DeMasters (2001) would be important in documenting structural brain abnormalities in a given case, but the functional significance, and clinical diagnostic significance in the case of leukoencephalopathy specifically, would likely need to be confirmed by neuropsychological test findings.

Findings from ancillary test results also can aid in determining the very important considerations of biological and clinical plausibility of the patient's symptoms. As mentioned already, the usual expectation in a case of toxic-induced disorder is to find behavioral impairments that are consistent with bilateral involvement of the central nervous system, as opposed to a more focal presentation. Findings on neuropsychological tests that included clear impairment in verbal learning and memory in the face of intact nonverbal learning and memory would be contrary to this expectation. When coupled with findings from MRI that showed abnormalities that also were limited to the dominant hemisphere, the conclusion that the patient's problem was something other than a toxicant-induced disorder should be strongly confirmed. Similarly, most disorders that result from acute chemical intoxication tend to improve following removal from further exposure, or at the least to show no further deterioration of the patient's condition. Neuropsychological findings of worsened performance over time, then, would lack biological and clinical plausibility. In this instance, a finding from MRI or CT of increased atrophy in temporal/parietal brain regions would increase suspicion that the patient was suffering from a neurodegenerative disease. Although there are always exceptions to rules such as these just mentioned, consistent findings from multiple test approaches greatly strengthen the conclusions.

The importance of the patient history and interview

We discussed the importance and other details of the patient history and interview, especially in chapters 4, 5, and 6 of volume I. A few additional comments here reflect aspects of the clinical evaluation that result directly from a careful interview and history. While an effort always should be made to obtain formal historical records, including past educational and work-related records, the interview provides an opportunity to hear this history from the patient's viewpoint. Discrepancies between the two sources of information can be noted, and an attempt can be directly made to reconcile these report differences. Even when it is decided that the patient may be a poor or unreliable historian, the information obtained can be critical to the diagnostic conclusions. We said earlier that it is not the intent of the clinician to "catch" the patient in a lie. It is important, however, to know when the facts as presented by various sources are contradictory, or when they are consistent. While most clinicians do not want to think that their patients might not be totally forthright, the reality is that misrepresentation does occur. The choice is to either accept all that is reported as truthful or to acknowledge that the "lie" is another aspect of behavior that needs to be recognized and included impartially in the process of forming a diagnostic conclusion. We included "lie" in quotation marks because not all report inaccuracies are necessarily motivated attempts to mislead. In fact, it may be impossible to know if conscious intent is involved. Misinformation might reflect altered memories, for instance, or simply the patient's, or another's, unique view of events. The important point is that the errors in reporting be recognized and considered. In the *case presentation*, information was obtained from the patient that reflected both types of accuracy, consistent and contradictory across sources. Both were important to the diagnostic process. The patient's complaint about anxiety around issues of CO exposure was consistent with other records, for instance. Among other things, he had taken unusual steps to avoid what he viewed as the possibility for further CO exposure (e.g., changing his heating system). The apparent validity of these reports fit with test findings that were positive for anxiety as well, such that this information served to document the presence of PTSD as a verifiable disorder suffered by the patient. At the same time, the observed discrepancies between his denials of prior physical, emotional, or work-related problems and historical records that reflected the presence of such difficulties helped to determine that there had likely been no clinically significant change in symptoms other than PTSD as a result of his exposure. This diagnosis led to treatment of the mild symptoms associated with his PTSD, which, in turn, led to professional attention to his more general, long-standing, and unresolved emotional difficulties. Information from the clinical interview and history was critical in reaching this end.

Establishing causation in clinical neurotoxicological investigations

Repeatedly in these volumes, we have emphasized the need to approach causal determination separate from diagnosis. We discussed the concept of causation a number of times in these volumes, and chapter 8 of volume I deals exclusively with the topic. Here, we approach the topic by using the *case pesentation* in order to share our approach to establishing causation in what on the surface appears to be a very complicated case.

The diagnosis indicates whether or not the patient's symptoms and signs result from illness and the nature of that illness when it is found to be present. The etiology (cause) gives the reason for the illness. It is common to be able to establish a clinical diagnosis without being able to determine the cause for the disorder. Alzheimer's disease (AD), for instance, is a disorder that is clinically diagnosable even though we do not know its cause. With regard to diagnostic conclusions in the present *case presentation*, the patient can be described as having low general intellect. The discrepancies noted between his report of history in interview and the information contained in formal records leave him unreliable as a historian (see Table 19.2), but together the information from these sources leaves it possible to draw the conclusions described here. Granting that his potential ability might be higher than his scores on formal tests would suggest that owing to his examination in a non-native language and culture, there is nothing in his history or in the pattern of his test results to suggest that he ever functioned much differently than measured on the occasion of his present examination. His poor performance on a test of effort also suggests that his scores are an underestimate of his actual ability. The low (English) Vocabulary and (USA culturally based) Information scores are consistent with his apparent language, cultural, and educational history. His reading recognition score is most likely consistent with his educational background. Abstract conceptualization and problem solving appeared to be normal and consistent with a low general ability level. As in the neurological examination described earlier, he was slow and deliberate on task performance. Beyond this, he was particularly slow with the right hand on a fine motor skill task, but normal with the nondominant hand and on problem-solving tasks. While his scores on memory tests were low, they were no lower than would be predicted by his general ability level, considered within the context of poor effort. Also, his better performance on delayed recall than in initial learning can be seen as consistent with poor effort and possibly variable attention. Emotionally, he appeared anxious in interview, and his scores on formal tests in this area reflected mild to moderate levels of anxiety and depression.

Our final diagnostic conclusion was presented with comment on the contribution from cultural, language, educational, and motivational factors to the patient's functional status. In terms of formal diagnoses, he was found to be suffering from PTSD, superimposed on a general anxiety disorder with depressive components.

In applying causal criteria to these findings, his PTSD was attributed to his experience of having been exposed to CO in the workplace. The general anxiety disorder was seen as long standing and predating the exposure incident. His relatively low ability level was seen also as long standing and unrelated to the exposure. How did we arrive at these causal conclusions? First, with regard to the diagnosis of PTSD, he met the DSM criteria for this disorder, including recurrent thoughts and verifiable changes in behavior in reaction to his concerns (e.g., changing his heating system). There was no evidence that he suffered from these relatively specific symptoms before his exposure, and he described his symptoms as having improved although not entirely remitted in the time since his exposure. Importantly, anxiety was evidenced by observation and in terms of formal test results. That he was exposed to CO had been documented by laboratory testing at the time of his hospitalization. There is documentation in the professional and scientific literature that this type of disorder can occur as result of exposure and that the time course of such symptoms can match that reflected by the patient. It is true that we know almost nothing of the circumstances of his exposure or whether he experienced it at the time as being of a traumatic nature. The truth is that individual emotional reaction to a potentially traumatic event is always likely to be a matter of deduction, hopefully based on the presence of objective data rather than outright speculation. The important questions to ask about such an event include whether or not the event occurred and, once documented, if it carried the potential for physical injury or death. In addition, the clinician needs to determine that the patient's response to the experience involved some aspect of intense fear or anxiety. In this instance, the first of these questions, i.e., the occurrence of the event, was answered by documented history. The second was answered by the substantial scientifically derived database that documents the potential adverse effects of CO exposure, and the final question was answered through clinical interview, history, and neurobehavioral test findings.

No pathology other than the patient's PTSD could be attributed to his exposure to CO. The various complaints the patient attributed to CO exposure during the interview were documented to exist prior to his exposure. While his examination findings contained instances of low intellectual and cognitive functioning, these were consistent with extraneurological explanations with histories predating the exposure, or they were instances of less than optimal effort or normal variations. The poor fine motor performance on one test in the neuropsychological examination was not mirrored in the neurological examination findings and the focal nature of the finding would not fit with a neurotoxic hypothesis. His normal CT and MRI scans were consistent with extraneurological explanations for the findings as well.

Controversial neurotoxic disorders involving the central nervous system

In chapter 15 of the present volume, we discussed the topic of the neurobehavioral effects of solvent exposure. We described this topic as among the most controversial in neurobehavioral toxicology. In fact, there are many topics in neurobehavioral toxicology that lend themselves to controversy, the contentiousness most often revolving around some aspect of the overall issue.

Controversy surrounds the hypothesis of chronic low-dose exposures. In the case of solvents, much of the controversy has surrounded the notion of whether or not chronic, low-dose exposure to these substances, as opposed to high-dose, acute exposure, leads to neurotoxic induced dysfunction (e.g., *painters' encephalopathy*). We believe that the fact that efforts to explore hypotheses related to a potential problem, i.e., that long-term exposure to low doses of various chemicals by workers would eventuate in neurobehavioral dysfunction in those workers, is not in itself a basis for the controversy. Some of the methods employed might have been critiqued and even criticized by other scientists interested in these same topics, and the reported outcomes from studies, positive or negative, would be expected to lead to reasoned debate. Such is the nature of scientific work. Controversy, on the other hand, can arise from the willingness of some to accept as scientifically documented fact what most would consider to be incompletely answered questions. It has been our experience that many controversies in neurobehavioral toxicology result from this phenomenon, presuming a hypothesis as if its probability has been established when it has not.

Especially in scientific fields where fact and reason serve as foundations for their work, the notion of "controversy" seems paradoxical. So, how can well-meaning and capable scientists disagree? The answer to this question, of course, is that the scientist is first a human being. Science is a methodology, something the scientist does, not what he or she is. Most of us have a tendency to confuse the scientist with the person. It is not easy to maintain the distinction in roles between acting as a scientist and being a person. In science, something is possible, probable, or not available to the scientific method at the time of inquiry. From this perspective, anything not yet shown to be probable is possible. As a person, the scientist, as everyone else, has other alternatives. For example, he or she can "believe" something to be true, including things not susceptible to scientific inquiry. As a scientist, however, he or she must live in a world where much remains unknown, perhaps even unknowable, except for those things that can be approached by scientific methodology. This world can conflict with those who may want to know now; e.g., the physician who must treat a patient, an attorney attempting to prove that some substance injured their client, another attorney wanting to prove that it did not, or the scientist him- or herself who wants something to be true or false. This interface between science and other methodologies is where controversy is likely to arise, and it will most often occur around those things that are possible but not yet shown by science to be probable; that is, presuming a hypothesis to be true when its probability has not yet been scientifically established.

Controversy as distinct from scientific argument

We would make a distinction between controversy in neurotoxicological disorders and problems that are possible but not yet scientifically resolved. An example of such a scientific problem is found in Feldman (1998) who argued that since exposure to OP pesticides depresses cholinesterase activity, which then returns over time (weeks to months) to its baseline levels, the exposed individual is at increased risk to develop symptoms at lower doses than would ordinarily produce such symptoms as a result of repeated OP exposures. Feldman's hypothesis provides a good rationale for predicting that chronic or repeat exposures to OP pesticides could lead to OP poisoning at doses lower than would otherwise be the case (see discussion on *delayed neurotoxicity* later in this chapter). On the other hand, Richardson, Moore, Kayyali, and Randall (1993) have shown the development of tolerance as a result of repeat exposures to OP compounds, a finding that could pose a challenge to Feldman's postulation. Tolerance, e.g., suggests that a nonlinear relationship exists between dose and effect such that increasing dose levels over time will be required in order to achieve an effect observed at the time of the initial dose. The scientific debate surrounding this issue is likely to continue for some time, and science requires the patience to proceed step by step in addressing the relevant questions. For those without such patience, controversy might well result.

Controversy based on misunderstandings or misinterpretations

Also at times, controversy can develop as a result of misunderstanding or misinterpretation of the results of scientific research. Methodological weaknesses, e.g., can lead to apparent findings that in fact are erroneous. Despite the recognition by most researchers that multiple, potential confounders must be accounted for before concluding that a causal relationship exists between two study variables, confounding variables often are either unrecognized or inadequately controlled in a given study. This is especially true in cross-sectional studies where practically it may be impossible to control all relevant factors, and this fact serves as a rationale for the priority assigned to longitudinal epidemiological studies in addressing issues of causality. The problem is pronounced especially when the statistical design calls for regression analyses, and we earlier cited an example in which historical, cumulative exposure was found to be significantly correlated with aspects of neuropsychometric outcome (see volume I). In that example, it was found that aging accounted for both cumulative dose and behavioral outcome, with no causal implications between dose and behavior. This situation serves to remind us of the basic lesson in introductory statistics classes, that correlation does not reflect causality. Yet, whether through overzealousness, carelessness, or other reasons, many rely on such data to form conclusions about causal relationships. When this occurs, controversy is bound to result.

The controversy of delayed neurotoxicity

There are times when a patient complains of an abnormality some time after an exposure incident. It is not unusual that these "late" complaints are seen as possibly related to the previous exposure. When biologically plausible, the possibility of a connection between the patient's illness and prior exposure should be seriously considered. Since symptoms of toxicant exposure are known in some instances to occur following a period of delay, controversy can develop that is focused on whether it did, or can, occur in a given situation. In fact, there is some confusion in the published literature as to what constitutes a "delay." Here, we define "delayed effects" as adverse effects that appear at a later time even though no adverse effect was apparent at the time of the initial exposure (see volume II for additional discussion on this topic). In contrast to malignancies that result from exposure to carcinogens whose effects may occur long after the initial exposure, few proven models exist of delayed onset neurotoxicity. Four examples of delayed onset central nervous system disorder include radiation induced neuronal degeneration, 1-methyl-4-phenyl-1,2,3,6-tetrahydropyridine (MPTP)–induced parkinsonism, late progression of old poliomyelitis, and boxers' parkinsonism and dementia (*dementia pugilistica* or, at times, *chronic traumatic encephalopathy* [Rowland, 1989]). Another example of delayed effects following neurotoxicant exposure is organophosphate-induced delayed neurotoxicity (OPIDN), which was discussed in volume II. OPIDN differs from the other examples given in that the delay is generally very short, a few weeks after exposure, although MPTP-induced parkinsonism may appear almost immediately after exposure (hours), depending on the dose. The short-term delay can be contrasted with the other conditions listed where the delay involves the central nervous system and can be years, even decades, after the initial exposure.

MPTP-induced parkinsonism represents the best understood model of central nervous system delayed neurotoxicity, even though paradoxically it is typically a disorder with rapid onset neurotoxicity. Delayed effects, however, do occur and can be explained on the basis of subclinical injury to a population of neurons. MPTP enters the central nervous system and following oxidative transformation induces neuronal damage in the zona compacta and substantia nigra (Calne, Eisen, McGeer, & Spencer, 1986). MPTP is a dopamine neuron neurotoxin and exposure to MPTP can induce rapid onset of parkinsonism with dose-dependent levels of severity, and this fact unfortunately was well documented in the early 1980s when about 400 people voluntarily took the drug for recreational purposes (Albin, 2000). Some of these individuals, however, evidenced delayed effect neurotoxicity. The most likely mechanism underlying the delay in these cases involved MPTP exposure at doses sufficient to produce neurological damage but insufficient to produce neurological symptoms and signs (i.e., subclinical injury). Individuals who used the drug and who initially were apparently asymptomatic showed evidence of abnormally low numbers of striatal dopamine terminals (Calne et al., 1985). Over time, these same individuals were found to show progressive loss of striatal dopamine neurons (Vingerhoets et al., 1994), and at least some of these subsequently developed (delayed) evidence of parkinsonism (Calne et al.). How long a delay between exposure and manifestation of clinical symptoms and signs depends on a number of factors, including the extent of initial neuronal loss, the size of the individual's neuronal pool (neuronal reserves), individual variations in susceptibility to neuronal loss (which, in turn, might reflect ability to detoxify or transform noxious agents into inactive toxins), and individual rate of neuronal attrition.

The syndrome of late progression of old poliomyelitis, another example relevant to clinical neurotoxicology, might be explained by mechanisms that are somewhat similar to MPTP-induced delayed neurotoxicity. In poliomyelitis, a motor neuron disease (bulbar motor neurons and anterior horn cells) of viral etiology, patients develop paralyses or profound weakness of some but not all muscle groups. Functional improvement over time characterized those who survived the initial infection. The mechanism for improved strength involved reinnervation of denervated muscle fibers through collateral sprouting of surviving neurons. Nevertheless, over time a number of these "improved" patients evidenced recurrent and progressive weakness. This late, or delayed, disease progression likely reflects the normally expected neuronal attrition of motor neurons. The normal person can tolerate the loss of many motor neurons without consequence to innervated muscle, including the loss attributed to normal age-related neuronal attrition. For the person with a prior poliomyelitis and a markedly reduced motor neuron pool, however, the loss of even a few anterior horn cells can have profound effects, e.g., recurrence and progression of muscle weakness.

Although there are similarities, the mechanism for delayed onset of symptoms and signs of parkinsonism and dementia in dementia pugilistica can be contrasted to those described for MPTP-induced delayed neurotoxicity and late progression of old poliomyelitis. In dementia pugilistica, the normal attrition of central nervous system neurons is accelerated by a series of discrete traumatic events, perhaps similar to the increased vulnerability to injury from repeat head trauma of any type (e.g., concussions experienced during team sports or as result of motor vehicle accidents) (Levin, Benton, & Grossman, 1982; Rowland, 1989; U.S. Department of Health and Human Services [DHHS], 2005). In part because of the protectiveness of strong social and professional lobbying in support of boxing, little is known about this condition, and there is need for prospective epidemiological studies (Rowland, 1989). What is known comes from only relatively few studies. The average length of time from beginning a career in boxing and onset of symptoms and signs of dementia pugilistica for those affected is said to be 16 years, with pathologic findings that include hypothalamic anomalies, substantia nigra degeneration, widespread neurofibrillary changes, and cerebellar folia scarring (Rowland, 1989). The limited number of individuals who suffer from this condition is a factor that has limited the opportunity for formal epidemiological studies, limiting inquiries to case reports and cross-sectional comparisons of clinical cases between individuals diagnosed with dementia pugilistica and patients diagnosed with other dementias, e.g., AD. Studies that have been done have reported both similarities and differences between the two types of dementia, AD and dementia pugilistica (Erlanger, Kutner, Barth, & Barnes, 1999; Hof et al., 1992; Roberts, Allsop, & Bruton, 1990).

Here, we presented examples that are known to include the possibility for onset of clinical effects that is delayed for some period following an initial exposure or injury. Also, the examples were chosen because there is considerable scientific evidence that is sufficient to document the occurrence of delayed onset in these conditions, including knowledge about the neuropathology involved in each condition. A presumption common to all of the examples given is that there is some threshold in terms of neuronal pool, below which normal neurological function ceases and the affected individual becomes symptomatic. Since neuronal and related attrition occurs with the process of aging, it would be expected that all who live long enough will become symptomatic at some point in response to such loss. From an optimistic viewpoint, and with normal variations, the neuronal pool is sufficiently large under normal circumstances to last a person's lifetime. From the perspective discussed here, neurobehavioral toxicology is interested in those non-normal circumstances that speed the process of attrition. Not yet discussed is the accelerated attrition associated with some chronic, cumulative disorders. Although the cause remains unknown, progressive dementia such as AD fits a chronic model. It is well documented that symptoms of AD manifest much earlier in the course of this disease than was previously thought (Berent et al., 1999). For all of these models, diagnosable abnormality occurs at the point that neuronal and related attrition intersects with the threshold for developing clinically evident signs. The fact that this threshold is reached sometime after the exposure or other injury to the central nervous system first initiated the enhanced process of attrition makes it a delayed effect.

Controversies surrounding nonspecific symptoms

The nonspecific nature of symptoms in neurotoxic disorders involving the central nervous system itself leads to controversy. Headache, dizziness, difficulties with vision, sleep difficulties, feeling low, feeling wound up, fatigue, aches and pains, and a multitude of other complaints might result from exposure to various toxicants; however, other pathological and normal conditions have the capacity to produce such complaints. We could add to a list of possible causes for nonspecific complaints the various psychopathologies (e.g., depression, anxiety, and other psychological and psychiatric conditions) that can accompany exposure to toxicants but also can develop independent of any exposure or may be of unknown etiology. A reliance on symptoms alone, or on the presence of pathology temporally related to exposure to conclude a neurobehavioral toxicological cause, is inappropriate. The best way to avoid controversy that is likely to develop as a result of such practice is to approach the diagnosis independent of cause and use objective criteria in forming conclusions about both.

Controversies surrounding subclinical impairments

Disease can be defined as a specific illness or disorder that is clinically manifest, ideally with the presence of symptoms and signs. Diagnostic and causal conclusions rest on the integration and analyses of history, observation, examination, consideration of laboratory test results, and other information relevant to the case at hand. The analysis considers the results from all sources in conjunction with objective criteria that are to be met in reaching final diagnostic and etiological conclusions. Unfortunatley, these requirements can be, and at times are, distorted by individuals for a variety of reasons, e.g., to support a personal belief. One way is to ignore some component in the clinical process, e.g., relying solely on symptoms or solely on test results to make a diagnostic conclusion. A somewhat more sophisticated, but still eroneous, route is to rely on novel definitions for some aspect of the required diagnostic criteria. Calne and Calne (1988), for instance, called attention to what they saw as a trend to alter the threshold for abnormality by equating "normal" with an ideal state of health rather than employing the traditional departure from average by some standard of variation (e.g., a score of 2 SD below the mean on a standard test of intelligence as the cutoff for intellectual deficiency).

There are times when one may conclude that an abnormality is "subclinical." Subclinical is another term that can be imprecise. As a result, it is a term that is subject to error or misuse on occasion. As properly used, subclinical refers to a condition that produces neither symptoms nor signs on clinical examination but is demonstrated on some recognized and appropriate diagnostic test. The concept of "subclinical disorder" can be beneficial clinically in a number of ways, e.g., providing an objective baseline for monitoring the future course of disease or disorder. At times, however, the term has been defined in a slightly different way, as referring to a disease or abnormal condition that is so mild as to produce few positive clinical findings (Anderson, 1994; Merck Source, 2005). Problems can arise when this term is used loosely as a specific diagnostic category and used to label positive findings from some part of the evaluation (e.g., symptoms) but not from all findings (e.g., absence of signs or corroborative findings from other laboratory tests or study results).

There are occasions when subclinical can be employed in a documentable fashion, e.g., someone with a history of documented symptoms and signs of toxicant-induced disorder who through the normal reparative processes has improved to the extent that only some mild symptoms remain. An underlying premise in the present work is that neurobehavioral impairment reflects the nature and extent of central nervous system dysfunction. It should also be recognized that central nervous system dysfunction can exist at molecular levels or in systems that otherwise remain inaccessible to clinical inquiry by the present state of technology. Thus, a patient who has recovered grossly from previous injury may still reflect symptoms or findings on some laboratory tests while clinically manifest signs may be apparently absent. Whether limited to test results or manifest in mild clinical findings, the determination of residual findings from prior acute exposure requires a history of prior symptoms and signs. Even when such historical information is available, the current clinical manifestations may be non-existent or so minor as to lack any clinical significance, the patient having recovered from the prior illness. Recovery from a severe motor neuropathy, for example, typically is accompanied by no clinical evidence of weakness or incoordination but on electrophysiological examination may evidence slow nerve conduction showing regeneration of motor axons, a finding of no clinical significance.

Consider the following. A patient is being evaluated to establish baseline level of functioning before inclusion in a research project. The neurological examination, including brain imaging studies and other laboratory tests, are normal. Neuropsychological examination reveals relative impairments in verbal and visual delayed recall with normal results in the rest of the examination. While the patient described meets the definition used previously for subclinical disorder, the question must be asked: subclinical for what? This example suggests an extensive differential diagnosis, and none of the possible disorders on this list is ruled in or out by the clinical evaluation provided. The neuropsychological examination results serve to verify the presence, nature, and pattern of the patient's memory functioning. Beyond this, however, the results provide little more than the establishment of baseline functioning, a worthwhile accomplishment that might serve the patient well in the future. However, the results do not provide a basis for making a definitive clinical diagnosis, determining the cause of the complaints, suggesting treatment, or rendering a clinical prognosis. Applying the term, subclinical, to the diagnostic conclusion adds nothing of clinical value. On the contrary, such a label could mislead others and delay a future and more detailed diagnosis because it may connote an answer to the "subclinical for what" question posed earlier, i.e., that the findings are below the clinical threshold for some suspected disorder.

In a series of studies that evaluated middle-aged volunteers from the local community (e.g., Berent et al., 1999), a subset of subjects who showed psychometric evidence for impaired learning was chosen for further clinical studies. Exclusion criteria included a host of medical and neurological illnesses, alcohol and other substance abuse, as well as evidence of impaired mental status or outright dementia. The subjects included in the sample for further study were classified as having "Isolated Memory Impairment" (IMI) because of the relatively narrow pattern of positive findings in the screening measures. These volunteers subsequently were re-evaluated over a several year period. Some were found on re-examination to have abnormal brain imaging studies, and some did not. Approximately half of these subjects developed diagnosable "probable AD" after two years, but some improved in their test results while others were discovered to have conditions other than AD that explained the initial test findings. The subjects entering this study who had no complaints could have been described as having subclinical disorder. But, what disorder? Despite extensive steps to exclude those with conditions known to cause cognitive impairment, some of the subjects were found ultimately to have clinical explanations, or normal variations, that explained the findings. While a primary interest involved identification of AD early in the course of the disorder, the findings were not 100% specific for AD. In other words, the subclinical findings in this situation were of limited value in terms of arriving at a specific, final clinical diagnosis.

To give one additional brief illustration, the topic of intellectual deficiency was mentioned earlier and within the context of statistical thresholds in determining abnormality. As a construct, "intellectual deficiency" can be defined operationally on the basis of (valid) neuropsychological test results. We employed a similar model to classify IMI. In fact, such constructs are used routinely clinically to classify patients' neuropsychological performance. Also, the criteria presented for a given clinical diagnosis may specify such constructs as necessary for making the diagnosis. However, because the criteria associated with a given construct are met, does not imply that such information is sufficient to make the final clinical diagnosis. In AD, verification of cognitive impairment with objective neurobehavioral testing is listed as a diagnostic criterion. Because objectively establishing the presence of cognitive impairment is necessary for the diagnosis does not mean that such verification is sufficient to conclude the diagnosis. Similarly, consider the diagnosis of *mental retardation* (MR). Establishing the presence of sub-average intellect (defined as indicated earlier) is but one of several criteria that must be met in order to make this diagnosis (American Psychiatric

Association, 1994). While the clinician could correctly describe, even classify, the patient with intellectual deficiency on the basis of test results, it would be wrong to diagnose mental retardation solely on these data. And, in terms of cause, the possible causes for MR will be many even when diagnosed correctly (e.g., heredity, early developmental anomalies, perinatal problems, early life medical illnesses, environmental influences, to name but a few).

Summary

Disorders seldom occur in isolation. That is, every individual brings to the clinical evaluation a unique personal background, and a medical history that may reflect past, or current, illness or injury, the symptoms of which might mirror those that are associated with a presently suspected diagnosis. Regardless of the relationship to toxicant exposure, behavioral abnormalities are included in the final diagnosis. However, whether normal or not, these various behaviors, as we have discussed repeatedly, can affect the clinical presentation, at times to the extent that an otherwise sensible clinical diagnosis can be obscured. Also, normal variations in behavior influence the nature of communication between doctor and patient and, therefore, the nature of the clinical evaluation. The clinician interested in neurobehavioral toxicology, therefore, will need to maintain knowledge of these behavioral factors and remain sensitive to their occurrence and impact on the clinical evaluation. In the research arena, many of these factors call for inclusion in the study design, as independent variables for study or as potential confounders that need to be considered in making research conclusions.

Since behavior varies between individuals, with a fairly high range of possible normal expressions, and since these manifestations are important diagnostically, how does one go about determining their normality? We discussed in some detail the processes involved in determining normality and abnormality in volume 1, and we indicated that it is among the most important things to accomplish in clinically evaluating an individual. The various methodologies to be employed in making these conclusions can be summarized as including statistical and qualitative approaches as well as analyses of patterns revealed in the formal (metric) and informal (clinical observations) as to their clinical sensibility. For example, a patient who appears unable to perform successfully on formal neuropsychological tests of learning and memory in one portion of the psychometric examination while evidencing intact memory on another task that differs only in not being an obvious test of memory is displaying a pattern that is neither biologically nor psychologically sensible. So, too, is the patient who fails to recall information learned in the examination setting but who displays good recall for recently learned information during the clinical history and interview. Such observations do not mean necessarily that the patient is feigning impairment, but it does mean that the clinician must consider extraneurological explanations for observed test scores. Whether based in neurological dysfunction or not, a qualitative approach suggests that abnormality is present when the patient's symptoms are found to produce a change in the patient's efficiency (in personal or vocational roles), is sufficiently unusual and lacking in social context as to be described as bizarre, or produce significant discomfort, e.g., the "pain" of depression or anxiety (Berent & Trask, 2000).

While the statistical approach to determining normality remains the most objective because of its reliance on quantification, it is important to remember that the behaviors being measured in evaluation of the central nervous system, especially on the neuropsychological examination, are for the most part under the volitional control of the patient. As such, they are subject to influence from all of the behavioral variations discussed in this chapter and elsewhere in these volumes. It is for this reason, as much as any other, that we have stressed that the formal neuropsychological examination is but one facet of the neuro-behavioral evaluation, albeit an important one. While the statistical approach is desirable because of its quantification and objectivity, a powerful application of the principles and methods of physical measurement to the evaluation of behavior, its reliance on normative data is a weakness as well as strength. There may often be some question, for instance, with regard to the suitability of normative data for the specific patient being compared. This may be especially relevant when evaluating a patient from special or esoteric backgrounds or, as in the *case presentation*, someone with unique backgrounds in education, language, culture, and other individual difference variables.

The employment of ancillary tests and historical information is also important in making a complete clinical evaluation. In some cases, e.g., in the diagnosis of seizure disorder or a specific type of dementia or encephalopathy, the diagnostic criteria will specify the necessity for such tests (American Academy of Neurology, 2001; Filley & Kleinschmidt-DeMasters, 2001; Sackellares & Berent, 1996). In other cases, good clinical sense dictates the consideration of these extra-examination findings. For example, a pattern on the neuropsychological examination results that includes abnormally low reading and vocabulary in the face of normally appearing general intellectual ability might suggest failure of that individual to profit maximally from past educational pursuits. If a review of the person's school records revealed that the patient actually did well in school, the clinician would need to look further into the clinical explanation for these test outcomes. Diagnostically important, the clinician would have to now consider a finding that suggests an onset of disorder that occurred sometime after completing his education, as opposed to a long-term, if not lifelong, condition.

Notes

1   Details of the history have been modified to preserve the anonymity of the patient and the patient's family.

2   In the 1993 movie, *True Romance* (Tarantino & Scott, 1993), the mobster (Christopher Walken) interrogates the father (Dennis Hopper) and tells him that there are 17 things that a person can do to reveal that he is not telling the truth. Although these 17 things were not specified in the movie, one of them has to be inconsistency of fact from one statement to the next. While the purpose of the

clinical interview is not to catch the patient in a lie, the clinician needs to listen carefully to the patient and at some point ask for clarification of seeming inconsistencies. In the present instance, the clinician would wish to ensure that the seeming inconsistency was not simply the result of lack of language mastery.

3   A history is taken during the course of interview, to include the patient's primary complaints, review of systems, demographic and exposure details, and other information reviewed earlier in these volumes (see chapters 5 and 6 of volume I). In addition, records are obtained to the extent possible that reflect the patient's history in areas of school performance, work, past medical injuries, conditions, and treatments; and other information with relevance to a given case. To the extent that records are unavailable, the report of findings should indicate in what ways the missing records limit or otherwise qualify the interpretations and conclusions that can be made.

References

Albin, R. L. (2000). Basal ganglia neurotoxins. In J. W. Albers & S. Berent (Eds.), *Clinical neurobehavioral toxicology* (pp. 665–680). Philadelphia: W. B. Saunders.

American Academy of Neurology. (2001). Clinical diagnostic guidelines: Internet Communication. PDF retrieved from http://www.aan.com/professionals/practice/guidelines/pda/Dementia_diagnosis.pdf

American Psychiatric Association. (1994). *Diagnostic and Statistical Manual of Mental Disorders* (4th ed.). Washington, DC: Author.

Anderson, K. N. (1994). *Mosby's medical dictionary*, 4th ed. St. Louis, Mosby Press.

Ardila, A. (2003). Language representation and working memory with bilinguals. *Journal of Communication Disorders, 36*, 233–240.

Baum, A. (1991). Toxins, technology, and natural disasters. In G. R. VandenBos & B. K. Bryant (Eds.), *Cataclysms, crises, and catastrophes* (pp. 9–53). Washington, DC: American Psychological Association.

Beck, C. T., & Gable, R. K. (2003). Postpartum depression screening scale: Spanish version. *Nursing Research, 52*, 296–306.

Berent, S., Giordani, B., Foster, N., Minoshima, S., Lajiness-O'Neill, R., Koeppe, R., et al. (1999). Neuropsychological function and cerebral glucose utilization in isolated memory impairment and Alzheimer's disease. *Journal of Psychiatric Research, 33*, 7–16.

Berent, S., & Trask, C. L. (2000). Human neuropsychological testing and evaluation. In E. Massaro (Ed.), *Neurotoxicology Handbook* (Vol. 2, pp. 551–576). Totowa, NJ: Humana press.

Binder, L. M. (1993). Assessment of malingering after mild head trauma with the Portland Digit Recognition Test. *Journal of Clinical and Experimental Neuropsychology, 15*, 170–182.

Bolla, K. I., & Roca, R. (1994). Neuropsychiatric sequelae of occupational exposure to neurotoxins. In M. L. Bleeker & J. A. Hansen (Eds.), *Occupational neurology and clinical neurotoxicology* (pp. 133–159). Baltimore: Williams & Wilkins.

Bowden, A., & Fox-Rushby, J. A. (2003). A systematic and critical review of the process of translation and adaptation of generic health-related quality of life measures in Africa, Asia, Eastern Europe, the Middle East, South America. *Social Science and Medicine, 57*, 1289–1306.

Brown, D. L., Smith, T. L., & Knepper, L. E. (1998). Evaluation of five primitive reflexes in 240 young adults. *Neurology, 51*, 322.

Calne, D. B., & Calne, J. S. (1988). Normality and disease. *Canadian Journal of Neurological Sciences, 15,* 3–4.

Calne, D. B., Eisen, A., McGeer, E., & Spencer, P. (1986). Alzheimer's disease, Parkinson's disease, and motoneurone disease: Abiotrophic interaction between ageing and environment? *Lancet, 2,* 1067–1070.

Calne, D. B., Langston, J. W., Martin, W. R., Stoessl, A. J., Ruth, T. J., Adam, M. J. et al. (1985). Positron emission tomography after MPTP: Observations relating to the cause of Parkinson's disease. *Nature, 317,* 246–248.

D'Elia, L., Satz, P., & Schretlen, D. (1989). Wechsler Memory Scale: A critical appraisal of the normative studies. *Journal of Clinical and Experimental Neuropsychology, 11,* 551–568.

Erlanger, D. M., Kutner, K. C., Barth, J. T., & Barnes, R. (1999). Neuropsychology of sports-related head injury: Dementia Pugilistica to Post Concussion Syndrome. *Clinical Neuropsychologist, 13,* 193–209.

Feldman, R. G. (1998). *Occupational and environmental neurotoxicology.* Philadelphia: Lippencott-Raven.

Fiedler, N., Feldman, R. G., Jacobson, J., Rahill, A., & Wetherell, A. (1996). The assessment of neurobehavioral toxicity: SGOMSEC joint report. *Environmental Health Perspectives, 104*(Suppl. 2), 179–191.

Filley, C. M., & Kleinschmidt-DeMasters, B. K. (2001). Toxic leukoencephalopathy. *New England Journal of Medicine, 345,* 425–432.

Folia, V., & Kosmidis, M. H. (2003). Assessment of memory skills in illiterates: Strategy differences or test artifact? *Clinical Neuropsychologist, 17,* 143–152.

Folstein, M. F., Folstein, S. E., & McHugh, P. R. (1975). "Mini-mental state." A practical method for grading the cognitive state of patients for the clinician. *Journal of Psychiatric Research, 12,* 189–198.

Fortuny, L., & Mullaney, H. A. (1997). Neuropsychology with Spanish speakers: Language use and proficiency issues for test development. *Journal of Clinical and Experimental Neuropsychology, 19,* 615–622.

Frazer, A., & Hensler, J. G. (1999). Serotonin. In G. J. Siegel, B. W. Agranoff, R. W. Albers, S. K. Fisher, & M. D. Uhler (Eds.), *Basic neurochemistry: Molecular, cellular and medical aspects* (6th ed., pp. 263–292). Philadelphia: Lippincott-Raven.

Frederick, C. J. (1991). Psychic trauma in victims of crime and terrorism. In G. R. VandenBos & B. K. Bryant (Eds.), *Cataclysms, crises, and catastrophes* (pp. 59–108). Washington, DC: American Psychological Association.

Gil, E. F., & Bob, S. (1999). Culturally competent research: An ethical perspective. *Clinical Psychology Review, 19,* 45–55.

Hendrickson, S. G. (2003). Beyond translation…cultural fit. *Western Journal of Nursing Research, 25,* 593–608.

Hof, P. R., Bouras, C., Buee, L., Delacourte, A., Perl, D. P., & Morrison, J. H. (1992). Differential distribution of neurofibrillary tangles in the cerebral cortex of dementia pugilistica and Alzheimer's disease cases. *Acta Neuropathologica, 85,* 23–30.

Jacobs, L., & Gossman, D. (1980). Three primitive reflexes in normal adults. *Neurology, 30,* 184–188.

Jacobs, D. M., Sano, M., Albert, S., Schofield, P., Dooneief, G., & Stern, Y. (1997). Cross-cultural neuropsychological assessment: A comparison of randomly selected, demographically matched cohorts of English- and Spanish-speaking older adults. *Journal of Clinical and Experimental Neuropsychology, 19,* 331–339.

Kalechstein, A. D., Newton, T. F., & van Gorp, W. G. (2003). Neurocognitive functioning is associated with employment status: A quantitative review. *Journal of Clinical and Experimental Neuropsychology, 25,* 1186–1191.

Karzmark, P. (2000). Validity of the serial seven procedure. *International Journal of Geriatric Psychiatry, 15,* 677–679.

La Rue, A., Romero, L. J., Ortiz, I. E., Liang, H. C., & Lindeman, R. D. (1999). Neuropsychological performance of Hispanic and non-Hispanic older adults: An epidemiologic survey. *Clinical Neuropsychologist, 13,* 474–486.

Lee, T. M., Cheung, C. C., Chan, J. K., & Chan, C. C. (2000). Trail making across languages. *Journal of Clinical and Experimental Neuropsychology, 22,* 772–778.

Levav, M., Mirsky, A. F., French, L. M., & Bartko, J. J. (1998). Multinational neuropsychological testing: Performance of children and adults. *Journal of Clinical and Experimental Neuropsychology, 20,* 658–672.

Levin, H. S., Benton, A. L., & Grossman, R. G. (1982). *Neurobehavioral consequences of closed head injury.* New York: Oxford University Press.

Lindzey, G., Hall, C., & Thompson, R. F. (1975). *Psychology.* New York: Worth Publishers.

Lupien, S. J., & McEwen, B. S. (1997). The acute effects of corticosteroids on cognition: Integration of animal and human model studies. *Brain Research—Brain Research Reviews, 24,* 1–27.

Marshall, S. C., Mungas, D., Weldon, M., Reed, B., & Haan, M. (1997). Differential item functioning in the Mini-Mental State Examination in English- and Spanish-speaking older adults. *Psychology and Aging, 12,* 718–725.

Matsui, Y., Ohbu, S., & Yamashina, A. (1996). Hospital deployment in mass sarin poisoning incident of the Tokyo subway system—an experience at St. Luke's International Hospital, Tokyo. *Japan-Hospitals, 15,* 67–71.

McEwen, B. S., de Kloet, E. R., & Rostene, W. (1986). Adrenal steroid receptors and actions in the nervous system. *Physiological Reviews, 66,* 1121–1188.

Merck Source (2005). *Dorland's medical dictionary online.* Internet: http://www.mercksource.com

Merriam-Webster, A. (1993). *Merriam-Webster's collegiate dictionary* (10th ed.). Springfield, MA: G & C Merriam Company.

Mkoka, S., Vaughan, J., Wylie, T., Yelland, H., & Jelsma, J. (2003). The pitfalls of translation—a case study based on the translation of the EQ-5D into Xhosa. *South African Medical Journal, 93,* 265–266.

Morita, H., Yanagisawa, N., Nakajima, T., Shimizu, M., Hirabayashi, H., Okudera, H. et al. (1995). Sarin poisoning in Matsumoto, Japan. *Lancet, 346,* 290–293.

Moruzzi, G., & Magoun, H. W. (1949). Brain stem reticular formation and activation of the EEG. *Neurophysiology, 1,* 455–473.

Murphy, G. (1949). *Historical introduction to modern psychology.* New York: Harcourt, Brace and World.

Nisenson, L. G., Pepper, C. M., Schwenk, T. L., & Coyne, J. C. (1998). The nature and prevalence of anxiety disorders in primary care. *General Hospital Psychiatry, 20,* 21–28.

Penley, J. A., Wiebe, J. S., & Nwosu, A. (2003). Psychometric properties of the Spanish Beck Depression Inventory-II in a medical sample. *Psychological Assessment, 15,* 569–577.

Reis, A., Guerreiro, M., & Petersson, K. M. (2003). A sociodemographic and neuropsychological characterization of an illiterate population. *Applied Neuropsychology, 10,* 191–204.

Rey, A. (1964). *l'examen clinique en psychologie*. Paris: Presses universitaires de France.

Richardson, R. J., Moore, T. B., Kayyali, U. S., & Randall, J. C. (1993). Chlorpyrifos: Assessment of potential for delayed neurotoxicity by repeated dosing in adult hens with monitoring of brain acetylcholinesterase, brain and lymphocyte neurotoxic esterase, and plasma butyrylcholinesterase activities. *Fundamental and Applied Toxicology, 21*, 89–96.

Roberts, G. W., Allsop, D., & Bruton, C. (1990). The occult aftermath of boxing. *Journal of Neurology, Neurosurgery and Psychiatry, 53*, 373–378.

Rosal, M. C., Carbone, E. T., & Goins, K. V. (2003). Use of cognitive interviewing to adapt measurement instruments for low-literate Hispanics. *Diabetes Educator, 29*, 1006–1017.

Rowland, R. W. (1989). *Merritt's textbook of neurology* (8th ed.). Philadelphia: Lea & Febiger.

Sackellares, J. C., & Berent, S. (1996). *Psychological disturbances in epilepsy*. Boston: Butterworth-Heinemann.

Sailer, U., Flanagan, J. R., & Johansson, R. S. (2005). Eye-hand coordination during learning of a novel visuomotor task. *Journal of Neuroscience, 25*, 8833–8842.

Schlag, J., & Schlag-Rey, M. (1982). Functional significance of visually triggered discharges in eye movement related neurons. In C. D. Woody (Ed.), *Conditioning: Representation of involved neural functions* (pp. 375–387). New York: Plenum Press.

Spurgeon, A., Gompertz, D., & Harrington, J. M. (1997). Non-specific symptoms in response to hazard exposure in the workplace. *Journal of Psychosomatic Research, 43*, 43–49.

Stewart, A. L., & Napoles-Springer, A. M. (2003). Advancing health disparities research: Can we afford to ignore measurement issues? *Medical Care, 41*, 1207–1220.

Tarantino, Q., & Scott, T. (1993). *True romance*. USA, Warner Brothers.

Trueblood, W., & Schmidt, M. (1993). Malingering and other validity considerations in the neuropsychological evaluation of mild head injury. *Journal of Clinical and Experimental Neuropsychology, 15*, 578–590.

U.S. Department of Health and Human Services (DHHS), C. f. D. C. a. P. C. (2005). Traumatic brain injury (TBI): Topic home. Retrieved from http://www.cdc.gov/node.do/id/0900f3ec8000dbdc

Uttl, B., & Van Alstine, C. L. (2003). Rising verbal intelligence scores: Implications for research and clinical practice. *Psychology and Aging, 18*, 616–621.

VandenBos, G. R., & Bryant, B. K. (1991). *Cataclysms, crises, and catastrophes*. Washington, DC: American Psychological Association.

Vingerhoets, F. J., Snow, B. J., Tetrud, J. W., Langston, J. W., Schulzer, M., & Calne, D. B. (1994). Positron emission tomographic evidence for progression of human MPTP-induced dopaminergic lesions. *Annals of Neurology, 36*, 765–770.

Woodworth, R. S., & Schlosberg, H. (1938). *Experimental psychology (1938 edition)*. New York: Rinehart and Winston.

Woodworth, R. S., & Schlosberg, H. (1964). *Experimental psychology*. New York: Rinehart and Winston.

World Health Organization. (2001). *International classification of functioning, disability and health (ICF)*. Geneva: Author.

Appendix

Table A Explicit questions used to verify a clinical diagnosis.

Does the proposed diagnosis
Explain all clinical findings (adequacy)?   If not, does it explain the most important findings?   Best fit the illness pattern (primacy or dominance)?   Fit the observed or implied pathophysiology (coherence)?   Provide the simplest explanation for the illness (parsimony)?   Escape disproof (robustness)?   Best anticipate the subsequent clinical course (prediction)?

Modified from "Users' Guides to the Medical Literature: XXIV. How to Use an Article on the Clinical Manifestations of Disease. Evidence-Based Medicine Working Group," by W. S. Richardson, M. C. Wilson, J. W. Williams, Jr., V. A. Moyer, and C. D. Naylor, 2000, *The Journal of American Medical Association, 284*, p. 869.

Table B The "Bradford Hill" criteria.

Questions useful in establishing a toxic etiology

Is the timing of exposure and onset of signs appropriate (temporality)?
 Is there a high relative risk based on sound epidemiology studies or case reports (strength of association)?
 Is the proposed cause–effect relationship biologically plausible (plausibility)?
 Is there an anticipated dose–response relationship (biological gradient)?
 Has the association been observed repeatedly among studies conducted by different persons, at different times, and in different settings (consistency/replication)?
 Is the cause–effect relationship such that associations are relatively limited to specific groups of exposed individuals and to particular diseases (specificity)?
 Does the association conflict with generally known facts (coherence)?
   Does removal from exposure modify the adverse effect?
   Are there analogous problems caused by similar agents?
   Has an animal model been established?
 Have other potential explanations been investigated and eliminated (differential diagnosis)?

"The Environment and Disease: Association or Causation," by A. B. Hill, 1965, *Proceedings of the Royal Society of medicine, 58*, p. 295.

References

Hill, A. B. (1965). The environment and disease: Association or causation. *Proceedings of the Royal Society of medicine, 58,* 295–300.

Richardson, W. S., Wilson, M. C., Williams, J. W., Jr., Moyer, V. A., & Naylor, C. D. (2000). Users' guides to the medical literature: XXIV. How to use an article on the clinical manifestations of disease. Evidence-Based Medicine Working Group. *The Journal of American Medical Association, 284,* 869–875.

Index